Post-crisis Fiscal Policy

Post-crisis Fiscal Policy

edited by Carlo Cottarelli, Philip Gerson, and Abdelhak Senhadji

The MIT Press
Cambridge, Massachusetts
London, England

MIT Press books may be purchased at special quantity discounts for business or sales promotional use. For information, please email special_sales@mitpress.mit.edu.

This book was set in Sabon LT Std by Toppan Best-set Premedia Limited. Printed and bound in the United States of America.

Library of Congress Cataloging-in-Publication Data
Post-crisis fiscal policy / edited by Carlo Cottarelli, Philip Gerson, and Abdelhak Senhadji.
    pages cm
Includes bibliographical references and index.
ISBN 978-0-262-02718-2 (hardcover : alk. paper) 1. Fiscal policy. 2. Financial crises. 3. Global Financial Crisis, 2008-2009. 4. International Monetary Fund. I. Cottarelli, Carlo. II. Gerson, Philip R. III. Senhadji, Abdelhak.
HJ192.5.P68 2014
339.5'2–dc23
                                2013038917

10 9 8 7 6 5 4 3 2 1

Contents

Acknowledgments

First and foremost, we would like to thank our contributing authors, whose hard work and dedication made this book possible. The ideas in the book have been shaped by many stimulating discussions with our colleagues in the Fund, counterparts in member countries, and conference participants. While the list is too long to mention everyone by name, we owe them a great deal of gratitude. We are particularly grateful to our current and former colleagues from the Fiscal Affairs Department for making the department a stimulating environment for such an endeavor.

We are grateful to the IMF's External Relations Department and the MIT Press for their advice and efficient management of the production process. In particular, we would like to thank Sean Culhane and Patricia Loo at the IMF's External Relations Department, and Jane Macdonald and Dana Andrus at the MIT Press.

We are very grateful to Maria Tramuttola for outstanding editorial and logistical support.

The views expressed in the book are those of the authors and editors, and should not be attributed to the International Monetary Fund.

Foreword

For many countries the global financial crisis also turned into a fiscal crisis. Policy makers had to confront an extraordinarily challenging environment with fewer than usual economic weapons in their arsenals. In particular, monetary policy—the main traditional stabilization tool—was constrained, leaving fiscal policy to shoulder an unusually large burden. A combination of fiscal stimulus, collapse in output and fiscal revenues, along with, in some cases, expensive packages to rescue the financial system, strained public finances and resulted in higher government debt.

The unprecedented magnitude and scope of the crisis led to a broad rethinking of policy advice, including a call for a globally coordinated fiscal policy response. Later, as the macroeconomic outlook improved, policy makers shifted their attention to the task of reining in the surge in public debt—which can often be a lengthy undertaking. The issues covered in this book will therefore remain at the forefront of the fiscal policy debate for many years. *Post-crisis Fiscal Policy* is the first book by IMF staff entirely devoted to fiscal policy and the global crisis. It reflects the Fund's unique vantage point, gathered from helping our membership navigate the policy challenges of the past tumultuous years. It brings together much of the analysis that has guided the IMF's position on the evolving role of fiscal policy. In particular, it underscores how the global financial crisis has reshaped our understanding of the role of fiscal policy and has refocused the attention of the economics profession on fiscal sustainability issues.

While the analysis is deeply rooted in analytical work, the book is mostly non-technical and written with a wide audience in mind. I expect it to be of interest to policy makers and to those in think tanks, academe, and the financial media. I hope it contributes to an informed and productive public dialogue within our member countries as they confront the fiscal challenges of the future.

Christine Lagarde
Managing Director
The International Monetary Fund

Introduction

Carlo Cottarelli, Philip Gerson, and Abdelhak Senhadji

Fiscal policy makers have had to operate in an extraordinarily challenging environment over the last few years. First, they were confronted with an exceptionally large output shock, the biggest since the 1930s. Second, reflecting in large part the size of the shock but also the relatively weak fiscal position in many advanced economies in the period before the financial crisis, they quickly found their policy options constrained by spiraling deficits and a rapid buildup of public debt, which rose in some advanced economies to dizzying levels not seen since the end of the Second World War. Before long, policy options were further constrained by a loss of confidence in the ability of some countries to pay back their debts, as evidenced by a return to risk premia that had not been seen in advanced economies for many years. And throughout this period, the task for policy makers was further complicated by the need for fiscal policy to shoulder an unusually large share of the burden in responding to developments, with various factors conspiring to limit the capacity of monetary policy to deal with the shock.

In these unprecedented circumstances, the International Monetary Fund (IMF) advocated a policy response that was, for it, likewise unprecedented. At the outset of the crisis, in 2008, the IMF for the first time in its history called for a global fiscal expansion across all countries able to afford it, seemingly abandoning its long-held position that monetary policy, not fiscal policy, was the appropriate response to a deceleration in economic activity. Three considerations lay behind this change of view about the role of fiscal policy.

- The magnitude of the shock to the world economy was deemed so large that without a coordinated fiscal support, the world economy would not merely sink into recession but plunge into depression.
- While the recession had originated in a house-price boom and misbehavior in the financial sector, it soon evolved into a demand-deficiency recession. Lack of demand, abetted by uncertainty and rising unemployment, was driving output further and further down. Keynes's *General Theory* was the relevant textbook.

- With credit markets dysfunctional and private sector overhang in several advanced economies, the monetary lever ceased to work as well: even at close-to-zero money market rates, private sector demand remained weak.

As the global economy gradually improved and signs of tensions in some government paper markets became apparent, a process of fiscal adjustment started in 2010, first in emerging economies and then in advanced economies. Here, again, the IMF's views on how fiscal adjustment should be implemented reflected the specific challenges of the new situation. The Fund stressed that the speed of adjustment should vary across countries, reflecting, in particular, (1) the state of their public finances (countries with larger imbalances had to move more quickly), (2) market pressures (because of lower credibility, countries under market pressure had to move faster), and (3) the state of the economy and the impact that fiscal adjustment would have on it. Altogether, in countries that were not facing market pressures and had adopted credible medium-term fiscal adjustment plans, the IMF has recommended proceeding with deficit reduction at a steady, gradual pace, thus taking an intermediate position between the fiscal doves (who have argued that fiscal adjustment could be postponed altogether to provide continued support to demand) and the fiscal hawks (who have held that a front-loaded adjustment was needed to prevent a fiscal crisis or even—in some versions—to provide a burst of confidence that would jolt the private sector back to life). Two factors underpinned the Fund's emphasis on gradualism:

- First, as in the current environment, multipliers are likely to be high when output is demand-determined and the transmission mechanism of monetary policy is weak; indeed, in principle, it would be better to postpone adjustment to a time when private-sector demand is too strong, not too weak. However, a full postponement would not be credible with financial markets, which could eventually lose faith in promises that they would be repaid in better days (especially given the failure of many advanced economies to tighten fiscal policy during the "better days" that preceded the current crisis).
- Second, there is risk of too much of a good thing: fiscal adjustment leading to significant output deceleration can be counterproductive as markets, alarmed about the impact that continued falls in GDP would have on a country's creditworthiness, could push interest rates higher not lower, as confirmed by some econometric evidence on interest rate determinants (Cottarelli and Jaramillo 2012).

Of course, not all of the Fund's policy prescription is new. There is still a role for monetary policy, with the IMF arguing that fiscal adjustment should be accompanied by continued monetary relaxation, to help cushion the negative impact that even gradual deficit reduction will have on growth. Indeed, fiscal dominance should be avoided: relaxed monetary policy is not a substitute for fiscal adjustment. And the Fund continues to encourage countries to undertake structural reforms that boost potential output over the medium term, as strong growth has shown to greatly facilitate fiscal consolidation (World Economic Outlook, October 2012, IMF).

Unfortunately, the crisis in advanced economies is not yet over, and it is therefore too early to write its definitive history. Fiscal deficits and debt ratios remain high in many advanced economies, while output growth is still weak and unemployment in many countries at unacceptable levels. It is not, however, too early to begin drawing from the fiscal policy experience of the last few years, to help inform policy makers as they face the continued challenges from the crisis. This book comprises five parts, each containing several chapters. After part I provides the overarching analytical framework for the book, part II continues with a chronological review of the buildup of fiscal vulnerabilities that started well before the crisis. Part III presents the policy response during the crisis, and part IV the outlook and policy challenges ahead. Part V concludes with lessons learned and suggestions about the way forward.

Part I Assessing Fiscal Sustainability: An Analytical Framework

The five chapters in part I provide the analytical basis to the remainder of the book. Chapter 1 by Carlo Cottarelli develops a framework of rollover risk that integrates three dimensions: (1) the baseline projections of fiscal variables (stock and flow variables, asset and liability structure, and long-term age-related fiscal spending), (2) fiscal risks surrounding the baseline scenario (macroeconomic and fiscal policy shocks), and (3) other salient variables (nonfiscal variables and risk appetite). This framework is then used to discuss what triggers fiscal crises.

Chapter 2 by Carlo Cottarelli and Julio Escolano develops various practical methods to assess the sustainability of fiscal policies. Broadly, they fall into three categories: (1) gap measures based on the difference between the actual value of a fiscal magnitude, such as the primary balance, and the notional value that would meet specific criteria, such as hitting a target debt ratio in a specified time or satisfying the intertemporal budget constraint (IBC) of the government; (2) estimates of fiscal policy reaction functions (FPRF) that allow testing the consistency of these FPRFs with the IBC condition or the absence of Ponzi-game explosive debt dynamics; and (3) fiscal vulnerability indicators that can flag the likelihood of a future fiscal crisis or stress episode when prespecified threshold values are crossed (typically based on the past predictive power of the indicators). Finally, the chapter presents extensions of basic debt dynamics methodology for the treatment of government assets and the dynamics of net debt, and the methodological adjustments necessary to deal with foreign currency-denominated and inflation-indexed debt.

Julio Escolano in chapter 3 discusses the behavior of the interest-rate growth differential (IRGD), an essential variable in the dynamics of the public debt-to-GDP ratio. Economic growth theory suggests that the IRGD should be positive in economies on, or near, their balanced growth path. In advanced economies the IRGD has been indeed generally positive, close to 1 percentage point on average in the twenty years preceding the crisis. Any increase in the IRGD raises the primary balance required to stabilize the debt. In contrast, among emerging and developing economies, negative IRGDs predominate, often well below −10 percentage points. As a result many of these economies have been able to maintain a stable or a downward trend in their debt ratios despite persistent large primary deficits. The policy room provided by strongly negative IRGDs may, however, contract over time as a consequence of financial development and globalization. The chapter argues that negative IRGDs are not rooted in a long-term income catch-up process but in negative real interest rates brought about by financial repression that stunts economic growth.

Chapter 4 by Li Zeng first reviews some stylized facts about the primary fiscal balance and finds that while achieving a large primary fiscal surplus is not unusual, sustaining it over an extended period is quite uncommon. The chapter then estimates the empirical relationship between the primary fiscal balance and its underlying determinants, using both country fixed-effect and dynamic-panel data methods. Real economic growth is found to have a significant positive impact on the primary fiscal balance. There is also evidence that countries tend to run higher primary fiscal balances when faced with higher debt-to-GDP ratios. These findings are quite robust to sample selection, various model specifications, and the interest rate and forward-looking growth measures used in the regressions. Evidence is lacking, however, to support the conjecture that countries act more aggressively on fiscal consolidation when the public debt exceeds a certain threshold. Finally, the chapter illustrates how its empirical findings could be applied to predict a country's primary fiscal balance on the basis of its economic fundamentals. The predicted primary fiscal balance benchmark could be a helpful input in assessing whether, based on historical experience, government consolidation plans are realistic.

The fifth and last chapter in part I by Manmohan Kumar and Jaejoon Woo empirically investigates the extent to which large public debts will adversely impact investment, productivity, and growth, a critical question in the current environment of high debts in many advanced economies. In doing so, it pays particular attention to a variety of methodological issues, including reverse causality and simultaneity bias. The results suggest an inverse relationship between initial debt and subsequent growth, controlling for other determinants of growth. On average, a 10 percentage point increase in the initial debt-to-GDP ratio is associated over the medium to long run with a slowdown in real per capita GDP growth of around 0.2 percentage points per year, with the impact somewhat smaller in advanced economies than in emerging market economies. Some evidence suggests nonlinearity, with higher levels of initial debt having a proportionately larger negative effect on subsequent growth. Moreover, when a country's economic and financial position vis-à-vis the rest of the world is weak or the share of its foreign-currency denominated debt is large, the adverse impact of initial public debt on subsequent growth tends to be much more pronounced than when these factors are at more moderate levels.

Part II Buildup of Fiscal Vulnerabilities Prior to the Crisis

The four chapters of part II examine when and how fiscal vulnerabilities started to build up prior to the crisis. In doing so, these chapters also put the current crisis in historical perspective. Chapter 6 by Jiri Jonas and Iva Petrova examines the state of fiscal accounts in advanced and emerging economies from the postwar period until the outburst of the 2007 crisis, identifying some early symptoms of fiscal profligacy that eventually degenerated into fiscal stress. These symptoms include a secular upward trend in spending and a tendency to confuse temporary upswings in revenues as structural changes, leading to unanticipated revenue losses and deficit explosion during the crisis. In G7 countries, general government expenditures grew persistently, from 25 percent of GDP in 1950 to 40 percent in the early 1990s. Initially, increasing expenditures were paid for by increasing revenues, but these were eventually accommodated by wider deficits and growing debt. After reaching a postwar low of 35 percent of GDP in the mid-1970s, helped by a negative interest-growth differential, the debt-to-GDP ratio stood at 84 percent by the time the crisis erupted. The reduction in fiscal deficits in advanced economies just before the crisis reflected largely temporary factors: equity prices added about 1.5 percent of GDP to revenues in advanced G20 countries, while housing prices, at their peak prior to the crisis, improved revenues in several EU countries by about 2 percent of GDP. Overall, the underlying fiscal balance in many advanced economies was not as strong as it appeared and reduced the fiscal space to absorb the shock of the crisis. Pre-crisis improvements in the fiscal positions of emerging market economies were generally more robust. Moreover they were helped by lower borrowing costs and, in some cases, by high commodity prices.

Chapter 7 by S. Ali Abbas, Nazim Belhocine, Asmaa El-Ganainy, and Anke Weber takes an even longer view than the previous chapter to analyze the ongoing debt buildup in advanced countries in historical perspective, with a view to identifying significant drivers of debt accumulation and subsequent debt reductions. The findings suggest that the Great Accumulation episode of the 2000s reflected a mix of primary deficits, higher real interest rates, and stock-flow adjustments related to the banking and currency crisis, while unfavorable interest-growth differentials played a major role in the debt accumulation of the Great Depression of the 1930s. For large debt reductions since 1880, the primary balance did the heavy lifting, except in the post–World War II period, when negative interest-growth differentials in the context of capital controls and financial repression contributed favorably.

Chapter 8 by S. Ali Abbas, Nathaniel Arnold, Petra Dacheva, Mark De Broeck, Lorenzo Forni, Martine Guerguil, and Bruno Versailles focuses on the sovereign debt crisis in the euro area (EA). The chapter's goal is to identify the roots of the EA sovereign debt crisis with particular emphasis on why it affected the EA but not other large advanced economies. The chapter starts by documenting the considerable cross-country heterogeneity in fiscal performance across the EA in the pre-crisis era and identifies specific institutional and market failures that hampered fiscal convergence and amplified vulnerabilities. Deepening intra-EA imbalances and rising fiscal vulnerabilities in the first decade of the euro had planted the seeds of the crisis. When it broke, delays in elaborating a regional response undermined confidence in the EA's capacity to act as a policy entity. A concentration on fiscal adjustment, combined with banking sector weaknesses and lagging growth-supporting structural reforms, engendered negative feedback loops among fiscal consolidation, banks' balance sheets, and growth. The consolidation effort was further complicated by the adoption of nominal targets in the context of the EU fiscal framework, which emphasized fiscal policy's procyclical bent. The chapter concludes with observations on lessons learned and on the way forward for the EA.

Chapter 9 by John Norregaard, Aqib Aslam, Dora Benedek, and Thornton Matheson shows that current tax systems distort saving and financing behavior of individuals and firms by providing incentives for higher leverage, risk-taking, and the promotion of complicated financial instruments. Although tax policy did not directly cause the financial crisis, tax distortions increased the exposure to shocks and probably delayed recovery. The chapter discusses the channels through which tax policies may have caused this delay and suggests reform measures that should be considered to eliminate distortions in tax systems and promote economic stability. In particular, the debt bias in corporate finance represents a key tax distortion in most countries. While debt-financing costs are usually deductible from the corporate income tax base, returns on equity are not. This asymmetry provides a tempting incentive for excessive leverage. Similarly the differential tax treatment of capital income across various financial assets encourages risk-taking, including risks associated with complex and opaque financial instruments. Prevalence of low-tax jurisdictions also fosters excessive leverage by providing incentives for tax avoidance. Moreover executive compensations schemes are frequently designed in a way that promotes excessive risk-taking. Finally, favorable tax treatment of homeownership, reflected in elevated housing prices in many countries, contributed to a housing bubble and unsustainable mortgage-based borrowing. Tax reform measures are therefore needed in many countries to mitigate these adverse consequences and to help prevent future financial distress. Along with growth-friendly revenue mobilization efforts, new financial-sector taxes could be designed to correct existing externalities and to raise revenue.

Part III Management of Fiscal Policy during the Crisis

Part III is devoted to fiscal policy during the crisis. Chapter 10 by Thomas Baunsgaard, Alejandro Guerson, and Kyung-Seol Min analyzes how countries employed activist fiscal policies in response to the crisis. It provides an in-depth analysis of the timing, size, and composition of fiscal stimulus packages in advanced and emerging market economies and discusses issues related to their implementation. Contrary to widespread public belief, the fiscal stimulus was not the main reason for the substantial rise in fiscal deficits and debt ratios. By quantifying the relative contribution of various factors, the chapter finds that a decline in government revenues and, to a lesser extent, government support to the financial sector were the main factors behind the surge in deficits and debt ratios. Stimulus packages were well diversified across various revenue and expenditure instruments and were generally well coordinated, at least in the first phase of the crisis. Although fiscal stimulus packages varied across countries, an econometric analysis shows that these differences were generally consistent with each country's economic fundamentals, including available fiscal space, the severity of the downturn in domestic economic activity, the ability and space to use monetary policy, and the degree of trade openness that dilutes the effect of fiscal stimuli on the domestic economy.

Martine Guerguil, Marcos Poplawski-Ribeiro, and Anna Shabunina discuss in chapter 11 low-income African economies that seem to have been able to escape the procyclical fiscal bias that had plagued them for many decades. This helped mitigate the impact of the global crisis in the region. However, overall fiscal numbers mask two diverging and potentially troubling trends: current spending has been in most cases above budget plans, while capital outlays have been largely below. Empirical analysis suggests that the quality of governance and of budgetary institutions explains a sizable part of the difference between intended and observed current expenditure. In contrast, the under-execution of investment projects seems mostly due to political factors. This implementation gap between current and capital spending casts a shadow over future fiscal space, as the growing weight of not easily reversed current outlays intensifies spending rigidity and likely contributes to the observed drift in deficits even as growth has recovered. Further strengthening of the institutions and processes governing public investment is needed to avoid a return to fiscal procyclicality.

The Great Recession has refocused attention on the effectiveness of fiscal policy as a countercyclical tool and has revived the debate about the size of fiscal multipliers, the topic of chapter 12 by Aiko Mineshima, Marcos Poplawski-Ribeiro, and Anke Weber. The chapter underscores the continued lack of consensus about the size of fiscal multipliers, which measure the impact of fiscal policy on output. Although there seems to be broad agreement that expansionary fiscal policy has a positive impact on growth, at least in the short term, it is unclear whether fiscal multipliers are larger or smaller than unity. Based on a comprehensive survey of the literature, the chapter concludes that the size of first-year government spending multipliers lies between 0.3 and 1.0 during normal times, with revenue multipliers being significantly smaller. The size of multipliers tends to be influenced by various factors, however, including the state of the economy, monetary policy stance, degree of openness, level of debt, and types of fiscal instruments used. In particular, recent studies, including original work summarized in this chapter, suggest that multipliers could be significantly larger during economic downturns than during economic expansions. The finding has important policy implications for the design of fiscal adjustment plans. In particular, it suggests that when feasible, a gradual adjustment is preferable to a frontloaded one.

Chapter 13 by Mika Kortelainen, Douglas Laxton, and Jack Selody uses the International Monetary Fund's Global Integrated Monetary and Fiscal Model (GIMF) to illustrate the increased effectiveness of expansionary fiscal policy when monetary policy accommodates the shock, such as was the case in the 2008 to 2009 coordinated fiscal expansion. To accomplish this, the authors introduce simple fiscal policy and monetary policy rules into the model to show the dynamics of policy coordination. They also show how features such as financial accelerators affect the dynamics of policy coordination. The chapter examines three scenarios. The first simulates an expansionary fiscal policy when the monetary policy rate has not reached its lower bound and shows that fiscal policy is much more effective when accommodated by monetary policy. The second scenario highlights that even when the policy rate is at its lower bound, an expansionary fiscal policy could be still quite effective if accompanied by unconventional monetary policy easing. Finally, the third scenario illustrates the counterproductive nature of expansionary fiscal policy when markets perceive the debt path to be unsustainable.

Chapter 14 by Ceyla Pazarbasioglu, Uffe Mikkelsen, and Suchitra Kumarapathy examines financial sector support during the crisis with a particular emphasis on the extent to which costs differed across countries. More specifically, it describes the types of central bank and government support provided to the financial sector during the crisis, quantifies the initially pledged and actually utilized government support measures across countries, and compares the costs of current crisis interventions with costs during earlier episodes. The chapter shows that extensive public support has been provided to restore confidence in the financial system. As the crisis unfolds, its fiscal costs remain uncertain, but so far it is evident they have differed widely across countries. Compared to previous crises, governments to date have relied more on containment—through central bank liquidity provision and guarantees of bank liabilities—and less on restructuring banks' assets. This approach has given rise to large contingent liabilities as risks are transferred from private to government balance sheets, but in most cases the approach has limited initial fiscal outlays. Importantly, this approach delays the much needed restructuring of banking and corporate sectors, critical for their viability and profitability. This risks transferring the costs of the crisis into the future and extending the economic downturn.

Chapter 15 by Borja Gracia, Jimmy McHugh, and Tigran Poghosyan assesses the impact of the global crisis on subnational governments (SNGs) using disaggregated state level data for eight large highly decentralized countries—namely Australia, Brazil, Canada, China, Germany, Mexico, Spain, and the United States. The chapter finds that the crisis adversely affected SNGs in advanced countries, primarily through a steep reduction in output, which in turn generated a decline in own revenues. SNGs in emerging economies were less affected as economic activity held up comparatively well. The chapter also examines the short-run policy response of SNGs. In general, SNGs operated countercyclical policies, maintaining and in some cases increasing expenditure levels, compared to the pre-crisis period, owing to transfers from the central government in the context of national stimulus packages. At the same time, there was some limited relaxation of SNG budget rules and borrowing constraints. The crisis exacerbated long-run sustainability challenges for many SNGs. A considerable part of revenue declines was structural. Given the current plans of central governments to withdraw the stimulus packages, SNGs should put in place reforms to tackle the structural gap between the higher post-crisis level of expenditures and permanently lower revenues.

Part IV Post-crisis Fiscal Outlook

Part IV of the book covers the post-crisis fiscal outlook and risks in advanced and emerging economies, highlighting both short- and long-term fiscal challenges and risks to fiscal sustainability. Chapter 16 by Laura Jaramillo and Pablo Lopez-Murphy uses scenario analysis to illustrate the fiscal challenges facing advanced and emerging economies. The financial crisis left many countries, especially advanced economies, with a dangerous combination of high debt and high fiscal deficits. Over the medium term, even as crisis-related measures are unwound, headline deficit-to-GDP ratios are not expected to return to pre-crisis levels without fiscal adjustment measures. Although revenues are expected to recover from their current cyclical weakness, they are not projected to resume their original (pre-crisis) path because of what has been regarded as a permanent loss of potential GDP, a feature of most financial sector crises. Correspondingly, expenditure is expected to remain high in terms of GDP, despite sizable expenditure cuts, owing to a combination of lower expected potential GDP and new spending pressures, including debt servicing costs and age-related spending. As overall balances are expected to narrow only gradually, debt ratios are expected to remain high over the medium term, especially in several large advanced countries. Debt is expected to take a downward path in emerging economies, supported by relatively strong GDP growth. Nonetheless, underlying this positive outlook for emerging market economies are relatively benign assumptions regarding interest rates and growth trends. Therefore, looking ahead, all countries face important risks that could derail debt reduction. These risks include policy implementation challenges, greater macroeconomic uncertainty—over interest rates, growth, and the exchange rate—and the possibility that large contingent liabilities materialize.

Chapter 17 by Lorenzo Forni and Marialuz Moreno Badia analyzes what the goal of fiscal adjustment should be and the extent to which other nonconventional measures can help in restoring and maintaining market confidence. It argues that despite considerable adjustment, many countries still have a long way to go. Thus it is essential to calibrate the pace of adjustment for the long haul, taking into account the state of the economy and funding pressures. Central banks also have a role to play by implementing supportive monetary policies and ensuring the proper working of credit markets. On the other hand, financial repression (with or without inflation) is unlikely to produce a large payoff as a captive domestic investor base may be difficult to achieve in a globalized world. The privatization of nonfinancial assets promises a somewhat larger potential to reduce the debt burden, although it may be difficult to realize in the short term. Finally, debt restructuring may be unavoidable in some cases, but this could have large costs particularly if public debt is in the hands of domestic residents.

Chapter 18 by Xavier Debrun and Andrea Schaechter examines the *Institutional Reforms and Fiscal Adjustment*. It reviews recent developments in the establishment of institutions specifically aimed at fostering fiscal discipline and counter-cyclicality. The chapter argues that the mixed results obtained with fiscal policy rules in the run-up to the 2008 to 2009 crisis have favored the emergence of a new generation of institutions. First, fiscal rules are now designed to better respond to cyclical output movements and are equipped with explicit enforcement mechanisms. Second, the growing number of independent fiscal councils signals countries' interest in other forms of legitimate constraints on fiscal discretion, involving better operation of checks and balances in the political system and greater awareness by the electorate. Third, these new institutions are backed by public financial management reforms aimed at a stronger medium-term orientation of the budget. While welcome, these developments are no panacea. The implementation of more complex rules raise significant challenges, and experience with fiscal councils remains too limited to distill credible best practice.

In chapter 19 Baoping Shang and Mauricio Soto focus on public spending on pensions and health care; they discuss the rapid growth and projected increase of these costs, respectively, by 3.5 and 2 percentage points of GDP in advanced and emerging economies over the next two decades. Such increases will add to the already urgent need for fiscal adjustment in many countries. For countries with large projected spending increases and limited fiscal space, the challenge is to contain the growth of public pension and health spending without adversely affecting the social objectives of these programs. The viable options to contain pension spending include curtailing eligibility (e.g., by increasing the retirement age), reducing benefits, or increasing contributions. While all of these options involve apparent trade-offs, increasing the retirement age has many advantages. Containing public health spending requires a mix of macro-level controls, such as imposing budget caps, and micro-level efficiency-enhancing reforms, such as strengthening market mechanisms. For countries where coverage is still limited and with available fiscal space to increase spending, the challenge is to expand coverage while keeping the systems on a fiscally sustainable path. While these countries also need to improve the efficiency of current spending, they could consider providing basic pension and health benefits to the entire population financed by general tax revenues.

In chapter 20 Mika Kortelainen, Douglas Laxton, and Jack Selody examine the general equilibrium model outlined in chapter 13. This chapter illustrates how combining fiscal consolidation with structural reform and coordinated fiscal policy can reduce public-sector indebtedness, encourage growth, and lower global imbalances for all participating countries. On the one hand, fiscal consolidation is typically associated with shrinking current-account deficits and slowing growth. On the other hand, structural and fiscal reform creates the potential for the world economy to grow while rebalancing global demand. The potential for a virtuous circle to arise is illustrated in two parts. First, structural and fiscal reforms are combined with fiscal consolidation in deficit countries to show that even without monetary policy, easing the result of coordinated policy action is positive for participating countries. Then, fiscal consolidation is combined with monetary easing to show that coordinating these actions is positive for the world economy and does not generate inflation in the major developed economies, even in the absence of increased potential growth from structural and fiscal reforms.

Chapter 21 concludes with some policy lessons from the crisis.

Reference

Cottarelli, C., and L. Jaramillo. 2012. Walking hand in hand: Fiscal policy and growth in advanced economies. Working Paper 12/137. International Monetary Fund, Washington, DC. Available via the Internet: http://www.imf.org/external/pubs/cat/longres.aspx?sk=25946.0.

Part I

Assessing Fiscal Sustainability: An Analytical Framework

1

Fiscal Sustainability and Fiscal Risk: An Analytical Framework

Carlo Cottarelli

1.1 Introduction

Developments over the last few years have evidenced the damaging effects of fiscal crises on economic activity. The term "fiscal crisis" here refers to the difficulty the government experiences in rolling over its debt. This difficulty shows up in forms of varying intensity, from the need to pay higher interest rates on government paper to a complete loss of market access. These difficulties reverberate through the economy, as higher risk premia are applied also to private sector borrowers and as increased uncertainty on future prospects discourages investment and consumption. Inevitably, economic growth suffers as evidenced by the experience of several euro area countries during 2011 to 2012, and of several emerging economies during the past decades. This chapter discusses the factors that affect markets' perceptions of the risk of a fiscal crisis, or of rollover problems. Clearly, this perception does not depend on any single fiscal indicator, certainly not just on the level of debt: interest rates, which should reflect the average perception of investors about the rollover risks, are currently very different across advanced economies with the same debt ratio. As another example, debt tolerance has traditionally been seen to be lower for emerging economies, involving lower debt thresholds in assessing their exposure to risk. Thus things are more complicated.

The objective of this chapter is to provide a sort of "checklist" or a way of framing the analysis of the relevant factors, rather than to provide a specific quantitative assessment of what affects the perception of rollover risks, and hence risk premia. In the process, I will comment on the key challenges that economies are facing following the deterioration of the fiscal accounts in 2008 to 2009, thus providing a "road map" for the entire volume. Section 1.2 will review some basic concepts and present the conceptual framework used to discuss rollover risks, breaking down the analysis into factors affecting the baseline fiscal projections, the risks around those projections, and other relevant factors affecting the perception of rollover risks. These three components (baseline, risks around the baseline, and other

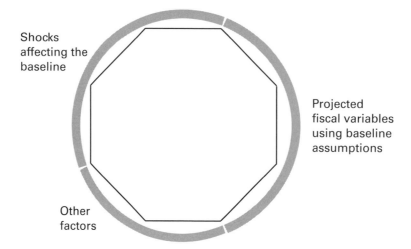

Shocks affecting the baseline

Projected fiscal variables using baseline assumptions

Other factors

Figure 1.1
Risk octagon

factors) will then be discussed in turn in the next three sections. Section 1.6 concludes.

1.2 Some Basic Concepts

The factors affecting rollover risks will be summarized in a "risk octagon," with each side of the octagon representing one risk dimension (figure 1.1). What are the key risk dimensions?

Figure 1.1 identifies three main risk areas referring to (1) the baseline fiscal projections (with three different risk dimensions); (2) fiscal risks, that is, the risks that the baseline fiscal projections will not materialize (also with three risk dimensions); and (3) other factors (two additional dimensions).

Let us consider the first area. What are the most relevant fiscal variables that affect the perception of rollover risks? Borrowers can face difficulties in rolling over their debt for a number of reasons, not necessarily related to their economic and financial conditions. Lenders can, for example, become illiquid and require the repayment of their debt. Illiquidity problems can also arise because of monetary policy: a monetary tightening would raise interest rates.

We are here, however, concerned about rollover problems arising from the markets' perception that the government may be unable to service all its debt. For a sovereign operating in relatively developed and liquid financial markets, these rollover problems necessarily involve doubts about government solvency.[1] The term "government insolvency" refers to a balance sheet condition in which the net worth of the government, in the absence of debt repudiation, is negative.[2]

Thus a good starting point to assess the factors affecting the perception of rollover risks is the government solvency condition, stating that the net present value of its non-interest revenues minus its non-interest expenditures—or, alternatively, the net present value of its primary balance—is equal to (or higher than) its net debt.[3] While a more detailed treatment of this condition is given in chapter 2, it is worth here recalling that in cases where the interest rate on government debt is higher than the growth rate of the economy, the intertemporal budget constraint of the government is always met when the public (net) debt-to-GDP ratio is stable. In turn, the latter is stable when the primary balance, in relation to GDP, is equal to the differential between the interest rate on public debt and the growth rate of the economy (scaled by one plus the GDP growth rate) times the debt ratio:[4]

$$pb = [(i - g)/(1+g)]d,$$

where d is the stock of net debt at the end of the previous period, pb is the primary balance during the current period, i is the average nominal interest rate on public debt, and g is the nominal growth rate of GDP.[5] All this implies that assessing solvency risks, given a certain initial debt stock, requires, as a starting point, looking at baseline projections for the primary balance, the interest rate on public debt, and the growth rate of GDP (what we will call "fiscal fundamentals"). It should be underscored that what matters is not only the current values of these variables but their future values too.

One clarification is in order, though. The interest rate on government debt reflects in itself markets' assessment of rollover risks. It is therefore the variable that needs to be explained. It is important to focus on what affects the interest rate. Among these factors is the composition of government assets and liabilities, as well as the strength of its investors' base.

Altogether, the first risk area of the octagon (baseline projections for fiscal variables) includes three dimensions of risk: (1) short-term projections on fiscal fundamentals, (2) longer term projections on fiscal fundamentals, and (3) asset and liability management variables, affecting, other conditions being the same, the interest rate on government debt.

The second area refers to shocks that may move fiscal outcomes away from the baseline, or, in the jargon of public financial management, what we call "fiscal risks."[6] These are relevant because the higher the uncertainty around the baseline (particularly the higher is the likelihood of negative shocks), the higher will be the risk premium required by markets to cover the rollover risk. Three kinds of shocks will be considered: macroeconomic shocks (essentially on output and inflation), shocks from contingent liabilities, and policy shocks.

Finally, the third area includes two residual dimensions: the first one refers to non-fiscal variables that can influence the perception of rollover risks; the second refers to the market's attitude toward risk-taking.

1.3 Baseline Fiscal Projections

1.3.1 Short-Term Fiscal Fundamentals

As noted, assessing rollover risks requires forming a view on how the primary balance will evolve over time, in relation to an initial debt stock.

Observers of fiscal variables and interest rates spreads in 2011 may soon reach the conclusion that fiscal fundamentals do not matter much. Among advanced economies, the two countries with the highest primary deficit in 2011 were Japan and the United States. Yet these countries could borrow at low rates in both real and nominal terms.[7] Definitely, this shows that current key fiscal variables are not the only thing that matters in affecting risk perception. But do they matter at all?

Econometric evidence suggests that current fiscal variables are important (e.g., see Cottarelli and Jaramillo 2012; Baldacci et al. 2011; Ardagna 2009). The point, however, is fairly evident by simple data inspection. Figure 1.2 reports primary balance gaps (the difference between the primary balance and the primary balance that would stabilize the debt-to-GDP ratio at the current interest and growth rates) and debt ratios for advanced economies in 2011. The size of each country balloon is proportional to the ten-year CDS spread for that country. All large balloons cor-

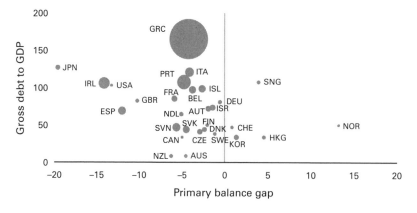

Figure 1.2

Advanced economies: Primary balance gap versus debt-to-GDP ratio, 2011. The primary balance gap is the difference between the actual primary balance in 2011 and the primary balance that would stabilize debt at 2011 level. CDS spreads are for end-period. Net debt for Australia, Canada, Japan, and New Zealand.

Sources: IMF, *Fiscal Monitor,* October 2012; Markit

respond to a combination of high primary gap and high debt. Also there are some small balloons in that area, suggesting that if a combination of high primary deficit and high debt is not a sufficient condition to be under market pressure, it is at least a necessary condition.

The sharp deterioration in primary balances during 2008 and 2009, particularly in advanced economies, is documented in chapter 7. How large should the primary balance adjustment be? And would such a correction be feasible and sustainable?

From a technical point of view, restoring fiscal solvency simply requires bringing the primary balance to a level that stabilizes the debt-to-GDP ratio, given certain assumptions on the interest-rate–growth differential. Debt stability, even at a very high level, is all that is needed. However, there are various reasons why the goal of fiscal adjustment cannot just be the stabilization of the debt ratio at any level. First, the higher the debt level is, the more a country is exposed to interest rate and growth shocks: when debt is high, an increase in interest rates requires a higher adjustment in the primary balance to absorb it, and this exposure raises the premium that a country has to pay to roll over its debt. Second, and related, several (although not all) empirical studies show an inverse relationship between public debt and growth (see chapter 5), at least beyond a certain debt threshold. All this points at the need to improve the primary balance with the goal not only of stabilizing the debt ratio but also of lowering it (see medium-term adjustment scenarios discussed in IMF 2012a).

As to whether a correction would be feasible and sustainable, there are two issues:

- The first relates to the magnitude of the correction and the cost that a fiscal tightening would have for economic activity. The evidence suggests that the fiscal multiplier can be sizable when output is below potential and when the economy is in a liquidity trap (see chapter 12) so that the cost of a fiscal tightening, in term of forgone output, can be sizable. Financial markets seems to have focused quite a lot on this link between fiscal adjustment and growth during 2011 and 2012, which is one key reason why interest rates remained high for countries undertaking sizable fiscal adjustments (e.g., see the discussion in Cottarelli and Jaramillo 2012). This said, a fiscal tightening caused only a temporary deceleration in growth (and even the effect on the level of output should eventually fade away).
- The second relates to the economic and political difficulty of keeping the primary balance at a high level for a prolonged period of time. This takes us to the second dimension of the risk octagon.

1.3.2 Future Developments in Fiscal Variables

The second dimension of the risk octagon refers to the future evolution of the primary balance, as well as the future growth rate. Given the intertemporal nature of the government's budget constraint, the current deficit should play only a minor role in assessing fiscal solvency risks. What matters is the future level of primary balances, since this affects the long-term dynamics of the debt ratio. This has several implications for assessing fiscal solvency risks.

First, it is important to correct the primary balance for any temporary factors that may affect its current level, hence the importance of looking at cyclically adjusted primary balances. Correcting fiscal balances for the output cycle is by now fairly common practice. Less common, regrettably, is to correct the primary balance for the effect of other cyclical factors (e.g., asset price and commodity price cycles) as well as for a host of other temporary factors (e.g., temporary revenues or spending) (Bornhorst et al. 2011). Primary balances should also, of course, take into account announced policy changes if they are credible enough to affect the baseline.

Second, factors affecting long-term spending and revenue trends should be closely considered. Among spending trends, those related to spending for pension and health care are particularly important, given the magnitude of the projected increase (see chapter 19). Among revenue trends, of particular importance for emerging economies are trends in revenues from exhaustible resources.[8] One issue is the relative importance of these long-term spending trends vis-à-vis short- and medium-term developments. The empirical evidence that some of these long-term trends affect interest rates is at present very limited. For example, we are not aware of studies showing that spending trends in health care and pension spending affect interest rates or yields. On the contrary, Cottarelli and Jaramillo (2012) show that markets seem to primarily focus on current fiscal variables such as the current public debt and deficit ratios. It is, however, true that poor trends in entitlement spending are often quoted by market analysts as signaling severe fiscal weaknesses. Thus more work is needed in this area to quantify the impact of these long-term trends on measures of risk perception. In any case, even if the impact is limited in the short run, addressing these challenges would still be important to avoid future increases in interest rates when they eventually materialize.

Finally, and perhaps more crucial, is the issue of the economic and political sustainability of keeping the primary balance at high levels for a prolonged time. Keeping the primary balance high means keeping taxation and public spending at respectively higher and lower levels than in other countries, with negative effects on competitiveness and growth, with related political difficulties. Chapter 4 discusses the evidence of what affects the primary balance in the medium term in normal circumstances, thus providing a benchmark for assessing the difficulty of running primary balances above the norm. One important factor is growth, as there is evidence that higher growth rates tend to be associated with higher primary balances, although it is less clear whether this effect goes beyond cyclical factors in a significant way.[9] Altogether, concerns about public debt sustainability hinge on whether markets believe countries will do what it takes to keep the primary balance at a sufficiently high level to stabilize or, as discussed, lower the debt ratio. If they perceive the absence of an adequate resolve to do so, fear of debt restructuring will arise with negative implications for rollover risks. [10]

One final comment relates to various factors that can affect the perception that medium-term fiscal trends will be benign despite the difficulties inherent in fiscal adjustment. Among these, one should include fiscal institutions promoting fiscal rectitude (see the discussion below on the likelihood of fiscal policy shocks). More generally, perceptions that fiscal rectitude is a core value for the population can also affect market perceptions that adjustment will eventually take place.[11]

1.3.3 Assets and Liability Structure and the Investor Base

While, in principle, the analysis of solvency can be conducted in terms of net debt, in practice, the likelihood of a rollover crisis depends a lot on the composition of assets and liabilities in terms of maturity, currency denomination, and characteristics of the investor base.

Maturity is important because it affects the borrowing requirement that the government has to face in each period: this matters because the lower the financing requirements are, the lower the risk that underlying fiscal solvency concerns will lead to a rollover crisis before they can be addressed though policy actions. Maturity is also important because it affects the speed at which a shock on market interest rates carries over to the average interest rate on government debt. In this respect, the situation of some advanced countries that have been under financial market pressure during 2010 and 2012 would have been much worse if these countries had entered the crisis with shorter debt maturity (figure 1.3).

Currency composition matters because the revenues of the government are usually denominated in domestic currency. If debt is denominated in foreign currency, the government can be exposed to exchange-rate risk: for example, real exchange-rate depreciation would make it more difficult for the government to meet its intertemporal budget constraint, since the debt stock would increase without a commensurate increase in its revenues. A second and perhaps more important reason (which may explain some of the features of the recent crisis in the euro area) is that if debt is denominated in a currency that the government cannot print through its central bank, the government paper market will not benefit from the existence of a lender of last resort, in case doubts arise about the government's ability to service its debt (see below).

The characteristics of the investor base are relevant because they affect the stability of the investment decision and hence the likelihood that a rollover crisis arises. In this respect, several considerations are relevant:

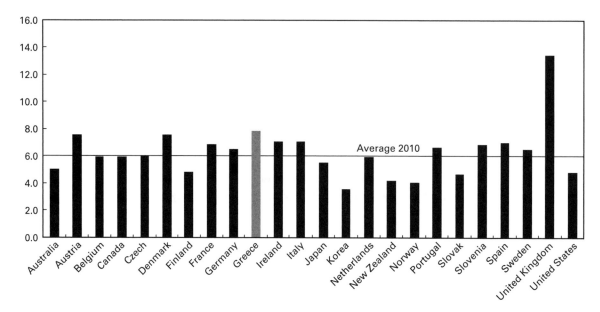

Figure 1.3
Maturity of government debt, August 2010 (years)
Sources: Bloomberg; IMF, *Fiscal Monitor,* November 2010

- The first is the split between domestic and foreign residents. Domestic residents are perceived to be less volatile, which can be explained by home bias effects (including moral suasion) and by the fact that defaulting on government debt is much less attractive if debt is held by residents (as noted above, default/restructuring is also a tax). This can be a decisive factor and is probably the key reason why interest rates on Japanese government paper are relatively low despite very high deficit and debt ratios.

- Financial repression can greatly enhance the stability of the investor base and thus lower governments' borrowing costs. This is a key reason why many developing economies benefit from low real interest rates and are thus able to have favorable debt dynamics with weak primary balances (chapter 4).

- Institutional investors (like insurance companies) are also perceived to be less volatile.

- The presence of foreign official investors can lower the perception of risk under certain conditions. Official lending is likely to be less affected by the vagaries of market sentiment, but it may be affected by political considerations. An additional consideration is whether official lending receives a preferred creditor status with respect to ordinary investors. If it does, an increase in the share of official lending could reduce the likelihood of a crisis but does increase the cost for the private sector of a crisis if that occurs. Increased recognition of this effect, for example, the restructuring of Greek debt in 2011, has reduced the beneficial effect of official lending in the most recent period.

- Foreign central banks play a special role. If a currency has achieved "reserve currency" status, foreign central banks will invest in it. This will increase the investor base and can greatly lower the cost of borrowing. This is indeed one key reason why interest rates in the United States remain so low despite the weakening in their fiscal accounts in recent years: the share of US Treasury paper held by foreign central banks has reached about one-third in 2012 (against about one-fifth at the end of the 1990s).

- Finally, the presence in the market of the central bank can significantly lower the borrowing costs for the government, as long as this does not affect inflation expectations. As discussed in Cottarelli and Jaramillo (2012), this occurs for two reasons. First, there is a direct quantitative effect: the larger the share of central bank purchases, the lower is the amount of debt that needs to be sold outside the public sector. Second, there is a key liquidity effect: the presence of the central bank ensures that a rollover crisis cannot happen, since the central bank has inexhaustible resources to repay government debt coming due. The catch, of course, is that if the presence of the central bank leads to a loss of confidence in the value of the currency, nominal interest rates would start reflecting not only a higher inflation expectation but also an inflation/devaluation risk premium, which can be quite high. So it is critical that the use of the printing press does not lead to a higher inflation expectation. In the context of a surge in demand for liquidity after 2009, these conditions have been met and the financing of increased amounts of government debt since then has been greatly facilitated by the intervention of central banks in the government paper market (as in the United Kingdom and the United States).

1.4 Fiscal Risks

The second risk area concerns possible sources of shocks to the baseline. I focus explicitly on three sources of shocks: shocks from contingent liabilities (particularly those arising from the financial sector), macroeconomic shocks, and policy shocks.

1.4.1 Shocks from Contingent Liabilities
Traditionally, fiscal analysis has focused on contingent liabilities arising from contractual obligations of governments, such as public-private partnerships. But it is now clear that noncontractual commitments are also critical. And those arising from the financial sector can have devastating effects on the fiscal accounts, as was seen during the recent crisis. The direct support to the financial system provided by the

eight countries most affected by the financial crisis ranges from 3 percent of GDP in the United States to 38 percent of GDP in Ireland, after taking into account the recovery (so far) of what was initially injected. The range is very large, as a result of a number of factors discussed in chapter 14.

1.4.2 Macroeconomic Shocks

The second source of shock relates to macroeconomic assumptions, particularly growth, interest-rate, and exchange-rate assumptions. These shocks can operate by affecting revenues and spending, or by affecting the value of government assets and liabilities. Long-lasting shocks are, of course, more relevant. As discussed, growth is especially important because it affects not only the debt-to-GDP dynamics, given a certain primary balance, but also the primary balance, given certain policy settings.

The traditional approach followed in this area is to look at fan charts describing how certain fiscal variables, such as the debt-to-GDP ratio, are affected by shocks. These shocks are typically distributed around a baseline assumed to be unbiased, with the magnitude of the fan charts reflecting the volatility of shocks around past regression lines. However, in assessing forward-looking risks, it is also important to keep in mind that the baseline may be biased. Here it is worth mentioning two factors that are particularly important in assessing current medium-term fiscal projections (as discussed in chapter 16).

The first is that current IMF (as well as consensus) baseline projections are based on the assumption that the crisis led to a major loss of potential output that is not going to be recovered even in the medium term. Figure 1.4 reports the *World Eco-*

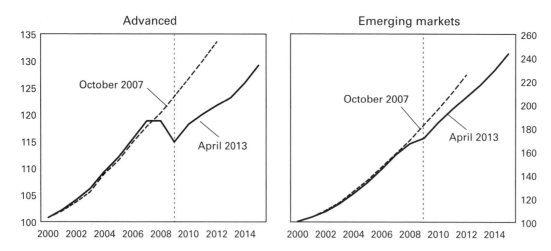

Figure 1.4
Real GDP in advanced and emerging economies.
Sources: IMF, *World Economic Outlook*, October 2007 and April 2013

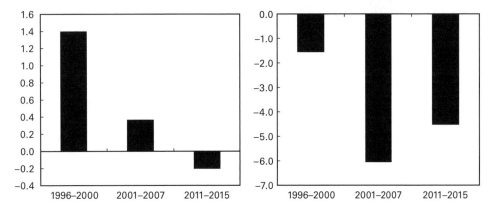

Figure 1.5
Interest-rate–growth differential (in percent)
Sources: IMF, *Fiscal Monitor,* November 2010; IMF staff estimates

nomic Outlook (WEO) projections for advanced and emerging economies before the crisis. These are compared with the fall 2010 WEO projections: output levels never catch up with the original baseline. The corresponding revenue loss for advanced economies equals about 3 percentage points of GDP, a huge amount. This output projection is based on the experience of the previous financial crisis, but there were exceptions in the past. With this evidence some commentators have argued that particularly with respect to the United States, the current concerns about fiscal prospects are much too pessimistic: the fiscal deficits were caused by the economic crisis and will go away when the crisis is over.

The second factor relates to possible overoptimism on baseline interest rate projections. In the fall 2012 WEO projections, the interest-rate–growth differential in the coming five years is quite low by historical standards, indeed negative on average (figure 1.5). This is possible in a period of still low growth and ample liquidity provided by the central bank to financial sector markets (and, for some countries, directly to the government paper market, as discussed above). But, at the same time, the debt stock has increased rapidly for advanced economies since 2007, and this will over time put pressure on interest rates.

The interest-rate–growth differential is also a source of uncertainty for emerging economies. The favorable fiscal outlook for these countries discussed in chapter 16 is premised on the continuation of a largely negative differential. As discussed above, there is an economic puzzle here. Economic theory tells us that this differential cannot be negative for a long time because, otherwise, agents could borrow and invest more, financing the capital accumulation with increased income later (which should drive up interest rates). And yet the differential has been negative, on average, for emerging economies for decades. This issue and its political implications are discussed in chapter 3.

1.4.3 Fiscal Policy Shocks

The third kind of shock relates to fiscal policy itself, namely to the possibility that policies deviate from those underlying the baseline. The traditional approach in discussing this risk is to rely on estimates of fiscal policy reaction functions and to use the residuals of such estimates to assess the risks of significant deviations from the projected baseline. However, this is where it is important to take into account also the possibility that changes in fiscal institutions affect the way policies are implemented.

Strengthening of budgetary institutions, introducing fiscal rules, and setting up independent fiscal councils to monitor fiscal developments can reduce the risk of deviations of policies from initial policy announcement (e.g., see Debrun et al. 2009, and chapter 18). In the same vein, credible reporting of fiscal data is essential: the ex post discovery that earlier fiscal reporting was incorrect can damage credibility and results in higher interest rates (for more details, see IMF 2012b), as evidenced by the recent experience of some euro area countries (particularly Greece). Country-specific political shocks are also critical in assessing the likelihood of possible changes in the fiscal policy course reflected in the baseline, and they may affect market perceptions of debt sustainability quite sharply. Last, but definitely not least, good communication of policy intentions is critical in affecting market perception of policy risk. Many of the problems that have emerged in the last few years, for individual countries and the whole euro area, have reflected difficulties in presenting policy intentions in a convincing way.

1.5 Other Risk Dimensions

The last risk area includes risk dimensions that are not directly fiscal but can affect indirectly the perceived risk in investing in government paper.

1.5.1 Nonfiscal Fundamentals

It is now apparent that the likelihood of a fiscal crisis also depends not only on the public sector balance sheet but also on the overall conditions of the economy, including the availability of overall saving to finance it, the growth rate of the economy, and the likelihood of spillovers from the rest of the economy to the public sector via contingent liabilities.

Two additional channels are worth discussing. The first relates to the magnitude of private-sector debt. There seems to be growing consensus that high levels of private debt increase the risk of speculative attack against government paper. This could be due not only to the fact that high private debt can lead to contingent liabilities for the government but also to the possibility that a private-sector debt crisis leads to lower growth and to an increase of country risk with inevitable spillovers for the public sector.

The second relates to the existence of an external imbalance: countries facing twin deficits are more likely to suffer speculative attacks, which could also lead to a run out of government paper. The reason could be that an external imbalance signals an overvalued exchange rate, and real exchange-rate depreciation would make it more difficult to service external debt. This happens regardless of whether the equilibrium is restored through a nominal depreciation or through an internal devaluation: in the case of a nominal depreciation, the public debt-to-GDP ratio increases as the exchange rate is depreciated without a commensurate improvement in the primary balance. In the case of an internal devaluation, the debt ratio also increases because the GDP deflator declines. Again, the experience of some euro area countries with sizable external imbalances in the last few years illustrates how markets are sensitive to this issue.

1.5.2 Risk Appetite

The last dimension of risk is essentially what we could call general (i.e., not fiscal specific) market sentiment or risk appetite. Given all other variables that we have discussed, and risks surrounding these variables, a higher propensity by markets to take up risk reduces the likelihood of a crisis in all countries. This is tricky, though, as, with respect to a *worsening* in risk appetite, we need to distinguish between two groups of countries. On the one hand, there are those that are considered as safe havens. These are countries where the risk of a crisis is, for whatever reason, regarded as low and that may therefore attract investments in government paper from other countries. In the recent past this effect has benefited the US and German government paper markets. Other countries would, to varying degree, suffer from these outflows. The overall result is that cross-country differences in risk perception—as signaled by interest-rate differentials—would deepen when overall risk appetite weakens. More work is needed to evaluate what makes a country a "safe haven." It seems that some underlying strength based on the evaluation of the risk factors discussed above is what gives a country a safe haven status and makes it easier to finance its deficit, particularly at times of low risk appetite. But one point seems clear, namely that the status of safe haven is not something that is cast in bronze and countries cannot abuse it in the long run by exploiting their possibility to borrow at low rates: countries benefit from this status as long as they do not abuse it.

1.6 Conclusions

The discussion above confirms the complexity of the factors affecting the perception of rollover risks and explains why it is often difficult to draw conclusions based on a limited number of indicators. In principle, the various risk dimensions could be quantified and overall risk developments could be followed through like a "cobweb" expanding within the risk octagon. This said, several caveats need to be considered in applying that framework, especially if one intends to move from a multidimension approach to a single summary indicator of risk.

First, the risk dimensions are not independent from each other, including with respect to fiscal policy decisions. For example, a weakening in the fiscal baseline can reflect the expected materialization of some risks, and therefore be accompanied by an improvement in some risk dimensions, and vice versa. Second, various elements of risks could move in the same direction: for example, a weakening of market sentiment can lead not only to a weakening in the corresponding dimension but also to a reduction in maturity composition, and hence a weakening in the asset and liability management dimension.

Second, further work is needed to assess the relative importance of the various dimensions. This will not be easy: econometric regressions require necessarily parsimonious specifications. Yet it would be important to identify more precisely the relative contributions of the various factors described by the octagon, a necessary step to summarize the risk assessment with a single indicator.

The third caveat relates to the policy implications of any work on rollover risk. Reducing rollover risk is not the only thing that matters in shaping fiscal policies. Otherwise, it would be sufficient to aim at the lowest degree of risk. Things are more complicated in reality as fiscal policy has its own ends: to provide public services, for example, while avoiding excessively distortionary taxation. Fiscal policy should also play a role in reducing output fluctuations, typically through automatic stabilizers but, in some cases, also through countercyclical policies. Always aiming at reducing fiscal deficit is unlikely to be optimal.

This is indeed at the core of the policy debate on how fiscal policy should be handled currently, especially in advanced countries (the so-called austerity debate), something that we will return to in the last chapter of this book.

Notes

1. The term "liquid" includes two dimensions: one is the depth of the government paper market (i.e., the fact that the market has a sufficient size so that the sale of government paper for individual investors can easily be absorbed); the second has to do with the conditions in the monetary base market, as already noted. One important consideration to bear in mind is that the assessment of rollover risks in terms of solvency, which is followed in the text, focuses on the markets' *perception* of solvency. Situations may arise where the

market perceives the government to be insolvent as a result of an excessively pessimistic assessment of the fiscal outlook. In such a situation interest rates may end up being higher than their "fundamental" value. One can refer to this situation as one of "illiquidity" for the government rather than of "insolvency." However, in a way, this is just semantics: "multiple equilibria" situations can arise where, in the bad equilibrium, illiquidity problems turn into solvency problems. It is in this case that the availability of a lender of last resort, like the IMF or the central bank, becomes particularly important to avoid unwarranted increases in interest rates that would not be sustainable over time.

2. The concept of fiscal solvency needs also to be contrasted with the concept of fiscal sustainability. The term "fiscal sustainability" refers to the possibility of sustaining over time the same fiscal policy stance—that is, the fiscal policy parameters affecting fiscal outcomes—without incurring fiscal solvency problems. A country can be solvent even if the fiscal stance is not sustainable because markets expect that the policy stance would at one point be changed. Fiscal unsustainability should not be confused with debt unsustainability: debt unsustainability arises as a particular case of fiscal unsustainability, that is, when restoring fiscal sustainability requires some form of debt restructuring rather than an adjustment in other fiscal policy parameters (see "Modernizing the framework for fiscal policy and public debt sustainability analysis," International Monetary Fund, paper prepared by the Fiscal Affairs Department and the Strategy, Policy, and Review Department, August 5, 2011).

3. The analysis can be (and often is, for simplicity) conducted also in terms of gross debt, in which case the primary balance has to be defined as total revenues minus non-interest spending.

4. One digression is needed to discuss the case of countries with a negative interest-rate–growth differential, which is common in emerging economies. A negative differential allows countries to stabilize, or even lower, their debt ratio while running negative primary balances. Moreover the standard prescription for debt stabilization—the primary balance should be larger, the higher is the debt level—does not hold if the differential is negative: stabilizing the debt ratio requires a weaker (more negative) primary balance the higher the debt level (and, for a dynamic perspective, the debt will eventually stabilize for any negative primary balance). This said, a negative differential is inconsistent with efficiency considerations, and it is unlikely to persist over the longer run (particularly in the absence of financial repression), and particularly if the debt ratio starts rising, limiting the possibility of abuse of the negativity of the interest-rate–growth differential. The differential, while often negative on average, has indeed been more volatile in emerging economies than in advanced ones (Escolano, Shabudina, and Woo 2011). Thus, even for a negative differential, the primary balance remains an important indicator of the health of public finances, including their ability to withstand shocks to the differential.

5. If the interest rate on assets differs from the interest rate on liabilities, this formula no longer applies. Note also that the term debt here includes also the liabilities of the government toward the central bank. If the balance sheets of the government and the central bank are consolidated, a term including base money would also appear in this relationship as distinct from other debt (base money is not debt in the sense that it does not require servicing).

6. The term "fiscal risks" is often used to indicate the risk of a fiscal crisis. In line with the public financial management literature, the term is here instead used in the meaning indicated in the text.

7. For example, in the United States, the ten-year nominal bond yield at the end of 2011 was 1.875 percent, whereas the yield of the ten-year inflation-indexed bond was −0.12

percent. For Japan, the corresponding rates for the seven-year bonds at end 2011 were 0.55 and 0.78 percent, respectively (source: Bloomberg, LP).

8. A host of other factors are, of course, important in affecting long-term fiscal trends, such as increased spending needs to fight global warming, or the potential erosion in revenues arising from increased tax competition.

9. Of course, the growth of the economy is also important for fiscal sustainability because it enters directly the debt-stability equation.

10. This said, debt restructuring also involves a correction in the "primary balance": from an economic perspective it involves a tax on bond-holders, and if that tax were classified as such, the primary balance in the year of debt restructuring would surge to very high levels, with contractionary effects on the economy, whose effects would depend, among other things, on the distribution of bonds between domestic and foreign holders.

11. Formal tests of debt sustainability, following Bohn (1998) indeed rest on testing whether, based on history, the primary balance was adjusted in response to increases in the stock of debt. One difficulty in applying this approach to current circumstances is that many countries never had a public debt ratio as high as the current one and therefore the past may be an untrustworthy guide, given the possibility of nonlinearities in the relationship between public debt and the desired primary balance.

References

Ardagna, S. 2009. Financial market's behavior around episodes of large changes in the fiscal stance. *European Economic Review* 53: 37–55.

Baldacci, E., S. Gupta, and A. Mati. 2011. Political and fiscal risk determinants of sovereign spreads in emerging markets. *Review of Development Economics* 15 (2): 251–63.

Bohn, H. 1998. The behavior of U.S. public debt and deficits. *Quarterly Journal of Economics* 113 (3): 949–63.

Bornhorst, F., F. Dobrescu, A. Fedelino, J.Gottschalk, and T. Nakata. 2011. When and how to adjust beyond the business cycle? A guide to structural fiscal balances. Technical note. Fiscal Affairs Department, IMF, Washington, DC.

Cottarelli, C., and L. Jaramillo. 2012. Walking hand in hand: Fiscal policy and growth in advanced economies. Working paper 12/137. IMF, Washington, DC. Available via the Internet: http://www.imf.org/external/pubs/cat/longres.aspx?sk=25946.0.

Debrun, X., D. Hauner, and M. Kumar. 2009. Independent fiscal agencies. *Journal of Economic Surveys* 23 (1): 44–81.

Escolano, J., A. Shabunina, and J. Woo. 2011. The puzzle of persistently negative interest rate–growth differentials: Financial repression or income catch-up. Working paper 11/260. IMF, Washington, DC.

International Monetary Fund. 2012a. *Fiscal Monitor: Taking stock: A Progress Report on Fiscal Adjustment*. Washington, DC: IMF. Available at: http://www.imf.org/external/pubs/ft/fm/2012/02/fmindex.htm.

International Monetary Fund. 2012b. Fiscal transparency, accountability, and risk. Policy paper. IMF, Washington, DC. Available at: http://www.imf.org/external/np/fad/trans/.

2

Debt Dynamics and Fiscal Sustainability

Carlo Cottarelli and Julio Escolano

2.1 Introduction

This chapter presents the analytical relationships that describe government debt dynamics and underpin the sustainability of fiscal policies. A fiscal policy plan is understood here as a plan for revenue and expenditure, or more succinctly, for the resulting primary balances. Sustainability of fiscal policy plans underlies the discussion of debt dynamics. In loose terms, a fiscal policy plan is sustainable if it can be implemented without the government becoming unable to roll over its debt and having to resort to extreme measures such as default or hyperinflation.[1] In more technical terms, a fiscal policy plan can be defined as sustainable if it is compatible with an economic equilibrium—where markets clear, given the policy plan and the characteristics of the economy, including preferences of economic agents, available technology, and market institutions.[2]

The discussion here focuses on features of fiscal policy plans and associated debt dynamics that can point to their sustainability or unsustainability on the basis of observed evidence. Section 2.2 lays out the key concepts of debt dynamics used throughout the chapter and discusses the importance of long-term government solvency (the intertemporal budget constraint) and a stable debt ratio under the different scenarios of the differential between interest rates and growth. Section 2.3 discusses, in this light, various practical methodologies to assess the sustainability of fiscal policies. Some of these methodologies are eminently heuristic, while others are set within an explicit probabilistic setting. Finally, section 2.3 presents some extensions to deal with the debt dynamics in special cases.

2.2 An Overview of Debt Dynamics

The basic identity describing the movement of government debt states that debt at the end of the year (or any other conventional period) is given by the debt at the end of the previous year augmented by interest payments and reduced by the primary balance during the period:

$$D_t = (1 + i_t)D_{t-1} - P_t. \tag{2.1}$$

In this identity, D_t is the debt at the end of year t, and P_t is the primary balance in year t—both in national currency units (e.g., current dollars).[3] Most of the discussion here will be conducted in terms of gross debt (i.e., without netting out asset holdings), and under the assumption that there is no indexed or foreign currency-denominated debt. Extensions for the treatment of net debt, or debt denominated in foreign currency or indexed, will be discussed at the end of this chapter. The interest rate i_t in equation (2.1) is the average effective interest rate paid by the government in year t.[4] Given that governments typically have outstanding debt issued at different dates in the past, the average effective interest rate is not the market yield of government debt in year t.[5] Rather, the current market yield is the rate that the government would have to pay on an additional unit of debt (i.e., the marginal interest rate). As the interest rate varies over time, the average and marginal interest rates will not generally be the same. However, since the time variation of i_t plays only a secondary role in the discussion that follows, it will be assumed to be constant ($i_t = i$). As equation (2.1) is an identity, it conveys no information on the sustainability of the public finances. A discussion of sustainability requires additional structure.

As discussed in chapter 1, the concept of sustainability (as defined above) is closely related to the concept of solvency. It is therefore natural to start an analysis of sustainability by looking at the conditions under which a government can be regarded as solvent based on its ability to meet its budget constraint. When evaluating the economic viability of a specific ongoing investment project, it is common to require that the investment returns be sufficient, by the end of the project, to fully service existing debt (principal and interest) as well as any other debt incurred along the way. The economic operations of a government, however, involve ongoing recurrent revenue and expenditure for general purposes and do not have a natural end point or deadline when all debt must be paid off. Thus a similar characterization of the viability of a fiscal policy plan is given by the government's intertemporal budget constraint (IBC), which considers an infinite horizon: it states that the present value of all future primary balances (discounted at the discount rate i) must equal the initial debt

$$\text{IBC (nominal currency units): } D_0 = \sum_{t=1}^{\infty} \frac{P_t}{(1+i)^t}. \tag{2.2}$$

The IBC is not an accounting identity, since it rules out a large set of fiscal policy plans. Specifically, the policies that it rules out are the Ponzi games:[6] policies where debt and interest are systematically paid by issuing new debt. Equivalently these policies are also ruled out explicitly by the no-Ponzi game condition (NPG):

NPG (nominal currency units): $\lim\limits_{t\to\infty}\dfrac{D_t}{(1+i)^t}=0.$ $\qquad\qquad\qquad$ (2.3)

It can indeed be shown that the IBC is formally equivalent to the NPG—if either holds, so does the other.[7] Loosely speaking, the NPG states that in the long run, debt cannot grow at a rate equal or higher than the interest rate. This implies that debt service cannot be financed exclusively by issuing more debt because in that case the debt would accumulate at least at the rate of interest. In particular, under policy plans that do not meet the IBC/NPG, the snowball effect (i.e., $(1+i)D_{t-1}$, the first term in the right-hand side of equation 2.1) dominates the dynamics of debt in the long term. This is because under these policy plans either the primary balance is not positive (i.e., is not in surplus) or, if it is positive, it does not keep pace with the stock of debt. Given their equivalence, we will henceforth refer just to the IBC.

While the IBC rules out the Ponzi game type of policy plans, it does not imply that debt must be eventually paid in full. For example, a policy plan that sets the primary balance at the level that is just enough to pay the interest bill ($P_t = iD_0$) will keep debt constant at its initial level (which hence will never be paid back), but it will meet the IBC condition.

As noted, the IBC is written in "dollar" terms, not in relation to GDP. Why then is fiscal solvency often assessed by looking at the behavior of the debt to GDP ratio?

Through algebraic manipulation, equation (2.1) can be expressed as a proportion of (nominal) output:

$$d_t = \frac{(1+i_t)}{(1+\gamma_t)}d_{t-1} - p_t, \qquad\qquad\qquad (2.4)$$

where lowercase letters d_t and p_t represent now the corresponding magnitudes as a ratio to GDP in year t, and γ_t is the growth rate of nominal GDP. We also define the interest-rate–growth differential (IRGD) λ_t as follows:

$$\lambda_t = \frac{i_t - \gamma_t}{1+\gamma_t} = \frac{r_t - g_t}{1+g_t}, \qquad\qquad\qquad (2.5)$$

$$1+\lambda_t = \frac{1+i_t}{1+\gamma_t} = \frac{1+r_t}{1+g_t}, \qquad\qquad\qquad (2.6)$$

where r_t and g_t are the real interest and growth rates (both adjusted by the GDP deflator). [8] For ease of notation, we will assume from now on that the IRGD is constant over time ($\lambda_t = \lambda$), as well as the underlying growth and interest rates. Under the representation of debt as a ratio to GDP, the identity describing the movement of the debt ratio, the government intertemporal budget constraint (IBC) and the no-Ponzi game (NPG) condition can be expressed respectively as follows:

$$d_t = (1+\lambda)d_{t-1} - p, \qquad (2.7)$$

$$\text{IBC (ratios to GDP)} \quad d_0 = \sum_{t=1}^{\infty}(1+\lambda)^{-t}p_t, \qquad (2.8)$$

$$\text{NPG (ratios to GDP)} \quad \lim_{N \to \infty}(1+\lambda)^{-N}d_N = 0. \qquad (2.9)$$

Notice, however, that these are completely identical to equations (2.1) to (2.3). The dynamics of debt can indeed also be expressed as a ratio to any other magnitude through formally similar equations—such as debt as a ratio to private financial wealth (as an indicator of potential demand for debt), government assets (as an indicator of collateral coverage), and any other magnitude (rainfall in Texas). Critically, changes in γ (including when the latter is the growth rate of GDP) would be irrelevant for meeting the IBC. So, why is the behavior of d (which definitely depends on the growth rate of GDP, other things being the same) regarded as key to solvency?

To answer this question, we have to consider that the "dollar" value of primary balances typically depends on the level of GDP, as the latter is the base for taxation; that is, the base for the resources that can be used to service debt. So a higher growth rate of GDP implies that revenues rise more rapidly.

Let's focus therefore on fiscal plans in which p_t is constant and equal to p (or p_t rises up to a level that is the maximum sustainable for the economy, i.e., the primary balance in relation to GDP is bounded). Assume also, for the moment, that the interest rate is larger than the growth rate of the economy, meaning $\lambda > 0$, a common occurrence in mature economies.[9]

In this case the stability of d ensures that the IBC condition is met:[10] the two conditions are mathematically equivalent (e.g., see Bartolini and Cottarelli 1994). The intuition is simple: if p is such that d is constant, nominal debt is rising at the GDP growth rate and is therefore rising at a rate below the interest rate, which is the essence of the IBC. Conversely, if the interest rate is higher than the GDP growth rate—or is expected to become so over the long term—the IBC condition, jointly with the observation that the primary surplus as percentage of GDP cannot grow indefinitely, imply a bounded debt-to-GDP ratio. And if the maximum amount of resources—as measured by the primary balance—that a government can potentially mobilize to service its debt is roughly proportional to the size of the GDP, then the debt ratio must be stable if it is to meet the IBC condition (Escolano 2010).[11]

Things are, however, different when the interest rate is lower than the growth rate.[12] A GDP growth rate in excess of the interest rate exerts a powerful stabilizing force on the debt ratio. Essentially it allows persistent primary deficits while maintaining a stable or even declining debt ratio. But with primary deficits the ICB condition cannot be met: the stability of the debt ratio will therefore not be sufficient to ensure that the IBC condition is met. Such stability is therefore a milder solvency condition than the IBC.[13] That is, under a nonpositive IRGD, a constant debt ratio is a Ponzi game. It would be, however, what is sometimes called "an honest Ponzi game," in the sense that the growth of debt is still bounded by the growth of what is ultimately its "collateral," namely GDP, the source of government revenues. That is ultimately why, even if the IBC condition is not met, a stable debt ratio is regarded as sustainable.

2.3 Debt Sustainability Indicators

The definition of sustainability above hinges on the IBC condition or, at least, the stability of the debt ratio, and it has given rise to a number of relevant indicators. An even partial coverage of the increasingly abundant literature on this topic is beyond the scope of this chapter.[14] Instead, we will focus on a few methodologies that are widely used, offering some comments in light of the conceptual discussion above. In general terms, these methodologies fall into three broad categories: (1) *gap measures*, which are based on the difference between the actual value of a fiscal magnitude, such as the primary balance, and the notional value that would meet specific criteria, such as hitting a target debt ratio in specified time or satisfying the IBC condition; (2) estimates of fiscal policy reaction functions (FPRF), which allow testing the consistency of these FPRFs with the IBC condition or the absence of Ponzi-game type explosive debt dynamics; and (3) *fiscal vulnerability indicators*, which flag the likelihood of a future fiscal crisis or fiscal stress when pre-specified values are crossed (often based on their past predictive power).

2.3.1 Fiscal Gap Measures

Debt-Stabilizing Primary
Possibly the simplest indicator of debt sustainability is the gap between the primary balance ratio to GDP that would stabilize the current debt ratio and the actual primary balance ratio (Blanchard 1990; Blanchard et al. 1990). Given a value of the IRGD (λ^*, possibly estimated on the basis of a historical average or a projection), the primary balance ratio that stabilizes the debt ratio at a given level (d^*) is $p^* = \lambda^* d^*$. Thus comparing p^* (often calculated at the current debt ratio) with the actual primary balance ratio (possibly cyclically adjusted to capture its underlying level) provides a measure of the adjustment that would be necessary to stabilize the debt ratio.

The $s1$ Indicator
An alternative indicator of sustainability is the gap between the primary balance ratio that would bring the debt ratio to a pre-specified level within a given period and the present actual primary balance ratio (European Commission 2009). This

indicator is often called the "$s1$" indicator and it is regularly used in the European Union to assess the sustainability of fiscal policy in member countries—with a target debt ratio of 60 percent and a period consistent with the surveillance horizon under the Stability and Growth Pact. The following formula can be used to calculate the primary ratio (p^*) that must be maintained for N years to reach a target debt ratio of d_N^* if the initial debt ratio is d_0:

$$p^* = \frac{\lambda}{(1+\lambda)^{-N} - 1}\left[(1+\lambda)^{-N} d_N^* - d_0\right].$$

A similar approach has been used in the IMF's *Fiscal Monitor* to calculate adjustment needs benchmarks for advanced and emerging economies.[15] The $s1$ indicator, however, requires a choice, to some extent arbitrary, of the target debt ratio (d_N^*) and of the time allowed for hitting the target (N).

The $s2$ Indicator

The $s2$ indicator aims at benchmarking the long-term sustainability of a fiscal policy plan. Typically, this policy plan comprises a short- to medium-term period for which policies are specified in detail and a subsequent long-term projection that keeps the primary balance ratio to GDP constant except for the effects of some variables of interest for which long-term projections are available—such as health and pension expenditure, or fiscal revenue from natural resources subject to depletion. This indicator is regularly used in the European Union to measure long-term adjustment needs of member economies taking into account long-term trends in age-related expenditure (European Commission 2009, 2011).

Given a path of projected primary balances for all future periods ($\{p_t\}_{t=1}^{\infty}$), the sustainability indicator $s2$ is defined as the fixed annual addition at perpetuity (expressed as a ratio to the contemporaneous GDP) to the projected primary balances that would be necessary to meet the IBC condition. Thus, using the IBC equation (2.8), we can define the $s2$ indicator implicitly as follows:

$$d_0 = \sum_{t=1}^{\infty}(1+\lambda)^{-t}(p_t + s2),$$

or by its equivalent explicit formula

$$s2 = \lambda d_0 - \lambda \sum_{t=1}^{\infty}(1+\lambda)^{-t} p_t.$$

Since there is no presumption that the shape of the projected sequence of primary balances is optimal or that a fixed annual addition is the best policy approach, the indicator should be considered a benchmark and not necessarily a policy recommendation or a measure of the adjustment needed in any particular year.

2.3.2 Sustainability Tests Based on the Fiscal Policy Reaction Function (FPRF)

This strain of sustainability tests aims at estimating whether the fiscal policy re-action function, as revealed by the past behavior of fiscal variables, is consistent with debt sustainability—provided that the same policy reaction function is maintained in the future. A FPRF specifies the behavior of the key fiscal policy instruments (typically, the primary balance ratio) as a function of the debt ratio and other relevant variables—such as the output gap. Sustainability tests are useful to reveal the need for change in the way fiscal policies are conducted (i.e., a change in the FPRF) before the debt dynamics becomes explosive. Also sustainability tests have been used to assess the risk of adverse market reactions in the near future—the size of the "fiscal space" available. Thus, if the estimated policy reaction function leads to explosive debt dynamics, the distance between the current debt ratio and the point at which its dynamics become explosive can be used as a measure of the available fiscal space.

Many of the proposed tests aim at detecting a co-integrating relationship linking the primary balance—or primary expenditure and revenue separately—and the outstanding stock of debt. Under some conditions these co-integrating relationships are sufficient for the IBC to hold. Specifically, most sustainability tests follow different variations of the methodology proposed by Bohn (1998, 2005, 2007). This methodology produces an explicit estimate of the FPRF—which can be itself of independent interest. It posits the existence of a FPRF as follows:

$$p_t = \alpha d_{t-1} + \beta X_t + v_t, \tag{2.10}$$

where p_t and d_t are, as before, the primary and debt ratios respectively; X_t is a vector of exogenous variables influencing the primary balance (e.g., the output gap, trade openness, terms of trade, fixed effects); v_t is a random shock; and α and β are parameters to be estimated. The coefficient α measures the forcefulness with which government policies react to an increase in the debt ratio: other things equal, an increase in the debt ratio of Δd will prompt an increase in the primary balance ratio of $\alpha \Delta d$. It is commonly assumed that the stochastic process $\beta X_t + v_t$ is bounded and that the IRGD is positive ($\lambda > 0$).[16] Using the FPRF given by equation (2.10) and the identity describing the movement of the debt ratio (equation 2.7), the dynamics of the debt ratio is given by the following:

$$d_t = (1 + (\lambda - \alpha))d_{t-1} - \beta X_t - v_t. \tag{2.11}$$

In this setting, whether the debt path meets the IBC condition hinges on the value of α, which can be statistically estimated and tested. It is clear, from equation (2.11) that the asymptotic rate of growth of the debt ratio is $\lambda - \alpha$, since the last two right-hand-side terms are bounded. Thus, when $\alpha > 0$ (and therefore $\lambda - \alpha < \lambda$), the debt ratio will meet the NPG (equation 2.9), and a fortiori the IBC (Bohn 1998).

Taking into account the existence of a maximum primary surplus ratio, Ostry, Ghosh, Kim, and Qureshi (2010) and Ghosh, Kim, Mendoza, Ostry, and Qureshi (2011) estimate a nonlinear policy reaction function—with a nonlinear $\alpha(d_{t-1})$ replacing αd_{t-1} in equation (2.10). They find cross-country evidence that the primary balance reacts increasingly less to higher values of the debt ratio and even declines after some point.[17] Based on the estimated nonlinear policy reaction function, they calculate a "point of no return" for the debt ratio. Beyond that point, the debt ratio sets on an explosive dynamics that the increasingly weaker reaction of the primary balance (because the nonlinearity) is impotent to stop. They propose that the difference between this point of no return and the actual debt ratio can be seen as a measure of the fiscal space available for a country.[18]

2.3.3 Sustainability Indicators

This approach to measuring the sustainability of fiscal policy aims a systematizing the use of a broad variety of fiscal and macroeconomic indicators to flag the risk of a fiscal crisis. It builds on the literature on early warning system models—until recently, covering mainly external and financial crises.[19] We will focus here on the methodology proposed by Baldacci, McHugh, and Petrova (2011), Baldacci et al. (2011), and IMF (2011b).[20] Rather than testing the IBC condition or estimating the deviation with respect to that condition, this methodology starts with a large set of indicators, and identifies those that have shown a past capacity to predict subsequent episodes of fiscal stress. Then, these indicators are aggregated into a single index which can be viewed as a summary indicator of the likelihood of a fiscal distress episode. Both the definition of fiscal stress episodes and the choice of indicators are based on the conceptual framework of Cottarelli (2011), which is discussed in the opening chapter of this book.[21]

The first step in this methodology is choosing the features that define episodes of fiscal stress, characterized as periods of extreme government funding difficulties, such as debt default, or extremely high inflation or sovereign yields. In the second step, a threshold value is chosen for each indicator which, when crossed, signals that the indicator predicts a crisis. For each indicator, the threshold is chosen to minimize a combination of false positives (type I errors) and false negatives (type II errors).[22] Then, associated to each indicator, a dummy 0–1 variable is constructed according to whether the indicator sends a crisis signal (1) or a non-crisis signal (0). These variables, weighted by their predictive power (one minus the total misclassification error ratio), are aggregated into an index. In this way, variables are assigned a higher weight the higher their forecasting accuracy.

This methodology is valuable in building early warning systems, aiming to flag the potential for fiscal crises in the short term. Also it has the virtue of letting data speak for themselves, imposing little a priori structure as to the causal nexus between specific policies and eventual fiscal outcomes. It is ill-suited, however, to identify an unsustainable current fiscal stance that could result in a fiscal crisis only in the medium or long term or to single out the specific fiscal policy features that need to be changed.

2.4 Some Special Issues

2.4.1 Foreign Currency-Denominated and Inflation-Indexed Debt
The discussion of debt dynamics in this chapter, as in most of the literature, assumes that all debt is denominated in domestic currency and nonindexed. In practice, however, many countries issue sovereign debt denominated in foreign currencies or indexed to inflation. We develop here the expressions of the debt ratio dynamics focusing on the case of foreign currency-denominated debt, and then we point out how these expressions can be adapted to inflation-indexed debt.

The law of movement of the debt ratio (equation 2.7) when there is foreign currency-denominated debt is formally identical to the case when all debt is denominated in domestic currency. The only difference is that the IRGD (λ) must be replaced by an adjusted IRGD ($\hat{\lambda}$) that takes into account the change in the stock of debt and interest payments due to the variation of the exchange rate. To this end, the interest rate (i) must be replaced by an adjusted return rate (ρ) that incorporates these exchange rate effects:

$$\hat{\lambda}_t = \frac{\rho_t - \gamma_t}{1 + \gamma_t},$$ (2.12)

$$d_t = \left(1 + \frac{\rho_t - \gamma_t}{1 + \gamma_t}\right) d_{t-1} - p_t = \left(1 + \hat{\lambda}_t\right) d_{t-1} - p_t.$$ (2.13)

In these expressions, d_t represents the stock of debt at the end of year t as a ratio to GDP (with foreign currency-denominated debt valued in domestic currency at the end-year exchange rate). As before, γ_t is the nominal growth of GDP and p_t is the primary balance ratio to GDP, both in year t.

Let α_t be the proportion of total debt denominated in foreign currency (measured in domestic currency equivalent) at the end of year t and let ε_t be the depreciation of the exchange rate (measured as units of domestic currency per unit of foreign currency) in year t. Also let i^d and i^f be, respectively, the interest rates on domestic currency-denominated and foreign currency-denominated instruments. Then the expressions for the adjusted return on debt (ρ) and associated adjusted interest rate ($\hat{i}$) are as follows:

$$\rho_t = \hat{i}_t + \alpha_{t-1}\varepsilon_t,$$ (2.14)

$$\hat{i}_t = (1 - \alpha_{t-1})i_t^d + \alpha_{t-1}(1 + \varepsilon_t)i_t^f = \frac{\text{Total budget interest bill in } t}{\text{Total debt at end of } t - 1}. \tag{2.15}$$

Notice that as in the domestic currency debt case, $\hat{i}_t$ can be easily calculated as the interest bill reported in the budget divided by the stock of debt at the end of the previous year.[23]

This treatment is easily generalized to debt in several foreign currencies by extending the second term in equations (2.14) and (2.15) with additional terms, one for each foreign currency, weighted by the relative proportion of total debt denominated in that currency (replacing the weighting α_{t-1} above). Since the law of movement of the debt ratio with and without foreign currency-denominated debt (equations 2.13 and 2.7) are formally the same, other debt dynamics expressions and conclusions also carry through with the appropriate replacement of the adjusted IRGD ($\hat{\lambda}$) for the domestic-currency IRGD (λ) and of the adjusted return on debt (ρ) for the domestic interest rate (i).

When some debt is denominated in domestic currency but indexed to inflation, equations (2.12) through (2.15) still apply with appropriate re-interpretations and modifications of the variables. This is because inflation-indexed debt is formally similar to debt indexed to a notional "foreign currency" that maintains its real value.[24] Specifically, α_t represents the proportion of indexed debt (measured at its current inflation-indexed value) relative to total debt; i^f represents the (real) interest rate paid on indexed debt; and ε_t represents the inflation rate according to the appropriate price index. The adjusted return on debt (ρ) then corresponds to the interest payments reported in the budget divided by debt outstanding at the end of the previous year—if budget accounts report interest actually paid as well as accrued though increase of the principal due to indexation, in accordance with international standards of budget accounting and reporting.[25] If the budget reports only interest due for payment during the year, but not the uplift of the principal (cash accounting), the budget interest bill divided by debt outstanding at the end of the previous year corresponds to the adjusted interest rate ($\hat{i}_t$). Finally, the factor $(1 + \varepsilon_t)$ in equation (2.15) should be dropped in most cases, depending on the contractual arrangements for the payment of interest.[26]

2.4.2 Gross and Net Debt

Debt dynamics and sustainability analyses are usually conducted on the basis of gross debt—as is done in the rest of this chapter. However, a more comprehensive government solvency analysis requires the consideration of assets as well as liabilities.[27] Also full consistency between flow variables (e.g., budget balance) and stocks (e.g., government's financial net worth) can only be achieved by taking into account the asset side of the government's balance sheet. Incorporating the asset side in debt dynamics analyses is particularly important when governments own large financial assets,[28] but also in more common situations such as when the debt management office pre-finances future expenditure needs well in advance to lock in favorable market conditions.

Factors that hinder the consideration of assets as part of a more comprehensive net debt analysis include the paucity of governments' balance sheet data and the heterogeneous nature of assets in a government's balance sheet—in contrast with liabilities, which are often relatively homogeneous. Specifically, assets have different levels of liquidity and marketability, and they are available to meet government financial obligations in different degrees (e.g., because their sale may require legal reforms or overcoming severe political constraints). As in other financial analyses, the type of assets that is appropriate to net out against debt obligations depends on the purpose of the analysis. Thus countries differ in the assets they consider in their calculations of net debt: ranging from none to liquid financial assets, all financial assets, all financial and nonfinancial assets, and so on. Moreover government assets are often hard to value (e.g., if they are not traded).

The discussion that follows presents the basic relationships that underlie the dynamics of net debt. Let a_t denote the value of assets at the end of year t as a ratio to GDP. Also the superscript a (respectively, d) will indicate that a variable (e.g., interest, interest-rate–growth differential) corresponds to assets (respectively, debt). Thus, for example, i^a (i^d) represents the nominal rate of return earned on assets (rate of interest paid on debt). Finally, p^g and p^n represent the gross and net primary balance ratios to GDP.[29] The gross primary balance is revenue less expenditure before interest paid on debt, while the net primary balance is revenue less expenditure before both receipts of returns on assets and interest paid on debt.[30] All other symbols retain their meanings from previous sections. Specifically, the following reflects the relationship between net and gross primary balance ratios:

$$p_t^g = p_t^n + \frac{i_t^a}{1 + \gamma_t} a_{t-1}. \tag{2.16}$$

The laws of movement of asset and debt ratios in terms of the net and gross primary ratios are given by the following equations (the counterparts of equation 2.4):

$$d_t - a_t = (d_{t-1} - a_{t-1}) + \lambda_t^d d_{t-1} - \lambda_t^a a_{t-1} - p_t^n, \tag{2.17}$$

$$d_t - a_t = (d_{t-1} - a_{t-1}) + \lambda_t^d d_{t-1} + \frac{\gamma_t}{1 + \gamma_t} a_{t-1} - p_t^g, \tag{2.18}$$

where the IRGD is now different for assets and debt,

$$\lambda_t^a = \frac{i_t^a - \gamma_t}{1 + \gamma_t} = \frac{r_t^a - g_t}{1 + g_t}, \quad \lambda_t^d = \frac{i_t^d - \gamma_t}{1 + \gamma_t} = \frac{r_t^d - g_t}{1 + g_t}. \tag{2.19}$$

When assets are brought into the light, it is clear that in analyses based on gross debt, it is often implicitly assumed that nominal assets remain unchanged[31]—and thus that asset ratios decline with the growth of GDP. This follows from implicitly assuming that primary surpluses are used to reduce debt (and not to build up assets) and primary deficits are financed by debt (and not by asset sales). This can be seen by rearranging equation (2.18):

$$d_t = \left(1 + \lambda_t^d\right)d_{t-1} - p_t^g + \left(a_t - \frac{1}{1+\gamma_t}a_{t-1}\right). \tag{2.20}$$

This equation differs from equation (2.7), where assets were not considered, by the addition of the last term, which equals the increase in nominal assets as a ratio to GDP. Thus both equations are equivalent (and equation 2.7 holds) if and only if the last term is zero $(a_t = a_{t-1}/(1+\gamma_t))$: that is, the nominal value of assets remains unchanged and the asset ratio to GDP declines at the rate $1/(1+\gamma)$, reflecting the growth in GDP.

For the same reason, the (net or gross) primary balance that stabilizes both the asset and debt ratios at given levels (e.g., a^* and d^*) exceeds the (net or gross) primary balance that stabilizes only the debt ratio—by the asset buildup necessary for the asset ratio to keep pace with the growing GDP. Thus a country that targets a stable net debt (or financial net worth) needs to maintain a tighter fiscal stance than would be necessary to pay just the growth-adjusted gross interest bill $(p^g = \lambda^d d^*)$. In particular, the net and gross primary balances that stabilize both the asset and debt ratios are the following (assuming constant interest rates):

$$p^{n^*} = \lambda^d d^* - \lambda^a a^*,$$

$$p^{g^*} = \lambda^d d^* + \frac{\gamma}{1+\gamma}a^* = p^{n^*} + \frac{i^a}{1+\gamma}a^*.$$

Notes

1. While a policy plan may be unviable for reasons other than the debt dynamics it generates (e.g., because it introduces large economic distortions and impedes economic growth), it will most often lead eventually to a loss of government access to credit markets and to difficulties in financing its operations.

2. Of course, the practical interests of markets and policy makers are in assessing the sustainability of policy plans in which the key parameters are not changed in the too distant future. In principle, any policy plan for a finite (and hence observable) period can become, in theory, a sustainable plan by adding to it, in an arbitrarily distant future, the necessary remedial policy actions. But this is uninteresting. Indeed, very often the interest lies in assessing the sustainability of the current policy setting.

3. The variable P_t is interpreted here as the fiscal primary balance (revenue less expenditure before interest payments), but it can be defined, if pertinent, to include also debt-changing

below-the-line operations. The value of these debt-changing below-the-line operations is often computed as a residual (the difference between the change in debt and the overall balance) and it is referred as the "stock-flow adjustment." The stock-flow adjustment may not be zero, inter alia, owing to privatization receipts used to redeem debt, other net acquisition or disposal of financial assets (e.g., financial sector support operations) financed with debt, or accounting adjustments. If the effective interest rate is adjusted for exchange rate-driven valuation changes in the foreign currency-denominated debt (as discussed below), the stock-flow adjustment should not include these valuation changes. The stock-flow adjustment is occasionally a result of deliberate attempts to obfuscate the true deficit (see IMF 2011b; Irwin 2012; Weber 2012). In the analysis that follows we abstract from debt monetization and seigniorage.

4. The average effective interest rate in year t is typically computed as the quotient between actual budgetary interest payments in t and the debt outstanding at the end of year $t-1$.

5. Moreover outstanding debt consists of instruments with various maturities that typically carry different interest rates.

6. Named after Charles Ponzi (1882–1949), a colorful although eventually unsuccessful swindler.

7. See proposition 1 in Escolano (2010).

8. Based on the identities $1 + \gamma_t = (1 + g_t)(1 + \pi_t)$ and $1 + i_t = (1 + r_t)(1 + \pi_t)$, where π_t is the growth of the GDP deflator in year t.

9. This condition, when postulated for a balanced growth path, is often called the "modified golden rule." Growth theory suggests that if the economy uses resources efficiently and private economic agents prefer current to future consumption, then the modified golden rule must hold, at least asymptotically over the long term for an economy that approaches a balanced growth path (see Blanchard and Fischer 1989). This is because, otherwise, private agents could always choose a strictly preferred alternative consumption-saving plan by reducing their holdings of assets (e.g., government debt) or increasing their liabilities. Essentially, in an equilibrium balanced growth path, the modified golden rule must hold, since otherwise economic agents would need to reinvest yearly at perpetuity all the return they obtain on their assets or more (since in a balanced growth path assets grow at the same rate as GDP; a rate that would be equal or higher than the interest rate). Individual price-taking agents would prefer, for example, to consume all their assets initially and avoid investment altogether. Even though this would violate aggregate feasibility, it shows that $\lambda \leq 0$ cannot be a balanced growth competitive equilibrium.

10. That is, the debt ratio may rise and fall, but it must remain within a stable range. It cannot grow unboundedly forever.

11. If p is not constant and can increase without bound, then, in principle, the IBC condition, under a positive IRGD, represents a weaker sustainability concept than the boundedness of the debt ratio. Under the IBC condition, the debt cannot grow at a rate equal or higher than the interest rate—that is, the government must service a proportion of the debt through primary surpluses. However, the debt can still grow faster than GDP, since the interest rate exceeds the GDP growth rate. For example, debt could grow at a rate intermediate between the GDP growth rate and the interest rate. So, in principle, an increasing debt ratio is compatible with the IBC condition. However, this would require an unbounded rise of p_t, which is unreasonable. The existence of a maximum level of the primary surplus-to-GDP

ratio is an eminently reasonable condition, and in practice, the feasible maximum primary surplus is likely to be only a few percentage points of GDP—owing either to Laffer curve effects or, probably before that, to political constraints. As pointed out in Keynes (1924) "when the State's contractual liabilities, fixed in terms of money, have reached an excessive proportion of the national income . . .. The active and working elements in no community, ancient or modern, will consent to hand over to the *rentier* or bond-holding class more than a certain proportion of the fruits of their work" (p. 64).

12. As discussed in a subsequent chapter, this happens in most developing economies; see also Escolano, Shabunina, and Woo (2011).

13. This is because a constant debt ratio will imply that debt grows at the same rate as GDP and thus that its rate of increase will exceed or be equal to the interest rate, implying a violation of the IBC condition.

14. European Commission (2011) contains a recent stocktaking of different methodologies. See also Chalk and Hemming (2000), Trehan and Walsh (1991), Quintos (1995), and Bohn (2005, 2007).

15. See IMF (2012) statistical tables 13a and 13b. The *Fiscal Monitor*, however, considers cyclically adjusted primary balances and a gradual adjustment for about ten years followed by ten years of constant primary balance at the required (high) level to hit the debt target. It also considers varying IRGD for advanced economies, taking into account the endogenous effects of high debt on interest rates and growth (Poghosyan 2012; Kumar and Woo 2010).

16. The assumption that the stochastic process $\beta X_t + v_t$ is bounded is not particularly restrictive if the control variables in X_t are the output gap, the trade balance as a ratio to GDP, dummy variables representing institutional features, annual percentage changes in the terms of trade, and so on, all of which are naturally bounded. The main results, however, also hold under weaker conditions: "almost surely" (i.e., for all realizations of the stochastic process except possibly for a set of probability zero) if $\beta X_t + v_t$ is almost surely bounded (with the bound depending on the realization); or in an expected value sense if $\beta X_t + v_t$ is stationary.

17. The empirical evidence from the literature, however, is still mixed on whether the fiscal response may vary when debt ratios are unusually high (European Commission 2011), on whether emerging and advanced economies (or indeed any two different economies) follow broadly similar FPRFs, or on the stability of FPRFs over time.

18. Note, however, that the point of no return for individual countries is based on panel estimates that involve the same reaction function for all countries, and that empirically only few observations exist describing the reaction at very high debt levels, as these have not been experienced by most countries.

19. See Baldacci, McHugh, and Petrova (2011), Baldacci et al. (2011), and European Commission (2011), and references therein.

20. See the discussion on fiscal sustainability risks in IMF (2011a, app. 3)), in particular, on deriving a fiscal sustainability risk map.

21. See also Schaechter et al. (2012) for a set of indicators for advanced economies compiled based on this conceptual framework.

22. This combination is typically the total misclassified error ratio, defined as the proportion of non-crisis years that were misclassified as crisis years plus the ratio of crisis years that were misclassified as non-crisis years.

23. This is because budget reporting is typically done in domestic currency units, with interest payments on foreign currency-denominated debt converted into domestic currency at the exchange rate of the date when the payment was made. This also corrects for the fact that interest is not always due at the end of the year (as assumed in the formulas) but at different dates throughout the year. Notice, however, that under standard fiscal accounting, the variation in the value of outstanding debt due to exchange rate changes is not reported as interest payments (it is a "below-the-line" holding gain or loss). Hence it is useful to distinguish ρ, which includes the exchange rate-induced increase in principal owed, from $\hat{i}$, which does not include it. Thus $\hat{i}$ closely corresponds to the fiscal accounting concept of interest and can be calculated based on the budget-reported interest bill.

24. Inflation-indexed debt, however, is different from foreign currency-denominated debt in other important respects not covered in this discussion. For example, a country that issues its own currency can always redeem inflation-index debt by issuing domestic currency (i.e., monetizing the debt). This expedient may not be feasible if the debt must contractually be redeemed in foreign currency and the country lacks the necessary foreign reserves and has no access to international credit markets.

25. See IMF (2001, para. 6.42–6.49).

26. The mentioned factor should be dropped if interest in year t is paid on the indexed value of the debt at the end of the previous year. It should be kept if interest is paid on the value of the debt after increasing it by the inflation in year t.

27. See IMF (2011b, app. 3) on the importance of monitoring gross and net debt.

28. For example, in the cases of Norway or Japan.

29. For the purposes of this discussion and the use of these formulas, any holding gains (losses) on assets can be added to (subtracted from) the primary balance to calculate p_t (net or gross). As before, holding gains (losses) on debt could also be added (subtracted) to the primary balance.

30. The gross primary balance has been denoted simply as "primary" balance in the rest of this chapter, where "debt" referred to gross debt.

31. Except for holding gains and losses. It is typically also assumed that the primary balance includes interest receipts (i.e., that it is the gross primary balance).

References

Baldacci, Emanuele, James McHugh, and Iva Petrova. 2011. Measuring fiscal vulnerability and fiscal stress: A proposed set of indicators. Working paper 11/94. IMF, Washington, DC. Available at: http://www.imf.org/external/pubs/ft/wp/2011/wp1194.pdf.

Baldacci, Emanuele, Iva Petrova, Nazim Belhocine, and Gabriela Dobrescu. 2011. Assessing fiscal stress. Working paper 11/100. IMF, Washington, DC. Available at: http://www.imf.org/external/pubs/ft/wp/2011/wp11100.pdf.

Bartolini, Leonardo, and Carlo Cottarelli. 1994. Government Ponzi games and the sustainability of public deficits under uncertainty. *Ricerche Economiche* 48: 1–22.

Blanchard, O. J., and Stanley Fischer. 1989. *Lectures on Macroeconomics*. Cambridge: MIT Press.

Blanchard, O. J. 1990. Suggestions for a new set of fiscal indicators. Working paper 79. OECD Economics Department, Paris. Available at: http://dx.doi.org/10.1787/435618162862.

Blanchard, O. J., C. Chouraqui, R. P. Hagemann, and N. Sartor. 1990. The sustainability of fiscal policy: New answers to an old question. Economic Studies 15 (autumn). OECD, Paris. Available at: www.oecd.org/eco/outlook/34288870.pdf.

Bohn, Henning. 1998. The behavior of U.S. public debt and deficits. *Quarterly Journal of Economics* 113 (3): 949–63.

Bohn, Henning. 2005. The sustainability of fiscal policy in the United States. Working paper 1446. CESifo, Munich. Available at: http://www.cesifo-group.de/ifoHome/CESifo-Group/cesifo.html.

Bohn, Henning. 2007. Are stationarity and cointegration restrictions really necessary for the intertemporal budget constraint? *Journal of Monetary Economics* 54 (7): 1837–47.

Chalk, Nigel Andrew, and Richard Hemming. 2000. Assessing fiscal sustainability in theory and practice. Working paper 00/81. IMF, Washington, DC. Available at: http://www.imf.org/external/pubs/ft/wp/2000/wp0081.pdf.

Cottarelli, Carlo. 2011. The risk octagon: A comprehensive framework for assessing sovereign risks. Presented at University of Rome "La Sapienza," January. Available at: http://www.imf.org/external/np/fad/news/2011/docs/Cottarelli1.pdf.

Escolano, Julio. 2010. A practical guide to public debt dynamics, fiscal sustainability, and cyclical adjustment of budgetary aggregates. Technical Notes and Manuals 2010/02. IMF, Washington, DC. Available at: http://www.imf.org/external/pubs/ft/tnm/2010/tnm1002.pdf.

Escolano, Julio, Anna Shabunina, and Jaejoon Woo. 2011. The puzzle of persistently negative interest rate–growth differentials: Financial repression or income catch-up? Working paper 11/260. IMF, Washington, DC. Available at: http://www.imf.org/external/pubs/ft/wp/2011/wp11260.pdf.

European Commission. 2009. Sustainability report 2009. *European Economy* no. 9/2009. Available at: http://ec.europa.eu/economy_finance/publications/european_economy/index_en.htm.

European Commission. 2011. Public finances in EMU. *European Economy* no. 3/2011. Available at: http://ec.europa.eu/economy_finance/publications/european_economy/index_en.htm.

Ghosh, Atish R., Jun I. Kim, Enrique Mendoza, Jonathan D. Ostry, and Mahvash Qureshi. 2011. Fiscal fatigue, fiscal space and debt sustainability in advanced economies. Working paper 16782. NBER, Cambridge, MA.

IMF. 2001. *Government Finance Statistics Manual 2001 (GFSM 2001)*. Available at: http://www.imf.org/external/pubs/ft/gfs/manual/index.htm.

IMF. 2011a. *Fiscal Monitor*, April. Available at: http://www.imf.org/external/ns/cs.aspx?id=262.

IMF. 2011b. *Fiscal Monitor*, September. Available at: http://www.imf.org/external/ns/cs.aspx?id=262.

IMF. 2012. *Fiscal Monitor*, October. Available at: http://www.imf.org/external/ns/cs.aspx?id=262.

Irwin, Timothy C. 2012. Accounting devices and fiscal illusions. Staff discussion note 12/02. IMF, Washington, DC. Available at: http://www.imf.org/external/pubs/ft/sdn/2012/sdn1202.pdf.

Keynes, John M. 1924. *A Tract on Monetary Reform*. London: Macmillan.

Kumar, Manmohan S., and Jaejoon Woo. 2010 Public Debt and Growth. Working paper 10/174. IMF, Washington, DC. Available at: http://www.imf.org/external/pubs/ft/wp/2010/wp10174.pdf.

Ostry, Jonathan David, Atish R. Ghosh, Jun Il Kim, and Mahvash Saeed Qureshi. 2010. Fiscal space. Staff position note 2010/11. IMF, Washington, DC. Available at: http://www.imf.org/external/pubs/ft/spn/2010/spn1011.pdf.

Poghosyan, T. 2012. Long-run and short-run determinants of government bond yields in advanced economies. Working paper 12/271. IMF, Washington, DC. Available at: http://www.imf.org/external/pubs/ft/wp/2012/wp12271.pdf.

Quintos, Carmela E. 1995. Sustainability of the deficit process with structural shifts. *Journal of Business and Economic Statistics* 13 (4): 40917.

Schaechter, Andrea, Emre Alper, Elif Arbatli, Carlos Cáceres, Giovanni Callegari, Marc Gerard, Jiri Jonas, Tidiane Kinda, Anna Shabunina, and Anke Weber. 2012. A toolkit for assessing fiscal vulnerabilities and risks in advanced economies. Working paper 12/11. IMF, Washington, DC.

Trehan, Bharat, and Carl E. Walsh. 1991. Testing intertemporal budget constraints. *Journal of Money, Credit and Banking* 23: 20623.

Weber, Anke. 2012. Stock-flow adjustments and fiscal transparency: A cross-country comparison. Working paper 12/39. IMF, Washington, DC. Available at: http://www.imf.org/external/pubs/ft/wp/2012/wp1239.pdf.

3

The Determinants of the Interest-Rate–Growth Differential

Julio Escolano

3.1 Introduction

The interest-rate–growth differential (IRGD) is a key determinant of the dynamics of the ratio of government debt to GDP (the debt ratio, for short). Essentially, the IRGD is the difference between the interest rate paid on government debt and the growth rate of GDP.[1] The IRGD drives the inertial or "snowball" dynamics of the debt ratio. For any given primary balance, higher interest rates result in larger rollover refinancing needs, while higher growth reduces the ratio of debt to GDP by increasing the latter.[2] Thus the IRGD represents the rate at which the debt ratio would increase (or decrease, when the IRGD is negative) if the primary budget was balanced. Also, from a different angle, the IRGD determines the primary balance necessary to keep the debt ratio constant (the debt-stabilizing primary), which is the IRGD times the debt ratio.

An economy with a high IRGD will require the allocation of large budgetary resources to debt service if the debt ratio is to be kept in check. Conversely, an economy with a negative IRGD can incur sustained primary deficits and still experience a stable, or even declining, debt ratio. This will occur when the growth-induced reduction in the debt ratio exceeds its increase owing to the interest bill plus the primary deficit which need to be financed with additional debt.

I explore in this chapter the cross-country and temporal patterns of the IRGD. In this analysis, I follow closely Escolano, Shabunina, and Woo (2011) (henceforth ESW). I first discuss and quantify the snowball effect on debt driven by the IRGD. This effect turns out to be large but generally of opposite sign in advanced and nonadvanced economies. In the latter, a large negative snowball effect—rooted in negative IRGDs—has allowed sustained significant primary fiscal deficits without exploding debt ratios. The next section shows that IRGDs are associated with GDP per capita, with persistently negative IRGDs in many nonadvanced economies. I suggest then the reasons for this anomalous behavior of IRGDs in nonadvanced economies and discuss whether such behavior is caused by the income catch-up process or by financial repression. I conclude the chapter with some implications for the design of medium-term fiscal policies in nonadvanced economies.

3.2 How Large Is the Impact of the IRGD on Debt Dynamics?

The change in the government debt ratio during a given period can be split into two conceptually different components: on the one hand, the effect of on- and off-budget operations driven by policies, and, on the other hand, the snowball effect driven by the IRGD and the inherited debt ratio, which is arguably less subject to the direct control of fiscal policies. The first component can be gauged by the sum of the primary balance and the stock-flow residual. The primary balance summarizes the budget policy decisions on revenue and primary spending. The stock-flow residual is the difference between the change in debt and the overall budget balance (revenue less expenditure, including interest payments). It reflects financial operations (e.g., sales or acquisition of stocks, bank recapitalizations) that affect the debt stock.[3] The second component, the snowball effect, is determined by the size of the existing debt stock, the associated interest bill, and the growth of the economy. While these latter variables are influenced by the policy environment, they are not under the direct control of policy makers.

Formally, the increase in the debt ratio of a country during N years between two dates (t and $t + N$) is given by the following expression (Escolano, 2010).

$$d_{t+N} - d_t = \sum_{i=t+1}^{t+N} \lambda_i d_{i-1} + \left(\sum_{i=t+1}^{t+N} -p_i + \sum_{i=t+1}^{t+N} e_i \right), \tag{3.1}$$

where d_t represents the debt ratio to GDP at the end of year t; λ_t represents the IRGD, defined as $\lambda_t = (i_t - \gamma_t) / (1 + \gamma_t)$, where i_t is the (nominal) average effective interest rate paid on government debt and γ_t is the growth rate of (nominal) GDP, both in year t; p_t is the primary budget balance (revenue less expenditure before interest payments) as a ratio to GDP; and e_t is the stock-flow residual measured as a ratio to GDP.[4] **Equation (3.1)** decomposes the change in the debt ratio as the sum of the contribution from the snowball effect, and the contribution from budgetary resources (the primary balance ratio) plus the stock-flow residual. Each of these contributions is the aggregation over the N periods of the corresponding annual values.

For most countries, the size of the snowball effect on debt, driven by the IRGD, is of a first order of magnitude compared with the effect of budgetary and off-budget financial operations—often exceeding them. Table 3.1 shows the contribution to changes in the debt ratio for a sample of countries during 2000–2011 from the IRGD snowball effect versus the contribution from the fiscal and financial operations summarized by the primary balance and the stock-flow residual.

Table 3.1
Decomposition of changes in the debt ratio, 2000 to 2011

	Change in the debt ratio (% GDP)	Of which:		IRGD (geometric annual average) (%)
		Due to primary and stock-flow residual (% GDP)	Due to IRGD (snowball effect) (% GDP)	
Advanced economies				
Australia	4.66	5.75	−1.09	−0.81
Austria	6.10	−2.74	8.84	1.22
Belgium	−9.97	−23.22	13.25	1.21
Canada	3.30	−12.34	15.64	1.86
Czech Republic	22.72	23.48	−0.76	−0.51
Denmark	−16.31	−24.67	8.36	1.52
Estonia	0.92	3.49	−2.57	−4.66
Finland	5.33	2.01	3.33	0.88
France	28.61	19.51	9.10	1.28
Germany	20.37	5.70	14.67	2.10
Greece	61.97	44.69	17.28	0.85
Iceland	58.17	53.75	4.41	−0.14
Ireland	68.97	61.69	7.28	0.44
Israel	−10.21	−37.89	27.67	2.75
Italy	11.63	−14.35	25.97	2.18
Japan	89.47	50.67	38.79	1.94
Korea	16.16	21.37	−5.21	−1.81
Netherlands	11.36	3.80	7.56	1.21
New Zealand	6.37	3.02	3.35	1.41
Norway	16.95	29.00	−12.05	−2.07
Portugal	59.46	43.60	15.86	2.01
Slovak Republic	−6.99	1.09	−8.08	−1.83
Slovenia	17.34	21.12	−3.79	−1.36
Spain	9.74	11.77	−2.03	−0.39
Sweden	−15.38	−15.25	−0.13	−0.03
Switzerland	−13.03	−9.14	−3.88	−0.52
United Kingdom	40.87	35.33	5.54	0.97
United States	48.10	44.41	3.68	0.52
Nonadvanced economies				
Argentina	−0.68	81.96	−82.65	−7.63
Brazil	−1.71	−0.62	−1.08	−0.13
Bulgaria	−59.83	−38.99	−20.85	−4.53
Chile	−2.00	−1.03	−0.97	−0.35

(continued)

Table 3.1
(*continued*)

| | Change in the debt ratio (% GDP) | Of which: | | IRGD (geometric annual average) (%) |
		Due to primary and stock-flow residual (% GDP)	Due to IRGD (snowball effect) (% GDP)	
China	9.40	32.09	−22.69	−10.50
Colombia	−2.12	−1.88	−0.25	0.09
Egypt (2002–2011)	−13.99	41.62	−55.61	−7.15
Hungary	24.90	22.33	2.57	0.00
India	−5.73	35.58	−41.31	−4.92
Indonesia	−70.65	−22.34	−48.31	−9.03
Jordan	−30.08	30.40	−60.49	−7.01
Kenya	−4.26	21.01	−25.27	−4.59
Latvia	25.41	29.18	−3.77	−4.43
Lithuania	14.96	19.46	−4.50	−1.96
Malaysia	17.56	31.87	−14.31	−2.81
Mexico	1.26	1.69	−0.42	−0.16
Morocco	−19.33	−12.25	−7.07	−1.10
Nigeria	−66.95	−9.03	−57.92	−10.62
Pakistan	−22.82	25.05	−47.87	−6.79
Peru	−21.51	−8.05	−13.46	−3.55
Philippines	−16.87	−9.72	−7.16	−1.19
Poland	19.55	21.87	−2.32	−0.28
Romania	3.44	26.45	−23.01	−9.18
Russia	−47.90	−12.79	−35.11	−11.62
Saudi Arabia	−81.14	−55.92	−25.22	−5.40
South Africa	−4.47	0.00	−4.48	−1.14
Thailand	−14.76	5.61	−20.38	−3.86
Turkey (2001–2011)	−38.69	−28.12	−10.57	−1.30
Ukraine	−9.30	28.50	−37.80	−13.06

Source: World Economic Outlook Database

The magnitude of the snowball effect on debt dynamics is particularly large among nonadvanced economies, often dwarfing primary on-budget and off-budget operations. Among the sample of advanced economies in table 3.1,[5] the IRGD averaged about 0.4 percentage point and the snowball effect contributed on average about 7 percentage points of GDP to an average change in debt of 19 percentage points of GDP.[6] Among nonadvanced economies, the average contribution of the snowball effect to changes in the debt ratio was substantially larger than among advanced economies and of the opposite sign (i.e., debt-reducing). This contribution averaged −23 percentage points of GDP, toward an average change in the debt ratio of −14 percentage points of GDP. In other words, among nonadvanced economies, the large debt-reducing snowball effect more than offset the debt-increasing contribution of the combined net primary budgetary operations and net off-budget financial operations—which averaged 9 percentage points of GDP.

The cause of the large debt-reducing contribution from the snowball component in nonadvanced economies is the pervasive presence of negative IRGD values among these economies—as evidenced by the last column in table 3.1.[7] In contrast to the advanced economies, virtually all the nonadvanced economies in the sample had negative average IRGDs during the period—the exceptions (Colombia and Hungary) had IRGDs very close to zero.[8]

The important factual point is that the IRGD-driven snowball effect is generally negative (i.e., debt-stabilizing) and large among nonadvanced economies—exerting a powerful downward thrust on the dynamics of their debt ratios. This downward pull on debt ratios among economies with a negative IRGD has allowed them to maintain broadly stable and often strongly declining debt ratios, even in the presence of substantial primary deficits or large debt-augmenting off-budget operations. The reasons underpinning the pattern of variation of IRGDs across countries and whether they should be expected to persist form the topic of the following sections.

3.3 The IRGD and Income Levels

The evidence of widespread negative IRGDs among nonadvanced economies is an aspect of a broader stylized fact: IRGDs show a positive correlation with (relative) income per capita (figure 3.1).[9] Among advanced economies, the IRGD has averaged about 1 percentage point in recent decades (table 3.2). Blanchard et al. (1990) and ESW find values within this range for the OECD as a whole in the 1980s and for the advanced G20 economies in 1999 to 2008, respectively. The IRGD in some advanced economies, such as the United States, has been occasionally very low or even negative for long periods before the 1970s. However, Reinhart and Sbrancia (2011) provides evidence that these low IRGDs were caused by temporary episodes

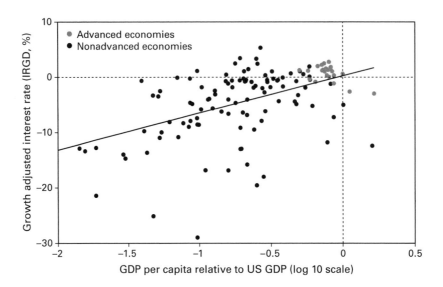

Figure 3.1
IRGD and income levels
Source: Escolano, Shabunina, and Woo (2011)

of financial repression (associated with the reduction of large public debt ratios after the Second World War and other exceptional debt surges).

In contrast, nonadvanced economies have generally low IRGDs, many of them substantially negative. The average IRGD annual observation during 1999 to 2008 was about –4 percentage points among emerging market economies, and below –7 percentage points for the whole ESW sample of nonadvanced economies. Nonadvanced, nonemerging economies, which correspond to the lower income level group, had an average IRGD of about –8.5 percentage points, and a substantial part of these observations were well below –10 percentage points. As shown in figure 3.2, these extremely low average values of the IRGD among nonadvanced economies are not driven by a few outliers.

3.4 Why Is the IRGD So Low in Nonadvanced Economies?

Economic growth theory suggests that the IRGD should be positive in economies that operate along a path of balanced growth (Blanchard and Fischer 1989)—that is, when over sufficiently long periods, the main macroeconomic aggregates (output, capital stock, consumption, wages, etc.) broadly grow at the same rate, and key ratios (growth, interest rate, savings rate, etc.) are approximately constant. This is the so-called "modified golden rule."[10] A balanced growth path is thought to de-

Table 3.2
Interest-rate–growth differential (IRGD), advanced economies (geometric average over the period, in percentage points)

Country	Nominal interest rate		Nominal growth	Interest-rate–growth differential[a]	
	Effective[b]	Long-term bond[c]		Effective[b]	Long-term bond[c]
Australia (1990–2011)	8.6	6.9	5.1	3.4	1.7
Austria (1991–2011)	5.3	5.2	3.9	1.4	1.2
Belgium (1991–2011)	5.9	5.4	3.8	2.0	1.5
Canada (1985–2011)	9.2	6.5	5.2	3.8	1.3
Denmark (1991–2011)	6.6	5.4	3.7	2.9	1.7
Finland (1991–2011)	6.1	5.8	3.7	2.3	2.0
France (1985–2011)	6.1	6.1	4.0	2.1	2.1
Germany (1992–2011)	5.4	4.8	3.5	2.7	2.1
Greece (1992–2011)	8.1	9.6	9.4	0.8	2.3
Ireland (1991–2011)	5.4	6.0	7.1	−1.6	−1.1
Italy (1985–2011)	8.0	7.9	5.4	2.5	2.4
Japan (1985–2011)	3.4	3.0	1.6	1.8	1.4
Luxembourg (1991–2011)	5.4	5.0	6.9	−1.4	−1.8
Netherlands (1991–2011)	6.0	5.1	4.4	1.5	0.6
Norway (1998–2011)	4.6	4.7	6.5	−1.8	−1.7
Portugal (1991–2011)	7.4	6.8	5.5	1.8	1.3
Spain (1995–2011)	5.4	5.2	5.8	−0.3	−0.5
Sweden (1995–2011)	4.8	4.9	4.4	0.3	0.5
Switzerland (1985–2011)	3.3	3.7	3.4	0.0	0.3
United Kingdom (1991–2011)	6.4	5.8	4.7	1.6	1.0
United States (1985–2011)	6.1	6.0	5.1	1.0	0.9
Average[d]	6.1	5.7	4.9	1.3	0.9

Sources: AMECO and World Economic Outlook Databases
a. IRGD, defined as $(a − b)/(1 + b)$; where a is the interest rate and b is the growth rate.
b. Interest payments in year t as a ratio to debt outstanding at the end of year $t − 1$.
c. Ten-year benchmark central government bond, when available; closest bond available otherwise.
d. Unweighted arithmetic average.

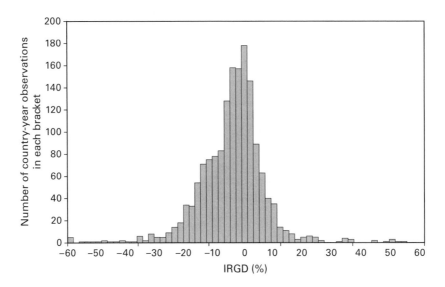

Figure 3.2
Interest-rate–growth differential: Nonadvanced economies, 1999 to 2010
Source: Escolano, Shabunina, and Woo (2011)

scribe well the main medium-term macroeconomic growth features of advanced economies—and indeed the IRGD is generally positive among advanced economies, as discussed above. Standard economic growth theory, however, is by and large silent about the values of the IRGD that should be expected in economies that are not at, or near, the balanced growth path (King and Rebelo 1993)—other than predicting that over the long term these economies will converge toward this path, and that as a consequence the IRGD will then eventually be positive.

Thus, in practice, it is often implicitly assumed by public finance analysts and practitioners that IRGDs well below those prevailing in advanced economies are a feature of the income catch-up process of emerging and low income economies. Under this benign view, high growth due to rapid accumulation of human and physical capital drives down the IRGD and erodes debt ratios, allowing these economies to sustain substantial primary fiscal deficits without adverse consequences. If very low—in many cases, strongly negative—IRGDs are an intrinsic feature of the income catch-up process, one can expect them to stay for many years to come. And by the time these IRGDs start trending up and the debt dynamics becomes a problem because the income catch-up is close to completion, the affected economies will have the capability and resources to rebalance their fiscal stance.

Unfortunately, under scrutiny, this view turns out to be strongly counterfactual. The gap in IRGD between advanced and nonadvanced economies is predominantly

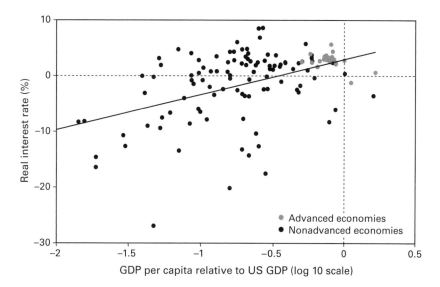

Figure 3.3
Real interest rates and income levels: Country averages, 1999 to 2008
Source: Escolano, Shabunina, and Woo (2011)

due to lower interest rates—not mainly to higher growth—in the latter economies than in the former. For example, during 1990 to 2010, the average IRGD gap between nonadvanced and G7 economies was 8 percentage points (the IRGD was –5.7 among nonadvanced economies and 2.4 in the G7). Of this gap, about two-thirds was due to lower real interest rates (by 5.3 percentage points) in nonadvanced economies, and about one-third was due to higher growth (by 2.8 percentage points). Like the IRGD, real interest rates are correlated with (relative) per capita income levels (figure 3.3) and their predominant role in explaining the IRGD gap is a widespread feature across time and regions (figure 3.4).

While higher growth in nonadvanced economies than in advanced economies is an intrinsic feature of the income catch-up process, lower real interest rates are not. On the contrary, the income per capita catch-up process can be expected to result in higher, not lower, interest rates among nonadvanced economies. It is higher marginal productivity of capital—implying higher rates of return—that drives capital accumulation and causes faster GDP per capita growth in nonadvanced economies.[11] External borrowing could, in principle, circumvent high closed-economy interest rates, lowering the average effective interest rate on sovereign (and private) debt. But the interest rate should still be higher than that of advanced economies by the liquidity, risk, and other premia. For example, the spread between emerging market sovereign debt and US treasury bills (as measured by the EMBI Global spreads) averaged 451

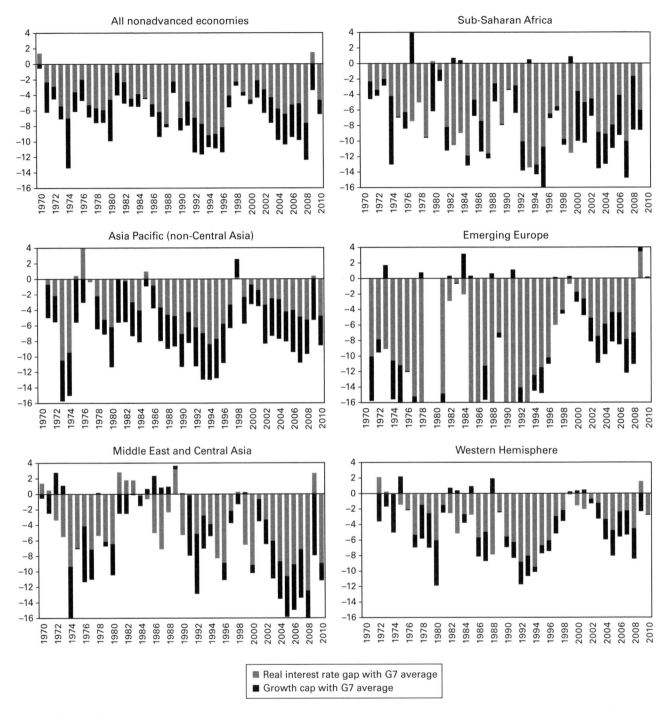

Figure 3.4
IRGD gap between nonadvanced economies and G7, with decomposition by *r* and *g*. The real interest rate is corrected by exchange rate effects. The sample size varies with time, depending on data availability. Database updated to 2010.
Source: Escolano, Shabunina, and Woo (2011)

basis points over 2000 to 2011—reflecting this market-determined overall premium. Moreover, in practice, the typical nonadvanced economy pays a lower average effective interest rate on its domestic debt than on its external borrowing (after adjusting for exchange rate gains and losses). Thus the capacity of some sovereigns to tap international capital markets does not explain the lower interest rates paid by nonadvanced economies.

While the evidence militates against the hypothesis that low IRGDs are rooted in the income catch-up process, it points instead to severe distortions and financial repression. The relevant financial market distortions include captive savings markets, high barriers to cross-border financial flows (particularly of retail savings operations), government-directed lending and administrative allocation of savings (often directly through public ownership of major financial institutions and pension funds), interest rate controls, and bans or severe restrictions on hedging means (e.g., inflation-indexed or foreign currency-denominated financial instruments). As documented in Reinhart and Sbrancia (2011), financial repression, particularly when combined with persistent (although not necessarily very high) inflation, has proved to be an effective means of reducing IRGDs and of eroding public debt ratios—via real interest rates well below their notional competitive market equilibrium and often negative for long periods of time.

Stylized facts as well as formal econometric testing suggest that financial repression is at the basis of the abnormally low real interest rates in nonadvanced economies. Sustained low real interest rates are associated with indicators of financial repression (figure 3.5) and with steady but persistent inflation (figure 3.6). Financial liberalization reforms in the 1980s and 1990s spurred growth in some emerging economies, but they also ended the previous period of negative real interest rates (figures 3.7 and 3.8), as these rates rose pari passu with indicators of financial development.

ESW formally explores this hypothesis through a panel regression model. Their model seeks to determine the significance and size of the influence that financial repression exerts on real interest rates. After controlling for standard determinants of interest rates,[12] they find that a variety of financial repression indicators are statistically significant and of a size that can explain the large deviations of real interest rates with respect to their notional market-determined levels in many nonadvanced economies. Among the most significant indicators are commercial bank assets as a ratio to commercial and central bank assets, private credit, financial liberalization index, external capital account openness, and inflation. Given that financial repression can take a variety of forms, they also extract the two first principal components (explaining 70 percent of the variance) from their set of indicators. The first principal component turns out to capture the presence of financial distortions, while the second principal component closely reflects the presence of inflation. All these

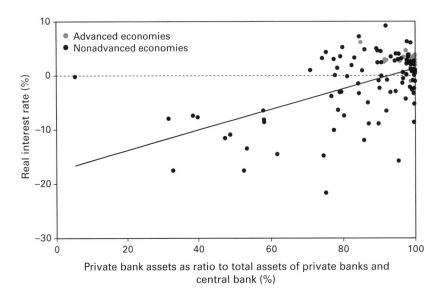

Figure 3.5
Financial repression and real interest rates
Source: Escolano, Shabunina, and Woo (2011)

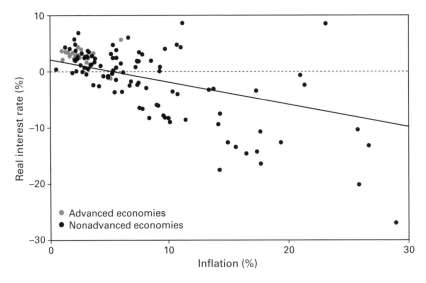

Figure 3.6
Inflation and real interest rates
Source: Escolano, Shabunina, and Woo (2011)

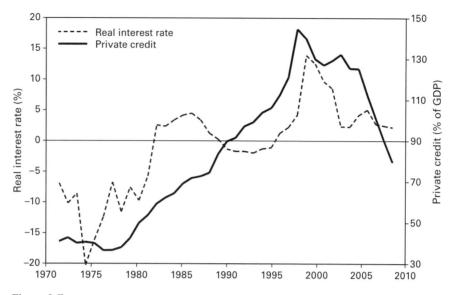

Figure 3.7
Korea: Real interest rates and private credit
Source: Escolano, Shabunina, and Woo (2011)

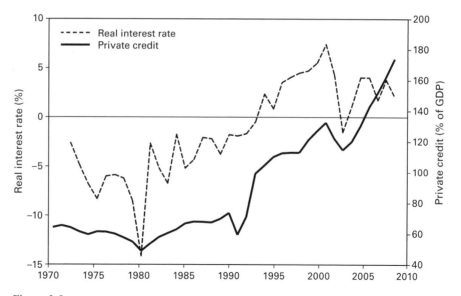

Figure 3.8
South Africa: Real interest rates and private credit
Source: Escolano, Shabunina, and Woo (2011)

indicators are found to be statistically significant and of a size that makes them economically meaningful.

3.5 Conclusions

Persistent negative values of the IRGD, often well below −10 percentage points, are a pervasive feature of the public debt dynamics of many nonadvanced economies. These negative IRGDs exert a sizable downward pressure on government debt ratios, allowing stable or even declining debt ratios in the presence of sustained primary fiscal deficits. But these negative IRGDs are unlikely to be a serendipitous side effect of the income catch-up process of these economies. The evidence strongly suggests that they are, by and large, the result of equally pervasive distortions and repression of financial activity, which keep average effective real interest rates paid on public debt well below their market-determined equilibrium levels. In association with persistent inflation, real interest rates are negative for extended periods in many cases.

In these conditions the favorable fiscal policy environment is likely to dissipate well before these countries complete their income catch-up process—perhaps in a few years—as a consequence of financial development and increasing financial globalization. During the 2000s, emerging Europe and some leading performers in Latin American and Asia have already experienced a significant erosion of the financial barriers that kept IRGDs and real interest rates artificially low in the past. Countries that envisage an increasing integration into the world economy will need to consider their medium-term fiscal stance in light of a likely increase of the IRGD toward market equilibrium levels.

Even if a country were able to keep pervasive restrictions on its domestic financial intermediation system, this would probably not be a desirable policy. Exploring the channels through which financial development is an intrinsic component of income growth is beyond the scope of this chapter.[13] However, most of the literature (as well as practitioners' experience) suggests that efficient mobilization and allocation of domestic savings becomes at some point incompatible with channeling a large part of these savings toward public debt yielding severely distorted returns. At that point many countries may in fact risk that farsighted growth-enhancing policies be discarded in favor of the short-term expedience of maintaining the financial distortions to ensure the financing of public debt at an artificially low cost.

Notes

1. More precisely, the IRGD is the difference between the interest rate and the GDP growth rate (adjusted if necessary for valuation gains or losses on foreign-currency or indexed debt),

divided by one plus the GDP growth rate. For a detailed discussion, see chapter 2 on debt dynamics in this book.

2. Output growth can also reduce the debt ratio indirectly by increasing the primary budget balance: higher growth typically raises tax revenue (as a percentage of GDP), and it can reduce expenditure by lowering the cost of safety net programs (e.g., unemployment). This endogenous impact of growth on the budget can be altered by discretionary policies. The discussion here takes the primary balances as given, and it does not deal with these indirect effects of growth. For a discussion of the determinants of the primary balance, see chapter 4 in this book.

3. This stock-flow residual may arise because accounting adjustments or because debt-changing financial operations. The latter could be sales of financial assets used to reduce debt, or acquisition of financial assets, such as financial sector support operations, financed by debt issuance. Unfortunately, the stock-flow residual also arises because debt-financed fiscal operations are often transferred off-budget in an attempt to reduce the reported headline budget deficit or to avoid budget disclosure of the details of these operations (see Irwin 2012; Weber 2012).

4. The (nominal) average effective interest rate is typically calculated as budgetary interest paid in year t divided by the stock of debt at the end of year $t - 1$. ESW also corrects the effective interest rate for exchange rate related valuation changes in the debt stock (see chapter 2 on debt dynamics in this book)—as I do whenever possible throughout this chapter. This is appropriate from an economic perspective, since these valuation changes are part of the cost of servicing the foreign currency-denominated debt. However, under standard fiscal accounting, these valuation changes are reflected in the value of the debt stock, but (unlike those arising on inflation-indexed debt) they are not part of the budgetary interest bill. Instead, they are implicitly part of the stock-flow residual. If the effective interest rate is adjusted to include valuation changes, these valuation changes should be subtracted, for consistency, from the stock-flow residual term.

5. Unless otherwise noted, the classification of economies as advanced, emerging, and so forth, follows the statistical appendix of the IMF *Fiscal Monitor* (http://www.imf.org/external/ns/cs.aspx?id=262). However, when the database of ESW is quoted, some countries that are currently classified advanced economies are counted as emerging economies if they were classified as such during most of the sample period (1999–2008). This reclassification includes Korea and new EMU members.

6. All cross-country averages are simple averages.

7. A large snowball effect could also be, in principle, the result of a large debt stock, even with an IRGD of small absolute value. However, the average initial debt ratio was similar for advanced and nonadvanced economies, at about 56 percent of GDP.

8. Many of the advanced economies with negative IRGDs are Central and Eastern European economies that were not classified as advanced for a significant part of the sample period.

9. Whenever it is not otherwise stated, the data used here are from the database of Escolano, Shabunina, and Woo (2011). This database is an unbalanced annual panel of 128 advanced and nonadvanced economies covering 1999 to 2008, after eliminating those with concessional debt exceeding 50 percent of their external public or publicly guaranteed debt (about

one-third of the original sample). For nonadvanced economies, the interest rate is adjusted for currency depreciation effects on foreign currency-denominated debt. The database has been updated through 2010.

10. The modified golden rule follows from the basic features of a competitive equilibrium. If the IRGD were negative, the return on investment (the interest rate) would be lower than the rate of increase of the capital stock (which equals the GDP growth rate along the balanced growth path). Thus each and every year, economic agents would be investing more than what they obtain from their investments. However, no individual economic agent would choose such an intertemporal investment–consumption pattern, since investment would reduce her consumption now without increasing it at any time in the future.

11. King and Rebelo (1993) find that in standard growth models that are realistically parameterized, the transition toward the balance growth path from low initial levels of capital (the income catch-up process) will result in very high real interest rates. In their simulations, both model-based real interest rates and IRGDs during the catch-up process were well in excess of their values when the transition is completed.

12. The controls include public debt ratios, fiscal deficits, output growth, population aging, domestic private saving ratios, and world interest rates. Some of these controls could have been caused or facilitated by financial repression (high debt and deficits, inefficiently high savings rates, low growth). In those cases, this would bias downward the size and significance estimates of the impact of financial repression indicators on real interest rates.

13. See Levine (1997, 2005) and Khan and Senhadji (2000).

References

Blanchard, O. J., C. Chouraqui, R. P. Hagemann, and N. Sartor. 1990. The sustainability of fiscal policy: New answers to an old question. Economic Studies 15, Autumn. OECD, Paris. www.oecd.org/eco/outlook/34288870.pdf.

Blanchard, O. J., and Stanley Fischer. 1989. *Lectures on Macroeconomics*. Cambridge: MIT Press.

Escolano, Julio. 2010. A practical guide to public debt dynamics, fiscal sustainability, and cyclical adjustment of budgetary aggregates. IMF Technical Notes and Manuals 2010/02. IMF, Washington, DC. http://www.imf.org/external/pubs/ft/tnm/2010/tnm1002.pdf.

Escolano, Julio, Anna Shabunina, and Jaejoon Woo. 2011. The puzzle of persistently negative interest rate–growth differentials: Financial repression or income catch-up? Working paper 11/260. IMF, Washington, DC. http://www.imf.org/external/pubs/ft/wp/2011/wp11260.pdf.

Irwin, Timothy C. 2012. Accounting devices and fiscal illusions. Staff discussion note 12/02. IMF, Washington, DC. http://www.imf.org/external/pubs/ft/sdn/2012/sdn1202.pdf.

Khan, Mohsin S., and Abdelhak S. Senhadji. 2000. Financial development and economic growth: An overview. Working paper 00/209. IMF, Washington, DC. http://www.imf.org/external/pubs/ft/wp/2000/wp00209.pdf.

King, R. G., and S. T. Rebelo. 1993. Transitional dynamics and economic growth in the neoclassical model. *American Economic Review* 83 (4): 908–31.

Levine, Ross. 1997. Financial development and economic growth. *Journal of Economic Literature* 35: 688–726.

Levine, Ross. 2005. Finance and growth: Theory and evidence. In Philippe Aghion and Steven Durlauf, eds., Handbook of Economic Growth, vol. 1. Amsterdam: Elsevier, 865–934.

Reinhart, C., and B. Sbrancia. 2011. The liquidation of government debt. Working paper 16893. NBER, Cambridge, MA.

Weber, Anke. 2012. Stock-flow adjustments and fiscal transparency: A cross-country comparison. Working paper 12/39. IMF, Washington, DC. http://www.imf.org/external/pubs/ft/wp/2012/wp1239.pdf.

4

Determinants of the Primary Fiscal Balance: Evidence from a Panel of Countries

Li Zeng

4.1 Introduction

The primary fiscal balance is a key determinant of public debt dynamics. Together with the level of the public debt stock and the differential between the interest rate on public debt and GDP growth, it forms the basis for projecting the future path of a country's public debt. This chapter first reviews some stylized facts about the primary fiscal balance. It then tries to empirically identify the most important underlying determinants of the primary fiscal balance, using cross-country panel data. The final section of the chapter provides an illustrative example showing how to apply the empirical findings to predict a country's primary fiscal balance on the basis of fundamentals.

4.2 Stylized Facts

In view of the need for major fiscal adjustment in the years ahead, especially among the advanced economies, a natural question to ask is how challenging such required adjustments will be by historical standards. Some stylized facts about the primary fiscal balance can help to put in perspective the magnitude of the challenge. Appendix table A4.1 provides the summary statistics for the historical primary fiscal balance of 87 countries during the past few decades.[1] Figure 4.1 shows the frequency plots of the highest primary fiscal surplus for each country.

The first two panels in figure 4.1 show that achieving large primary fiscal surplus in one year is not an unusual event. Over 40 percent of the countries (37 out of 87, or 14 out of 32 advanced economies) had a maximum one-year primary fiscal surplus exceeding 5 percent of GDP.

Nonetheless, a high level of primary fiscal surplus has been maintained over an extended period less frequently, as demonstrated by the next four panels in figure 4.1. Out of the 87 sample countries, only 14 recorded an average primary fiscal surplus higher than 5 percent of GDP over a five-year period.[2] A further look into these

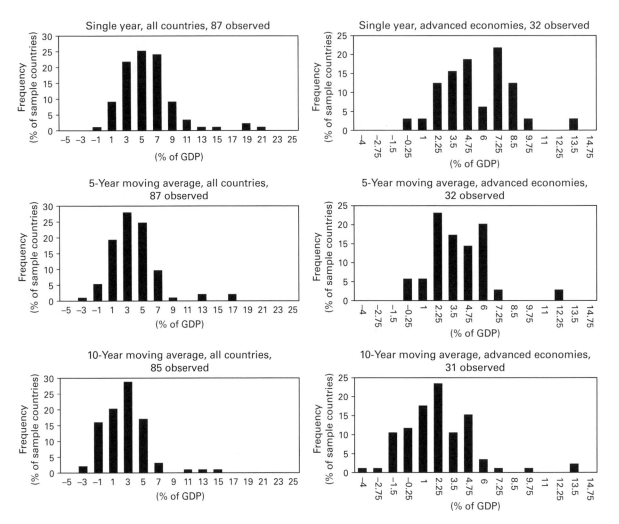

Figure 4.1

Frequency plots of maximum fiscal balance, by country, annual data, 1956 to 2009. The sample excludes oil and primary product exporters, as defined by the WEO, and HIPC MDRI beneficiary countries. Data are available beginning in 1956 for Japan, in the 1960s and 1970s for another 15 advanced economies, in the 1980s for about 30 countries, and in the 1990s for the bulk of the sample. The total number of country-year observations is 2,061.

Source: World Economic Outlook Database

Table 4.1
Episodes of sustained, large primary surpluses

Need to finance large interest bill stemming from high public debt	Revenue boost from natural resource exports and other factors	Strong overall performance, coupled with fiscal prudence
Jamaica * (1988–92, 15.1, 107)	Botswana * (1984–88, 16.5, 32)	Singapore * (1991–95, 11.6, 73)
Seychelles * (1988–92, 8.8, 80)	Egypt * (1993–97, 5.8, 97)	New Zealand * (1993–97, 6.0, 51)
Belgium * (1998–2002, 6.3, 110)	Lesotho *[a] (2004–2008 11.1, 62)	Denmark * (1985–89, 5.7, 62)
Dominica (2003–2007, 5.3, 107)		Turkey * (2003–2007, 5.3, 53)
Israel (1987–91, 5.1, 140)		Canada (1997–2001, 5.1, 90)
Panama (1990–94, 5.1, 77)		

Note: Reported in the table are five-year episodes during which countries achieved an average primary fiscal balance above than 5 percent of GDP. The starred countries have recorded more than one such episode. Nonetheless, only the episode with the highest average primary fiscal balance is listed. Reported in the parentheses are (time period / average primary balance as percentage of GDP / average public debt as percent of GDP).
a. The high primary balance of Lesotho during the period 2004 to 2008 was, to a large extent, explained by the receipts from the Southern African Customs Union, which repeatedly exceeded the budget forecast, thanks mostly to buoyant revenues from South Africa.

countries (table 4.1) shows that such large fiscal surpluses by three of them were actually connected to exogenous factors that would be difficult for other countries to replicate—large increases in revenues related to natural resources (Botswana and Egypt) or transfers arising from custom union membership (Lesotho).[3] The remaining 11 countries account for less than 15 percent of the sample. If the averaging horizon is lengthened to ten years, then only 4 countries (Belgium, Jamaica, Singapore, and Seychelles), aside from Botswana and Lesotho, recorded an average primary surplus higher than 5 percent of GDP.

It is worth pointing out, though, that having not achieved high levels of primary fiscal balance over an extended period of time does not necessarily mean that the country is incapable of doing so—it may simply have never needed to. For example, countries with low debt-to-GDP ratios, low borrowing costs, and healthy growth would not need to run large primary surpluses. Nevertheless, measuring the required primary fiscal balance for reducing debt against historical benchmarks may be suggestive of how challenging the needed adjustments will be. Investigation of the 14 countries that achieved a five-year moving average primary fiscal balance higher than 5 percent of GDP reveals that most of them were facing high public debts, exceeding 60 percent of GDP, at the time when they ran large primary surpluses. This is broadly consistently with the notion that countries facing higher debt pressure tend to run higher primary fiscal balance. The effect of debt pressure on the primary fiscal balance will be studied more carefully through regression analysis in the next section.

The role of rapid GDP growth in facilitating large primary surpluses can also be explored through simple charts. The top left-hand side panel in figure 4.2 plots the maximum single-year primary fiscal balance of each country against the real GDP growth of the same period. While most countries registered their best primary fiscal balance when their economies were growing, this cross-country chart seems to suggest that a country's ability to run high primary fiscal balance does not critically

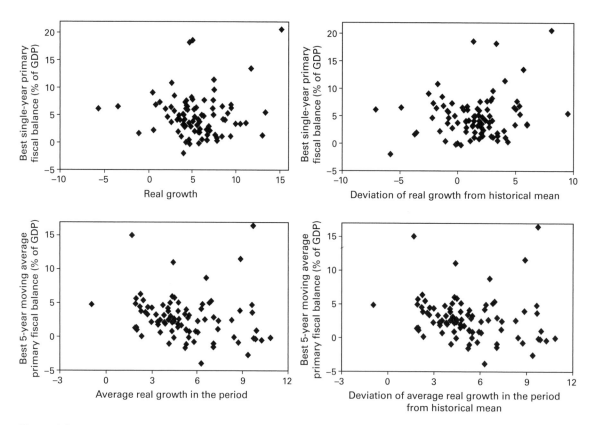

Figure 4.2
Best primary fiscal balance versus growth. The sample consists of 87 countries, with data for 1956 to 2009, subject to availability.
Source: World Economic Outlook Database

hinge upon its GDP growth. The top right-hand side panel in figure 4.2 replaces the real GDP growth in the first chart with its deviation from the countries' historical mean. It shows that more than one-fourth of the countries had their best primary fiscal balance when real growth was below the countries' historical average.

Do such patterns hold at the medium-term frequency? To answer this, the bottom two panels of figure 4.2 report the best primary balance and real growth for five-year (moving) averages. The patterns shown are similar to those seen in the top panels. While most countries achieved their best five-year average primary fiscal balance when the economies were growing, there is no clear cross-country positive correlation between such best five-year average and the corresponding average real growth. The bottom right-hand side panel shows that even in the medium run, more than one-fifth of the countries had their best five-year average primary fiscal balance when the average real growth of the period was below the countries' historical mean.

While figure 4.2 indicates that a country's ability to run large primary fiscal surpluses is not critically constrained by its GDP growth, it should *not* be interpreted as evidence against the positive impact of growth on the primary fiscal balance. There are several reasons. First, figure 4.2 only reports cross-country comparisons of the cases when countries had their best primary fiscal balance. Second, other important determinants of the primary fiscal balance, such as countries' public debt levels, are not taken into account in figure 4.2. Finally, figure 4.2 does not address the potential dual causality between the primary fiscal balance and growth. Thus a more accurate gauge of the growth impact on the primary fiscal balance will require rigorous econometric analysis, incorporating additional time-series perspective, taking cases other than the best-performing episodes into consideration, controlling for other determinants of the primary fiscal balance, and dealing with the endogeneity between growth and the primary fiscal balance carefully. The next section seeks to meet these goals.

4.3 Determinants of the Primary Fiscal Balance

The discussion thus far has focused on the maximum primary fiscal balance that countries have achieved. Such "boundary cases" provide useful references for measuring the challenges facing countries that need large fiscal adjustments. However, a more general question is, in a given environment, what level of primary fiscal balance should reasonably be expected.

This section and the next will try to shed light on this question by first empirically identifying the key underlying determinants of the primary fiscal balance and gauging their quantitative impact through regression analysis, and then providing illustrative examples on how to apply the regression results to relate a country's primary fiscal balance to its fundamentals.

4.3.1 Modeling the Primary Fiscal Balance

This chapter uses two methods to estimate the empirical relation between the primary fiscal balance and its underlying determinants. The first one is the country fixed-effect (FE) model:

$$pb_{i,t} = \alpha_0 + \alpha_i + \beta \cdot X_{i,t} + \varepsilon_{i,t}, \tag{4.1}$$

where $pb_{i,t}$s country i's primary fiscal balance, as a share of GDP, in period t; α_0s a constant; α_is the country fixed effect; $X_{i,t}$ a vector of underlying determinants for the primary fiscal balance; and $\varepsilon_{i,t}$s an error term.

The second method is the dynamic panel data (DPD) model, where the first lag of the primary fiscal balance, $pb_{i,t-1}$ is added to the right hand side of the equation as a regressor:

$$pb_{i,t} = \alpha_0 + \alpha_i + \gamma \cdot pb_{i,t-1} + \beta \cdot X_{i,t} + \varepsilon_{i,t}. \tag{4.2}$$

The lagged dependent variable is included to capture the persistence in the primary fiscal balance. Indeed, it is well known that when a country needs to improve its primary surplus, a given adjustment is often phased in over several years.

4.3.2 Determinants of Primary Fiscal Balance

The previous literature has suggested a wide range of factors that may affect a country's primary fiscal balance (e.g., see Woo 2003).

• *Real GDP Growth* (g)

There are different channels through which economic growth can affect the primary fiscal balance. One is the automatic fiscal stabilizers. For instance, in an economy with a share of revenues equivalent to, say, 40 percent of GDP, a 1 percentage point increase in economic growth would, other things equal, result in a 0.4 percent of GDP improvement in the fiscal balance, under the assumption that government expenditure is inelastic to growth and revenues have unit elasticity vis-à-vis output. In addition to the cyclical factors, the trend of growth may also affect the primary fiscal balance, for example, through its influence on how difficult it is politically to run large primary fiscal balance.[4]

• *Debt-Stabilizing Primary Fiscal Balance* (dspb)

This is the level of primary fiscal balance that a country needs to run to stabilize its public debt as a percent share of GDP. It is the product of the stock level of public debt and the differential between the interest rate on public debt and GDP growth. It captures the impact of the debt stock, the financing conditions and the economic growth in measuring the public debt pressure facing a country. Because countries tend to be forward-looking in assessing their debt pressure, this chapter tries to reflect that by constructing the interest-rate and growth differential using, for country i at period t, the average of the WEO vintage forecast on growth for periods $t+1$ to $t+5$.[5] Ideally, the same should be done for the interest rate as well, so that the constructed differential is fully forward-looking. Unfortunately, doing so would render a loss of too many observations; as a result the implied contemporaneous interest rate on public debt is used in the baseline specification instead.

• *Public Debt Stock as a Share of GDP (d)*
This is another debt pressure measure, included to compliment the debt-stabilizing primary fiscal balance. On the one hand, countries with low initial debt levels might have space to let the public debt grow without causing immediate concerns over sovereign solvency. On the other hand, for countries already burdened with very high public debt stocks, stabilizing the debt may not be enough—they need to run a larger primary fiscal balance to reduce the debt stock over time.[6]

• *Private Savings as a Share of GDP (prisav)*
Private savings may affect a country's primary fiscal balance through financing channels. While for countries with perfect financial market access, the interest rate, a price measure by itself, could be a good indicator of the public financing tightness, quantity measures, such as the private savings, are also needed to give a more complete public financing picture for countries with constrained market access. Higher private savings give the government more room for financing its deficits, and thus could lead to a lower level of primary fiscal balance.

• *Inflation*
The theoretical prediction on how inflation would affect the primary fiscal balance is more ambiguous. On the one hand, as pointed out by Abiad and Ostry (2005), when inflation rises, the primary fiscal balance may improve, because of the Patinkin effects, if expenditures are fixed in nominal terms, or the bracket-creep effects on tax revenues.[7] On the other hand, higher inflation, as an alternative method for government to lower its real debt burden, could reduce the need to run a high primary fiscal surplus and thus lead to a smaller primary fiscal balance. Which factor is dominant remains an empirical question.

• *ICRG Composite Risk Index (comprisk)*[8]
The primary fiscal balance may be affected by political and institutional factors as well. Political stability and high-quality institutions tend to be associated with high primary fiscal balance. The ICRG composite risk index, where a higher value indicates a more stable political and economic environment, is included to capture such effects.

Compared with the many factors that have been discussed in the literature, only a small set of determinants are included in the regressions here. It is also worth discussing some regressors that are excluded here.

• *Government Revenues as a Share of GDP*
The revenue-to-GDP ratio was used by some early studies as a proxy for a country's revenue-generating capacity and therefore a determinant for the primary fiscal balance. In estimations not reported (for the sake of brevity), the contemporaneous ratio was highly correlated with the primary surplus, but the link was fragile when the lagged revenue ratio or its moving average were used instead, in spite of the high correlation among these series. This suggests that the significant relation between the primary fiscal balance and government revenues might be mainly driven by the direct accounting relation between the two.

• *Other Economic, Political, and Demographic Variables.*
Other economic variables—such as terms of trade—political variables— such as corruption index and the checks-and-balances index— and demographic variables— such as population ratio of age 65 and older—did not seem to bring extra explanatory power to the baseline specifications where the previously discussed determinants were all included. This is possibly due to the high collinearity among these variables.

4.3.3 Sample and Data
The regressions use a panel of 61 countries, comprising 29 advanced economies, 22 emerging market economies and 10 low income countries. The observations used for the baseline specifications range from 1990 to 2007. More detailed information can be found in appendix table A4.1. There are two special notes about the sample.

First, the following countries or episodes, where the primary fiscal balance was largely driven by special factors, are excluded: (1) oil and other primary product exporters;[9] (2) the Multilateral Debt Relief Initiative (MDRI) beneficiary countries;[10] (3) high-inflation episodes, with inflation rate higher than 35 percent per annum; and (4) three annual observations prior to any fiscal stress episode.[11]

Second, this study takes advantage of the newly available Historical Public Debt Database (HPDD), compiled by the Fiscal Affairs Department of the IMF, resulting in wider sample coverage than earlier studies. The baseline regressions have over 700 observations, more than double the sample size of IMF (2003) and of Abiad and Ostry (2005). The summary statistics and construction details of the data are provided in appendix table A4.2.

Estimation Results and Robustness Check
One of the concerns in estimating equations (4.1) and (4.2) is the two-way causality between the primary fiscal balance and growth. To alleviate such concerns, all the

fixed-effect models are estimated using the instrumental variable method, with the real growth for each country instrumented by the average growth rate of its largest trade partners. The dynamic panel models are estimated using the Arellano–Bond GMM method, with the real growth treated as endogenous and the average growth rate of the countries' largest trade partners included as an additional instrumental variable.

Baseline Results and Main Robustness Tests

Tables 4.2 and 4.3 report the estimation results of the baseline specifications using the two methods, along with some robustness tests based on simpler specifications or alternative models, including a pooled-data OLS regression and a random-effect model.

The baseline result of the fixed-effect model, in column 1 of table 4.2, shows a significant positive impact of real growth on the primary fiscal balance. It suggests that when the real GDP grows faster by 1 percentage point, the primary fiscal balance is 0.53 percentage point of GDP higher. This result does not seem to be affected

Table 4.2
Fixed-effect model: Baseline and some robustness check

Dependent variable: Primary balance (% of GDP)	(1) Baseline	(2) Simpler specifications	(3)	(4)	(5) Alternative models	(6)
Estimator	FE	FE	FE	FE	OLS	RE
Real GDP growth	0.530***	0.544***	0.550***	0.586***	0.702***	0.536***
	(0.082)	(0.082)	(0.084)	(0.088)	(0.114)	(0.079)
Debt-stabilizing primary fiscal balance	0.287***	0.290***	0.275***	0.264***	0.281***	0.285***
	(0.057)	(0.057)	(0.057)	(0.061)	(0.062)	(0.055)
Debt stock at beginning of period	0.018***	0.014**	0.016**	0.011	0.033***	0.020***
	(0.007)	(0.006)	(0.007)	(0.007)	(0.004)	(0.006)
Private savings	−0.243***	−0.247***	−0.227***		−0.129***	−0.224***
	(0.026)	(0.026)	(0.026)		(0.019)	(0.024)
Inflation	0.083***	0.069***		0.053**	0.108***	0.080***
	(0.022)	(0.022)		(0.024)	(0.025)	(0.022)
ICRG composite risk index	0.064***		0.045**	0.073***	0.133***	0.075***
	(0.022)		(0.022)	(0.024)	(0.016)	(0.020)
Observations	793	793	793	793	793	793
Number of countries	61	61	61	61	61	61
R-squared	0.567	0.558	0.553	0.499	0.082	

Note: Standard errors are in parentheses; *** $p < 0.01$, ** $p < 0.05$, and * $p < 0.1$.

Table 4.3
Dynamic panel data model: Baseline and some robustness check

Dependent variable: Primary balance (% of GDP)	(1) Baseline	(2) Simpler specifications	(3)	(4)
Estimator	DPD	DPD	DPD	DPD
Real GDP growth	0.226*** (0.018)	0.247*** (0.023)	0.231*** (0.013)	0.237*** (0.018)
Debt-stabilizing primary fiscal balance	0.212*** (0.018)	0.226*** (0.018)	0.214*** (0.034)	0.206*** (0.016)
Debt stock at beginning of period	0.030*** (0.004)	0.024*** (0.004)	0.024*** (0.002)	0.029*** (0.003)
Private savings	-0.131*** (0.009)	-0.136*** (0.008)	-0.133*** (0.009)	
Inflation	0.062*** (0.007)	0.057*** (0.005)		0.057*** (0.005)
ICRG composite risk index	0.040*** (0.006)		0.015*** (0.004)	0.052*** (0.007)
First lag of primary balance	0.594*** (0.017)	0.571*** (0.022)	0.554*** (0.023)	0.659*** (0.038)
Observations	744	744	744	744
Number of countries	61	61	61	61

Note: Standard errors are in parentheses; *** $p < 0.01$, ** $p < 0.05$, * $p < 0.1$.

much by either dropping some regressors from the specification, columns 2 to 4, or switching to an alternative model, columns 5 and 6 in the table. In fact, the coefficient on real growth would increase to slightly over 0.7, if the pooled-data model is adopted.

The baseline result of the dynamic panel data model, column 1 of table 4.3, also suggests a significant positive growth impact on the primary fiscal balance. The implied steady state coefficient on real growth, 0.56, is indeed close to what was seen in table 4.2, although the immediate growth impact, 0.23, appears to be much smaller.[12] Similar to the fixed-effect model, this result does not seem to be affected much by dropping some regressors from the specification.

The estimation results in tables 4.2 and 4.3 also show that countries tend to respond to higher debt pressure by running a larger primary fiscal balance. The two variables associated with debt pressure, the debt-stabilizing primary fiscal balance and the public debt stock, both have significant positive coefficients under the baseline specifications.

The fixed effect model (table 4.2) suggests that when the debt-stabilizing primary fiscal balance rises by 1 percentage point, countries tend to raise their primary fiscal balance by 0.3 percentage point. The dynamic panel data model (table 4.3) shows a smaller short-term response in the primary fiscal balance to the same shock, 0.2 percentage point; but at the same time it implies a larger steady state impact of a half percentage point.

The coefficient on the public debt stock ranges between 0.01 to 0.02 in the fixed-effect model. The dynamic panel data model indicates a 0.03 short-term impact of debt increase on the primary fiscal balance, which implies a steady state coefficient of 0.07.

The private savings and the ICRG composite risk index both have significant coefficients with expected signs in tables 4.2 and 4.3. The comparison between the results of the two estimation methods indicates a consistent pattern for these two variables: they both seem to have smaller short-term impact but larger steady state influence in the dynamic panel data model than in the fixed-effect model.

While economic theories suggest mixed effects of inflation on the primary fiscal balance, its coefficients in tables 4.2 and 4.3 are all positive and significant. This seems to indicate that, empirically, inflation's primary-balance-enhancing effect dominates its primary-balance-substitute effect. One possible reason for such results is that episodes with high inflation, when its substitution effect for running a primary fiscal balance is most significant, are excluded from the estimation sample.[13]

4.3.4 Further Robustness Check: Outliers and Alternative Samples

This part runs more robustness tests to check whether the baseline results are driven by outliers or whether they would change substantially with alternative estimation samples.

To test whether the estimation results are driven by outliers, the baseline specifications are re-estimated excluding those observations with tail residuals. The chapter applied three different thresholds for identifying outliers, 1 percent, 2 percent, and 5 percent. Since the results are similar, only the estimations excluding 2 percent observations are reported in tables 4.4 and 4.5. Comparisons with the baseline results show that they are qualitatively the same and quantitatively close.

Another robustness test is to re-estimate the baseline specifications while dropping one sample country at a time. The purpose is to check whether the baseline results were driven by the observations of any specific country. The result summary of those estimations, reported in table 4.6, shows that all the coefficients remain in a reasonably small range around those obtained with the full sample. This finding suggests that the baseline results were not driven by any specific country in the sample.

The baseline regressions excluded three annual observations prior to each fiscal stress episode. To test whether such selection on the sample had a critical impact

Table 4.4
Fixed-effect model: Excluding outliers and with alternative samples

Dependent variable: Primary balance (% of GDP)	(1) Exclude 2% outliers	(2) Exclude 10 annual observations prior to fiscal stress episodes	(3) Not exclude obs. prior to fiscal stress episodes	(4) Include 2008–2009 observations	(5) Exclude major political conflict episodes
Real GDP growth	0.588***	0.583***	0.478***	0.454***	0.515***
	(0.082)	(0.099)	(0.072)	(0.036)	(0.083)
Debt-stabilizing primary fiscal balance	0.346***	0.308***	0.295***	0.268***	0.274***
	(0.053)	(0.064)	(0.051)	(0.050)	(0.058)
Debt stock at beginning of period	0.020***	0.026***	0.023***	0.022***	0.017**
	(0.006)	(0.009)	(0.006)	(0.006)	(0.007)
Private savings	−0.246***	−0.278***	−0.228***	−0.190***	−0.248***
	(0.024)	(0.030)	(0.023)	(0.023)	(0.029)
Inflation	0.077***	0.090***	0.071***	0.062***	0.085***
	(0.021)	(0.030)	(0.019)	(0.020)	(0.023)
ICRG composite risk index	0.057***	0.078***	0.070***	0.084***	0.060**
	(0.020)	(0.025)	(0.020)	(0.021)	(0.025)
Observations	779	657	888	904	709
Number of countries	61	57	61	61	54
R-squared	0.615	0.569	0.576	0.589	0.556

Note: Standard errors are in parentheses; *** $p < 0.01$, ** $p < 0.05$, * $p < 0.1$.

on the estimation results, the models are re-estimated with two alternative selection criteria: exclude 10 annual observations prior to each fiscal stress episode, or exclude no observations at all. The results are reported in columns 2 and 3 of tables 4.4 and 4.5. The estimations in column 4 of the two tables include observations of 2008and 2009, while those in column 5 exclude major political conflict episodes from the sample.[14] Although the coefficients based on these alternative samples exhibit different sizes, with mixed patterns, from the baseline results, the qualitative conclusions always remain unchanged.

4.3.5 Further Robustness Check: Alternative Interest-Rate Measures

Table 4.7 tests the baseline results using alternative interest-rate measures.

As discussed earlier, countries are, or should be, forward-looking in assessing their debt sustainability. However, owing to limited data availability, the implied contemporaneous nominal interest rate on public debt was used to construct the interest-rate and growth differential, in the calculation of the debt-stabilizing primary fiscal balance. In columns 1 and 3 of the table, this interest rate for period t is replaced by

Table 4.5
Dynamic panel data model: Excluding outliers and with alternative samples

Dependent variable: Primary balance (% of GDP)	(1) Exclude 2% outliers	(2) Exclude 10 annual observation prior to fiscal stress episodes	(3) Not exclude observations prior to fiscal stress episodes	(4) Include 2008–2009 observations	(5) Exclude major political conflict episodes
Real GDP growth	0.206***	0.228***	0.213***	0.281***	0.275***
	(0.013)	(0.014)	(0.016)	(0.014)	(0.021)
Debt-stabilizing primary fiscal balance	0.174***	0.218***	0.251***	0.336***	0.229***
	(0.015)	(0.020)	(0.020)	(0.046)	(0.016)
Debt stock at beginning of period	0.039***	0.045***	0.032***	0.039***	0.019***
	(0.003)	(0.005)	(0.004)	(0.006)	(0.005)
Private savings	−0.107***	−0.148***	−0.129***	−0.117***	−0.141***
	(0.010)	(0.006)	(0.007)	(0.010)	(0.009)
Inflation	0.063***	0.069***	0.045***	0.069***	0.079***
	(0.005)	(0.006)	(0.005)	(0.005)	(0.007)
ICRG composite risk index	0.048***	0.063***	0.037***	0.072***	0.039***
	(0.006)	(0.008)	(0.006)	(0.013)	(0.005)
First lag of primary balance	0.582***	0.567***	0.522***	0.573***	0.513***
	(0.035)	(0.026)	(0.026)	(0.025)	(0.036)
Observations	732	612	832	855	667
Number of countries	61	57	61	61	54

Note: Standard errors are in parentheses; *** $p < 0.01$, ** $p < 0.05$, * $p < 0.1$.

the average of periods t, $t + 1$ and $t + 2$. This implicitly assumes that the government has perfect foresight on its future interest rate and brings more forward-looking aspect to the calculated debt-stabilizing primary fiscal balance. The regressions reported in columns 2 and 4 of the table are similar, but they use the moving average interest rate of period $t - 1$, t and $t + 1$ instead. The estimation results based on these specifications are again qualitatively the same as, and quantitatively close to, the baseline results.

4.3.6 Further Robustness Check: Alternative Debt Pressure Measures
Tables 4.8 and 4.9 reports more robustness test results with alternative debt pressure measures.

In columns 1 to 3, the average of the contemporary vintage of the *WEO* forecast for economic growth, used to calculate the interest-rate and growth differential, is replaced by the average of actual future growth. This alternative approach is

Table 4.6
Result summary of estimations dropping one sample country at a time

Variable	Number of estimations	Mean	Standard deviation	Min	
Fixed-effect model					
Real GDP growth rate	61	0.529	0.014	0.499	0.596
Debt-stabilizing primary fiscal balance	61	0.286	0.019	0.178	0.317
Stock of public debt	61	0.018	0.003	0.012	0.036
Private savings	61	−0.242	0.009	−0.267	−0.194
Inflation	61	0.083	0.004	0.068	0.095
ICRG composite risk index	61	0.064	0.006	0.042	0.085
Dynamic panel data model					
Real GDP growth rate	61	0.239	0.019	0.202	0.298
Debt-stabilizing primary fiscal balance	61	0.219	0.018	0.165	0.263
Stock of public debt	61	0.030	0.004	0.020	0.038
Private savings	61	−0.135	0.006	−0.147	−0.121
Inflation	61	0.064	0.005	0.055	0.078
ICRG composite risk index	61	0.042	0.004	0.031	0.052
First lag of primary fiscal balance	61	0.576	0.022	0.521	0.618

equivalent to assuming that the country's authorities have perfect foresight regarding its future economic growth. The interest rates used in these three columns correspond to the baseline specification and the two alternative interest-rate measures used in table 4.7, respectively. As shown in the tables, the coefficients on real growth, private savings, inflation and ICRG composite risk index, all remain highly significant and close in size to those under the baseline specifications. The coefficients for the debt-stabilizing primary fiscal balance, while showing more variation in size, also remain highly significant with the expected signs.

Estimations in column 4 of tables 4.8 and 4.9 use the interest-rate and growth differential, together with the public debt stock, to gauge the debt pressure facing a country. Those in column 5 again use the debt-stabilizing primary fiscal balance, but it is set to zero when it has negative values. This is to test whether the frequent sign switch of the debt-stabilizing primary fiscal balance in some countries, which happens when the interest rate and growth are close to each other, have significant impact on the regression results. The results for all other regressors turn out to be similar to those under the baseline specifications. The previous conclusion that countries tend to raise their primary fiscal balance when facing increased debt pressure is also confirmed by the significant positive coefficients on the new debt pressure variables.

Table 4.7
Alternative interest-rate measures

Dependent variable: Primary balance (% of GDP)	(1) FE[a]	(2) FE[b]	(3) DPD[a]	(4) DPD[b]
Real GDP growth	0.514***	0.537***	0.232***	0.229***
	(0.081)	(0.083)	(0.015)	(0.022)
Debt-stabilizing primary fiscal balance (alternative 1)	0.260***		0.195***	
	(0.063)		(0.020)	
Debt-stabilizing primary fiscal balance (alternative 2)		0.226***		0.151***
		(0.057)		(0.022)
Debt stock at beginning of period	0.018***	0.012*	0.032***	0.024***
	(0.007)	(0.007)	(0.004)	(0.007)
Private savings	−0.239***	−0.232***	−0.135***	−0.126***
	(0.026)	(0.027)	(0.010)	(0.008)
Inflation	0.086***	0.080***	0.067***	0.069***
	(0.023)	(0.024)	(0.005)	(0.006)
ICRG composite risk index	0.061***	0.068***	0.045***	0.045***
	(0.022)	(0.023)	(0.008)	(0.007)
First lag of primary balance			0.566***	0.552***
			(0.018)	(0.037)
Observations	792	775	743	727
Number of countries	61	61	61	60
R-squared	0.565	0.554		

Note: Standard errors in parentheses; *** $p < 0.01$, ** $p < 0.05$, * $p < 0.1$.
a. In calculation of the debt-stabilizing primary balance, the contempraneous real interest rate is replaced by the moving averaing of periods t, $t + 1$, and $t + 2$.
b. In calculation of the debt-stabilizing primary balance, the contempraneous real interest rate is replaced by the moving averaing of periods $t − 1$, t, and $t + 1$.

4.3.7 Nonlinearity in Debt Stock

The regressions reported in table 4.10, by introducing nonlinearity in d to the models, try to test the notion that countries would act more aggressively to reduce the public debt after it exceeds a certain threshold. The regressions in columns 1 and 3 achieve this by including a higher order term of d as an additional regressor, while those in columns 2 and 4 add a spline for d at the threshold of 60 percent of GDP, a widely used indicative level for a more vigilant watch on a country's debt sustainability.

There seems to be little evidence of nonlinearities in the relationship between the primary fiscal balance and the debt-to-GDP ratio. For the fixed-effect model, both coefficients on the public debt and its square are insignificant in column 1. In column 2, contrary to what one would expect, the coefficient on the over-threshold part of

Table 4.8
Fixed-effect model: Alternative measures of debt pressure

Dependent variable: Primary balance (% of GDP)	(1) FE[a]	(2) FE	(3) FE[a,c]	(4) FE	(5) FE[d]
Real GDP growth	0.502***	0.498***	0.517***	0.550***	0.519***
	(0.080)	(0.080)	(0.082)	(0.085)	(0.083)
Debt-stabilizing primary fiscal balance	0.113***				
	(0.040)				
Debt-stabilizing primary fiscal balance (alternative 1)		0.083**			
		(0.042)			
Debt-stabilizing primary fiscal balance (alternative 2)			0.077*		
			(0.043)		
Interest-rate and growth differential				0.178***	
				(0.038)	
Nonnegative debt-stabilizing primary balance					0.268***
					(0.093)
Debt stock at beginning of period	0.024***	0.021***	0.018**	0.017**	0.014**
	(0.007)	(0.007)	(0.007)	(0.007)	(0.007)
Private savings	−0.233***	−0.232***	−0.226***	−0.246***	−0.249***
	(0.026)	(0.026)	(0.027)	(0.026)	(0.027)
Inflation	0.074***	0.075***	0.072***	0.084***	0.066***
	(0.022)	(0.022)	(0.024)	(0.023)	(0.022)
ICRG composite risk index	0.066***	0.065***	0.066***	0.073***	0.071***
	(0.022)	(0.022)	(0.023)	(0.022)	(0.022)
Observations	792	792	775	793	793
R-squared	0.563	0.561	0.552	0.561	0.558

Note: Standard errors are in parentheses; *** − < 0.01, ** $p < 0.05$, * $p < 0.1$.
a. Perfect foresight is assumed in calculating forward-looking real growth.
b. Contemporaneous real interest rate is replaced by the moving average of periods t, $t + 1$, and $t + 2$.
c. Contemporaneous real interest rate is replaced by the moving average of periods $t − 1$, t, and $t + 1$.
d. Negative forward-looking debt-stabilizing primary balance is replaced by zero.

Table 4.9
Dynamic panel data model: Alternative measures of debt pressure

Dependent variable: Primary balance (% of GDP)	(1) DPD[a]	(2) DPD[a,b]	(3) DPD[a,c]	(4) DPD	(5) DPD[d]
Real GDP growth	0.250***	0.223***	0.207***	0.221***	0.238***
	(0.020)	(0.019)	(0.016)	(0.015)	(0.019)
Debt-stabilizing primary fiscal balance	0.137***				
	(0.023)				
Debt-stabilizing primary fiscal balance (alternative 1)		0.120***			
		(0.028)			
Debt-stabilizing primary fiscal balance (alternative 2)			0.127***		
			(0.022)		
Interest-rate and growth differential				0.109***	
				(0.013)	
Nonnegative debt-stabilizing primary balance					0.203***
					(0.037)
Debt stock at beginning of period	0.032***	0.031***	0.037***	0.031***	0.026***
	(0.005)	(0.005)	(0.005)	(0.039)	(0.020)
Private savings	−0.122***	−0.126***	−0.136***	−0.140***	−0.143***
	(0.008)	(0.006)	(0.010)	(0.009)	(0.008)
Inflation	0.067***	0.066***	0.065***	0.055***	0.056***
	(0.008)	(0.006)	(0.005)	(0.005)	(0.004)
ICRG composite risk index	0.042***	0.036***	0.037***	0.044***	0.042***
	(0.007)	(0.005)	(0.006)	(0.006)	(0.005)
First lag of primary balance	0.576***	0.564***	0.606***	0.575***	0.573***
	(0.023)	(0.030)	(0.014)	(0.039)	(0.020)
Observations	768	768	751	744	744
Number of countries	61	61	60	61	61

Note: Standard errors in parentheses; *** $p < 0.01$, ** $p < 0.05$, * $p < 0.1$.
a. Perfect foresight is assumed in calculating forward-looking real growth.
b. Contemporaneous real interest rate is replaced by the moving average of periods t, $t + 1$, and $t + 2$.
c. Contemporaneous real interest rate is replaced by the moving average of periods $t − 1$, t, and $t + 1$.
d. Negative forward-looking debt-stabilizing primary balance is replaced by zero.

Table 4.10
Nonlinearity in debt stock

Dependent variable: Primary balance (% of GDP)	(1) FE	(2) FE	(3) DPD	(4) DPD
Real GDP growth	0.530***	0.527***	0.242***	0.242***
	(0.083)	(0.083)	(0.016)	(0.024)
Debt-stabilizing primary fiscal balance	0.287***	0.287***	0.230***	0.228***
	(0.057)	(0.056)	(0.017)	(0.020)
Debt stock at beginning of period	0.017		0.060***	
	(0.018)		(0.007)	
Debt stock at beginning of period (squared)	0.001		−0.016***	
	(0.010)		(0.003)	
Debt below 60% of GDP		0.023*		0.050***
		(0.014)		(0.006)
Debt above 60% of GDP		0.017**		0.025***
		(0.008)		(0.005)
Private savings	−0.243***	−0.242***	−0.141***	−0.126***
	(0.026)	(0.026)	(0.008)	(0.010)
Inflation	0.083***	0.083***	0.062***	0.070***
	(0.022)	(0.022)	(0.005)	(0.009)
ICRG composite risk index	0.064***	0.065***	0.045***	0.049***
	(0.022)	(0.022)	(0.005)	(0.008)
First lag of primary balance			0.551***	0.571***
			(0.037)	(0.027)
Observations	793	793	744	744
Number of countries	61	61	61	61
R-squared	0.567	0.568		

Note: Standard errors are in parentheses; *** $p < 0.01$, ** $p < 0.05$, * $p < 0.1$.

the public debt is actually smaller than the one on the below-threshold debt. For the dynamic panel data model, the coefficient on d^2 is negative in column 3, which seems inconsistent with the view that higher debt has an increasingly strong and positive impact on the primary balance. Similar to the fixed-effect model, the estimation result in column 4 shows a smaller coefficient for the over-threshold part of debt than the below-threshold portion.

4.3.8 Subsample Results
Tables 4.11 and 4.12 report the estimation results for subsamples separating the advanced economies from other countries. There are some interesting differences between the estimated coefficients for the two subsamples.

Table 4.11
Fixed-effect model: Subsample results

Dependent variable: Primary balance (% of GDP)	(1) FE	(2) FE	(3) FE	(4) FE	(5) FE	(6) FE	(7) FE	(8) FE
	Advanced economies				Other countries			
Real GDP growth	0.690***	0.697***	0.667***	0.770***	0.397***	0.423***	0.431***	0.434***
	(0.097)	(0.096)	(0.096)	(0.105)	(0.123)	(0.125)	(0.129)	(0.132)
Debt-stabilizing primary fiscal balance	0.331***	0.306***	0.409***	0.011	0.375***	0.384***	0.370***	0.416***
	(0.115)	(0.115)	(0.115)	(0.117)	(0.065)	(0.066)	(0.066)	(0.069)
Debt stock at beginning of period	−0.012	−0.013	−0.022***	−0.014	0.065***	0.054***	0.063***	0.057***
	(0.009)	(0.009)	(0.008)	(0.010)	(0.010)	(0.009)	(0.010)	(0.010)
Private savings	−0.341***	−0.351***	−0.321***		−0.189***	−0.186***	−0.178***	
	(0.044)	(0.044)	(0.044)		(0.031)	(0.032)	(0.032)	
Inflation	0.243***	0.230***		0.188**	0.052**	0.035		0.036
	(0.071)	(0.071)		(0.076)	(0.021)	(0.022)		(0.023)
ICRG composite risk index	0.077*		0.060	0.117**	0.085***		0.071***	0.081***
	(0.046)		(0.046)	(0.049)	(0.024)		(0.024)	(0.025)
Observations	433	433	433	433	360	360	360	360
Number of countries	29	29	29	29	32	32	32	32
R-squared	0.646	0.643	0.638	0.581	0.558	0.524	0.531	0.487

Note: Standard errors are in parentheses; *** $p < 0.01$, ** $p < 0.05$, * $p < 0.1$.

Table 4.12
Dynamic panel data model: Subsample results

Dependent variable: Primary balance (% of GDP)	(1) DPD	(2) DPD	(3) DPD	(4) DPD	(5) DPD	(6) DPD	(7) DPD	(8) DPD
	Advanced economies				Other countries			
Real GDP growth	0.399***	0.446***	0.398***	0.383***	0.095**	0.193***	0.113***	0.168***
	(0.037)	(0.036)	(0.030)	(0.020)	(0.042)	(0.048)	(0.036)	(0.052)
Debt-stabilizing primary fiscal balance	0.160	0.468***	0.299**	0.159	0.337***	0.291***	0.296***	0.301***
	(0.099)	(0.158)	(0.120)	(0.282)	(0.038)	(0.016)	(0.026)	(0.018)
Debt stock at beginning of period	0.033***	0.038***	0.041***	0.042***	0.071***	0.044***	0.058***	0.050***
	(0.009)	(0.011)	(0.011)	(0.014)	(0.012)	(0.010)	(0.008)	(0.007)
Private savings	-0.177***	-0.216***	-0.122***		-0.121***	-0.113***	-0.116***	
	(0.031)	(0.027)	(0.017)		(0.011)	(0.011)	(0.009)	
Inflation	0.107***	0.044		0.063**	0.029**	0.026**		0.040***
	(0.021)	(0.029)		(0.026)	(0.014)	(0.013)		(0.013)
ICRG composite risk index	0.030		0.012	0.058**	0.070***		0.044***	0.061***
	(0.022)		(0.021)	(0.024)	(0.017)		(0.015)	(0.013)
First lag of primary balance	0.658***	0.669***	0.784***	0.774***	0.418***	0.283***	0.342***	0.336***
	(0.054)	(0.080)	(0.069)	(0.115)	(0.066)	(0.058)	(0.086)	(0.112)
Observations	405	408	405	405	339	341	339	339
Number of countries	29	29	29	29	32	32	32	32

Note: Standard errors in parentheses; *** $p < 0.01$, ** $p < 0.05$, * $p < 0.1$.

On the one hand, under both the fixed-effect and dynamic panel data models, the positive impact of growth on the primary fiscal balance is estimated to be larger in the subsample consisting of the advanced economies than for the other countries. This could be an indication that the automatic fiscal stabilizers are larger in the advanced economies or that their fiscal policies are more countercyclical than those in other countries. On the other hand, the primary fiscal balances of the advanced economies seem to be less responsive to debt pressure. This is particularly evident if one compares the coefficients on the public debt stock for the two groups of countries. The advanced economies consistently have smaller coefficients, which even turn negative under the fixed-effect model, albeit mostly insignificant. The advanced economies also receive smaller coefficients on the debt-stabilizing primary fiscal balance under most specifications. Overall, these results seem to be broadly consistent with the common wisdom that, under normal circumstances, the advanced economies have better access to the financial markets and can therefore handle debt pressure with less urgency than other countries.

Under all specifications in the two tables, the size of the coefficient on the private savings is larger (more negative) for the advanced economies than for the other country group. This seems consistent with the fact that financial markets are better developed in the advanced economies, which makes it easier for their governments to tap domestic private savings for public financing. The regression results also show that inflation has a larger positive impact on the primary fiscal balance in the advanced economies than in other countries. While this seems contradictory to the view that inflation is less of a public financing tool in the advanced economies than in the emerging and low income countries, it is actually consistent with the recent finding by Reinhart and Sbrancia (2011) that inflation was an important channel for the advanced economies to liquidate their public debt. Since most advanced economies have a relatively stable political environment and high quality institutions, one would expect the ICRG composite risk index to matter less among them. The results shown in the tables appear to be consistent with this: while the coefficient for the ICRG composite risk index is positive and significant under all specifications for the emerging and low-income country group, it is statistically insignificant in half of the specifications for the advanced economies.

4.4 Application: Predicting the Primary Fiscal Balance on the Basis of Fundamentals

The previous section identified important determinants for the primary fiscal balance and estimated their quantitative impact. This section illustrates one application of these results—to project primary fiscal balance benchmark for countries, that is, the level of primary fiscal balance that countries are expected to run given their fundamentals.

The application using the fixed-effect model is straightforward: for any period t, plugging the set of fundamentals $X_{i,t}$ into equation (4.1′) will produce the model-based primary balance benchmark $\widehat{pb}_{i,t}$:

$$\widehat{pb}_{i,t} = \hat{\alpha}_0 + \hat{\alpha}_i + \hat{\beta} \cdot X_{i,t}. \tag{4.1′}$$

If the dynamic panel data method is used, there are two possible ways to proceed. Supposing that forecasts on the underlying determinants are available for each year within the projection horizon, the future primary fiscal balance can be computed out recursively using equation (4.2′):

$$\widehat{pb}_{i,t} = \hat{\alpha}_0 + \hat{\alpha}_i + \hat{\gamma} \cdot pb_{i,t-1} + \hat{\beta} \cdot X_{i,t}. \tag{4.2′}$$

The other way to apply the dynamic panel data method is based on the steady state relation implied by the model, which directly projects the medium-term primary fiscal balance benchmark, pb_i^* by plugging the medium-term fundamental forecast, X_i^* into equation (4.3):

$$pb_i^* = \frac{\hat{\alpha}_0}{1-\hat{\gamma}} + \frac{\hat{\alpha}_i}{1-\hat{\gamma}} + \frac{\hat{\beta}}{1-\hat{\gamma}} \cdot X_i^*. \tag{4.3}$$

For illustration purpose, this chapter takes its medium-term forecasts of the fundamentals from the last available projection by the *WEO* and predicts the primary fiscal balance benchmark for each country in the sample by applying the second method for the dynamic panel data model.[15] To show how the underlying determinants are driving the projections, table 4.13 reports the summary forecasts, along with the decomposition by contributions of the determinants, for four country groups: advanced economies and the other countries are considered separately, and each of these groups is further subdivided depending on whether the model predicts a positive or negative primary fiscal balance benchmark for the country.

The table shows some interesting contrasts between the advanced economies and the rest countries. On the one hand, since the emerging market and low income countries are expected to grow faster in the medium term and tend to have higher inflation, the model predicts that they should run higher primary fiscal balances than the advanced economies. On the other hand, other factors work in the opposite direction. For instance, the emerging market and low income countries are projected to face, on average, smaller public debt pressure than the advanced economies, as indicated by both the debt-stabilizing primary fiscal balance and the level of public debt stock. In addition the political environment and institution quality tend to be less favorable in these countries. Both factors suggest that they might run lower primary fiscal balances than the advanced countries.

There are also interesting comparisons between the countries with negative primary balance benchmarks and those with positive benchmarks. Table 4.9 indicates

Table 4.13
Country group comparison: Projected medium-term primary fiscal balance benchmark

Country group	Medium-term primary fiscal balance benchmark	Contribution of each component to the primary fiscal balance benchmark							
		Real GDP Growth	Debt-stabilizing primary fiscal balance	Debt stock at beginning of period	Private savings	Inflation	Composite risk index	Country effect	Constant
	(1)	(2)	(3)	(4)	(5)	(6)	(7)	(8)	(9)
Advanced economies w. negative benchmarks	-1.5	1.4	0.0	1.4	-5.1	0.2	5.0	-1.5	-2.9
Advanced economies w. positive benchmarks	2.3	1.3	0.1	1.3	-4.4	0.2	5.2	1.5	-2.9
Other countries w. negative benchmarks	-2.1	2.5	-0.3	0.9	-5.4	0.3	4.4	-1.7	-2.9
Other countries w. positive benchmarks	1.6	2.6	-0.3	0.8	-3.7	0.4	4.3	0.5	-2.9

that the countries with negative primary balance benchmarks on average have higher private savings rates, and they tend to have poorer historical performance, as reflected by the smaller country fixed effects.

Having computed the primary fiscal balance benchmarks on the basis of fundamentals, one could carry out additional exercises by comparing them to other references. For instance, the predicted benchmark can be compared to the debt-stabilizing primary fiscal balance. If the predicted primary fiscal balance benchmark is above what is required to stabilize the debt, one could be more inclined to expect that stabilizing the debt would not require extraordinary efforts compared with the past. Conversely, if the predicted benchmark is below the debt-stabilizing primary fiscal balance, this is an indication by the model that additional adjustment policies may be needed to stabilize the country's public debt. The predicted benchmark can also be compared to the primary fiscal balance projections obtained through other methods, including those by IMF country desk economists or other forecasters. While the model takes a cross-country perspective and projects the primary fiscal balance based on historical experience, the forecasts by IMF desk economists, for example, tend to take more country specific factors into consideration, especially planned reforms.

Appendix

Table A4.1
Historical primary fiscal balance information

IFS Code	Country	First observed	Last observed	Total observed	Min	Max	Mean	Standard deviation	In regression sample[a]
111	United States	1960	2009	50	−10.88	4.20	−00.34	2.37	Yes
112	United Kingdom	1979	2009	31	−10.02	3.21	−1.06	2.84	Yes
122	Austria	1978	2009	32	−4.20	2.24	−0.41	1.45	Yes
124	Belgium	1979	2009	31	−7.38	6.85	2.39	3.71	Yes
128	Denmark	1976	2009	34	−6.42	8.25	2.06	3.21	Yes
132	France	1970	2009	38	−5.01	1.89	−0.53	1.46	Yes
134	Germany	1977	2009	33	−2.09	4.11	0.02	1.39	Yes
136	Italy	1980	2009	30	−5.85	6.10	0.18	3.45	Yes
137	Luxembourg	1980	2009	30	−3.01	6.42	2.16	2.21	Yes
138	Netherlands	1980	2009	30	−2.54	5.15	0.76	1.97	Yes
144	Sweden	1980	2009	30	−11.67	4.94	−0.73	4.37	Yes
146	Switzerland	1983	2009	27	−1.88	4.11	1.09	1.53	No
156	Canada	1961	2009	49	−5.26	6.01	0.54	3.10	Yes
158	Japan	1956	2009	54	−9.20	3.16	−1.47	2.99	Yes
172	Finland	1976	2009	32	−8.59	7.81	1.16	3.96	Yes
174	Greece	1988	2009	22	−6.82	4.65	0.10	3.41	Yes
176	Iceland	1973	2009	37	−7.48	6.74	0.37	2.78	Yes
178	Ireland	1976	2009	34	−14.48	6.27	−1.27	5.96	Yes
181	Malta	1995	2009	15	−6.82	1.10	−2.78	2.83	Yes
182	Portugal	1980	2009	30	−4.21	2.34	−0.72	1.81	Yes
184	Spain	1980	2009	30	−10.90	3.33	−0.74	2.96	Yes
186	Turkey	1991	2009	19	−2.63	6.56	1.94	3.03	Yes
193	Australia	1970	2009	40	−3.28	3.98	0.10	1.99	Yes
196	New Zealand	1984	2009	26	−1.72	7.61	2.91	2.72	Yes
199	South Africa	1980	2009	30	−3.36	3.83	0.30	2.48	Yes
213	Argentina	1992	2009	18	−1.35	5.31	1.36	1.96	Yes
223	Brazil	1996	2009	14	−0.89	4.18	2.62	1.73	Yes
233	Colombia	1989	2009	21	−1.92	3.69	1.54	1.61	Yes
238	Costa Rica	1993	2009	17	−2.41	5.02	1.91	1.80	Yes
243	Dominican Republic	1980	2009	30	−5.54	3.39	−1.26	1.96	Yes
253	El Salvador	1990	2009	20	−5.00	0.49	−1.43	1.58	Yes
283	Panama	1982	2009	28	−2.94	6.85	2.90	2.59	Yes

(*continued*)

Table A4.1
(*continued*)

IFS Code	Country	First observed	Last observed	Total observed	Min	Max	Mean	Standard deviation	In regression sample[a]
288	Paraguay	1977	2009	33	−3.29	5.73	0.74	2.10	Yes
298	Uruguay	1993	2009	17	−1.86	3.57	0.45	1.65	Yes
313	Bahamas	1991	2009	19	−3.92	2.99	0.46	1.50	Yes
316	Barbados	1985	2009	25	−4.82	6.13	1.09	3.41	No
321	Dominica	1986	2009	24	−5.56	7.69	1.40	3.84	No
343	Jamaica	1983	2009	27	−5.06	18.21	8.55	5.19	No
362	St. Lucia	1983	2009	27	−4.76	5.49	0.19	2.66	No
423	Cyprus	1988	2009	22	−3.06	6.54	0.75	2.33	Yes
436	Israel	1987	2009	23	−2.83	9.62	1.89	2.53	No
439	Jordan	1993	2009	17	−4.06	5.93	0.51	2.70	Yes
446	Lebanon	1992	2009	18	−19.00	2.81	−3.80	6.99	Yes
469	Egypt	1984	2009	26	−19.07	7.31	−3.32	8.13	Yes
514	Bhutan	1993	2009	17	−8.39	4.66	−0.92	4.03	No
518	Myanmar	1995	2009	15	−7.41	−1.95	−4.11	1.50	No
522	Cambodia	1996	2009	14	−4.22	0.43	−1.61	1.45	No
524	Sri Lanka	1986	2003	18	−6.74	0.04	−2.51	1.74	Yes
532	Hong Kong SAR	2005	2009	5	−3.31	7.70	1.95	4.18	Yes
534	India	1991	2009	19	−4.81	1.13	−2.51	1.45	Yes
542	Korea	1979	2009	31	−0.91	4.22	1.60	1.32	No
548	Malaysia	1995	2009	15	−3.35	6.19	−0.21	3.05	Yes
556	Maldives	1979	2007	29	−21.62	4.10	−5.75	6.31	No
564	Pakistan	1994	2009	16	−2.51	2.90	0.36	1.52	Yes
576	Singapore	1990	2009	20	1.79	13.49	7.36	3.39	Yes
616	Botswana	1980	2009	30	−9.64	20.61	5.90	7.11	No
624	Cape Verde	1986	2009	24	−17.48	0.85	−5.49	4.65	No
664	Kenya	1980	2009	30	−4.06	6.14	0.85	2.54	Yes
666	Lesotho	1980	2009	30	−16.25	18.59	0.35	8.57	No
684	Mauritius	1980	2009	30	−8.76	3.56	−0.94	2.94	No
686	Morocco	1970	2009	40	−15.42	5.02	−1.25	4.72	Yes
718	Seychelles	1983	2009	27	−14.29	11.44	1.31	6.77	No
728	Namibia	1993	2009	17	−4.26	6.32	−0.52	2.67	No
734	Swaziland	1980	2009	27	−3.45	8.52	0.38	3.31	No
744	Tunisia	1981	2009	29	−5.64	10.84	0.22	2.99	Yes
819	Fiji	1990	2009	20	−3.97	7.32	0.19	2.88	No
846	Vanuatu	1981	2007	27	−7.25	9.09	−0.91	3.73	No
913	Belarus	1996	2009	14	−2.52	1.97	0.00	1.33	No

Table A4.1
(*continued*)

IFS Code	Country	First observed	Last observed	Total observed	Min	Max	Mean	Standard deviation	In regression sample[a]
914	Albania	1994	2009	16	−8.97	−0.16	−3.28	2.85	Yes
915	Georgia	1995	2009	15	−8.42	3.77	−2.68	3.39	No
917	Kyrgyz Republic	1995	2009	15	−16.53	1.38	−5.28	4.68	No
918	Bulgaria	1999	2009	11	0.09	4.80	3.20	1.43	Yes
921	Moldova	2001	2009	9	−6.32	4.99	1.17	3.14	Yes
923	Tajikistan	2005	2009	5	−7.96	2.16	−3.93	3.95	No
924	China	1984	2009	26	−3.04	1.32	−1.46	0.93	Yes
926	Ukraine	1998	2009	12	−4.50	1.83	−0.89	1.95	Yes
935	Czech Republic	1996	2009	14	−5.53	0.55	−2.88	1.85	Yes
936	Slovak Republic	1996	2009	14	−4.62	−0.27	−1.89	1.32	Yes
939	Estonia	1995	2009	15	−3.80	3.40	0.31	2.29	Yes
941	Latvia	1994	2009	16	−11.33	1.10	−1.69	2.91	Yes
944	Hungary	1990	2009	18	−5.37	6.52	0.67	3.68	No
946	Lithuania	1994	2009	16	−9.12	0.33	−2.55	2.73	Yes
960	Croatia	1994	2009	16	−5.55	2.44	−1.34	2.01	Yes
961	Slovenia	1994	2009	16	−4.99	2.04	0.10	1.49	Yes
963	Bosnia & Herzegovina	1998	2009	12	−6.62	2.93	−1.84	2.73	No
964	Poland	1993	2009	17	−3.51	1.37	−0.96	1.60	Yes
968	Romania	1996	2009	14	−5.75	1.67	−1.01	2.13	Yes
	All	1956	2009	2061	−21.6	20.6	0.02	4.07	

Note: Summarized here is the general government primary fiscal balance, defined as the general government overall fiscal balance excluding net interest payments. The data are retrieved from the IMF World Economic Outlook Database (line GGBXI).

a. The regression sample starts from 1990.

Table A4.2
Summary statistics of data

Variable	Number of observations	Mean	Standard deviation	Min	Max
Sample for baseline regressions[a]					
Primary fiscal balance (percent of GDP)[b]	793	0.7	3.1	−14.0	13.5
Real GDP growth rate	793	3.9	3.0	−10.9	14.2
Debt-stabilizing primary fiscal balance (percent of GDP)[c]	793	−0.1	2.4	−19.8	14.6
Stock of public debt (percent of GDP)[d]	793	58.5	31.2	3.7	191.6
Private savings (percent of GDP)	793	19.7	6.4	3.0	44.6
Inflation	793	4.7	5.1	−1.4	34.5
Composite risk index	793	75.9	8.9	43.5	94.0
Average real growth rate of largest trade partners[e]	793	3.5	1.6	−0.9	9.3
Extended sample[a]					
Primary fiscal balance (% of GDP)[b]	1008	0.4	3.2	−14.0	13.5
Real GDP growth rate	1008	3.5	3.7	−18.5	14.2
Debt-stabilizing primary fiscal balance (% of GDP)[c]	1008	−0.2	2.3	−19.8	14.6
Stock of public debt (% of GDP)[d]	1008	56.9	32.1	3.7	217.6
Private savings (% of GDP)	1008	19.2	6.7	−7.9	45.2
Inflation	1008	5.0	5.3	−1.6	34.5
Composite risk index	1008	75.2	9.0	37.0	94.0
Average real growth rate of largest trade partners[e]	1008	3.1	2.2	−11.0	9.3

a. The sample for baseline regressions covers the period 1990 to 2007, and it excludes three annual observations prior to any fiscal stress episodes. The extended sample, used for various robustness tests, covers the period 1990 to 2009, and it does not exclude any observations prior to fiscal stress episodes.
b. Due to limited data availability, especially for the emerging market economies and low income countries in the sample, the headline primary fiscal balances, rather than cyclically adjusted figures, are used for the estimations.
c. In calculation of the debt-stabilizing primary fiscal balance, the interest-rate and growth differential is calculated as the following: $rminug_{i,t} = r_{i,t} - \overline{fwdg_{i,t}}$, where $r_{i,t} = 100 * \dfrac{Interest\ payment_{i,t}}{End\text{-}of\text{-}period\ public\ debt\ stock_{i,t-1}}$ is the implied nominal interest rate on public debt for country i at period t, and $\overline{fwdg_{i,t}}$ is the average of country i's WEO vintage forecasts on nominal GDP growth at period t for periods $t + 1$ to $t + 5$.
d. The public debt data, retrieved from the Historical Public Debt Database (HPDD), are gross debt for general government, except for countries where only the central government debt information is available.
e. For each country, the five largest trade partners based on 2007 total bilateral trade are selected for the calculation.
Data sources: (a) World Economic Outlook (WEO) Database, IMF; (b) Historical Public Debt Database (HPDD), IMF; (c) Direction of Trade Statistics (DOTS), IMF; (d) International Country Risk Guide (ICRG)

Notes

The author is very grateful to his colleagues in the Fiscal Affairs Department at the IMF, especially Paolo Mauro for close guidance and Ricardo Velloso and Fuad Hasanov for helpful discussions. He also wishes to thank Kathleen Ngangoue for her help with data preparation.

1. Summarized in the table is the *general government* primary fiscal balance, defined as the general government overall fiscal balance excluding the *net* interest payments. The data are retrieved from the IMF World Economic Outlook Database (line GGBXI).

2. Some countries achieved such outcome more than once.

3. Botswana and Egypt are not classified as primary commodity exporters by the WEO.

4. In some trial regressions, growth was separated into trend and cyclical components. While both appeared to play a role in most (but not all) specifications, the results were fragile to changes in specifications. Even so, real growth was a robust determinant.

5. Note that, as a result, this is a different variable from the contemporaneous growth rate (g) mentioned above.

6. See Bohn (1998) for an early study on the relationship between the primary fiscal balance and the debt-to-GDP ratio in the United States.

7. The Patinkin effect refers to the negative relationship between the inflation rate and real government expenditures. See Patinkin (1993).

8. The International Country Risk Guide (*ICRG*) is compiled by the PRS Group. More detailed information on the database can be found at http://www.prsgroup.com/.

9. Following the 2009 update of the WEO Group Aggregates.

10. See IMF Factsheet, The Multilateral Debt Relief Initiative (www.imf.org/external/np/exr/facts/pdf/mdri.pdf). The MDRI beneficiary countries are excluded for two reasons. First, the large one-time debt relief received by these countries caused abnormal movements in their primary fiscal balance. Second, and more important, it is highly likely that these countries had already been on unsustainable debt paths prior to the debt relief. Including them would thus cause bias in the estimation that is intended to predict what an appropriate primary surplus would be.

11. The reason for excluding observations prior to a fiscal stress episode is that if the estimation is used to predict what an appropriate primary surplus would be, based on fundamentals, it is important to leave out those observations where policies were clearly headed in the wrong direction. In the empirical implementation, the chapter follows the definition of fiscal stress episodes by Baldacci, McHugh, and Petrova (2011) and Baldacci et al. (2011).

12. $0.56 = 0.226/(1 - 0.594)$.

13. In some trial regressions, the chapter collapsed the annual observations from 1990 to 2007 into averages for three 6-year periods (1990–1995, 1996–2001, and 2002–2007) and estimated the fixed-effect model using those averages. While the coefficients on inflation were still positive in most cases, many of them became less significant or insignificant, suggesting that the primary balance-enhancing effect might be weaker in the medium term. To ensure that the empirical results were not driven by the inclusion of inflation, all

the robustness check regressions reported in later part of this section were also estimated with inflation excluded. The conclusions on other determinants remained qualitatively unchanged.

14. The data on major political conflict episodes are obtained from the Major Episodes of Political Violence (MEPV) database complied by the Center for Systemic Peace (http://www.systemicpeace.org). The chapter defines major political conflict episodes as periods with the ACTOTAL score greater than 4.

15. This exercise used the April 2011 vintage of the IMF's *WEO* projections on real growth, the public debt stock and other fundamentals for 2016. *Comprisk* for a country takes the value of its latest observation.

References

Abiad, Abdul, and Jonathan D. Ostry. 2005. Primary surpluses and sustainable debt levels in emerging market countries. Policy discussion paper 05/6. IMF, Washington, DC.

Baldacci, E., N. Belhocine, G. Dobrescu, J. McHugh, and I. Petrova. 2011. Assessing fiscal stress. Working paper 11/100. IMF, Washington, DC.

Baldacci, E., J. McHugh, and I. Petrova. 2011. Measuring fiscal vulnerability and fiscal stress: A proposed set of indicators. Working paper 11/94. IMF, Washington, DC.

Bohn, Henning. 1998. The behavior of U.S. public debt and deficits. *Quarterly Journal of Economics* 113 (3): 949–63.

International Monetary Fund. 2003. Public debt in emerging markets: Is it too high? *World Economic Outlook*. Washington, DC: IMF, 113–52.

Patinkin, Don. 1993. Israel's stabilization program of 1985,or some simple truths of monetary theory. *Journal of Economic Perspectives* 7 (spring): 103–28.

Reinhart, Carmen M., and M. Belen Sbrancia. 2011. The liquidation of government debt. Working paper 16893. NBER, Cambridge, MA.

Woo, Jaejoon. 2003. Economic, political, and institutional determinants of public deficits. *Journal of Public Economics* 87 (3–4): 387–426.

5

The Relationship between Debt Levels and Growth

Manmohan S. Kumar and Jaejoon Woo

5.1 Introduction

This chapter empirically investigates a critical policy question of the extent to which large public debts are likely to have an adverse effect on investment, productivity, and growth. From a theoretical point of view, this can occur through a variety of channels including higher long-term interest rates, possibly higher future distortionary taxation, higher inflation, greater uncertainty, vulnerability to crises, and reduced scope for countercyclical fiscal policies. Despite the importance of the issue, there is little systematic evidence in the literature.

The chapter provides empirical evidence on the impact of high public debt on subsequent growth of real per capita GDP in a panel of advanced and emerging market economies during 1970 to 2008. Building on large empirical growth literature (e.g., see Barro and Sala-i-Martin 2003; Aghion and Durlauf 2005), it pays particular attention to a variety of methodological issues, including reverse causality and simultaneity bias, resulting from the possibility that while high debt may have an adverse effect on growth, low growth—for reasons unrelated to debt—could also lead to high debt, or that government debt and growth might be jointly determined by a third variable. In addition it explores nonlinearities and threshold effects—that is, whether there is a certain level of debt only beyond which debt begins to have an adverse effect on growth.

The empirical results of the analysis, based on a range of econometric techniques, suggest an inverse relationship between initial debt and subsequent growth, controlling for other determinants of growth: on average, a 10 percentage point increase in the initial debt-to-GDP ratio is associated over the medium to long run with a slowdown in real per capita GDP growth of around 0.2 percentage points per year, with the impact being somewhat smaller in advanced economies than in emerging market economies. There is some evidence of nonlinearity with higher levels of initial debt having a proportionately larger negative effect on subsequent growth. Moreover, when a country's economic and financial position vis-à-vis the rest of the world is weak or the share of its foreign-currency denominated debt is large, the adverse impact of initial public debt on subsequent growth tends to be much more pronounced than when these factors are at more moderate levels.

The rest of the chapter is organized as follows: Section 5.2 discusses the channels through which high debt may affect growth, and summarizes related existing studies. Section 5.3 describes data and some stylized facts relating to public debt and growth; Section 5.4 presents the main panel regression results on the relationship between debt and growth, including an analysis of the relationship between international financial integration and the impact of high public debt on growth. Section 5.5 concludes.

5.2 Channels and Existing Studies

Public debt has important influence over the economy both in the short and the long run. The conventional view is that debt increases (reflecting deficit financing) can stimulate aggregate demand and output in the short run but crowds out private capital and reduces output in the long run (see Elmendorf and Mankiw 1999 for a literature survey). This chapter focuses on the long-run effects of public debt.

Standard growth theory predicts that an increase in government debt leads to slower growth—temporary decline in growth along the transition path to a new steady state in the neoclassical model, such as the Solow model, and a permanent decline in growth in the endogenous growth model (Saint-Paul 1992). Building on Barro's (1990) endogenous growth model with public goods externalities, Aizenman et al. (2007) further show that with effective upper bound on tax revenue due to distortions and imperfect tax enforcement, an increase in initial debt lowers productive government spending, which reduces the return to capital and growth subsequently.

There are several channels through which high debt could adversely impact medium- and long-run growth that have received attention in the literature: high public debt can adversely affect capital accumulation and growth via higher long-term interest rates (Gale and Orzag 2003; Baldacci and Kumar 2010), higher future distortionary taxation (Barro 1979; Dotsey 1994) and lower future public capital spending (Aizenmann et al. 2007), higher inflation (Sargent and Wallace 1981; Cochrane 2010), and greater uncertainty about prospects and policies. In more extreme cases of a debt crisis, by triggering a banking or currency crisis, these effects can be magnified (Burnside et al. 2001; Hemming et al. 2003). High debt is also likely to constrain the scope for countercyclical fiscal policies, which may result in higher volatility and further lower growth (see Aghion and Kharroubi 2007, on the effects of countercyclical fiscal policy on growth, and Woo 2009, on the effects of procyclicality and volatility of fiscal policy on growth).[1]

Despite these considerations, there has been little systematic analysis of the impact on GDP growth of high public debt in advanced or emerging market economies until very recently—the notable exceptions are Kumar and Woo (2010) for 46 advanced and emerging economies in 1970 to 2007, Checherita and Rother (2010) for 12 euro economies for 1970 to 2008, Cecchetti et al. (2011) for 18 OECD countries for 1980 to 2006, and Balassone et al. (2011) for Italy for 1890 to 2009. Kumar and Woo (2010) was the first study that provided systematic econometric evidence on the negative effects of public debt on long-run growth by employing rigorous statistical techniques that took into account determinants of growth, reverse causality, endogeneity, and other issues. Using long historical data (since the early 1800s), Reinhart and Rogoff (2010) find that the difference in average growth rates of GDP between low debt (below 30 percent of GDP) and high debt (above 90 percent of GDP) groups is 4.2 percentage points in advanced economies (also see Reinhart et al. 2012). Their study, however, only considers correlations between debt and growth and does not take into account other determinants of growth as well as other issues such as reverse causality.[2]

A number of other studies have looked at the impact of external debt on economic growth in developing economies. Most of these studies were motivated by the "debt overhang" hypothesis—a situation where a country's debt service burden is so heavy that a large portion of output accrues to foreign lenders and consequently creates disincentives to invest (Krugman 1988; Sachs 1989). Imbs and Ranciere (2007) and Pattillo, Poirson, and Ricci (2002, 2004) find a nonlinear effect of external debt on growth: that is, a negative and significant impact on growth at high external debt levels (typically over 60 percent of GDP), but an insignificant impact at low debt levels.

5.3 Data and Stylized Facts

Data for the key variables such as GDP, population, and investment are obtained from Penn World Table 7.0 (Heston et al. 2011). Fiscal data including government debt are from the IMF's World Economic Outlook Database, and other variables are from World Bank's World Development Indicators and Barro and Lee (2011). The main econometric analysis is based on a panel of 38 large and medium-sized advanced and emerging economies (defined as an economy with a population of over five million) for the period 1970 to 2008, although we also present the results using the full sample of 79 countries (advanced, emerging, and developing countries) without population size restriction (see the appendix at the end of this chapter for the country list).

First, data on government debt and growth clearly show a negative relationship between *initial* government debt and *subsequent* growth of real per capita

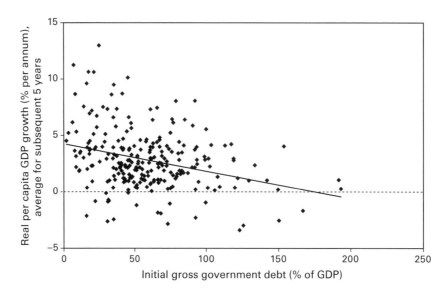

Figure 5.1
Initial government debt and subsequent growth of per capita real GDP over five-year periods
Source: Authors' calculation

GDP. Figure 5.1 shows a scatter plot of initial debt against subsequent growth of real per capita GDP over five-year periods in the sample of countries with population of over five million. According to the OLS fitted line, the coefficient of initial debt is −0.024. Taken at face value (i.e., ignoring the potential endogeneity problem, and not controlling for other growth determinants), it suggests that a 10 percentage point increase in initial debt-to-GDP ratio is associated with a subsequent slowdown in per capita GDP growth of 0.24 percentage points.[3] At shown below, this magnitude turns out to be surprisingly consistent with that obtained using robust econometric analysis. Similarly *initial* debt is negatively associated with *subsequent* domestic investment over five-year periods (figure 5.2).

Second, the *subsequent* growth rate of per capita GDP over five-year periods following high *initial* debt episodes (above 90 percent of GDP) is on average lower than that following low *initial* debt episodes (below 30 percent of GDP) (figure 5.3). In advanced economies, the difference in the average growth rates between low initial debt and high initial debt episodes is 0.9 percentage points; in emerging economies, it is more than twice that (1.7 percentage points). Similarly the average growth differential in G7 countries between low and high initial debt periods is 1.7 percentage points. In the full sample (including developing countries) the growth differential is 2.8 percentage points.

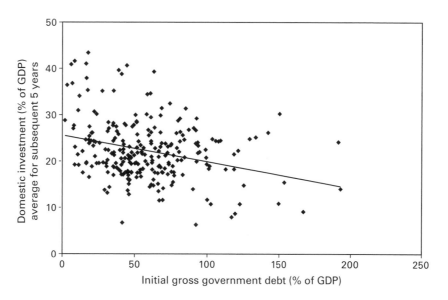

Figure 5.2
Initial government debt and subsequent domestic investment over five-year periods
Source: Authors' calculation

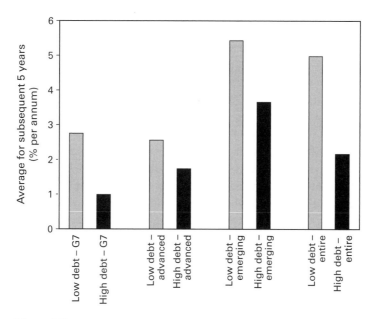

Figure 5.3
Subsequent growth of real GDP per capita and high and low initial government debt (low debt <30 percent of GDP, and high debt >90 percent of GDP)
Source: Authors' calculation

5.4 Econometric Analysis

5.4.1 Model Specification

The econometric analysis focuses on the medium- and long-run relationship between initial government debt and subsequent economic growth, while exploiting both cross-sectional and time-series dimensions of the data. Our panel spans 39 years from 1970 to 2008, and comprises eight nonoverlapping five-year periods (1970–1974, 1975–1979, . . ., 2000–2004, 2005–2008), except for the last period spanning four years. Additionally cross-country OLS regressions were estimated for longer time periods (see appendix tables A5.2 and A5.3).

The baseline panel regression specification is as follows:

$$y_{i,t} - y_{i,t-\tau} = \alpha y_{i,t-\tau} + X_{i,t-\tau}\beta + \gamma Z_{i,t-\tau} + \eta_t + v_i + \varepsilon_{i,t}, \tag{5.1}$$

where a period is a five-year time interval (i.e., $\tau = 4$); t denotes the end of a period and $t - \tau$ denotes the beginning of that period; i denotes country; y is the logarithm of real per capita GDP; v_i is the country-specific fixed effect; η_t is the time-fixed effect; $\varepsilon_{i,t}$ is an unobservable error term; $X_{i,t-\tau}$ is a vector of economic and financial variables; $Z_{i,t-\tau}$ is the initial government debt (as percentage of GDP).[4]

We consider a core set of explanatory variables that have been shown to be consistently associated with growth in the empirical literature (e.g., Sala-i-Martin et al., 2004). The variables X in the baseline specification are as follows: (1) initial level of real GDP per capita, to capture the catching-up process; (2) log of average years of secondary schooling in the population over age 15 in the initial year (taken from Barro and Lee 2011); (3) initial government size (as measured by government consumption share of GDP);[5] (4) initial trade openness (sum of export and import as a percentage of GDP); (5) initial financial market depth (liquid liabilities as a percentage of GDP); (6) initial inflation as measured by CPI inflation (to be precise, logarithm of (1+ inflation rate)); (7) terms of trade growth rates (averaged over each time period); (8) banking crisis incidence, since banking crises typically result in slow growth; (9) fiscal deficit , which includes the finding that fiscal deficits are negatively associated with long-run growth (see Fischer 1993; Baldacci et al. 2004).

To check the robustness of results, some prudent specifications were tried and additional variables also considered: these included population (a proxy of country size), age-dependency ratio (a proxy for population aging), investment,[6] fiscal spending volatility, urbanization, private saving, and checks and balances or constraints on executive decision-making (as a proxy for institutionalized constraints; see Glaeser et al. 2004).[7]

5.4.2 Econometric Estimation and Sources of Bias

A number of sources of biases can cause inconsistent estimates of the coefficients in panel growth regressions using differing estimation techniques. The first is the omitted-variables bias (so-called heterogeneity bias) resulting from possible correlation between country-specific fixed effects (v_i) and the regressors, affecting the consistency of pooled OLS and BE (between estimator) estimates. The second is the endogeneity problem due to potential correlation between the regressors and the error term, which would affect the consistency of pooled OLS, BE, and FE (fixed effect panel regressions). Specific to dynamic panels, there is a dynamic panel bias that will make FE estimates inconsistent.[8] The third is the classical measurement errors (errors in variable) in the independent variables, which affects the consistency of pooled OLS, BE, and FE estimator, although the bias tends to be exacerbated in FE and moderated in BE.

Different estimation techniques have their own pros and cons: on the one hand, the BE estimator (which applies the OLS to a single cross section of variables averaged across time periods) tends to reduce the extent of measurement error via time averaging of the regressors but does not deal with the omitted-variables bias. On the other hand, pooled OLS and BE suffer from both omitted-variables bias and measurement errors but will reduce the heterogeneity bias because, other things equal, measurement errors tend to reduce the correlation between the regressors and the country fixed effects. Separately, FE addresses the problem of the omitted-variables bias via controlling for fixed-effects but tends to exacerbate the measurement error problem, relative to BE and OLS. The measurement error bias under FE tends to get even worse when the explanatory variables are more time-persistent than the errors in the measurement (Hauk and Wacziarg 2009).[9] Furthermore, in the dynamic panel setting, the within-transformation in the estimation process of FE introduces a correlation between transformed lagged dependent variable and transformed error, which also makes FE inconsistent.

Theoretically, the dynamic panel GMM estimator addresses a variety of biases such as the omitted-variables bias, endogeneity, and measurement errors (e.g., as long as instruments are uncorrelated with the errors in measurement, if they are white noise as in the classical case), but it may be subject to a weak instruments problem (Roodman 2009; Bazzi and Clemens 2009). While the SGMM (system GMM) that is used in this chapter is generally more robust to weak instruments than the difference GMM, it can still suffer from weak instrument biases.[10] In sum, it is difficult to see a priori which estimator yields the smallest *total bias* in the presence of various sources of bias.

However, an important conclusion from the Monte Carlo study of growth regressions by Hauk and Wacziarg (2009) is that the BE performs the best among the four estimators (pooled OLS, BE, FE, and difference GMM) in terms of the extent of *total bias* on each of the estimated coefficients in the presence of both potential heterogeneity bias and a variety of measurement errors.[11] Therefore the BE and SGMM estimators are the preferred estimation techniques in this chapter, although we present results using other techniques also.

5.4.3 Basic Results

The main results for advanced and emerging economies are presented in table 5.1. Columns 1 through 4 show that the coefficients of initial debt are negative and are significant at the 1 to 5 percent levels, with their values ranging from −0.015 to −0.030 across the various estimation techniques.[12] The BE regression in column 1 suggests that a 10 percentage points of GDP increase in initial public debt is associated with a slowdown in subsequent growth in real GDP per capita of around 0.25 percentage points per year. The pooled OLS and FE in columns 2 and 3 yield results similar to those of the BE regression, although their estimates of initial debt coefficient become somewhat smaller (around −0.02). The SGMM estimate of initial debt coefficient is also in a similar range (−0.03) and significant at the 1 percent level.

The coefficients on other explanatory variables (initial income per capita, average years of schooling, financial market development, inflation, banking crisis, and fiscal deficit) have the expected sign and are mostly significant at conventional levels across various estimation techniques. The OLS and FE estimators are likely to be biased in the opposite direction in the context of lagged dependent variables in short panels, with OLS biased upward, and FE downward. The *consistent* GMM estimator should lie between the two (Bond 2002). In the growth regressions, this means that the OLS understates the convergence rate (reflected by the coefficient of initial income per capita), while the FE estimator overstates it. Consistent with this reasoning, the OLS coefficient of initial real per capita GDP is −1.88, whereas the FE coefficient is −3.92. The SGMM coefficient of the initial income per capita (−2.34) is between those two estimates, indicating that the reported SGMM estimate in column 4 is likely to be a *consistent* parameter estimate of the convergence rate.

Consistency of the SGMM estimator depends on the validity of the instruments. We consider two specification tests, suggested by Arellano and Bover (1995) and Blunedell and Bond (1998). The first is a Hansen *J*-test of overidentifying restrictions, which tests the overall validity of the instruments by analyzing the sample analogue of the moment conditions used in the estimation process. This indicates that we cannot reject the null hypothesis that the full set of orthogonality conditions are valid (*p*-value = 0.65).[13] The second test examines the hypothesis that the error term $\varepsilon_{i,t}$ is not serially correlated. We use an Arellano–Bond test for autocorrelation, and find that we cannot reject the null hypothesis of no second-order serial correlation in the first-differenced error terms (*p*-value = 0.24).[14]

The regressions in columns 2 to 4 do not include the time-fixed effects. It is possible that global factors can simultaneously affect both domestic growth and public debt, which may bias the results toward finding a stronger relationship between debt and growth. At the same time, however, as global factors can be correlated with domestic fiscal or economic variables, one can expect that the inclusion of time-

Table 5.1
Baseline panel regression: Growth and initial government debt, 1970 to 2008 (five-year period panel)

Sample: Advanced and emerging economies (with population of over 5 million);
Dependent variable: Real per capita GDP growth (%)

Explanatory variables	(1) BE	(2) Pooled OLS	(3) FE	(4) SGMM	(5) Pooled OLS	(6) FE	(7) SGMM
Initial real GDP per capita	-2.123***	-1.877**	-3.924***	-2.336***	-1.707**	-4.744**	-2.229***
	(-5.02)	(-2.54)	(-2.74)	(-3.47)	(-2.14)	(-2.36)	(-2.95)
Initial years of schooling	4.813***	3.143**	3.388	4.508*	3.136**	2.394	3.161
	(3.94)	(2.57)	(1.64)	(1.93)	(2.55)	(1.07)	(1.55)
Initial inflation rate	2.151	-2.100***	-2.630***	-2.666**	-2.457***	-2.454***	-2.678**
	(0.82)	(-3.32)	(-5.38)	(-2.49)	(-3.21)	(-5.81)	(-2.05)
Initial government size	0.109**	0.109**	0.147	0.162	0.111**	0.055	0.138
	(2.06)	(2.43)	(1.68)	(1.36)	(2.38)	(0.70)	(1.23)
Initial trade openness	-0.002	-0.004	0.023*	-0.013**	-0.005	0.023	-0.004
	(-0.43)	(-0.78)	(1.73)	(-2.03)	(-1.11)	(1.57)	(-0.57)
Initial financial depth	0.022**	0.020**	0.001	0.035***	0.023**	0.006	0.027**
	(2.15)	(2.13)	(0.07)	(3.18)	(2.50)	(0.64)	(2.31)
Terms of trade growth	0.204**	-0.013	0.009	-0.032	-0.017	-0.003	-0.044*
	(2.33)	(-0.52)	(0.33)	(-1.14)	(-0.70)	(-0.13)	(-1.97)
Banking crisis	-1.077	-0.617	-0.638***	-1.033	-0.612*	-0.513*	-1.838
	(-0.61)	(-1.58)	(-2.96)	(-1.55)	(-1.75)	(-1.98)	(-1.24)
Fiscal deficit	0.028	-0.044***	-0.047***	-0.046***	-0.045***	-0.035***	-0.062***
	(0.80)	(-4.27)	(-4.07)	(-2.96)	(-4.72)	(-3.50)	(-3.10)
Initial government debt	-0.025**	-0.022***	-0.015**	-0.030***	-0.018**	-0.004	-0.019*
	(-2.28)	(-3.29)	(-2.17)	(-4.14)	(-2.34)	(-0.67)	(-1.89)
Arellano–Bond AR(2) test p-value[a]				0.65			0.45
Hansen J-statistics (p-value)[b]				0.24			0.29
Number of observations	166	166	166	166	166	166	166
R^2	0.68	0.51	0.39		0.58	0.51	
Time-fixed effects	N/A	No	No	No	Yes	Yes	Yes

Note: Heteroskedasticity and country-specific autocorrelation consistent *t-statistics* are in parentheses. Time dummies are not reported. Levels of significance: *** 1 percent, ** 5 percent, * 10 percent. In the OLS regressions, dummies for OECD, Asia, Latin America, and sub-Saharan Africa are also included in each regression (not reported to save space). FE refers to the fixed-effects panel regressions and BE is the between estimator. For the dynamic panel estimation, a two-step system GMM (SGMM) with the Windmeijer's finite-sample correction for the two-step covariance matrix.
a. The null hypothesis is that the first-differenced errors exhibit no second-order serial correlation.
b. The null hypothesis is that the instruments used are not correlated with the residuals.

fixed effects may understate the estimated effects of these variables. Columns 5 to 7 include time-fixed effects in the regression to allow for global factors. The pooled OLS and SGMM coefficients of initial debt remain significant at 5 to 10 percent, and the size of those coefficients is reduced as expected. The estimates suggest that a 10 percentage point increase in the initial debt-to-GDP ratio is associated with a slowdown in growth of per capita GDP around 0.2 percent per year.

In contrast, the FE results on initial debt turn out to be sensitive to whether time-fixed effects are included or not in the regression (compare column 6 with column 3). The FE coefficient of initial debt is now insignificant and reduced to −0.004. It is well known in the literature that the FE can bias toward zero the slope estimates on the determinants of the steady-state level of income—the accumulation and depreciation variables in the Solow model (Islam 1995). Given that the FE estimator tends to identify parameters on the basis of within-country variation, compared to cross-sectional alternatives such as pooled OLS and BE, it is not surprising that the within-country variation in each of regressors (especially time-persistent variables) is further reduced once time-fixed effects are accounted for.[15] Moreover the measurement error bias can also be exacerbated under FE. With these caveats, time-fixed effects are included in the remaining regressions.

5.4.5 Robustness of Results

A variety of robustness checks were conducted. First, to account for the possibility that there may have been structural changes over the sample period, including changes in global trend growth or global risk factors, time-fixed effects were included. In addition we restricted the sample to the second half of the period to check whether there are significant changes in the estimated coefficients. Thus columns 1 to 4 in table 5.2 repeat the same sets of regressions (BE, pooled OLS, FE, and SGMM) for the period 1990 to 2008. The results are quite similar to those for the entire period. Except for the FE estimate, the impact of initial debt is significant, ranging from −0.020 to −0.024, indicating that a 10 percentage point increase in initial debt-to-GDP ratio is associated with decline in per capita GDP growth of around 0.2 to 0.24 percent per year.

Second, columns 5 to 8 and 9 to 12 of table 5.2 replicate the regression exercises for 46 advanced and emerging economies and the full sample of 79 countries (which includes 33 developing countries in addition to the 46). Again, the results are broadly similar to those in table 5.1, although the size of the debt coefficients becomes slightly smaller.

Third, we run a single cross-country regression of the type that is most commonly used in the empirical growth literature for longer time periods. One might be concerned that the five-year time interval in our panel data may not be long enough to smooth out the short-term business cycle fluctuations. The results are remarkably similar to the panel regression results in table 5.2 (appendix tables A5.2 and A5.3).

Table 5.2
Baseline panel regression: Robustness checks on time periods and sample

Dependent variable: Real per capita GDP growth (%)

Explanatory variables	(1) BE	(2) Pooled OLS	(3) FE	(4) SGMM	(5) BE	(6) Pooled OLS	(7) FE	(8) SGMM	(9) BE	(10) Pooled OLS	(11) FE	(12) SGMM
	Period: 1990–2008 sample: OECD and emerging economies				Period: 1970–2008 sample: OECD and emerging economies without population size restriction				Period: 1970–2008 sample: Full sample (including developing countries) without population size restriction			
Initial real GDP per capita	−1.794***	−1.711**	−3.325*	−2.376**	−1.796***	−1.074*	−5.843***	−2.072*	−0.962***	−1.021**	−4.495**	−1.566**
	(−4.67)	(−2.22)	(−1.99)	(−2.21)	(−4.37)	(−1.80)	(−3.09)	(−1.96)	(−2.79)	(−2.09)	(−2.13)	(−2.12)
Initial years of schooling	3.815***	3.491***	−0.784	3.903	3.768***	1.809*	4.629**	2.956	1.550*	0.887	2.624	2.346*
	(3.35)	(2.78)	(−0.17)	(0.92)	(3.10)	(1.68)	(2.56)	(0.87)	(1.79)	(0.98)	(1.11)	(1.79)
Initial inflation rate	1.258	−2.918***	−2.308***	−1.717	2.227	−1.201*	−2.262***	−1.112	2.727	0.324	−0.899	−0.251
	(0.51)	(−3.19)	(−4.33)	(−1.14)	(0.92)	(−2.14)	(−5.37)	(−0.93)	(1.14)	(0.46)	(−1.12)	(−0.33)
Initial government size	0.120**	0.119**	0.074	0.205*	0.030	−0.018	−0.039	−0.180*	−0.020	−0.026	−0.023	−0.092
	(2.41)	(2.45)	(0.68)	(1.73)	(0.77)	(−0.44)	(−0.56)	(−1.75)	(−0.63)	(−1.00)	(−0.41)	(−1.23)
Initial trade openness	0.001	−0.007	0.030*	−0.006	0.009**	0.003	0.015	0.003	0.003	0.004	0.002	0.000
	(0.19)	(−1.55)	(1.76)	(−0.72)	(2.38)	(0.78)	(1.63)	(0.24)	(0.83)	(1.29)	(0.15)	(0.03)
Initial financial depth	0.016*	0.027**	0.002	0.032	0.002	0.001	0.007	−0.001	−0.000	−0.004	−0.006	0.006
	(1.71)	(2.68)	(0.13)	(1.66)	(0.27)	(0.07)	(0.76)	(−0.06)	(−0.05)	(−0.60)	(−0.54)	(0.74)
Terms of trade growth	0.223***	−0.016	−0.018	−0.049	0.187**	−0.001	0.008	−0.046	−0.033	0.028	0.062**	0.024
	(2.79)	(−0.29)	(−0.36)	(−0.94)	(2.14)	(−0.04)	(0.31)	(−1.03)	(−0.64)	(0.92)	(2.05)	

(continued)

Table 5.2
(*continued*)

Dependent variable: Real per capita GDP growth (%)

Explanatory variables	(1) BE	(2) Pooled OLS	(3) FE	(4) SGMM	(5) BE	(6) Pooled OLS	(7) FE	(8) SGMM	(9) BE	(10) Pooled OLS	(11) FE	(12) SGMM
	Period: 1990–2008 sample: OECD and emerging economies				Period: 1970–2008 sample: OECD and emerging economies without population size restriction				Period: 1970–2008 sample: Full sample (including developing countries) without population size restriction			
Banking crisis	0.632	−0.358	−0.576	−1.233	−1.445	−0.867**	−0.837***	−1.003	−3.566**	−1.357***	−1.026***	−1.861***
	(0.38)	(−0.68)	(−1.15)	(−0.90)	(−0.80)	(−2.23)	(−2.80)	(−1.16)	(−2.32)	(−3.85)	(−3.53)	(−3.21)
Fiscal deficit	0.009	−0.055***	−0.046***	−0.057*	0.050*	−0.037***	−0.045***	−0.045**	−0.028**	−0.034***	−0.041***	−0.035***
	(0.27)	(−4.18)	(−2.92)	(−1.71)	(1.72)	(−3.40)	(−4.25)	(−2.46)	(−2.32)*	(−3.80)	(−5.50)	(−2.13)
Initial government debt	−0.024***	−0.020**	−0.008	−0.023*	−0.019*	−0.020**	−0.011*	−0.021*	−0.021***	−0.017***	−0.011*	−0.016*
	(−2.85)	(−2.26)	(−0.65)	(−2.02)	(−1.94)	(−2.62)	(−1.78)	(−1.74)	(−3.22)	(−3.31)	(−1.66)	(−1.83)
Arellano–Bond AR(2) test *p*-value[a]				0.42				0.59				0.59
Hansen *J*-statistics (*p*-value)[b]				0.13				0.98				0.36
Number of observations	124	124	124	124	208	208	208	208	297	297	297	297
R²	0.72	0.61	0.44	N/A	0.56	0.44	0.51	N/A	0.37	0.36	0.43	N/A
Time-fixed effects	N/A	Yes	Yes	Yes	N/A	Yes	Yes	Yes	N/A	Yes	Yes	Yes

Note: Heteroskedasticity and country-specific autocorrelation consistent *t-statistics* are in parentheses. Time dummies are not reported. Levels of significance: *** 1 percent, ** 5 percent, * 10 percent. In the OLS regressions, dummies for OECD, Asia, Latin America, and Sub-Saharan Africa are also included in each regression (not reported to save space). FE refers to the fixed-effects panel regressions and BE is the between estimator. For the dynamic panel estimation, a two-step system GMM (SGMM) with the Windmeijer's finite-sample correction for the two-step covariance matrix.

a. The null hypothesis is that the first-differenced errors exhibit no second-order serial correlation.

b. The null hypothesis is that the instruments used are not correlated with the residuals.

5.4.6 Nonlinearities and Differences between Advanced and Emerging Economies

To explore potential nonlinearities, table 5.3 (columns 1–4) shows regressions that include the interaction terms between initial debt and dummy variables for three ranges of initial debt ratio: Dum_30 for low debt (below 30 percent of GDP), Dum_30–90 for medium debt (30–90 percent of GDP), and Dum_90 for high debt (over 90 percent of GDP). The coefficients of low initial debt (i.e., initial debt*Dum_30) are all insignificant and of the positive sign, which seems to suggest that relatively low levels of public debt are not significantly harmful to growth. In the OLS the coefficient of medium level of debt (initial debt*Dum_30–90) is significant at 5 percent, and its estimated coefficient is –0.028. But they are all insignificant in other estimations (BE, FE and SGMM). By contrast, the coefficients of high debt (initial debt*Dum_90) are negative and significant at 1 percent under OLS, and SGMM.

Interestingly, the negative effect of initial debt on growth in advanced economies tends to be smaller than that in emerging economies. Columns 5 to 8 in table 5.3 use the interaction terms between initial debt and dummy variables for advanced and emerging economies.[16] The coefficients of both interaction terms are negative and significant at various levels, except for the FE results and the coefficient of the initial debt*Dum_advanced term in BE. Under BE, OLS, and SGMM, the coefficients of initial debt in advanced economies range from –0.012 to –0.017, whose absolute size is smaller than that of emerging economies (–0.038 to –0.044): a 10 percentage point increase in initial debt-to-GDP ratio is associated with growth slowdown around 0.12 to 0.17 percent in advanced economies, compared to 0.38 to 0.4 percent in emerging economies. This may reflect limited borrowing capacity of emerging economies due to less-developed domestic financial markets, and/or inadequate access to international capital markets, with both factors leading to greater adverse effect on private investment and growth compared to the advanced economies.

5.4.7 International Financial Integration and Impact on Growth

An important question that arises is whether and to what extent the impact on growth of initial public debt is conditional on a country's economic and financial position vis-à-vis the rest of the world. For example, does the NFA (net foreign asset) position of a country or aggregate foreign liabilities matter for the magnitude of the relationship between public debt and growth?[17] Is it the case that the adverse impact of high debt on growth would be low if at the same time the aggregate foreign liabilities of a country are relatively low? This could be related to the fact that high public debt is being financed by private domestic savings rather than from abroad. Conversely, excessive foreign liabilities may compound the fiscal vulnerability arising from public debt per se, to the extent that foreign creditors may be more sensitive to changes in global risk appetite, or they may have shorter time horizons. Another

Table 5.3
Panel regression: Different levels of initial debt and advanced versus emerging economies

Dependent variable: Real per capita GDP growth (%)

Explanatory variables	(1) BE	(2) Pooled OLS	(3) FE	(4) SGMM	(5) BE	(6) Pooled OLS	(7) FE	(8) SGMM
Initial real GDP per capita	-2.014***	-1.875***	-4.912**	-2.227***	-2.796***	-2.539***	-4.705**	-2.897***
	(-5.13)	(-2.79)	(-2.65)	(-3.14)	(-4.51)	(-2.96)	(-2.35)	(-4.07)
Initial years of schooling	4.377***	3.185***	2.260	3.988	4.691***	3.127***	2.232	2.074
	(3.77)	(3.10)	(1.00)	(1.42)	(3.91)	(2.79)	(1.03)	(1.06)
Initial inflation rate	1.551	-2.773***	-2.329***	-2.352**	0.503	-3.213***	-2.390***	-9.852**
	(0.59)	(-3.67)	(-5.06)	(-2.65)	(0.18)	(-3.17)	(-5.17)	(-2.31)
Initial government size	0.135**	0.127***	0.033	0.199**	0.096*	0.086*	0.056	0.293**
	(2.65)	(3.06)	(0.40)	(2.03)	(1.82)	(2.02)	(0.70)	(2.65)
Initial trade openness	-0.003	-0.005	0.026*	-0.007	-0.002	-0.005	0.023	-0.005
	(-0.65)	(-1.37)	(1.77)	(-1.02)	(-0.30)	(-1.18)	(1.56)	(-0.76)
Initial financial depth	0.023**	0.023***	0.006	0.026***	0.022**	0.024***	0.005	0.032***
	(2.18)	(3.02)	(0.68)	(2.84)	(2.24)	(2.87)	(0.57)	(3.06)
Terms of trade growth	0.183*	-0.018	-0.003	-0.038	0.235**	-0.008	-0.002	-0.050**
	(1.93)	(-0.65)	(-0.18)	(-1.23)	(2.66)	(-0.32)	(-0.10)	(-2.26)
Fiscal deficit	0.011	-0.046***	-0.033***	-0.045**	0.019	-0.050***	-0.034***	-0.059***
	(0.32)	(-4.75)	(-3.14)	(-2.23)	(0.53)	(-4.94)	(-3.24)	(-3.69)
Banking crisis	-1.270	-0.563	-0.468	-0.612	-0.992	-0.588*	-0.506*	-1.163
	(-0.72)	(-1.60)	(-1.61)	(-0.83)	(-0.57)	(-1.75)	(-1.94)	(-1.13)

Initial debt*Dum_below30	0.016	0.0002	0.017	0.030				
	(0.17)	(0.01)	(0.65)	(1.25)				
Initial debt*Dum_30_90	-0.037	-0.028**	0.007	-0.015				
	(-1.43)	(-2.66)	(0.79)	(-1.26)				
Initial debt*Dum_above90	-0.010	-0.015***	-0.001	-0.015***				
	(-0.79)	(-2.79)	(-0.08)	(-2.91)				
Initial debt*Dum_advanced					-0.017	-0.012**	-0.005	-0.014*
					(-1.35)	(-2.19)	(-0.75)	(-1.95)
Initial debt*Dum_emerging					-0.044**	-0.042***	0.001	-0.038*
					(-2.62)	(-2.97)	(0.08)	(-1.95)
Arellano–Bond AR(2) test p-value[a]				0.34				0.14
Hansen J-statistics (p-value)[b]				0.86				0.85
Number of observations	166	166	166	166	166	166	166	166
R^2	0.75	0.62	0.52	0.52	0.7	0.61	0.51	0.51
Time-fixed effects	N/A	Yes	Yes	Yes	N/A	Yes	Yes	Yes

Note: Heteroskedasticity and country-specific autocorrelation consistent *t-statistics* are in parentheses. Time dummies are not reported. Levels of significance: *** 1 percent, ** 5 percent, * 10 percent. In the OLS regressions, dummies for OECD, Asia, Latin America, and sub-Saharan Africa are also included in each regression (not reported to save space). FE refers to the fixed-effects panel regressions and BE is the between estimator. For the dynamic panel estimation, a two-step system GMM (SGMM) with the Windmeijer's finite-sample correction for the two-step covariance matrix.
a. The null hypothesis is that the first-differenced errors exhibit no second-order serial correlation.
b. The null hypothesis is that the instruments used are not correlated with the residuals.

channel could be in terms of signaling: high public debt when foreign liabilities are also high may indicate that the imbalances facing a country are broader than just the public sector and hence there are greater underlying vulnerabilities. Similar arguments could be used with regard to the NFA, rather than only foreign liabilities per se.

In order to investigate this issue, we considered the NFA and foreign liabilities (as a percentage of GDP) as an additional variable, as well as an interactive term. The empirical analysis indicates that the bilateral correlation between government debt and the NFA or foreign liabilities is low (correlation coefficients are –0.10 and 0.11, respectively), and neither the NFA nor foreign liabilities are significant in growth regressions, as shown in columns 1 to 4 of table 5.4 (the results on foreign liabilities are not reported). However, the logic of the above argument would suggest that the interaction of initial public debt with NFA or liabilities might be more important than the simple correlations. This was assessed by examining the interaction of debt with a dummy that took a value of 1 if the NFA exceeded the sample median value (–17 percent of GDP), or if foreign liabilities were greater than the 75th percentile (89 percent of GDP), and 0 otherwise. The results are shown in columns 5 to 8 and 8 to 12 of table 5.4, respectively. The results appear to bear out the basic hypothesis: when foreign liabilities are high or NFA low, the adverse impact of public debt on growth is about *one and a half to two* times as large as is the case otherwise. These results are striking from an economic perspective, and statistically significant. Perhaps what they are really alluding to is the notion that if the economy as a whole is operating essentially outside its means, the impact of high public debt on growth is substantially worse than when it is operating within it.

Next, we turn to the question of whether the currency composition of public debt also matters. The larger the portion of foreign-currency denominated debt as a share of total public debt, the larger the extent of exposure to foreign currency risk. This is related to the "Original Sin" problem highlighted by Eichengreen and Hausmann (1999), whereby the debt is denominated in foreign currency, which could have adverse macroeconomic consequences. If a country affected by "Original Sin" has net foreign debt, then it is likely to have a currency mismatch in its national balance sheet. Large swings in the real exchange rate will thus likely have an effect on aggregate wealth and on the country's ability to service its debt. As a consequence "Original Sin" tends to make debt riskier, increase volatility, and affect a country's ability to conduct an independent monetary policy. Table 5.5 shows the results when we included the interaction of debt with a dummy that took a value of 1 if the domestic-currency portion exceeded the sample median value (89 percent of total debt), or if it is greater than the 25th percentile (59 percent of total debt), and 0 otherwise. The regression coefficients of the interaction terms are mostly significant and of the expected sign. *Importantly, they suggest that when the foreign-currency debt*

Table 5.4

Panel regression: Different levels of initial NFA and foreign liabilities

Dependent variable: Real per capita GDP growth (%)

Explanatory variables	(1) BE	(2) Pooled OLS	(3) FE	(4) SGMM	(5) BE	(6) Pooled OLS	(7) FE	(8) SGMM	(9) BE	(10) Pooled OLS	(11) FE	(12) SGMM
Initial real GDP per capita	-2.127***	-1.698**	-4.772**	-1.852**	-2.273***	-1.863**	-4.754**	-2.182***	-1.909***	-1.816**	-4.949**	-1.881***
	(-4.95)	(-2.23)	(-2.29)	(-2.51)	(-5.43)	(-2.66)	(-2.38)	(-3.86)	(-4.40)	(-2.35)	(-2.46)	(-2.78)
Initial years of schooling	4.760***	3.044**	2.345	2.580	4.458***	3.076***	2.396	3.749***	5.066***	3.308***	2.250	1.592
	(3.81)	(2.51)	(1.04)	(1.11)	(3.72)	(2.92)	(1.08)	(2.77)	(4.22)	(2.76)	(1.04)	(0.67)
Initial inflation rate	2.019	-2.397***	-2.483***	-1.402	2.874	-2.098***	-2.418***	-1.905	-0.277	-2.621***	-2.527***	-2.514**
	(0.75)	(-3.20)	(-5.82)	(-1.21)	(1.12)	(-3.06)	(-5.53)	(-1.58)	(-0.09)	(-3.57)	(-5.84)	(-2.15)
Initial government size	0.108*	0.115**	0.057	0.142	0.096*	0.115**	0.059	0.114	0.117**	0.117*	0.053	0.111
	(2.00)	(2.44)	(0.73)	(1.50)	(1.86)	(2.70)	(0.74)	(0.68)	(2.26)	(2.61)	(0.67)	(1.32)
Initial trade openness	-0.003	-0.006	0.023	0.008	0.0003	-0.004	0.024	-0.007	-0.001	-0.002	0.026*	0.003
	(-0.50)	(-1.28)	(1.51)	(1.07)	(0.06)	(-1.17)	(1.58)	(-1.40)	(-0.13)	(-0.39)	(1.90)	(0.28)
Initial financial depth	0.019	0.021**	0.006	0.018	0.014	0.021**	0.006	0.027**	0.020*	0.022**	0.006	0.021*
	(1.47)	(2.18)	(0.66)	(1.24)	(1.29)	(2.62)	(0.66)	(2.33)	(1.98)	(2.26)	(0.64)	(1.66)
Terms of trade growth	0.199**	-0.016	-0.003	-0.034	0.167*	-0.021	-0.004	-0.034	0.161*	-0.022	-0.007	-0.051***
	(2.22)	(-0.62)	(-0.13)	(-0.77)	(1.92)	(-0.90)	(-0.17)	(-0.99)	(1.81)	(-0.95)	(-0.28)	(-2.75)
Fiscal deficit	0.028	-0.044***	-0.035***	-0.034	0.021	-0.045***	-0.035***	-0.044	-2E-04	-0.050***	-0.039***	-0.067***
	(0.79)	(-4.80)	(-3.59)	(-1.44)	(0.62)	(-5.40)	(-3.52)	(-1.59)	(-0.00)	(-5.03)	(-3.55)	(-2.78)
Banking crisis	-0.943	-0.570	-0.525*	-2.219*	-1.468	-0.510	-0.489*	-1.077	-0.672	-0.550	-0.485*	-0.427
	(-0.52)	(-1.66)	(-1.88)	(-1.96)	(-0.85)	(-1.46)	(-1.83)	(-1.19)	(-0.38)	(-1.56)	(-1.81)	(-0.54)
Initial government debt	-0.024**	-0.017**	-0.004	-0.015*								
	(-2.14)	(-2.40)	(-0.72)	(-1.81)								
Initial NFA (net foreign assets)	0.003	0.005	-0.002	-0.013								
	(0.39)	(0.84)	(-0.21)	(-1.26)								

(continued)

Table 5.4
(continued)

Dependent variable: Real per capita GDP growth (%)

Explanatory variables	(1) BE	(2) Pooled OLS	(3) FE	(4) SGMM	(5) BE	(6) Pooled OLS	(7) FE	(8) SGMM	(9) BE	(10) Pooled OLS	(11) FE	(12) SGMM
Initial debt*Dum_NFA_above_median[a]					-0.020*	-0.015**	-0.004	-0.023*				
					(-1.80)	(-2.64)	(-0.60)	(-1.84)				
Initial debt*Dum_NFA_below_median					-0.042***	-0.029***	-0.006	-0.029*				
					(-2.88)	(-3.17)	(-0.70)	(-1.95)				
Initial debt*Dum_Foreign_Liabilities_below_75percentile[b]									-0.013	-0.015*	-0.003	-0.017*
									(-0.99)	(-1.98)	(-0.38)	(-1.85)
Initial debt*Dum_Foreign_Liabilities_above_75percentile									-0.036***	-0.025***	-0.010	-0.025*
									(-2.81)	(-2.74)	(-1.19)	(-1.71)
Arellano–Bond AR(2) test p-value[c]				0.16				0.28				0.36
Hansen J-statistics (p-value)[d]				0.47				0.16				0.90
Number of observations	166	166	166	166	166	166	166	166	166	166	166	166
R^2	0.68	0.59	0.51		0.71	0.61	0.51		0.7	0.59	0.52	
Time-fixed effects	N/A	Yes	Yes	Yes	N/A	Yes	Yes	Yes	N/A	Yes	Yes	Yes

Note: Heteroskedasticity and country-specific autocorrelation consistent *t-statistics* are in parentheses. Time dummies are not reported. Levels of significance: *** 1 percent, ** 5 percent, * 10 percent. In the OLS regressions, dummies for OECD, Asia, Latin America, and sub-Saharan Africa are also included in each regression (not reported to save space). FE refers to the fixed-effects panel regressions and BE is the between estimator. For the dynamic panel estimation, a two-step system GMM (SGMM) with the Windmeijer's finite-sample correction for the two-step covariance matrix.

a. The median value of NFA in the sample of 36 advanced and emerging economies is –17 percent of GDP.
b. The 75 percentile level of foreign liabilities in the sample of 36 advanced and emerging economies is 89 percent of GDP.
c. The null hypothesis is that the first-differenced errors exhibit no second-order serial correlation.
d. The null hypothesis is that the instruments used are not correlated with the residuals.

Table 5.5
Panel regression: Domestic versus foreign currency-denominated portion of public debt

Dependent variable: Real per capita GDP growth (%)

Explanatory variables	(1) BE	(2) Pooled OLS	(3) FE	(4) SGMM	(5) BE	(6) Pooled OLS	(7) FE	(8) SGMM
Initial real GDP per capita	-2.531***	-2.092***	-4.927**	-2.337**	-2.178***	-1.856**	-4.818**	-2.688**
	(-4.79)	(-2.96)	(-2.32)	(-2.29)	(-4.40)	(-2.44)	(-2.35)	(-2.37)
Initial years of schooling	5.311***	3.293***	3.195	4.209	5.054***	3.110**	3.030	2.578
	(4.01)	(3.10)	(1.32)	(1.54)	(3.63)	(2.52)	(1.22)	(0.74)
Initial inflation rate	0.946	-2.471***	-2.393***	-3.002**	2.136	-2.652***	-2.401***	-2.521*
	(0.30)	(-3.53)	(-5.90)	(-2.28)	(0.69)	(-2.98)	(-4.73)	(-1.67)
Initial government size	0.081	0.091*	0.086	0.182	0.111*	0.112**	0.095	0.118
	(1.30)	(2.01)	(1.19)	(1.64)	(1.80)	(2.32)	(1.24)	(1.05)
Initial trade openness	-0.002	-0.005	0.025	-0.012*	-0.001	-0.004	0.026	0.001
	(-0.32)	(-0.93)	(1.51)	(-1.72)	(-0.18)	(-0.90)	(1.48)	(0.12)
Initial financial depth	0.018	0.017**	0.005	0.026*	0.022	0.023**	0.004	0.024*
	(1.40)	(2.08)	(0.50)	(1.84)	(1.54)	(2.36)	(0.41)	(1.97)
Terms of trade growth	0.211**	0.004	0.003	-0.032	0.212**	-0.018	-0.000	-0.040*
	(2.27)	(0.14)	(0.10)	(-0.99)	(2.18)	(-0.72)	(-0.00)	(-1.70)
Banking crisis	-1.613	-0.832*	-0.588*	-0.501	-0.547	-0.612	-0.577*	-2.577
	(-0.67)	(-2.03)	(-2.00)	(-0.34)	(-0.23)	(-1.33)	(-1.98)	(-1.48)
Fiscal deficit	0.008	-0.051***	-0.036***	-0.074***	0.028	-0.047***	-0.035***	-0.063***
	(0.19)	(-4.36)	(-3.24)	(-4.01)	(0.66)	(-4.61)	(-3.11)	(-4.43)
Initial debt*Dum_domdebt_below25pctile[a]	-0.047**	-0.054***	-0.039***	-0.060*				
	(-2.35)	(-2.86)	(-2.79)	(-1.94)				

(continued)

Table 5.5
(continued)

Dependent variable: Real per capita GDP growth (%)

Explanatory variables	(1) BE	(2) Pooled OLS	(3) FE	(4) SGMM	(5) BE	(6) Pooled OLS	(7) FE	(8) SGMM
Initial debt*Dum_domdebt_above25pctile	-0.021*	-0.017**	-0.004	-0.023*				
	(-1.72)	(-2.50)	(-0.77)	(-1.74)				
Initial debt*Dum_domdebt_belowMedian[b]					-0.025	-0.028**	-0.011	-0.033**
					(-1.63)	(-2.71)	(-1.04)	(-2.24)
Initial debt*Dum_domdebt_aboveMedian					-0.025*	-0.018**	-0.006	-0.019**
					(-1.90)	(-2.40)	(-0.87)	(-2.20)
Arellano–Bond AR(2) test p-value[c]				0.68				0.89
Hansen J-statistics (p-value)[d]				0.41				0.55
Number of observations	151	151	151	151	151	151	151	151
R^2	0.7	0.63	0.51		0.67	0.6	0.51	
Time-fixed effects	N/A	Yes	Yes	Yes	N/A	Yes	Yes	Yes

Note: Heteroskedasticity and country-specific autocorrelation consistent *t-statistics* are in parentheses. Time dummies are not reported. Levels of significance: *** 1 percent, ** 5 percent, * 10 percent. In the OLS regressions, dummies for OECD, Asia, Latin America, and sub-Saharan Africa are also included in each regression (not reported to save space). FE refers to the fixed-effects panel regressions and BE is the between estimator. For the dynamic panel estimation, a two-step system GMM (SGMM) with the Windmeijer's finite-sample correction for the two-step covariance matrix.

a. The 25 percentile level of domestic currency-denominated public debt portion in the sample 36 advanced and emerging economies is 59 percent of total public debt.

b. The median level of domestic currency-denominated public debt portion in the sample 36 advanced and emerging economies is 89 percent of total public debt.

c. The null hypothesis is that the first-differenced errors exhibit no second-order serial correlation.

d. The null hypothesis is that the instruments used are not correlated with the residuals.

portion is large, the negative impact of public debt on growth can be more than twice as large as is the case otherwise.

5.5 Summary and Concluding Remarks

This chapter has provided systematic empirical evidence on the impact of high initial debt on subsequent growth for a panel of advanced and emerging market economies over nearly four decades. The chapter builds on the large empirical literature on the determinants of long-term growth and a much more limited literature, pertaining primarily to low-income countries, that explores the impact of high external debts on growth via crowding out and the debt overhang. In the empirical estimation, the chapter employs a variety of econometric techniques and pays particular attention to a range of estimation issues including reverse causality, endogeneity, and outliers. In addition it explores nonlinearities and threshold effects.

The results, based on a range of econometric techniques, suggest an inverse relationship between *initial* public debt and *subsequent* growth, controlling for other determinants of growth: on average, a 10 percentage point increase in the initial debt-to-GDP ratio is associated with a slowdown in real per capita GDP growth of around 0.2 percentage points per year, with the impact being smaller (around 0.15) in advanced economies and larger when (net) foreign liabilities are relatively high. There is some evidence of nonlinearity, with only high (above 90 percent of GDP) levels of debt having a significant negative effect on growth. As shown in Kumar and Woo (2010), this adverse effect largely reflects a slowdown in labor productivity growth, mainly due to reduced investment and slower growth of the capital stock per worker. On average, a 10 percentage point increase in initial debt ratio is associated with a decline of investment by about 0.4 percentage points of GDP, with a larger impact in emerging economies. The analysis also suggests that when foreign liabilities are high or NFA low, or the share of foreign currency denominated debt is large, the adverse impact of public debt on growth is substantially greater. Various robustness checks yield largely similar results. The results underline the need to take measures that would over the medium- to long-term not just stabilize public debts but place them on a downward trajectory to avoid adverse effects on growth.

Appendixes: Country List

The sample of countries is dictated by the availability of data. The following 38 advanced and emerging economies with a population of over 5 million are included in the baseline panel regressions.

Table A5.1

Country	Country
Australia	Japan
Austria	Korea
Belgium	Malaysia
Brazil	Mexico
Canada	Netherlands
Chile	Pakistan
China	Peru
Colombia	Philippines
Czech Republic	Poland
Denmark	Portugal
Egypt	Russian Federation
France	Slovak Republic
Germany	South Africa
Greece	Spain
Hong Kong	Sweden
Hungary	Switzerland
India	Turkey
Indonesia	United Kingdom
Italy	United States

Note: 1. Eight additional countries are also available in the panel regressions for all available 46 advanced and emerging economies without the over five-million population size restriction: Finland, Iceland, Ireland, Israel, Jordan, Norway, New Zealand, and Singapore. 2. Thirty-three developing countries that are included in the full sample of 79 countries are Barbados, Bolivia, Bulgaria, Costa Rica, Croatia, Cyprus, Ecuador, Gambia, Guinea-Bissau, Guyana, Honduras, Iran, Jamaica, Kuwait, Lesotho, Mauritania, Mauritius, Mozambique, Nicaragua, Panama, Romania, Rwanda, Senegal, Slovenia, Sri Lanka, Sudan, Swaziland, Syria, Togo, Trinidad and Tobago, Tunisia, Uganda, and Uruguay. 3. The list of advanced economies includes Australia, Austria, Belgium, Canada, Denmark, Finland, France, Germany, Greece, Iceland, Ireland, Italy, Japan, Netherlands, New Zealand, Portugal, Spain, Sweden, Switzerland, the United Kingdom, and the United States, which were the OECD member nations as of 1990, except for Turkey, which is classified as an emerging market economy.

Table A5.2
Cross-country regression: Government debt and long-term growth of advanced and emerging economies (without restriction on population size)

Dependent variable: Real per capita GDP growth (%)

Explanatory variables	(1) OLS 1975–2008	(2) OLS 1985–2008	(3) OLS 1990–2008	(4) OLS 1995–2008	(5) OLS 2000–2008	(6) OLS 1990–2008	(7) OLS 1995–2008	(8) OLS 2000–2008
Initial real GDP per capita	1.862	−2.928*	−2.464***	−1.726**	−0.480	−1.353	−1.121*	−0.494
	(1.91)	(−2.00)	(−4.44)	(−2.37)	(−0.58)	(−1.63)	(−1.84)	(−0.61)
Initial years of schooling	0.393	0.576	2.462**	2.944**	1.021	1.419	2.204**	1.286
	(0.38)	(0.50)	(2.66)	(2.08)	(0.63)	(1.15)	(2.09)	(0.82)
Initial inflation rate	8.395**	−1.578	0.400	8.932**	1.628	−0.059	2.831**	1.300
	(4.37)	(−0.77)	(0.99)	(2.12)	(0.43)	(−0.38)	(2.19)	(0.38)
Initial government size	−0.127*	−0.024	−0.027	0.021	0.114**	−0.020	0.020	0.101*
	(−2.86)	(−0.40)	(−0.85)	(0.58)	(2.25)	(−0.72)	(0.57)	(1.96)
Initial trade openness	0.012*	0.016	0.010**	0.014***	0.001	0.008	0.004	−0.0002
	(3.93)	(1.39)	(2.18)	(3.04)	(0.21)	(1.43)	(0.81)	(−0.04)
Terms of trade growth	0.039	−0.036	−0.192	−0.189*	0.071	−0.195	−0.124	0.049
	(0.54)	(−0.20)	(−1.13)	(−1.97)	(0.78)	(−1.31)	(−1.60)	(0.61)
Banking crisis			−0.428	−0.728	0.061	0.082	−0.825	−0.044
			(−1.26)	(−1.33)	(0.11)	(0.22)	(−1.60)	(−0.08)
Initial government debt	−0.020**	−0.009	−0.018***	−0.029***	−0.020			
	(−4.49)	(−1.07)	(−3.29)	(−3.73)	(−1.65)			
Government debt, average						−0.021**	−0.022**	−0.018*
						(−2.21)	(−2.68)	(−1.83)
Number of observations	10	20	30	37	44	42	46	46
R^2	0.99	0.60	0.85	0.67	0.63	0.53	0.51	0.62

Note: Heteroskedasticity-consistent *t-statistics* are in parentheses. Levels of significance: *** 1 percent; ** 5 percent; * 10 percent. An intercept term and dummies for OECD, Asia, Latin America, and sub-Saharan Africa are included in each regression, except for column 1 in which the number of observations is small relative to the number of covariates (not reported to save space).

Table A5.3
Growth accounting and cross-country growth regression: Advanced and emerging economies (without restriction on population size)

Explanatory variables	(1) OLS 1990–2008	(2) OLS 1995–2008	(3) OLS 1990–2008	(4) OLS 1995–2008	(5) OLS 1990–2008	(6) OLS 1995–2008	(7) OLS 1990–2008	(8) OLS 1995–2008	(9) OLS 1990–2008	(10) OLS 1995–2008	(11) OLS 1990–2008	(12) OLS 1995–2008
	Dependent variable: Growth of real output per worker				Dependent variable: Growth of TFP				Dependent variable: Growth of capital stock per worker			
Initial real GDP per capita	-2.278***	-1.490**	-1.219	-1.033	-1.810***	-1.070**	-1.276**	-1.001***	-1.438*	-1.080	-0.041	-0.119
	(-4.35)	(-2.19)	(-1.44)	(-1.68)	(-5.14)	(-2.57)	(-2.52)	(-2.87)	(-1.89)	(-1.21)	(-0.04)	(-0.16)
Initial years of schooling	2.653***	3.076**	1.692	2.620**	2.972***	2.810***	2.352***	2.790***	1.350	2.387	0.004	1.300
	(2.90)	(2.10)	(1.40)	(2.17)	(4.37)	(3.04)	(3.12)	(3.79)	(0.86)	(1.24)	(0.00)	(0.85)
Initial inflation rate	0.739*	11.195**	0.079	3.680*	0.762**	7.907***	0.239	2.529**	0.029	8.876	-0.440	2.710
	(1.89)	(2.54)	(0.33)	(1.91)	(2.84)	(3.08)	(1.41)	(2.04)	(0.05)	(1.23)	(-1.39)	(0.98)
Initial government size	-0.030	0.038	-0.033	0.015	-0.026	0.038*	-0.026	0.019	-0.037	0.006	-0.038	-0.012
	(-0.87)	(1.10)	(-1.01)	(0.40)	(-1.51)	(1.86)	(-1.24)	(0.84)	(-0.68)	(0.13)	(-0.99)	(-0.25)
Initial trade openness	0.010**	0.013**	0.007	0.002	0.011***	0.011***	0.009**	0.005	-0.002	0.004	-0.006	-0.008
	(2.35)	(2.64)	(1.14)	(0.35)	(3.47)	(4.05)	(2.30)	(1.54)	(-0.32)	(0.60)	(-0.94)	(-1.27)
Terms of trade growth	-0.063	-0.187*	-0.089	-0.171**	-0.054	-0.165**	-0.031	-0.138**	-0.082	-0.071	-0.176	-0.098
	(-0.43)	(-1.80)	(-0.64)	(-2.29)	(-0.59)	(-2.64)	(-0.38)	(-2.66)	(-0.33)	(-0.44)	(-1.07)	(-1.00)
Banking crisis	-0.014	-0.628	0.432	-0.837	0.030	-0.467	0.372	-0.299	-0.345	-0.204	0.092	-1.295*
	(-0.04)	(-1.01)	(1.15)	(-1.55)	(0.14)	(-1.28)	(1.59)	(-0.93)	(-0.62)	(-0.23)	(0.18)	(-1.75)
Initial government debt	-0.021***	-0.029***			-0.012***	-0.018***			-0.020*	-0.027*		
	(-3.33)	(-2.86)			(-3.93)	(-3.21)			(-1.77)	(-1.80)		
Government debt, average			-0.020**	-0.017**			-0.010	-0.008			-0.026**	-0.026**
			(-2.08)	(-2.20)			(-1.68)	(-1.68)			(-2.33)	(-2.69)
Number of observations	30	36	44	45	30	36	44	45	30	36	44	45
R^2	0.85	0.64	0.48	0.46	0.87	0.69	0.56	0.51	0.65	0.42	0.45	0.38

Note: Heteroskedasticity-consistent *t-statistics* are in parentheses. Levels of significance: *** 1 percent, ** 5 percent, * 10 percent. An intercept term and dummies for OECD, Asia, Latin America, and sub-Saharan Africa are included in each regression (not reported to save space).

Notes

This chapter heavily draws on Kumar and Woo (2010, 2012).

1. There is some evidence that high initial debt is associated with weaker recovery strength during the recovery phase in 54 advanced and emerging economies during 1970 to 2009 (Woo et al., 2013).

2. Herdon, Ash, and Pollin (2013) show that some of Reinhart and Rogoff (2010)'s "average" result when debt is above the 90 percent debt threshold was incorrect due to a coding error. Yet they also obtain the similar result that high debt is associated with lower growth, although the corrected growth rate (2.2 percent) when debt is above 90 percent is higher than that (−0.1 percent) originally reported in Reinhart and Rogoff (2010). Then again, Panizza and Presbitero (2012) suggest that there is no a causal relationship from high debt to slow growth using an IV regression, while confirming a negative relationship between debt and subsequent growth in the OLS regression, in a sample of OECD countries. However, significant caution is needed in interpreting their result, as their instrumental variable (IV), valuation effects (product of foreign currency debt portion of public debt and exchange rates), seems problematic and invalid. There is no convincing economic rationale as to why such an IV could satisfy the exclusion restriction condition (a key condition required of an acceptable IV) nor support the empirical test.

3. Also there is evidence that high *initial* debt at the start of recession is associated with weaker strength of recovery as well as longer duration from trough to end of the recession-recovery cycle for the advanced and emerging economies during 1970 to 2009. See Woo et al. (2013).

4. To be precise, the average growth rate of real per capita GDP per year over the period $t\text{-}\tau$ and t is $(y_{i,t} - y_{i,t\text{-}\tau})/\tau$, which is actually used in the empirical application of **equation (5.1).** All the explanatory variables in $X_{i,t\text{-}\tau}$ are measured at the beginning of period, except for the terms of trade growth, incidences of banking crisis, and fiscal deficit that are measured over the period $t - \tau$ and t.

5. Also it can be motivated by a consideration of fiscal sustainability. Huang and Xie (2008) derive a fiscal sustainability frontier in an endogenous growth framework and show that higher levels of government spending reduce the sustainable level of government debt. This implies that estimating a threshold effect on growth based on a widely used single-dimensional perspective of fiscal sustainability such as debt in excess of a particular level may be difficult. What matters is the ability to finance any given level of debt, which in part depends on the availability of savings and the preferences of the savers. Related, Woo (2003) finds that financial market depth is one of the robust determinants of public deficits for various estimation techniques and extensive robustness checks including an extreme-bounds analysis. Thus a measure of financial depth is included in the baseline regression.

6. The *proximate* causes of growth, such as investment or capital per worker, are not included in the core set of growth determinants, but are examined in the growth accounting exercises instead. Nonetheless, we check whether including investment in the regression changes the estimated coefficients of initial government debt.

7. Results are not shown here to save space. See Kumar and Woo (2010).

8. To see this more clearly, rewrite **equation (5.1)** as $y_{i,t} = (1 + \alpha)y_{i,t-\tau} + X_{i,t-\tau}\beta + \gamma Z_{i,t-\tau} + \eta_t + v_i + \varepsilon_{i,t}$. The endogeneity bias (often called dynamic panel bias) arises due to inevitable correlation between $y_{i,t-\tau}$ and v_i in the presence of lagged dependent variable because $y_{i,t-\tau}$ is endogenous to the fixed effects (v_i) in the error term. In the FE, the fixed effects (v_i) are eliminated via within-transformation, but there is now a correlation between the transformed lagged dependent variable and the transformed error term, causing the FE to be inconsistent and biased downward.

9. Intuitively, the within-transformation (i.e., demeaning) under FE may exacerbate the measurement error bias by decreasing the signal-to-noise ratio (Grilliches and Hausman 1987; Hauk and Wacziarg 2009).

10. A standard test of weak instruments in dynamic panel GMM regressions does not currently exist (Bazzi and Clemens, 2009). See Stock, Wright, and Yogo (2002) on why the weak instrument diagnostics for linear IV regression do not carry over to the more general setting of GMM.

11. The BE estimator applies the OLS to perform estimating of the following equation: $\overline{y_i} - y_{i,-1} = \alpha \overline{y_{i,-1}} + \overline{X_{i,-1}}\beta + \gamma \overline{Z_{i,-1}} + v_i + \overline{\varepsilon_i}$, where the upper bar indicates the average of each variable across time periods (up to eight periods), for example, $\overline{X_{i,-1}} = \sum_t X_{i,t-\tau} / T_i$. Thus time-fixed effects are not appropriate and suppressed by the BE. As one can see, the BE estimator does not correspond to the cross-sectional estimator most commonly used in the literature in which the dependent and explanatory variables are averaged, say, over 1970 to 2008, except for the initial income level in 1970. Hauk and Wacziarg (2009) show that the properties of the cross-sectional estimators are very similar to the properties of the BE estimator, but that BE performs slightly better.

12. In the OLS and robust regressions, dummies for OECD, Asia, Latin America, and sub-Saharan Africa are included. Results for robust regressions are similar to those of pooled OLS, so they are not reported to save space.

13. Importantly, the difference-in-Hansen tests of exogeneity of instrument subsets do not reject the null hypothesis that the instrument subsets for the level equations are orthogonal to the error (p-value = 0.34), that is, the assumption that lagged differences of endogenous explanatory variables being used as instruments in levels are uncorrelated with the errors. This is the additional restriction that needs to be satisfied for the SGMM estimator.

14. The dynamic panel GMM can generate too many instruments, which may overfit endogenous variables and run a risk of a weak-instruments bias (Roodman 2009; Bazzi and Clemens 2009). Given that one recommendation, when faced with a weak-instrument problem, is to be parsimonious in the choice of instruments. Roodman (2009) suggests restricting the number of lagged levels used in the instrument matrix or collapsing the instrument matrix or combining the two. The reported SGMM results in our chapter are obtained by combining the "collapsed" instrument matrix with lag limits.

15. With the time-fixed effects included, the coefficients of years of schooling and initial debt are often insignificant under FE in contrast to those under SGMM, as one can see throughout this chapter.

16. See Table A5.1 for the list of advanced and emerging economies.

17. Recent sovereign debt crisis in Europe suggests that there is a strong correlation between the NFA positions and sovereign yields, indicating the market perceptions of fiscal risks (e.g.,

debt default and fiscal unsustainability) stemming from high debt may depend on the NFA position.

References

Aghion, P., and S. Durlauf. 2005. *Handbook of Economic Growth,* vol. 1A and 1B. Amsterdam: North-Holland.

Aghion, P., and E. Kharroubi. 2007. Cyclical macro policy and industry growth: The effect of countercyclical fiscal policy. Working paper. Harvard University, Cambridge.

Aizenman, J., K. Kletzer, and B. Pinto. 2007. Economic growth with constraints on tax revenues and public debt: Implications for fiscal policy and cross-country differences. Working paper 12750. NBER, Cambridge, MA.

Arellano, M., and O. Bover. 1995. Another look at the instrumental variables estimation of error-components models. *Journal of Econometrics* 68: 29–51.

Balassone, F., M. Francese, and A. Pace, 2011. Public debt and economic growth in Italy. *Quaderni di Storia Economica*, Banca d'Italia, no. 11, October.

Baldacci, E., A. Hillman, and N. Kojo. 2004. Growth, governance and fiscal policy transmission channels in low-income countries. *European Journal of Political Economy* 20: 517–49.

Baldacci, E., and M. Kumar. 2010. Fiscal deficits, public debt and sovereign bond yields. Working paper 10/184. IMF, Washington, DC.

Barro, R. 1979. On the determinants of the public debt. *Journal of Political Economy* 85 (5): 940–71.

Barro, R. 1990. Government spending in a simple model of endogenous growth. *Journal of Political Economy* 98 (5): S103–25.

Barro, R., and J. Lee. 2011. A new data set of educational attainment in the world, 1950–2010. Working paper 15902. NBER, Cambridge, MA.

Barro, R., and X. Sala-i-Martin. 2003. *Economic Growth*. Cambridge: MIT Press.

Bazzi, S., and M. Clemens. 2009. Blunt instruments: On establishing the causes of economic growth. Working paper 171. Center for Global Development, Washington, DC.

Blundell, R., and S. Bond. 1998. Initial conditions and moment restrictions in dynamic panel data models. *Journal of Econometrics* 87 (1): 115–43.

Bond, S. 2002. Dynamic panel data models: A guide to micro data methods and practice. Working paper 09/02. Institute for Fiscal Studies, London.

Burnside, C., M. Eichenbaum, and S. Rebelo. 2001. Prospective deficits and the Asian currency crisis. *Journal of Political Economy* 109 (6): 1155–97.

Cecchetti, S., M. Mohanty, and F. Zampolli. 2011. The real effects of debt. Working paper 352. BIS, Basel.

Checherita, C., and P. Rother. 2010 The impact of high and growing government debt on economic growth: An empirical investigation for the euro area. Working paper 1237. European Central Bank, Frankfurt.

Cochrane, J. 2010. Understanding policy in the Great Recession: Some unpleasant fiscal arithmetic. Working paper. University of Chicago.

Dotsey, M. 1994. Some unpleasant supply side arithmetic. *Journal of Monetary Economics* 33: 507–24.

Eichengreen, B., and R. Hausmann. 1999. Exchange rates and financial fragility. Paper presented at the Symposium New Challenges for Monetary Policy, August 26–28, Jackson Hole.

Elmendorf, D., and N. G. Mankiw. 1999. Government debt. In J. B. Taylor and M. Woodford, eds., *Handbook of Macroeconomics*, vol. 1C. Amsterdam: North-Holland, 1615–69.

Fischer, S. 1993. The role of macroeconomic factors in growth. *Journal of Monetary Economics* 32 (3): 485–512.

Gale, W., and P. Orszag. 2003. The economic effects of long-term fiscal discipline. Discussion paper 8. Urban-Brookings Tax Policy Center, Washington, DC.

Glaeser, E., R. La Porta, F. Lopez-de-Silanes, and A. Shleifer. 2004. Do institutions cause growth? *Journal of Economic Growth* 9: 271–303.

Hauk, W., and R. Wacziarg. 2009. A Monte Carlo study of growth regressions. *Journal of Economic Growth* 14 (2): 103–47.

Hemming, R., M. Kell, and A. Schimmelpfennig. 2003. Fiscal vulnerability and financial crises in emerging market economies. Occasional paper 218. IMF, Washington, DC.

Heston, A., R. Summers, and B. Aten. 2011. Penn World Table Version 7.0. Center for International Comparisons of Production, Income and Prices at the University of Pennsylvania.

Herndon, T., M. Ash, and R. Pollin. 2013. Does high public debt consistently stifle economic growth? A critique of Reinhart and Rogoff. Working paper. University of Massachusetts at Amherst.

Huang, H., and D. Xie. 2008. Fiscal sustainability and fiscal soundness. *Annals of Economics and Finance* 9 (2): 239–51.

Imbs, J., and R. Ranciere. 2007. Overhang hangover. Working paper. Universite de Lausanne.

Islam, N. 1995. Growth empirics: A panel data approach. *Quarterly Journal of Economics* 110 (4): 1127–70.

Krugman, P. 1988. Financing versus forgiving a debt overhang. *Journal of Development Economics* 29: 253–68.

Kumar, M. S., and J. Woo. 2010. Public debt and growth. Working paper 10/174. IMF, Washington, DC.

Kumar, M. S., and J. Woo. 2012. Public debt and growth: An update. Unpublished working paper. IMF, Washington, DC.

Panizza, U., and A. Presbitero. 2012. Public debt and economic growth: Is there a causal effect? Unpublished working paper. Università Politecnica delle Marche.

Pattilo, C., H. Poirson, and L. Ricci. 2002. External debt and growth. Working paper 02/69. IMF, Washington, DC.

Pattilo, C., H. Poirson, and L. Ricci. 2004. What are the channels through which external debt affects growth? Working paper 04/15. IMF, Washington, DC.

Reinhart, C., V. Reinhart, and K. Rogoff. 2012. Debt overhangs: Past and present. Working paper 18015. NBER, Cambridge, MA.

Reinhart, C., and K. Rogoff. 2010. Growth in a time of debt. *American Economic Association Papers and Proceedings* 100 (2): 1–9.

Roodman, D. 2009. A note on the theme of too many instruments. *Oxford Bulletin of Economics and Statistics* 71 (1): 135–58.

Sachs, J. 1989. The debt overhang of developing countries. In G. A. Calvo, R. Findlay, P. Kouri, and J. B. de Macedo, eds., Debt Stabilization and Development. Cambridge, MA: Basil Blackwell, 80–102.

Saint-Paul, G. 1992. Fiscal policy in an endogenous growth model. *Quarterly Journal of Economics* 107 (4): 1243–59.

Sala-i-Martin, X., G. Doppelhofer, and R. Miller. 2004. Determinants of long-term growth: A Bayesian averaging of classical estimates (BACE) approach. *American Economic Review* 94 (4): 813–35.

Sargent, T., and N. Wallace. 1981. Some unpleasant monetarist arithmetic. *Quarterly Review* (Fall), Federal Reserve Bank of Minneapolis.

Stock, J. H., J. H. Wright, and M. Yogo. 2002. A survey of weak instruments and weak identification in generalized method of moments. *Journal of Business and Economic Statistics* 20 (4): 518–29.

Woo, J. 2003. Economic, political and institutional determinants of public deficits. *Journal of Public Economics* 87 (3): 387–426.

Woo, J. 2009. Why do more polarized countries run more procyclical fiscal policy? *Review of Economics and Statistics* 91 (4): 850–70.

Woo, J., T. Kinda, and M. Poplawski-Ribeiro. 2013. Economic recovery from recessions, fiscal policy, and structural reforms. Working paper. IMF, Washington, DC, forthcoming.

Part II

Buildup of Fiscal Vulnerabilities prior to the Crisis

6

Fiscal Trends and Fiscal Stress prior to the Crisis

Jiri Jonas and Iva Petrova

6.1 Introduction

This chapter traces the evolution of fiscal aggregates in advanced and emerging economies prior to the crisis. The long-term trend of public finances in the advanced economies illustrates gradual buildup of vulnerabilities over time. In the postwar period until the early 1990s, the long-term fiscal picture shows steadily expanding expenditures, initially paid for by increasing revenues, but eventually accommodated by wider deficits and growing debt. During the 1950 and 1960s, unanticipated postwar inflation and negative interest-rate–growth differential contributed to a rapid reduction in public debt, even as expenditure growth picked up in the 1960s. However, in the mid-1970s, the wearing off of favorable debt dynamics factors and relentless increase in pension and health care expenditures placed the debt ratio on the rise again. While expenditure growth eventually slowed and its ratio to GDP stabilized, it remained at a high level. Even periods of rapid economic growth did not result in a significant reduction in the debt ratio.

A more detailed look at the fiscal positions in the period preceding the crisis that contrasts developments in advanced and emerging economies reveals a lack of effort in advanced economies to reverse these trends, eventually magnifying fiscal challenges to distress levels in some countries. In the years before the crisis, advanced economies' headline fiscal balance improved. However, this improvement was less pronounced than in emerging economies, and partly reflected temporary cyclical factors rather than lasting structural improvements in fiscal positions. As a result vulnerabilities built up earlier were not much reduced, and the public sector balance sheets were left with an insufficient capacity to absorb the impact of the crisis, possible future shocks, and future aging-related pension and health care spending pressures.

6.2 Gradual Buildup of Fiscal Vulnerability in Advanced Countries

The 2007 crisis found most advanced economies in a weak fiscal position.[1] Even though there had been some stabilization or even reduction of public debt and expenditure ratios in the period preceding the crisis, it was not enough to reverse the significant deterioration that took place mainly during the second half of the 1970s and the 1980s. As a result the G7 public debt reached a historically high level of 84.2 percent of GDP in 2005 (figure 6.1). In 2005 the public debt ratios of France, Germany, and Japan also peaked. Despite short episodes of stabilization or temporary reversal, particularly during the 1990s when the US debt ratio fell notably, the G7 debt ratio grew steadily from the bottom it reached in 1974 (35 percent of GDP) and more than doubled by 2007 (84 percent of GDP). During the period of declining debt ratio, in 1950 to 1974, the G7 deficit averaged 0.5 percent of GDP. After a sharp increase in 1975, the deficit did not return to the pre-1975 levels (with a brief exception of in 2000), and averaged 3.5percent of GDP during the period 1975 to 2006 (figure 6.2).

Particularly remarkable is the increase in Japan's debt ratio during that period, from 20 percent of GDP to almost 190 percent of GDP. Italy managed to stabilize and partly reverse the debt ratio around the time of euro entry, but its debt ratio never fell below 100 percent of GDP. Among the few G7 countries that tackled the debt challenge, Canada reversed the trend of growing debt by implementing a consolidation program in the 1990s.[2] The United Kingdom maintained a declining debt ratio from a postwar peak of over 200 percent of GDP to around 40 percent during the 1990s and 2000s, by far the lowest among the G7 countries.

The postwar period was characterized by growing government expenditures (figure 6.3). The average G7 total government expenditures rose from less than 25 percent of GDP in 1950 to close to 40 percent by early 1990s. Most of the increase in the G7 government total and primary expenditures reflects rapid growth in health care and pension expenditures. In most countries the rise in public debt also led to increasing interest payments, gradually opening the gap between primary and total expenditures. Government expenditure ratio fell slightly during the second half of the 1990s but was back close to the postwar record high by 2007.

During the 1950s and 1960s the G7 debt ratio was falling. Even though the growth in government expenditures picked up in the 1960s, revenues grew rapidly and G7 countries generally maintained positive primary positions (table 6.1, figure 6.4). A negative interest-rate–growth differential, reflecting partly unexpected inflation and financial repression, also helped erode the real value of debt (Masson and Mussa 1995; Shigehara 1995).

However, in the second half of the 1970s primary deficits began to rise in frequency at the same time as inflation expectations caught up with actual inflation

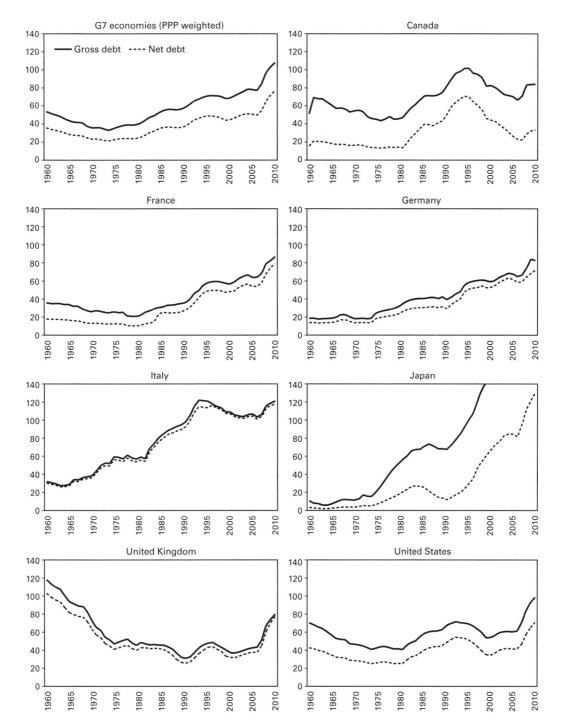

Figure 6.1
Government debt ratios in G7 economies, 1960 to 2011
Sources: Cottarelli and Schaechter (2010); projection from *Fiscal Monitor*, September 2011

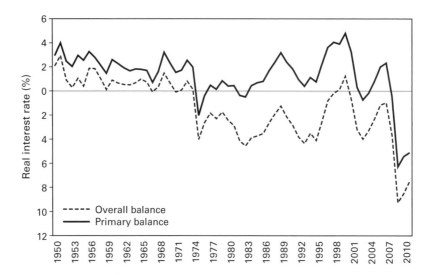

Figure 6.2
General government balance in G7 countries, 1950 to 2011
Source: Fiscal Monitor Database

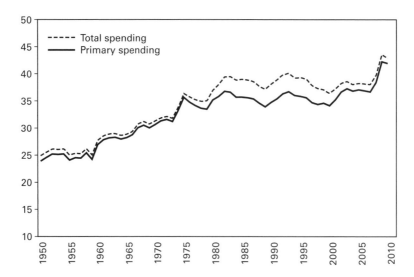

Figure 6.3
Government expenditure ratios in G7 economies, 1950 to 2011
Source: Cottarelli and Schaechter (2010)

Table 6.1
Long-term debt dynamics factors in G7 economies, 1950 to 2007

Overall balance	1950–1974		1975–2007		
	Average overall balance	Percent years with surplus	Average overall balance	Percent years with surplus	
Canada	0.1	60.0	−3.4	39.3	
France	0.4	87.5	−2.8	0.0	
Germany	−7.9	6.7	−1.6	10.7	
Italy	−3.2	0.0	−7.2	0.0	
Japan	0.9	89.5	−2.3	21.4	
United Kingdom	−1.7	24.0	−0.1	42.9	
United States	0.4	52.0	−0.5	32.1	
Average	**−0.8**	**50.5**	**−1.6**	**24.4**	
Primary balance	1950–1974		1975–2007		1980–2007
	Average primary balance	Percent years with surplus	Average primary balance	Percent years with surplus	Interest-rate–growth differential
Canada	3.2	96.0	4.0	82.1	4.6
France	1.7	100.0	−0.1	46.4	2.0
Germany	−7.0	13.3	1.4	92.9	2.9
Italy	−1.5	33.3	0.7	60.7	3.0
Japan	1.4	100.0	1.1	60.7	1.7
United Kingdom	2.6	72.0	3.4	85.7	1.8
United States	2.3	96.0	3.6	92.9	−4.0
Average	**1.0**	**65.3**	**2.1**	**72.1**	**2.2**

Sources: Cottarelli and Schaechter, 2010; Fiscal Monitor Database; Wyplosz, 2012
Note: Fiscal balance data for France begins in 1959, Germany in 1962, Italy in 1960, and Japan in 1956.

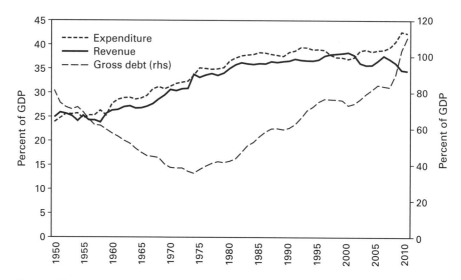

Figure 6.4
G7 economies: Revenue expenditure and gross debt, 1950 to 2010
Source: Cottarelli and Schaechter (2010), Fiscal Monitor Database

and bond yields increased.[3] This prompted a rise in interest payments and impaired governments' ability to achieve strong overall fiscal positions. The frequency of overall deficits increased relative to the postwar period. The interest-rate–growth differential also moved to a positive territory, exacerbating debt dynamics. Consequently, even though in some countries primary balances were on average higher than in the postwar period (Germany and Italy), they were not sufficiently high to offset the adverse effect of the interest-rate–growth differential.

6.3 Improved Fiscal Balances before the Crisis: Less Than Meets the Eye?

In this section we look in greater detail at fiscal developments during the years preceding the crisis.[4] This was a period of generally robust economic growth and low inflation, as well as strong house and stock price growth. Headline fiscal balances improved in both advanced and emerging economies. However, the fiscal improvement in emerging economies was more pronounced and solid than in advanced economies. As a result most advanced economies achieved little during these boom years to reverse the postwar debt buildup and remained ill-prepared to absorb the fiscal costs of the crisis. This also does not bode well for their ability to handle future adverse fiscal shocks, as well as the potential rise in pension and health care spending as the number of retirees grows.

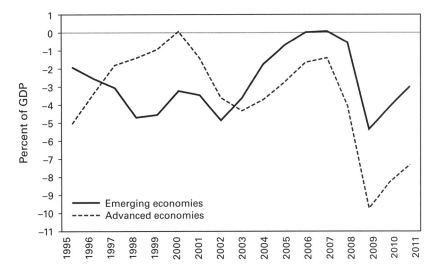

Figure 6.5
Advanced and emerging economies: Overall balance, 1995 to 2011. Averages are PPP-GDP weighted using rolling weights and are based on data availability.
Source: Fiscal Monitor Database

6.3.1 Headline Balances Improved . . .

In the benign environment of strong growth, low inflation, and booming asset prices, fiscal positions in both advanced and emerging economies improved before the crisis, though to a different extent. The overall fiscal balance improved by 4.5 percent of GDP in emerging economies during 2002 to 2007, and by a more modest 2.7 percent of GDP during 2003 to 2007 in advanced economies (figure 6.5). Thus, despite similar initial balances in 2002 to 2003, deficit reduction in emerging economies was nearly twice as large as in advanced economies. In fact the aggregate emerging economies' fiscal balance reached a small surplus in 2006 and 2007, the strongest position since the 1990s. In contrast, advanced economies' overall fiscal balance stayed well below the previous strongest position—a 0.1 percent surplus reached in 2000

6.3.2 . . . Driven by Rising Revenue and Falling Expenditures

Both increasing revenues and falling expenditures (as a percentage of GDP) contributed to narrowing fiscal deficits before the crisis (figure 6.6). In advanced economies, the expenditure ratio fell by about 4 percent of GDP between 1995 and 2001, and remained almost unchanged at around 39 percent of GDP after 2001.[5] Primary expenditures remained also broadly stable during that period. General government revenues grew moderately in the second half of the 1990s, helping to close the deficit,

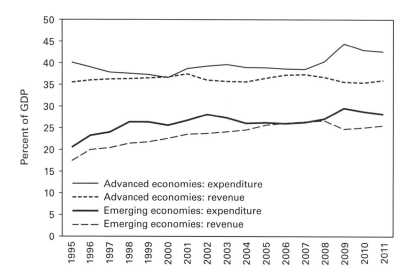

Figure 6.6
Advanced and emerging economies: Revenue and expenditure, 1995 to 2011. Averages are PPP-GDP weighted using rolling weights and are based on data availability.
Source: Fiscal Monitor Database

but declined during the brief recession of the early 2000s and slowly recovered by 2007.

In emerging economies, general government revenues displayed a remarkably steady growth between mid-1990s and 2007, from 17 to 26 percent of GDP, bringing the gap relative to advanced economies' revenues from about 20 percent of GDP in mid-1990s down to 11 percent of GDP by 2007. During that period, emerging economies' expenditures peaked in 2002, at 28 percent of GDP, and then fell a bit, despite continued robust revenue growth. This decline is due to a sharp fall in interest expenditures, while primary expenditures rose by over 1 percent of GDP in 2004 to 2007.

Aggregate numbers hide differences in the expenditure level before the crisis in individual countries (figure 6.7). In some countries, general government expenditures as a percentage of GDP were well below the maximum during 1995 to 2007. In Canada and Germany, expenditures were about 10 percent of GDP below the peak.[6] On the other side of the spectrum, in the United States, expenditures as a percentage of GDP reached their highest level in 2007, and in others (Australia, France, the United Kingdom), they were close to the pre-crisis peak.

While interest expenditures were declining during the 2000s in all advanced economies, public health and pensions expenditures as a percentage of GDP increased the most, with the exception of Germany (figure 6.8). In countries where total

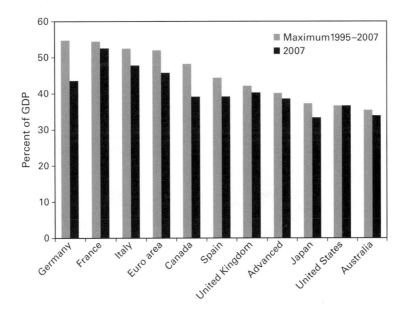

Figure 6.7
Advanced economies: Expenditures, 1995 to 2007. Averages are PPP-GDP weighted using rolling weights and are based on data availability.
Source: Fiscal Monitor Database

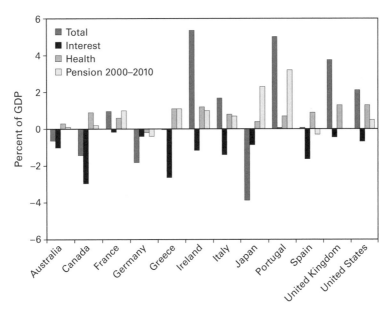

Figure 6.8
Advanced economies: Change in expenditures, 2000 to 2007
Sources: Fiscal Monitor Database; IMF (2010, 2011)

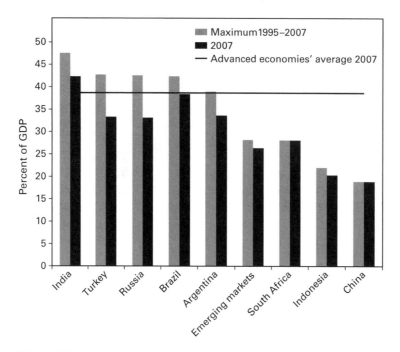

Figure 6.9
Emerging economies' expenditures, 1995 to 2007. Averages are PPP-GDP weighted using rolling weights and are based on data availability.
Source: Fiscal Monitor Database

expenditures ratio increased, this was entirely or mostly explained by higher pension and health spending; nevertheless, pension and health expenditure ratio rose even in countries where the total expenditure ratio fell. While advanced economies' primary expenditures fell by about 0.5 percent of GDP between 2000 and 2007, average pension and health expenditures rose over 1 percent of GDP, pointing to the continuation of longer term trend discussed in section 6.2.

Emerging economies show a similar picture (figure 6.9). In some countries (Argentina, Russia, Turkey), 2007 expenditures were below the previous peak, while in China and South Africa, they were at the peak. In Brazil and India, despite declining from their pre-crisis peak, general government expenditures were still higher than the average for advanced economies (the horizontal line).

6.3.3 Debt Paths in Advanced and Emerging Economies Diverged
The difference in fiscal balance developments in advanced and emerging economies shapes divergent paths of gross general government debt in the two sets of countries

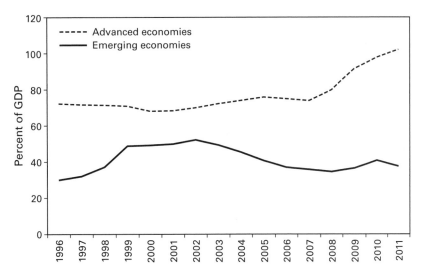

Figure 6.10
Advanced and emerging economies' gross government debt, 1996 to 2011. Averages are PPP-GDP weighted using rolling weights and are based on data availability.
Source: Fiscal Monitor Database

during the pre-crisis period (figure 6.10). In emerging economies, the debt-to-GDP ratio peaked in 2002, around 52 percent of GDP, before declining steadily to 35 percent of GDP in 2007, yet still above the mid-1990s level. In advanced economies, the debt-to-GDP ratio was stable and even fell slightly in the late 1990s and 2000, but rose gradually again by 2005. At the crisis onset, advanced economies' debt was close to 75 percent of GDP, and the difference in debt-to-GDP ratio between advanced and emerging economies had almost doubled, from about 20 percent of GDP in 2002 to close to 40 percent of GDP in 2006 and 2007.

For advanced economies as a group, the level of 2007 general government gross debt approached the maximum level reached during the 1996 to 2007 period (figure 6.11), despite the period of a relatively robust economic growth prior to 2007. With the exception of Australia, Canada, Spain, and to a lesser extent Italy, debt levels in advanced economies were close to—or at, in the case of Portugal—their previous peak. Relatively little—if any—reduction in the debt ratios had been accomplished under very favorable pre-crisis conditions of strong growth, booming revenues, and very low financing costs.

In contrast, the 2007 public debt level of emerging economies was notably below the 1980 to 2007 peak, and about half of that in the advanced economies (figure 6.12). The decline in the aggregate emerging economies' debt ratio was driven

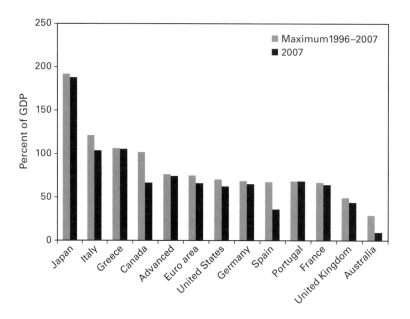

Figure 6.11
Advanced economies' gross government debt, 1995 to 2007. Averages are PPP-GDP weighted using rolling weights and are based on data availability.
Source: Fiscal Monitor Database

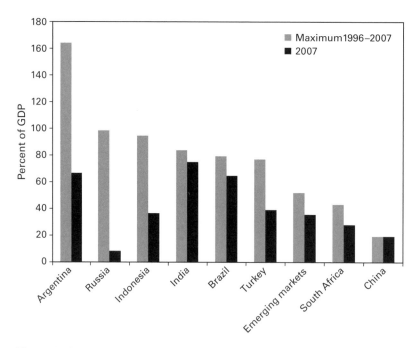

Figure 6.12
Emerging economies' gross government debt, 1995 to 2007. Averages are PPP-GDP weighted using rolling weights and are based on data availability.
Source: Fiscal Monitor Database

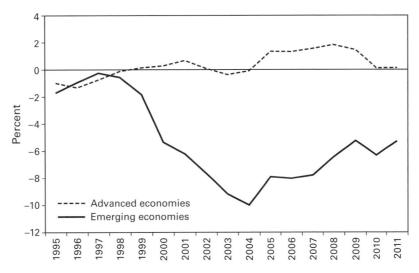

Figure 6.13
Interest–growth differential. The decline in the interest–growth differential in advanced economies after 2008 is due to monetary easing in the largest countries.
Sources: IMF, *Word Economic Outlook (WEO)*; International Finance Statistics (IFS); IMF staff calculations

mainly by several countries with high debt in the 1990s—Argentina, Indonesia and Russia. In Brazil and India the decline in the 2007 debt ratio compared to the peak was less pronounced.

The debt dynamics also reflected the interest-rate–growth differential of advanced and emerging economies (figure 6.13). In the advanced economies, the differential was mostly positive, and reached a peak in 2008 as growth collapsed. In emerging economies, the interest-rate–growth differential slumped in the late 1990 and helped reduce the debt ratio rapidly. This was driven both by strong growth and other factors, such as still existing financial isolation.[7] A reversal in this trend started in mid-2000s driven mostly by the European emerging economies.

The improvement in headline fiscal balances prior to the crisis has not always reflected sustained fiscal adjustment and the improvement in underlying fiscal fundamentals, particularly in advanced economies. To a large extent it reflected temporary factors. We look at three such factors in greater detail: booming economy, falling borrowing costs, and growing asset prices.

6.3.4 Strong Economic Growth Helped Reduce Deficits . . .
Following subdued economic activity in the early 2000s, real GDP growth accelerated after 2003. In advanced economies, average growth picked up from 1.7

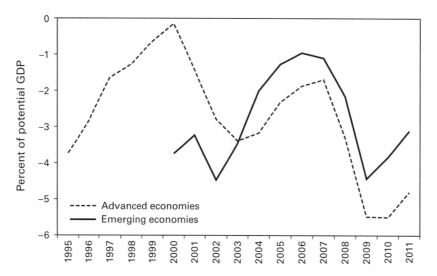

Figure 6.14
Advanced and emerging economies' cyclically adjusted overall balance, 1995 to 2011. Averages are PPP-GDP weighted using rolling weights and are based on data availability.
Source: Fiscal Monitor Database

percent in 2000 to 2003 to 2.9 percent in 2004 to 2007; and in emerging economies, from 5.6 percent to 8.5 percent in the same period. In 2002 to 2003, output gaps were usually negative but swung to positive values by 2007. The strong economic growth in 2004 to 2007, in both advanced and emerging economies, led to larger improvement of the overall fiscal balance than of the cyclically adjusted balance (figure 6.14). [8]

In advanced economies the overall balance improvement was almost one-half larger than the cyclically adjusted balance, while in emerging economies it was only about one-third larger. Thus the improvement of the overall fiscal balance driven by cyclical factors was more pronounced in advanced than in emerging economies. Still, even after adjusting for cyclical factors, the overall balance improvement in emerging economies remained stronger than in advanced economies. In 2006 and 2007 emerging economies had reached by far the strongest cyclically adjusted fiscal balance since at least late 1990s—when the aggregated data for this group are available—while advanced economies' cyclically adjusted balance remained well below the peak achieved in 1997 to 2001.

6.3.5 . . . And So Did Falling Costs of Borrowing . . .
During the 2000s, falling costs of government borrowing helped improve overall fiscal positions. Prompted by abundant global liquidity, the effective interest rate

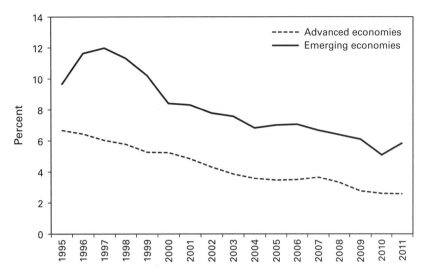

Figure 6.15
Advanced and emerging economies' effective interest rates. Averages are PPP-GDP weighted using rolling weights and are based on data availability. The effective interest rate is measured as a ratio of general government interest payments and general government gross debt.
Source: Fiscal Monitor Database

(interest expenditure divided by debt) kept falling during most of that period (figure 6.15). As a result, in advanced economies, interest expenditures fell significantly between mid-1990s and mid-2000s, by over 2 percent of GDP, quite remarkable given that the debt ratio was generally trending upward (figure 6.16).

In emerging economies, the picture was very much the same. Interest expenditures fell from a peak of 5 percent of GDP in 1999 to close to 2 percent of GDP in 2007 (figure 6.17). Unlike in the advanced economies, the reduction in interest expenditures was also supported by sliding debt-to-GDP ratio.

The decline in emerging economies' borrowing costs reflected a confluence of several factors, including (1) improved domestic policies and policy frameworks, (2) favorable external conditions (high growth, rising commodity prices), and (3) increased investors' interest in emerging economies.[9] Foreign investors, including institutional investors, increased their exposure to emerging economies, including to locally issued sovereign bonds. Sovereigns in emerging economies were able to borrow in their own currency, while at the same time extending debt maturities, thus reducing the exposure to exchange rate and interest rate risks (redemption from "original sin").[10] The EMBI spreads fell rapidly, and so did emerging economies' bond yields, even when at times in 2006 and 2007 the benchmark US ten-year Treasury yield was on the rise (figure 6.18).

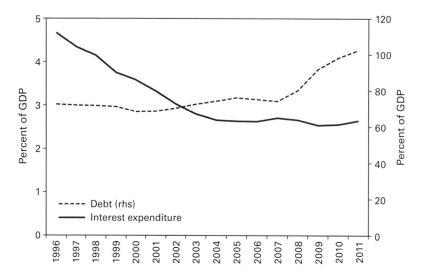

Figure 6.16
Advanced economies' gross debt and interest expenditures. Averages are PPP-GDP weighted using rolling weights and are based on data availability.
Source: Fiscal Monitor Database

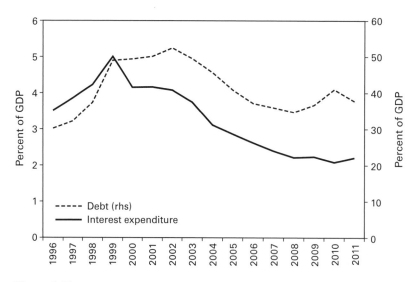

Figure 6.17
Emerging economies' gross debt and interest expenditures. Averages are PPP-GDP weighted using rolling weights and are based on data availability.
Source: Fiscal Monitor Database

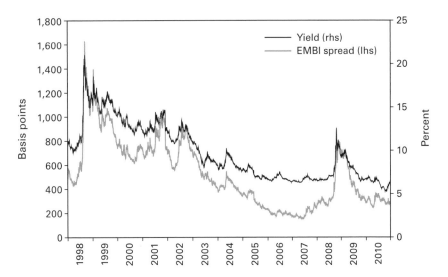

Figure 6.18
EMBI yields and spreads
Source: Datastream

Primary fiscal position adjusted for the business cycle developed in line with the cyclically adjusted overall balance in advanced economies, improving by 1.5 percent of GDP (figure 6.19). In emerging economies, reflecting the above-mentioned significant decline in interest expenditures, the cyclically adjusted primary balance strengthened notably less (2.0 percent of GDP) than the cyclically adjusted overall balance (3.5 percent of GDP). Nonetheless, emerging economies showed prolonged and sustained improvement in the cyclically adjusted primary balance since late 1990s, with six years of surplus, peaking at 1.6 percent of GDP in 2006. In contrast, advanced economies experienced much shorter and smaller improvement, leading to only one year of a tiny cyclically adjusted primary surplus in 2007.

The different extent of improvement of different fiscal balance measures in advanced and emerging economies before the crisis reflects the effect of lower interest costs captured by the cyclically adjusted primary balance (figure 6.20). This effect was almost zero in advanced economies (interest expenditures as percent of GDP were basically flat in 2004 to 2007), but more important than the impact of the business cycle in the emerging economies.

6.3.6 . . . And Rising Asset Prices and Other Temporary Factors
In addition to strong growth and falling costs of borrowing and interest expenditures, fiscal performance before the crisis was also boosted by temporary factors that are beyond the reach of fiscal policy makers and not always perfectly correlated with

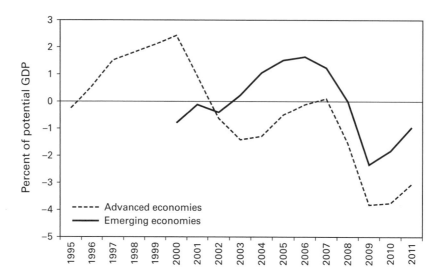

Figure 6.19
Advanced and emerging economies' cyclically adjusted primary balance. Averages are PPP-GDP weighted using rolling weights and are based on data availability.
Source: Fiscal Monitor Database

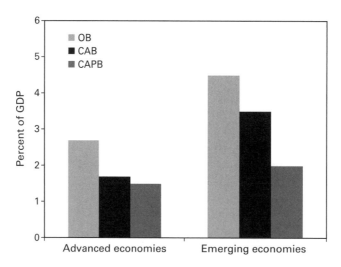

Figure 6.20
Advanced and emerging economies' fiscal balance improvements (bottom to peak before 2007)
Source: Fiscal Monitor Database

Box 6.1
Structural fiscal balances

The structural fiscal balance is the underlying fiscal position after stripping out one-off and temporary factors that affect revenues and expenditures. To estimate the structural balance, adjustment of fiscal aggregates is done sequentially by identifying one-off effects, the output gap effect, and additional transitory effects. One-off effects are identified separately for revenue and expenditure items as outliers—observations standing 2 standard deviations from the average value of the revenue or expenditure ratio to GDP.

The adjustment for the output gap uses revenue and expenditure elasticities identified by Girouard and André (2005). Disaggregated revenues and expenditures are used where available to fine-tune the adjustment. Output composition effects also take account of the deviation of the direct and indirect tax bases—as well as domestic absorption (the current account balance)—from their normal (ten-year moving average) values.

Additional effects are identified with respect to the gaps of (1) equity and housing prices, with elasticities estimated by Price and Dang (2011); (2) terms of trade effects, with elasticities as in Turner (2006); and (3) commodity price effects, with elasticities approximated by equity price elasticities. These gaps are defined as deviations from the normal values of equity, commodity, and housing prices, and terms of trade, which are estimated using HP filtering. For robustness, moving averages have also been used to estimate the gaps, broadly confirming the conclusions.

the business cycle (box 6.1).[11] Such factors include growing equity and real estate prices, feeding directly into income or property taxes, or indirectly boosting household wealth and increasing VAT and other taxes on goods and services.[12] Other sources of transient revenues stemmed from rising commodity prices, especially in emerging economies, or from external imbalances with lush imports raising government revenues from taxes on goods and international trade.

In advanced economies, equity and housing prices added sizable revenues, especially in the fifteen years after the mid-1980s (when financial regulations were eased and capital controls dismantled in a number of economies, and securitization flourished (figure 6.21).[13] Early in that period, windfall revenues from equity prices were strong in North America, the United Kingdom, and Ireland—exceeding 2 percent of GDP in the late 1980s. Equity prices picked up again in the late 1990s, causing large fiscal effects across many advanced economies. At the peak, these effects exceeded 2 percent of GDP in the United Kingdom, Germany, and France and were close to this amount in a number of other European countries. In general, windfall revenues from asset prices were somewhat higher in Europe than in other advanced economies until 2000.

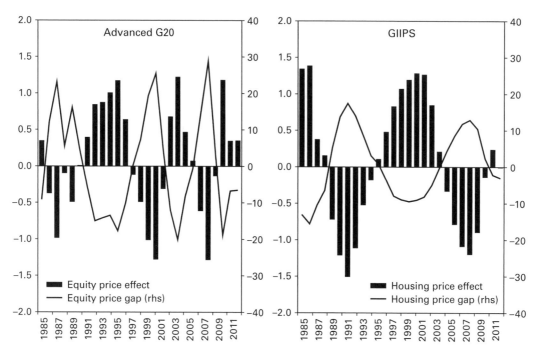

Figure 6.21
Advanced economies' transient fiscal effects (percent of potential GDP) and asset price gap (percent), 1985 to 2011.
PPP-GDP weights were used to calculate weighted averages. Positive transient effects drive the temporary improvement in the headline (unadjusted) balance. GIIPS denotes Greece, Ireland, Italy, Portugal, and Spain.
Sources: IMF, *World Economic Outlook (WEO)*; Bank for International Settlements (BIS); Organisation for Economic Co-operation and Development (OECD); IMF staff calculations

The boom in the equity market that started in early 2000s caused a sizable increase in tax buoyancy (tax collection as percentage of GDP) in the United States, Canada, and Japan in 2004 to 2006.[14] Windfall revenues from asset prices were practically negligible in other countries in Asia and Pacific. In Europe, equity price effects reached 1.5 percent of GDP, but exceeded 3 percent of GDP in Ireland.

Windfall revenues from housing prices were on average in the positive territory after the mid-1980s, especially in northern Europe, where they exceeded 2 percent of GDP and reached 3 to 3.5 percent of GDP at the peak of the real estate boom. After 2000, housing prices picked up rapidly throughout all advanced economies. Housing prices rallied in peripheral Europe, improving headline balances by about 2 percent of GDP in Spain and some of the smaller EU countries. This is consistent with other studies, which find significant equity price effects in the run-up of the dot.com bubble and large house price effects prior to the 2008 financial crisis.

Hence advanced economies, especially in Europe and North America, enjoyed periods during which financial and real asset valuation contributed to strong headline fiscal balances. The persistence of these effects made the assessment of underlying fiscal positions very challenging, as asset prices were notoriously difficult to project and known to exhibit random walk properties. Persistently strong revenues were more likely to be considered permanent, altering the understanding of where the underlying fiscal position stood relative to a sustainable fiscal balance. Only the loss of asset price related revenue in the wake of the 2008 financial crises revealed their transient nature.

While much less sensitive to share and household prices, emerging economies' fiscal performance has not been spared from their effects. The dynamics of the transient revenue effects in emerging economies has mirrored those in advanced economies. Strong stock returns in advanced economies have been combined with a growing demand for commodities, which have boosted fiscal revenues in emerging economies, especially the resource rich ones.

Overall, the boom in commodity prices during the 2000s contributed to strong improvement in overall fiscal balances in emerging economies. IMF (2012) found that unlike the previous commodity boom during the 1970s, during the 2000s commodity boom, average fiscal balance (both overall and cyclically adjusted) improved for exporters in all commodity groups. Machinea (2012) estimates that in Latin America, revenues from export represent about 1/4 of total public sector revenue, and during the boom, additional revenues were used to reduce public debt and increase social spending. However, in developing countries, Spatafora and Samake (2012) found an ambiguous impact of commodity price shocks on fiscal outcomes during the period 1990 to 2010, as higher revenues led to higher spending.

Our results show that in emerging economies of the Middle East and Latin America, commodity revenues have been the primary driver of headline fiscal revenues, with underlying revenues and structural positions becoming increasingly weaker (figure 6.22). In the Middle Eastern countries, temporary commodity revenues have peaked above 10 percent of GDP. In Latin America, the robust commodity exports have boosted revenues by more than 2 percent of GDP has and have driven an inflow of capital in domestic stock and real estate markets.[15] The wealth effects of commodity and capital inflows have also supported domestic demand and created absorption-led revenue increase in the years preceding and during the financial crisis in advanced economies.

Asset and consumption-driven growth in taxes on goods and services has characterized the headline fiscal position in European emerging economies, exposing them to fiscal weaknesses during capital flow reversal. These absorption effects reached 1.5 to 2 percent of GDP in countries with large current account deficits, where consumption-lead revenues boomed before declining abruptly in 2008 and 2009.

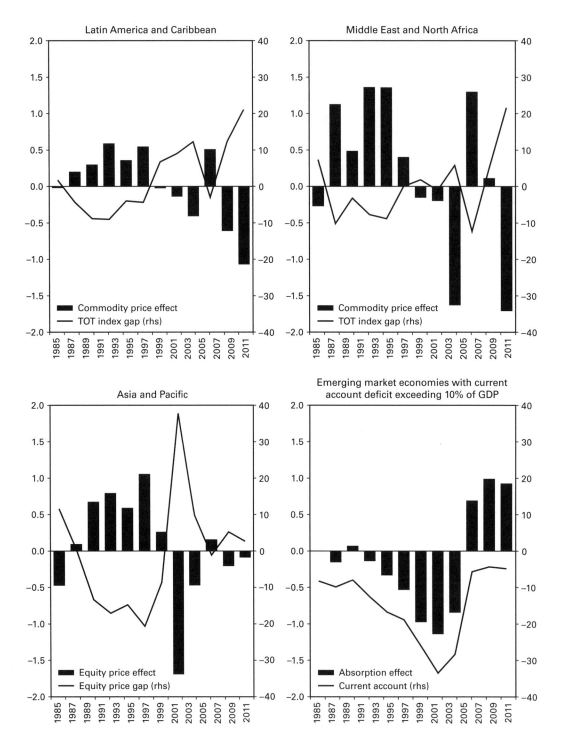

Figure 6.22
Emerging economies' transient fiscal effects (percent of potential GDP), 2000 to 2011. PPP-GDP weights were used to calculate weighted averages. Positive transient effects drive the temporary improvement in the headline (unadjusted) balance. Sources: IMF, *World Economic Outlook (WEO)*; Bank for International Settlements (BIS); Organisation for Economic Co-operation and Development (OECD); IMF staff calculations

The underlying fiscal position has consistently improved only in emerging econo-mies in Asia, where negative commodity gaps and export-led output growth have minimized windfall fiscal revenues. Nonetheless, revenues driven by elevated equity and housing prices have exceeded 1.25 percent of GDP since 2000 even in these economies.

6.3.7 Fiscal Pressures Projected to Increase in the Future

Not only was the present state of public finance at the time of the eruption of the cri-sis weaker than meets the eye. In addition, a number of countries face the prospects of increasing future fiscal pressures because of projected higher spending on public pensions and health care (see IMF 2010; Clements 2012).

In advanced economies, public health spending is projected to increase by 3 per-cent of GDP from 2011 to 2030, with the United States facing the largest projected increase, by over 5 percent of GDP. In seven European countries, the spending is projected to increase by over 3 percent of GDP. Longer term projection for 2011 to 2050 shows more than twice higher increase in advanced economies' public health spending, by 6.5 percent of GDP. In emerging economies, the projected 2011 to 2030 increase is much less, by 1 percent of GDP on average. As for pension spending, the projected increase is similar for advanced and emerging economies, about 1 percent of GDP in 2010 to 2030, but with substantial variation across the countries (and with some countries' pension spending such as Italy's projected to decline). Look-ing further to the future, the projected increase in spending on public pensions and health care by 2050 is even higher. However, these projections are subject to consid-erable uncertainty.

6.3.8 The Upshot: Smaller Fiscal Space, Greater Fiscal Risks

On the face of it, fiscal space at the time of the eruption of the crisis seemed abun-dant (figure 6.23, box 6.2). In advanced economies, despite elevated debt stocks the low-interest rate environment provided ample opportunity to extend debt maturi-ties and reduce financing needs. In emerging economies—especially after the Asian crisis—improved fiscal balances, better debt structure, and strong growth combined with low global interest rates led to favorable debt dynamics. These contributed to healthy fiscal indicators and seemingly low exposure to fiscal stress.

However, while on aggregate fiscal pressures remained subdued and fiscal space continued improving, pressures started mounting in some advanced economies in early 2000s (figure 6.24). The secular trend in health spending was putting fiscal pressures uniformly across all regions. Yet the turnaround had regional origins (fig-ure 6.25). The burden of pension spending and aging pressures—dependency ratio and the projected thirty-year increase in pension spending—were more pronounced in Europe (Slovenia, Ireland, Belgium, Greece, and Spain) and Asia and the Pacific

Box 6.2
Deriving fiscal stress and fiscal space

Fiscal stress and fiscal space indexes used in this chapter follow Baldacci, McHugh, and Petrova (2011) and Baldacci et al. (2011).

The indexes are built as signals of distress.
Forty-one distress events are identified in advanced economies and 135 events in emerging market economies during 1970 to 2010. Stress episodes arise when a government is exposed to the possibility of failure to achieve its policy objectives because of exceptional rollover problems. This may reflect outright debt default or restructuring, exceptionally high levels of inflation reducing the debt level in real terms, large financing needs forcing a country to request official assistance under an IMF-supported program with a high quota share (above 100 percent), or a large spike in bond yields making debt service extremely difficult.

A parsimonious set of indicators has strong signaling power.
Twelve fiscal indicators—among a set of more than 40—were selected for their signaling power. These variables include the difference between GDP growth and the imputed interest rate on government debt, cyclically adjusted primary balance, general government gross debt, gross financing needs, short-term debt to total debt, foreign currency denominated debt to total debt for emerging economies/debt held by nonresidents to total debt for advanced economies, weighted average maturity of government debt, short-term external debt to international reserves for emerging economies, deviation of fertility rate from replacement rate, old-age dependency ratio, and projections of long-term change in public pension and health spending. The variables' critical thresholds signaling fiscal stress were determined using a univariate, nonparametric method aiming to minimize the sum of type I (false positive) and type II (false negative) errors of identifying fiscal stress one period ahead.

The indexes are normalized averages of the indicators.
To build the fiscal stress index, the thresholds are used to assign each variable a 0 or 1 value signaling the potential for distress. These values are weighted by the predictive power of the individual indicators and aggregated into an index. To generate the fiscal space index, space is defined as a fiscal indicator's normalized distance from its fiscal stress threshold. The weighted by the indicators' predictive power distances are aggregated into an index.

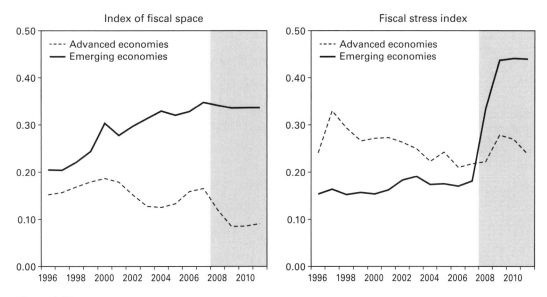

Figure 6.23
Fiscal space and fiscal stress, 1996 to 2010. PPP-GDP weights were used to calculate weighted averages.
Source: IMF staff calculations

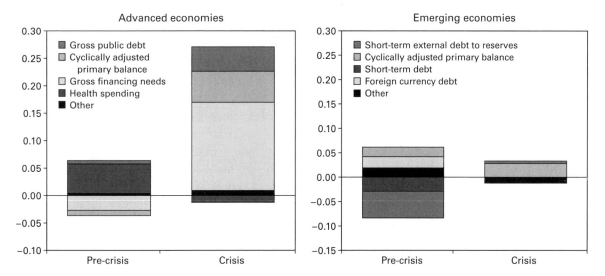

Figure 6.24
Contribution of the fiscal stress index components, 2000 to 2011. PPP-GDP weights were used to calculate weighted averages. "Pre-crisis" denotes the 1996 to 2007 period; "Crisis" denotes the 2008 to 2011 period. The dynamics of the overall index is presented in figure 6.23.
Source: IMF staff calculations

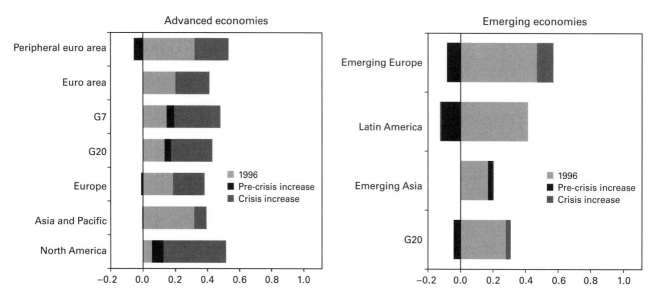

Figure 6.25
Regions and fiscal stress accumulation. PPP-GDP weights were used to calculate weighted averages. "Pre-crisis" denotes the 1996 to 2007 period; "Crisis" denotes the 2008 to 2011 period.
Source: IMF staff calculations

(Japan, Korea, and New Zealand) than in peers. Some peripheral euro area countries and Asia were also carrying greater public debt burdens, which in combination with unfavorable interest–growth differentials, engendered financing need ratios beyond the stress threshold several years before the outset of the financial crisis. Countries in emerging Europe also showed signs of fiscal vulnerability as their fiscal positions, financing conditions, public debt levels and structures remained more onerous during the pre-crisis period than in peers.

The emergence of the crisis has exposed weaknesses in handling contingent liabilities from the financial system and the fiscal stress consequences of a sharp turnaround in risk appetite in advanced economies. Financing needs have increased with the first signs of the crisis as governments swiftly committed to supporting financial institutions, and skyrocketed with the collapse in revenues prompted by the decline in economic activity and asset prices. Fiscal support aiming to mitigate second round effects on the economy further widened fiscal imbalances and placed debt at a new high.

This has also led to an abrupt change in the composition of fiscal space (figure 6.26). In advanced economies, the decline in fiscal space has come as a result of a sharp increase in gross financing needs, deterioration in cyclically adjusted primary balances, and debt accumulation. In emerging economies, fiscal space remains large-

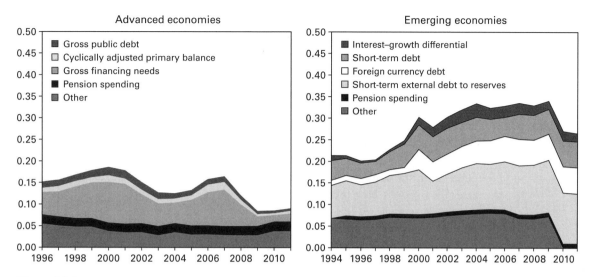

Figure 6.26
Fiscal space, 1996 to 2011. PPP-GDP weights were used to calculate weighted averages.
Source: IMF staff calculations

ly dependent on international liquidity, providing a buffer for short-term external payments, as well as prudent debt structures with low ratios of foreign currency and short-term debt.

6.4 Conclusions

What is the main takeaway from fiscal developments before the crisis?

First, in the postwar period, government role in advanced economies expanded significantly, and while higher tax revenues initially financed a large part of this expansion, eventually fiscal deficits increased and public debt began to accumulate. Between mid-1990s and 2007 government expenditures as a percentage of GDP stabilized and even declined, and the debt ratio increased only moderately during that period. However, at the start of the crisis, the government size and debt ratio still remained near the postwar high in a number of advanced economies.

Second, the reduction in fiscal deficits overstated the structural fiscal improvement particularly in advanced economies, and did not always signal an appropriate fiscal policy conduct. In 2007, the overall fiscal deficit exceeded 2 percent of GDP in France, Japan, United Kingdom, and United States. This indicated insufficient fiscal adjustment in the preceding period of strong economic growth. Prior to the crisis, fiscal policy tended to be insufficiently counter-cyclical in a number of countries, even though this was masked by improving headline balances as a result of strong economic growth, negative output gaps, as well as credit-driven booming asset prices and related tax revenues.

Governments often treat temporary revenues as permanent and use them to boost expenditures, rather than to cut deficits.[16]The EC (2008) notes the strong aggregate fiscal figures for 2007 mask underlying weaknesses and sums up presciently: "The expenditure overruns confirm a discomfiting pattern observed over many years. Considering that a significant part of the extra revenues recorded in 2006 and 2007 is likely to vanish as economic activity decelerates and that the cyclical position may have been underestimated, the tendency to overspend is liable to limit the room for maneuver in the coming years."[17] With the benefit of hindsight, it is clear that fiscal authorities should have pursued "more ambitious fiscal targets in good times, to provide governments with an ability to respond in times of financial crisis."[18]

Third, though above-discussed problems of temporarily inflated revenues apply to some extent to emerging economies as well, fiscal improvement in these countries before the crisis appeared generally to be on a more solid ground. Two mutually supportive developments contributed to this outcome: (1) improvement in the fiscal policy framework and fiscal policy conduct[19] and (2) improved structure of government financing with an extension of debt maturities that increased borrowing in domestic currency and that broadened the set of investors. As a result, when the crisis struck, emerging economies were in much stronger position to engage in countercyclical fiscal easing than during previous episodes of weak growth (see Frankel, Végh, and Vuletin 2011). The strengthening of emerging economies' fiscal position was not limited to central government. As noted in Canuto and Liu (2010), many subnational governments in emerging economies entered the crisis in a strong position thanks to extensive fiscal consolidation before the crisis.[20]

Fourth, as a result of relatively high debt and limited improvements in underlying fiscal balances, the eruption of the crisis led quickly to serious deterioration of advanced countries' fiscal position, squeezing the fiscal space and resulting in many cases to markets' doubts about fiscal sustainability. The consequence was that in a number of countries, the room for using fiscal policy to mitigate the weak private demand and output decline was limited in extent and duration, and countercyclical fiscal easing could not always be maintained long enough to allow economic activity pickup.

The inadequacy of fiscal improvements prior to the crisis appears even starker when taking into account the projected future fiscal challenges, particularly the projected increase health care and pension costs (see chapter 19 in this volume). As the full fiscal implication of the crisis become more clear (IMF 2011c), the room of many advanced economies' public sectors (and some emerging economies) to absorb the projected increase in health and pension costs has become more limited. While past reforms helped limit the past and projected increase in health care and pension costs, without further reforms, these costs are still likely to increase substantially. This underscores the urgency of putting in place credible plans to mitigate the impact on public finance of projected population aging and, even more important, to arrest the sustained rapid growth of health care costs. The at best limited improvement in advanced economies' fiscal position before the crisis makes this task even more challenging, as governments have to navigate between two objectives: (1) to provide near-term support to economic activity and (2) at the same time putting in place credible plans to repair the public sector balance sheets even while simultaneously dealing with the projected future pension and health care spending pressures.

Notes

1. The analysis in this section is based on Cottarelli and Schaechter (2010).

2. See Sansak, Liu, and Nakata (2011).

3. In some countries (e.g., Italy), financial liberalization also contributed to increasing deficits.

4. In this section we look at all advanced countries rather than just the G7 countries. We focus on the period 1995 to 2007 partly because of an increased coverage of countries in aggregate data of advanced and emerging economies starting in 1995.

5. As discussed above, the G7 total expenditure ratio returned back close to the postwar height in 2007, but in the broader sample of all advanced economies, it remained almost 2 percent of GDP below the record high. Thus the decline in non-G7 expenditure ratio was even more pronounced.

6. In Germany, the Netherlands, and Japan, there was a reclassification in 1995 of some expenditures, which resulted in a large spike in expenditure ratio in that year in Germany and the Netherlands. See Joumard et al. (2008).

7. See Escolano, Shabunina, and Woo (2011).

8. However, at that time, estimates of output gap differed significantly from the current ones, preventing a correct assessment of cyclical component of the improvement.

9. See IMF (2007).

10. See Jeanne and Guscina (2006).

11. A cyclically adjusted fiscal balance is corrected for the effects of the business cycle. A structural balance in addition is corrected for other one-off or temporary effects, whose cycle may be offset from the business cycle or have different amplitude.

12. For a detailed description of the factors affecting fiscal positions beyond the business cycle, see Bornhorst et al. (2011). The structural balances presented in this analysis use the template published at http://www.imf.org/external/np/fad/strfiscbal/index.htm.

13. Gorton and Metrick (2011).

14. The analysis has shown that this increase was driven by several temporary factors: (1) growth in capital gains, (2) growth in corporate profits in excess of GDP growth, and (3) stronger income growth of high-income individuals, which in combination with progressive tax system boosted tax revenue. See Swiston, Mühleisen, and Mathai (2007).

15. IMF (2011a).

16. Eichengreen et al. (2011) note that the rising public debt in the euro zone prior to the crisis reflected ever increasing public services and transfers. Figure 6.6 shows aggregate expenditure in advanced economies gradually declining or flat before the crisis. However, to a large extent, this reflects a 3.6 percent of GDP expenditure decline in Germany between 2005 and 2007.

17. European Commission (2008, p. 12). It should be noted that the overspending means relative to the plan. It does not preclude the decline in spending as a percentage of GDP.

18. Ceccheti (2011).

19. See Frankel, Végh, and Vuletin (2011). Relevant to the European problems, the authors note that in Chile, the cyclically adjusted fiscal rule that has been successfully followed since 2001 ensured that temporarily high fiscal revenues are not spent but saved. Other countries in the region have been improving fiscal policies following Chile's example.

20. Canuto and Liu (2010).

References

Baldacci, Emanuele, James McHugh, and Iva Petrova. 2011. Indicators of fiscal vulnerability and fiscal stress. Working paper 11/94. IMF, Washington, DC.

Baldacci, E., I. Petrova, N. Belhocine, G. Dobrescu, and S. Mazraani. 2011. Assessing fiscal stress. Working paper 11/100. IMF, Washington, DC.

Bornhorst, Fabian, Gabriela Dobrescu, Annalisa Fedelino, Jan Gottschalk, and Taisuke Nakata. 2011. When and how to adjust beyond the business cycle? A guide to structural fiscal balances. Technical Notes and Manuals /11/02. IMF, Washington, DC.

Canuto, O., and L. Liu. 2010. Subnational debt finance and the global financial crisis. *Economic Premise, No. 13*. Washington: World Bank.

Cecchetti, Stephen. 2011. Fiscal policy and its implications for monetary and financial stability. Remarks at the 10th BIS Annual Conference, Lucerne, June 23–24.

Clements, Benedict J., ed. 2012. The Challenge of Public Pension Reform in Advanced and Emerging Economies. Washington, DC: IMF.

Cottarelli, Carlo, and Andrea Schaechter. 2010. Long-term trends in public finances in the G-7 economies. Staff position note 10/13. IMF, Washington, DC.

Eichengreen, B., R. Feldman, J. Liebman, J. von Hagen and C. Wyplosz. 2011. Public debts: Nuts, bolts and worries. *Geneva Reports on the World Economy*. Geneva: International Center for Monetary and Banking Studies.

Escolano, Julio, Anna Shabunina, and Jaejoon Woo. 2011. The puzzle of persistently negative interest rate–growth differentials: Financial repression or income catch-up? Working paper 11/260. IMF, Washington, DC.

European Commission. 2008. *Public Finance in EMU*. Brussels: European Commission.

Frankel, J., C. A. Végh, and C. Vuletin. 2011. On graduation from fiscal procyclicality. Working paper 17619. NBER, Cambridge, MA.

Girouard, Nathalie, and Christophe André. 2005. Measuring cyclically adjusted budget balances for OECD countries. Working paper 434. Economics Department, OECD, Paris.

Gorton, Gary, and Andrew Metrick. 2011. Getting up to speed on the financial crisis: A one-weekend-reader's guide. Working paper 17778. NBER, Cambridge, MA.

International Monetary Fund. 2007. *Global Financial Stability Report, September 2007.* Washington, DC: IMF.

International Monetary Fund. 2010. Macro-fiscal implications of health care reform in advanced and emerging economies. Policy paper. IMF, Washington, DC.

International Monetary Fund. 2011a. Shifting winds, new policy challenges. *Regional Economic Outlook.* Western Hemisphere Department. IMF, Washington, DC.

International Monetary Fund. 2011b. *Fiscal Monitor: Addressing Fiscal Challenges to Reduce Economic Risks.* Washington, DC: IMF.

International Monetary Fund. 2012, *World Economic Outlook.* Washington, DC: IMF.

Jeanne, Olivier, and Anastasia Guscina. 2006. Government debt in emerging market countries: A new data set. Working paper 06/98. IMF, Washington, DC.

Joumard, Isabelle, Makoto Minegishi, Christophe André, Chantal Nicq, and Robert Price. 2008. Accounting for one-of operations when assessing underlying fiscal positions. Working paper 642. Economics Department, OECD, Paris.

Machinea, José L. 2012. Latin America's commodity windfall. http://www.project-syndicate.org/commentary/latin-america-s-commodity-windfall.

Masson, Paul, and Michael Mussa. 1995. Long-term tendencies in budget deficits and debt. Presented at Budget Deficits and Debt: Issues and Options Symposium sponsored by the Federal Reserve Bank of Kansas City, August 31–September 2, Jackson Hole, WY.

Price, Robert, and Thai-Thanh Dang. 2011. Adjusting fiscal balances for asset price cycles. Working paper 868. Economics Department, OECD, Paris.

Sansak, C., L. Liu, and T. Nakata. 2011. Canada: A success story. In P. Maoro, ed., Chipping away at Public Debt. Hoboken, NJ: Wiley, 1–30.

Shigehara, Kumiharu. 1995. Commentary: Long-term tendencies in budget deficits and debt. Presented at Budget Deficits and Debt: Issues and Options Symposium sponsored by the Federal Reserve Bank of Kansas City, August 31–September 2, Jackson Hole, WY.

Spatafora, Nikolia, and Issouf Samake. 2012. Commodity price shocks and fiscal outcomes. Working paper 12/112. IMF, Washington, DC.

Swiston, A., M. Mühleisen, and K. Mathai. 2007. U.S. revenue surprise: Are happy days here to stay? Working paper 07/143. IMF, Washington, DC.

Turner, David. 2006. Should measures of fiscal stance be adjusted for terms of trade effects? Working paper 519. Economics Department, OECD, Paris.

Wyplosz, Charles. 2012. Fiscal rules: Theoretical issues and historical experiences. Working paper 17884. NBER, Cambridge, MA.

7

Current Debt Crisis in Historical Perspective

S. Ali Abbas, Nazim Belhocine, Asmaa El-Ganainy, and Anke Weber

7.1 Introduction

The simultaneity and scale of debt accumulations in a number of advanced countries in the wake of the global financial crisis and the accompanying so-called Great Recession have renewed attention and interest in the historical behavior of public debt in advanced economies, and first research on this topic has already emerged, such as Reinhart and Rogoff (2011), Abbas et al. (2011), IMF (2012), and Reinhart et al. (2012).

These studies have indicated, consistent with figure 7.1, that the current debt buildup is certainly not unique in its scale if the entire past century is considered.[1] Debt ratios in 19 advanced economies, 14 of which are European, underwent a number of major spikes (followed by reversals) since the early 1900s.[2] The most notable of these relate to World Wars I and II, when the weighted-average debt ratio rose to about 90 and 130 percent, respectively.[3] Major debt buildups during peacetime, which would constitute a more relevant comparator for the ongoing debt surge, occurred around the Great Depression (1929 to 1932) and over the four decades leading up to the current crisis (1970 to 2007). During the Great Depression, 15 out of 19 countries witnessed increases of 10 percentage points of GDP or more in their public debt ratios, with the weighted-average increase recorded at 23 percent of GDP. By comparison, during the period 1970 to 2007, public debt ratios in 14 out of 19 countries registered increases of more than 10 percent of GDP, with a weighted-average increase of 45 percent of GDP.

However, a number of important questions related to historical episodes of debt buildup merit further attention. For example, what is the *explanation* for the relative size and composition of past debt surges (i.e., contribution of cumulative primary deficits vs. interest-rate–growth differential) when compared with the current debt buildup? In particular, why is the debt increase in the Great Recession larger than that observed during the Great Depression despite the fact that the growth decline has been much smaller this time around? To what extent did a larger initial debt and

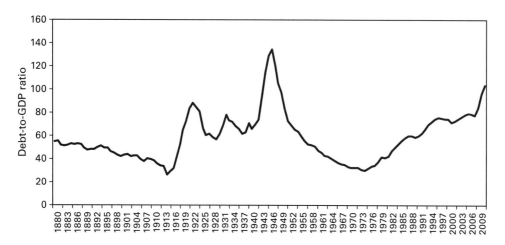

Figure 7.1
Public debt in 19 advanced countries, 1880 to 2009
Sources: Historical Public Debt Database; authors' calculations

size of state contribute to this anomalous result? Similarly, what were the key drivers of the seminal debt increase witnessed over the period 1970 to 2007, and to what extent were these constant through the decades? What insights can be gleaned regarding the *composition* of stock-flow adjustments, which Abbas et al. (2011) highlighted as an important driver of past debt surges?

A second set of questions relates to what we can learn from past debt reductions. While examining the debt buildups related to the World Wars may not be that interesting from a policy perspective, their unwinding certainly is. Debt is debt, whether created out of military spending or financial crisis, and policy makers confronted with high debt could benefit from an analysis of the factors guiding postwar debt reductions which, incidentally, remain unprecedented in scale and scope: during 1945 to 1970, debt ratios in the advanced economies fell in weighted-average terms by about 90 percentage points, with large reductions in each of the cases of the United Kingdom, the United States, and Japan. The key policy issue here is whether debt reduction strategies adopted during that period, such as financial repression (Reinhart et al. 2011), can be realistically replicated in today's globalized financial markets, and given the markedly different holder profiles of public debt.

This chapter attempts to shed light on these questions that have clear policy relevance for debt sustainability and prospects for debt reduction in today's advanced economies. The rest of the chapter is organized as follows: Section 7.2 presents our analytical framework and a brief literature review. Section 7.3 analyzes the ongoing debt buildup in advanced economies, drawing comparisons with the Great Depression and identifying key distinguishing features. Section 7.4 examines the gradual but pervasive debt increase during 1970 to 2007 (the so-called Great Accumulation), identifying both the evolution of the relative contributions of the primary deficit and interest–growth differential components, as well as analyzing the role of large stock-flow adjustments linked to currency and banking crises. Section 7.5 sheds light on major successful debt reduction episodes in the immediate aftermath of World War II (WWII), highlighting the role of negative real interest rates, and presenting a contrast with debt reductions during periods of greater financial liberalization.

7.2 Analytical Framework and Literature Review

A standard framework for decomposing large debt ratio increases (decreases) is represented by the following equation (Escolano 2010):

$$d_T - d_0 = \sum_{t=1}^{T} \frac{i_t - \gamma_t}{1 + \gamma_t} d_{t-1} + \sum_{t=1}^{T} p_t + \sum_{t=1}^{T} sfa_t. \tag{7.1}$$

Equation (7.1) states that the total episode change in the debt-to-GDP ratio ($d_T - d_0$) is the sum of three components, each cumulated over the episode years: (1) the product of the lagged debt ratio and the differential between the effective interest rate on debt (i_t) and the nominal GDP growth rate (γ_t), (2) the primary deficit (p_t), and (3) a residual stock-flow adjustment term (sfa_t).[4] It is important to note up front that this decomposition likely understates the true contribution of economic growth to debt reduction, since high growth eases the political constraints on improving the primary fiscal balance.

Using a similar methodology, a number of cross-country studies have attempted to explain the sources of changes in public debt, although lack of long time series data has limited the time coverage of most of these studies to the post-1970 period. For instance, Campos, Jaimovich, and Panizza (2006) examine public debt changes in 117 countries over the period 1972 to 2003 and find that traditional factors (i.e., primary balances and interest–growth differentials) largely explained the debt buildups (and reductions) changes in advanced economies, whereas stock-flow adjustments were critical for developing economies.[5] Easterly (2001) invokes the debt decomposition framework to highlight the role of real economic growth in driving large debt changes. He argues that that the buildups in the 1980s and 1990s in advanced economies were caused by an unanticipated growth slowdown and a delay in calibrating fiscal policies to that slowdown.

Abbas et al. (2011) is the only study, however, to systematically apply this framework to historical debt increases in advanced economies over a sufficiently long time period. They identify 60 major episodes of debt ratio increases (of 10 percentage

Table 7.1
Debt ratio increases for 60 large debt ratio increases in 19 advanced economies, 1880 to 2007 (in percent of GDP unless otherwise indicated; averages across episodes)

Large debt increases	Number of episodes	Starting debt ratio	Ending debt ratio	Total increase	Components (as share of total increase)				
					Primary deficit	Interest–growth differential $(i - \gamma)$	i	$-\gamma$	Debt-increasing stock-flow adjustment
War	16	71.4	109.5	38.0	45.3	5.0	47.1	−42.0	49.7
Peacetime	44	46.7	92.5	45.8	30.0	24.1	67.0	−45.0	45.9
Nonrecession	16	39.6	86.4	46.8	38.5	−11.5	81.5	−95.9	72.9
Recession	28	50.8	96.0	45.2	25.0	45.1	58.4	−14.9	29.9
All (simple average)	60	53.3	97.0	43.7	33.6	19.7	62.4	−44.3	46.8
All (median)	60	43.5	81.3	32.5	21.4	31.4	57.1	−31.5	44.4

Source: Abbas et al. (2011)

points or more) for 19 advanced countries over 1880 to 2007 (reported in appendix table A7.1 of this chapter), the largest of which were Greece (169 percentage points, 1886–1894, and 78 percentage points, 1979–1993) United Kingdom (149 percentage points, 1940–1946), Italy (95 percentage points, 1963–1994), Austria (56 percentage points, 1974–1996), Switzerland (56 percentage points, 1928–1944), and Spain (56 percentage points, 1974–1996). The mean (median) debt increase was sized around 44 (33) percentage points; while the median speed was about 6 percentage points of GDP per year.

The identified episodes were then divided into different subsamples according to their timing (e.g., coincidence with periods of military conflict, global recession), as shown in table 7.1. Interestingly, and while wartime debts accumulated faster than those during peacetime, the rapid increase in advanced economies' debts during the Great Recession represents an exceptional feature of the current debt crisis. Moreover, although wartime debt increases started from higher debt levels and were associated with larger primary deficits, they were smaller in size than peacetime debt increases. The key driver of this anomalous result appears to be the interest–growth differential component, the contribution of which was relatively modest in wartimes (5 percent of the debt increase), but sizable in peacetimes (24 percent); during global recessions (prior to 2007), it rose to 45 percent. Another interesting result they report is that debt increases during nonrecessionary periods were slightly larger than those during global recessions. The key contributors to these good time debt surges were fiscal profligacy, but also SFAs. While the average contribution of SFAs over all

60 debt buildup episodes amounted to 47 percent, they were noticeably larger during nonrecessionary episodes (73 percent).

In the next section, we extend the debt decomposition exercise to analyze the ongoing debt build up in advanced economies (i.e., during the Great Recession) and contrast it to the surge witnessed during the Great Depression, the last time advanced economies together experienced a large, negative, and sustained shock to output during peacetime.

7.3 A Tale of Two Crises: Debt Buildups during the Great Recession and the Great Depression

7.3.1 Debt Buildup during the Great Recession, 2007 to 2013

Table 7.2 shows the results of the decomposition exercise of debt changes for the 17 advanced economies whose debt ratios increased by more than 10 percentage points of GDP during 2007 to 2013. The episodes were defined using trough-to-peak debt ratios, so in some cases the start- and end-years were different from 2007 and 2013, respectively (although the horizon in all cases was bounded within 2007 to 2013). In addition to the standard components driving debt ratio increases (primary deficit and interest–growth differential), currency depreciation effects and financial asset buildups (defined as the difference between changes in gross and net debt), both of which feed into the SFA, are also examined. The main findings are as follows:

- The weighted-average debt increase is about 40 percent of GDP, with the largest surges witnessed in Ireland (93 percentage points), Japan (58 percentage points), Greece (54 percentage points), Portugal (50 percentage points), Spain and the United Kingdom (about 47 percentage points each), and the United States (45 percentage points). All other countries registered debt increases exceeding 10 percent of GDP, except Sweden and Switzerland, whose debt ratios actually declined.

- Sixty-five percent of the weighted-average debt increase was accounted for by cumulative primary deficits, 25 percent by the interest–growth differential component, and 10 percent by SFAs.

- Structural primary deficits account for about 60 percent of the headline primary deficits, although several countries (Belgium, Canada, Finland, Germany, and Italy) ran cumulative structural surpluses during the period.

- In the cases of the larger debt increases noted above, the structural primary deficit contributed, on average, more than 75 percent to the deterioration in the primary deficit.

- The contribution of the interest–growth differential was divergent across countries, broadly mirroring the evolution of interest and growth rates over the period 2007 to 2013 (figure 7.2).[6] Several groups of countries emerge:

Table 7.2
Decomposition of debt ratio increases in advanced economies during the Great Recession (in percent of GDP, cumulative over the episode years)

Large debt increases	Starting debt ratio	Ending debt ratio	Increase	Components Primary deficit	Of which: Structural primary deficit	Interest-growth differential $(i - \gamma)$	Debt-increasing stock-flow adjustment	Of which: Buildup in financial assets[a]	Residual
Australia	9.7	24.8	15.1	10.4	10.7	1.3	3.3	-2.3	5.6
Austria	60.2	75.8	15.5	3.2	1.2	5.4	7.0	1.8	5.2
Belgium	84.1	98.7	14.6	0.2	-2.3	7.7	6.7	4.0	2.6
Canada	66.5	86.7	20.2	-0.2	-4.1	6.3	14.1	6.3	7.9
Finland	33.9	54.2	20.3	2.6	-6.9	1.6	16.0	21.0	-5.0
France	64.2	93.1	28.9	17.0	5.8	7.9	3.9	1.2	2.7
Germany	65.2	83.2	18.0	-0.2	-3.4	6.3	11.9	11.6	0.4
Greece	105.4	159.3	53.9	23.2	28.2	28.3	2.5	0.0	2.5
Ireland	24.8	118.2	93.3	59.1	29.8	22.8	11.4	-3.0	14.4
Italy	103.1	126.6	23.5	-10.0	-15.6	28.8	4.8	5.4	-0.6
Japan	188.6	246.8	58.2	37.6	29.5	28.5	-7.9	-9.4	1.6
Netherlands	45.3	71.2	25.9	9.9	6.2	7.7	8.3	9.8	-1.5
New Zealand	17.4	37.7	20.3	12.4	8.5	2.2	5.7	1.8	3.8
Portugal	68.3	118.6	50.3	13.5	11.6	22.8	14.0	-0.3	14.3
Spain	36.1	84.0	47.9	31.9	22.9	12.6	3.5	2.7	0.8
United Kingdom	43.9	90.3	46.4	32.0	23.2	4.7	9.7	-1.6	11.3
United States	67.2	112.0	44.8	37.3	22.3	4.3	3.2	6.0	-2.8
PPPGDP-weighted average[b]	80.5	120.6	40.1	26.2	16.0	10.1	3.7	3.1	0.6
Memo items:									
Sweden[c]	40.2	33.8	-6.4	-9.0	-11.3	-0.2	2.8	-4.5	6.8
Switzerland[c]	55.9	47.5	-8.4	-11.3	-11.0	1.3	1.7	-1.4	3.0

Sources: World Economic Outlook; authors' calculations.
Note: The Great Recession period was bound to 2007 to 2013 for all countries except Finland (start-year is 2008); Germany (end-year is 2010); Greece (end-year is 2011); and Australia, Belgium, Canada, and New Zealand (end-year is 2012) in order to capture the largest debt increase for each country during the Great Recession.
a. Positive values imply accumulation/acquisition of financial assets.
b. Computed using 2007 PPPGDP weights.
c. Debt-to-GDP ratios for Sweden and Switzerland declined during 2007 to 2013.

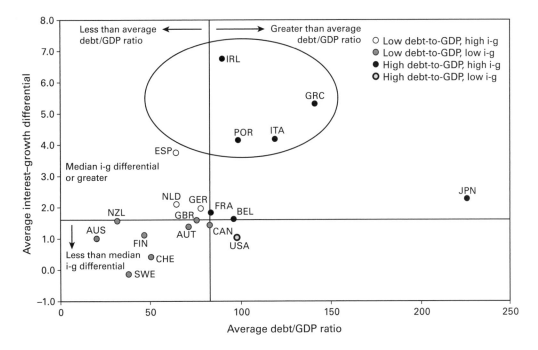

Figure 7.2
Scatterplot of interest–growth differential and debt ratio in advanced economies, 2007 to 2013
Source: Authors' calculations

- The "stress zone," which included Greece, Ireland, Italy, Spain, and Portugal, had high average debt ratios during the period (with the exception of Spain, whose average debt ratio was moderate at about 65 percent of GDP), and high average interest–growth differentials (about 5 percent).

- The "comfort zone," featuring Australia, Finland, New Zealand, Sweden, and Switzerland, had low average debt ratios over the period and favorable interest–growth differential (ranging between 0 and 1.5 percent).

- The "middle kingdoms," comprising countries in between the two extremes above, include Austria, Belgium, Canada, France, Germany, Netherlands, and the United Kingdom.

- Two "special cases," where debt ratios were high but the interest–growth differential was low, were (1) Japan, which has a large net foreign assets position, big domestic savings pool, and high domestic ownership of debt, and (2) the United States, because of its reserve currency status, coupled with the very substantial monetary policy easing since the crisis.[7]

- Finally, currency valuation effects were found to be negligible as the foreign-currency denominated share of debt was close to zero (in most cases), but financial asset buildups were significant, accounting for most of the SFA. The majority of these buildups reflected financial sector support operations in the wake of the crisis (e.g., Belgium, Germany, Netherlands, Spain, and the United States; IMF 2011), including through loans to support the housing sector (e.g., Canada).

7.3.2 Comparison with Debt Buildup during the Great Depression, 1928 to 1933

It is instructive to compare the current debt buildup with that witnessed during the Great Depression, the last time several advanced economies entered a prolonged economic downturn collectively. Table 7.3 reports the debt increase decomposition for the same countries covered above.[8] Two observations stand out:

- *Debt buildup during the Great Depression was smaller.* The weighted-average increase was 23 percent of GDP, suggesting that the surge in debt ratios over 1928 to 1933 was almost half of the 40 percent of GDP debt increase observed this time around. The result is not driven by a few large countries: debt buildups in 9 of the 17 cases shown in table 7.2 were larger than the corresponding debt ratio increases during the Great Depression.

- *Primary deficits played no role in the accumulation of debts.* Unlike the current debt increase, where the primary deficit contribution was 65 percent, the Great Depression debt surge was accounted for entirely by the interest–growth differential component.[9] The cumulative primary balance was, on a weighted-average basis, a surplus of 2.2 percent of GDP with 10 of the 19 countries registering surpluses. Although the United States ran a small cumulative primary deficit through 1933, the US government's primary fiscal response to the Depression was procyclical, and became expansionary only from 1933 onward, and this expansion too was offset partly by tight fiscal policy at the state and local government levels (Romer 2012).[10]

7.3.3 Identifying Key Distinguishing Factors

At first glance these observations appear somewhat counterintuitive. The Great Depression was accompanied by a much larger drop in output and surge in unemployment than the Great Recession. Indeed, in our sample of countries, real output fell 18 percent, in weighted-average terms, from peak-to-trough during the Depression, as opposed to a 4 percent fall during the Great Recession. Similarly median unemployment in 12 advanced economies (for which data were available) had risen to almost 25 percent at the height of the Great Depression but has remained in single digits this time around.

Figure 7.3 helps us understand the two key drivers of these results:

- *Initial level of debt.* The level of public indebtedness at the beginning of the global financial crisis was much higher (weighted average of 80 percent of GDP)

Table 7.3
Decomposition of debt ratio increases in advanced economies during the Great Depression (in percent of GDP, cumulative over the episode years)

	Starting debt ratio	Ending debt ratio	Increase	Components		
				Primary deficit	Interest–growth differential ($i - g$)	Debt-increasing stock-flow adjustment
Australia	62.3	98.2	35.8	−9.2	40.8	4.2
Austria	15.4	36.5	21.0	29.0	11.7	−19.8
Belgium	79.1	98.3	19.2	−6.5	12.4	13.4
Canada	53.2	117.9	64.7	1.2	59.1	4.3
Finland	10.8	16.1	5.4	2.9	8.0	−5.5
France	138.6	172.7	34.1	−6.6	58.8	−18.1
Germany	9.3	23.9	14.6	2.8	10.0	1.7
Greece	80.4	105.9	25.5	11.5	30.5	−16.5
Ireland	14.9	31.4	16.5	−3.3	4.0	15.8
Italy	97.4	106.6	9.2	0.4	16.6	−7.7
Japan	39.1	62.2	23.1	−2.7	6.4	19.5
Netherlands	74.2	116.1	41.9	0.3	33.4	8.2
New Zealand	163.3	246.6	83.3	−11.2	89.9	4.5
Portugal	42.5	45.8	3.2	−38.8	40.2	1.8
Spain	61.4	65.1	3.6	−12.8	10.7	5.8
Sweden	18.4	29.6	11.2	3.1	7.8	0.2
Switzerland	22.7	26.7	4.0	−5.5	9.4	0.1
United Kingdom	170.5	194.0	23.4	−29.5	47.4	5.6
United States	16.3	40.0	23.6	5.3	18.0	0.3
PPPGDP-weighted average	**56.9**	**80.0**	**23.1**	**−2.2**	**24.7**	**0.6**

Source: Abbas et al. (2011)
Note: The SFA component is adjusted for the currency depreciation component for France (−7.1 percent of GDP) and the United Kingdom (7.0 percent of GDP).

than what prevailed at the start of the Great Depression (weighted average of 57 percent of GDP). This result is not driven by a few large economies: for about two-third of the countries in our sample, debt levels in 2007 were higher than they were in 1928. Therefore the consequent snowball effects during the Great Recession for the same output and unemployment shock could be expected to be quantitatively larger than those that obtained during the Great Depression.

• *Government size.* The reported weighted-average size of the state in 2007 (general government expenditure of 40 percent of GDP) was four times the

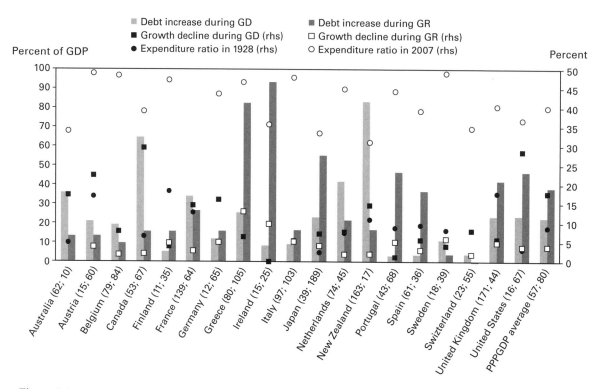

Figure 7.3
Debt surge, growth decline, and the size of the state: Great Depression (GD) versus Great Recession (GR). Numbers in parentheses after country name refer to the debt-to-GDP ratio at the start of the Great Depression (in 1928) and at the start of the Great Recession (in 2007), respectively.
Sources: Historical Public Debt Database; authors' calculations

average size of government in 1928 (9 percent of GDP).[11] This is a well-established phenomenon (see Holsey and Borcherding 1997; Tanzi and Schuknecht 2000), which is explained by the so-called Wagner's law: as an economy experiences economic growth, the relative government size increases. A key implication of this phenomenon is that the (small) governments at the time of the Great Depression were incapable of running very large deficits as a *share of GDP*—either via automatic stabilizers or countercyclical fiscal expansion, despite proportionally large swings in nominal revenues and expenditures (30 percent, in weighted-average terms). In the current episode, nominal revenues fell by a much smaller proportion (7.5 percent, in weighted-average terms), although expenditures still increased by 30 percent (in weighted-average terms); but, the overall deficit (and hence debt) impact of these shifts was larger as a *share of GDP* given the markedly bigger government size in relation to the economy.

It is important to note some caveats and trade-offs involved in making the argument that the larger debt buildup during the Great Recession appeared to be associated with a larger government this time around. One key caveat is the differential policy reactions to the Great Depression and the global financial crisis. As mentioned earlier, fiscal policy responded to the Great Depression procyclically; even automatic stabilizers were not allowed to fully operate (see Chandler 1970). The policy response following the global financial crisis was the opposite: not only were automatic stabilizers allowed to fully operate but a substantial coordinated fiscal stimulus was implemented by advanced countries. These differential policies are likely to have been an important explanatory factor for the observed differences in growth and unemployment outcomes across the two episodes.

Another caveat is that with all macro and fiscal variables fully endogenous to one another, it does not follow that a smaller government in 2007 would have resulted in a smaller increase in debt ratios. As noted by many researchers (e.g., see Baunsgaard and Symansky 2009), larger governments are associated with bigger automatic stabilizers, which cushion the fall in output and employment. When supported by monetary accommodation—as was the case this time around—the resulting interest–growth differential turned out to be quite favorable for several advanced economies.[12]

The key trade-off is that a larger government partly buffers private agents from the adverse consequences of an economic slowdown or collapse. The cost in terms of deteriorating public finances must therefore be weighed against the welfare gain implied by softening the adjustment burden on private sector incomes and consumption. This softening is achieved both passively, via increased automatic stabilizers (lower taxes and higher social transfers), and actively, via the support that countercyclical fiscal policy provides to growth and employment. More generally, there may be a second-order welfare gain from a larger government size to the extent that the latter is negatively associated with output volatility (e.g., see Gali 1994; Debrun et al. 2008).

As discussions over the optimal government size (and degree of policy interventionism) are necessarily complex, we focus on the other distinguishing factor (explaining the larger debt increase during the Great Recession) identified above: namely the higher level of public debt prevailing at the start of the Great Recession. The next section studies the gradual but massive buildup of this debt across advanced economies over 1970 to 2007—a period we refer to as the Great Accumulation.

7.4 Analysis of Pre-crisis Vulnerabilities: The Great Accumulation

As mentioned above, the 2007 to 2013 episode is characterized by weaker initial conditions relative to previous debt accumulation periods, particularly with respect to the high starting debt ratios at the onset of the financial crisis in 2007. This section explores the causes of the large initial debt levels in 2007 by looking closely at the gradual but pervasive debt increases in advanced economies over the period 1970 to 2007. In order to shed some light on how the relative contributions of the various components to debt increases have changed over time, the pre-crisis period is split into three subsamples: 1970 to 1984, 1985 to 1992 and 1993 to 2007. These subsamples are chosen to correspond to the beginning of the great moderation in the United States in the mid-1980s (Bernanke 2004) and in other countries, such as the United Kingdom, by end 1992 (Benati 2007).

7.4.1 The Great Accumulation: from Bretton Woods to the Great Moderation

The weighted-average debt increase during 1970 to 2007 was 45 percent of GDP, slightly larger than the average debt increase during the Great Recession. The increase was gradual and pervasive and took place over more than thirty-five years. In light of this, the pre-crisis debt buildup period can be described as the Great Accumulation, although this was by no means a homogeneous period. The period prior to the mid-1980s was marked by the oil price shock of the early 1970s, alongside the collapse of the Bretton Woods System of exchange rates, and the stock market crash in advanced economies that led to a recession marked by a remarkable rise in unemployment and rising inflation. It was also characterized by intermittent recessions in the early 1980s with higher oil prices in the context of the second oil price shock in 1979. From the mid-1980s more contractionary monetary policy in the United States and the United Kingdom exacerbated the general slowdown in growth relative to the post-WWII decades (Easterly 2001). In the 1990s growth picked up with the IT boom in the United States, while interest rates came down as markets internalized the low inflation environment. In the latter part of the decade and beginning of the new millennium, significant post–euro convergence growth was observed in Europe. The period as a whole also saw rising government expenditure over time not matched by a commensurate increase in revenue (especially structural revenues). While in 1970, the weighted-average public expenditure-to-GDP ratio in advanced countries amounted to about 30 percent of GDP; it had increased to 40 percent by 2007, reflecting higher government outlays on health care, pension, and social protection (Cottarelli and Schaechter 2010).

The contribution of the various components to changes in debt evolved significantly over the course of the Great Accumulation in line with the developments above (figure 7.4). While the period prior to 1985 was characterized by large contributions of stock-flow adjustments and primary deficits, the interest–growth differential became a more important determinant of debt increases over 1985 to 1992 in line with monetary policy developments in the largest advanced economies and the general growth slowdown. Despite favorable growth developments on the back of the IT boom in the United States and post–euro convergence growth in

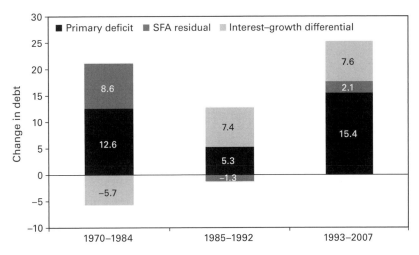

Figure 7.4
Sources of debt increases in advanced countries during the Great Accumulation, by subperiods (in percent of GDP)
Source: Authors' calculations

Europe, the largest debt increases that averaged 25 percentage points of GDP, in weighted-average terms, were observed between 1993 and 2007. Primary deficits contributed 62 percent to this debt increase. The greater role of primary deficits in debt increases likely reflects, among other factors, the rising share of government expenditure over time. The role of stock-flow adjustments in explaining debt changes decreased significantly after the mid-1980s, perhaps reflecting greater macroeconomic stability, in particular, less volatile exchange rate movements than in the 1970s. However, looking at weighted averages understates the importance of these SFAs for public debt developments. As shown in table 7.4, stock-flow adjustments, in a number of countries, contributed significantly to large debt increases in the post-1985 periods.

7.4.2 Large Stock-Flow Adjustments: Size and Composition
Further decomposing the unexplained changes in public debt seems to suggest that during the 1970s, SFAs were primarily explained by valuation effects. The pre-1985 period was characterized by a significant number of currency crises and a significant share of foreign-currency denominated debt (figures 7.5 and 7.6). Although by World War II the "original sin" had greatly diminished with countries borrowing mainly in their own currencies, some pressures to borrow in foreign currency reemerged in the late 1970s, with the average share of "foreign" debt amounting to about 8 percent. The combination of this together with currency crises could have led to significant valuation effects leading to discrepancies between the change

Table 7.4
Episodes of large unexplained changes in public debt (in percent of GDP)

	1970–1984				1985–1992				1993–2007			
	Increase in debt	SFA	Interest–growth differential	Primary deficit	Increase in debt	SFA	Interest–growth differential	Primary deficit	Increase in debt	SFA	Interest–growth differential	Primary deficit
Austria	31.2	17.3	-1.5	15.4	13.6	5.5	2.8	5.3				
Belgium					10.2	1.9	12.0	-3.7				
France	8.3	5.0	-1.7	5.0								
Germany					2.5	2.0	0.6	0.0				
Greece	19.7	13.4	-15.1	21.4	33.4	22.7	-14.4	25.1	9.5	20.8	-9.9	-1.4
Italy	37.8	34.1	-62.2	65.9					6.2	2.8	4.9	-1.5
Japan	55.2	34.1	-8.8	29.9	5.5	5.3	2.6	-2.3	114.9	16.8	34.8	63.3
Portugal	24.3	35.8	-26.9	15.3	3.0	5.6	0.7	-3.3	19.8	8.9	3.2	7.7
Spain	29.8	11.7	-14.0	32.1	5.8	2.4	-0.5	3.9	11.4	2.9	4.1	4.4
Sweden	44.7	31.4	0.5	12.9	27.0	14.8	6.6	5.6				
Switzerland					14.1	10.8	-0.2	3.5	22.7	9.9	6.6	6.2
United Kingdom	5.0	6.9	-7.4	5.5					14.5	5.2	2.1	7.2

Source: Authors' calculations

Note: The table shows the maximum increase in debt (from trough to peak) observed in any of the subsamples and the contribution of the SFA residual to this increase. Only episodes in which the SFA contribution exceeds 15 percent of the change in debt are listed.

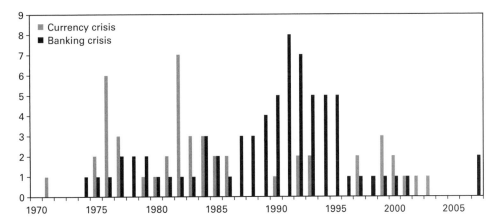

Figure 7.5
Banking and currency crises in advanced economies during the Great Accumulation. Shown are the number of countries in the sample of advanced economies experiencing banking and/or currency crises.
Source: Reinhart and Rogoff (2011)

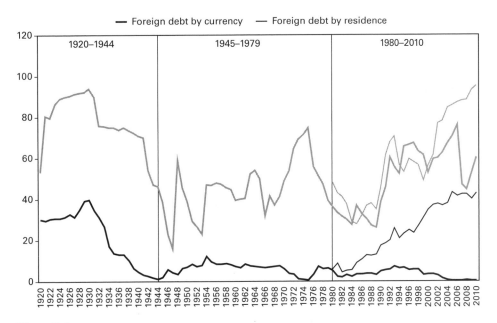

Figure 7.6
Median and maximum shares of foreign debt by currency and residence in advanced countries, 1920 to 2010. The black line represents the median, and the gray line the maximum. Data on foreign curreney residence is only available for 1980 to 2010.
Sources: WEO; various official publications

in public debt and the deficit. It is interesting that since the 1980s a new vulnerability emerged, namely a rising share of nonresident borrowing, often associated with a less stable investor base since private nonresidents may be more willing to shift their investment out of the country than are domestic investors.

Since the 1980s, stock-flow adjustments were mainly the result of significant accumulations of financial assets. Looking at the total accumulation of stock-flow adjustments shows that changes in financial assets account for a large proportion of them between 1980 and 2007, although in some countries (Greece, Ireland, and Portugal) significant stock-flow adjustments net of financial assets are observed (figure 7.7). Some of the financial asset accumulations are likely linked to banking crises, the frequency of which greatly increased in the mid-1980s (figure 7.5). However, this may not be the case for all countries and all periods. There are at least two other potential explanations for these financial asset accumulations. Some countries may invest their budget surpluses into financial assets instead of paying back debt (Finland, Sweden, and New Zealand). In Japan the large accumulation of financial assets

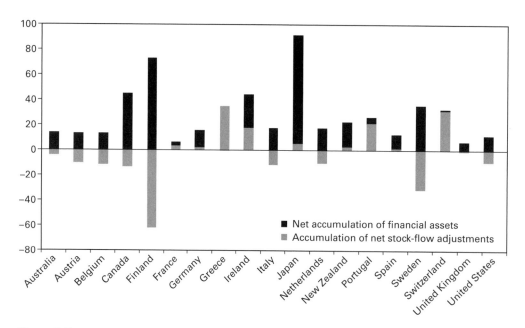

Figure 7.7
Stock-flow adjustments and the accumulation of financial assets, 1980 to 2007. The accumulation of net stock-flow adjustments measures the sum of net stock-flow adjustments between 1981 and 2007, as a percentage of 2007 GDP. Net stock-flow adjustments are defined as the difference between the change in the level of annual net debt minus the overall budget balance (in levels). Thus they measure gross stock-flow adjustments net of transactions in financial assets. The net accumulation of financial assets then corresponds to the difference between cumulative gross stock-flow adjustments and net stock-flow adjustments.
Sources: Country authorities; IMF staff calculations

Table 7.5
Unbalanced fixed effects panel regressions with stock-flow adjustments as the dependent variable, 1970 to 2007 (in percent of GDP)

Dependent variable	Coefficient and standard errors		
	1970–2007	Pre-1985	Post-1985
Constant	2.65	4.02	1.89
	0.12***	0.13***	0.17***
Valuation effect	0.30	1.27	0.13
	0.26	0.61**	0.29
Banking crises	0.70	0.25	0.96
	0.34**	0.52	0.45**
R^2 (within)	0.03	0.06	0.03
Number of observations	274	95	179

Sources: World Economic Outlook; Reinhart and Rogoff (2011)

Note: The dependent variable is defined as $\dfrac{SF_t}{NGDP_t} = \dfrac{Debt_t - Debt_{t-1}}{NGDP_t} - \dfrac{Deficit_t}{NGDP_t}$, where *Debt* denotes gross debt, *Deficit* denotes overall budget deficit, SF denotes the stock-flow adjustment, and *NGDP* denotes nominal GDP; * denotes significance at 10 percent level, **denotes significance at 5 percent, and ***denotes significance at 1 percent. Valuation effect denotes the percentage change in the nominal effective exchange rate interacted with the public sector debt denoted in foreign currency (in percent of GDP); a positive change denotes exchange rate depreciation. Banking crises takes a value of 1 during banking crisis.

is likely linked to its large public pension fund. Moreover some countries may have had an incentive to shift expenditure below the line, by injecting capital into public companies, thereby pushing spending to entities excluded from the fiscal accounts (Von Hagen and Wolff 2006).

Results from a fixed effects panel regression confirm that valuation effects were a key determinant of stock-flow adjustments prior to 1985, whereas the role of banking crises increased after the mid-1980s (table 7.5). However, running two sub-sample regressions and dividing the sample into pre- and post-1985 periods, shows that valuation effects very significantly contributed to stock-flow adjustment prior to 1985. Similarly comparing the post-1985 period to the whole sample period shows that banking crises become an even more important determinant of stock-flow adjustments since 1985.

7.4.3 Fiscal Transparency on the Rise

The problem of large discrepancies between the change in public debt and deficits in general seems to have diminished over the pre-crisis period. While some stock-flow adjustments are perfectly legitimate owing to accounting issues, large and persistent stock-flow adjustment could point to an inappropriate recording of budgetary operations and, if positive, lead to ex post upward revisions of deficit levels (IMF 2011). Greater fiscal transparency may have played a role in explaining the diminishing role of SFAs over the pre-crisis period. While there are no data showing the evolution of fiscal transparency over time, it is likely that openness toward the public at large about government structure and functions, fiscal policy intentions, and public sector accounts has increased since the 1970s in advanced economies. Greater fiscal transparency allows better scrutiny of government accounts and would make it harder for government to engage in deceptive fiscal stratagems. It should also enhance the quality of fiscal data and thereby decrease SFAs arising from measurement errors. Using an index of fiscal transparency that was constructed for most countries for 2007, it is possible to look at the contribution of SFAs to debt changes between 1980 and 2007 in countries that experience above and below average fiscal transparency.[13] Interestingly, in countries with above average fiscal transparency the contribution of stock-flow adjustments to increases in debt is significantly smaller than in countries with below average fiscal transparency (figure 7.8). Thus greater fiscal

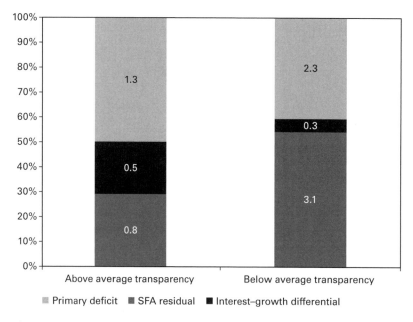

Figure 7.8
Sources of debt increases and fiscal transparency. Debt increases denote any positive change in gross debt between 1980 and 2007. Data labels denote the mean of the components of debt increases (in percent of GDP). Higher values of the transparency index denote greater fiscal transparency. Above (below) average denotes group of countries with a fiscal transparency index above (below) the average of its peer group (advanced economies). The fiscal transparency index is extracted from the Report on Observance of Standards and Codes (ROSC; see Hameed 2005).
Sources: Country authorities; authors' calculations

transparency overall may be an important factor behind the comparatively smaller contribution of SFAs during the debt surge prior to the Great Recession.

7.5 Analysis of Episodes of Successful Debt Reductions

This section motivates a discussion of the prospects for achieving lower debt levels in today's advanced economies by documenting the drivers of successful large debt reductions over the past century and a half. Most research in this area has focused on the post-WWII period, but with fairly divergent results for different subperiods. For the 1945 to 1970 period—when the largest documented debt reductions occurred—Reinhart et al. (2011) identify artificially low real interest rates as the main debt "liquidating" vehicle. For the post-1970 period, Abbas et al. (2010) find that primary surpluses did all the heavy lifting. IMF (2012) examined fifteen episodes of debt reductions in a number of advanced countries during 1884 to 1995 and also find that debt reduction ultimately requires primary surpluses—this was indeed the case in the post-1980s debt reductions, including that of Italy in 1992 to join the European Monetary Union; and of Canada in 1995 to address fiscal imbalances of the early 1980s. Below we take a closer look at the post-WWII debt reductions, contrasting them with episodes from earlier and later periods, with a view to extracting policy conclusions for policy makers facing high debts today.

7.5.1 Debt Reductions in the Aftermath of World War II

Large reductions in the public debt-to-GDP ratio in selected advanced economies in the aftermath of WWII are decomposed following the same approach detailed in section 7.2. The key results are as follows (table 7.6):

- Debt reduction was accounted for primarily by the interest–growth differential, with primary surpluses playing a smaller role.[14] The differential contributed over three-fourth of the 86 percent of GDP average debt reduction, thus eroding the debt stock at a rate of about 4 percent of GDP per year.
- The contribution of the primary surplus varied across episodes, as well as subperiods of episodes. For instance, primary balances contributed to almost half of the debt reduction in the United States over the period 1946 to 1974. In the United Kingdom the share was lower (one-fourth) but fluctuated through the decades: primary surpluses accounted for about half the debt reduction in the late 1960s but only about one-sixth in the first half of the 1970s, when inflation surged to 12 percent per annum (figure 7.9).
- The favorable interest–growth differential during the pre-1980 period arose from low and often negative real interest rates and was supported by rapid economic growth. The median annual growth rate was about 4.5 percent over

Table 7.6

Major post-WWII debt-to-GDP reductions in advanced economies (in percent of GDP, cumulative over the episode years, except last three years columns, which are in percent)

	Start year	End year	Duration (years)	Starting debt ratio	Ending debt ratio	Debt reduction	Primary balance	Growth–interest differential component	Unexplained debt reduction	Average real GDP growth	Average effective real interest rate	Average inflation rate
Australia	1946	1963	17	92.5	29.3	63.2	19.1	67.0	-22.9	4.6	-2.3	5.7
Canada	1945	1957	12	155.5	58.7	96.7	43.1	69.6	-16.0	4.3	-1.4	4.0
France	1949	1969	20	44.3	14.4	29.9	9.5	42.4	-21.9	5.3	0.8	3.7
New Zealand	1946	1974	28	147.6	40.6	107.0	-63.9	157.2	13.7	3.9	-2.9	4.9
Sweden	1948	1954	6	41.6	28.7	12.9	-12.8	12.3	13.4	3.7	-3.9	6.5
Switzerland	1945	1962	17	78.9	12.0	66.9	5.5	28.0	33.4	5.1	1.6	1.3
United Kingdom	1946	1975	29	270.0	47.0	223.0	60.4	182.9	-20.4	2.6	-1.5	5.5
United States[a]	1946	1974	28	121.2	32.2	89.0	48.1	60.6	-19.7	3.5	0.2	3.4
Average (unweighted)			19.6	119.0	32.9	86.1	13.6	77.5	-5.1	4.1	-1.2	4.4
Average (PPPGDP-weighted)[b]			25.5	127.9	33.1	94.8	42.0	71.3	-18.5	3.7	-0.2	3.8
Median[c]			18.5	92.5	29.3	66.9	23%	77%		4.1	-1.5	4.5

a. Overlaps with the 1951 conversion of short-term marketable US Treasury debt for 29-year nonmarketable bonds.
b. Computed using 2007 PPPGDP weights.
c. For the debt decomposition component columns, the median share in the "explained" portion of debt reduction is reported.

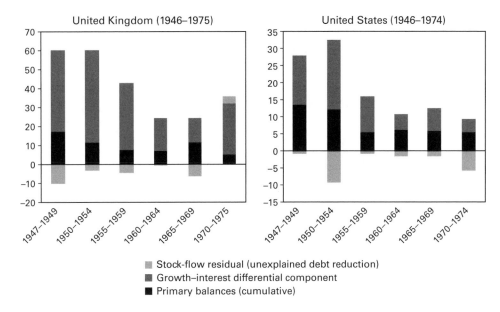

Stock-flow residual (unexplained debt reduction)
Growth–interest differential component
Primary balances (cumulative)

Figure 7.9
Postwar debt reductions in the United Kingdom and the United States
Source: Authors' calculations

the period, led by strong postwar reconstruction and investment activity in some countries, and by catch-up effects in others. While this pace of growth was healthy by historical standards, the real hallmark of this period was *negative* real effective interest rates (median of –1.5 percent). As a result the interest–growth differential was significantly negative during this period, reaching a median of 5.1 percent (figure 7.10).

• Negative real interest rates were fostered by a range of financial repression instruments, including widespread capital controls. It appears that the liquidating force of "financial repression, accompanied by a steady dose of inflation" was at play during the post-WWII period (Reinhart et al. 2011; IMF 2012).[15] These instruments— presented as prudential regulation—included interest rate ceilings and reserve requirements on banks, directed financial sector credit to government, prudential floors on pension fund assets to be held as government securities, caps on deposit rates to boost retail demand for government bonds, and restrictions on cross-border foreign exchange transactions. Their ubiquity across advanced economies, combined with widespread capital controls, helps explain their persistence and success through this period (Reinhart et al. 2011).

• Central bank holdings of government paper were high, and to the extent that these represented a monetization of fiscal deficits, they are likely to have enabled

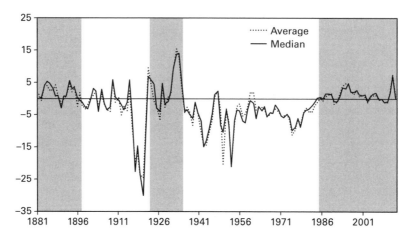

Figure 7.10
Interest–growth differential, 1881 to 2010
Source: Authors' calculations

the maintenance of moderate to high inflation rates. It is clear from figure 7.11 that by historical standards, the central bank share of government securities was quite high (6.5 percent of GDP and 11 percent of gross debt) in the United States during 1945 to 1980. For euro area countries as well, the central bank share of securities was noticeably high in the aftermath of WWII before falling sharply (except for Greece, Italy, and Portugal, which continued to rely on substantial central bank funding until later).

7.5.2 Debt Reductions during Periods of Greater Financial Liberalization

We now turn to an analysis of debt reductions during periods whose degree of financial interlinkages and capital account liberalization more closely resemble present realities than does the immediate post-WWII period. Two such period include 1880 to 1914, or the first era characterized by large capital flows; and the post-1980 period of financial liberalization. We find that the factors explaining debt reductions during these two periods align closely but diverge substantially from the pattern of post-WWII debt reduction discussed above. Most important:

- Primary surpluses did the heavy lifting. The contribution of the interest–growth differential to overall debt reduction was, on average, one-fourth during 1880 to 1914, one-third during 1914 to 1944, and nil post-1980 (table 7.7). This pattern also holds for other large debt reductions reported in IMF (2009) and in Abbas et al. (2011). For instance, the decline in the United Kingdom's national debt from a peak of 288 percent of GDP in 1821 (at the end of the Napoleonic wars)

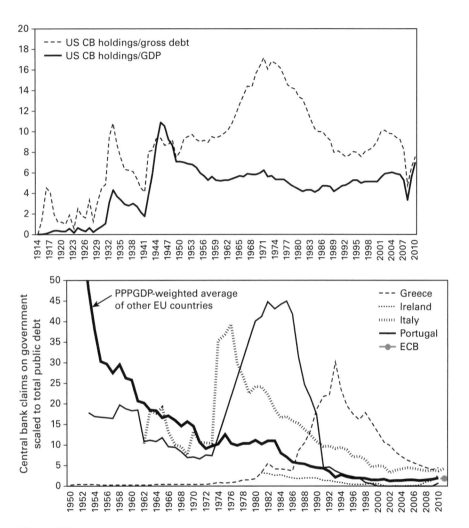

Figure 7.11
Central bank holdings of government securities in advanced economies
Sources: Balance sheets of the Federal Reserve System; *International Financial Statistics*

Table 7.7
Decomposition of large debt reductions in different historical periods (in percent of GDP, cumulative over the episode years, simple averages)

Period	Number of episodes	Starting debt ratio	Ending debt ratio	Debt reduction	Primary surplus	Growth–interest differential component	Unexplained debt reduction
Pre-1914	14	101.7	61.1	40.6	20.1	10.2	10.3
Inter-war	17	127.2	80.9	46.3	22.2	16.1	7.9
Post-WWII	8	119.0	32.9	86.1	13.6	77.5	−5.1
Post-1980	17	76.1	47.3	28.7	24.9	−1.3	5.1

Source: Authors' calculations

to 27 percent of GDP in 1914 was accounted for by consistently large peacetime primary surpluses.

- However, the aforementioned dominant primary surplus contributions usually occurred in the context of strong growth. Beyond the experience of the United Kingdom after the Napoleonic wars, this is also true of other pre-WWI debt reductions, such as Japan (1887–1898), the United States (1880–1916), Italy (1897–1913), and Austria (1892–1899): annual economic growth averaged almost 4 percent during these episodes (Abbas et al. 2011). For the post-1980 debt reduction episodes—such as Belgium (1993–2007), Ireland (1987–2002), Spain (1996–2007), Canada (1996–2008), Sweden (1996–2008), and New Zealand (1986–2001)—annual growth averaged 3.5 percent (Abbas et al. 2010). That conventional fiscal adjustment and growth have led the way in periods of global financial integration is intuitive as well as consistent with previous studies (e.g., IMF 2010). As mentioned earlier, it is important to keep in mind that high growth rates ease the political constraints on consolidation which facilitates the generation and maintenance of large primary surpluses.

7.5.3 Prospects for Debt Reduction in Today's Advanced Economies

A number of factors may complicate a rapid reduction of debts in advanced economies.[16] First, despite the substantial fiscal consolidation in train, the residual required adjustment needs to bring debt down to prudent levels (e.g., 60 percent of GDP) remain very significant.[17] Second, long-term structural factors related to aging (e.g., pension and health care) will weigh on fiscal space in a way that they did not in the past. Third, the growth lever, which proved very important in lowering debt levels (and which relaxes the political constraints on consolidation), is expected to be less strong today compared to the post-WWII period. Fourth, achieving improvements via negative real interest rates as witnessed during the post-WWII period will prove difficult given the current context of independent central banks, and the large syn-chronized supply of government bonds by a number of advanced economies in the face of more elastic demand for government paper (given highly integrated capital markets). Even if resort to higher inflation were possible, debt ratio simulations, given the current maturity and currency structure of public debt, suggest that the liquidation impact of such higher inflation will be limited (appendix table A7.2).

Looking ahead, the pursuit of unconventional options, such as liquidation of debt through financial repression and/or inflation (or outright restructuring), will likely prove difficult and may come with high costs and uncertainty (Cottarelli et al. 2010). A gradual, but steady, adjustment would appear to be the right course of action. Indeed history presents several episodes of orderly adjustment in the context of sustained medium-term growth. This suggests that there is a premium on both implementing structural measures that improve competitiveness and the business environment, and designing fiscal adjustment in a manner that minimizes the drag on growth.

APPENDIX A: Episodes of Debt-to-GDP Increases by Country

Table A7.1
Episodes of debt-to-GDP increases by country

Number	Country	Start year	End year	Duration	Starting level	Ending level	Increase
1	Austria	1880	1886	6	69.6	84.1	14.6
2	Austria	1929	1935	6	15.4	40.4	25.0
3	Austria	1974	1996	22	12.8	68.4	55.6
4	Belgium	1881	1886	5	31.8	47.3	15.5
5	Belgium	1890	1898	8	41.9	54.0	12.0
6	Belgium	1974	1979	5	38.8	49.4	10.6
7	Belgium	1982	1987	5	98.8	128.1	29.3
8	Finland	1990	1994	4	14.1	57.7	43.6
9	France	1882	1887	5	90.1	117.1	26.9
10	France	1891	1895	4	103.9	114.5	10.5
11	France	1929	1932	3	138.6	172.7	34.1
12	France	1980	1998	18	20.7	59.4	38.7
13	Germany	1880	1894	14	25.4	47.0	21.6
14	Germany	1973	2005	32	18.1	68.0	49.9
15	Greece	1886	1894	8	48.2	217.0	168.8
16	Greece	1898	1990	2	181.0	218.1	37.1
17	Greece	1960	1963	3	11.6	22.6	11.0
18	Greece	1965	1972	7	16.5	26.5	10.0
19	Greece	1979	1993	14	22.6	100.5	77.9

(continued)

Table A7.1
(*continued*)

Number	Country	Start year	End year	Duration	Starting level	Ending level	Increase
20	Ireland	1973	1987	14	35.1	87.1	52.0
21	Ireland	1989	1991	2	77.4	94.5	17.2
22	Italy	1880	1884	4	91.6	117.2	25.6
23	Italy	1963	1994	31	27.2	121.8	94.7
24	Netherlands	1920	1923	3	62.0	88.9	26.9
25	Netherlands	1929	1936	7	74.2	122.2	48.0
26	Netherlands	1977	1993	16	37.8	78.5	40.7
27	Netherlands	1982	1987	5	53.7	73.0	19.3
28	Portugal	1920	1921	1	45.0	66.9	21.9
29	Portugal	1974	1985	11	13.5	56.5	43.0
30	Portugal	2000	2007	7	48.5	68.3	19.8
31	Spain	1884	1889	5	73.1	83.6	10.5
32	Spain	1893	1896	3	79.7	95.9	16.2
33	Spain	1897	1902	5	91.4	123.6	32.2
34	Spain	1974	1996	22	11.4	67.4	56.0
35	Sweden	1930	1933	3	18.4	29.6	11.2
36	Sweden	1967	1971	4	16.1	29.3	13.2
37	Sweden	1976	1984	8	26.1	70.8	44.7
38	Sweden	1990	1996	6	46.3	84.4	38.0
39	Switzerland	1928	1944	16	22.7	78.9	56.2
40	Switzerland	1989	1998	9	31.0	63.7	32.7
41	Switzerland	2000	2005	5	61.1	72.2	11.2
42	United Kingdom	1929	1933	4	170.5	194.0	23.4
43	United Kingdom	1940	1946	6	121.1	269.8	148.7
44	United Kingdom	1991	1997	6	38.0	57.9	19.9
45	Australia	1925	1932	7	55.3	98.2	42.9
46	Australia	1942	1946	4	62.0	92.5	30.5
47	Canada	1928	1933	5	53.2	117.9	64.7
48	Canada	1937	1945	8	87.9	155.5	67.5
49	Canada	1979	1996	17	45.3	101.7	56.4
50	Japan	1919	1936	17	22.6	63.5	40.9
51	Japan	1937	1944	7	57.0	204.0	146.9
52	Japan	1970	1987	17	11.9	74.1	62.2
53	Japan	1974	1987	13	18.9	74.1	55.2
54	Japan	1991	2005	14	67.9	191.6	123.8
55	New Zealand	1921	1933	12	117.7	246.6	128.9
56	New Zealand	1940	1946	6	128.1	147.6	19.5
57	United States	1916	1919	3	2.7	33.3	30.5
58	United States	1929	1934	5	16.3	41.0	24.6
59	United States	1941	1946	5	38.6	121.2	82.6
60	United States	1981	1995	14	41.4	71.1	29.7

Note: Debt increases that started from 2007 onward due to the financial crisis are excluded from this list, with the exception of debt increases that were already in place (defined as debt increases above 5 percent of GDP) by the time the financial crisis struck.

APPENDIX B: Simulating the Impact of Higher Inflation on Debt Ratios

We simulate the impact on debt ratios if inflation were to average 4, 6, or 8 percent annually over 2011 to 2016, rather than the average of 1.7 percent over 2011 to 2016 (as per *World Economic Outlook,* WEO*)* baseline projections for the eight largest advanced economies over the medium term.[18] As shown in table A7.1, raising the average inflation rate to 8 percent annually—about six percentage points higher than in the WEO baseline—would only reduce the 2016 debt-to-GDP ratio for the sample by 14 percentage points. This is despite the fact that medium- and long-term, nonindexed, domestic currency-denominated debt—exactly the type of debt that should be easiest to inflate away—accounts for almost two-thirds of the government debt stock in many of the advanced economies.

Table A7.2
Impact of higher inflation on debt ratios in advanced economies, 2011 to 2016

	2001		2011–16	2016			
				Total debt, with average inflation equal to:			
	Total debt	MT-LT debt[a]	Inflation, WEO[b]	WEO	4 Percent[c]	6 Percent[c]	8 Percent[c]
Australia	24.1	17.3	2.0	20.6	19.6	18.4	17.3
Canada	84.2	33.0	2.2	72.6	70.7	68.6	66.6
France	87.6	65.6	1.8	86.7	82.5	78.0	73.9
Germany	80.1	71.0	1.1	71.9	67.5	62.8	58.5
Italy	120.3	103.5	2.0	118.0	111.2	103.9	97.2
Japan	229.1	169.7	−0.1	250.5	239.4	227.4	216.3
United Kingdom	83.0	59.5	2.9	81.3	77.7	73.8	70.1
United States	99.5	65.1	1.5	111.9	107.2	102.1	97.4
Simple Average	**101.0**	**73.1**	**1.7**	**101.7**	**97.0**	**91.9**	**87.2**

Sources: IMF, WEO; OECD; Fund staff estimates
Note: WEO inflation figures reported in percent; all other figures are percentages of GDP.
a. Medium- and long-term debt in domestic currency, nonindexed.
b. GDP deflator inflation, average over the period as projected in the WEO.
c. This could imply an increase in inflation by 2.3, 4.3, and 6.3 percentage points, respectively, over projected average inflation of 1.7 percent.

Notes

The authors would like to thank Malin Hu for her outstanding research assistance, Luis Catao (IMF Research , Department) for providing historical exchange rate data on advanced economies, and Keiko Takhashi (Ministry of Finance, Japan) and Oliver Bush (Bank of England) for supplying historical public debt composition data for Japan and the United Kingdom, respectively.

1. The average increase (in PPPGDP-weighted terms) in the public debt ratio in 19 advanced economies by 2013 is projected at 40 percent of GDP relative to 2007 (pre-crisis) levels, with 17 out of the 19 countries covered in this chapter registering debt surges of more than 10 percentage points of GDP.

2. The 19 countries covered in this chapter are: Australia, Austria, Belgium, Canada, Finland, France, Germany, Greece, Ireland, Italy, Japan, Netherlands, New Zealand, Portugal, Spain, Sweden, Switzerland, the United Kingdom, and the United States. The choice of countries is guided primarily by constraints on the availability of historical data.

3. Throughout this chapter, "weighted-average" refers to averages in PPPGDP-weighted terms, whereas "average" refers to simple averages.

4. The SFA is defined as the difference between the annual change in public debt and the budget deficit. Such discrepancies could reflect valuation effects operating on foreign currency debt, time of recording effects (deficits are often measured in accrual terms while debt is a cash concept), and other below-the-line operations, such as assumption of debts of non-governmental entities, debt restructuring or default, privatization, drawdown and buildup of government deposits, transactions in financial assets, as well as measurement errors.

5. The result is also confirmed by Weber (2012), who finds that the relative contribution of stock-flow adjustments to large debt increases in advanced economies has diminished over time in line with greater fiscal transparency.

6. Over the sample period, the average interest–growth differential is about 2 percent.

7. The size of the Federal Reserve System's balance sheet rose by about 10 percentage points of GDP from Q2-2008 to end-2010, double the increase observed over the same period in the balance sheets of the Bank of Japan and the European Central Bank. This has contributed to both record-low US Treasury yields, and the return of growth, producing a negative interest–growth differential for the United States.

8. As in the case of the Great Recession, the start and end-years of the episodes were bounded between 1928 and 1933 (i.e., trough-to-peak increases identified during this period) to ensure that we captured the impact of the Great Depression and not other developments.

9. SFAs appear to play a negligible role during the Great Depression, on average, but are quite large for some individual episodes. We were able to (partially) identify the sources of these SFAs in some cases. For example, the sterling's depreciation added 7 percent of GDP to the UK debt burden, while in France, the franc's appreciation knocked off a similar amount of the debt. For the remaining cases, the large SFAs likely reflect a combination of data quality issues, mismatch between concepts used for stock vs. flow reporting, or lack of fiscal transparency.

10. Chandler (1970) and Romer (1992) document the implementation of a large tax increase via the Revenue Act of 1932, which was followed by the modestly countercyclical fiscal expansion (New Deal) initiated under US President Roosevelt.

11. Although data are mostly available on central government expenditure during the Great Depression, spending outside central government cannot explain this 31 percentage point of GDP gap in the size of the state in 1928 and its size in 2007.

12. Of course, policy accommodation has its limits and if debt keeps growing, interest–growth differentials would ultimately begin to rise as well (as indicated by recent research; e.g., Kumar and Woo 2010; Baldacci and Kumar 2010).

13. The starting year for the analysis is 1980 in order to avoid large data gaps for some of the debt changes components in some advanced countries.

14. Note that in the case of debt reductions, the interest–growth differential more conveniently captures the contribution of the (negative of the) interest growth differential.

15. In this regard, the experience of advanced economies at that time appeared similar to that of emerging economies, where the interest–growth differential has turned out negative for the most part of the past few decades (IMF 2011).

16. For a more detailed discussion, see chapter 16 on the post-crisis fiscal outlook.

17. As documented in IMF (2011), the projected weighted-average adjustment of 3.5 percent of GDP between 2010 and 2016 amounts to less than half of what is needed through 2020. Post-2016 gaps are larger than 3 percent of GDP, in weighted-average terms, for several advanced economies, including Belgium, Ireland, Japan, Spain, and the United States.

18. This scenario is based on the latest available WEO projections of October 2011. The simulations assume that the structure of government debt (shares of medium- and long-term debt; average maturity; and portion that is foreign currency denominated) remains constant over time; economic growth rates are unaffected by changes in inflation; and interest rates on newly issued debt adjust one-for-one (full Fisher effect) to increases in inflation. If nominal interest rates on domestic currency, nonindexed, short-term debt in 2012 to 2013 adjust between 2012 and 2013 only by half of the increase in inflation between 2012 and 2013, but a full Fisher effect resumes thereafter (without compensating for the temporary decline in the real interest rate), then the overall impact of inflation on the debt ratio by 2016 is larger, but only by 1 percent of GDP.

References

Abbas, S. M. A., O. Basdevant, S. Eble, G. Everaert, J. Gottschalk, F. Hasanov, J. Park, C. Sancak, R. Velloso, and M. Villafuerte. 2010. *Strategies for Fiscal Consolidation in the Post-crisis World*. IMF Fiscal Affairs Department. Washington, DC: International Monetary Fund.

Abbas, S. M. A., N. Belhocine, A. El-Ganainy, and M. Horton. 2011. Historical patterns and dynamics of public debt: Evidence from a new database. *IMF Economic Review* 59 (4): 717–42.

Baldacci, E., and M. Kumar. 2010. Fiscal deficits, public debt, and sovereign bond yields. Working paper 10/184. IMF, Washington, DC.

Baunsgaard, T., and S. Symansky. 2009. Automatic fiscal stabilizers: How can they be enhanced without increasing the size of government? Staff position note 09/23. IMF, Washington, DC.

Benati, L. 2007. The great moderation in the United Kingdom. Working paper 769. ECB, Frankfurt.

Bernanke, B. 2004. The Great Moderation. *federalreserve.gov*. http://www.federalreserve.gov/BOARDDOCS/SPEECHES/2004/20040220/default.htm.

Campos, C., D. Jaimovich, and U. Panizza. 2006, "The Unexplained Part of Debt," Inter-American Development Bank, Research Department, Working Paper No., 554 (Washington, Inter-American Development Bank)

Chandler, Lester V. 1970. *America's Greatest Depression: 1929–1941*. New York: Harper Row.

Cottarelli, C., L. Forni, J. Gottschalk, and P. Mauro. 2010. Default in today's advanced economies: Unnecessary, undesirable and unlikely. Staff position note 10/12. IMF, Washington, DC.

Cottarelli, C., and A. Schaechter. 2010. Long-term trends in public finances in the G-7 economies. Staff position note 10/13. IMF, Washington, DC.

Debrun, Xavier, Jean Pisani-Ferry, and André Sapir. 2008. Government size and output volatility: Should we forsake automatic stabilization? Working paper 08/122. IMF, Washington, DC.

Easterly, William R. 2001. Growth implosions and debt explosions: Do growth slowdowns cause public debt crises. *Contributions to Macroeconomics* 1 (1): 1–26.

Escolano, J. 2010. *A Practical Guide to Public Debt Dynamics, Fiscal Sustainability, and Cyclical Adjustment of Budgetary Aggregates*. Washington, DC: IMF.

Gali, Jordi. 1994. Government size and macroeconomic stability. *European Economic Review* 38: 117–32.

Hameed, F. 2005. Fiscal transparency and economic outcomes. Working paper 05/225. IMF, Washington, DC.

Holsey, Cheryl M., and Thomas E. Borcherding. 1997. Why does government's share grow? An assessment of the recent literature on the U.S. In Dennis C. Mueller, ed., Perspectives on Public Choice: A Handbook. New York: Cambridge University Press, 562–91.

International Monetary Fund. 2009. Fiscal implications of the global economic and financial crisis. Occasional paper 269. Fiscal Affairs Department. IMF, Washington, DC.

International Monetary Fund. 2010. Strategies for fiscal consolidation in the post-crisis world. Departmental paper 10/04. Fiscal Affairs Department. IMF, Washington, DC.

International Monetary Fund. 2011. *Fiscal Monitor. Shifting Gears: Tackling Challenges on the Road to Fiscal Adjustment* (April).. Washington, DC: IMF.

International Monetary Fund. 2012. *World Economic Outlook. The Good, the Bad, and the Ugly: 100 Years of Dealing with Public Debt Overhangs* (October). Washington, DC: IMF, 101–27.

Kumar, M., and J. Woo. 2010. Public debt and growth. Working paper 10/174. IMF, Washington, DC: IMF.

Reinhart, M. C., J. F. Kirkegaard, and M. B. Sbrancia. 2011. Financial repression redux. *Finance and Development* 48 (2): 22–26.

Reinhart, M. C., and K. Rogoff. 2011. From financial crash to debt crisis. *American Economic Review* 101: 1676–1706.

Reinhart, M.C., V. R. Reinhart, and K. S. Rogoff. 2012. Public debt overhangs: Advanced-economy episodes since 1800. *Journal of Economic Perspectives* 26 (3): 69–86.

Romer, Christina D. 1992. What ended the Great Depression? *Journal of Economic History* 52 (December): 757–84.

Romer, Christina D. 2012. An interview with Christina Romer on *Learning from the Great Depression.* http://fivebooks.com/interviews/christina-romer-on-learning-great-depressionAccessed on October 2, 2013.

Tanzi, Vito, and L. Schuknecht. 2000. *Public Spending in the 20th Century.* Cambridge: Cambridge University Press.

Von Hagen, J., and G. B. Wolff. 2006. What do deficits tell us about debt? Empirical evidence on creative accounting with fiscal rules in the EU. *Journal of Banking and Finance* 30 (12): 3259–79.

Weber, A. 2012. Stock-flow adjustments and fiscal transparency: A cross-country comparison. Working paper 12/39. IMF, Washington, DC: IMF).

8

The Other Crisis: Sovereign Distress in the Euro Area

S. Ali Abbas, Nathaniel Arnold, Petra Dacheva, Mark De Broeck, Lorenzo Forni, Martine Guerguil, and Bruno Versailles

8.1 Introduction

The sovereign crisis that has engulfed the euro area (EA) since 2009 was largely unexpected. In early fall 2008, before the collapse of Lehman triggered what is now known as the Great Recession, the EA appeared to be in a relatively sheltered position. The area's macroeconomic indicators were faring well compared to those of other advanced economies. Its banks looked relatively less exposed to the worst effects of the subprime or other toxic assets. And an institutional framework was in place to facilitate cross-border policy coordination. However, once Greece, a member with a relatively small economic weight in the EA, began to face financing difficulties in late 2009/early 2010, a sovereign debt crisis erupted, and since then the EA has struggled with financial pressures and confidence loss.

This chapter tries to identify the causes of this unexpected turn of event, the obstacles that have hampered a quicker resolution of the crisis, and the way forward. Its main findings are these:

- The seeds of the sovereign debt crisis in the EA were planted well ahead of the Great Recession. Partly as the result of institutional gaps, intra-EA imbalances deepened and vulnerabilities built up in the first decade of the euro, even if they were not fully recognized until the crisis broke. The Great Recession did not generate these imbalances and vulnerabilities, but it amplified them and brought them sharply to the fore.

- Difficulties in elaborating a regional response to the crisis undermined confidence in the EA as a policy entity. Early actions were mostly a collection of national plans, weakening their impact while fueling doubts about the credibility of the EA.

- Crisis management processes had not been envisaged in the design of institutional arrangements for the eurozone. Against the background of a global financial crisis and nervous markets, the absence of a lender of last resort sharply aggravated fiscal distress in some EA members, fueled contagion, and raised serious concerns about the viability of the currency union.

- The policy response initially focused on the fiscal front and, to some degree, neglected weaknesses in the banking sector and growth-supporting structural reforms, encouraging the development of negative feedback loops between fiscal consolidation, banks' balance sheets, and growth.

More specifically regarding fiscal policy, three lessons can be drawn:

- The institutional design of the EA, an incomplete monetary union, puts an inordinate share of the adjustment burden on national fiscal policies. With rapid financial integration, however, fiscal levers proved insufficient to prevent or reverse the emergence of intra-EA imbalances. The announcement in the summer of 2012 by the European Central Bank (ECB) of its readiness to provide the financing needed to prevent undue sovereign debt distress was a major step in alleviating market pressures. Although the elaboration of EA-wide banking and financial supervision policies should further even out the adjustment burden going forward, it remains to be seen whether the currency union will be able to prosper without more elaborate common risk-sharing or stabilization instruments.

- In an environment of high uncertainty, the adoption of nominal (non-cyclically adjusted) targets has tended to give fiscal policy a procyclical bent. The move to structural targets should leave space for countries to navigate unexpected surprises, but it raises nontrivial technical and communicational issues.

- With financial globalization, the two-way links between a sovereign and the domestic banks have become tighter and can quickly unleash hard-to-control negative feedback loops. This was particularly evident in the EA setting, but also resonates for countries outside the EA with large banking systems, such as the United Kingdom. Large, internationally active banks can potentially generate large contingent liabilities for a sovereign. In addition to strengthened regulation, including in the macroprudential area, these countries have strong incentives to build larger fiscal buffers in quiet times, in order to increase their response capacity in case of a crisis.

After a period of trials and errors, important steps have been taken to restore confidence in the capacity of the EA to overcome this crisis, but further efforts are needed to strengthen its ability to define and implement economic policies with a truly regional dimension. As long as the union remains incomplete, the design of fiscal policy in member states will remain a particular challenge.

8.2 Before the Fall: Fiscal Policy and the Buildup of Intra-Euro Area Vulnerabilities

Up to 2009, few would have seen the EA as a stage for fiscal drama. Its average overall fiscal deficit between 1999 and 2007, around 2 percent of GDP, was lower than in Japan or the United States. At end-2007, the gross government debt-to-GDP ratio was also lower than in these two countries (figure 8.1). Other indicators similarly pointed to a reasonably well-behaved fiscal position for the EA as a whole. For example, primary expenditure as a percentage of GDP was lower in 2007 than in 1999, and the fiscal stance did not seem to be particularly procyclical in good times (figure 8.2).

8.2.1 Growing Fiscal Gaps

However, this relatively good aggregate outturn masked significant heterogeneity among EA countries. A number of them had chronically large deficits both in headline and cyclically adjusted terms. For instance, the general government deficit of Greece and Portugal exceeded the Maastricht ceiling every year during 1999 to 2007. The largest EA countries did not perform much better, with Italy exceeding the ceiling six times, Germany five times, and France three times. But Finland, Ireland, Luxembourg, and Spain achieved sustained fiscal surpluses.

Fiscal heterogeneity continued to be an issue on the eve of the Great Recession (figures 8.3 and 8.4). In 2007, six EA members still had large deficits, while eight EA members registered fiscal surpluses, some of which resulted from strong consolidation efforts. In particular, Germany's general government balance had swung into surplus as fiscal tightening efforts begun several years earlier paid off. But consolidation in other deficit countries was much less advanced or had not yet been initiated. The gap in fiscal performances within the EA in 2007 is well illustrated by the distance between Finland's 5.3 percent surplus and Greece's 6.5 percent deficit, measured as a share of GDP and in headline terms.

The heterogeneity of fiscal balances largely reflects strong expenditure growth in many EA countries.[1] Expenditure growth was particularly fast in countries that later faced a sovereign debt crisis. For instance, over 1999 to 2007, primary expenditures as a share of GDP rose by 2.8 percentage points in Portugal, 4.1 percentage points in Ireland, and 5.5 percentage points in Greece. In real terms and corrected for cyclical factors, primary expenditures in Ireland almost doubled in this period. In these three countries, the increase in expenditures was heavily skewed toward transfers (IMF 2008; Lemgruber and Soto 2013; Abbas 2012). The share of the government wage bill expanded too, further increasing spending rigidity. Primary expenditures as a share of GDP also rose by more than 1 percentage point in Italy and by around 1 percentage point in Belgium and the Netherlands during this period as room from falling interest payments was used to increase other spending.

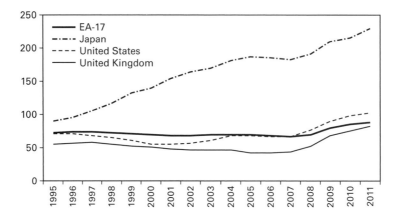

Figure 8.1a
Advanced economies' key fiscal indicators, 1995 to 2011; general government gross debt (percent of GDP)
Sources: AMECO Database; IMF Historical Public Debt Database; World Economic Outlook (WEO) Database

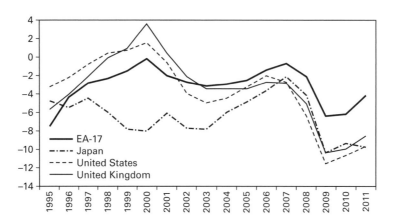

Figure 8.1b
Advanced economies' key fiscal indicators, 1995 to 2011; general government overall balance (percent of GDP)
Sources: AMECO Database; IMF Historical Public Debt Database; World Economic Outlook (WEO) Database

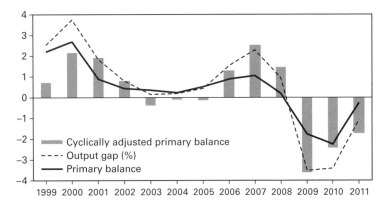

Figure 8.2
Fiscal position and the output gap in the euro area-17, 1999 to 2011
Source: AMECO Database

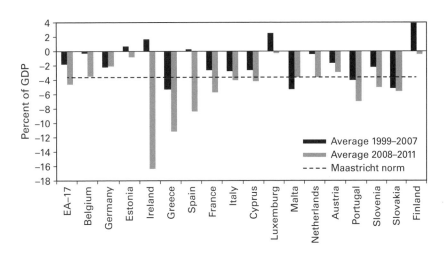

Figure 8.3
General government overall balance, euro area-17, 1999 to 2011 (percent of GDP)
Source: AMECO Database

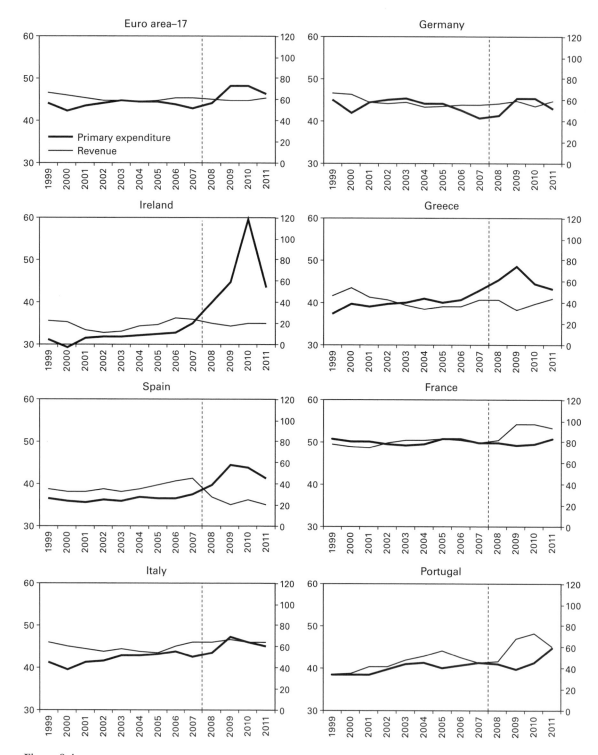

Figure 8.4
Euro area's expenditures and revenue as share of GDP, 1999 to 2011
Source: AMECO Database

As many countries reduced tax rates or narrowed their tax base through tax exemptions, revenue growth, in turn, was lagging or ephemeral. In the EA as a whole, the revenue-to-GDP ratio dropped by around 1.25 percentage points during 1999 to 2007, reflecting a decline in Germany, in particular, but also in Belgium and the Netherlands. Among the chronic excessive deficit countries, revenue in Greece, as a percentage of GDP, was around 2 percentage points lower in 2007 than at the time of euro introduction. Portugal managed to increase its revenue in tandem with its primary expenditures, but not by enough to achieve a primary surplus. In Ireland and Spain, a large share of the seemingly strong revenue growth was due to credit and real estate booms, making public finances vulnerable to a downturn.[2] Already in 2007 there were warnings that as much as three-quarters of Spain's increase in government revenue would disappear when the real estate boom came to an end (Martinez-Mongay et al. 2007).

With hindsight, in a number of EA countries government balances adjusted for the cycle and corrected for asset price effects were weaker than originally thought during most of 1999 to 2008, thus unknowingly permitting a loosening of the fiscal stance. However, capturing asset price effects in real time raises a number of methodological challenges that are not yet fully addressed—and even less so before the crisis. Furthermore, balances adjusted for asset price effects using ex post data and recently improved methodologies continue to show strong heterogeneity in fiscal outcomes within the EA.[3]

Differences in the debt position at the time of euro adoption, divergent fiscal balances, and different growth and interest-rate conditions all contributed to substantial heterogeneity of debt ratios. Greece, but also Belgium and Italy, entered the EA with general government debt above 100 percent of GDP, substantially more than the Maastricht ceiling and more than double Finland's and Ireland's debt ratios at the same point in time. Following euro adoption, the debt ratio further increased in Greece, as the country failed to maintain primary surpluses and had to take on hidden liabilities, and also in Portugal, where primary balances remained in deficit. Belgium and Italy, on the other hand, made further progress toward debt reduction through a primary surplus policy. Interest-rate–growth differentials also mattered. They contributed importantly to the reduction of the debt ratio in Ireland and Spain during 1999 to 2007, but also explain in part why the ratio went up in the two largest EA countries, France and Germany, in this period.

The large and continued policy divergence was possible in part because of important flaws in the EA fiscal surveillance framework.

- *Weaknesses in design.* The Stability and Growth Pact (SGP) rules were fundamentally asymmetric, with alarm bells and sanctions if countries breached the ceilings, but no incentives for building fiscal buffers in good times (see ECB

2011; Larch et al. 2010). With minimal buffers, even a mild slowdown (as in 2002 to 2003) was sufficient to activate the Excessive Deficit Procedure (EDP) for a number of EA members.

- *Weaknesses in enforcement.* The SGP could not effectively enforce fiscal discipline. Germany and France, by ignoring the fiscal adjustment requirements of the EDP rules in 2002 to 2003, undermined the SGP's credibility. The 2005 reform of the SGP increased policy flexibility, but without introducing stronger enforcement mechanisms. Compliance was further hampered by the complexity of the ESA 95 rules for reporting of general government balances[4] coupled, in the case of Greece, with outright misreporting.

In the defense of EA authorities, measuring output gaps and one-off revenue effects at a time of large cyclical upswings and asset bubbles was also methodologically challenging. Up until the end of 2008, the European Commission's (EC) earlier estimates of cyclically adjusted balances were systematically revised upward for the EA as a whole, as well as for all individual countries.

Also, contrary to the expectations embedded in the EMU's design, market discipline was ineffective in controlling fiscal policies. Because the European monetary union was born as a compromise, with limited centralization of functions beyond the monetary authority, market forces were expected to complement institutional arrangements in ensuring fiscal discipline. Explicit provisions in the Treaty on the Functioning of the European Union (TFEU) sought to limit moral hazard by prohibiting the monetary financing of public debt (Article 123[5]), while the no bailout clause (Article 125[6]) specifically stated that a member facing financial difficulties should not expect assistance from the Union or other member states. Both provisions provided an unambiguous signal that the ECB would not step in to alleviate budget distress and gave markets the responsibility to price in the risk of sovereign default. In practice, however, sovereign borrowing costs converged rapidly after the adoption of the euro, with spreads over Germany (considered the benchmark) shrinking to negligible levels for all EA members.

This in large part reflected investors' expectations that a sovereign default in the EA would be too costly not to trigger some form of support, either from the ECB or from other members. The absence of predefined bankruptcy or restructuring arrangements for sovereigns also left a degree of ambiguity regarding the actual application of the no bailout clause. Bank accounting practices reinforced the perception that sovereign default was not an option in the EA, as both bank regulators and the ECB, in their collateral policy, considered all government bonds risk-free (Buiter and Sibert 2005). Government debt managers adjusted their issuance strategies and risk management practices to the new low-spread regime, leaving the sovereign vulnerable to rollover and re-pricing risks if market expectations of official support to EA members in distress were not to be met and spread compression was undone.

8.2.2 Widening Nonfiscal Gaps

Imbalances also built up in nonfiscal areas after the introduction of the common currency. Nominal interest rates converged quickly, well before inflation rates. The resulting negative real interest rates in higher inflation countries fueled internal demand and credit booms, as well as an unprecedented increase in private debt in some countries (Ireland, Spain) and in public debt in some others (Greece, Portugal). The fast expansion in bank balance sheets—in some countries, such as Ireland, banks' assets grew up to five times of GDP—was matched by a parallel increase in crossborder banking investment. Some countries (Greece, Portugal, Spain) already had large external imbalances at the time of euro introduction, and reported a further widening after the launch of the common currency (figure 8.5). These countries entered the EA with relatively weak external competitiveness indicators, which continued to deteriorate subsequently.

In contrast with the fiscal area, EA-wide rules and incentives to monitor and correct nonfiscal adverse dynamics were very much lacking. By design, the EA policy framework was intended to control public sector imbalances, under the assumption that market forces would be sufficient to correct any excess in private demand before it would reach destabilizing levels. As a result limiting or curbing the emerging imbalances in private sector balance sheets was not seen as a central or urgent policy goal. The Lisbon Strategy, set up in 2000, did seek to foster structural convergence, but it largely relied on market and peer pressure to encourage the implementation of structural reforms. In practice, reforms were implemented, at best, in a piecemeal manner. Progress remained uneven across areas, with key labor market reforms

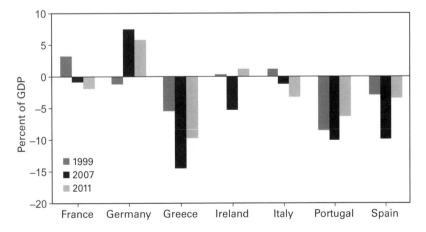

Figure 8.5
Current account balance developments in selected euro area countries
Source: World Economic Outlook (WEO) Database

particularly lacking. The growth performance in countries with a weak structural reform record was overall disappointing.

Most important, banking supervision and regulation remained under the national umbrella. Notwithstanding the quick integration of financial systems across the euro area, member states remained individually responsible for deposit insurance schemes and the fiscal costs of domestic bank resolution, which exposed them to substantial contingent risks.

Further tightening this adverse bank–sovereign loop, the share of own-government bonds in bank holdings remained relatively high. In some EA countries, banks have historically been important holders of domestic government debt (figure 8.6). In Belgium, for example, the share of own-government debt held by banks at the time of

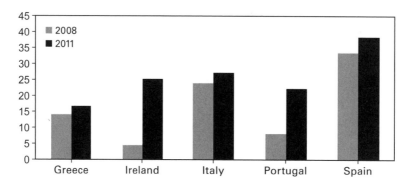

Figure 8.6a
Public debt held by domestic banks (percent of total public debt)
Source: Arslanap and Tsuda (2012)

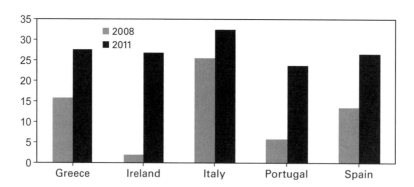

Figure 8.6b
Public debt held by domestic banks (in percent of GDP)
Source: Arslanap and Tsuda (2012)

euro introduction was as high as 40 percent. As the EMU spurred the integration of previously segmented national sovereign debt markets, the share of own-government bonds in bank holdings generally declined, but by less than what effective risk-sharing would have suggested. Banks with a relatively high share of own-government securities in their portfolios were exposed to important market value losses if sovereign yields were to come under pressure. In turn, EA countries with relatively high own public debt held by banks were exposed to banking sector distress.

In all, initial expectations that the combination of a EA institutional framework, which was kept to a minimum, and the free play of corrective market forces would be powerful drivers of economic and policy convergence and business-cycle harmonization did not materialize. Rather, large imbalances emerged in public sector as well as private sector balance sheets. Abundant financing and market exuberance in the pre-Lehman era papered over these cracks, giving policy makers the confidence that the EA framework was sufficiently strong to ensure the viability of the union.

8.3 In the Lion's Den: Fiscal Policy in the First Phase of the Crisis

The Great Recession came to the EA somewhat later and initially less severely than to the United Kingdom and the United States. The EA did not immediately face strong headwinds when the first signs of pressures in international financial markets emerged in August 2007, in part because EA financial institutions were overall less directly exposed to toxic financial products. Recession struck the United States already in the first quarter of 2008, with the United Kingdom following in the second quarter, but the EA only entered it in the third quarter. The fall of Lehman Brothers in September 2008 shook international financial markets profoundly, and this time the EA was not immune. Interbank markets froze and some major European banks lost access to funding. In the wake of the global financial turmoil in the fourth quarter of 2008, the United Kingdom, the United States and all EA countries experienced a very deep recession in 2009, with broadly similar output contractions (figure 8.7).

Deeper cracks became apparent within the euro area shortly after the Lehman event. First, the recession in Ireland took a somewhat different shape than in the rest of the EA. Because of its strong trading links with the United States and the United Kingdom, Ireland entered the recession in early 2008, earlier than the rest of the EA. Moreover, the external shock served as the detonator of a severe banking crisis. Largely because of an abundance of low-cost foreign funding combined with lax domestic oversight, Irish banks became overextended and overexposed to domestic residential and commercial real estate. The banking system collapsed under the combination of sharply increasing funding costs and falling asset prices (by end-2009, house prices had declined by 21 percent), pushing the country into a deep recession (real GDP contracted by 8 percent over 2008 to 2010).

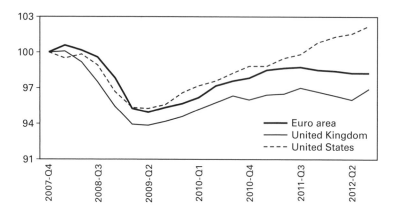

Figure 8.7
Level of real GDP (seasonally adjusted, 2007-Q4 = 100)
Source: Eurostat

Second, financial markets began to differentiate among EA members. Although the initial post-Lehman "flight to safety" pushed all EA nominal bond yields down, there was a significant contemporaneous widening in both bond spreads over Germany and CDS spreads in fall 2008. By early 2009, a 250 basis point spread over Germany had emerged for both Greece and Ireland, reflecting growing market concerns about the soundness of both countries' fiscal accounts.

Markets also began to internalize the transfer of risk from banks' to sovereigns' balance sheets, as evidenced by the falling CDS spreads for the banks and rising CDS spreads for sovereigns in late 2008, following the announcement by the ECB of important banking support measures. The opposite movement of bank and sovereign spreads came to an end in 2009, as rising sovereign spreads began to be transmitted to bank spreads, while news about financial sector stress continued to push up sovereign spreads (Mody and Sandri 2011).

Conversely, persistent imbalances appeared in Target 2, the euro area large-value cross-border payment and settlement system, as banks from EA countries that were not under pressure (mostly German banks) began to liquidate their claims, including interbank claims, in EA countries under pressure. Nonetheless, the imbalances remained relatively small (€100 to 200 billion) through 2008 to 2009. There were no indications yet that these tensions would intensify and culminate in a collapse in investor confidence and major sell-off in peripheral countries' sovereign debt markets.

8.3.1 Policy Response to Financial Shock

Understandably, the immediate policy focus in the aftermath of the financial shock was on avoiding a financial sector meltdown. The response of the ECB, the European Commission and national authorities was swift. The ECB slashed policy rates and eased liquidity. The fiscal authorities were equally quick in providing support to the financial sector, including guarantees and capital injections. In fall 2008, 11 EA countries, including all the larger ones, announced bank support schemes to reassure markets about the solvency of their banking systems.

The size (and composition) of the ECB's balance sheet expansion was much less ambitious than that witnessed contemporaneously in the United States and the United Kingdom, in part reflecting the limits set to the ECB's capacity to intervene in sovereign debt markets. For the EA as a whole, the cost of financial sector support in that first phase was relatively limited, although its nature, scale and impact varied considerably across countries. A clear outlier was Ireland, where the introduction of a blanket guarantee on large bank liabilities implied massive on- and off-balance sheet exposure for the sovereign. In other countries, financial sector support programs only led to a marginal widening of general government deficits (by less than half a percentage point of GDP). The increase in related contingent liabilities was also contained; it remained below 10 percent of GDP in all EA members except Ireland, Belgium, and the Netherlands—well below the impact observed in the United Kingdom (figures 8.8 and 8.9). From that view point, EA policy makers could thus conclude that, except for a few country-specific problems, the eurozone as a whole was relatively sheltered from the worst effects of the financial crisis.

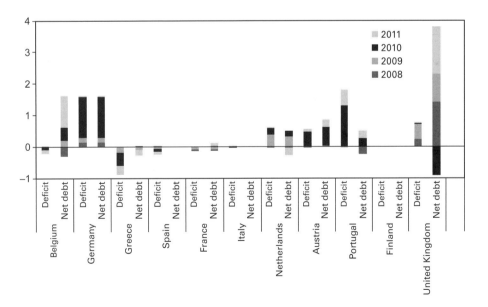

Figure 8.8
Impacts of financial sector support on general government deficit and net debt in euro area-11 and the United Kingdom (percent of GDP)
Source: Eurostat

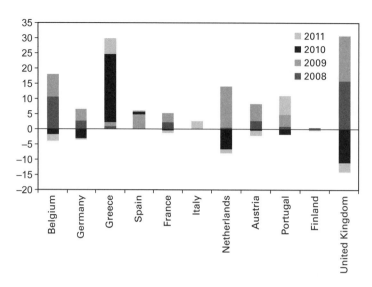

Figure 8.9
Contingent liabilities arising from financial sector support in euro area-11 and the United Kingdom
(percent of GDP)
Source: Eurostat

8.3.2 Fiscal Policy: from Stimulus to Consolidation

The economic slowdown in the fourth quarter of 2008 prompted calls for a coordinated, timely, targeted, and temporary countercyclical fiscal expansion in advanced economies. The November 2008 European Economic Recovery Plan provided for an EU-wide stimulus of €200 billion, or 1.5 percent of EU GDP, one-fifth of which would be contributed by the European Investment Bank and the remaining four-fifth by national governments. However, the depth of the 2009 recession and its impact on the fiscal position were initially very much underestimated. For instance, the EC in fall 2008 projected still some positive growth for 2009, whereas the actual outturn was –4.5 percent. Then, as signs emerged in early 2010 that global growth was rebounding faster than initially expected, the focus of concerns shifted to the state of public finances. Between 2007 and 2009, government balances deteriorated by almost 8 percentage points of GDP and debt ratios jumped by almost 14 percentage points of GDP in the EA as a whole, significantly more than expected. The EC emphasized the need for timely exit from excessive deficits and, in high-debt countries, for steady debt reduction through ambitious consolidation in line with SGP targets. The policy stance thus moved relatively quickly, for the whole of the EA, to fiscal consolidation. In most cases planned stimulus plans were not implemented in full (table 8.1).

Table 8.1
Discretionary fiscal response to the 2008 to 2009 financial crisis in the euro area, the United Kingdom, and the United States

	Announced stimulus[a]	Cumulative growth decline in 2009–2010[b]		Sovereign bond yield[c]	Initial and projected government debt[d]			Projected government deficit (average over 2008–10)	
	2008–10	Projected	Actual	Sep'08–Apr'09	End-2008 level (actual)	2008–10 buildup (projected)	2008–10 buildup (actual)	Projected	Actual[e]
Belgium	0.8	3.7	0.4	4.2	90	11	6	3.9	3.5
Spain	4.8	4.2	4.2	4.1	40	27	21	7.4	8.4
Ireland	0	11.4	6.5	4.8	44	39	48	11.6	17.4
Italy	0	4.3	4.0	4.5	106	11	13	4.0	4.1
Netherlands	1.9	3.9	2.2	3.9	58	7	5	2.8	3.4
Germany	3.3	5.1	1.2	3.4	66	11	16	3.3	2.4
Finland	3.4	4.5	6.0	3.8	34	13	15	-0.2	0.4
France	1.1	3.2	1.6	3.8	67	15	14	5.7	6.0
Austria	3.6	4.1	1.9	4.1	63	1	8	3.3	3.2
Portugal	1.0	4.5	1.6	4.4	66	18	22	5.3	7.9
Greece	0	0.8	8.2	5.3	99	26	35	5.3	12.1
EA-11 average[f]	2.1	4.3	2.6	4.0	70	15	16	4.6	5.0
United Kingdom	1.5	3.7	2.3	3.8	52	28	27	6.5	8.9
United States	4.9	2.8	0.8	3.0	71	27	23	9.1	9.9

a. Cumulative impact of discretionary stimulus measures (in percent of GDP), as reported in the Spring 2010 *Fiscal Monitor*.
b. Projections and actuals are as per the EC spring 2009 and autumn 2012 forecasts (in percent).
c. Ten-year sovereign bond yield (in percent).
d. Projections and actuals are as per the EC spring 2009 and autumn 2012 forecasts (in percent of GDP).
e. Projections and actuals are as per the EC spring 2009 and autumn 2012 forecasts (in percent of GDP).
f. Excludes bank support costs of 1.3, 1.3, and 20.2 percent of GDP in 2010 for Germany, Portugal, and Ireland.
f. PPPGDP weighted.

In the event, the size of the stimulus in this period varied considerably across the EA, but it was not a contributing factor to the subsequent sovereign debt crisis. Sovereigns facing widening spreads (Italy, Greece, and Ireland) did not implement a stimulus in 2009 and 2010 but rather focused on its opposite, fiscal tightening. In the rest of the EA, the stimulus was relatively small: about 2.1 percent of GDP for the larger EA countries as a whole, comparable to the United Kingdom, but less than half the size of the US stimulus, despite the fact that growth forecasts at the time of the announcement/finalization of these stimulus packages showed a steeper decline in GDP growth in the EA than in the United States (where growth had already suffered more in 2008). The stimulus package was particularly modest taking into account that monetary conditions were tighter in the EA than in the United Kingdom or the United States—in part reflecting the institutional constraints on the ECB's interest-rate policy and financial sector support measures.

The high degree of uncertainty, particularly about the growth outlook, weighed on the design of fiscal policy. With rapidly changing estimates of the output gap, implementation lags weakened the initial impact of stimulus measures. The EC's focus on using nominal deficit and debt ceilings as fiscal anchors undercut the mitigating role of automatic stabilizers.[7] A few EA members faced additional fiscal pressures to adjust to widening sovereign spreads.

8.3.3 Fragmented, Continually Narrow Policy Focus

The EA policy response in the first phase of the crisis already exhibited some limiting features that would continue to haunt it and hamper the resolution of the subsequent sovereign crisis. First, with the exception of initial liquidity provision to banks by the ECB, policies were designed mainly from a national perspective, and only loosely coordinated at the euro level. Partly because of the absence of established euro-wide policy levers, efforts to mitigate the impact of the external shock on European banks were more a juxtaposition of individual national actions than a well-articulated EA-wide response. Similarly, even though cross-border activities raised significant risks of intra-euro area spillovers, the Irish authorities were left to bear alone the largest share of the costs of the banking crisis. The reliance on national responses in the face of such a systemic event may have begun to undermine confidence in the EA as a policy entity. Even more, the insistence on the strict separation between monetary and fiscal management and the prohibition on the ECB from providing any support to an EA sovereign, even as markets turned jittery, may have planted the doubts that would later come to question the sustainability of the monetary union itself.

Also the policy stance at the EA level remained narrowly focused on fiscal adjustment, leaving other imbalances and their institutional roots somewhat aside. In particular, the absence of euro-wide regulatory and supervisory arrangements for the banking sector was not initially perceived as an urgent problem. Similarly structural reforms, notably those aimed at fostering a change in relative intra-EA prices, were often put on a back burner. Overall, the onset of the Great Recession did not prompt a reconsideration of the underlying EA policy framework. As a result intra-EA private sector imbalances were not yet a major policy concern. The current account deficits in the countries under pressure did narrow somewhat, but more as the result of the higher borrowing costs and demand compression than of a structural shift. On reflection, the adjustment appears asymmetric, as it was largely limited to the countries with deficits, while the surpluses in other EA members did not come down.

8.4 In the Eye of the Storm: Sovereign Debt Crisis

Triggered by a loss of investor confidence in Greece and the ensuing emergence of serious fiscal vulnerabilities in other euro members, a sovereign debt crisis engulfed the EA in 2010. The crisis spread across EA countries in successive, widening waves (see detailed timeline in appendix A at the end of this chapter).

- The EA sovereign debt crisis is generally considered to have originated with the loss of investor confidence following the substantial upward revision of Greek deficit and debt figures in late 2009. Concerns about the large cross-country exposure of EA banks to sovereign risk, public discord among EA leaders on how to respond to increasing financial pressures on Greece, and the possibility, muted by some policy makers, of a Greek debt restructuring further weakened confidence. Initial signs of contagion to Ireland and Portugal emerged in spring 2010, and EA leaders for the first time discussed the possible need for new mechanisms to support sovereigns facing rising and potentially unsustainable borrowing costs.

- The crisis entered a new phase with the May 2010 agreement on an adjustment program and financial assistance for Greece, and the announcement of new EU support mechanisms, most notably the European Financial Stability Facility (EFSF).[8] The ECB launched a Securities Markets Program (SMP) to purchase government bonds in the secondary market with the aim of restoring the proper functioning of dysfunctional market segments and the monetary policy transmission mechanism. But discord on how to activate the new mechanisms, questions about the commitment of EA leaders to a durable resolution of the crisis, and renewed discussion of a possible private creditor bail-in for Greece resulted in a quick return of severe market pressures. Ireland and Portugal were particularly affected this time and also had to seek international financial assistance. Sharply widening sovereign spreads further exacerbated the negative feedback loop between sovereign risk and bank risk in a number of EA countries.

- The focal point of the EA sovereign debt crisis returned to Greece in the second half of 2011 as the country was unable to meet reform and fiscal consolidation commitments and output contracted much faster than forecast. The announcement that a restructuring of private sector holdings of Greek public debt would be part of a second program and disagreements among EA leaders on the scope of the restructuring dealt a new blow to already very low investor confidence. Contagion affected Italy and Spain. It was further fueled by these countries' deteriorating growth prospects and the realization that the SMP was too small and its conditions too restrictive to stabilize their sovereign bond markets. The ECB responded by cutting interest rates and putting in place a €1 trillion long term liquidity facility for banks (the long-term refinancing operation, or LTRO), which established an effective lender-of-last resort function for banks; it also aimed, indirectly, at improving the liquidity of sovereign debt markets.

- By mid-2012, concerns regarding the capacity of the Spanish authorities to support ailing banks pushed spreads to new record levels and triggered new waves of contagion. Investor confidence was undermined by the perception that EA sovereigns would remain vulnerable to self-fulfilling debt runs and contagion as long as a lender of last resort function for sovereign debt was not put in place.[9] In response, decisive reforms were introduced that addressed the institutional weaknesses at the core of the crisis and considerably improved investor sentiment toward the EA as a whole. Most important, the ECB announced in July that it saw the euro project as irreversible and that it stood ready to do "whatever it takes" to preserve the monetary union. In September, it announced the replacement of the SMP with the Outright Monetary Transactions (OMT) facility, which could be used to intervene, in potentially unlimited amounts and for as long as necessary, to stabilize secondary sovereign debt markets.

Beyond crisis management, other important reforms were adopted in the banking and fiscal areas. Proposed banking reforms included a framework for sharing the burden of bank recapitalizations, the creation of a single bank supervisory mechanism in the hands of the ECB, and the agreement to establish a Banking Union. Fiscal reforms, under the so-called Fiscal Compact, included three key elements that in combination should facilitate the convergence of fiscal policy over the medium term: the use of a structural budget target, which combines the sustainability goal with room for adjustment to the economic cycle; the intent to anchor firmly fiscal governance at the national level, through the inclusion of the structural target in national legislation; and the strengthening of supranational oversight (box 8.1). Both the Banking Union and the Fiscal Compact are meaningful structural decisions that give the EMU institutional framework a noticeably broader, more ambitious dimension.

Two striking features of the EA sovereign debt crisis have been how quickly and broadly it spread (in less than three years, it went from Greece, a country accounting

Box 8.1
The fiscal compact

The Treaty on Stability, Coordination, and Governance in the Economic and Monetary Union, also known as the Fiscal Compact, was adopted in March 2012 by 25 EU members and entered into force in January 2013, after it was ratified by 17 members; it complements and reinforces earlier EU fiscal governance reforms introduced as part of the "six pack," which took effect in December 2011.

The Compact aims at reinforcing the union's fiscal governance by focusing on implementation of the fiscal rules and commitments at the national level. It includes, in particular, a requirement to include in national legislation a rule that limits annual structural deficits to a maximum of 0.5 percent of GDP (1 percent of GDP for countries with debt levels significantly below 60 percent and low long-term fiscal sustainability risks). Countries are also required to design automatic correction mechanisms that will be triggered in the event of deviations from the structural budget balance rules. The European Court of Justice is to verify the transposition of structural budget balance rules to national legislation. The Fiscal Compact also includes a defined path to lower debt ratios to the threshold of 60 percent of GDP (at an annual pace of no less than one-twentieth of the distance between the observed level and the target) as well as stronger enforcement procedures (including the use of a reverse qualified majority, rather than simple majority, to assess noncompliance).

for 2.5 percent of the EA's GDP, to four more countries– Ireland, Portugal, Spain, and Cyprus–with a cumulative share of 15 percent of the EA's GDP) and how long it took for a comprehensive solution to take shape. Two elements can help explain why this happened. First, the explicit prohibition on the ECB to provide support to distressed sovereigns fueled contagion, raising the risk of a breakup of the currency union. A second limiting factor was the policy setup that had crystallized in the first phase of the crisis, with its focus on national decision-making and fiscal consolidation. As a result the EA policy response remained for a long time excessively focused on fiscal consolidation, delaying the emergence of necessary broader, EA-wide policy reforms.

8.4.1 No Lender of Last Resort

As mentioned earlier, the European monetary union was designed as an incomplete union, explicitly excluding fiscal risk-sharing, either by the ECB or other members (Articles 123 and 125 of the TFEU). Similarly the EMU did not include a unified system of financial oversight. Bank supervision remained a national prerogative and crisis management, in case of banking distress, a national responsibility. This meant that in a crisis, there was no explicit lender of last resort, neither for the banks nor for the sovereign.

Specifically, and in sharp contrast with countries issuing in their own currency, national fiscal authorities in EA members could not benefit from the standard (even if implicit) central bank guarantee that cash would always be made available to repay government debt issued in domestic currency, and banks could not rely on a credible guarantee from their sovereign. This set EA members markedly apart from other countries where the central bank was able to purchase a significant share of government debt issues through the crisis. Illustrating the limitations of the SMP, at end-2012, ECB purchases under the program amounted to somewhat less than 4 percent of outstanding long-term securities issued by EA sovereigns. By comparison, gilts acquired by the Bank of England under its purchasing facility accounted for nearly 30 percent of the end-2012 gilt stock, and the comparable ratio for the Federal Reserve was somewhat less than 14 percent. While no bonds have yet been purchased, the new OMT arrangement is expected to function as a lender of last resort in case the need arises, conditional upon a country agreeing to an ESM program.

The two institutional gaps fed upon each other. As concerns about fiscal sustainability began to surface, sovereign debt markets became prone to recurrent liquidity crises and strong contagion effects. Higher borrowing costs undermined the soundness of public finances and raised doubts about the capacity of fiscal authorities to support ever more vulnerable banking systems. These adverse feedbacks led markets to increasingly question the ability of some EA members to remain in the currency union. This was reflected, in particular, in the sharp increase in the Target 2 claims of countries not under pressure, which rose to more than €700 billion by mid-2012, not only because of shifts in asset balances from countries under pressure to countries not under pressure but also because of strategic cash movements by banks to protect against perceived redenomination risk (Cecchetti et al. 2012).

There has been a debate on whether the existence of Target 2 aggravated the crisis by allowing some countries to postpone bank and private-demand rebalancing (Sinn and Wollmershäuser 2012). However, a unionwide payments and settlements system is integral to a monetary union; its key role is precisely to facilitate between union member countries the financial flows that are inherent in the monetary union. In periods when individual member countries suffered financial stress, the system allowed a smooth reduction of cross-border interbank claims and liquidation of external holdings of crisis-country sovereign debt through matching liquidity flows between central banks. This inherent feature of a monetary union and its implications for crisis management were, however, not fully appreciated before the crisis.

8.4.2 Slow, Complicated Decision-Making Process

The emergence of a collective policy response was further complicated by the lack of an effective economic policy coordinating body for the EA and by the overlap of national and supranational decision levels. Monthly meetings of euro group finance ministers did not provide a proper forum for timely responses to new developments. Major decisions and initiatives had to be deferred to meetings of EU heads of states, which were sometimes contentious and where domestic political considerations often played an important and divisive role. In some cases, great importance was given to decisions by national institutions (e.g., the German constitutional court), at the expense of room for maneuver for supranational institutions. Coordination between national authorities and the ECB also proved challenging at times.

As a result the policy response to the sovereign crisis followed a jerky and piecemeal path that could neither calm market nor restore confidence in a lasting manner. In EA policy makers' defense, the depth of the Greek crisis came as a surprise to most (the deficit had been underreported by a factor of four) and the institutional arrangements had not been designed with an internal failure of that size in mind. In the event, the principle of EA assistance to member countries in distress was agreed upon relatively quickly. But it proved difficult to find consensus on its form and scope. In practice, financial support was explicitly constrained ex ante but reluctantly increased ex post, once programmed targets were missed and market tensions intensified. Notwithstanding the increased virulence of the crisis, emergency liquidity provision mechanisms were established only gradually and in a halting manner. The provision of emergency liquidity to banks through national central banks came first. When it proved insufficient, the ECB stepped in by providing extensive liquidity to banks and easing related collateral requirements, but its interventions were kept deliberately limited in amount and time. The ECB's Long-Term Refinancing Operations in late 2011 and early 2012, while meant to provide liquidity to EA banks, allowed for the use of government bonds as collateral and, as a result, increased the available liquidity in peripheral countries' sovereign debt markets. However, the credit risk from the sovereign debt remained with the financial institutions, intensifying sovereign-bank links. Only after pressures resumed, and two years after the beginning of the euro crisis, did the ECB affirm its readiness to intervene in sovereign debt markets as needed to safeguard the monetary union, thereby calming fears of a possible breakup of the eurozone.

Formal crisis resolution mechanisms were put in place at a similarly halting pace. The EFSF, set up at the time of the approval of the first Greek program, was temporary in nature, and it was soon realized that its lending capacity fell far short of what was needed to meet the potential financing needs of EU members under pressure. Its successor, the ESM, sought to permanently strengthen the EU's crisis response capacity, but the scope of its activities, while wider than that of the EFSF, remains to be fully clarified. Indicative of the slow pace at which new EU institutional initiatives have been developed and the time it takes for different member states to approve them, the ESM, announced in December 2010, was finally ratified only in September 2012. Agreement on concrete steps to strengthen fiscal governance has also been long in coming, in spite of the well-understood reform needs.

8.4.3 Narrow Fiscal Focus

Possibly because instances for EA level policy discussions were more developed in this field, the main focus of the policy response to the crisis remained in the fiscal area. Reforms to the EU fiscal framework through the Fiscal Compact, "six packs," and "two packs" were expected to strengthen the incentives for fiscal prudence. However, the framework remained directed toward bringing down budget deficits to below 3 percent of GDP and public debt to below 60 percent of GDP as quickly as possible.[10] The focus on fixed headline (noncyclically adjusted) deficit and debt ceilings lent a strong procyclical bent to consolidation efforts. In an environment of pervasive uncertainties, fiscal multipliers were often underestimated and the targets missed, unleashing a negative feedback effect whereby additional tightening measures were introduced, further depressing near-term growth and complicating the attainment of the targets.[11] Even though the ambitious headline targets were often missed, in a context of negative growth and high multipliers, the repeated adjustment efforts resulted in larger than expected consolidation when measured in cyclically adjusted terms. By 2012, most EA countries had implemented substantial fiscal adjustments. In fact, a comparison of the improvement in the CAB projected at the onset of the sovereign debt crisis with the outcome shows that the improvement was in most cases larger than planned during 2010 to 2012, with a positive surprise on the order of about 1 percentage point of GDP for the EA as a whole (figure 8.10).

In contrast, growth disappointed, as the outcome during 2010 to 2012 fell around 2.5 percentage points short of the projection for the EA on average, suggesting that the negative growth impact of the consolidation efforts was underestimated. The weakening growth did raise doubts about EA countries' capacity to implement their adjustment plans. As a result confidence effects were elusive and borrowing costs often increased in the near term as markets were more responsive to lower growth prospects than to fiscal consolidation efforts (Cottarelli and Jaramillo 2012). Immediate financial payoffs were thus limited: while the level of budget deficits started to gradually converge, spread dispersion remained high.

The protracted resolution of banking difficulties was also a drag on growth. Although bank runs were forestalled through the provision of EA liquidity, no supervisory authority was in place to rigorously assess banks' overall risk exposure and deal with distressed banks. In the absence of a cross-border resolution mechanism, national authorities were reluctant to recapitalize parent banks and assume all the related fiscal costs, even after stress tests revealed significant capital shortfalls. As a result many problem banks were kept afloat without prospect for a lasting solution. This not only intensified adverse sovereign-bank loops, but also constrained credit supply, putting the brakes on the recovery in peripheral countries. Only in mid-2012 was a plan floated for a Banking Union with a common supervision and resolution

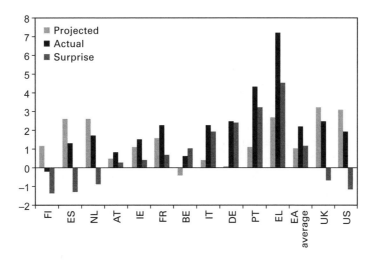

Figure 8.10
Projected and actual improvements in the cyclically adjusted balance, 2010 to 2012 (percent of GDP).
Bank supports costs have been excluded from outturns for Ireland, Portugal, and Germany.
Sources: European Commission Economic Forecasts (spring 2010 for projections; autumn 2012 for
out-turns)

mechanism. Even then, reaching agreement on its actual modalities has proved to be a slow and difficult process.

Since the crisis, intra-EA current account imbalances and relative price differences have continued to unwind. However, the jury is still out on whether these developments are of a temporary nature, mainly driven by the recession-induced import compression, or reflect deeper structural changes. Unit labor costs have fallen significantly in the countries that entered the crisis with high external deficits (Greece, Ireland, Portugal, and Spain), under the joint impact of job-shedding-driven productivity gains and of wage adjustment. But lasting structural adjustment cannot simply rely on wage and price restraints; it must be supported by broader gains in productivity and nonprice competitiveness. Several countries have initiated important labor market reforms whose effects are not yet fully felt and may yield benefits down the road. The EU has put in place a framework to monitor broader macroeconomic imbalances and formulate policies to eliminate excessive imbalances, which over time may facilitate broader policy convergence.

8.5 Concluding Remarks: Safer Harbor in Sight?

The global financial crisis has had a dramatic impact on the EA as it unveiled what would become a full-blown and EA-wide sovereign debt crisis. This chapter has explored why a sovereign debt crisis hit the EA, but not other advanced economies with similar fiscal imbalances. It points to institutional weaknesses in the original EMU design that allowed the buildup of macro-financial imbalances within the EA before 2008. Once the global financial crisis brought those into the open, institutional gaps and political economy constraints then combined to delay the capacity of the European authorities to define policy responses with a broad enough scope, both geographically and topically, to restore confidence in the EA project.

After a searching period, sizable progress has been made to address these shortcomings. New and important steps were taken in the summer of 2012, almost three years after the initial events in Greece that triggered the sovereign debt crisis. These included a proposed framework for sharing the burden of bank recapitalizations, an agreement in principle on a proposal to form a Banking Union, and a strengthening of fiscal governance. Most important, to address fears about the viability of the euro itself, the ECB announced both its intention "to do whatever it takes" to preserve the EMU and the creation of the Outright Monetary Transactions Facility to stabilize EA sovereign debt markets. In the fiscal area, the Fiscal Compact "six packs" and "two packs" introduce binding fiscal rules at the national level. These initiatives go a long way to address the institutional gaps at the core of the crisis and indeed considerably improved investor sentiment toward the EA as a whole.

Still EA leaders have yet to agree on the specifics of important elements of the new construction, including the scope for a joint deposit insurance scheme and bank resolution mechanism and room for additional risk-sharing through pooling of national budget resources. More important, they still have to build a credible and recognized economic decision making instance for the EA as a whole. Some of the recent decisions go in that direction. It is to be hoped that this crisis, like past crises in the process of European economic integration, will served as engine for further institutional changes toward a more complete union.

On the fiscal front, three general policy lessons emerge from the EA experience through the crisis.

- *Fiscal policy in times of global stress needs to show a high degree of flexibility.* The higher than usual uncertainty around growth forecasts and the volatility of market sentiment complicate the design of fiscal policy. The challenge is exacerbated by the fact that fiscal multipliers are likely to be higher than average in a recession, and that most trading partners are also consolidating. In such circumstances, a gradual but steady path of consolidation will have more chances of success than heavy frontloading or backloading. Structural or cyclically adjusted targets can help rebuild confidence while leaving space for the operation of automatic stabilizers. But the calculation of structural balances, or even of output gaps, raises nontrivial technical difficulties. Such targets also are tricky to explain to the general public, and thus more prone to suspicions of manipulation. Combining sufficient flexibility in the targets with credibility in the direction of the fiscal stance is thus the first challenge for fiscal policy.

- *Countries with large banking systems may need stronger fiscal buffers.* Financial globalization tightens the links between banks and their sovereigns by increasing the size of banks' balance sheets and making them potentially more vulnerable to developments outside a country's natural supervision perimeter. The possibility that hard-to-control negative feedback loops between the banks and their sovereign unleash quickly was particularly evident in the EA setting. But this possibility also resonates for countries outside the EA with large, internationally active banks, such as, for example, the United Kingdom. The first response is strengthened regulation, including macroprudential regulation, in coordination with supervisors in partner countries. But these countries could also consider building larger fiscal buffers in quiet times, to increase their response capacity in case of a crisis.

- *The institutional design of the EA, an incomplete monetary union, puts an inordinate share of the adjustment burden on national fiscal policies.* Other macroeconomic management policies, such as monetary or exchange rate policies, have limited, if any, power to mitigate the impact of shocks. With rapid financial integration, however, the fiscal levers are insufficient to prevent or reverse the emergence of broader intra-EA imbalances. In addition the small size of the EU common budget severely restricts the space for smoothing shocks across member states. The announcement by the ECB of its readiness to provide financing to prevent undue fiscal distress was a major step in alleviating pressure on national budgets. The elaboration of EA-wide banking and financial policies should further even out the adjustment burden going forward. However, it remains to be seen whether the currency union will be able to prosper without more elaborate common risk-sharing or stabilization instruments.

Appendix A: Ten-Year Sovereign Bond Yields and Crisis Timeline

The appendix figure and the more detailed account of market and policy events in the EA below provide a timeline of the crisis and document related sovereign spread movements.

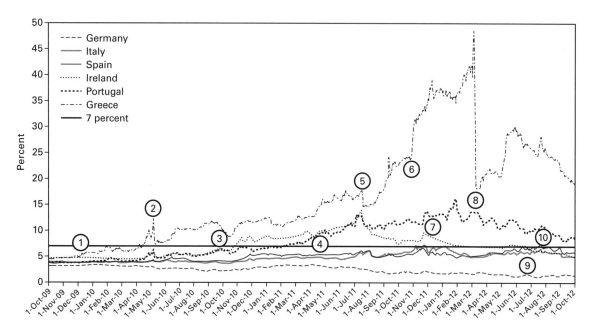

Figure A8.1
Ten-year sovereign bond yields and crisis timeline: (1) Yields rise after initial Greek credit rating downgrade following revelations of much higher than expected 2009 deficit; (2) yields spike after Greece rating downgraded to "junk" then fall after €110 billion Greek bailout and ECB SMP announced; (3) Irish yields jump after government announces large increase in bank bailout costs, with Irish government bailout agreed in late November; (4) Portugal requests bailout after contagion drives up its yields following Irish bailout; (5) initial second Greek bailout announced, with relatively mild PSI component (21 percent haircut); (6) yields spike in response to revised second Greek bailout, with more financing (€130 bn) and more costly PSI (50 percent haircut); (7) the ECB announces two 25 bp rate cuts and the LTRO worth €1 trillion to counterfinancial fragmentation in the EMU; (8) even larger second Greek bailout announced (€174 bn), followed by final agreement on Greek PSI (more than 50 percent haircut); (9) after its yields rise to 7 percent, Spain seeks funds for banking sector bailout and EA leaders agree to create the Banking Union; (10) Draghi states that the ECB is "ready to do whatever it takes" to preserve the EMU, and markets appear convinced as yields fall.
Source: Datastream

Table A8.1
Timeline of key market and policy events since Lehman's collapse

	Market events	Policy events
September 2008	• Lehman Brothers holdings incorporated files for Chapter 11 bankruptcy protection, Bank of America agrees to buy Merrill Lynch for $50 billion. • Dow Jones Industrial Average plunges 504 points to 10,917 (15/09/2008).	• US government sponsored mortgage firms, Fannie Mae and Freddie Mac, are rescued by the US government (07/09/2008). The Fed and Treasury agree to bailout for AIG. • The Fed makes its first interest-rate cut of 0.5 to 4.75% since 2003. • One of the biggest insurance and banking companies in Europe, Fortis, is given a $16.4 billion capital injection from the governments of Netherlands, Luxembourg, and Belgium. Dexia follows shortly, helped by Belgian, French and Luxembourg governments ($9 billion). • Ireland's Finance Minister Brian Lenihan announces sweeping guarantee of bank deposits and debt. (30/09/2008).
October 2008	• Banks all over Europe and US struggle as EU leaders discuss bank rescue plans along the lines of those in US and UK. • The IMF says more European banks may fail as freeze inter-bank lending occurs (22/10/2008).	• US Congress passes the "Emergency Economic Stabilization Act of 2008," commonly known as TARP, a $700 billion rescue package to aid the financial sector (03/10/2008). • RBS, Lloyds TBO, and HBOS among other banks receive a bailout from the UK government. • The IMF, World Bank and the European Union offer Hungary a loan of $25.1 billion. It is the biggest rescue package for an emerging economy since the start of the crisis, exceeding Hungary's quota 10 times (29/10/2008).
November 2008		• IMF rescue packages approved for Iceland ($2.1 billion), Pakistan ($7.6 billion), and Ukraine ($16.5 billion). • Chinese government offers a big stimulus package of $586 billion, about 7% of its GDP. • G20 summit in Washington to discuss measures to strengthen growth and aid the financial system. • The European Commission unveils €200 billion economic recovery plan to stimulate spending and boost confidence. • US Fed announces liquidity injection of $800 billion to stabilize financial system. AIG receives $150 billion in additional bailout support from Fed and Treasury, while TARP funds used to buy preferred shares to bolster capital, and guarantees on bank assets and senior debt provided for a number of major US banks.

(continued)

Table A8.1
(*continued*)

	Market events	Policy events
December 2008	• Central banks around the world cut rates and introduce measures to support lending.	• Following Spain's announcement of a fiscal stimulus in November, France, Germany, and Sweden announce stimulus plans in early December. • President Bush announces that $17.4 billion of TARP funds will be used for a bailout of major carmakers. • The Irish government announces plans to provide €9 billion to recapitalize listed banks.
January–March 2009	• Stock markets continue to fall and unemployment rises in US and other countries.	• US Congress approves a $787 billion stimulus package. • GDP growth projections revised downwards for a number of countries. G20 finance ministers pledge "sustained effort" to restore the world economy to growth. • In March the IMF announces reforms to lending procedures for member countries and with the EU agree to provide a rescue package worth €20 billion to Romania.
April–August 2009	• World stock markets gradually begin to recover after bottoming out in March. • Stringent bank stress tests performed for the largest US banks and results released in May. Large US banks found to have too little capital forced to raise private capital or accept additional support from TARP funds. A number of US banks announce plans to raise private capital by issuing equity, which helps restore market confidence in US banks. • Two of the three major US car makers are taken through an accelerated government supported bankruptcy.	• Revised growth figures for 2008Q4 show GDP fell more than previously thought and GDP continued to contract in 2009Q1, while growth estimates for 2009 are revised downwards again. • The IMF calls for European banks to be subject to stress tests similar to those in the US.
July–September 2009	• Unemployment numbers come out lower than expected and the economic outlook is optimistic. • The decline in GDP growth in many advanced countries begins to slow. According to Ben Bernanke, the US recession is most likely over.	• Debt continues to rise and US Treasury officials suggest that the cap to public borrowing may need to be raised from the current $12.1 trillion. • Despite confidence that the US is nearing an end to the recession, the deficit hits a record $1.4 trillion (08/10/09).

Table A8.1
(*continued*)

	Market events	Policy events
October 2009		• The Socialist party wins elections in Greece. George Papandreou becomes prime minister and soon after announces that the projected deficit for 2009 will be much higher than previously projected.
December 2009	• Greece is downgraded to triple B+ with negative outlook following revelations in October and November of much higher than expected deficits for 2009. S&P changes the outlook of Portugal and Spain to negative.	• Greek budget deficit is revised from 3.7% to ultimately 13.6% of GDP.
January–March 2010	• Spanish government performs a successful 6.9 billion bond issuance.	• Greek government announces multiple austerity plans to increase tax revenue, cut spending, and cut salaries in the public sector. • Portugal announces a privatization plan, tax increases on high income, and limit to public-sector wages.
April–August 2010	• S&P cuts Greece's rating to "junk" on April 27, drives yields to unsustainable levels. • Comments by Merkel about restructuring sovereign debt after bailout agreed led to spike in Greek yields and contagion in Ireland and Portugal, motivating ECB announcement of SMP and EA leaders agreement on EFSF (May 10, 2010)	• Announcement of €110 billion bailout for Greece (May 2).
September–December 2010	• Disagreements between euro area leaders and proposals to restructure sovereign debt (generating contagion to Spain), as well as government resistance to accepting bailout drove up yields in late October/early November. • Yields still rose as discussions of proposals aired to include restructuring/PSI in ESM (ESM agreed on November. 28) rescues.	• Irish government announces bank bailout costs in excess of €30 billion and fiscal deficit of 32% of GDP (Portugal's track Ireland's until then). • Irish government agrees bailout November 21.

(*continued*)

Table A8.1
(*continued*)

	Market events	Policy events
January–June 2011	• ECB raises rates 25 basis points (May 6)	• Portugal requests bailout after contagion drives up yields following Irish bailout. (May 5). Official loan is approved on May 16 at €78 billion. It will be equally split between the EFSF, ESM, and the IMF.
July 2011	• Yields in Greece, Ireland, and Portugal have risen to unprecedented levels, with Spain and Italy's yields rising too, though less. • Moody's slashes Greek credit rating shortly after (July 25), cites PSI as default.	• Second Greek bailout announced, with relatively mild PSI component (21% haircut).
August 2011	• US federal government takes a credit-rating hit, being downgraded by S&P from AAA to AA+. Still, US yield fell by two 2 bp to 2.54% the next day.	
September–October 2011	• Yields spike in response to bailout and Greek PM's referendum proposal (withdrawn).	• Revised second Greek bailout announced, with more financing (€130 billion) and more costly PSI (50% haircut).
December 2011	• After performing stress tests on more than 70 banks, the European Banking Authority says more than 30 banks in 12 countries must come up with a total of €114.7 billion ($153.8 billion) in new capital by next June.	• ECB announces second 25 bp cut (first on November 3) and the LTRO, which provides €1 trillion of 3-year collateralized loans to banks (first half in December 2011, second half in February 2012).
January–March 2012	• Sharp drop in Greek and Portuguese yields, only temporary in the case of Greece as election-related uncertainty and comments by EA leaders that a Greek exit from the EMU would be manageable drove yields back up.	• Even larger second Greek bailout announced February 21 (€174 billion), followed by final agreement on Greek PSI, with more than 50% haircut.
April–June 2012	• Uncertainty about implementation and comments from some euro area leaders after Banking Union announced, suggesting this would not apply to legacy assets, undermine the effort to break sovereign–bank link as Spain's yields keep rising.	• Spain seeks support for bailout of banking sector, without formal bailout program, and two days later euro area leaders announce agreement to create Banking Union and allow the ESM to recapitalize banks directly.

Table A8.1
(*continued*)

	Market events	Policy events
July–September 2012	• Yields for peripheral countries fall, even before the announcement of the details of the mechanism that will be used.	• Draghi states that yields no longer reflect fundamentals, but instead convertibility risk, impeding monetary policy transmission. Draghi states that the ECB is "ready to do whatever it takes" to preserve the EMU and that "it will be enough." • The OMT program announced in September to allow unlimited buying of sovereign bonds by ECB as long as country is applies for some type of program with ESM that comes with conditionality attached and monitored by IMF. • US Fed announces third round of quantitative easing (QE), involving purchasing $85 billion Treasury bonds and mortgage-backed securities per month for the foreseeable future.
October–December 2012	• Yields on Italian sovereign debt rose less than half a percentage point in December following the resignation of Mario Monti, who led a technocratic government for 13 months.	• ESM activated in October. • Official creditors agree to extend maturity of loans and reduce interest rates on loans. Further reduction in Greek debt held by private sector achieved by buying back its debt at prices less than face value. • Negotiations with Cyprus over bailout request continue. • In December, EU finance ministers agree on a key component of a Banking Union, the Single Supervisory Mechanism (SSM) for banks in the euro area, with the ECB assuming supervisory responsibility for large banks by 2014. Agreement proves elusive on other key features of the Banking Union.
January–June 2013	• Despite some short-term gyrations in yields of peripheral countries, overall markets remain subdued. • Ireland issues €5 billion in 10-year bonds. • Global financial markets roiled by statements that US Fed may start tapering QE program in September.	• Cyprus reaches initial bailout agreement with the Troika in late March, but a provision to haircut all bank deposits causes the Parliament to reject the agreement. Revised bailout plan includes haircuts on deposits above €100,000 at the two largest banks and the wind-down of one of the banks. Capital controls are imposed to prevent capital flight from Cyprus that would cause the collapse of the entire financial sector. • The ECB lowers rates on main refinancing operations and marginal lending facilities.
July–September 2013	• Yields on Portuguese debt rise due to resignations of key ministers.	• The ECB introduces a form of "forward guidance"–committing to keep rates low for an extended period–in July. • The US Fed decides to delay the start of QE tapering.

Notes

Asad Zaman provided superb research assistance.

1. See Turrini (2008) for a more in-depth analysis of the procyclical stance of euro area fiscal policies in economic good times, driven mainly by expenditure developments.

2. Price and Dang (2011) show how asset price movements can be incorporated into cyclically adjusted balances (CABs) and show that the effect was particularly pronounced for Spain and Ireland.

3. The estimates in Price and Dang (2011) indicate that, as a share of GDP, Finland's surplus and Greece's deficit were even farther apart in 2007 when adjusted for the cycle and corrected for asset prices rather than in headline terms.

4. This complexity reflects, among other factors, the interpretation of the boundaries of general government, consolidation issues, and the use of accrual accounting.

5. "Overdraft facilities or any other type of credit facility with the European Central Bank or with the central banks of the Member States (hereinafter referred to as 'national central banks') in favor of Union institutions, bodies, offices or agencies, central governments, regional, local or other public authorities, other bodies governed by public law, or public undertakings of Member States shall be prohibited, as shall the purchase directly from them by the European Central Bank or national central banks of debt instruments" (Article 123, TFEU).

6. "The Union shall not be liable for or assume the commitments of central governments, regional, local or other public authorities, other bodies governed by public law, or public undertakings of any Member State, without prejudice to mutual financial guarantees for the joint execution of a specific project. A Member State shall not be liable for or assume the commitments of central governments, regional, local or other public authorities, other bodies governed by public law, or public undertakings of another Member State, without prejudice to mutual financial guarantees for the joint execution of a specific project"(Article 125, TFEU).

7. Larger automatic stabilizers and countercyclical fiscal rules could help mitigate the risk that implementation lags significantly weaken the effectiveness of fiscal stimulus (Blanchard et al. 2010; Kumhof and Laxton 2009; Baunsgaard and Symansky 2009).

8. The EFSF was agreed by the 27 member states of the European Union with the objective of preserving financial stability in Europe by providing financial assistance to eurozone states in economic difficulty, selected interventions in primary and secondary debt markets, and recapitalizations of financial institutions through loans to governments. The EFSF is backed by guarantee commitments from the eurozone member states for a total of €780 billion and has a lending capacity of €440 billion.

9. For an analysis of the mechanisms that can create the conditions for self-fulfilling debt runs in a monetary union, see De Grauwe (2012).

10. In program countries (Greece, Ireland, Portugal, and Cyprus) the pace and size of fiscal consolidation efforts were determined largely by financing constraints.

11. See Baum and others (2012), Blanchard and Leigh (2013), and Eyraud and Weber (2013).

References

Abbas, S. Ali. 2012. Medium-term fiscal consolidation in Ireland: Growth-friendly, targeted, sustainable. Ireland: Selected Issues. Country report 12/265. IMF, Washington, DC.

Arslanap, Serkan, and Takahiro Tsuda. 2012. Tracking global demand for advanced economy sovereign debt. Working paper 12/284. IMF, Washington, DC.

Baum, Anja, Marcos Poplawski-Ribeiro, and Anke Weber. 2012. Fiscal multipliers and the state of the economy. Working paper 12/286. IMF, Washington, DC.

Baunsgaard, Thomas, and Steven Symansky. 2009. Automatic fiscal stabilizers. Staff position note 2009/23. IMF, Washington, DC.

Blanchard, Olivier, Giovanni Dell'Ariccia, and Paolo Mauro. 2010. Rethinking macroeconomic policy. Staff position note 2010/03. IMF, Washington, DC.

Blanchard, Olivier, and Daniel Leigh. 2013. Growth forecast errors and fiscal multipliers. Working paper 13/01. IMF, Washington, DC.

Buiter, Willem, and Anne Sibert. 2005. How the eurosystem's treatment of collateral in its open market operations weakens fiscal discipline in the eurozone (and what to do about it). Downloadable from http://willembuiter.com.

Cottarelli, Carlo, and Laura Jaramillo. 2012. Walking hand in hand: Fiscal policy and growth in advanced economies. Working paper 12/137. IMF, Washington, DC.

Cecchetti, Stephen, Robert McCauley, and Patrick McGuire. 2012. Interpreting Target 2 balances. Working paper 393. BIS, Basel.

De Grauwe, Paul. 2012. The governance of a fragile eurozone. *Australian Economic Review* 45 (3): 255–68.

ECB, 2011. Ensuring fiscal sustainability in the euro area. *ECB Monthly Bulletin* (April): 61–77.

Eyraud, Luc, and Anke Weber. 2013. The challenge of debt reduction during fiscal consolidation. Working paper 13/67. IMF, Washington, DC.

International Monetary Fund. 2008. Greece: 2007 Article IV consultation—Staff report. IMF Country report 08/148. IMF, Washington, DC.

Kumhof, Michael, and Douglas Laxton. 2009. Simple, implementable fiscal policy rules. Working paper 09/76. IMF, Washington, DC.

Larch, Martin, Paul van den Noord, and Lars Jonung. 2010. The stability and growth pact: Lessons from the Great Recession. European economy economic paper 429. European Commission, Brussels.

Lemgruber, Andrea, and Mauricio Soto. 2013. Fiscal consolidation in Portugal: Designing growth-friendly and sustainable fiscal reforms. Portugal: Selected issues paper. Country report 13/19. IMF, Washington, DC.

Martinez-Mongay, Carlos, Luis-Angel Maza Lasierra, and Javier Yaniz Igal. 2007. Asset booms and tax receipts: The case of Spain, 1995–2006. European economy economic paper 293. European Commission, Brussels.

Mody, Ashoka, and Damiano Sandri. 2011. The eurozone crisis: How banks and sovereigns came to be joined at the hip. Working paper 11/269. IMF, Washington, DC.

Price, Robert, and Thai-Thanh Dang. 2011. Adjusting fiscal balances for asset price cycles. Working papers 868. OECD Economics Department, Paris.

Sinn, Hans-Werner, and Timo Wollmershäuser. 2012. Target loans, current account balances and capital flows: The ECB's rescue facility. *International Tax and Public Finance* 19 (4): 468–508.

Turrini, Alessandro. 2008. Fiscal policy and the cycle in the euro area: The role of government revenue and expenditure. European economy economic paper 323. European Commission, Brussels.

9

Has Taxation Contributed to the Crisis?

John Norregaard, Aqib Aslam, Dora Benedek, and Thornton Matheson

9.1 Introduction

A broad consensus has emerged on the view that tax policy was not a direct cause of the financial meltdown during 2008.[1] Yet tax distortions—by providing incentives for higher leverage, risk taking, and the use of tax arbitrage through complicated financial instruments—may well have exacerbated its severity and prolonged its duration.[2] Recently, implemented and planned policy initiatives also point to the fact that tax policy reform is an essential part of the broader macroeconomic strategy for addressing the adverse consequences of the crisis in several countries.

This chapter surveys and discusses the different, and often very complex, channels through which current tax policy is believed to have distorted the savings and financing behavior of individuals and businesses in the run-up to the recent financial crisis. Most such channels have been long recognized, but few countries have actively sought to address them in a sustained and effective manner. While a survey of this nature is primarily backward-looking, the discussion here acknowledges the key role for tax policy in the aftermath of a crisis—to restore and maintain fiscal sustainability. The chapter therefore presents and discusses tax policy options for achieving the dual objectives of mitigating or eliminating distortions, particularly those that encourage excessive leverage—thus making tax structures more conducive to growth—and mobilizing additional revenue. Meeting both objectives is a prerequisite for effectively returning to fiscal sustainability over the medium term. Given the central role of the financial sector in the recent crisis, a section is devoted to the possible adoption of financial taxes on a broader international scale. This area is currently high on most policy agendas and warrants special attention including from the point of view of preventing future financial crises.

In discussing these issues, the chapter synthesizes a large body of recent analytical work carried out within the IMF's Fiscal Affairs Department,[3] supplemented where relevant with work by the EC, OECD, other institutions, and academe. It also highlights shortcomings in our current understanding of the role of tax policy in generating vulnerabilities—or addressing them—in the broader financial markets, and thus provides some guidance concerning potential areas where future research could generate a high return.

Section 9.2 reviews the key channels through which tax distortions are believed to have contributed to excessive leverage and other financial market problems that surfaced during the crisis, and policy measures available to remedy these distortions. Section 9.3 outlines the key tax policy options open to governments to reorient their tax systems toward growth and improved revenue-raising, while mitigating risks of future crises. In this regard, taxation of the financial sector is central, and is discussed in section 9.4. Section 9.5 concludes.

9.2 Key Channels of Tax Distortions

9.2.1 Debt Bias in Corporate Finance

Income tax systems affect corporate financing decisions as they typically treat debt and equity financing in different ways.[4] While interest payments are usually deductible from the corporate income tax (CIT) base, returns on equity—such as dividends paid to shareholders or capital gains on shares—are not. This asymmetry introduces a bias toward debt financing by providing an incentive for firms to issue debt up to the point where tax savings are offset by an increased cost of capital from a higher risk of default. Overborrowing by banks in turn implies further distortions to the financial sector.

Personal income taxes (PIT) on interest, dividends, and capital gains may also influence the choice between debt and equity financing. Taxing interest income at the personal level reduces the debt bias at the corporate level. Financing by retained earnings raises share prices, which may trigger capital gains tax (CGT) at the personal level; high CGT rates therefore discourage this type of financing. Dividend taxation, however, increases the cost of financing by new equity. Nevertheless, with mobile capital the impact of PIT may be unclear and most analyses focus only on CIT.

Table 9.1 shows the required before-tax return on an investment that a company needs to earn in order to meet the after-tax return required by investors. Cost of capital is presented for the three alternative financing sources—retained earnings, new equity, and debt—in the United States, Japan, and EU27 (unweighted average and range of lowest and highest in the group) in 2007. The cost of capital for equity differs for PIT-taxed and PIT-exempt investors and reflects differing tax consequences of the assumed alternative of investing in risk free debt, which is subject to PIT on interest.

Keen et al. (2010) show that the tax advantage to debt finance has declined since 1990, in line with a decreasing trend of the CIT rate. As De Mooij (2011) points out,

Table 9.1
Cost of capital for alternative sources of finance

	PIT-exempt investor			PIT-taxed investor at top rate		
	Retained earnings	New equity	Debt	Retained earnings	New equity	Debt
United States	9.2	9.2	4.8	5.8	6.5	4.9
Japan	10.4	10.4	5.6	9.5	15.4	5.6
EU-27 average[a]	6.8	6.9	4.6	5.6	6.4	4.7
<range>	<5.0; 9.0>	<5.6; 9.0>	<3.9; 5.3>	<3.5; 6.9>	<3.0; 9.3>	<4.0; 5.6>

Source: De Mooij (2011)
Note: The after-tax return is assumed to be 5 percent and inflation 2 percent. The numbers are unweighted averages of calculations for five different assets featuring different depreciation rates: intangibles, buildings, machinery, financial assets, and inventories. Data refer to 2007.
a. Unweighted average.

several countries have made efforts to limit this bias by regulation and introduced rules in recent years that do not allow the deduction of interest payments over a certain threshold of the debt–equity ratio (thin capitalization rules).

However, divergence of the CIT rates across countries also increased over the last decades, which has strengthened the incentive of multinationals to shift debt into high-tax countries. The spread of leveraged buyouts has contributed to high levels of indebtedness, further eroding CIT receipts (see box 9.1 for further discussion).

High levels of leverage make firms more vulnerable to economic shocks and increase the probability of bankruptcy. Therefore, while leverage in itself is not necessarily a problem, in times of financial distress excessive debt levels—of financial as well as nonfinancial companies—can contribute to escalating the crisis by raising the probability of default. While exact welfare costs of excessive debt financing are difficult to quantify, the recent crisis has demonstrated that they can be substantial.

9.2.2 Addressing the Debt Bias[5]

There are no compelling economic arguments for treating debt more favorably than equity for tax purposes.[6] A broadly accepted benchmark is tax *neutrality* according to which tax provisions should be designed not to impact corporate financing decisions. Along this line of thinking, tax-induced distortions of corporate financing structures will ultimately generate efficiency losses. Hence an argument in favor of the present unequal treatment of debt and equity would be valid only in the case where clearly identified externalities would rationalize the use of less equity and more debt finance. Existing externalities, however, seem if anything tilted in the opposite direction: when corporations borrow, they are likely to internalize expected bankruptcy costs that they themselves would incur but not the impact of their own failure on others—a negative externality that in principle could be corrected by a *tax penalty* on borrowing. An externality that is particularly large for systemically important financial institutions.[7] Other government policies could conceivably exacerbate the effect of interest deductibility such as guarantees on deposits or corporate debt.[8]

While hard to quantify accurately, existing evidence does seem to support the notion that high leverage—for example, as measured by high *debt–equity ratios*—is associated with greater output losses in post-crisis periods.[9] Although this may provide further support to the idea of a penalty on debt, setting the appropriate penalty level under existing circumstances would be fraught with difficulties—leaving a move toward neutrality as a more pragmatic and realistic policy objective.[10]

Elimination of the debt bias could conceptually be realized through two different routes, both of which have been tried (in some form) in practice: first, the present favorable tax treatment of interest could be curtailed or eliminated, thus treating interest for tax purposes more like dividends; and second, keeping full interest deductibility as it is now but introducing a notional deduction from taxable profits for return to equity, thus basically treating dividends as interest.

Limiting or eliminating full deductibility of interest can be implemented in different fashions:

• Many countries apply already *thin capitalization* or *earnings stripping provisions* that, respectively, deny deductibility for (excess) interest payments in case the debt–equity ratio exceeds a certain level (e.g., 3:1), or for interest payments exceeding a certain limit measured as a percentage of before-tax profits. While fairly straightforward to administer, such "one-size fits all" limitations do not always take account of borrowing needs and capacities of individual companies.

• A particular model, originally developed by the US Treasury, the *comprehensive business income tax* (CBIT),[11] would disallow interest deductibility altogether (but eliminate its taxation at the investor level), but has not been adopted by any country so far.

• *Real-base cash-flow corporate income taxes* allow—in different forms—a full and immediate deduction for investment while disallowing a deduction for interest. This type of corporate taxation, which would tax only excess profits, imposes a zero marginal tax rate on new investment, and does not distort financing decisions. It has so far been adopted only in East Timor (in 2008) and, as a minimum CIT, in Mexico.

Many governments have been trying, also recently, to better counter the abuses that interest deductibility may invite, while at the same time attempting to ensure that their countries remain attractive destinations for multinational corporations to

Box 9.1
Recent restrictions on interest deductions[12]

The behavior of private equity funds with respect to buying domestic companies, frequently using so-called debt push-down, was the impetus for the Dutch and Danish interest deduction reforms.[13] In *Denmark*, new rules came into force in July 2007 with the objective of preventing future use of leveraged acquisitions financing structures: interest deductions above a threshold were capped as a percentage of operating assets, and with a second cap set at 80 percent of before-tax earnings. In the *Netherlands*, interest deduction restrictions aimed specifically at takeovers of Dutch companies came into effect on January 1, 2013, covering both related-party and third-party debt. The interest deduction will be limited to the filing group's profits after deduction of the target's profit, with some further restrictions.

New strict interest deductibility rules—broader in their applicability than just to acquisitions—came into force in *Germany* in 2008 aimed at stimulating the use of equity capital (and prompted by a European Court of Justice ruling that resident and nonresident companies be treated equally in this respect). They would deny deductibility of interest on *all* (not just intra-group) debt in excess of 30 percent of income before consideration of interest payable (with exemptions for smaller enterprises and specific circumstances), but interest expenses denied can be carried forward indefinitely.

Italy subsequently introduced provisions similar to the new German rules, and *France* is considering doing so, possibly phasing-in the cap for interest deductions starting at 80 percent of earnings with a final target of 30 percent. Furthermore the French Finance Law 2012 extended present thin capitalization rules by introducing limits on interest rates and debt–equity ratios for certain acquisition debt (applied on a separate entity basis). In the same vein, *Ireland's* Finance Act 2011 disallowed deduction of debt for acquisitions by a related-party as well as some intra-group lending (Ireland has no thin capitalization rules). In *Sweden*—having one of the most "liberal" interest deduction regimes with no thin capitalization or debt–equity rules—a proposal for new interest deduction restrictions is expected in November 2013.

invest in, or at least channels through which to route income. While policy initiatives in this domain are related to interest deductibility, they also typically address more specific individual country concerns as illustrated by the examples in box 9.1.

An alternative option, as noted, is to maintain deductibility of interest but allow a notional deduction for the "normal" return to equity finance, also called an *allowance for corporate equity* (or ACE).[14] A CIT in the form of an ACE taxes only profits in excess of the required rate of return of investors and is therefore fully neutral.[15] A number of countries have adopted in recent years different versions of the ACE,[16] mostly with some positive experience, although its design and effects are not completely unproblematic.

By eliminating the debt bias at corporate level (and thereby moving the CIT closer to a tax on economic profits), introduction of an ACE would be expected to lead to reduced debt–equity ratios—a presumption that is, indeed, supported by some empirical evidence.[17] Furthermore, specifically relating to banks,[18] an ACE could provide an incentive for accumulating additional capital reserves and thus help recapitalize banks.

There are two key difficulties associated with the introduction of an ACE. First, a choice must be made regarding the notional "normal" rate of return to equity, with strong arguments, including that of simplicity, favoring a single, uniform proxy for a risk-free rate of return (e.g., the interest on long-term government bonds).[19] Second, and perhaps more important under present circumstances, introducing an ACE implies a decline in CIT revenue—an effect that has been estimated to be potentially quite significant;[20] and with considerations of tax competition constraining the scope for recuperating any loss through (unilateral) CIT rate increases. This adverse revenue effect could, however, be mitigated by two important second-order effects.[21] Removal of the debt bias will reduce the subsidy to debt finance, and to the extent that the incidence of the CIT falls on labor,[22] eliminating the tax on the normal rate of return to equity should increase labor income. The additional wages may be taxed directly in order to compensate for the loss in CIT revenue while still leaving labor better off.[23] Moreover the immediate revenue impact of an ACE could be mitigated by providing relief only for equity generated after some initial date.

9.2.3 Complexity, Tax Havens, and Risk Taking

Besides corporate finance, taxation of other instruments potentially contributed importantly to the crisis. This subsection considers specific tax attributes that may have contributed to exacerbating risk taking and the opacity of financial arrangements, with four features being of particular interest.

Innovative financial instruments, the design and use of which are in some cases driven by tax considerations as well as the primary aim for an improved (re)allocation of risks. Examples include a spectrum of derivatives such as swaps and securitized financial instruments. Securitization—or the pooling of loans into an investment vehicle and then selling securities (e.g., mortgage-backed securities (MBS)) backed by the repayments of these loans—allows investors to offset capital losses from high risk investment against ordinary income, while also allowing banks to share part of this tax advantage through a lower cost of borrowing.[24] A more uniform tax treatment of capital income would appear to be the appropriate policy response to address this issue involving, inter alia, levying CGT on an accrual rather than a realization basis.

The prevalence of low-tax jurisdictions, including tax havens, that tax in particular mobile capital income at low rates, could also have encouraged excessive leverage and thus contributed to the crisis, by creating incentives for avoidance and evasion schemes. Profit-shifting operations of this nature could also be affected through other devices such as transfer pricing and location decisions for corporate headquarters. Companies can also take advantage of double-tax treaties providing favorable tax rates, through low-tax jurisdictions. Measures to address these issues would include often technically complex and politically sensitive full information exchange agreements[25] and, even more challenging and unprecedented, a much stronger tax cooperation to reduce or eliminate the potential for tax arbitrage of this nature.[26]

A long-known effect of taxation is that it may lead to *higher investment in risky assets*[27]—an effect that is discouraged if loss offset is imperfect, as is the case in most countries. Such asymmetries in the treatment of losses could create arbitrage opportunities and may also hamper corporate restructuring in case a company acquiring a loss-making company is denied the use of the loss for tax purposes. The appropriate policy response to counter the effect of taxation in the form of *higher investment in risky assets* is in principle straightforward. While potentially costly in (immediate) revenue terms, a more "liberal" tax treatment of losses would be the right policy response, including facilitating corporate restructuring for which the potential revenue losses should be balanced against the costs of corporate failures that may follow if acquisitions are not forthcoming because of restrictive loss provisions.[28]

High executive compensation, in part performance related (bonuses and stock options), has attracted considerable attention in the wake of the crisis, in part because the structure of compensation may well have induced higher risk taking (particularly the prevalence of stock options). Generally, however, tax reliefs appear to have been fairly limited in most countries relative to the tax treatment of the salary component, with some exceptions.[29] High executive compensation, with the potential for higher risk taking (particularly the prevalence of stock options) that it entails, should be addressed by not providing any special tax reliefs for executive pay packages relative to the tax treatment of the salary component.[30]

A central question regarding the role that tax measures should be accorded in addressing risk taking and excess leverage—particularly as it relates to the role of financial institutions—is the appropriate balance between financial regulation versus financial taxation, a question to which there are no easy answers and one that clearly deserves further research.

9.2.4 The Tax Treatment of Housing

Most accounts of the 2008 financial crisis present the dynamics of the US housing market and the related financial structure as a key trigger of the crisis (e.g., Hemmelgarn et al. 2011). Tax provisions, in addition to loosening monetary policies in the wake of the dot-com bubble and lax regulatory provisions, contributed to a housing bubble that ended in a credit crunch. Between 2001 and 2005 the number of houses sold in the United States increased by 41.3 percent, the average price rose by 39.3 percent, and the proportion of subprime mortgages soared from 7.2 to over 20 percent

(Hemmelgarn and Nicodème 2010). While the number of transactions sharply decreased after 2005, housing prices continued to increase. Higher volatility, together with the formation of expectations for continued increases in housing prices, can detach prices from fundamentals and generate a housing bubble.

Favorable tax treatment of homeownership is likely to be reflected in house prices. In the short term, when the physical stock of housing is virtually fixed, most taxes will be fully captured by housing prices. For example, a reduction in the capital gains tax on housing is expected to increase house prices. In the longer term, supply will adjust to the new tax rules, but important effects can remain. Furthermore distortions affecting one part of the market more directly may induce substitution effects, leading to further distortions in other segments. Tax effects can also substantially affect the user cost of housing and subsequently demand. In the United States, for example, mortgage interest deductibility and other tax features on average provide a tax reduction equivalent to around 19 percent of the user cost, the difference greater for high-income households (Poterba and Sinai 2008).

While governments might have socially motivated preferences for promoting home ownership, from an economic point of view the expected cost of owning a house in equilibrium should be equal to the cost of renting it. Therefore the tax system should seek neutrality in the owner/renting dimension. This means full taxation of imputed rents and capital gains on housing, and deductibility of mortgage interest payments. Table 9.2 summarizes tax treatments for a subset of European countries and the United States.

Table 9.2
Taxation of owner-occupied houses in Europe and the United States

	Taxation of imputed rents	Mortgage interest tax relief	Capital gains tax
Belgium	Yes	Tax deductibility with limit	No
France	No	Tax credit for the first 5 years with a limit	No
Germany	No	No	No
Ireland	No	Tax credit for the first 7 years with a limit	No
Italy	No	Tax credit with a limit	No
Netherlands	Yes	Tax deductibility without limit	No
Spain	No	Tax credit with a limit on the amount of housing costs	No
United Kingdom	No	No	No
United States	No	Tax deductibility with a limit on the amount of mortgage principal ($1 million)	No (if CG<$500,000)

Source: Hemmelgarn et al. (2011)

In practice, this neutrality of tax treatment is hardly ever present. In most countries imputed rents and capital gains on primary residences are untaxed. Few countries tax imputed rents (e.g., Belgium and the Netherlands; in Italy, while imputed rent is taxable, an offsetting deduction is provided) and some countries tax capital gains on owner-occupied housing (e.g., Republic of Korea, not included in table 9.2), but usually under favorable provisions (e.g., a high threshold or low rate). Tax relief for mortgage interest costs is given in all countries except Germany and the United Kingdom. In the Netherlands, Belgium, and the United States interest expense is deductible from the tax base, so the tax advantage depends on the marginal tax rate of the owner. In the other countries the tax relief mainly takes the form of a tax credit (for a detailed discussion of country examples, see Hemmelgarn et al. 2011). Distortions make investment in housing more favorable than in other assets. This generates a bias toward ownership over renting, and also provides incentives for greater leverage than under a neutral tax system.

Attempts to scale back generous tax provisions for home ownership are generally met with fierce political opposition, in part because a neutral tax treatment would—fully or partly—be capitalized in property prices resulting in a one-off capital loss for present owners. The United Kingdom, however, provides a good example of tapering off these tax advantages gradually. An alternative policy route that could achieve broadly similar objectives would be to strengthen recurrent property taxation based on property market values. These taxes are considered less distortionary than other taxes (including property transfer taxes) with an incidence that rests mainly on the well-off.[31]

A more neutral tax treatment of housing markets would improve efficiency and help avoid macroeconomic imbalances, but it could also in the short term result in reduced house prices and possibly construction activity, and so should be carefully designed and sequenced. Potential reform measures in this area that should be coordinated with broader tax reform efforts include in particular the following:

- Removal of *transaction taxes* could be a shorter term measure with a number of positive effects: it would remove an impediment to efficient trading, increase prices, potentially speed up clearance of any excess supply, support labor mobility, and remove an incentive for collusion between buyers and sellers to under-declare sales prices. Transaction taxes are, however, easy to collect and a potential source of buoyant revenue, and they have been claimed to counter housing price volatility although this effect has not yet been validated.

- Strengthening *recurrent property taxes*, while efficient in its own right, could also help offset the revenue losses from phasing out transfer taxes. These taxes are appealing, since they serve in part as user charges reflecting the location-specific value of local public goods, and are therefore neutral with regard to saving and financing decisions of individuals and businesses.

- *Taxing imputed rent as well as capital gains* would remove substantial sources of distortions in the housing market, but strong political opposition persists in many places.
- If the exemption of imputed rent is maintained, *phasing out mortgage interest relief* should be implemented, as was done in the United Kingdom.
- *Taxing first sales of residences under the VAT* (already in place in some countries) would remove distortions of consumption decisions and could also serve as a proxy for income taxation of imputed rent.

9.3 Tax Policies for Fiscal Consolidation and Growth

Tax policy will play a central role in addressing the adverse consequences of the crisis. Two recent developments illustrate this point: first, the debate on ways to tax financial institutions and financial transactions to generate revenue and correct for distortions, is ongoing and intense, as clearly reflected in section 9.4; and second, efforts by many countries to strengthen taxation in order to bring down budgetary deficits, for example, by increasing VAT rates and broadening the VAT base in the wake of the crisis.[32] The primary means for regaining fiscal sustainability in many countries will be to secure economic growth in tandem with continued deficit reductions. The two subsections that follow discuss different but interrelated aspects of the role that tax policy may play in achieving these objectives.

9.3.1 Developing Efficient and Growth-Friendly Tax Structures

Aside from eliminating the possible distortions and incentives inherent in most current tax systems as discussed in section 9.2, it is useful to revisit more generally those elements of a tax system that have the strongest impact on economic growth. The link between taxation and economic growth is, however, both controversial and complex. The overall burden of taxation, as well as the way different taxes are designed and combined (the "tax structure"), can have a number of implications for both the level and growth rate of GDP per capita.

Growth theory provides fairly strong yet somehow conflicting predictions about the effects of taxation on growth and against this opaque theoretical backdrop, the empirical evidence on the strength and direction of tax effects on growth is not much clearer.[33] The traditional theoretical framework for analyzing tax policy has been the "neoclassical" growth model, and subsequently models of "endogenous growth." The former provide only external factors as the primary driver of long-run growth, while the latter allow for certain key characteristics of the technology process assumed for producing goods to generate long-run growth automatically, for example, through spillovers and increasing returns to scale. Endogenous growth models have been particularly important, since modeling the processes by which growth is generated has allowed the effects of taxation upon individual decision-making to be traced. As a result these models have provided the basis of key results in optimal taxation, for example, that capital income should be taxed at a zero rate (Lucas 1990). However, if the results from optimal taxation are accepted as ideal, then actual tax systems are typically far from what optimal policy prescribes. The possibility for tax reform to raise the rate of growth should therefore exist even once the distortions discussed earlier have been corrected.[34]

In view of the relatively limited guidance that growth theory offers for operational policy, the question is what *empirical evidence* can be brought to bear on policy formulation. Most empirical studies focus, however, on advanced economies with ambiguous results, much like the theory.[35] The preference within the empirical literature has been for "tax regressions" which suffer the same pitfalls as the ubiquitous "Barro growth regressions" upon which they are based.[36] Nevertheless, within the context of cross-country growth regressions, the tax regression literature has raised its own set of issues, leading to various different avenues of research.

The measure used to represent tax rates is an important issue in empirical work. The implication of standard microeconomic theory is that the marginal tax rate is more relevant to an individual's decision-making than the average tax rate, since optimal choices are determined at the margin.[37] Therefore using the average tax rate to understand growth does not capture this distortionary feature of taxation. However, obtaining an estimate for marginal tax rates is more complex than estimating average tax rates. Easterly and Rebelo (1993) review growth regressions using 13 different measures for marginal tax rates, yielding coefficients that are not significant save for one negative significant coefficient on the tax rate. This suggests that the effects of marginal tax rates on growth are inconclusive. The public finance literature remains divided.[38]

The OECD (2010) examined more generally taxes and their impact on the primary drivers of growth, such as employment, total factor productivity, and investment, ranking taxes on the basis of their distortionary effects on per capita GDP. Broadly, the report concluded that broad-based consumption taxes and property taxes appear to be—as theory would suggest (since they do not reduce the return to saving and investment)—less harmful to growth than income taxes.[39]

Corporate income taxes are considered the most harmful for growth, by discouraging investment in capital and productivity improvements, both of which are important for growth. In particular, Lee and Gordon (2005) identify entrepreneurial activity as a major driver of growth and investigate the effects of the top marginal personal and corporate income tax rates on growth. They show that lower corporate income taxes, relative to personal taxes, can encourage risk taking by providing an incentive to incorporate, whereas a progressive tax schedules can discourage risk taking, harming growth prospects. However, excessive risk taking has been cited as one of the key distortions in the run-up to the recent crisis (see section 9.2 on key channels of tax distortions), so that this aspect of the role of the corporate income taxes needs to be re-examined.

Broadly consistent with OECD's work on the tax structure, some research has suggested that the tax mix—the balance between direct and indirect taxation—is important in driving growth. Empirical results of Martinez-Vazquez, Vulovic, and Liu (2010) suggest that a higher ratio of direct taxes to indirect taxes is harmful to growth in developed economies (thus supporting the OECD results), but the results are not significant for developing countries.[40]

Governments find themselves dealing increasingly with relatively more mobile tax bases. Tax policy can therefore have implications for growth due to international competitiveness, for example, in the case of fiscal devaluation.[41] Though tax is clearly not the only factor feeding in to where a company determines the location of its operations, corporate income taxes are key for some countries as a means of securing capital and business.

When thinking of fiscal consolidation, studies have shown different impacts of growth to changes in taxes and/or expenditure. Taking the government's fiscal stance as given, Alesina and Ardagna (2010) find that fiscal stimuli based upon tax cuts are more likely to increase growth than those based upon spending increases. However, the IMF (2010b) found that episodes of consolidation are clearly contractionary: a fiscal consolidation equivalent to 1 percent of GDP leads on average to a 0.5 percent decline in GDP after two years, and to an increase of 0.3 percent in the unemployment rate.[42]

Ultimately the issue of a lack of structural modeling in growth regressions comes back to haunt tax regressions. Simultaneity and reverse causality can cause bias in the estimated coefficients. For example, in the standard regressions of growth (left-hand side) on the tax ratio (right-hand side), theory and experience provide convincing arguments that causality can run in the opposite direction; countries that grow rapidly tend to experience rapid growth in tax collection, as well as government spending (another possible right-hand side variable).

The growth effects of tax policy are wide-ranging and—perhaps with the exception of the proposed ranking order of different taxes with respect to their growth effect—broadly inconclusive. Despite this, there remains an entrenched belief that taxes must be damaging for growth and that the evidence will eventually confirm this fact. What is clear is that tax policy cannot operate in a vacuum, given its obvious interaction with compliance, administration, and politics. Any strategy for consolidation will require an understanding of the nature of taxes available and their potential for mobilizing revenue with the least impact on efficiency and growth—an issue to which we turn next.

9.3.2 Options for Mobilizing Revenue[43]

It is important to gauge which instruments are best placed to help mobilize revenues for the purposes of reducing fiscal deficits. The means for raising revenues should ideally adhere to some broad principles of sound tax policies that in addition to addressing the distortions discussed above would include the following:

- A fair distribution of the tax burden is essential, not least because equity concerns have increased in recent years as inequality within countries has grown but also owing to the risks of avoidance in countries with weak compliance structures.

- Strengthening of internationally coordinated tax setting is also required since lack of coordination can lead to collectively inefficient outcomes and lower revenue collection given the mobility of capital, goods, and labor.[44] In its absence, the case for higher reliance on taxing relatively immobile bases, in particular consumption, real estate and natural resources, is further strengthened.

- Finally, alongside international collaboration, enhanced simplicity of tax systems is essential to strengthen compliance and tax administrations.

Raising those taxes with the lowest marginal cost of public funds (MCPF) is the natural choice for raising revenue.[45] There is no consensus on the precise MCPFs of alternative tax instruments, but there is nevertheless, broad consensus on those taxes that could be further exploited in the move toward fiscal consolidation, such as consumption-based taxes over income taxes, as discussed earlier.

The *VAT* is one of the most important taxes across almost all G20 and emerging countries. However, exemptions and excessive rate differentiation continue to compromise its effectiveness and implementation and there remains substantial scope for improving its revenue performance in almost all countries in which it has been deployed, even without increasing the standard rate. In general, the scope for administrative improvement in the VAT is especially large in emerging countries, while that for policy improvement (unifying rates and removing exemptions) is greater in advanced countries.[46]

Excises are also relatively underexploited in many advanced economies. And they can represent an important means of raising revenues in many countries in a period of consolidation. Excise receipts are lower in the emerging G20, where the arguments for cigarette taxation, in particular, may be especially strong. In advanced economies, their yield is in trend decline reflecting not just changing consumption patterns but also falling real tax rates. Policy makers have moderated rate increases partly for fear of triggering excessive cross-border shopping and smuggling. In addition, the low level of fuel taxation in some advanced countries means that the potential revenue gains from more efficient tax levels, as well as excise types (e.g., congestion charges), are substantial.[47]

In developing countries, consumption taxes generally present much greater opportunities for revenue mobilization relative to other taxes, notably trade taxes on which low income countries (LICs) are particularly dependent. The purpose of replacing trade taxes with domestic consumption taxes is principally to improve macroeconomic stability and to introduce the benefits of free trade to developing economies without jeopardizing competitiveness.

Environmental taxes fall within the same sphere as excises. While the primary role of such taxes may not be revenue mobilization, but the correction of negative externalities, the use of environmentally related taxation and emission trading systems is growing in the OECD. An expanding number of jurisdictions are using taxes and charges in areas like waste disposal and on specific pollutants. Moreover governments are making their existing environmental taxes more efficient. The issue, however, is that the tax base is typically narrow and so not much revenue (with a few exceptions) is mobilized. Tax rates can also be low but the potential for revenue particularly from carbon taxes and emissions trading schemes is large over the medium term.[48]

Property taxes remain a promising source of increased revenue for some countries, but there can be many practical obstacles.[49] Efficiency and fairness are strong arguments for the use of property taxes: they are relatively benign for growth, as discussed above; they raise few issues of international coordination; and while their incidence is still not fully understood, they fall disproportionately on the wealthy. Administrative complexities and costs (including the development of efficient cadastre and valuation mechanisms) limit their use, as do unpopularity due to their high visibility. However, significant progress has been made in recent years in developing a range of administrative arrangements that allow stronger reliance on property taxation even in middle- and low-income countries.[50] Assigning property taxes predominantly to lower levels of government may pose challenges for increased revenue-raising. This, though, is another area with clear potential for significant and relatively efficient medium-term revenue enhancement in several countries.[51]

Concerning *direct taxes*, corporate income taxes remain one of the largest sources of revenue (particularly in developing countries) and a natural candidate for reform in any fiscal consolidation as the business environment deteriorates. However, the strength of CIT revenue particularly in developed countries also reflected a large contribution from the financial sector that has now shrunk substantially, and could be further compressed by regulatory reform. While there remains scope for base-broadening in many countries, potential revenue gains from this seem fairly modest.

In addition, out of all of the taxes, the *corporate income tax* is relatively more hostage to trade-offs: a sound corporate income tax needs to encourage an appropriate amount of risk taking and innovation, but also raise sufficient revenues, while not being uncompetitive relative to rates elsewhere. The corporate income tax also serves as a backstop to PIT and remains a relatively efficient tax on economic rents. However, given the ease with which profits can be shifted to low-tax jurisdictions, it can play this role fully only if policies are coordinated across countries.

Personal income taxes are generally considered key to the pursuit of equity in the tax system, though the effectiveness of this is tempered by its incentive effects on both real activity, compliance, and labor and capital mobility. There is a significant scope in some countries, however, for base-broadening and simplification, which could raise substantial revenue. And in those countries that are heavily reliant on the personal income tax and in need of large fiscal adjustment, there may be little choice but to raise intermediate marginal rates in the personal income tax schedule. Furthermore countries are increasingly looking to taxpayers at the top of the wealth or income scale who make a significant economic contribution to society and account for a large part of total income tax. Targeting this segment through wealth taxes is an increasingly popular measure as part of consolidation.

9.4 Financial Sector Taxation

The 2008 financial crisis and its aftermath have caused policy makers to scrutinize not only financial sector regulation but taxation as well. New financial sector taxes could be designed to correct existing distortions either in tax codes, such as the CIT debt bias, or in financial markets, such as the "too big to fail" externality. Also the explosive growth in financial sector profits and compensation since the 1980s suggests that the sector could provide a fair and efficient source of revenue.[52] This section reviews the major tax instruments proposed since the crisis to raise revenue and/or improve incentives in the financial industry.

9.4.1 Bank Levies

The most common form of new financial sector tax enacted since the 2008 crisis has been a charge on bank balance sheet leverage.[53] Twelve countries have thus far introduced such levies, predominantly in Europe, where the taxes raise an average of 0.2 percent of GDP.[54] In addition to counteracting the debt bias introduced by the CIT, bank levies can help internalize the social cost of bank failure, which likely exceeds the private cost to the bank's owners and directors, particularly for larger, systemically important financial institutions (SIFIs). They also help correct the lower borrowing costs that markets extend to the largest SIFIs owing to their implicit government guarantee: the so-called "too big to fail" externality. IMF (2010c) estimates this funding advantage at 20 to 65 basis points.

Addressing the social cost of failure and too-big-to-fail externalities prescribes certain design features for bank levies. Because these problems are likely to be more acute for larger institutions, a significant asset size threshold and a progressive rate structure above the threshold appear appropriate. The base of the tax should comprise all debt liabilities not subject to an (adequate) insurance scheme. The appropriate rate for each type of liability should take into account its duration vis-à-vis the bank's assets, with more stable and longer term liabilities like (insured) deposits taxed at a lower rate than potentially volatile short-term liabilities, such as interbank loans (repos).

Enacted bank levies vary widely in their features. The top rates are generally low relative to the IMF-recommended rate of 10 to 50 basis points; Germany, for example, charges 2 to 4 basis points and Sweden 3.6 basis points. Liability caps, which have the effect of reducing the marginal tax rate for affected banks to zero,[55] also undercut the tax's desired behavioral effects. While most bank levies apply to uninsured liabilities, a wide variety of bases is used, including deposits (Belgium and Denmark) and risk-based assets (France). Hungary and Sweden exempt interbank loans, excluding an important source of short-term debt. Two countries, the United Kingdom and Korea, vary their tax rate according to the term of the liability.

A major concern regarding bank levies is the potential for double taxation of cross-border institutions. Because bank levies are not income taxes, existing networks of tax treaties do not apply. All existing European levies tax domestic subsidiaries of foreign banks and foreign branches of domestic banks; however, some countries (Austria, Hungary, and the United Kingdom) tax domestic branches of foreign banks, while other countries (France and the United Kingdom) tax foreign subsidiaries of domestic banks, creating risk of double taxation. The European Union has proposed bank levy harmonization in which countries would limit their tax bases to entities that they regulate. France and the United Kingdom have pioneered a tax treaty that gives the home country tax primacy, with a credit issued for host country taxes—the opposite treatment from most double income tax treaties.

9.4.2 Financial Activities Tax

Another tax proposed to raise revenue and correct distortions in the financial sector is the financial activities tax (FAT), a value-added tax levied on financial institutions' wages and profits. Since many credit-invoice VATs, particularly those within Europe, exempt financial services, a low-rate, broad-based FAT can be seen as correcting the undertaxation of financial services. A more narrowly based FAT could be targeted at taxing financial sector rents and/or discouraging excessive risk taking (IMF 2010c).[56]

The broadest-based version (FAT1) would apply to all financial sector value added—the sum of wages and profits at the firm level. In contrast to a credit-invoice VAT, FAT credits would not be given to financial service purchasers, so like the VAT exemption it would increase the net cost of financial inputs for business purchasers, causing some cascading. However, this increase in costs would be appropriate for consumer purchases of financial services, which are undertaxed under VAT exemption. Several examples of FAT1-type taxes predate the financial crisis, including a subtraction-method VAT on financial services in Israel and a payroll tax in VAT-exempt sectors (largely financial services) in France, Denmark, and Iceland.

Two narrower versions of the FAT are aimed at taxing excess profits and curbing risk-taking incentives. "FAT2" would apply only to labor compensation above some (high) level, as well as to total financial sector profits; ideally the compensation base would include all financial sector returns to labor above what could be earned in the next most lucrative profession. "FAT3" would apply only to profits in excess of normal equity returns in nonfinancial industries, as well as to high remuneration. Such excess profits earned in good years likely represent high-risk bets placed with a view to putting the resultant losses to the taxpayer in bad years. Taxing away these abnormal returns would help neutralize the incentive for too-big-to-fail financial firms to assume excessive risk.

In 2012 Iceland introduced the first FAT, levying a 5.45 percent tax on financial sector wages and a 6 percent tax on profits above ISK 1 billion.[57] Three other countries—Italy, France, and the United Kingdom —have introduced financial sector bonus taxes that can be viewed as partial FATs. The British and French taxes were temporary and did not significantly curb financial sector compensation. Italy in 2011 introduced a permanent surtax of 10 percent to be applied to financial sector bonuses in excess of 300 percent of wages. The EU has also proposed restrictions on financial sector bonuses,[58] according to which 50 percent of any bonus should be deferred for three to five years in order to discourage excessive tail risk assumption.

9.4.3 Financial Transactions tax

One of the most controversial proposals for taxing the financial sector that has emerged from the crisis is a securities transactions tax (STT): a tax levied on the principal amount of securities and/or derivatives each time they are sold.[59] STTs have been promoted by a broad range of civil society organizations as well as some governments and the European Union, who believe that—apart from being conceptually very simple—it has the power to both raise substantial revenue and reduce market risks by curbing short-term trading.

The EC has put forward a proposal for a broad-based STT that would impose a minimum tax rate of 10 basis points on stock and bond trades and a 1 basis point tax on the notional value of derivatives trades.[60] Revenues from the tax would be shared between country governments and the European Union. Currency spot market trading would be exempt, but foreign exchange derivatives would be taxed; loans and the initial issuance of stock and bonds would also be exempt. All transactions in which an EU-headquartered bank participates would be included in the base. The EU estimates that this proposal would raise EUR 57 billion in revenue and reduce GDP by 0.5 percent. The United Kingdom, home to Europe's largest and most liquid financial market, opposes the STT, along with Sweden and the Netherlands. In addition to raising revenue from the financial sector, the EC posits reduction of financial market risk as a principle rationale for the STT. While simple in concept, the EU proposal demonstrates that the STT is not without inherent administrative complexities.

In August 2012 France unilaterally introduced an STT of 10 bps on all purchases of stock in French-headquartered corporations with a market capitalization of at least EUR 1 billion, as well as an STT of 1 basis point on sovereign credit default swaps and high-frequency computerized trading. Expected revenues from the new tax are estimated at EUR 1.1 billion per year.

As a means of raising revenue, an STT offers the advantage of simplicity and administrability. Automation of most modern securities trading allows an STT to be easily collected by financial intermediaries.[61] However, the automation and integration of international financial markets also makes it easy for trading to migrate offshore in response to a national-level STT; this is a major consideration prompting the European Union to seek a multilateral STT.

The effectiveness of STTs as quasi-regulatory instruments is uncertain. While clear evidence exists that STTs reduce turnover (trading volume) and liquidity, the relationship between turnover and volatility is unclear. Some studies show that turnover is directly related to price volatility,[62] but other studies show that an increase in transaction costs raises price volatility.[63] The relationship may indeed be nonlinear: increased transaction costs raise volatility in thin markets but lower it in highly liquid markets.[64] A very low-rate tax on highly liquid market, as attempted by France, could in theory reduce volatility, but further empirical evidence is needed. Both theory and empirical evidence show that an increase in securities transaction costs, by reducing liquidity, increases the cost of capital.[65]

Though the STT is promoted as a tax on the financial sector, it is a controversial point whether its burden would actually fall on banks' shareholders and employees. Imposition of the STT would result in an initial drop in securities prices that would reduce the wealth of current capital owners. Going forward, issuers would pay a higher price for raising capital and/or investors would reap a lower rate of return, resulting in some combination of reduced investment and consumption. Financial intermediaries would likely be able to pass on the higher transaction costs of a broad-based STT to their customers; however, the resulting reduction in trading activity would in turn reduce profits and compensation for brokers and dealers, but many segments of financial activity will likely be unaffected.

In conclusion, if the goal is to raise revenue from financial sector profits and compensation, a broad-based FAT is arguably a better instrument than an STT. The financial taxation literature responding to the crisis—for example, Vella et al. (2011) and Shaviro (2011), as well as the European Commission's own analysis—tends to conclude that a FAT is a better instrument to raise revenue from financial sector profits than an STT. Where the goal is to reduce risk taking, a narrow-base FAT and/ or a bank levy are likely better instruments.

9.5 Concluding Remarks

This survey has discussed the role of tax policy in shaping the 2008 financial crisis as well as the central role that tax policy reform is playing—and will continue to play— in the aftermath of the crisis. It reflects the overall emphasis in the literature—but perhaps less so in policy circles—on the need to focus on eliminating "old" distortions, while introducing "new" taxes to address current shortcomings and encourage appropriate risk-taking behavior, such as bank levies and the financial activities tax. These will be key elements in a post-crisis tax reform strategy aimed at regaining fiscal sustainability—with prominent objectives being the adoption of more equitable and less distortive tax structures in support of economic growth and improved revenue mobilization, while assisting in the reduction of budgetary deficits.

Notes

The authors are grateful to Carlo Cottarelli, Michael Keen, Philip Gerson, and Abdelhak Senhadji for very helpful comments on an earlier draft.

1. See, for example, IMF (2009), Keen, Klemm, and Perry (2010), Shackelford, Shaviro, and Slemrod (2010), Alworth and Arachi (2012), and Ceriani et al. (2011).

2. Hemmelgarn and Nicodème (2010) provide a broad narrative of the monetary and regulatory policy loosening that amplified the effect of emerging new financial instruments (securitization in particular) in generating the property bubble in the run-up to the crisis.

3. As reported in three recent Fund Board Papers (IMF 2009, 2010a, 2011) and in IMF's report to the G20 (2010c).

4. For a formal derivation, see the appendix in Keen et al. (2010).

5. The discussion here focuses on corporate taxation; broader income tax reform aimed at removing all distortions to financial decisions would need to include also personal taxation of capital income.

6. A legalistic argument could be made that while lenders are considered as third parties to a corporation, with interest a "true" cost that should be deductible, shareholders are so entwined with the corporation that return to them in the form of dividends should not.

7. Keen and De Mooij (2012) provide some evidence that taxation does affect leverage also of banks.

8. Governments have traditionally limited the amount of leverage and other forms of risks assumed by financial institutions through regulation rather than taxation. Whether taxation or regulation is a better tool to internalize financial sector externalities will not be discussed further here (e.g., see Keen 2011 for a discussion).

9. See discussion in Keen et al. (2010, p. 53).

10. Although some limited moves in this direction in the form of bank levies are discussed in more detail in chapter 3, section 3.5, of this volume.

11. See US Department of the Treasury (1992).

12. An early discussion of such measures is provided in Norregaard and Khan (2007) while more recent examples are given by Sheppard (2011). See also De Mooij (2011) for a discussion of these policy measures.

13. According to Sheppard (2011), the use by multinationals of intra-group interest deductions to strip income out of European companies has been common, but when private equity funds started buying domestic companies, rules were tightened. "Debt push-down" has, according to Sheppard, been a common vehicle that private equity funds use to ensure that the operating companies that they buy do not pay tax to their countries of residence: purpose debt borrowed by a special-purpose acquisition vehicle is pushed down to the level of the target by means of a merger or restructuring. Some European governments (e.g., France, Italy, and Spain) have been taking these structures to court with varying levels of success.

14. See Griffith, Hines, and Sørensen (2010) for a discussion.

15. See De Mooij (2011) for a discussion of the ACE.

16. Croatia had an ACE from 1994 to 2001, Belgium adopted one in 2006; and variants were also applied in Brazil, Austria, and Italy.

17. Klemm (2007) and Keen and King (2002).

18. For which an ACE would be very similar to a deduction for a notional return on Tier 1 capital.

19. See Bond and Devereux (2003).

20. De Mooij and Devereux (2009) estimate that a unilateral adoption of an ACE by EU members would reduce corporate tax revenues by an average of 44 percent. For Croatia, the ACE may have reduced revenue by a third.

21. See Keen et al. (2010, pp. 55–56) for a discussion.

22. The argument being that in an open economy with highly mobile capital, the after-CIT rate of return to capital is fixed on world markets, and a tax on the normal return will then require a higher before-tax rate of return, which in turn will suppress the return to immobile factors such a labor (e.g., see Arulampalam, Devereux, and Maffini 2008 for a survey of the empirical evidence of this effect).

23. See also discussion in Keen et al. (2010, p. 56).

24. Hemmelgarn and Nicodème (2010) provide an account of the processes of—and different types of derivatives involved in—securitization. Using a formal model called Tax Arbitrage Feedback Theory, Eddins (2009) shows how differential tax treatment of market participants produce incentives that lead to instability and possible market bubbles.

25. As supported by OECD's harmful tax practice project and the Global Forum, which has seen some success in promoting exchange of information agreements.

26. For residence countries, perhaps a more promising measure would be to eliminate tax deferral, which is considered a key reason for the use of low-tax jurisdictions by multinationals.

27. If fully symmetric (i.e., with full and immediate deductibility for losses), tax reduces the variance of after-tax returns and will induce risk adverse investors to hold more of the risky asset—an effect that would be mitigated with a progressive tax.

28. Although a major reason why loss treatment tends to be restrictive is to prevent abuse.

29. The cap on the deductibility of salaries in the United States, for example, has provided a strong incentive for the use of performance-related pay.

30. See also the section on the financial activities tax (FAT) for discussion of bank bonus taxation.

31. The issue of strengthening recurrent property taxes as opposed to property transaction taxes is discussed in more detail in section 9.3.

32. For example, 14 OECD countries have increased their standard rate of VAT since 2010 with most of these countries also increasing reduced VAT rates.

33. The Solow (1956) growth accounting framework is the starting point for understanding how taxes can affect growth, where taxes should have no impact on long-term growth rates, but total factor productivity defines long-term potential growth and short-term distortions caused by tax policy are temporary. Changes to the tax structure can reduce the short-term growth rate. In the "endogenous growth" models steady state growth path can change over time owing to tax and expenditure policies, and as a results taxes can impact growth by distorting choices (see Stokey and Rebelo 1995). Theoretical papers using endogenous growth models usually find that reducing the distortionary effects of the current tax structure would permanently increase economic growth (see Engen and Skinner 1996 for a survey), but the magnitude of the increase is sensitive to key parameter assumptions. For example, on the one hand, Lucas (1990) reported that the tax effects on growth of revenue-neutral tax reforms that remove capital income taxes while increasing labor income taxes leaves growth rates broadly unchanged. On the other hand, Jones, Manuelli, and Rossi (1993) found that by lifting all distortionary taxes, average annual growth rates would increase by 4 to 8 percent.

34. Tax policies in developing countries are potentially further away from the recommendations of optimal tax policy in certain respects, and so if the conclusions from developed economies were to carry over to developing economies, then the potential benefits of tax reform in LICs should be even greater.

35. The literature on the empirical effects of tax on growth in developing economies is generally much sparser.

36. "Barro regressions" are growth regressions that were designed to test for convergence by regressing output growth on initial conditions for output and a number of other determinants of potential output. Durlauf, Johnson, and Temple (2005) survey the literature on such regressions.

37. As applied to labor markets, strictly speaking this is only true for the intensive margin (working hours), but not for the participation decision, and macro models tend to assume the participation margin is the more important one.

38. Aggregate time-series analysis provides differing conclusions, as do cross-country regression analysis and sector-specific studies of taxation and growth (see Engen and Skinner 1996).

39. Taxing consumption is equivalent to taxing accumulated assets, excess profits, and labor income: so it falls partly on a completely inelastic base—previously existing assets—and partly on a base less internationally mobile than capital income.

40. The results suggest that if the tax ratio of direct taxes to indirect taxes were to increase by 10 percent, then growth would fall by 0.56 percent. The same results apply for FDI flows: the panel of developed countries reports statistically negative effects of the ratio on FDI flows, while developing economies produce insignificant results.

41. Fiscal devaluation is discussed in De Mooij and Keen (2012).

42. This chapter does not discuss multiplier effects of tax incentives as this is discussed in another chapter of the book.

43. This section draws from IMF (2010a).

44. The discussion of financial sector taxation is a clear example.

45. At the margin, the welfare cost of changing some tax instrument to raise an additional dollar of revenue—its marginal cost of public funds (MCPF)—must be the same for all instruments; otherwise, welfare could be increased without loss of revenue by shifting from the instrument with a higher MCPF to one with a lower one.

46. For example, IMF (2010a) estimates that more efficient VAT policies (by reducing the exemption/rate "policy gap" by half) could raise nearly 2 percent of GDP for both emerging and advanced economies.

47. IMF (2010a) estimates that strengthening tobacco, alcohol, and fuel excises could on average (unweighted) raise an extra 0.6 percent of GDP in revenue in advanced G20 countries.

48. Globally efficient carbon pricing could raise US$50 to 660 billion annually, see IMF (2010a).

49. A general discussion of property taxes is provided in Norregaard (2013).

50. Such as Computer Assisted Mass Appraisal (or CAMA) systems that have significantly improved the basis for market value based property taxation.

51. IMF (2010a) estimates a potential average (unweighted) revenue gain from strengthened property taxation among advanced G20 countries of around 0.7 percent of GDP.

52. IMF (2010c).

53. The most common base for the tax is nondeposit debt liabilities. However, there is some variation: Hungary, for example, levies the tax on total assets less interbank debt liabilities.

54. The median tax raises 0.14 percent of GDP. Austria, Cyprus, France, Germany, Hungary, Iceland, Korea, Portugal, Romania, Slovenia, Sweden, and the United Kingdom have all enacted bank levies; Slovakia and the United States have also proposed versions of this tax.

55. Cyprus caps the liability at 20 percent of taxable profits; Germany caps it at 15 percent of net income; and Slovenia caps it at 0.167 percent of the loan balance.

56. Keen et al. (2013) and European Commission (2011) define three different types of FAT aimed at achieving these various goals.

57. The Iceland tax differs from an ideal FAT in that its profit tax base is accounting profits for which investment is depreciated, rather than cash flow profits for which investment would be expensed.

58. Directive 2010/76/EU. The US Federal Deposit Insurance Commission has proposed similar deferral rules for financial sector bonuses.

59. For a more in-depth discussion of FTTs, see Matheson (2012). For discussion of their administrative feasibility, see Brondolo (2011).

60. The STT would be levied on both purchaser and seller, for a total tax rate of 20 or 2 basis points in most trades.

61. For a more in-depth discussion of administrative issues regarding STTs, see Brondolo (2011).

62. For example, French and Roll (1986) and Barclay et al. (1990).

63. Hau (2006) and Jones and Seguin (1997).

64. Haberer (2004).

65. For a review of this literature, see Amihud et al. (2005).

References

Alesina, A., and S. Ardagna. 2010. Large changes in fiscal policy: Taxes versus spending. *Tax Policy and the Economy* 24: 35–68.

Alworth, Julian S., and Giampaolo Arachi. 2012. Introduction. In Julian Alworth and Giampaolo Arachi, eds., Taxation and the Financial Crisis. Oxford: Oxford University Press.

Amihud, Y., H. Mendelson, and L. H. Pedersen. 2005. Liquidity and asset prices. *Foundations and Trends in Finance* 1 (4): 269–364.

Barclay, M., R. Litzenberger, and J. Warner. 1990. Private information, trading volume and stock return variances. *Review of Financial Studies* 3 (2): 233–53.

Bond, S. R., and M. P. Devereux. 2003. Generalised R-based and S-based taxes under uncertainty. *Journal of Public Economics* 87 (5–6): 1291–1311.

Brondolo, J. 2011. Taxing financial transactions: An assessment of administrative feasibility. Working paper 11/185. IMF, Washington, DC.

Ceriani, Vieri, Stefano Manestra, Giacomo Ricotti, Alessandra Sanelli, and Ernosto Zangari. 2011. The tax system and the financial crisis. Occasional paper 85. Banca D'Italia, Rome.

De Mooij, R. A. 2011. Tax biases to debt finance: Assessing the problem, finding solutions. Staff discussion note 11/11. IMF, Washington, DC.

De Mooij, R. A., and M. Devereux. 2009. Alternative systems of business tax in Europe: An applied analysis of ACE and CBIT reforms. Taxation studies, 28. Directorate General Taxation and Customs Union, European Commission, Brussels.

De Mooij, R. A., and M. Keen. 2012. Fiscal devaluation and fiscal consolidation: The VAT in troubled times. Working paper 12/85. IMF, Washington, DC.

Easterly, W., and S. Rebelo. 1993. Marginal income tax rates and economic growth in developing countries. *European Economic Review* 37: 409–17.

Eddins, S. T. 2009. Tax arbitrage feedback theory. March 9. Available at: http://ssrn.com/abstract=1356159.

Engen, E. M., and J. Skinner. 1996. Taxation and economic growth. Working paper 5826. NBER, Cambridge, MA.

European Commission. 2011. Proposal for a Council Directive on a common system of financial transaction tax and amending directive 2008/7/EC. Staff working paper impact assessment accompanying the document COM 594, SEC 2011 final. EC, Brussels.

French, K., and R. Roll. 1986. Stock return variances: The arrival of information and the reaction of traders. *Journal of Financial Economics* 17: 5–26.

Gordon, R., and W. Li. 2009. Tax structures in developing countries: Many puzzles and a possible explanation. *Journal of Public Economics* 93: 855–66.

Griffith, R., J. Hines, and P. B. Sørensen. 2010. International capital taxation. In J. Mirrlees, S. Adam, T. Besley, R. Blundell, S. Bond, R. Chote, M. Gammie, P. Johnson, G. Myles, and J. Poterba, eds., Dimensions of Tax Design: The Mirrlees Review. Oxford: Oxford University Press, 914–1027.

Haberer, M. 2004. Might a securities transaction tax mitigate excess volatility? Some evidence from the literature. Discussion paper 04–06. CoFE, University of Konstanz.

Hau, H. 2006. The role of transaction costs for financial volatility: Evidence from the Paris Bourse. *Journal of the European Economic Association* 4 (4): 862–90.

Hemmelgarn, T., and G. Nicodème. 2010. The 2008 financial crisis and taxation policy. Taxation paper 20. EU, Brussels.

Hemmelgarn, T., Nicodème, G., and E. Zangari. 2011. The role of housing tax provisions in the 2008 financial crisis. Taxation paper 27. EU, Brussels.

International Monetary Fund. 2009. Debt bias and other distortions: Crisis-related issues in tax policy. Prepared by the Fiscal Affairs Department, June 12. Available at: https://www.imf.org/external/np/pp/eng/2009/061209.pdf.

International Monetary Fund. 2010a. From stimulus to consolidation: Revenue and expenditure policies in advanced and emerging economies. Fiscal Affairs Department. IMF, Washington, DC.

International Monetary Fund. 2010b. Will it hurt? Macroeconomic effects of fiscal consolidation. *World Economic Outlook* (October). Washington, DC: IMF

International Monetary Fund. 2010c. A fair and substantial contribution: A framework for taxation and resolution to improve financial stability. Report to the G20. IMF, Washington, DC.

International Monetary Fund. 2011. Revenue mobilization in developing countries. Fiscal Affairs Department. IMF, Washington, DC.

Jones, C., and P. J. Seguin. 1997. Transactions costs and price volatility: Evidence from Commission deregulation. *American Economic Review* 87 (4): 728–37.

Keen, M. 2011. Rethinking the taxation of the financial sector. *CESifo Economic Studies* 57 (1): 1–24.

Keen, M., and Ruud de Mooij. 2012. Debt, taxes, and banks. IMF Working paper 12/48. IMF, Washington, DC.

Keen, M., and J. King. 2002. The Croatian profit tax: An ACE in practice. *Fiscal Studies* 23 (3): 401–18.

Keen, M., A. Klemm, and V. Perry. 2010. Tax and the crisis. *Fiscal Studies* 31 (1): 43–79.

Keen, M., R. Krelove, and J. Norregaard. 2013. The financial activities tax. IMF Working paper, forthcoming.

Klemm, A. 2007. Allowances for corporate equity in practice. *CESifo Economic Studies* 53 (2): 229–62.

Lee, Y., and R. H. Gordon. 2005. Tax structure and economic growth. *Journal of Public Economics* 89: 1027–43.

Lucas, R. 1990. Supply-side economics: An analytical review. *Oxford Economic Papers* 42 (2): 293–316.

Martinez-Vazquez, J., V. Vulovic, and Y. Liu. 2010. Direct versus indirect taxation: Trends, theory and economic significance. Working paper 10–14. International Studies Program, Andrew Young School of Policy Studies, Georgia State University, Atlanta.

Matheson, T. 2012. Securities transaction taxes: Issues and evidence. *International Tax and Public Finance*. doi:10.1007/s10797-012-9212-5.

Norregaard, J. 2013. Taxing immovable property: Revenue potential and implementation challenges. Working paper 13/129. IMF, Washington, DC.

Norregaard, J., and T. Khan. 2007. Tax policy: Recent trends and coming challenges. Working paper 07/274. IMF, Washington, DC.

OECD. 2010. *Tax Policy Reform and Economic Growth*. Paris: OECD.

Poterba, J. M., and T. M. Sinai. 2008. Income tax provisions affecting owner-occupied housing: Revenue costs and incentive effects. Working paper 14523. NBER, Cambridge, MA.

Shackelford, Douglas A., Daniel N. Shaviro, and Joel Slemrod. 2010. Taxation and the financial sector. *National Tax Journal* 63: 781–806.

Shaviro, D. 2012. The financial transaction tax vs. the financial activities tax. Unpublished manuscript. New York University.

Sheppard, L. A. 2011. New restrictions on interest deductibility. *Tax Notes International* 64 (10): 684–87.

Stokey, N. L., and S. Rebelo. 1995. Growth effects of flat-rate taxes. *Journal of Political Economy* 103: 519–50.

US Department of the Treasury. 1992. Integration of the individual and corporate tax systems. US Treasury, Washington, DC.

Vella, J., C. Fuest, and T. Schmidt-Eisenlohr. 2011. The EU Commission's proposal for a financial transaction tax. *British Tax Review* 6: 607–21.

Part III

Management of Fiscal Policy during the Crisis

10

Fiscal Policy Response in Advanced and Emerging Market Economies

Elif Arbatli, Thomas Baunsgaard, Alejandro Guerson, and Kyung-Seol Min

10.1 Introduction

This chapter discusses the fiscal response to the sharp decline in global growth following the financial crisis that erupted in August 2007. The policy response to the financial crisis and economic recession was unprecedented, befitting the exceptional nature of the shock. The average fiscal deficit across all countries increased by 6.3 percent of GDP between 2007 and 2009, with a larger deterioration in advanced economies (figure 10.1). This reflected fiscal stimulus packages—the cyclically adjusted deficit increased by over 3 percent of GDP, the automatic stabilizers, the rescue packages for the financial sector, and a structural decline in revenues as a result of a decline in potential GDP. The relatively strong fiscal position of emerging and low-income countries allowed this group of countries to also implement expansionary fiscal measures.

Public debts increased significantly through 2008 to 2010, especially in advanced economies. For the world economy, general government gross debt rose to 70 percent of world GDP in 2010 (figure 10.1). In advanced economies, the level of general government debt reached about 100 percent of GDP and continued to increase to 108 percent in 2012. This was largely explained by the permanent loss of revenue mentioned above (which explains near half of debt accumulation through 2007 to 2011), and also by private debt bailouts, especially in the financial sector. The latter was needed for stabilization purposes and to shut down the negative feedback loop between the balance sheet of the financial sector and that of the government. Interestingly, the discretional fiscal stimulus was not the main factor behind the increase in public debt (explains about a quarter of debt accumulation through 2007 to 2011).

As debts continued to rise rapidly, it was clear that an exit strategy balancing the need to support growth in the short term, while ensuring long-term fiscal sustainability, became increasingly important. The effectiveness of fiscal stimulus would depend on many factors, including the size of the stimulus, its composition, the timing of

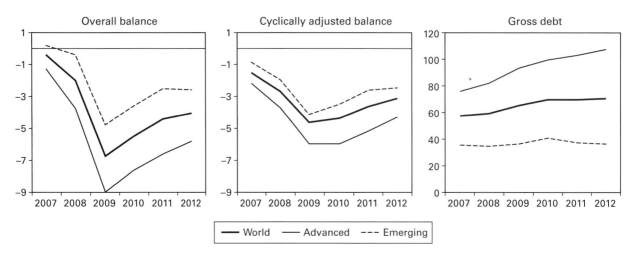

Figure 10.1
Global fiscal developments, 2007 to 2012: Overall balance, gross debt (in percent of GDP); cyclically adjusted balance (in percent of potential GDP)
Source: IMF, *Fiscal Monitor,* April 2012

the exit, and the consolidation plan following stimulus. Under current projections, debt ratios are expected to stabilize in advanced economies by 2015, although this outlook is vulnerable to fiscal slippages or shocks to the interest–growth differential (*Fiscal Monitor,* October 2012). While the average debt ratio in emerging and low-income country groups also initially rose, it fell back reasonably fast to only slightly above the pre-crisis level reflecting both fiscal consolidation and a quicker growth recovery.

This chapter analyzes how activist fiscal policies were used in response to the crisis. First, it summarizes some of the empirical evidence on whether an expansionary fiscal policy response was indeed appropriate. Some recent evidence indicates that a fiscal expansion was indeed appropriate in the conditions prevalent at the onset of the crisis of sharp and global growth decline and constrained room for monetary response, as policy rates were near the zero lower bound. Under such conditions, there is empirical evidence indicating that fiscal multipliers tend to be positive and large (see next chapter for a discussion on fiscal multipliers). This view, however, was not shared unanimously. An opposite view advocated fiscal consolidation. According to this view, supply-side propagation channels would dominate: further increases in fiscal deficits and public debts would be counterproductive as they would increase interest rates and risks to fiscal sustainability, crowding out private credit and ultimately reducing investment and employment.[1]

Second, the chapter evaluates the discretionary fiscal stimulus injected in the economy early in the crisis, based on size, composition, and international coordination.

Finally, the chapter describes the use of governments' balance sheet interventions as a stabilization instrument.

The remainder of this chapter explores in more detail the fiscal policy response. Section 10.2 will look at the fiscal policy response focusing on the G20 economies—the size and composition of the fiscal discretionary stimulus, the fiscal impulse in response to changes in the output gap, and how the different components contributed to the higher debt levels. Section 10.3 will present the main theoretical and empirical arguments in favor and against fiscal stimulus. Section 10.4 will briefly touch on selected issues related to the asset-liability management by governments during the crisis.

10.2 Fiscal Policy Response in G20 Economies

The fiscal policy response during the crisis can be better understood by decomposing the primary fiscal deficit. Given data availability, this will be done focusing on the largest advanced and emerging economies in the G20. Figure 10.2 breaks down the primary deficit for the G20 economies into the contribution from the automatic stabilizers, the discretionary fiscal stimulus, and other structural or discretionary fiscal effects not formally accounted for as part of the fiscal stimulus.[2] For the advanced G20 economies, the increase in the primary deficit in advanced economies was of broadly similar magnitude across the sources just mentioned. For the emerging G20

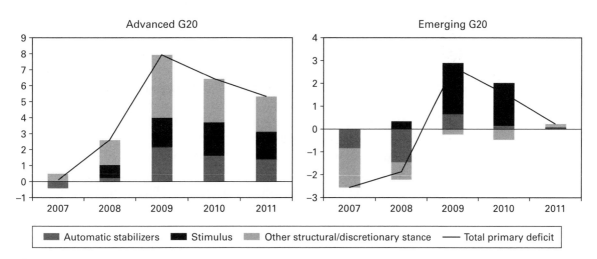

Figure 10.2
G20 economies' composition of the primary deficit (in percent of GDP, PPP-GDP weighted). The cyclical primary balance is presented in the chart as automatic stabilizers; the stimulus is as identified in the text below. The other structural/discretionary part is the unexplained residual.
Sources: IMF staff estimates; *Fiscal Monitor*, April 2012

economies on average, crisis-related fiscal stimulus measures dominated movements in the primary deficit.

10.2.1 Fiscal Stimulus Measures in G20 Countries

G20 countries implemented discretionary fiscal stimulus measures in response to the crisis of almost 2 percent of GDP annually in 2009 and 2010. This section will provide an overview of these measures for the G20 advanced and emerging countries.

Before discussing the size and composition of different stimulus measures, it is important to define the discretionary stimulus measures reported in this chapter. The stimulus includes only revenue and expenditure measures implemented or announced in response to the crisis up to 2012; in some countries it is difficult to track differences between announced and implemented measures. With respect to revenue measures, because it is often not possible to obtain actual data on implementation, the data are based on estimates by the country authorities or IMF staff. Identifying measures announced purely in response to the crisis involves some judgment and hence measures reported here may differ from other estimates owing to differences in the underlying baseline fiscal path. Finally, the stimulus measures used in this section do not include financial sector support measures (which is the topic of chapter 14 in this volume).

10.2.2 Advanced G20 Economies

The average annual fiscal stimulus in the advanced G20 countries during 2008 to 2010 was about 2 percent of GDP annually. Across individual countries, the stimulus packages differed in timing and size (figure 10.3). The largest packages were adopted in the United States and Japan, followed by Australia, Canada, Germany, and Korea. With limited fiscal space coming into the crisis, Italy was the only G20 country that did not provide fiscal stimulus as the expansionary spending measures were offset by revenue increasing measures. While the United States, the United Kingdom, Australia, Korea, and Japan provided some stimulus in 2008, the packages became generally effective starting only in 2009.

The composition of stimulus packages also differed across countries (figure 10.4). On average, advanced G20 countries adopted fiscal packages that relied slightly more on expenditure measures (3.7 percent of GDP), although revenue measures were also significant (2.8 percent of GDP). In Japan, Canada, and Australia fiscal stimulus was mainly provided by expenditure measures, whereas France, Korea, and the United States balanced revenue and expenditure measures. Germany and the United Kingdom had packages that concentrated mostly on revenue measures. The composition of spending changed over the course of the crisis with revenue measures becoming gradually more important: in 2008 stimulus came largely through revenue measures (about 45 percent of total stimulus in that year) but then

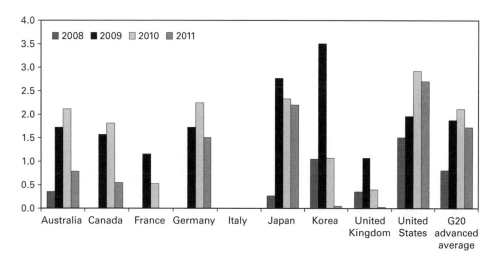

Figure 10.3
G20 advanced economies' fiscal stimulus (in percent of GDP)
Sources: Country authorities; IMF staff estimates

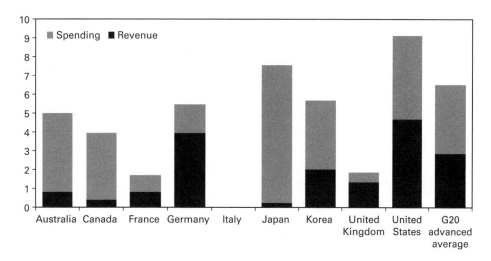

Figure 10.4
G20 advanced economies' composition of fiscal stimulus, 2008 to 2011 (cumulative in percent of GDP)
Sources: Country authorities; IMF staff estimates

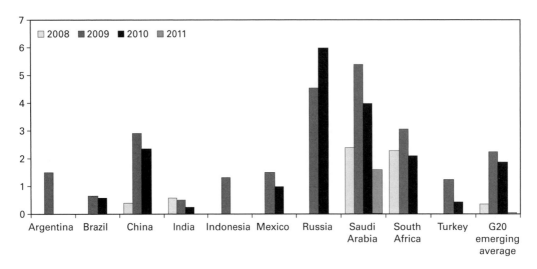

Figure 10.5
G20 emerging economies' fiscal stimulus, 2008 to 2011 (in percent of GDP)
Sources: Country authorities; IMF staff estimates

increased to about 64 percent of total stimulus in 2009 and remained at 60 percent in 2010.

10.2.3 Emerging G20 Economies

The average cumulative fiscal stimulus during 2008 to 2011 for emerging G20 economies was 4.5 percent of GDP, about two-thirds of the level in advanced countries (figure 10.5). The stimulus was concentrated in four countries: Saudi Arabia[3] and Russia provided the largest stimulus while South Africa and China also implemented relatively large packages. In other emerging economies the stimulus was more modest. The main stimulus measures were concentrated in 2009 to 2010, and no stimulus plan was announced for 2011 except for Saudi Arabia. In contrast to advanced economies, stimulus in emerging economies was dominated by expenditure measures, especially infrastructure spending (figure 10.6). The preference for expenditure-based stimulus measures may reflect emerging economies' higher infrastructure needs than in advanced economies, combined with lower capacity to increase revenues given more limitations in tax administration and also from tax evasion. In addition the response of private consumption to expenditure stimulus can be larger in emerging than in advanced economies, as a relatively larger share of the population is likely to be subject to liquidity constraints and to exhibit a hand-to-mouth consumption behavior.[4] Furthermore an increase in expenditure for social protection purposes is also warranted on social grounds, because, among other considerations, social protection systems are typically weaker.

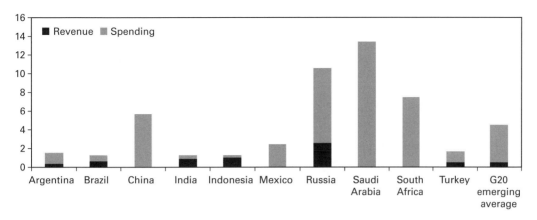

Figure 10.6
G20 emerging economies' composition of stimulus measures, 2008 to 2011 (in percent of GDP)
Source: Country authorities; IMF staff estimates

10.2.4 Fiscal Impulse during the Crisis

The fiscal impulse measures the demand impact of discretionary fiscal policy. It is estimated as the (negative of the) change in the cyclically adjusted primary balance. This captures the discretionary policy response by excluding the contribution from the automatic fiscal stabilizers (appendix B at the end of this chapter defines the fiscal policy terminology used). Notice that actual fiscal stimulus packages, as defined in policy records, would generally differ from the fiscal impulse calculated using statistical methods. First, stimulus packages need not in general include all fiscal measures in a given period. Second, the calculation of cyclically adjusted primary balances is subject to statistical error, including that from the difficulties in estimating potential GDP (particularly in the period under analysis), but also from other indicators that can affect the structural component of revenues, such as asset prices.

The evolution of the fiscal impulse during the crisis period provides additional insights. Figure 10.7 plots the fiscal impulse against the annual change in the output gap for G20 economies for 2008 to 2010.[5] Looking first at advanced G20 economies, in 2008, while the output gap worsened in all countries, it turned negative in only about half of the countries. In response, more than half of the countries injected fiscal impulse (most markedly in the United States and the United Kingdom). In 2009, all advanced economies had a negative output gap and responded with countercyclical fiscal impulse (albeit less so in Italy and Canada). In 2010, with signs of insipient recovery the output gap began closing in some countries, although it remained negative for all advanced G20 economies. The policy stance also started to diverge. Some countries began withdrawing fiscal impulse (the United Kingdom and Korea), others continued to provide fiscal impulse (Canada and Germany), while

Advanced economies

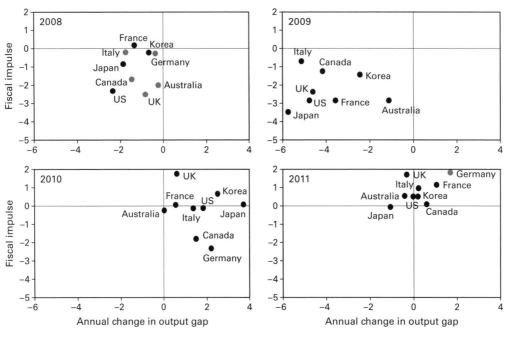

Emerging economies

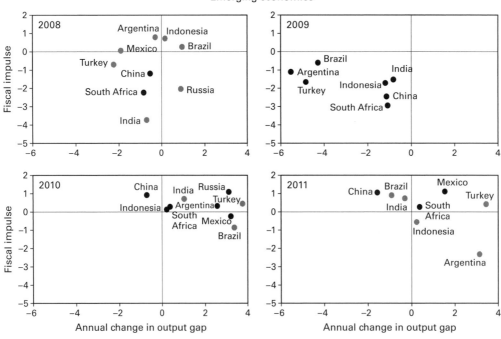

the remaining countries did neither inject nor withdraw fiscal stimulus. In 2011, the majority of advanced G20 economies began tightening fiscal policy by withdrawing fiscal stimulus.

Among G20 emerging economies, while a few countries began expansionary fiscal policies in 2008, only China and South Africa had a negative output gap at the time. However, by 2009, all emerging G20 economies had negative output gaps and provided fiscal impulse in response. In 2010 and 2011, both the economic conditions and the fiscal policy response became more diverse across countries. Although the economic recovery was stronger than in advanced economies (with fewer emerging economies having negative output gaps in 2011), there was seemingly less pressure to begin fiscal consolidation.

10.2.5 Decomposing the Increase in Government Debt in G20 Economies

As noted in the introduction, most advanced economies experienced significant and sustained increases in their debt levels, whereas emerging economies had relatively small increases that were eventually reversed. Looking specifically at G20 economies, the cumulative average increase in gross debt levels during 2007 to 2011 for advanced economies was about 31 percent of GDP, with the largest increases in Japan, United States, and United Kingdom (figure 10.8). In emerging G20 economies, on the other hand, average debt only increased by 1 percent of GDP with modest increases in some countries such as Mexico, China, and South Africa offset by declines in Argentina, Indonesia, and India.

By decomposing the increase in debt, the contributing factors to the higher debt level can be identified.[6] Over 60 percent of the debt increase in advanced economies can be attributed to the larger primary deficits (figure 10.8). This reflects the automatic stabilizers, the discretionary fiscal stimulus measures, as well as other economic factors not captured by the cyclical adjustment—for example, revenue declines associated with the sharp drop during the crisis in financial asset, housing, and commodity prices. Interestingly, fiscal stimuli were not the most important factor explaining the accumulation of debt. It was the decline in revenues, which was largely structural, that explains near half of the debt accumulation, particularly in G7 countries. The impact of slower growth and higher interest payments contributed

Figure 10.7
G20 economies' fiscal impulse and change in output gap, 2008 to 2011 (annual changes in percentage point of potential GDP). Bold dot countries are in positive (negative) output gap. The fiscal impulse is defined as the change in the cyclically adjusted primary balance. The following categories apply: first quadrant (output gap improving, fiscal balance improving), second quadrant (output gap deteriorating, fiscal balance improving), third quadrant (output gap deteriorating, fiscal balance deteriorating), fourth quadrant (output gap improving, fiscal balance deteriorating). Fiscal data for the United States reflect the structural primary balance.
Sources: *World Economic Outlook (WEO); Fiscal Monitor*, April 2012; IMF staff estimates

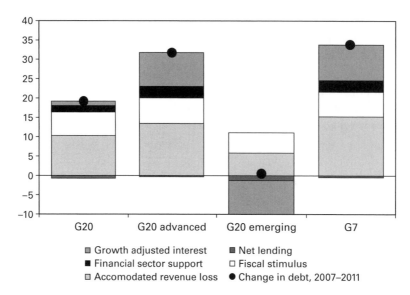

Figure 10.8
G20 economies' decomposition of the increase in government debt, 2007 to 2011
Sources: Country authorities; IMF staff estimates

about a quarter of the increase in debt levels. Financial sector support as well as net lending and other stock-flow adjustments played a lesser role.

The average hides significant differences across countries for the relative contribution to the higher debt of automatic stabilizers and discretionary stimulus measures. For instance, in France, United Kingdom, and Italy, the automatic stabilizers were relatively more important, whereas in Canada, Japan, and the United States, both the automatic stabilizers and discretionary stimulus mattered in explaining the increase in debt. In Germany, Australia, and Korea, the contribution from discretionary stimulus was relatively larger. All advanced countries, with the exception of Korea and Australia, had a significant contribution from adverse growth adjusted interest rate dynamics.

In emerging G20 economies, fiscal stimulus measures and revenue losses contributed to increase the debt level. However, in contrast to advanced economies, the interest growth dynamics actually reduced debt, almost offsetting the impact of discretionary fiscal measures and the loss of revenues. This reflected both the much faster recovery in economic growth, but also the historically favorable debt dynamics from growth and interest rates in many emerging economies.[7] This does not mean that these favorable debt dynamics will persist for ever (see discussion in chapter 1, section 1.2). Again the individual country experience was more diverse. While Saudi Arabia and Russia implemented large fiscal stimulus measures, these were offset by the revenue boost from higher oil prices. In China, favorable interest growth dynamics helped to partially offset the impact of large fiscal discretionary measures. In South Africa and Mexico stimulus measures were also large, contributing to an increase in their debt levels by about 7.4 and 2.5 percent of GDP, respectively, with less favorable interest growth dynamics.

10.3 Were the Fiscal Stimulus Measures Appropriate?

The crisis and the unprecedented fiscal measures implemented generated an active policy debate on the appropriate fiscal response to the crisis, the size of fiscal multipliers and the effectiveness of fiscal policy in general. Should governments have implemented a stronger fiscal policy response, or did they do too much? Part of the debate has become politicized, whereas other contributions have a more academic nature. This chapter will not undertake a review of the literature, but will include some references to key contributions that provide context.[8]

The issue of the appropriate fiscal response to the crisis ignited a heated debate. In broad terms, there were two main positions. On the one hand, there was the view that a fiscal expansion was needed, including some mix of expenditure increases and tax cuts. This view stressed the dominance of Keynesian propagation channels, including the possibility of coordination failure among consumers and investors that could result in a downward spiral of declining growth and deflation. The opposite view argued that a fiscal consolidation was the appropriate policy response, emphasizing supply-side effects and non-Keynesian propagation channels. According to this second view, a fiscal stimulus could be counterproductive and reduce investment and employment. The deterioration in government creditworthiness could increase sovereign premia that would spread to domestic interest rates. Growth expectations and investment would therefore decline, also from a possible increase in tax pressure (including the inflation tax) and credit crowding out at a later stage. This was compounded by the governments' bailout of private debts, particularly the banking sector's, of uncertain recovery value. This concern affected in particular some countries in the euro area under financing stress, which could not cushion the shock with currency depreciation.

A good example of the various views is a May 2009 debate in the *American Economic Review* on the role of fiscal policy in responding to the crisis. Auerbach (2009) argued that there are compelling circumstances for renewed fiscal policy activism, although for this to be effective more attention was needed to policy design. Taylor (2009), in contrast, found no empirical rationale for a revival of countercyclical discretionary fiscal policy. Feldstein (2009) cautiously accepted that rethinking the role of fiscal policy may be warranted in the exceptional crisis circumstances. More recently DeLong and Summers (2012) presented a framework contrasting fiscal policy in normal times—where fiscal policy should be determined more by supply-side rather than demand-side considerations—against fiscal policy in a severely depressed economy, with space for expansionary fiscal policy as a stabilization tool.

To this day, there is no consensus about which of the two views above is correct, either in academic or in policy makers' circles. The difficulties to reach a consensus are explained mainly by the mutual causation between growth and fiscal policy, which makes the identification of the impact of fiscal policy a complicated task. An existing strand of empirical literature finds evidence of expansionary fiscal contractions, notably Giavazzi and Pagano (1990 and 1996), Alesina and Perotti (1995 and 1997), and Alesina and Ardagna (1998).[9] In general, these studies argue that a fiscal consolidation can have a positive impact on growth if it is concentrated on politically sensitive expenditure categories, such as wages, transfers to households, and goods and services.

More recent empirical results, however, provide evidence supporting the view that a fiscal stimulus was crucial to aid growth under the conditions prevailing in 2008 to 2010. Based on a sample of advanced economies spanning the last thirty years, a study presented in the September 2010 *World Economic Outlook* (WEO) indicates that countercyclical fiscal policies have in general been expansionary.[10] Moreover this study also shows that a discretionary fiscal stimulus is more effective when the room for monetary policy is severely constrained, as it was the case in most of the advanced world at the onset of the crisis where policy rates were near zero. These results are consistent with those in Romer and Romer (2010) for the United States. In addition there was also evidence indicating that fiscal multipliers are positive and larger during recessions (see April 2010 *Fiscal Monitor*). Under such conditions fiscal adjustment could be delayed to support short-term growth.[11] Also too-fast adjustment can result in an increase in interest rates. Evidence from short-term credit default swap (CDS) spreads revealed that, if the fiscal multiplier is sufficiently large, fiscal consolidation would increase short-term spreads, even if the fiscal deficit declines, as a result of a decline in growth leading to an increase in the debt ratio.[12] In such a scenario, a fiscal consolidation could end up being self-defeating.

10.3.1 Assessment for an Appropriate Fiscal Stimulus

Some of the evidence reported above support the view that a fiscal stimulus was appropriate in broad terms. However, a more comprehensive assessment requires as well an analysis of its characteristics.[13] This subsection focuses on three main characteristics that are considered important: size, composition, and international coordination. The assessment of the appropriate size and composition of fiscal stimulus revived an old debate about the size of fiscal multipliers for the alternative revenue and expenditure policies and instruments. Policy reports published by the OECD argued that as tax multipliers were uncertain, appropriately designed spending measures with positive spillovers for long-term growth were desirable. The need for collective action and the importance of avoiding international trade protectionism, or other noncompetitive practices, were also highlighted in policy recommendations from international organizations such as the IMF and the OECD. Other considerations included the need to address employment and social protection needs.[14] This section provides a broad assessment of the application of fiscal stimulus in G20 economies.[15]

Size

In both advanced and emerging economies, the output gap remained large and protracted despite the fiscal stimulus. Based on this, in some larger advanced economies with initial fiscal space, more sizable initial fiscal stimulus packages could have better contributed to contain the decline in aggregate demand, at least at the margin, provided this were supported by low sovereign borrowing interest rates. However, it is not clear that significantly larger stimulus would have improved upon the observed results. Concerns about supply-side effects and also about debt sustainability mentioned above should not be underestimated. In emerging economies, output gaps were relatively smaller than in advanced economies while the applied relative fiscal stimulus was comparable in magnitude.

Figure 10.9 also shows how the size fiscal stimulus packages changed over time. Advanced G20s, on average, increased the size of the stimulus in 2010 relative to 2009 despite some recovery of output in that year. This could have been an outcome of implementation lags rather than policy design per se. Notable exceptions, however, are the cases of Italy, where there were no stimulus packages, and France and the United Kingdom, where the stimulus were reduced while output gaps remained negative. In the case of emerging G20s there was some reduction in the size of the stimulus packages in 2010 on average, possibly reflecting concerns about fiscal space in the face of uncertainty regarding the persistence of the global economic slowdown.

Fiscal sustainability was also taken into consideration in deciding the size of the fiscal stimulus and its intertemporal allocation. Countries with larger fiscal space (as indicated by a lower public debt and relatively lower fiscal deficits) and better access to financing in general opted for relatively larger fiscal stimulus packages (figure 10.11). The earlier withdrawal of stimulus packages in emerging G20s mentioned above relates in part to the need to preserve sovereign creditworthiness, as their sovereign spreads tend to be more volatile. In European countries under financial pressure, mainly Greece, Portugal, Ireland, Italy, and Spain, fiscal policy planning focused mainly on fiscal consolidation. In some countries, political opposition resulted in delays and limited the size of the stimulus relative to the government's intentions. One such example is the United States where fiscal stimulus execution was in part the responsibility of state and local administrations.

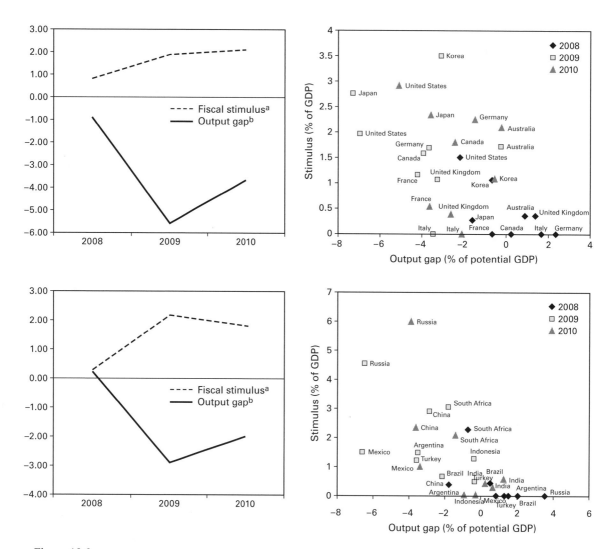

Figure 10.9
Fiscal stimulus and output gap (in percent of actual and potential GDP). (a) In percent of GDP, PPP-GDP weighted; (b) in percent of potential GDP, PPP-GDP weighted.
Sources: Country authorities; staff estimates

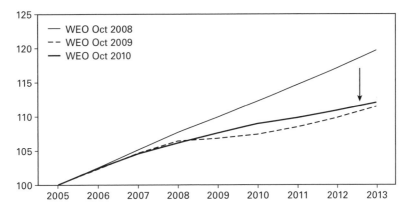

Figure 10.10
Potential GDP in advanced economies (median; 2005 = 100)
Sources: Country authorities; staff estimates

The uncertainty about the extent of decline in potential output and the corresponding permanent loss of revenues complicated an assessment of the appropriate size of the fiscal stimulus in real time. Potential GDP estimates were in fact reduced significantly since the crisis started (figure 10.10). Several countries introduced multiple stimulus packages, as policy makers continued to reassess the severity of the situation while the crisis unfolded. In particular, the processes of deleveraging and asset price deflation were likely to influence long-term revenue potential, a key input to assess the space for fiscal stimulus.

Composition

The composition of the stimulus packages was diversified across revenue and expenditure measures, especially in advanced economies. Given the uncertain nature of the global slowdown, the allocation of fiscal stimulus across various instruments was broadly appropriate. In the aggregate, more than three-fourths of the stimulus was based on expenditure measures, with a direct impact on aggregate demand. Moreover a large part of the expenditure stimulus was allocated to infrastructure investment and to safety nets. Many measures were targeted at credit-constrained households with a higher propensity to consume. Execution lags may have affected the effectiveness of infrastructure stimulus in the short term, but with a potentially protracted economic slowdown this is less problematic, particularly considering the long-term growth impact. Moreover expenditure measures have in most cases been designed to be transitory or self-unwinding, possibly given the need to address fiscal sustainability concerns. Increases in public wages have in general been avoided, appropriately so, as these are not well targeted and are difficult to reverse.

While tax measures provided diversification, better targeted measures may have had a stronger impact. Many measures focused on direct taxes on personal and corporate income. If growth expectations are low, income tax reductions would be less likely to stimulate consumption as precautionary savings would tend to increase.[16] Firms would also be less likely to pursue investments out of income tax reductions if they take a "wait-and-see" approach in an uncertain environment. In general, tax reductions targeted at households and firms that are more likely to be credit constrained, as opposed to across-the-board tax cuts, can be expected to better stimulate consumption and investment.

International Coordination

Especially in 2009, most countries contributed to the aggregate stimulus. However, this was followed by more divergent policy approaches. In the aggregate, G20 economies reacted concurrently and in synchronicity to the shock (figure 10.9). By 2009, G20s were already implementing fiscal stimulus packages of about 2 percent of GDP (PPP GDP-weighted), with median stimulus packages for advanced G20s at about 1.5 percent of GDP. The extent to which this syncronicity was due to international coordination, however, is difficult to assess. On the one hand, there were concrete efforts at coordination. The Group of Twenty (G20) cemented its role during the crisis as a key multilateral economic forum.[17] Through early 2012, six G20 summits[18] and more ministerial level meetings had been held, in which members committed to sustained fiscal stimulus to support growth and employment, and also to an exit strategy that ensures fiscal sustainability. On the other hand, the application of stimulus appears correlated with country-specific fundamentals (see the next subsection), including financing constraints and political willingness. This makes it difficult to assess if at least part of the fiscal stimulus responded to developments in the rest of the world. On the one hand, it is possible that large economies would have incentives to stimulate the global economy, as each economy's own growth could have a measurable impact on global output and result in a positive growth feedback effect. On the other hand, there was a potential for a "free-rider" problem: each economy would benefit from others' stimulus without incurring the costs related to increasing its own fiscal deficit and public debt.

10.3.2 Assessment against Cross-country Differences in Economic Fundamentals

Cross-country differences in fiscal stimulus were broadly consistent with country differences in economic fundamentals. Figure 10.11 shows that G20 countries with larger cumulative output gaps in general applied larger stimulus (measured as the cumulative stimulus through 2008 to 2010). The fiscal stimulus was larger in economies with more fiscal space (captured by a relatively lower pre-crisis public debt stock and stronger overall fiscal balance). More open economies applied less stimu-

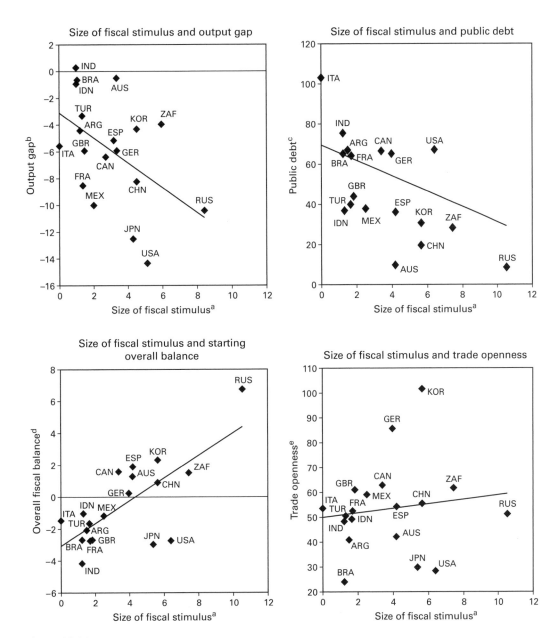

Figure 10.11
G20 economies' fiscal stimulus and economic fundamentals. (a) Cumulative fiscal stimulus from 2008 to 2010, in percent of GDP; (b) distance between nominal GDP and potential GDP accumulated through 2008 to 2010; (c) overall fiscal balance in 2007, in percent of GDP; (d) average of exports plus imports from 2008 to 2010, in percent of GDP.
Sources: Country authorities; staff estimates

Table 10.1
G20 Economies: Explaining country differences in fiscal stimulus

Variables	(1) OLS	(2) RE	(3) FE
Output gap (interaction with advanced economies)	−0.650***	−0.569**	−0.468*
	(0.140)	(0.232)	(0.273)
Output gap (interaction with emerging economies)	−0.300***	−0.317***	−0.355***
	(0.0787)	(0.113)	(0.124)
Automatic stabilizers (interaction with advanced economies)	−0.890***	−0.688	−0.705
	(0.331)	(0.457)	(0.522)
Automatic stab. (interaction with emerging economies)	0.0417	−0.00522	−0.280
	(0.423)	(0.317)	(0.367)
Lagged debt (interaction with advanced economies)	−0.00640***	−0.00659	0.0291
	(0.00216)	(0.00417)	(0.0198)
Lagged debt (interaction with emerging economies)	−0.0137*	−0.0157*	−0.0871**
	(0.00819)	(0.00937)	(0.0432)
Openness	−0.00400	−0.00664	−0.0647*
	(0.00617)	(0.00961)	(0.0336)
Constant	1.341**	1.524**	4.785**
	(0.617)	(0.759)	(1.905)
Observations	71	71	71
R-squared	0.414		0.480
Number of countries	18	18	18

Sources: Country authorities; staff estimates
Note: Standard errors in parentheses; *** $p < 0.01$, ** $p < 0.05$, * $p < 0.1$

lus, possibly reflecting the lower effectiveness of a given stimulus effort due to leakage compared to more closed economies.

A simple regression analysis supports the conclusion that the application of fiscal stimulus across countries was broadly in line with fundamentals. Table 10.1 shows the results of panel regressions that explain fiscal stimulus for G20 economies over 2008 to 2011, as a function of the output gap, the size of the automatic stabilizers, the lagged value of the debt-to-GDP ratio, and the degree of openness measured by the sum of imports and exports to GDP.[19] Interaction terms capture differences between advanced and emerging G20 economies.

The size of the fiscal stimulus was larger in countries with larger output gaps, with the response in advanced economies about twice as large compared to emerging economies (with significant coefficients in all regressions).[20] The relation between fiscal stimulus and the automatic stabilizers differs between the two country groups.

For advanced countries, a 1 percent of GDP increase in the deficit due to automatic stabilizers is associated with a decline in discretionary stimulus of between three-quarters to one percentage point (although the coefficient on automatic stabilizers is significant only for the OLS regression). For emerging markets, there is no clear relation between the automatic stabilizers and stimulus. Countries that had higher initial debt levels adopted smaller stimulus packages, with a larger impact for emerging economies. Finally, the effect of openness on the size of stimulus measures, albeit only significant for the fixed effects estimator, suggests that more open countries adopted smaller stimulus packages. These empirical results are consistent with Aizenman and Jinjarak (2010) which finds that across a larger sample of countries, "de facto fiscal space," which is measured by the inverse of the tax-years it would take to repay the public debt, is positively associated with fiscal stimulus. Their paper also finds higher trade openness was associated with lower fiscal stimulus and a higher level of depreciation during 2009 and 2010.

There was also a link between the fiscal and the monetary policy response. As mentioned above, central banks' policy rates in advanced G20s were already very close to the zero lower bound, and therefore there was limited room for action using traditional monetary policy instruments (indeed providing the key rationale for an activist fiscal policy). However, quantitative easing still allowed central banks to support aggregate demand.[21] Several advanced and emerging G20s significantly expanded their central bank balance sheets, most notably (but not exclusively) in the United States, but this has not been even across countries (figure 10.12). Several emerging G20s also relied on exchange rate depreciation to accommodate the economic slowdown (with the exception of China and Brazil), an instrument that was not available to several advanced G20 economies.

10.4 Selected Public Sector Asset and Liability Management Issues

The crisis resulted in a significant expansion of government balance sheets in advanced economies. In the advanced G20 economies, total liabilities averaged 90 percent of GDP at end-2010, an increase of almost 25 percentage points of GDP over 2007. However, one-quarter of the increase in liabilities was offset by the acquisition of financial assets, which reached about 40 percent of GDP on average at the end of 2010 (figure 10.13).

Governments used their balance sheets to limit the impact of the crisis, especially by supporting the financial sector. Examples of support for financial institutions were asset swaps/purchases (in Australia, Canada, Japan, Korea, Spain, United States, and Russia), bank recapitalization (in France, Italy, Japan, Korea, United Kingdom, United States, and Russia), and direct lending or crisis liquidity facilities (in Canada, Japan, Korea, United Kingdom, United States, Brazil, Russia, and Saudi Arabia).[22]

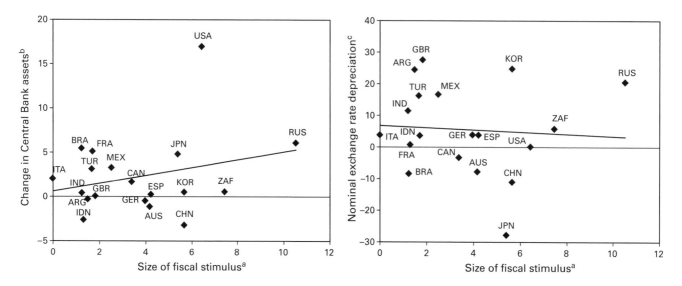

Figure 10.12
G20 economies' fiscal stimulus and monetary policy. (a) Cumulative fiscal stimulus from 2008 to 2010, in percent of GDP; (b) change in central bank total assets as a percent of GDP between 2008 and 2010; (c) cumulative increase in nominal effective exchange rate from 2008 to 2010.
Sources: Country authorities; staff estimates

Financial sector interventions were important to stabilize the financial markets and to prepare the ground for a credit-led recovery. For example, Laeven and Valencia (2013) find that for a sample of advanced and emerging economies, government support to bank capital during a crisis (when banks tend to be capital-crunched) has a positive effect on lending and contribute to the growth of firms that depend on financing. In addition there are both theoretical and empirical evidence that the economic recovery following significant growth decelerations can be protracted based on the extent to which financial sector frictions affect credit recovery (Bernanke and Gertler 1989; Greenwald and Stiglitz 1993; Kiyotaki and Moore 1997; Reinhart and Rogoff 2008b).[23] If balance sheet interventions protect financial institutions' ability to lend, then they could help not only to moderate the extent of output decline but also encourage the recovery afterward.

A critical caveat to keep in mind, however, is that fiscal sustainability also depends on the recovery value of the assets. Therefore there will be an increase in the public sector's exposure to risk going forward, given the uncertain recovery value of these assets. As sovereign creditworthiness is also an important determinant of economic growth (as it can affect interest rates), the recovery value of these assets is relevant for a full assessment of their impact on growth. This makes it important to set up appropriate asset-liability management (ALM) strategies to protect sovereign cred-

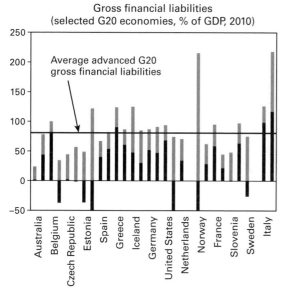

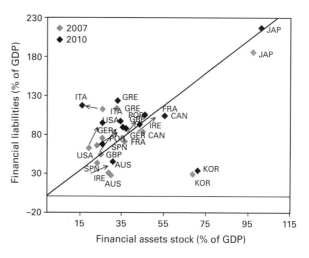

Figure 10.13
G20 economies' government assets and liabilities
Sources: Country authorities; staff estimates

itworthiness. An ALM should (1) be specified within a medium-term budget framework; (2) seek to maximize recovery rates through an orderly unwinding, timed according to the normalization of market conditions; (3) appropriately account and plan for the minimization and possible realization of contingent liabilities; and (4) identify and resolve risks from institutional deficiencies.

The expansion of government liabilities in most cases was in the form of bonds, but the increase in assets had a more diversified instrument base (figure 10.14). A large proportion of the governments' financial sector support took the form of purchase of bonds and issuance of loans. This allocation, other things constant, reduced the government's liquid position. Some governments might have compensated for this by increasing the holdings of liquid deposits. Some examples where this could have been the case are Germany, Italy, Mexico, and the United States.

Central banks' balance sheets have also expanded significantly in most G20s, including via holdings of government debt as part of a "quantitative easing" policy. This supported stabilization of asset prices in the face of possible sharp asset deflation processes, containing balance sheets' damage. Such interventions also provided time to develop fiscal plans seeking to improve sovereigns' creditworthiness and

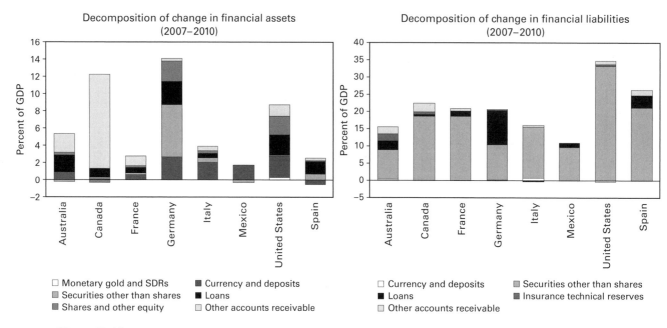

Figure 10.14
G20 economies' decomposition of government balance sheets
Sources: Country authorities; staff estimates

restore markets' confidence. The rationale was that such plans, if credible and comprehensive, would allow a decline in sovereign spreads, and in this way avoid unleashing the costs of a deterioration in the financial sector capital base, which could trigger a downward spiral on credit and growth.

Larger central bank interventions have taken place in the United States, Japan, France, and the United Kingdom, and also in Europe (by the European Central Bank). This is important as it implies that to the extent there is no need for sterilization,[24] the consolidated public sector debt including the central bank did not increase as much as that of the nonfinancial public sector (see April 2012 *Fiscal Monitor*, table 10.5). However, caution should be exerted in taking comfort from such financing operations, as the consolidated liabilities of the government (including bonds and also other liabilities such as deposits at the central bank or money base) have indeed increased. To the extent these cash and deposit holdings are demanded during periods of uncertainty as a store of value to protect balance sheets, it is to be expected that once economic recovery (and fiscal sustainability) have been established these government bonds would return to private balance sheets.

Several advanced G20 economies increased short-term debt financing through 2008 to 2010, unlike most emerging G20s. As figure 10.15 shows, Germany and France increased their short-term debt exposure, which is significant considering

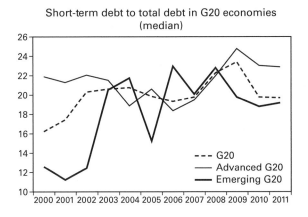

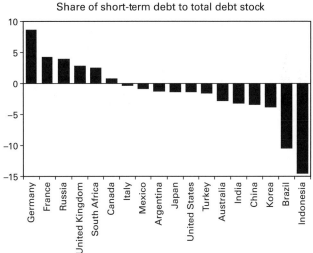

Figure 10.15
G20 economies' short-term government debt
Source: Bank of International Settlement

their high levels of gross debt and also the longer maturity of the acquired financial assets in the case of Germany. On the opposite end, several emerging G20s reduced their short-term debt share, especially Asian G20s, possibly as a result of better market liquidity conditions.

10.5 Conclusion

The fiscal policy response during the crisis was unprecedented. This reflected the exceptional nature of the financial crisis and the economic recession as well as the limited room for further monetary policy action.

The crisis opened a passionate policy debate about the role and effectiveness of fiscal policy. In broad terms, this debate focused on the appropriateness of a fiscal stimulus vs. a fiscal consolidation as a way out of the crisis. The empirical evidence, and a review of outcomes, indicates that some form of stimulus was critical to stop a downward spiral in growth and financial instability. But a deeper look at the fiscal responses presented in this chapter also shows that the response actually took into account the economic forces recognized in both positions. There was indeed a stimulus of close to 2 percent of GDP per year in 2009 to 2010, and it was diversified across various policy instruments. In most cases stimulus packages included a larger share of expenditure measures (particularly infrastructure investment which are generally associated with relatively high multipliers), but also a nontrivial share of revenue measures. The emphasis on the preservation of fiscal sustainability, however, was not absent at the time the stimulus was designed, and also later during the stimulus withdrawal phase. Fiscal stimuli size was contained, given the requirement to balance the need to avert a growth collapse vis-à-vis the risks involved in excessive borrowing. Stimuli typically included significant self-reversing (or easier-to-reverse) and transitory elements. Also, as the cross-country differences indicate, the stimulus was larger in countries in which the recession was deeper, had more fiscal space, and had less financial pressure. Finally, stimuli were larger in countries with less room for a monetary policy response, and less developed automatic stabilizers.

Arguably, the timing of the withdrawal of stimulus also took into account fiscal sustainability considerations. The stimulus was gradually withdrawn starting in 2011, as gross public debts reached about 70 percent of world GDP (and over 100 percent in advanced economies) and fiscal sustainability concerns took more preeminence. At that stage, given some signs of growth stability and financing constraints permitting, countries focused on managing the pace of fiscal consolidation. It became important to identify the delicate fiscal consolidation path that would ensure fiscal sustainability over the medium term while minimizing its negative near-term impact on growth. This withdrawal of stimulus was also broadly consistent with cross-country differences in economic fundamentals. Advanced economies, which had a more lasting decline in growth but also more fiscal space, maintained fiscal stimulus longer, while emerging economies potentially more susceptible to financing pressures withdrew stimulus earlier.

Government balance sheets were also impacted by the interventions during the crisis. The expansion of government liabilities has been partially matched by a corresponding increase in assets as a result of financial sector interventions. Still these operations have increased risks and uncertainty affecting government balance sheets. This calls for strengthening the management of public sector assets and liabilities in the coming years. A distinctive feature of interventions during the crisis was the widespread use of government (and in some cases also central banks) balance sheets to support financial markets, particularly the banking sector.

The crisis also highlighted the importance of building up fiscal space in good times to enable a response in bad times. On the positive side, the crisis improved policy coordination within the G20 group. Institutional progress was made in designing a framework for coordination and monitoring of macroeconomic and financial policies (the so-called G20 Mutual Assessment Process).

The road ahead remains challenging, and the need to secure fiscal sustainability is likely to continue to assume greater importance over time. In addition to additional fiscal consolidation needed to make public debt sustainability more stable and less vulnerable to shocks, key structural fiscal reforms remain critical, including reforms of health and pension schemes.

Appendix: Some Fiscal Policy Terminology and Definitions

Table A10.1
Fiscal indicators, 2007 to 2012
(Percent of GDP, except where otherwise noted)

	2007	2008	2009	Estimates 2010	Projections 2011	2012
Overall fiscal balance[a]						
World	−0.4	−2.0	−6.7	−5.5	−4.4	−4.0
Advanced economies	−1.3	−3.8	−9.0	−7.6	−6.6	−5.8
United States	−2.7	−6.7	−13.0	−10.5	−9.5	−8.2
Euro area	−0.7	−2.1	−6.4	−6.2	−4.2	−3.3
France	−2.7	−3.3	−7.6	−7.1	−5.4	−4.6
Germany	0.2	−0.1	−3.2	−4.3	−1.0	−0.8
Italy	−1.5	−2.7	−5.3	−4.5	−3.9	−2.8
Spain	1.9	−4.2	−11.2	−9.3	−8.5	−6.2
Japan	−3.0	−4.7	−10.8	−9.3	−10.1	−10.2
United Kingdom	−2.7	−4.9	−10.4	−9.9	−8.6	−7.9
Canada	1.6	0.1	−4.9	−5.6	−4.8	−4.2
Emerging economies	0.2	−0.4	−4.8	−3.6	−2.5	−2.6
China	0.9	−0.4	−3.1	−2.3	−2.0	−2.0
India	−4.2	−7.2	−9.7	−9.0	−8.3	−7.8
Russia	6.8	4.9	−6.3	−3.5	0.5	−0.8
Brazil	−2.7	−1.4	−3.1	−2.8	−2.6	−2.4
Mexico	−1.2	−1.1	−4.7	−4.3	−3.0	−2.6
South Africa	1.5	−0.5	−5.3	−5.1	−5.0	−4.8
Low-income economies	−1.7	−1.3	−4.0	−2.9	−2.5	−2.9
G20 economies	−1.0	−2.7	−7.6	−6.2	−5.1	−4.7
G20 advanced	−1.9	−4.4	−9.6	−8.2	−7.2	−6.3
G20 emerging	0.4	−0.2	−4.8	−3.5	−2.5	−2.6
General government cyclically adjusted balance (percent of potential GDP)						
World	−1.5	−2.6	−4.6	−4.4	−3.6	−3.1
Advanced economies	−2.1	−3.6	−5.9	−6.0	−5.1	−4.3
United States[b]	−2.8	−5.0	−7.5	−7.8	−7.0	−5.9
Euro area	−2.2	−3.1	−4.6	−4.7	−3.4	−2.0
France	−3.1	−3.0	−5.3	−5.2	−4.1	−3.4
Germany	−1.2	−1.3	−1.3	−3.5	−1.2	−0.4
Italy	−3.4	−3.6	−3.5	−3.4	−2.9	−0.8

(*continued*)

Table A10.1
(*continued*)

	2007	2008	2009	Estimates 2010	Projections 2011	2012
Spain	0.1	−5.4	−9.8	−7.8	−7.0	−4.0
Japan	−3.1	−4.1	−7.7	−7.8	−8.0	−8.6
United Kingdom	−4.0	−6.5	−9.0	−7.8	−6.3	−5.1
Canada	0.6	−0.5	−2.5	−4.0	−3.7	−3.1
Emerging economies	−0.8	−1.9	−4.1	−3.5	−2.6	−2.4
China	1.1	0.0	−2.4	−1.5	−0.7	−0.6
India	−5.8	−9.3	−10.8	−9.6	−8.7	−8.2
Russia	6.1	3.9	−3.3	−2.1	0.7	−1.1
Brazil	−3.1	−2.2	−2.2	−3.3	−2.7	−2.2
Mexico	−1.5	−1.3	−3.8	−3.8	−2.7	−2.4
South Africa	0.0	−2.0	−4.9	−4.6	−4.5	−4.1
G20 economies	−1.7	−3.0	−5.2	−5.1	−4.2	−3.7
G20 advanced	−2.4	−3.8	−6.0	−6.3	−5.5	−4.6
G20 emerging	−0.5	−1.7	−4.1	−3.4	−2.5	−2.5
General government gross debt						
World	57.4	59.3	65.7	69.9	70.0	70.8
Advanced economies	76.1	82.0	93.7	99.7	103.6	107.8
United States	67.2	76.1	89.9	98.5	102.2	108.0
Euro Area	66.4	70.1	79.8	85.6	88.5	91.0
France	64.2	68.3	79.0	82.4	86.3	89.1
Germany	65.2	66.7	74.4	83.2	81.5	81.5
Italy	103.1	105.8	115.5	118.4	121.0	124.9
Spain	36.1	39.9	53.6	60.8	70.6	78.2
Japan	188.6	196.2	216.3	219.0	233.4	241.0
United Kingdom	43.9	52.5	68.4	75.1	82.2	88.5
Canada	66.5	71.1	83.6	85.1	85.4	86.3
Emerging economies	35.8	34.6	36.6	40.7	37.7	36.2
China	19.6	17.0	17.7	33.5	26.6	23.3
India	75.4	74.7	74.4	68.1	66.6	66.1
Russia	8.5	7.9	11.0	11.7	10.6	10.7
Brazil	64.5	63.1	66.7	64.5	65.5	64.0
Mexico	37.8	43.1	44.7	42.9	44.1	43.4
South Africa	28.3	27.4	31.5	35.3	37.9	39.8
Low-income economies	41.8	38.6	41.9	39.7	38.7	39.2
G20 economies	63.9	66.4	73.2	78.1	77.8	78.5

Table A10.1
(*continued*)

	2007	2008	2009	Estimates 2010	Projections 2011	2012
G20 advanced	81.3	87.6	100.1	106.4	110.3	114.8
G20 emerging	36.3	34.6	35.8	40.7	37.1	35.2
Memorandum:						
World growth (percent)	*5.4*	*2.7*	*-0.6*	*5.2*	*3.8*	*3.4*

Source: IMF staff estimates and projections
Note: All country averages are PPP-GDP weighted using rolling weights and calculated based on data availability. Projections are based on IMF staff assessment of current policies.
a. For overall fiscal balance and cyclically adjusted balance, + indicates a smaller fiscal deficit; for gross debt, + indicates a larger debt.
b. Excluding financial sector support.

The overall balance in nominal terms (*OB*) can be written as the primary balance (*PB = T − E*) minus net interest expenditures (*INT*),

$$OB = PB - INT.$$

The distinction of the primary balance is important in that it identifies government policies, given that interest expenditures are in general out of the government control.

A **fiscal expansion (contraction)** is a decline (increase) in the *PB.* Notice that if a fiscal expansion is computed in percent of GDP (as opposed to computation in nominal terms), then it also captures changes in GDP.

The primary balance reflects a combination of factors, including from either the automatic budget responses (e.g., a decline in tax revenues during recessions, without a change in tax rates) or policy actions (e.g., a change in policy). To better identify these components, some specific indicators can be computed. The **cyclical primary balance** (*CPB*) is the share of the primary balance that results from cyclical economic developments. This is in general calculated by computing the component of revenues and expenditures that respond to the business cycle (see Fedelino et al. 2009). The **automatic stabilizers** are computed as the annual change in the *CPB,*[25]

$$AS = dCPB.$$

Removing the *CPB* from the *OB* results in the **cyclically adjusted primary balance** (*CAPB*),[26]

$$CAPB = PB - CPB.$$

The *CAPB* can be used to characterize fiscal policy: the **fiscal policy stance** is *procyclical* if the *CAPB* is in deficit (surplus) when the output gap is positive (negative) (Blejer and Cheasty 1993). A fiscal policy stance is *countercyclical* if the CAPB is in deficit (surplus) when the output gap is negative (positive).

Another important indicator to describe fiscal policy is the **fiscal impulse** (*FI*), which captures the impact of fiscal policy on aggregate demand relative to the past, as opposed to in relation to the state of the cycle as in the *CAPB* level. This is defined as the (negative of the) change in the *CAPB*,

$$FI = -dCAPB.$$

A fiscal impulse can be *procyclical* if *FI* is of the same sign as the output gap (e.g., a decrease in the CAPB when the output gap is positive, meaning the government is introducing an expansionary impulse during an economic boom), or *countercyclical* when *FI* has the opposite sign than the output gap.

A different concept is that of **fiscal stimulus** (*FS*). This terminology is used to refer to discretionary crisis-related fiscal policy actions introduced to support economic activity. These are in general a subset of the fiscal impulse, which might also include other measures that are either structural in nature or reflect the fiscal impact of other cyclical developments not captured by the economic cycle.

Notes

1. It is beyond the scope of this chapter to settle this debate.

2. The part of the primary deficit attributed to other structural or discretionary effects captures the underlying structural deficit (e.g., as a result of a change in the output gap from a decline in potential GDP, or arising from demographic pressures related to aging), financial sector support measures, and any additional fiscal impact of the crisis that is not captured by the cyclical adjustment. An example of the latter is revenue declines attributed to lower asset or housing prices (for a conceptual discussion, see *Fiscal Implications of the Global Economic and Financial Crisis*, app. V, IMF, 2009b).

3. The expenditure increase of Saudi Arabia mainly accelerated the implementation of existing development plans.

4. See Spilimbergo et al. (2009).

5. The output gap is defined as actual GDP minus potential GDP relative to potential GDP.

6. The change in debt is decomposed into the change in primary deficit, interest payments, the effects of growth dynamics (we report the effects of growth dynamics together with interest payments), net lending and other stock-flow adjustments, and financial sector support. This decomposition follows the methodology that has been applied in the September 2011 *Fiscal Monitor* for advanced G20 economies.

7. The differential between the effective interest rate and growth in emerging economies has historically been negative from 1990 to 2007 (*Fiscal Monitor*, April 2012).

8. A review of the size of fiscal multipliers would be provided in the next chapter.

9. A key reason that explains the opposing results is the difference in strategies used to identify discretionary fiscal consolidation episodes. The study in WEO identifies discretionary fiscal policy as the execution of announced stimulus packages. Most of the studies in the literature that argued that fiscal consolidation can increase growth use the change in the cyclically adjusted primary balance (i.e., a statistical concept) to estimate the magnitude of discretionary fiscal policy.

10. Exceptions occur typically in countries with high risks to fiscal sustainability.

11. See Baum, Poplawski-Ribeiro, and Weber (2012).

12. See Cottarelli (2012).

13. While there is no one definitive guideline for designing appropriate fiscal stimulus packages, some papers tried to identify guiding principles. One example is Spilimbergo et al. (2008). This paper proposes that to maximize the impact of discretionary fiscal policy, a stimulus package should be *timely* (given the urgent need for action), *large* (given the significant decline in demand), *lasting* (as the recession was expected to endure), *diversified* (given the uncertainty regarding which measures would be most effective), *contingent* (to ensure that further action would be taken if needed), *collective* (for all countries with fiscal space to contribute given the global nature of the shock), and *sustainable* (to avoid debt sustainability concerns triggering contractionary adverse effects in the short run).

14. See Khatiwada (2009) for a detailed discussion of labor market measures that were adopted.

15. Analyzing the appropriateness of stimulus packages at an individual country basis and with respect to considerations paid to social protection and labor market policies is beyond the scope of this chapter.

16. In the case of the United States, however, the fact that the payroll tax is capped might have resulted in a more stimulating impact as the cuts tend to benefit relatively more low- to middle-income earners.

17. The G20 comprises 19 countries (9 from advanced countries and 10 from emerging countries) and the European Union. To ensure global economic institutions work together, the International Monetary Fund, the World Bank, the Organisation for Economic Cooperation and Development (OECD), and others also participate in the G20 meetings.

18. Washington (November 2008), London (April 2009), Pittsburgh (September 2009), Toronto (June 2010), Seoul (November 2010), and Cannes (November 2011).

19. The results are robust to different estimation methods, including OLSs with panel-corrected standard errors, random effects estimator, and fixed effects estimator. Although, given the limited degrees of freedom, the evidence should only be considered indicative.

20. In principle, the application of stimulus would be correlated with lags of the output gap, but the regression results showed no statistically significant results under such specification. The reason is possibly that stimulus packages were applied with a lag of less than one year. As the shock took place in September 2007, the growth impact is observed in full in 2008, when fiscal stimulus started.

21. In Europe, the quantitative easing also included the ECB's balance sheet interventions, which are not included in figure 10.12.

22. See IMF Board paper SM/09/210.

23. Calvo, Izquierdo, and Talvi (2006a, b) provide evidence showing that, in the specific case of crisis or sharp output decelerations in the context of capital flow reversals ("sudden stops"), output recovery after crises in emerging economies has not been accompanied by a commensurate recovery in the stock of credit, a phenomenon they call "phoenix miracles." This result has been confirmed for industrial economies by Claessens, Kose, and Terrones (2008). Biggs, Mayer, and Pick (2009), however, argue that credit recovery does matter in order to explain output recovery, focusing on the distinction that what is required for growth to resume is that credit *flow* (new credit) recovers, even if the credit *stock* does not.

24. For example, in the United Kingdom the purchase by the Bank of England of government bonds from banks had an increase in banks' deposits at the central bank as a counterpart.

25. This equality holds in nominal terms. However, it is common to express the CPB as a share of potential GDP, and the PB as a share of GDP. As a result computing he difference above as share of the GDP under the usual conventions results in an (usually small) error, given the different denominators.

26. Given that the CPB measure is usually calculated based on the cyclical behavior of GDP, this measure includes the possibility of error if the cyclical components of revenues and expenditures respond to other variables that are not fully captured in GDP, such as terms of trade. Adjusting for other potential cycles (e.g., for commodity or asset prices) and for one-off measures give the structural balance (see Fedelino et al. 2009).

References

Aizenman, Joshua, and Yothin Jinjarak. 2010. De facto fiscal space and fiscal stimulus: Definition and assessment. Working paper 16539. NBER, Cambridge, MA.

Alesina, Alberto and Silvia Ardagna. 1998. Tales of fiscal adjustment. *Economic Policy* (October): 498–545.

Alesina, Alberto, and Roberto Perotti. 1995. Fiscal expansions and fiscal adjustments in OECD countries. *Economic Policy* 10 (21): 205–48.

Alesina, Alberto, and Roberto Perotti. 1997. Fiscal adjustments in OECD countries: Composition and macroeconomic effects. *IMF Staff Papers* 44 (June): 210–48.

Auerbach, A. J. 2009. Implementing the new fiscal policy activism. *American Economic Review* 99 (2): 543–49.

Baum, A., M. Poplawski-Ribeiro, and A. Weber. 2012. Fiscal multipliers and the state of the economy. Working paper 12/286. IMF, Washington, DC.

Bernanke, B. S., and M. Gertler. 1989. Agency costs, net worth, and business fluctuations. *American Economic Review* 79: 14–31.

Biggs, M., T. Mayer, and A. Pick. 2009. Credit and economic recovery. Working paper 218. DNB, New York.

Blejer, Mario, and Adrienne Cheasty, eds.,1993. *How to Measure the Fiscal Deficit*. Washington, DC: IMF.

Claessens, Stijn M., Ayhan Kose, and Marco E. Terrones. 2008. What happens during recessions, crunches and busts? Working paper 08/274. IMF, Washington, DC.

Cottarelli, Carlo, and Laura Jaramillo. 2012. Walking hand in hand: Fiscal policy and growth in advanced economies. Working paper 12/137. IMF, Washington, DC.

DeLong, J. Bradford, and Lawrence Summers. 2012. Fiscal policy in a depressed economy. Brookings Papers on Economic Activity (spring).

Fedelino, A., A. Ivanova, and M. Horton. 2009. Computing cyclically adjusted balances and automatic stabilizers. Technical notes and manuals 2009/05. IMF, Washington, DC.

Feldstein, Martin. 2009. Rethinking the role of fiscal policy. *American Economic Review* 99 (2): 556–59.

Giavazzi, Francesco, and Marco Pagano. 1990. Can severe fiscal contractions be expansionary? Tales of two small European countries. *NBER Macroeconomics Annual* 5: 75–122.

Giavazzi, Francesco, and Marco Pagano. 1996. Non-Keynesian effects of fiscal policy changes: International evidence and the Swedish experience. *Swedish Economic Policy Review* 3 (1): 67–103.

Greenwald, Bruce C., and Joseph E. Stiglitz. 1993. Financial market imperfections and business cycles. *Quarterly Journal of Economics* 108 (1): 77–114.

International Monetary Fund. 2009b. Fiscal implications of the global economic and financial crisis. Occasional paper 269. IMF, Washington, DC.

Khatiwada, Sameer. 2009. Stimulus packages to counter global economic crisis: A review. Discussion paper 196/2009. International Institute for Labour Studies, Geneva.

Kiyotaki, Nobuhiro, and Moore, John. 1997. "Credit Cycles." *Journal of Political Economy*, 1997, vol. 105, no. 2.

Laeven, Luc and Valencia, Fabián, 2013. "The Real Effects of Financial Sector Interventions during Crises," *Journal of Money, Credit and Banking*, Blackwell Publishing, vol. 45(1): 147-177, 02.

Ramey, Valerie A. 2009. Identifying government spending shocks: It's all in the timing. Working paper 15464. NBER, Cambridge, MA.

Reinhart, Carmen M., and Kenneth S. Rogoff. 2008b. Banking crises: An equal opportunity menace. Working paper 14587. NBER, Cambridge, MA.

Romer, Christina D. 2010. The macroeconomic effects of tax changes: Estimates based on a new measure of fiscal shocks. *American Economic Review* 100 (3): 763–801.

Romer, Christina D., and David H. Romer. 2010. The macroeconomic effects of tax changes: Estimates based on a new measure of fiscal shocks. *American Economic Review* 100 (3): 763–801.

Spilimbergo, A., S. Symansky, O. Blanchard, and C. Cottarelli. 2008. Fiscal policy for the crisis. Staff paper. IMF, Washington, DC. Available at: http://www.imf.org/external/pubs/ft/spn/2008/spn0801.pdf.

Spilimbergo, A., S. Symansky, and M. Schindler. 2009. Fiscal multipliers. Staff paper. IMF, Washington, DC. Available at: http://www.imf.org/external/pubs/ft/spn/2009/spn0911.pdf.

Taylor, J. B. 2009. The lack of an empirical rationale for a revival of discretionary fiscal policy. *American Economic Review* 99 (2): 550–55.

11

Fiscal Policy Response during the Crisis in Low-Income African Economies

Martine Guerguil, Marcos Poplawski-Ribeiro, and Anna Shabunina

11.1 Introduction

Fiscal policy has traditionally been procyclical in emerging market and developing economies; that is, government spending increases in good times but declines in bad times, possibly exacerbating the business cycle. A large and growing body of literature has linked this outcome to three main (and not inconsistent) factors: financial constraints, political distortions, and technical weaknesses.[1] Because of their limited access to financial markets, governments have no choice but to cut spending and raise revenues in bad times, while in good times, inadequate political and fiscal institutions make it difficult to resist pressures to increase expenditure and lower taxes. Growth forecast errors and weak implementation capacities add to these constraints. The resulting "procyclical bias" is likely to be particularly pronounced in low-income countries (LICs) in sub-Saharan Africa (SSA), given the smaller size of automatic stabilizers and more pervasive governance and administrative limitations.[2]

In the 2000s, a number of middle- and low-income countries began to graduate from this procyclical bias and conduct acyclical or countercyclical fiscal policies in the face of downturns. This change has been largely attributed to the strengthening of their fiscal frameworks and budget institutions.[3] As the global financial crisis broke out, many SSA LICs had built sizable fiscal buffers and were able to implement policies specifically aimed at mitigating the impact of the global slowdown on their economies. The authorities quickly designed ambitious stimulus packages. And international organizations were willing to provide the financing to that end.[4]

This chapter looks at the subsequent implementation of fiscal policies in SSA LICs. More specifically, it asks three questions. Were the fiscal policies implemented in response to the global crisis effectively countercyclical? Was implementation in line with the original plans? And if there were divergences, what were the causes? The answers to these questions feed into the ongoing debate on the role of fiscal policy in LICs and its potential contribution to macroeconomic stabilization, and can provide insights for its future design.

The chapter extends the finding of the literature in two ways. Following Thornton (2008), it is one of the few attempts to focus more specifically on the cyclicality of fiscal policy in low-income economies. SSA LICs have specific features that distinguish them from their higher income neighbors, such as South Africa or Botswana, and are likely to impact fiscal policy implementation, such as access to concessional financing, less diversified tax and public spending structures, and possibly weaker institutions. The chapter also builds on Lledó and Poplawski-Ribeiro (2011, 2013) by analyzing the determinants of budget execution separately for current and for capital spending. Isolating the impact of specific factors on implementation of public investment projects is particularly pertinent since closing the infrastructure gap is now a prominent policy goal in Africa.

We find that SSA LICs have been able to move away from procyclical fiscal policy during the global financial crisis, but the overall fiscal numbers mask two diverging and potentially bothersome trends: the large overexecution of current spending and the even larger underexecution of capital projects. Various factors contribute to this outcome. The quality of governance and budgetary institutions explains a significant part of the deviation between intended and observed current spending, while political factors seem to have more impact on the implementation of investment plans. A possible explanation is that democratically elected governments tend to receive a large share of aid, potentially above their actual implementation capacity, particularly when it comes to the execution of investment projects. This gap between execution of current and capital spending plans, if maintained, could reduce LICs' future fiscal space. Further strengthening of fiscal institutions, including efforts to increase the technical content of investment decisions, could help avoid a return to fiscal procyclicality.

The chapter is structured as follows. Section 11.2 briefly describes the impact of the global financial crisis on SSA LICs and the planned and observed fiscal policy responses. Section 11.3 examines whether the resulting fiscal stance was countercyclical as intended, and section 11.4 looks at the factors behind the deviation between fiscal plans and observed outcomes. Section 11.5 concludes.

11.2 Global Financial Crisis and Low-Income Africa

The decade prior to the global financial crisis witnessed noteworthy economic momentum in SSA. In a region previously plagued by dismal economic outturns, average annual growth accelerated to 5.3 percent over 2000 to 2007. Some low-income African countries even topped the world's growth charts, fueling talk of the emergence of "African lions" (McKinsey Global Institute 2010). The pre-crisis commodity boom explains only part of this new dynamism; activity accelerated across the continent and was observed even in countries where commodities did not account

Table 11.1
Real GDP growth (percent)

	2000–2007	2008	2009	2010	2011	2012
World	4.7	2.9	−0.6	5.0	3.6	3.1
Sub-Saharan Africa	6.3	5.6	2.8	5.3	5.1	5.1
Low-income sub-Saharan Africa	5.3	6.6	5.0	6.4	5.7	6.1

Source: *Fiscal Monitor*, October 2012
Note: Annual averages, weighted by GDP at PPP using 2009 weights and based on data availability.

for a large share of exports. Regained political balance and macroeconomic stability, the latter buttressed by far-reaching policy reforms including trade liberalization, privatization, and fiscal consolidation, were major factors behind this upswing.

The global financial crisis did break the trend. Growth in the region as a whole slowed to 2.8 percent in 2009, the lowest level in fifteen years. The effect on SSA LICs was more subdued, in good part because of their more limited integration with the world economy: the average shortfall in output was only 1.5 percentage points (table 11.1). However, the impact varied considerably across countries, reflecting the different strength of their external trade and financial links. About one-third of the countries (those more reliant on exports and remittances) suffered a substantial downswing, one-third a modest slowdown, while the remaining third was unaffected (some countries even benefitting from the reversal in the pre-crisis food price surge). Given the tenuous links of SSA LICs with international capital markets, very few suffered from financial strains in the aftermath of the crisis (see detailed table in appendix A at the end of this chapter).

The slowdown, when it happened, was also relatively short, with growth rebounding to pre-crisis levels in most cases as soon as 2010. This outcome was in sharp contrast with the slow and hesitant recoveries observed in the past (IMF 2009b) and the prolonged economic slump in advanced economies. The quick rebound in world trade and commodity prices helped, together with the resilience of aid flows (including those from international organizations). In all, the growth impact was significantly shallower, and the recovery faster, than initially anticipated (figure 11.1).

About 60 percent of SSA LICs designed ambitious fiscal stimulus packages to mitigate the impact of the expected negative shock, often with international support (table 11.2). The resulting widening of budget deficits (of about 1.5 percent of GDP over 2008 to 2009) was expected to be temporary. Revenue measures were included in about half the countries and sometimes involved lowering corporate taxes and royalties. Reductions in excise taxes and import duties on food and fuel products and/or increases in direct subsidies of these products were also common,

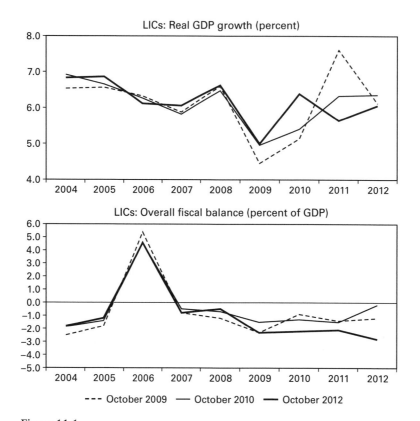

Figure 11.1
Successive vintages of growth and budget deficits forecasts. LICs: real GDP growth (percent); LICs: overall fiscal balance (percent of GDP). Annual averages are weighted by GDP at PPP using 2009 weights and based on data availability.
Sources: *Fiscal Monitor*, October 2012; *World Economic Outlook (WEO)*, October 2010 and October 2009

Table 11.2
Planned fiscal policy responses (percent of countries)

Planned countercyclical response	62
Of which:	
Planned tax measures	50
Planned changes in excise and custom duties or in fuel subsidies	44
Planned pro-poor spending measures	44

Source: IMF staff estimates

often as part of social support programs. Almost all countries in the group planned to step up capital spending (on average, by 3 percentage points of GDP over 2008 to 2010). These ambitious programs, mostly focused on road and energy projects, had been designed before the crisis as part of a drive to close an infrastructure deficit seen as a brake on potential growth. In contrast to experience with previous global slowdowns, when SSA LICs had been forced to trim spending in the face of an unexpected decline in revenue, most countries left their expenditure plans unchanged, thus combining long-term objectives (boosting potential growth) with short-term ones (stabilizing output). Capital spending was, in many cases, the largest element of the planned countercyclical response to the crisis (figure 11.2, upper panel).

In the event, the deficits ended up about 2 percentage points of GDP larger than projected. Revenue fell short of projections by an average of 2.5 percent of GDP, but overall spending was slightly below budget plans (by 0.5 percent of GDP). The degree of budget execution was noticeably different for current and capital spending (figure 11.3 and figure 11.2, lower panel). Capital projects were significantly underexecuted (an average gap of 1.9 percent of projected GDP, or 17 percent, with respect to the budget, with 70 percent of countries falling behind their plans) while current spending went in many cases over planned allocations (by 1.6 percent of projected GDP on average, or 9 percent over budget, in 70 percent of observations/country-years). The under execution of capital spending plans seems to have been noticeably smaller than that recorded in the pre-crisis period (33 percent on average, according to estimates in Briceño-Garmendia et al. 2008). Nevertheless, in practice, and contrary to initial plans, a large part of the stimulus was delivered via an increase in current spending and not through public investment.

11.3 A Shift to Countercyclical Fiscal Policies?

Although standard economic theory suggests that fiscal policy should ideally be countercyclical, many studies have shown that fiscal policy has been procyclical in most developing economies for most of the past decades. Gavin and Perotti (1997) and Thornton (2008) reach that conclusion for Latin America and low-income Africa, respectively, while Kaminsky, Reinhart, and Végh (2004), Akitoby et al. (2004), and Talvi and Végh (2005) show similar results for larger groups of developing economies across the world. This procyclical bias has been attributed to financial constraints, as developing countries are cut off from international credit markets in "bad times," forcing them to adjust (Gavin and Perotti 1997); political and institutional failures contributing to or failing to control overspending and rent-seeking activities in "good times" (Lane and Tornell 1999; Talvi and Végh 2005); and technical limitations including larger forecast errors and budget rigidities that narrow the scope for automatic stabilizers (Balassone and Kumar 2007).

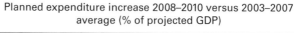

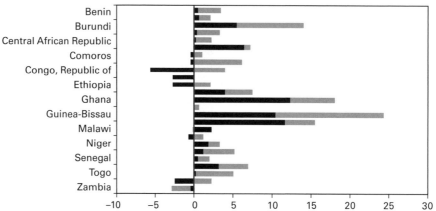

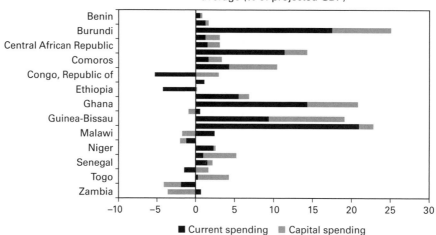

Figure 11.2
SSA LICs: planned versus executed current and capital spending, 2003 to 2008; planned expenditure increase 2008 to 2010 versus 2003 to 2007 average (percent of projected GDP); executed expenditure increase 2008 to 2010 versus 2003 to 2007 average (percent of projected GDP).
Source: IMF staff estimates

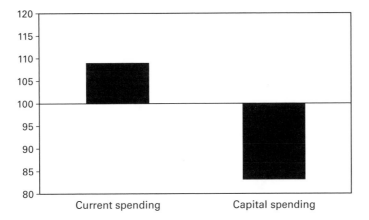

Figure 11.3
Capital and current spending implementation (percent of planned spending)
Source: IMF staff estimates

More recent papers have, however, indicated that a number of economies are moving away from the procyclical corner. Frankel, Végh, and Vuletin (2013) conclude that over the 2000s, about a third of developing economies have implemented countercyclical fiscal policies. Lledó, Yackovlev, and Gadenne (2011) find that procyclicality has declined in Africa since 2000. IMF (2010) reports preliminary data suggesting that two-thirds of SSA economies were able to implement a countercyclical response to the crisis in 2009. Our aim is to reassess this conclusion for the subset of SSA LICs in the context of the global financial crisis.

11.3.1 Methodology

Attempting to estimate business cycles in low-income Africa is challenging. One important limitation is the absence of high-frequency data; GDP is in most cases available only on an annual basis, which makes it difficult to obtain precise estimates of the output gap. In addition, output series in SSA tend to show a higher volatility, increasing the margins of error of any trend estimate. The problem is exacerbated here by the short period under consideration in this chapter, as the impact of the global financial crisis was, as mentioned, short-lived in SSA.

To mitigate the impact of these limitations we complement the traditional HP filter-based approach (that compares the level of the cyclically adjusted primary balance (CAPB) with that of the output gap and considers that fiscal policy is countercyclical if the correlation coefficient is positive)[5] with a nonparametric analysis that compares the growth of real primary government spending with that of trend output growth (the latter estimated as the average growth during the five years before the

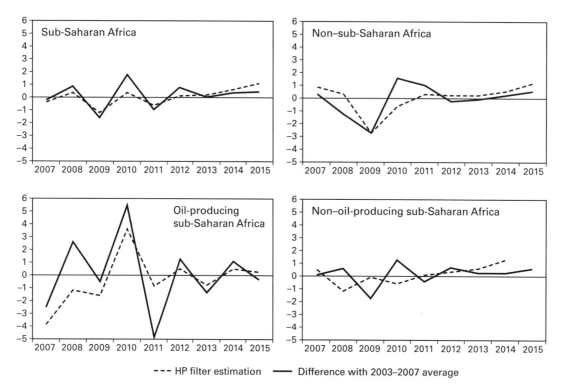

Figure 11.4
Output gap dynamics (percent of GDP) SSA; non-SSA; oil-producing SSA; non–oil-producing SSA.
Source: IMF staff estimates

crisis).[6] This additional test cannot, however, fully compensate for the weaknesses of the data, and the results should thus be taken as largely indicative.

11.3.2 Empirical Results

Estimates are computed for a group of 26 LICs in SSA (of which 3 are oil exporters) and a control group of 20 LICs in other regions. (Appendix B at the end of this chapter provides details on data and data sources as well as on the methodologies used in the different estimation exercises.) Figure 11.4 confirms that in LICs, the global financial crisis coincided with a brief but abrupt decline in the pace of activity to below its potential. The crisis hit in 2009, with the output gap at first widening markedly but narrowing shortly thereafter. In SSA LICs, and particularly in oil exporters, activity faltered again in 2011, but rebounded in the following year. These results are consistent across the two methodologies, although the HP filter, which uses a longer time period (1995 to 2017), shows a lesser change in the output gap in SSA.

Table 11.3
Share of country-years with countercyclical fiscal policy (percent)

	2003–2007	2008–2010
SSA total		
HP filter	42%	55%
Nonparametric 1	46%	50%
Non-SSA		
HP filter	40%	61%
Nonparametric 1	47%	56%

Source: IMF staff estimates

The closing of the output gap is also faster under the trend estimate, but in the case of SSA seems largely driven by the oil exporters. Notwithstanding the double dip, the overall shock to non–oil-producing SSA LICs was less destabilizing than in LICs in other regions (and considerably smaller than the shock to advanced economies), likely reflecting the lesser integration of SSA LICs in global trade.

11.3.3 Comparative Statistics
Table 11.3 shows simple estimates of the share of LICs implementing countercyclical fiscal policy. The data are split into two periods, 2003 to 2007 (before the crisis) and 2008 to 2010 (during the crisis), and estimated according to the two approaches described above. Prior to the crisis, well over half of the LICs followed procyclical policies. This proportion is, however, already significantly below that found in studies covering earlier decades, where the share of LICs undertaking countercyclical policies was often minimal. Interestingly, this proportion is roughly similar for the two methodologies and across regions—that is, the performance of SSA LICs is not noticeably different from that of LICs in other regions.

The table also shows that the share of countercyclical policy responses grew to well over half the total during the recent crisis. The increase is more pronounced for non-African LICs, but is still significant for SSA LICs. Again, both methods of estimation confirm this trend. A decomposition of the policy responses according to the type of shock (positive or negative) shows that in SSA as well as in other regions, the countercyclical response to negative shocks drives the trend (table 11.4). The movement is particularly pronounced for oil exporters, although this result should be treated with care given the small sample and the different nature of the cycle for commodity exporters. The share of countries following procyclical policies in good times also declined, suggesting that the change in policy responsiveness is not only due to the higher availability of financing.

Table 11.4
Asymmetrical fiscal policy response

HP filter Estimation	Countercyclical fiscal policy[a]			Procyclical fiscal policy[b]		
	Positive output gap shock	Negative output gap shock	Total	Positive output gap shock	Negative output gap shock	Total
2003–2007						
SSA total	21%	21%	**42%**	32%	26%	**58%**
SSA non–oil producers	21%	22%	**43%**	33%	24%	**57%**
SSA oil producers	0%	17%	**17%**	33%	50%	**83%**
Non-SSA	30%	10%	**40%**	33%	26%	**60%**
2008–10						
SSA total	19%	36%	**55%**	21%	24%	**45%**
SSA non–oil producers	19%	33%	**52%**	23%	25%	**48%**
SSA oil producers	17%	67%	**83%**	0%	17%	**17%**
Non-SSA	29%	32%	**61%**	13%	27%	**39%**

Source: IMF staff estimates
a. Share of cases (countries and years) in which countercyclical fiscal policy was conducted given the 0 output gap shock in the period- and country-group sample specified.
b. Share of cases (countries and years) in which procyclical fiscal policy was conducted given the output gap shock in the period- and country-group sample specified.

The exercise also confirms the small size of automatic stabilizers in LICs (table 11.5).[7] Reflecting relatively low tax ratio, automatic stabilizers on average account for barely 0.2 percent of GDP in SSA LICs. They are twice as large in LICs in other regions, mainly because their revenue-to-GDP ratios are higher. Automatic stabilizers are also considerably larger among oil exporters. The discretionary change in the primary balance has been on average substantially (1.5 to 3 times) larger than automatic stabilizers across all country groups.

11.3.4 Pooled Regressions

We try to formalize these results for SSA LICs by estimating the reaction function of the CAPB to the output gap. Given the small sample, regressions are estimated using panel fixed effects with ordinary least squares (FE-OLS) with White-heteroskedasticity corrected *t*-statistics. The results are shown in table 11.6. The coefficient beta shows the change in CAPB when the output gap increases by 1 percentage point; it is expected to have a positive sign when fiscal policy is countercyclical. We again split the sample in two time periods (before and after the crisis) and calculate the coefficients for both the planned CAPB and the observed CAPB.

Table 11.5
Automatic stabilizers (percent of GDP)

	SSA non–oil producers	Non-SSA	Oil producers
2003	−0.2	−0.3	−0.2
2004	−0.2	−0.2	0.2
2005	−0.1	−0.2	0.5
2006	−0.1	−0.1	0.7
2007	−0.1	0.1	−0.4
2008	0.0	0.4	−0.7
2009	−0.2	−0.3	−0.6
2010	−0.2	−0.4	0.2

Source: IMF staff estimates

Table 11.6
Fiscal policy and the business cycle in LICs

	CAPB			Planned CAPB
	1996–2007	2000–07	2008–10	2008–10
Output gap	−0.004	0.082	0.675**	
	(−0.046)	(0.875)	(2.291)	
Projected output gap				0.338**
				(1.754)
Previous year's debt	0.000	0.003	0.012	0.010
	(0.074)	(0.567)	(0.819)	(0.656)
Constant	−0.359	−0.665	−3.964**	−0.930
	(−0.362)	(−0.672)	(−2.273)	(−0.591)
Adjusted R^2	0.367	0.432	0.423	0.699
F	11.623	11.952	.	6.476
Number of observations	189	167	73	60

Source: IMF staff estimates
Note: All regressions are estimated using panel fixed effects with OLS (FE-OLS) with White heteroskedasticity corrected t-statistics in parentheses, rejection of the null hypothesis at *** $p < 0.01$, ** $p < 0.05$, * $p < 0.1$.

The data confirm the shift to countercyclical policies. The coefficient is negative but very small in the years prior to the crisis, suggesting that, on average, fiscal policy tended to be acyclical. In addition, the coefficient is not significant, which may reflect a large variance across countries in the sample. The coefficient becomes positive and significant for the planned as well as for the observed fiscal response to the crisis, thus confirming that the move toward countercyclical policy was both intended and achieved, and was rather widespread. The coefficient is higher for policy outcomes than for policy intent, suggesting that the countercyclical impact was actually larger than intended. This reflects the double impact of, on the one hand, the smaller-than-expected growth slowdown and, on the other hand, the larger-than-planned widening of the deficit—both effects increasing the measure of countercyclicality.[8] The next section attempts to identify the reasons behind this gap between planned and observed deficits.

11.4 What Explains the Difference between Fiscal Plans and Outcomes?

11.4.1 Theoretical Underpinnings

The literature has identified several factors that may contribute to gaps in the implementation of fiscal policy in LICs. Institutional, political, and capacity constraints figure prominently, but forecast errors also play a role:

- *Institutional and capacity constraints.* The implementation of fiscal policy is closely related to the quality of institutions, particularly those in the budgetary area. Weaker institutions tend to lengthen decision and implementation lags, while the absence of checks and balances gives government officials discretion to deviate from fiscal plans. High turnover and inadequate skills of public employees can also act as drags on implementation. Good governance and good institutions tend to go hand in hand. Gollwitzer and Quintyn (2010) confirm that sound budgetary institutions are most likely to be established in countries with a more effective rule of law for the elites. More recently IMF (2010) finds that planned fiscal adjustments or expansions are less likely to be implemented in SSA the larger they are, the more fragile the rule of law in the country, and the weaker the institutions framing the implementation of the annual budget (see also Lledó and Poplawski-Ribeiro 2013).

- *Political variables.* Electoral years, the political regime, and the length of time an administration has been in office may affect the implementation of fiscal policy. This is more likely to be the case in Africa where political transitions from one administration to another have often been challenging and conflicts have been more frequent than in other regions.

- *Differences between aid commitments and aid disbursements.* Aid has been found to be more volatile than fiscal revenue, and shortfalls in aid and domestic revenue have tended to coincide. Moreover the informational content of commitments made by donors is limited (Bulíř and Hamann 2003) and donors often have little flexibility to alter their disbursement schedules in the face of (positive or negative) shocks. Aid shortfalls can contribute to delays in public spending, particularly in highly aid-dependent countries, and to changes in spending composition, to the extent that aid was earmarked for specific purposes.

- *Errors in growth and inflation forecasts.* Deviations between projected and observed GDP growth and inflation may also affect the pace of policy implementation through the course of the fiscal year. Output forecast errors can be expected to be larger than in higher income countries, given the weaker forecasting capacity and the higher volatility of output. Forecast errors in CPI inflation may affect fiscal implementation through their impact on revenue.[9] Growth and inflation forecast errors are likely to affect the pace of budget execution in countries using cash budgeting, as is the case of many SSA LICs.

11.4.2 Methodology and Data

We try to identify separately the determinants of implementation gaps in current spending from those in capital spending. Section 11.2 showed how the rate of execution varied across these two categories, suggesting that different factors are at play in each case. We follow the methodology used by Beetsma, Giuliodori, and Wierts (2009) and Lledó and Poplawski-Ribeiro (2013) and look at the difference between planned and actual fiscal outcomes for each category and each country. As in this literature, differences between planned and actual spending in a given year *t* are here computed as a percent of projected GDP. The relationships are estimated in real time to proxy the information sets available to the policy makers at the time they made their decisions. In line with the literature, possible determinants include forecast errors (for growth, inflation, and grants), political variables (election years, the degree of democracy, and years the executive officer has been in office), and institutional variables (rule of law and government effectiveness). An interaction term is added to explore the combined effect of the quality of budgetary institutions (captured in largely time-invariant indicators) with overall government effectiveness. Details of the methodology and data sources are to be found in appendix A.

11.4.3 Empirical Results

Table 11.7 presents the descriptive statistics. As discussed in section 11.2, the current spending gap (here in levels) is negative on average (the observed level is higher than planned), while the capital spending gap (also in levels) is positive, reflecting underexecution. Grants fell short of projections, but by a relatively small amount. Inflation was lower than expected, but real GDP growth was higher. Reflecting the

Table 11.7
Descriptive statistics, 2008 to 2010 (percent of projected GDP, unless otherwise specified)

Variable	Mean	Standard deviation[a]	Minimum	Maximum	Observed
Current spending gap	−1.6	4.7	−16.5	13.3	83
Capital spending gap	1.9	4.0	−6.1	15.6	76
Real GDP gap	−0.3	2.9	−10.7	6.4	72
CPI gap	5.6	11.5	−18.1	39.8	84
Grants gap	0.4	4.0	−17.6	13.5	83
Planned current spending	17.4	6.9	9.3	49.5	83
Actual current spending	18.9	8.8	0.0	52.0	83
Planned capital spending	11.0	6.3	3.2	43.9	76
Actual capital spending	9.2	5.9	0.0	30.8	76
Realized capital spending[b]	8.4	5.1	0.0	27.4	76
Planned capital spending—previous year capital spending[c]	3.1	5.4	−5.6	34.1	76
Planned real GDP[d]	100	0	100	100	72
Actual real GDP[d]	65.1	33.7	0.1	146.4	72
Planned CPI inflation[d]	14.8	12.7	2.0	65.2	85
Actual CPI inflation[d]	8.7	8.4	−2.1	46.2	85
Planned grants	7.4	8.8	0.3	54.0	85
Actual grants	7.2	11.7	0.0	88.3	86
Degree of democracy (polity2)[e]	2.5	5.3	−9.0	10.0	84
Electoral year[e]	0.2	0.4	0.0	1.0	86
Executive years in office[e]	10.6	9.4	1.0	42.0	84
Index rule of law[e]	−0.7	0.6	−1.8	1.0	88
Index government effectiveness[e]	−0.7	0.6	−1.8	0.8	88
Overall categories × goverment effectiveness[e]	−1.0	1.0	−2.8	1.5	99
Overall stages × goverment effectiveness[e]	−1.0	1.0	−3.0	1.4	99
PIMI overall index × goverment effectiveness[e]	−0.8	0.8	−2.5	1.8	90

Source: IMF staff estimates
a. Cross-country and time standard deviation.
b. Variable in percent of actual GDP.
c. Variable in percent of respective (planned or actual) GDP.
d. Variable in percentage.
e. Scalar variable.

heterogeneity of the sample, standard deviations are sizable for about all variables in table 11.7.

Implementation of Current Spending

Table 11.8 displays the panel estimations for current spending. The results of the baseline regressions with only macroeconomic variables are shown in columns 1 and 2; those including political and governance institutions in columns 3 to 8; and the interaction with budgetary indexes in columns 9 and 10. The overall statistics are satisfactory, with significant *F*-tests. All variables enter with the expected signs, confirming their relevance for the estimations.

Forecast errors in real GDP and grants are closely associated with current spending plans deviations. As expected, the coefficients for forecast errors, both in real GDP and in grants, are positive and significant, although not very large. Forecast errors in inflation are generally nonsignificant.

Indicators of the quality of governance and fiscal institutions are found to be related to smaller deviations in current spending plans. Both the rule of law and government effectiveness are associated with better budget implementation, including times when they exist in combination (column 8) suggesting that strong governance and strong budget institutions do contribute to a better execution of current spending.[11]

The effect of political variables is also significant, but more complex. The dummy on electoral years has a positive and significant coefficient (columns 4 and 5), suggesting a stronger deviation from current spending plans in years when elections are held. In contrast, the indicator showing the number of years the chief executive has been in office yields a significant and negative coefficient, which suggests that the longer the executive has been in office, the smaller the deviations from plans.[12] The degree of democracy has a positive coefficient, suggesting that deviations from plans are more frequent in democracies, although it is only significant when the indicator of the number of years that the chief executive has been in office is also included in the regression.

The fact that the government time in office is inversely related to gaps in current spending is consistent with the positive coefficient for the level of democracy. By definition, democratic governments tend to stay less time in power. In addition, in SSA, the 2000s have seen the emergence of "new democracies" that often had to put in place new or reformed institutions, possibly raising near-term challenges to their implementation capacity.[13]

Implementation of Capital Spending Plans

The panel results for capital spending are shown in table 11.9. Forecast errors in grants again figure prominently, with a coefficient that is significantly larger than

Table 11.8
Panel estimation of determinants of execution of current spending plans

Variables	Baseline/economic			Political and governance institutional variables					Budgetary indexes	
	(1)	(2)	(3)	(4)	(5)	(6)	(7)	(8)	(9)	(10)
Constant	-1.594***	-1.518***	-1.412***	5.569***	5.421**	-6.364***	-9.585***	-11.671***	-9.448***	-8.844***
	(-5.68)	(-6.40)	(-3.74)	(2.46)	(2.49)	(-3.70)	(-2.61)	(-2.96)	(-2.48)	(-2.43)
Real GDP gap	0.261**	0.238*	0.272**	0.376***	0.442***	0.249*	0.184	0.202	0.246*	0.244*
	(1.97)	(1.66)	(2.20)	(2.67)	(2.67)	(1.93)	(1.31)	(1.57)	(1.83)	(1.78)
CPI inflation gap	0.071	0.026	0.035	-0.011	-0.003	0.038	0.032	0.040	0.031	0.031
	(1.50)	(0.55)	(0.82)	(-0.37)	(-0.11)	(0.79)	(0.69)	(0.84)	(0.57)	(0.57)
Grants gap		0.120***	0.116***	0.081**	0.075*	0.094**	0.114***	0.095**	0.180**	0.180**
		(2.75)	(3.79)	(1.98)	(1.76)	(2.24)	(2.91)	(2.35)	(2.02)	(2.04)
Degree of democracy (polity2)			0.106		0.278**					
			(0.90)		(2.56)					
Electoral year			-0.749	1.032**	1.320**					
			(-0.89)	(2.09)	(2.23)					
Executive years in office				-0.767***	-0.816***					
				(-2.99)	(-3.19)					

	(1)	(2)	(3)	(4)	(5)	(6)	(7)	(8)	(9)	(10)
Index rule of law						-6.276***		-4.620**		
						(-2.68)		(-2.07)		
Index government effectiveness							-9.405**	-7.678*		
							(-2.16)	(-1.85)		
Overall categories × goverment effectiveness									-6.104**	
									(-1.99)	
Overall stages × government effectiveness										-5.679*
										(-1.93)
Adjusted R^2	0.10	0.12	0.21	0.50	0.52	0.18	0.20	0.22	0.26	0.26
F-Test of the regression	1.31	9.80***	7.09***	4.53***	4.16***	5.97***	11.74***	5.74***	4.87***	4.83***
Number of countries	26	26	25	25	25	26	26	26	22	22
Number of observations	66	65	63	63	63	65	65	65	53	53

Source: IMF staff estimates

Note: All regressions are estimated using panel fixed effects with OLS (FE-OLS) with White heteroskedasticity corrected t-statistics in parentheses. ***, **, * rejection of the null hypothesis at 1 percent, 5 percent, and 10 percent level of significance, respectively.

Table 11.9
Panel estimation of determinants of execution of capital spending plans

Variables	Baseline/economic		Political and governance variables					Budgetary indexes and PIMI		
	(1)	(2)	(3)	(4)	(5)	(6)	(7)	(8)	(9)	(10)
Constant	1.507*	1.393***	−0.045	1.832	1.435	9.725**	18.094***	3.906	3.744	5.711*
	(1.93)	(2.85)	(−0.05)	(0.49)	(0.47)	(2.41)	(2.98)	(1.48)	(1.55)	(1.77)
Real GDP gap	0.384*	0.210	0.379**	0.259	0.417**	0.190	0.275	0.418**	0.418**	0.387***
	(1.79)	(0.98)	(2.29)	(0.96)	(2.32)	(0.84)	(1.42)	(2.33)	(2.33)	(2.76)
CPI inflation gap	0.159*	0.011	0.032	0.005	0.023	−0.009	−0.017	0.071	0.071	0.075
	(1.69)	(0.16)	(0.45)	(0.07)	(0.32)	(−0.18)	(−0.37)	(1.08)	(1.07)	(1.16)
Grants gap		0.724***	0.695***	0.701***	0.687***	0.764***	0.819***	0.466***	0.467***	0.591***
		(5.71)	(5.70)	(5.71)	(5.58)	(10.23)	(8.27)	(3.26)	(3.25)	(4.20)
Degree of democracy (polity2)			0.626**		0.663**					
			(2.24)		(2.22)					
Electoral year			1.230	0.994	1.679					
			(1.22)	(0.54)	(1.05)					
Chief executive years in office				−0.060	−0.176					
				(−0.15)	(−0.51)					
Index rule of law						11.336**	10.709**			
						(2.12)	(2.24)			

Index government effectiveness							4.369			
							(1.15)			
Overall categories × government effectiveness								1.602		
								(0.65)		
Overall stages × government effectiveness									1.479	
									(0.65)	
PIMI overall index										4.198
										(1.08)
Adjusted R^2	0.12	0.56	0.59	0.56	0.58	0.60	0.61	0.36	0.36	0.51
F-Test of the regression	2.13	10.11***	6.60***	9.59***	100.38***	39.14***	31.58***	7.72***	7.76**	8.17***
Number of countries	24	24	24	24	23	24	24	20	20	18
Number of observations	62	61	61	61	60	61	61	49	49	45

Source: IMF staff estimates
Note: All regressions are estimated using panel fixed effects with OLS (FE-OLS) with White heteroskedasticity corrected t-statistics in parentheses. ***, **, * rejection of the null hypothesis at 1 percent, 5 percent, and 10 percent level of significance, respectively.

that found for current spending. An absolute difference of 1 percent of projected GDP between expected and received grants is associated with a deviation of around 0.7 percent of projected GDP between planned and actual capital spending. This is in line with Bulíř and Hamann (2003), who argue that aid volatility accounts for higher spending volatility.

Indicators of the quality of institutions and governance play a much less prominent role in explaining deviations from capital spending plans than for current spending plans. Only the rule of law retains significance, while indicators of government effectiveness are not found to exert significant influence. This may reflect the fact that decisions on public investments are often taken at the political level, and may be less closely linked to the regular budget institutional process.

Among political variables, unlike in the case of current spending, only the degree of democracy is found to be significant, once more with a positive sign. The indicator for the number of years the chief executive or the party has been in power has again a negative sign, but it is not significant in any of the estimations. The fact that deviations from current as well as capital spending plans are more frequent in democracies is consistent with the "new democracy" hypothesis mentioned above. In addition, new governments may be inclined to embrace ambitious investment plans, while also facing large demand pressures, explaining why they may tend to overexecute current spending plans at the expense of capital spending plans. Finally, democratic countries tend to receive more aid than nondemocratic ones, irrespective of their implementation capacity. This is corroborated by table 11.10, which shows a positive correlation between the degree of democracy and the level of actual grants. Underexecution is likely to be more prominent for aid-financed capital spending than for aid-financed current outlays, given their longer execution time span and higher reliance on technical inputs (for project selection, engineering design, and procurement, among other steps).

Table 11.10
Correlation matrix between current and capital spending gaps, degree of democracy, and actual level of grants, 2008 to 2010

Variable[a]	Current spending gap	Capital spending gap	Degree of democracy	Actual grants
Current spending gap	1.00	0.29	−0.11	−0.31
Capital spending gap	0.29	1.00	0.08	0.04
Degree of democracy (polity2)	−0.11	0.08	1.00	0.22
Actual grants	−0.31	0.04	0.22	1.00

Source: IMF staff estimates
a. Cross-country and time standard correlation.

11.5 Concluding Remarks: The Once and Future Fiscal Space

This chapter brings some evidence that LICs in SSA have been able to move away from procyclical fiscal policy during the global financial crisis. Their fiscal policy response may have mitigated the impact of the crisis in the region, a noteworthy achievement. However, overall fiscal numbers mask two diverging and potentially bothersome trends: the overexecution of current spending and the underexecution of capital projects. The regression results suggest that both political and institutional variables may explain part of the deviation between intended and observed current spending, with good governance and institutions contributing to better execution, while political regime change may challenge implementation capacity. Institutional variables seem to have less effect on the implementation of capital spending plans, but political variables remain relevant, possibly reflecting the higher aid flows received by democratic governments, irrespective of their implementation capacity.

The gap between implementation of current and capital spending plans could reduce LICs' future fiscal space. Increases in current spending are often difficult to reverse, particularly in LICs where social safety nets tend to be underdeveloped. Higher current spending thus is most likely to reflect a higher wage bill or new price subsidies, which increase spending rigidity and reduce the capacity to use fiscal policy to respond to the next crisis. Figure 11.1 illustrates how, although growth remained above trend in 2011 and 2012, fiscal deficits did not narrow.

The underexecution of capital spending is a relatively common occurrence, including its occurrence in advanced economies. What is bothering in the case of SSA LICs is that the underspending occurred at a time of higher aid flows. Given the size of unmet demands, in the absence of strong firewalls, capital spending underexecution could thus end up feeding current spending overexecution.

Finally, the projected path of aid flows may also reduce fiscal flexibility in SSA LICs in the future (figure 11.5). Significant additional external financing was made available during the crisis, including augmented financing from the IMF and frontloaded disbursements from many donors. Aid helped the financing of fiscal stimuli in 2009 and 2010, but is projected to decline gradually, though steadily, in the years to come. Moreover the profile of concessional financing is also expected to change, with concessional project loans partially compensating for a pronounced decline in budget support loans. Given the trend in underexecuting investment projects, the change in the composition of aid could significantly constrain access to concessional resources in the near future. Further strengthening of fiscal institutions, including efforts to bring investment decisions under their purview, will be needed to avoid a return to fiscal procyclicality.

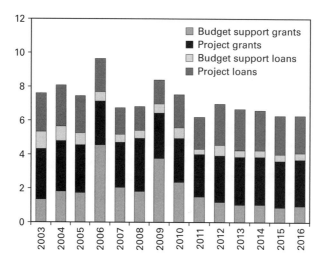

Figure 11.5
Concessional financing, composition, and projections (percent of GDP). Averages are for low-income countries and fragile states in Africa, with oil producers excluded.
Source: Authors' calculations; IMF staff estimates and projections

Appendix A: Real GDP Growth in Sample Countries

Table A11.1
Real GDP growth in sample countries (percent)

	1995	1996	1997	1998	1999	2000	2001	2002	2003	2004	2005	2006	2007	2008	2009	2010	2011	2012
Benin	6.0	4.3	5.7	4.0	5.3	4.9	6.2	4.4	4.0	3.1	2.9	3.8	4.6	5.0	2.7	2.6	3.5	3.5
Burkina Faso	5.7	11.0	6.3	7.3	6.2	2.9	6.6	4.4	7.8	4.5	8.7	6.3	4.1	5.8	3.0	7.9	4.2	7.0
Burundi	−7.9	−8.0	0.4	4.8	−1.0	−0.9	1.7	2.4	2.5	3.8	4.4	5.4	4.8	5.0	3.5	3.8	4.2	4.2
Cameroon	3.3	5.0	5.1	5.0	4.4	4.2	4.5	4.0	4.0	3.7	2.3	3.2	3.4	2.6	2.0	2.9	4.2	4.7
Central African Republic	4.9	−8.1	7.5	3.9	3.6	1.9	0.6	−0.6	−7.1	1.0	2.4	3.8	3.7	2.0	1.7	3.0	3.3	4.1
Chad	−0.8	2.1	5.7	7.0	−0.7	−0.9	11.7	8.5	14.7	33.6	7.9	0.2	0.2	1.7	−1.2	13.0	1.8	7.3
Comoros	3.6	−1.3	4.2	1.2	1.9	1.4	3.3	4.1	2.5	−0.2	4.2	1.2	0.5	1.0	1.8	2.1	2.2	2.5
Congo, Democratic Republic of	0.7	−1.1	−5.4	−1.7	−4.3	−6.9	−2.1	3.5	5.8	6.6	7.8	5.6	6.3	6.2	2.8	7.2	6.9	7.1
Congo, Republic of	4.0	4.3	−0.6	3.7	−2.6	7.6	3.8	4.6	0.8	3.5	7.8	6.2	−1.6	5.6	7.5	8.8	3.4	4.9
Côte d'Ivoire	5.6	8.1	5.7	4.5	1.8	−4.6	0.0	−1.6	−1.7	1.6	1.9	0.7	1.6	2.3	3.7	2.4	−4.7	8.1
Ethiopia	6.1	13.2	3.5	−4.0	6.0	5.9	7.4	1.6	−2.1	11.7	12.6	11.5	11.8	11.2	10.0	8.0	7.5	7.0
Gambia, The	−3.4	6.1	4.9	6.5	6.4	5.5	5.8	−3.2	6.9	7.0	−0.3	0.8	4.0	6.5	6.7	5.5	3.3	−1.6
Ghana	4.0	4.5	5.2	5.1	4.7	4.2	4.5	4.7	5.1	5.3	6.0	6.1	6.5	8.4	4.0	8.0	14.4	8.2
Guinea	4.7	5.2	5.2	4.6	4.5	2.9	3.8	4.2	1.2	2.3	3.0	2.5	1.8	4.9	−0.3	1.9	3.9	4.8
Guinea-Bissau	4.4	4.6	6.5	−27.2	7.6	7.5	2.0	−1.3	0.4	2.8	4.3	2.1	3.2	3.2	3.0	3.5	5.3	−2.8
Liberia	...	...	...	...	...	...	2.9	4.5	−28.4	4.1	5.9	9.0	13.2	6.2	5.3	6.1	8.2	9.0
Malawi	13.8	10.0	6.6	1.1	3.5	0.8	−4.1	1.7	5.5	5.5	2.6	2.1	9.5	8.3	9.0	6.5	4.3	4.3
Mali	2.4	7.4	5.3	4.4	5.7	−3.3	11.9	4.3	7.6	2.3	6.1	5.3	4.3	5.0	4.5	5.8	2.7	−4.5
Mozambique	2.2	14.8	11.1	11.8	8.4	1.5	12.3	9.2	6.5	7.9	8.4	8.7	7.3	6.8	6.3	7.1	7.3	7.5
Niger	−6.6	5.1	0.5	12.7	1.0	−2.6	8.0	5.3	7.1	−0.8	8.4	5.8	3.1	9.6	−0.9	8.0	2.3	14.5
Rwanda	24.5	11.6	14.9	8.3	5.1	6.5	8.5	13.2	2.2	7.4	9.4	9.2	5.5	11.2	4.1	7.2	8.6	7.7
Senegal	5.4	2.0	3.1	5.9	6.3	3.2	4.6	0.7	6.7	5.9	5.6	2.4	5.0	3.7	2.1	4.1	2.6	3.7
Tanzania	3.6	4.5	3.5	3.7	3.5	4.9	6.0	7.2	6.9	7.8	7.4	6.7	7.1	7.4	6.0	7.0	6.4	6.5
Togo	6.8	7.7	3.8	−2.3	2.6	−1.0	−1.6	−0.9	5.0	2.1	1.2	4.1	2.3	2.4	3.5	4.0	4.9	5.0
Uganda	11.3	9.1	5.5	3.8	8.2	5.4	7.0	7.6	6.6	6.6	8.6	9.5	8.6	7.7	7.0	6.1	5.1	4.2
Zambia	−2.8	6.9	3.3	−1.9	2.2	3.6	4.9	3.3	5.1	5.4	5.3	6.2	6.2	5.7	6.4	7.6	6.6	6.5
Average	**4.8**	**6.9**	**4.5**	**3.2**	**4.2**	**2.9**	**5.4**	**4.2**	**4.0**	**6.8**	**6.9**	**6.1**	**6.1**	**6.6**	**5.0**	**6.4**	**5.7**	**6.1**

Source: *Fiscal Monitor*, October 2012

Note: Country averages are weighted by GDP at PPP using 2009 weights and based on data availability.

Appendix B: Data Sources and Methodologies

Data and Data Sources

Actual (observed) macroeconomic variables for 26 SSA LICs and a control group of 20 LICs in other regions are taken for each year from 2008 to 2012 from the Fall *World Economic Outlook* (WEO) issues while planned (projected) variables come from a survey of authorities' intentions undertaken by the African Department of the IMF. Fall vintages of the WEO are used because by that period most countries already have a draft of the fiscal budget for the year ahead. One reason to use the previous-year forecast vintage of the WEO for planned changes in fiscal policy is that these forecasts embody the best IMF staff estimates of national authorities' feasible and sustainable fiscal plans. In line with international definitions, LICs are defined as countries with a per capita income below $1,160 (the cutoff level for access to concessional financing from IDA) during 2008 to 2010.

Political variables include the degree of democracy (extracted from the Polity IV dataset); years of the chief executive (or her party) in power (extracted from the updated version of the World Bank Database of Political Institutions; Beck et al. 2001); and a dummy for years of election (constructed with the information available at http://africanelections.tripod.com/index.html). Institutional variables include indicators of governance and of institutional capacity. Governance measures (rule of law and government effectiveness) come from the dataset of World Governance Indicators of the World Bank (see Kaufmann, Kraay, and Mastruzzi 2010). Institutional capacity indicators come from the datasets constructed by Dabla-Norris et al. (2010).

Methodologies for the Estimation of Cyclicality

The first approach is to estimate correlation coefficients between the level of the cyclically adjusted primary balance (CAPB, measured as a share of potential GDP) and that of the output gap. A co-movement between the change in the output gap and the change in the CABP is taken as indicative of a countercyclical fiscal policy. The output gap is estimated with the Hodrick–Prescott (HP) filter with the smoothing parameter of 100 over the period 1995 to 2017. Including five years of forecast reduces the problem of endpoints common to the HP filter. The CAPB is estimated as the difference between cyclically adjusted revenue (with a revenue elasticity of 1) and primary (noninterest) expenditure, a reasonable assumption for LICs given the quasi-inexistence of output-sensitive income support programs.

Given the small sample, regressions are estimated using panel fixed effects with OLS (FE-OLS) and White heteroskedasticity corrected *t*-statistics, as follows:

$$\widehat{capb}_{i,t} = \hat{\alpha}_i + \beta_1 ygap_{i,t} + \beta_2 d_{i,t-1} + \varphi_{i,t}, \tag{11.1}$$

where i denotes the country, $\widehat{capb}_{i,t}$ denotes the CAPB, $ygap_{i,t}$ denotes the output gap, and d denotes the lagged value of public debt. A positive change in the output gap corresponds to economic recovery and a negative value to economic recession; a positive change of the CAPB represents a strengthening of the fiscal accounts.

A similar formula is used to estimate the expected countercyclical effect of the budget plans designed before the crisis (compared to the projected output gap):

$$\widehat{capbBP}_{i,t} = \hat{\alpha}_i + \beta_1 ygapBP_{i,t} + \beta_2 d_{i,t-1} + \varphi_{i,t}, \tag{11.2}$$

where i denotes the country, $\widehat{capbBP}_{i,t}$ denotes the planned CAPB, $ygapBP_{i,t}$ denotes the projected output gap, and d denotes the lagged value of public debt.

The second approach, following Kaminsky, Reinhart, and Végh (2004) and IMF (2009b), compares the growth of real primary spending with that of trend output and assumes that fiscal policy is countercyclical in cases where real spending growth is positive but output growth is below trend. The measure of trend growth is free of the structural breaks that tend to distort HP-filtered results. To minimize risks of capturing such structural breaks, we take as trend growth the average real GDP growth in the five-year period prior to the crisis (2003 to 2007). Government spending (which is arguably more representative of the fiscal policy stance in LICs, given the low tax ratios and infrequent use of tax rates as short-term policy instruments) is deflated by the GDP deflator.

Methodology for the Estimation of Determinants of Deviations between Intended and Observed Fiscal Outcomes

The dependent variable in this case is the difference between planned and actual fiscal outcomes (*gap*). For each country, differences between planned and actual spending in a given year t are computed as a percentage of the projected GDP. The relationships are estimated in real time to proxy the information sets available for the policy makers at the time they made their decisions (see Cimadomo 2012):

$$gap_{j,t} = g^p_{j,t}(t, t^p) - g^a_{j,t}(t, t^a), \tag{11.3}$$

where j denotes the country; $g_{j,t}$ the type of government spending (current or capital), with $\left(g^p_{j,t}\right)$ the planned level, envisaged at the time the budget is formulated or $\left(t^p\right)$, and $\left(g^a_{j,t}\right)$ the actual level, based on the latest available fiscal outturns at $\left(t^a\right)$.

In view of the limited number of observations per country a panel setup is used. We start with a parsimonious specification where the implementation gaps (in absolute value, so that we capture both over- and underexecution) are only a function of the forecast errors in macroeconomic assumptions in growth, consumer price inflation, and grant (in percent of GDP). We then add political variables $(pol_{j,t})$ and institutional variables $(cap_{j,t})$ to this baseline. The empirical model can be described as follows:

$$abs(gap_{j,t}) = \alpha_j + \lambda_t + \beta_1 abs(x_{j,t}^p - x_{j,t}^a) + \beta_4 debt_{j,t-1} + \beta_6 pol_{j,t} + \beta_7 cap_{j,t} + \varepsilon_{j,t}, \quad (11.4)$$

where α_j and λ_t stand for the country and time fixed effects, respectively, and $x_{j,t'}^{t'}$ is a vector capturing the relevant macroeconomic variables in logs (real GDP growth, inflation, and grants). As before, superscripts indicate whether the variable is forecasted or corresponds to its actual (outturn) value, and subscripts indicate the country and the year to which the forecast/outturn is made. $\varepsilon_{j,t+1}$ is an i.i.d. error term.

As institutional indicators are largely time invariant, following Rajkumar and Swaroop (2008), an interaction term is introduced between the WGI index of government effectiveness and the indexes of quality of budgetary institutions. The underlying intuition is that the combination of an effective government with good budgetary procedures would allow an implementation closer to the initial plans (Burnside and Dollar 2000; Lledó and Poplawski-Ribeiro 2013).

The empirical model (11.4) is estimated using fixed effects ordinary least squares (FE-OLS). We use robust standard errors to avoid heteroskedasticity owing to potential measurement errors in the fiscal implementation gaps. A statistical procedure is also applied to identify outlier countries. When an observation (from either independent or dependent variables) is either above the sample average plus three times the sample standard deviation or below the sample average minus three times the sample standard deviation, it is excluded from the sample (replaced by a missing value).

Notes

We thank Nathalie Carcenac and Nancy Tinoza for excellent research assistance.

1. See, in particular, Akitoby et al. (2004); Kaminsky, Reinhart, and Végh (2005); Talvi and Végh (2005); Ilzetzki and Végh (2008); IMF (2009b).

2. Thornton (2008); Allen (2009).

3. Frankel, Végh, and Vuletin (2013); IMF (2010); Lledó, Yackovlev, and Gadenne (2011).

4. IMF (2009a).

5. See, for example, Fatás and Mihov (2003); Galí and Perotti (2003). Given the short sample period, we use level (rather than first differences) in the estimates.

6. See appendix B; Kaminsky, Reinhart, and Végh (2004); IMF (2009b).

7. Estimated as the difference between the headline and the cyclically adjusted primary balance.

8. The statistically insignificant coefficient for debt is among others related to the debt relief delivered to some countries in the sample during the period analyzed.

9. For an analysis of the relationship between fiscal policy and inflation in SSA, see Baldini and Poplawski-Ribeiro (2011); Cáceres, Poplawski-Ribeiro, and Tartari (2013).

10. These results are in line with Lledó and Poplawski-Ribeiro (2013). Further a horse race among other WGI governance variables is performed, and the results are available upon request.

11. The same robust result is obtained if one includes the number of years the government party is in office.

12. About half of the SSA countries in our sample changed political regime in the 2000s, and about one-third became democracies, according to the Polity IV dataset.

13. Hence any potential measurement error here concerns the deviation of the dataset from the policy makers' datasets, not the accuracy with which the data approximate the eventual outcomes of variables such as output.

References

Akitoby, Bernardin, Benedict Clements, Sanjeev Gupta, and Maria Gabriela Comboni. 2004. The cyclical and long-term behavior of government expenditures in developing countries. Working paper 04/202. IMF, Washington, DC.

Allen, Richard. 2009. The challenge of reforming budgetary institutions in developing countries. Working paper 09/96. IMF, Washington, DC.

Balassone, Fabrizio, and Manmohan Kumar. 2007. Cyclicality of fiscal policy. In Manmohan Kumar and Teresa Ter-Minassian, eds., Promoting Fiscal Discipline. Washington: IMF, 19–35.

Baldini, Alfredo, and Marcos Poplawski-Ribeiro. 2011. Fiscal and monetary determinants of inflation in low-income countries: Theory and evidence from sub-Saharan Africa. *Journal of African Economies* 20 (3): 419–62.

Beck, Thorsten, George Clarke, Alberto Groff, Philip Keefer, and Patrick Walsh. 2001. New tools in comparative political economy: The database of political institutions. *World Bank Economic Review* 15 (1): 165–76.

Beetsma, Roel, Massimo Giuliodori, and Peter Wierts. 2009. Planning to cheat: EU fiscal policy in real time. *Economic Policy* 24 (60): 753–804.

Briceño-Garmendia, Cecilia, Karlis Smits, and Vivien Foster. 2008. Financing public infrastructure in sub-Saharan Africa: Patterns and emerging issues. AICD background paper 15. World Bank, Washington, DC.

Bulíř, Ales, and A. Javier Hamann. 2003. Aid volatility: An empirical assessment. *IMF Staff Papers* 50 (1): 64–89.

Burnside, Craig, and David Dollar. 2000. Aid, policies and growth. *American Economic Review* 90 (4): 847–68.

Cáceres, Carlos, Marcos Poplawski-Ribeiro, and Darlena Tartari. 2013. Inflation dynamics in the CEMAC region. *Journal of African Economies* 22 (2): 239–75.

Cimadomo, Jacopo. 2012. Fiscal policy in real time. *Scandinavian Journal of Economics* 114 (2): 440–65.

Dabla-Norris, Era, Richard Allen, Luis Felipe Zanna, Tej Prakash, Eteri Kvintradze, Victor Lledo, Irene Yackovlev, and Sophia Gollwitzer. 2010. Budget institutions and fiscal performance in low-income countries. Working paper 10/80. IMF, Washington, DC.

Fatás, Antonio, and Ilian Mihov. 2003. On constraining fiscal policy discretion in EMU. *Oxford Review of Economic Policy* 19 (1): 112–31.

Frankel, Jeffrey A., Carlos A. Végh, and Guillermo Vuletin. 2013. On graduation from fiscal procyclicality. *Journal of Development Economics* 100 (1): 32–47.

Galí, Jordi, and Roberto Perotti. 2003. Fiscal policy and monetary integration in Europe. *Economic Policy* 37: 533–72.

Gavin, Michael, and Roberto Perotti. 1997. Fiscal policy in Latin America. *NBER Macroeconomics Annual* 12: 11–72.

Gollwitzer, Sophia, and Marc Quintyn. 2010. The effectiveness of macroeconomic commitment in weak(er) institutional environments. Working paper 10/193. IMF, Washington, DC.

Ilzetzki, Ethan, and Carlos A. Végh. 2008. Procyclical fiscal policy in developing countries: Truth or fiction? Working paper 14191. NBER, Cambridge, MA.

International Monetary Fund. 2009a. Fiscal policy in sub-Saharan Africa in response to the impact of the global crisis. Staff position note 2009/10. IMF, Washington, DC.

International Monetary Fund. 2009b. *Weathering the Storm, "Sub-Saharan Africa Regional Economic Outlook*. Washington, DC: IMF.

International Monetary Fund. 2010. *Back to Growth? Sub-Saharan Africa Regional Economic Outlook*. Washington, DC: IMF.

Kaminsky, Graciela L., Carmen M. Reinhart, and Carlos A. Végh. 2004. When it rains, it pours: Procyclical capital flows and macroeconomic policies. *NBER Macroeconomics Annual 2004* 19: 11–82.

Kaufmann, Daniel, Aart Kraay, and Massimo Mastruzzi. 2010. The worldwide governance indicators: Methodology and analytical issues. Policy Research working paper 5430. World Bank, Washington, DC.

Lane, Phillip, and Aaron Tornell. 1999. The voracity effect. American Economic Review 89: 22–46.

Lledó, Victor, and Marcos Poplawski-Ribeiro. 2011. Fiscal policy implementation in sub-Saharan Africa. Working paper 11/172. IMF, Washington, DC.

Lledó, Victor, and Marcos Poplawski-Ribeiro. 2013. Fiscal policy implementation in sub-Saharan Africa. *World Development* 46 (C): 79–91.

Lledó, Victor, Irene Yackovlev, and Lucie Gadenne. 2011. A tale of cyclicality, aid flows and debt: Government spending in sub-Saharan Africa. *Journal of African Economies* 20 (5): 823–49.

McKinsey Global Institute. 2010. *Lions on the Move: The Progress and Potential of African Economies*. New York: McKinsey.

Rajkumar, Andrew S., and Vinaya Swaroop. 2008. Public spending and outcomes: Does governance matter? *Journal of Development Economics* 86: 96–111.

Talvi, Ernesto, and Carlos A. Végh. 2005. Tax base variability and procyclical fiscal policy in developing countries. *Journal of Development Economics, Elsevier* 78 (1): 156–90.

Thornton, John. 2008. Explaining procyclical fiscal policy in African countries. *Journal of African Economies* 17 (3): 451–64.

12

Size of Fiscal Multipliers

Aiko Mineshima, Marcos Poplawski-Ribeiro, and Anke Weber

12.1 Introduction

The Great Recession has refocused attention on the effectiveness of fiscal policy. In the economic policy paradigm prevalent before the crisis, there was little room for fiscal policy activism. Monetary policy was considered more effective in managing short-run fluctuations, with fiscal policy contributing through automatic stabilizers. This implied that fiscal policy focused mainly on the medium and longer terms, enhancing potential growth through structural reforms, including reducing distortions in the economy, ensuring debt sustainability, and safeguarding the most vulnerable.

The reasons why fiscal policy took a backseat as a stabilization tool during the pre-crisis era are manifold.[1] First, there was wide skepticism about the effectiveness of fiscal policy, largely based on Ricardian equivalence arguments. Second, financial market developments increased the effectiveness of monetary policy, reducing incentives for politicians to use fiscal policy for economic stabilization. Third, in advanced economies, priority was given to stabilize and possibly decrease typically high debt levels; while in emerging market countries, the lack of depth of the domestic bond market limited the scope for countercyclical policy. Fourth, lags in the design and the implementation of fiscal policy, together with the short length of recessions, implied that fiscal measures were likely to come too late.[2] Fifth, fiscal policy, much more than monetary policy, was likely to be distorted by political constraints.

As the crisis deepened, nominal interest rates reached the "zero lower bound" in many advanced economies as a result of aggressive monetary easing. This, combined with a weakened transmission mechanism caused by an impaired financial system, limited scope for further maneuvering monetary policy. Attention thereby naturally shifted to the effectiveness of fiscal policy as a key crisis response. A number of countries passed fiscal stimulus bills aimed to fasten the economic recovery and ease the pain for their hardest hit citizens, although the size and composition of packages had considerable variations.[3] Once the global economy hit bottom, attention turned to the pace and the modalities of fiscal consolidation to reduced elevated public debt at unsustainable levels. These exceptional circumstances triggered a new wave of research on fiscal policy activism and fiscal multipliers.

Broad consensus about the size of fiscal multipliers can be summarized as follows. First, there is no "the" fiscal multiplier, or a unique size for fiscal multipliers. The size can be below or above unity, most likely depending on the country analyzed and the state of the economy. Second, fiscal multipliers tend to be materially larger during economic downturns than expansions and could exceed unity during recessions. The state dependency of fiscal multipliers is intuitive and supported by recent studies, including the empirical analysis in this chapter explicitly incorporating nonlinearities. During economic expansions, when employment and output are above potential levels, the crowding-out effects of a fiscal expansion tend to offset the direct impact of fiscal stimulus on aggregate demand, whereas during economic downturns, government spending better utilizes idle resources (i.e., unemployed labor and capital), further augmenting private consumption and/or investment.

The finding that fiscal multipliers tend to be larger during economic downturns gives support to the idea that governments could implement fiscal stimulus if the economy is in a deep recession and if there is the necessary fiscal space. The state dependency of multipliers also has an implication for the timing and pace of fiscal adjustment to unwind fiscal stimulus.

The structure of the chapter is as follows. Section 12.2 provides an overview of the evidence on the size of fiscal multipliers in the theoretical and empirical literature. Section 12.3 introduces recent empirical work exploring differences in the size of multipliers depending on the state of the economy. Section 12.4 concludes with policy implications coming out of the analysis in this chapter.

12.2 Debate on the Magnitude of Fiscal Multipliers

Fiscal multipliers are typically defined as the ratio of a change in output to an exogenous change in the fiscal deficit with respect to their respective baselines.[4]

The literature survey in this chapter indicates there is no unique size for fiscal multipliers. A plausible range of first-year multipliers, however, would comprise values around 0.5 to 0.9 for government spending and around 0.1 to 0.3 for revenue using linear models, although there are notable differences between the United States and European countries, as well as between the techniques used (table 12.1).[5] Linear models denote empirical and model-based approaches that do not distinguish between multipliers based on the underlying characteristics of the economy, such as whether the economy is at the zero lower bound or undergoing a recession. The range for spending multipliers is close to the findings of other literature surveys, such as Hall (2009), 0.5 to 1 with vector autoregressive approaches, and Boussard et al. (2012), 0.4 to 1.2, but is slightly lower than Ramey (2011b), 0.8 to 1.5. The differ-

Table 12.1
First-year fiscal multipliers: Summary of findings from previous literature (linear models)

a. Size of government spending fiscal multipliers

	All samples		United States		Europe	
	VAR	DSGE	VAR	DSGE	VAR	DSGE
Mean	0.8	0.7	1.0	0.7	0.8	0.6
Median	0.8	0.6	1.2	0.8	0.8	0.5
Maximum	2.1	1.7	2.1	1.6	1.8	1.2
Minimum	0.1	0.0	0.3	0.0	0.3	0.2
Plausible range[a]	0.5–0.9		0.7–1.1		0.5–0.7	

b. Size of government revenue fiscal multipliers

	All samples		United States		Europe	
	VAR	DSGE	VAR	DSGE	VAR	DSGE
Mean	0.2	0.3	0.7	0.5	0.1	0.2
Median	0.1	0.2	0.9	0.3	0.1	0.1
Maximum	1.4	1.3	1.4	1.3	0.7	0.7
Minimum	−1.5	0.0	−0.7	0.0	−0.5	0.0
Plausible range[a]	0.1–0.3		0.3–0.7		0.1–0.2	

Sources: Literature survey in the appendix; IMF staff estimates.
Note: Government spending excludes transfers for empirical models. VAR denotes summary statistics from linear vector autoregressive models, and DSGE denotes results from dynamic stochastic general equilibrium models. The summary statistics are calculated with the 20 studies that include estimated first-year multipliers, out of the total 41 studies shown in the appendix. The summary includes the maximum multipliers estimated with linear models from Auerbach and Gorodnichenko (2012b) because the study indicates the maximum values are observed between the first and fourth quarters after shocks. The summary excludes results from the DSGE studies that simulated the sizes of fiscal multipliers with zero lower bound of interest rates, and some outliers.
a. The upper and lower values of the mid 30 percent ranges, including VAR and DSGE, from box 12.1.

ence with respect to the latter could be partly explained by the fact that Ramey uses either cumulative multipliers for longer time horizons than one year or their peak values. Our range of revenue multipliers is broadly consistent with Boussard et al. (2012), who find that the size of first-year tax multipliers lies quite often below 0.7 and is frequently negative.

12.2.1 Estimation Techniques Used for Fiscal Multipliers

Multiplier estimates differ depending on the estimation techniques used as shown in table 12.1. The vector autoregressive (VAR) and dynamic stochastic equilibrium (DSGE) models are indeed very different, and both are subject to caveats as explained below.

12.2.2 Econometric Approaches

VAR models are widely used to quantify the size of fiscal multipliers. The key challenge relates to the difficulty of isolating exogenous movements in fiscal variables (endogeneity problem).[6] Since the seminal paper by Blanchard and Perotti (2002), a common approach has been to use a structural identification approach. This assumes that changes in fiscal variables could be due to (1) the automatic response of the fiscal balance to macroeconomic variables, (2) the discretionary response of fiscal policy to news in macroeconomic variables, and (3) truly exogenous shifts in fiscal policy, which are the shocks that need to be identified. The literature has typically used quarterly data, assuming that discretionary adjustment to fiscal policy in response to unexpected events is unlikely to be implemented within the same quarter.[7] Elasticities of revenue and expenditure items with respect to output can then be used to identify the automatic response of the fiscal balance to macroeconomic variables, namely point 1 above.

VAR models have been subject to various criticisms. First, the structural identification approach may fail to capture exogenous policy changes correctly because, for example, changes in revenues are not only due to cyclical developments and discretionary policy but also to asset and commodity price movements (IMF 2010). Other challenges for the VAR approach, like any other econometric analysis, relate to omitted variables,[8] limited identifying information (Romer 2011), and the elasticities used (Caldara and Kamps 2012). Moreover quarterly data, which are needed for the structural identification approach, are often not available for a long enough time span. For multicountry studies, using panel data also calls for caution as there is significant country heterogeneity in the effect of fiscal policy on output—with different debt dynamics, degree of openness, and fiscal reaction functions (Favero et al. 2011).

The "narrative" and "action-based" approaches are alternative methods to identify exogenous fiscal shocks. They seek to overcome the endogeneity and anticipatory biases through identifying policy shocks from government documents (e.g., budget documents) rather than data.[9] So far the narrative approach has only been applied using quarterly data for Germany (Hayo and Uhl 2014), the United Kingdom (Cloyne 2011), and the United States (Romer and Romer 2010). The IMF (2010) created a multiple country data sample based on this approach (see also Devries et al. 2011) but it only covers annual data.

12.2.3 Macroeconomic Model Approaches

New Keynesian macroeconomic models, particularly DSGE models, are commonly used for simulating the fiscal policy impact on growth. Analyzing fiscal multipliers with DSGE models also presents challenges, including the difficulty in modeling fiscal policy and incorporating nonlinearity. For example, unlike the Taylor rule for monetary policy, there is no widely accepted fiscal rule to be included in a DSGE model. In addition results of simulations using DSGE models tend to be sensitive to the size of parameters (e.g., degree of price and wage rigidities, habit persistence, investment adjustment cost), as well as structural features.[10] Furthermore incorporating nonlinearities, such as measuring the size of multipliers depending on the state of economy or when the zero lower bound is binding, in DSGE models is challenging. Fernández-Villaverde et al. (2012) discuss that the existing solutions have made simplifying assumptions that could have unexpected implications. For example, linearizing equilibrium conditions, such as the Euler equations, may hide nonlinear interactions between the zero lower bound and the policy functions of the agents, and linear approximations provide a poor description of the economy during deep recessions, such as the Great Recession. Furthermore they argue that in order to analyze the dynamics of the economy near or at the zero lower bound, models should allow time-varying expectations and variance of the number of additional periods at the zero lower bound.

12.2.4 Key Factors Influencing the Size of the Fiscal Multipliers

Multipliers not only differ across estimation techniques, but there are also a number of well-known factors influencing the size of multipliers, which are listed below.

Automatic Stabilizers

Automatic stabilizers tend to dampen the effect of a discretionary fiscal stimulus through the growth channel: a fiscal stimulus increases growth, which leads to higher taxes and lower transfers, hence reducing the fiscal multiplier (figure 12.1). The size of the automatic stabilizers is smaller for the United States than for Europe,[11] which could explain (at least partially) why the United States typically has larger fiscal multipliers.

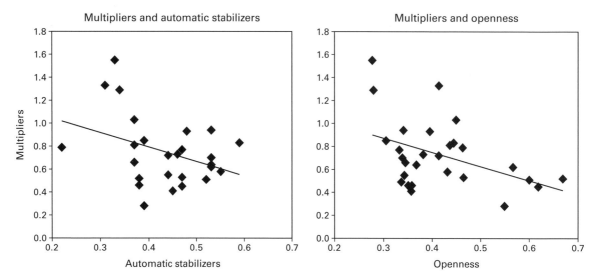

Figure 12.1

Fiscal multipliers relative to the automatic stabilizers and openness. Multipliers are based on the OECD (2009). Openness is measured by import penetration, that is the 2008 to 2011 average of Imports/(GDP – Exports + Imports) ×100. Automatic stabilizers are measured as the semielasticity of the budget balance and are extracted from Girouard and André (2005). The negative correlations in the panel are robust to outliers being removed using an automated Stata procedure.

Sources: IMF, Fiscal Affairs Department Fiscal Rules database and Fiscal Transparency database; Organisation for Economic Co-operation and Development (OECD); IMF staff estimates

Trade Openness

A country with a smaller propensity to import (i.e., large countries and/or countries only partially open to trade) has larger fiscal multipliers (Ilzetzki et al. 2011; IMF 2008; Barrell et al. 2012) (figure 12.1). This is because less of the additional demand generated by the stimulus will "leak" through imports, and this is probably another reason for why Europe has smaller fiscal multipliers than does the United States.

Exchange Rate Regimes

A country with a flexible exchange rate regime tends to have smaller fiscal multipliers than a country with a fixed regime because of the different monetary policy responses to a fiscal expansion.[12] Under a flexible exchange rate regime, the central bank does not change its monetary policy stance in response to a fiscal expansion—which increases output, raises interest rates, and attracts foreign capital—resulting in an appreciation of the real exchange rate and a reduction of net exports (leakages).[13] Under a fixed exchange rate regime, the central bank would have to expand the money supply to mitigate the appreciation pressures, resulting in a new equilibrium with larger output and unchanged interest rates.[14] Ilzetzki et al. (2011) show the fiscal multipliers are positive for countries with fixed exchange rate regimes while they are negative on impact and around zero in the long run for countries with flexible exchange rate regimes.

The discussion on the size of fiscal multipliers in a currency union is akin to that in a country with a fixed exchange rate regime. Nakamura and Steinsson (2011) argue that the relative monetary policy within a currency union—fixed relative nominal interest rate and exchange rate—is more accommodative than "normal" monetary policy of a country, which raises the real interest rate in response to inflationary shocks. Using state-level data for the United States, they find the "open economy relative multiplier"[15] to be roughly 1.5.[16] One caveat here is a possible spillover effect of fiscal stimulus. If the country in a currency union undertaking fiscal stimulus is large and not a price taker, and the stimulus is accompanied by monetary tightening to mitigate the inflationary pressures, other countries in the union are forced to follow suit and tighten monetary policy, negatively affecting their economic performance (Farhi and Werning 2012).

Fiscal Instruments

As shown in table 12.1, spending multipliers are usually larger than revenue multipliers in the short run.[17] This is largely because spending has a direct impact on aggregate demand while revenue has only an indirect impact on demand.[18] In this context, it is critical to make a distinction between the spending items that have a direct impact on aggregate demand (i.e., government investment and consumption) and those that have an indirect impact on aggregate demand. An example of the latter is a transfer to households, which impacts aggregate demand through its effects on household income and labor supply incentives. In other words, an increase in transfers to households plays a similar role as a reduction in taxes. Therefore much of the empirical literature excludes such transfers from government spending.

The size of multipliers for tax- and transfer-based stimulus tends to be highly dependent on the share of liquidity-constrained (hand-to-mouth) households and the relative distortions caused by fiscal instruments. Therefore short-run multipliers tend to become large if transfers are targeted to hand-to-mouth households, or if tax measures provide incentives to bring forward consumption or investment. Oh and Reis (2011) show that increases in targeted transfers are expansionary, raising both employment and output, through both a neoclassical wealth effect and a Keynesian aggregate demand effect. And although their gross impact is smaller than that of government purchases, the net impact on private consumption and investment is found significantly larger. Distortionary taxes to influence the timing of consumption or investment could also impact output, but they could exacerbate the crowding-out effects through increasing real interest rates.[19] In addition the longer term impact of distortionary tax measures should be carefully taken into account when a government decides on a tax-based economic stimulus.

Moreover the output implication of a deficit-financed temporary fiscal measure is likely different from that of a permanent fiscal measure. In general, a temporary measure tends to have a stronger effect than a permanent measure.[20] This is because a permanent measure, which would require a future increase in taxes, typically has a larger negative effect on households' lifetime wealth compared with a temporary measure, resulting in crowding out of private demand.

Debt Level

An increase in government spending in countries with high debt levels may act as a signal that fiscal tightening will be required in the near future, and the anticipation of such adjustment could have a contractionary effect that would offset any short-term expansionary effects. Ilzetzki et al. (2011) show that multipliers become lower, and eventually negative, as debt levels exceed a certain threshold.[21] Kirchner et al. (2010) also find that in the euro area, spending multipliers tend to be lower the higher is the level of public debt.

Financial Market Development

The degree of financial market development influences the size of fiscal multipliers through household liquidity constraints and the government's ability to finance the fiscal deficit. For example, Kirchner et al. (2010) indicate with time-varying parameter VAR models applied to the euro area that short-run spending multipliers decreased since the 1980s driven partly by increased access to credit during the period, which reduced household liquidity constraints and enhanced its behavior in line with the Ricardian equivalence.[22] However, the net impact of the degree of financial market development is ambiguous. Spilimbergo et al. (2009) suggest that, on the one hand, shallow financial markets limit the ability of the private sector to smooth consumption (and investment), thereby increasing the size of fiscal multipliers. On the other hand, governments with limited access to financial markets tend to face higher interest rates for their debt financing, thereby reducing the size of fiscal multipliers.

Development Stage and Size of Economy

The fiscal multipliers tend to be smaller in emerging economies than in advanced economies (IMF 2008; Ilzetzki et al. 2011). This could be due to credibility issues, especially related to debt concerns, triggering an adverse interest rate response. IMF (2008) also finds that revenue-based stimulus measures are more effective at boosting output than expenditure-based measures in emerging economies, perhaps reflecting concerns that increases in expenditures are politically difficult to reverse.

For advanced economies, fiscal multipliers tend to increase with the size of the economy. Barrell et al. (2012) argue that country size is an important distinguishing factor across multipliers, because changes in the real interest rate of a large economy triggered by discretionary fiscal policy actions have spillover effects to global interest rates. If an economy is a price taker, a relative decline in the real interest rate in the economy would cause depreciation pressures to the exchange rate, which in turn increases net exports and mitigates the adverse impact of the fiscal consolidation on the economy (the fiscal multiplier becomes smaller). However, because a large economy, such as the United States, is not a price taker, a decline in its real interest rate lowers global real interest rates, resulting in less impact on its relative real interest rates, exchange rates, and net exports, suggesting fiscal consolidation has large negative impact on its economy (the fiscal multiplier is large).[23]

Monetary Policy Stance

The monetary policy stance and coordination with fiscal policy are also key determinants of the size of fiscal multipliers. For example, if a central bank follows a Taylor rule, the nominal interest rate rises in response to an expansionary fiscal policy shock that puts upward pressures on output and inflation, which dampens the impact of the fiscal expansion (Christiano et al. 2009; DeLong and Summers 2012). However, if a central bank maintains accommodative monetary policy during a temporary fiscal expansion, the efficacy of such discretionary fiscal policy increases. Conversely, if the government proceeds with fiscal consolidation when the central bank operates a Taylor rule, the nominal interest rate declines to offset the contractionary impact of such adjustment. However, if the central bank keeps the nominal interest rate unchanged during fiscal consolidation, the adverse impact of fiscal contraction on output becomes larger (Barrell et al. 2012).

Role of Nonlinearities

More recent advances in the literature have explicitly incorporated nonlinearities when estimating fiscal multipliers. A first strand of research examined the impact of monetary policy on multipliers when monetary policy is constrained by the zero lower bound. A second and later strand of the literature has been investigating whether the impact of fiscal policy on growth differs in economic downturns and expansions. We look at the literature addressing both of these underlying nonlinearities in turn.

Zero Lower Bound

DeLong and Summers (2012) argue that in normal times central banks offset the effects of fiscal policy, which keeps the policy-relevant multiplier near zero. However, when interest rates are constrained by the zero lower bound, discretionary fiscal policy can be highly efficacious as a stabilization policy tool. Conversely, the existence

Table 12.2
Fiscal Multipliers and the Monetary Policy Stance

	Country	Methodology	No zero bound	Zero bound
Christiano et al. (2009)	United States	DSGE	0.8	3.4
Eggertsson (2006)	United States	DSGE	0.8	3.8

Note: For further details, see table A12.2.

of the zero lower bound deepens the contractionary impact of fiscal consolidation (Erceg and Lindé 2012a).

Several studies demonstrate government spending multipliers could be substantially larger than unity when the monetary policy stance is accommodative (see some examples in table 12.2). Eggertsson (2006) finds that government consumption multipliers are notably larger than unity (exceed 3) when monetary policy and fiscal policy are coordinated and the zero lower bound is binding. Christiano et al. (2009) also demonstrate with a DSGE model that fiscal multipliers become much larger than unity (sometimes over 3) whenever the zero bound on nominal interest rates is binding. Erceg and Lindé (2010) show with a DSGE model that the size of the fiscal multipliers increases with the duration of the liquidity trap.[24] Only a few empirical studies investigate fiscal multipliers under such conditions because episodes of nominal interest rates reaching the zero bound have been rare. Alumnia et al. (2010) analyzed with 1930s data for 27 economies, when interest rates were at or near the zero lower bound, and find that fiscal multipliers were about 1.6.

State of Economy

Several studies have investigated the dependency of fiscal multipliers on the state of the economy since the onset of the Great Recession. They found that the size of spending multipliers could be substantially larger than unity during economic recessions (table 12.3). IMF's (2012a) own analysis based on data for 28 advanced and emerging economies concludes that actual fiscal multipliers during the Great Recession might have been in the range of 0.9 to 1.7, significantly higher than previously thought. The IMF study suggests that multipliers may be well above unity given the environment of substantial economic slack, monetary policy constrained by the zero lower bound, and synchronized fiscal adjustment across numerous economies.[25] In a similar vein, Rendahl (2012) demonstrates with a DSGE model that the fiscal multiplier increases to 1.5 when unemployment exceeds the natural rate by 3 percentage points, but falls below one when the unemployment rate is below the natural rate plus two percentage points.[26]

The finding that multipliers are larger in downturns than expansions is in line with the prediction of the Keynesian theory. This is partly because during recessions

Table 12.3
Fiscal multipliers in economic recessions versus expansions

	Country	Methodology	Expansion	Recession
Auerbach–Gorodnichenko (2012b)	United States	VAR	0.6	2.5
Batini et al. (2012)	United States	VAR	0.3	2.2
	Euro area	VAR	0.4	2.6
Baum–Koester (2011)	Germany	VAR	0.3–0.4	1–1.3
Canzoneri et al. (2011)	United States	DSGE	0.9	2.2

Note: For further details, see tables A12.1 and A12.2.

government spending is less likely to cause an increase in interest rates and crowd out private consumption or investment.[27] In addition the proportion of hand-to-mouth households and firms is higher during recessions. Galí et al. (2007) find that the size of fiscal multipliers reflects the share of hand-to-mouth consumers in the economy and the degree of price stickiness.[28] In light of the recent Economic Stimulus Act of 2008, Parker et al. (2011) also find that responses to the 2008 tax rebates were larger for house holds with liquidity constraints or low income.

12.3 Fiscal Multipliers and State of the Economy[29]

As shown in the previous section, the crisis has renewed interest in the estimation of fiscal multipliers, which spurred a rapidly expanding body of literature in this area. As discussed above, fiscal multipliers may be significantly higher during periods of large negative output gaps, which is particularly relevant in the current global context.

This section explores how the effects of fiscal policy on output depend on whether the economy is in an expansion or a downturn. Country-by-country estimation allows the explanatory variables (government spending and revenue) to have differing regression slopes, depending on whether the chosen threshold variable—the output gap—is above or below a particular level, which is chosen to maximize the fit of the model.

Expansions and downturns are defined by the sign of the output gap (positive and negative, respectively). The choice of using the output gap as the threshold variable is motivated by several factors, including that under a negative output gap—independently of the sign of the GDP growth rate—excess capacities are available in the economy, reducing the crowding out of private investment following expansionary fiscal policy.

The section shows that the position in the business cycle affects the impact of fiscal policy on output: for an average of G7 economies, government spending and revenue multipliers tend to be larger in downturns than in expansions. Thus, depending on the phase of the business cycle, the size of multipliers (particularly on spending) is larger than the average estimated if one does not control for the cycle.

However, the value of the multipliers is found to differ significantly across countries, calling for a tailored use of fiscal policies and a country-by-country assessment of their effects. In those countries where spending impact multipliers are found to be statistically significant and sizable (Germany, Japan, and the United States), spending shocks have a significantly larger effect on output when the output gap is negative than when it is positive.

The results are generally less conclusive for revenue multipliers. The impact is more significant for Canada, France, Germany, and Japan. In Germany, revenue multipliers are slightly higher in "good times" than in "bad times," which could suggest that individuals and firms are more willing to spend additional income when market sentiment is positive, thereby becoming less Ricardian. In Canada and Japan, revenue measures work as a countercyclical tool only when the output gap is negative.

12.3.1 Methodology and Data

The econometric analysis conducts a nonlinear time-series estimation for six G7 countries (excluding Italy), applying a threshold vector autoregression (TVAR) methodology that closely follows Baum and Koester (2011). The threshold value is determined endogenously, allowing the data to find the value of the output gap that maximizes the fit of the model in both regimes.

This methodology contrasts with Auerbach and Gorodnichenko (2012a), who use a regime-switching structural vector autoregression (SVAR) in which the threshold value has to be determined exogenously. Furthermore Auerbach and Gorodnichenko (2012a) use a moving average presentation of the GDP growth rate as the threshold variable. Compared to Batini, Callegari, and Melina (2012), the main difference is the country sample used, as well as the choice of the threshold variable: Batini and others use output growth as the threshold variable.

The reasons to employ the output gap instead of the GDP growth rate are manifold. The output gap is the most common measure to identify economic cycles, seen not only as a reliable ex post but also as a reliable real-time indicator for policy makers. It is thus an appropriate choice given our focus on downturns and expansions. More important, one argument for fiscal policy being more effective in downturns than in expansions is that under a negative output gap, excess capacities are available in the economy, making the crowding out of private investment lower. This argument is expected to hold as long as the output gap is negative, and can hardly be captured by low or negative growth rates. The GDP growth rate has also the disadvantage that it can be positive after output has reached its trough, while a downturn can prevail for various further quarters (see Woo, Kinda, and Poplawski-Ribeiro 2014). Further the usual presence of positive serial correlation in GDP growth rates plays a role in explaining business cycles length. Business cycles are often estimated to last shorter when one uses the GDP growth rates (Harding and Pagan 2002).[30]

The countries included in our sample are Canada, France, Germany, Japan, the United Kingdom, and the United States.[31] For most countries we construct quarterly datasets since at least the 1970s. Data sources include the Organization for Economic Cooperation and Development (OECD) Economic Outlook, The IMF's *International Financial Statistics*, and Eurostat as well as national account data. Fiscal data cover the general government. There are some caveats regarding the data sources, as in the cases of Japan and France, for which data were interpolated for some years (see also Perotti 2005).

Along the lines of Blanchard and Perotti (2002, hereafter "BP"), the VAR includes three variables (real GDP, real net revenue, and real expenditure). Net revenue consists of general government revenues minus net transfers, and government spending comprises general government investment and general government consumption (but excludes transfers and subsidies). All series are deflated with the GDP deflator. For most of the countries—except for Germany, for which the HP filter is used (see Baum and Koester 2011)—output gap data are obtained directly from the OECD. (for a detailed description of the data, see Baum, Poplawski-Ribeiro, and Weber 2012, app. A).

The TVAR models change dynamics of a set of variables over two or more distinct regimes. The regimes are determined by a transition variable, which is either endogenous or exogenous (Hansen 1996, 1997; Tsay 1998). For simplicity, the model focuses on two regimes only, which can be represented as

$$y_t = \delta_1 X_t + \delta_2 X_t I\left[z_{t-d} \geq z^*\right] + u_t, \tag{12.1}$$

where z_{t-d} is the threshold variable determining the prevailing regime of the system, with a possible lag d, and $I[\bullet]$ is an indicator function that equals 1 if the threshold variable z_{t-d} is above the threshold value z^*, and 0 otherwise. The coefficient matrices δ_1 and δ_2, as well as the contemporaneous error matrix u_t, are allowed to vary across regimes. The delay lag d and critical threshold value z^* are unknown parameters and are estimated alongside δ_1 and δ_2.

Whether or not system (12.1) offers threshold behavior is determined by means of the Tsay (1998) multivariate threshold approach. The method applies a white noise test to predictive residuals of an arranged regression.[32] A detailed description of the testing procedure can be found in Tsay (1998), as well as in Baum and Koester (2011). This analysis further employs the BP structural identification procedure to identify the shocks for impulse response functions (IRFs). Such procedure accounts for the effect of automatic stabilization on revenues. Revenue elasticities with respect to GDP are obtained following OECD calculations (Girouard and André 2005). Subsequently the share of direct and indirect taxes, social security contributions, and social spending (transfers) in total net revenue are multiplied by their respective elasticities to construct quarterly weighted elasticities.

As discussed in section 12.2, the BP approach has been subject to criticisms, in particular that it fails to capture the exogenous policy changes correctly. However, the proposed alternative methods of the "narrative-" and "action-" based approaches have only been applied using quarterly data for the United Kingdom and the United States. The multiple country data sample based on the narrative approach created by IMF (2010) only covers annual data. Therefore, given the lack of quarterly data of comparable quality for the countries in our sample, the BP approach proved most useful in our study.[33]

In order to take previous criticism into account, the net revenue and expenditure series are corrected to eliminate, to the extent possible, those changes in government revenues and expenditure that are not necessarily linked to fiscal policy decisions and that cyclical adjustment methods may fail to capture (e.g., large movements in asset or commodity prices).[34] This removes the largest—but not all—measurement errors, as identified episodes in IMF (2010) refer to cases of fiscal consolidations and not expansions. Furthermore IMF (2010) only provides data on an annual basis (since the 1980s) and therefore covers only part of the dataset.[35] Hence especially the responses of output to revenue shocks have to be interpreted cautiously.

The IRFs reflect the nonlinearity of the model. They are computed using the method of generalized impulse response functions (GIRFs) developed by Koop, Pesaran, and Potter (1996), which are dependent on historical events . The GIRFs allow the shock impact to depend on the regime itself and the regime to switch after a shock has been implemented.[36] The latter is important, as output—and the output gap—evolves over time following a fiscal policy shock.

12.3.2 Country by Country Results

Figures 12.2 and 12.3 present four quarter cumulative multipliers for each country.[37]

Broad supportive evidence is obtained for a nonlinear impact of fiscal policy on output. Government spending shocks have a larger effect on output when the output gap is negative (Canada being the only exception). This is particularly true for those countries where spending multipliers are statistically significant on impact and sizable (Germany, Japan, and the United States).[38]

The results are generally less conclusive for revenue multipliers. The impact is statistically significant for Canada, France, Germany, and Japan. In Germany, revenue multipliers are slightly higher in "good times" than in "bad times," which could suggest that individuals and firms are more willing to spend additional income

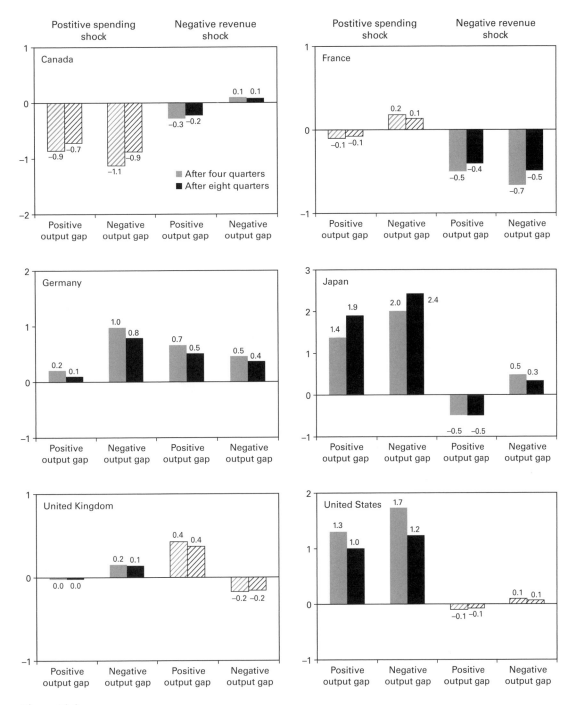

Figure 12.2
Cumulative fiscal multipliers: Fiscal expansion. The striped bars correspond to those measures for which no significant impact multiplier is found.
Source: IMF staff estimates

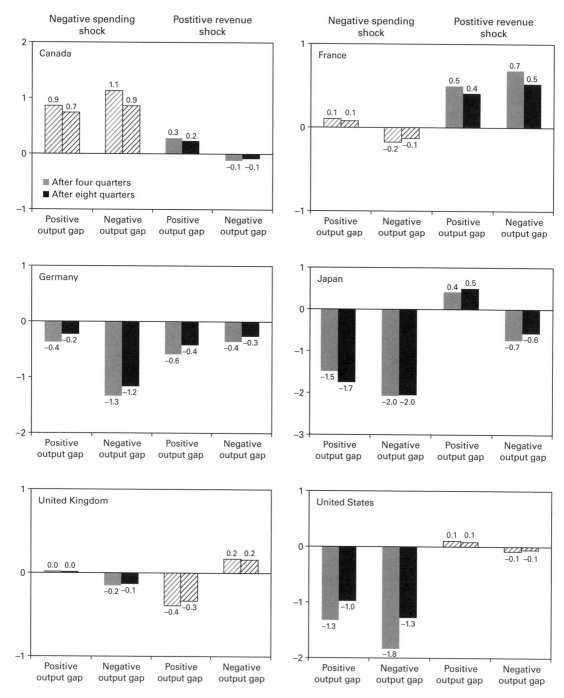

Figure 12.3
Cumulative fiscal multipliers: Fiscal contraction. The striped bars correspond to those measures for which no significant impact multiplier is found.
Source: IMF staff estimates

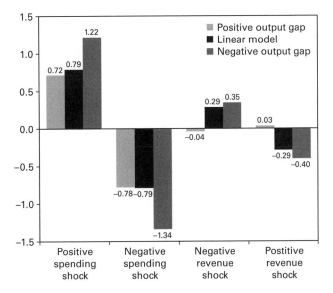

Figure 12.4
Fiscal multipliers in G7 economies. Cumulative multipliers are standardized multipliers over four quarters. Only statistically significant multipliers are included in the average. Average revenue multipliers exclude France, for which the outliers are large and data limitations are particularly severe. Italy is not included in the G7 average.
Source: IMF staff calculations

when market sentiment is positive, thereby becoming less Ricardian. In Canada and Japan revenue measures work as a countercyclical tool only when the output gap is negative.[39]

12.3.3 Results for the G7 Economies

Based on the country-by-country results, multipliers for an average of the G7 economies are shown in figure 12.4. They broadly support the above findings, with both consumption and revenue multipliers being significantly larger in times of negative output gaps than when the output gap is positive. Across countries, revenue multipliers are small (on average well below 0.5); whereas government purchases shocks, with the only exception of the United Kingdom, have sizable effects on real output.

Figure 12.4 also shows average multipliers estimated with a standard linear SVAR (based on the same BP identification as the TVAR). These multipliers from the linear model lie on average between the positive and negative regime multipliers and they are very much in line with averages identified in the literature discussed in the previous section.[40]

The linear model underestimates especially the effect of spending measures during downturns. In case of revenue measures, the linear model overestimates the

332 Aiko Mineshima, Marcos Poplawski-Ribeiro, and Anke Weber

discretionary impact in times of expansions. Assuming, consistent with recent fiscal adjustment packages in advanced economies, that two-thirds of the adjustment comes from spending measures, a weighted average of spending and revenue multipliers in downturns yields an overall fiscal multiplier of about unity.

12.3.4 Discussion and Caveats

The results indicate that multipliers vary by a large amount between and within countries. This calls for a tailored use of fiscal policies and a country-by-country assessment of their effects, which is in accordance with the other recent empirical literature (see Favero et al. 2011; Perotti 2005). The results also confirm the sizable spending multipliers found in the previous literature for the United States. For Canada and the United Kingdom, the low-expenditure multipliers are in line with Perotti (2005), who, using a structural identification à la Blanchard and Perotti (2002), finds that spending multipliers have decreased significantly since the 1980s.

The results are also mostly in line with the analyses that control for the state of the economic cycle (Auerbach and Gorodnichenko 2012a; Batini et al. 2012). They confirm the state dependency of fiscal multipliers and show that, especially for spending, multipliers are significantly larger in downturns than in expansions. Spending multipliers in the United States are found to be significantly above unity during downturns.

We find revenue multipliers are significantly smaller than spending multipliers, which is also broadly in line with the other literature. Revenue multipliers in the United States and the United Kingdom are found to be small and not statistically significant. This could be due to a change in the impact of revenue measures on output over time. Perotti (2005) shows that prior to the 1980s, tax cuts had a significant positive impact on GDP, but in the period after 1980, this effect became negative. These results contradict the findings of Romer and Romer (2010) and Cloyne (2011), who find significant and large revenue multipliers for the United States and the United Kingdom, respectively. However, recent work by Favero and Giavazzi (2012), as well as Perotti (2011), demonstrate that the estimation in Romer and Romer (2010) is subject to upward biases concerning the revenue multipliers.

Several important caveats apply to the analysis, as well as to most of the literature on fiscal multipliers. First, the model includes only three variables and does not take into account possible interactions with monetary policy and public debt. For instance, Auerbach and Gorodnichenko (2012b) find that the size of government debt reduces the response of output to government spending shocks. Thus the analysis could have overestimated fiscal multipliers, especially in high debt countries.[41] Second, some of the country heterogeneities may be the result of different data sources. Data limitations are particularly serious for France where true quarterly data are available only since the 1990s.

12.4 Conclusions and Policy Implications

This chapter has shown that there is no unique single size of fiscal multipliers: the size depends on various factors, including the state of the economy, monetary policy stance, fiscal leakages, and the types of fiscal instruments used. A comprehensive review of the studies covering mainly advanced economies provides guidance on the main factors that influence fiscal multipliers.

- Government spending has a higher multiplier while the tax multiplier is smaller in the short run.
- The United States tends to have larger multipliers than Europe, partly offsetting differences in the automatic stabilizers.
- Spending multipliers tend to be larger when the economy has large output gaps and when monetary policy is accommodative or ineffective (at the zero interest rate bound).
- Although the estimates are fewer, the multipliers for emerging markets and low-income countries tend to be lower than in advanced economies.

The original empirical work presented in this chapter explored in detail how fiscal multipliers differ depending on the state of the economy. The multipliers are nonlinear and vary over the business cycle: short-term spending multipliers are generally higher in economic downturns than in expansions. The size of spending multipliers during recessions could exceed unity, particularly for the United States, compared with the common range of spending multipliers around or below unity during normal times. This is in line with economic intuition: during expansions, or when unemployment and output are above potential levels, crowding-out effects of a fiscal expansion tends to offset the direct impact of fiscal stimulus on aggregate demand. The analysis also shows that first-year revenue multipliers are lower than spending multipliers, but the size of the multiplier varies significantly from country to country. This calls for a tailored approach when analyzing the impact of fiscal policy across countries.

The finding that the impact of fiscal policy on output depends on the underlying state of the economy has also important policy implications.

- Given that spending multipliers are large during economic recessions—they could exceed unity—it may make sense for a government to implement economic stimulus when the economy has a large negative output gap and the fiscal space.
- The pace of fiscal adjustment when an economy has a negative output gap should be carefully decided. As shown by the analysis in box 12.3, gradual fiscal adjustment may in some cases be preferable to a more upfront approach. For

example, when the output gap is negative initially, at the time the fiscal shock is implemented, a gradual negative spending adjustment will have a lower negative impact on output in the short term than an upfront reduction.[42] As Romer (2012) and DeLong and Summers (2012) argue, a dragged economic recovery could damage the economy permanently through lowering potential output and increasing the natural rate of unemployment (the hysteresis effects).[43] Furthermore, if the zero lower bound is binding, a scope for monetary policy to accommodate fiscal adjustment is limited, making the adverse impact of fiscal adjustment on the economy worse.[44] This suggests that when feasible, a more gradual fiscal consolidation is likely to prove preferable to an approach that aims at "getting it over quickly." More generally, policy makers should choose consolidation measures that are growth friendly and minimize the burden on the most vulnerable groups. A proper policy mix should be considered, including monetary policy and structural measures, in order to support growth as fiscal deficits go down.

• Designing a fiscal package calls for other factors in addition to the size of multipliers. Notably, consolidation measures should be underpinned by a credible medium-term plan up front, taking into account the long-term effects of specific fiscal adjustments. The measures should also take into account that the efficiency of tax and purchases changes depend on their preexisting levels and structure. For example, the current high tax pressures in some countries (particularly in Europe) suggest that the bulk of the fiscal adjustment should focus on the expenditure side (although revenue increases may be inevitable when the targeted adjustment is large).

• The trajectory of public-debt-GDP ratios in course of fiscal adjustment depends on several factors, including the initial debt level and the size of fiscal multiplier. In countries where the debt ratio is high and/or the fiscal multiplier is above average—both are likely in economic downturns—fiscal adjustment measures are unlikely to lower the public debt-to-GDP ratio initially as the direct effect of fiscal consolidation is likely to be offset by the indirect effect of a lower GDP.

Box 12.1
Sizes of fiscal multipliers—Literature survey

This box summarizes findings from a comprehensive survey of fiscal multipliers in the empirical literature, extending earlier work by Spilimbergo et al. (2009). The multipliers found in the literature using linear approaches are summarized in two categories based on the methodologies (i.e., VAR and DSGE). The main findings from the survey are as follows:

- Government spending multipliers are estimated to be positive, with a plausible range of 0.5 to 0.9, based on the mid 30 percent range of all samples. The spending multipliers for the whole sample range from 0.0 to 2.1, with the mean and median of 0.8 and 0.7, respectively.

- Tax multipliers are on average smaller than the spending multipliers, with a plausible range of 0.1 to 0.3, based on the mid 30 percent range of all samples. Some multipliers are negative with the tax multipliers for the whole sample ranging from –1.5 to 1.4, with mean and median of 0.2 and 0.2, respectively.

- The United States tends to have larger fiscal multipliers than Europe. The spending multipliers for the United States range from 0 to 2.1 with mean and median of 0.9 and 1, respectively, which are on average larger than the spending multipliers in Europe (ranging from 0.2 to 1.8 with mean and median of 0.6 and 0.5). As indicated by Coenen et al. (2012), this is probably because (1) Europe is more open, and therefore the leakage to imports is larger; (2) the degree of nominal rigidities is larger in Europe, and therefore the effect of expansionary fiscal actions on the rate of inflation is lower in Europe; and (3) automatic stabilizers play a larger role in Europe. Among these factors, Coenen et al. (2012) conclude that the higher nominal rigidity in Europe explains most of the difference in multipliers in Europe and in the United States.

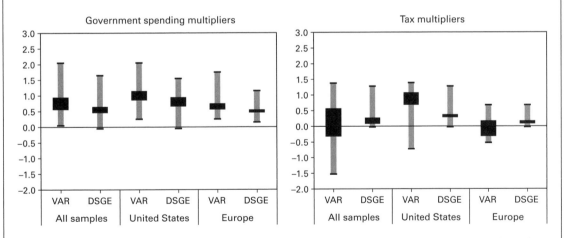

First-year fiscal multipliers from literature survey (linear approaches): DSGE includes New Keynesian models. Dark areas represent the mid-30 percent ranges (excluding top 35 percent and bottom 35 percent of the samples).
Sources: Literature survey in the appendix; IMF staff estimates

Box 12.2
What do economic theories predict about the size of fiscal multipliers?

Traditional Keynesian Approach

In the traditional Keynesian view, changes in aggregate demand, whether anticipated or unanticipated, have a positive short-run effect on real output and employment. The size of fiscal multipliers is dependent on the propensity to consume. The multiplier for government spending is calculated as $1/(1 - mpc)$ and that for taxes as $-mpc/(1 - mpc)$, where *mpc* indicates the marginal propensity to consume, under the assumption of a closed economy and constant interest rates. The *mpc* is assumed to be constant regardless of change in income, and is normally between 0 and 1; therefore the government spending multiplier is larger than unity. The criticism of the approach centers on the lack of microeconomic foundations of rational and optimizing agents.

Neoclassical Approach

The neoclassical approach is built on microeconomic foundations. The size of the fiscal multipliers is determined by intertemporal substitution of labor supply and wealth effects, and therefore varies depending on the nature of spending and the modalities of taxation used for financing the higher deficit.[a] For example, if households anticipate that an increase in government spending will be financed by debt, the neoclassical approach assumes they reduce spending now in anticipation of an increase in future taxes ("Ricardian equivalence"). Of course, in reality this may not always hold as beneficiaries of tax cuts today may not be paying off the debt within their lifetime (Blanchard 1985), and liquidity-constrained households that cannot borrow and therefore do not consume according to their permanent income (hand-to-mouth individuals) may increase consumption or investment if the liquidity constraint is eased (Coenen et al. 2012). The size of fiscal multipliers is typically smaller than unity, or even negative.[b]

New Keynesian Approach

The New Keynesian approach builds on the neoclassical approach but incorporates assumptions of sticky prices and other frictions (e.g., financial friction). The approach assumes that individuals and firms hold forward-looking, or rational, expectations while operating under some form of price and wage rigidity and liquidity constraint (Cogan et al. 2009). Because of the sticky-price assumptions, monetary policy can impact real output. The size of the fiscal multiplier depends on a number of factors, the most important being the type of fiscal instrument used and the extent of monetary accommodation.

a. See Baxter and King (1993) and Aiyagari et al. (1990).
b. Ramey (2011b) notes that short-run multipliers can be as large as 1.2, or as small as −2.5. Nakamura and Steinsson (2011) and Parker (2011) indicate that simple neoclassical models generally imply fiscal multipliers smaller than 0.5.

Box 12.3
Fiscal multipliers, the speed of adjustment and the nexus between consolidation and debt reduction: Some policy implications

The empirical findings suggest that during downturns fiscal multipliers are larger than during expansions. In the current environment, this has important implications for the desired speed of fiscal adjustment and the effect of fiscal consolidation on debt dynamics.

When the output gap is negative initially, at the time the fiscal shock is implemented a gradual negative spending adjustment will have a lower negative impact on output in the short term than an up-front spending reduction. The figure besides illustrates this for an average of the G7 economies in the sample. It shows the impact of a one

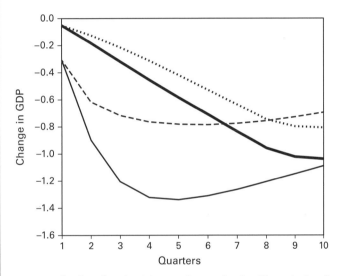

--- One "euro" up-front decrease in spending (positive output gap)

— One "euro" up-front decrease in spending (negative output gap)

····· One "euro" decrease in spending evenly spread over two years (positive output gap)

▬ One "euro" decrease in spending evenly spread over two years (negative output gap)

G7 economies: Cumulative impact on output from a negative discretionary fiscal spending shock. Estimates are from a threshold vector autoregression, with the output gap as the regime switching variable. A threshold of zero is endogenously determined within the model. Quarterly data from the 1970s are used. The figure shows average multipliers for G7 countries with significant impact multipliers.
Sources: Baum, Poplawski-Ribeiro, and Weber (2012); national sources; IMF staff estimates

(continued)

euro (or the relevant national currency) front-loaded improvement in the fiscal deficit versus a gradual improvement that is spread evenly over two years. When the output gap is negative initially, a more gradual fiscal adjustment hurts growth less in the first two and a half years of the simulation period.

Conversely, when the output gap is initially positive, a more front-loaded shock has a smaller cumulative impact on growth than under a negative regime (see IMF 2012b, annex 3). Accordingly, more front-loaded consolidation is preferable to a gradual deficit reduction approach after already around two years of gradual reduction (of the same amount spread out over two years).

An explanation for this finding lies in the nonlinear nature of the impulse response functions. They allow the regime to switch after the impact of the shock. Thus, if the shock initially occurs in a negative output gap regime, over the course of the tightening there is some probability of moving into a positive output gap regime in which multipliers are lower. With a longer fiscal consolidation period, the probability of this occurring is higher. Conversely, if the impact of the shock initially occurs in a positive output gap regime, then policy makers should use the favorable conditions (lower multipliers) and tighten upfront.

The discussion of up-front versus gradual adjustment is subject to some caveats. First, our results do not include anticipation effects. Especially in case of a gradual

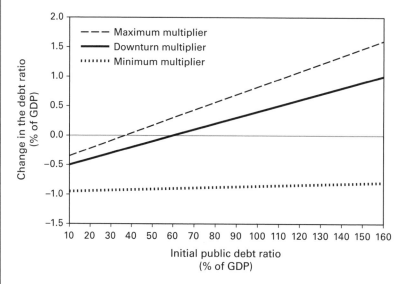

Impact on the debt ratio of a 1 percent of GDP discretionary tightening in the first year (relative to baseline). Multipliers are weighted averages of spending and revenue multipliers based on the previous literature and the observation that about two-thirds of recent fiscal adjustments in advanced economies rely on spending measures. The downturn multiplier is the weighted average of G7 multipliers in negative output gaps based on Baum, Poplawski-Ribeiro, and Weber (2012). The calculations assume that other factors remain constant, in particular interest rates.[a] For instance, with a multiplier of 0.6, the debt threshold would lie at about 120 percent of GDP. Source: Eyraud and Weber (2013)

adjustment, such effects could alter the growth forecast significantly. Second, a sharp up-front fiscal adjustment might be accompanied by further negative growth effects, which our model does not capture in the current specification (e.g., a further downward pressure on employment, human capital, and financial markets). Third, a sharp up-front adjustment may increase market confidence. Fiscal consolidation can in general calm markets, in which case the results of the up-front adjustment might be biased downward. However, in the current sovereign debt crisis the bond spreads seem largely driven by GDP growth prospects (Cottarelli and Jaramillo 2012).

Moreover, in countries where the debt ratio is high and/or the fiscal multiplier is above average, fiscal adjustment measures are unlikely to lower the public debt-to-GDP ratio initially as the direct effect of fiscal consolidation is likely to be offset by the indirect effect of a lower GDP. When the fiscal multiplier is 1 (a likely level in downturns), fiscal consolidation leads to an increase in the debt ratio in the first year in countries where the debt ratio initially lies above 60 percent. This debt threshold varies with the multiplier, which itself depends on the composition of the adjustment (spending vs. revenue) and other country-specific factors.[a]

a. The discussion here is based on Blanchard, Dell'Ariccia, and Mauro (2010).

Appendix

This appendix provides a summary of key papers that have estimated fiscal multipliers. It extends the earlier survey in Spilimbergo et al. (2009) with G indicating government spending, T indicating taxes, and Z indicating government investment.

Table A12.1
Literature survey on the size of fiscal multipliers: VAR approaches

Source	Methodology	Data sample	Country	Fiscal shock[a]			Fiscal multipliers			
							4 quarters	8 quarters	12 quarters	Cumulative
Afonso, Baxa, Slavik (2011)	Threshold VAR: measure the effects of fiscal developments associated with periods of financial crises. Results shown are for large fiscal shocks (2SD), which are normalized to the size of the initial fiscal shock set to 1% of GDP.	Quarterly data 1980:4–2009:4	United States	Debt-to-GDP ratio	Positive shock	High financial stress	0.1	0.2	0.2	0.4
						Low financial stress	0.1	0.2	0.2	0.5
					Negative shock	High financial stress	-0.1	-0.2	-0.2	-0.4
						Low financial stress	-0.1	-0.2	-0.2	-0.5
			United Kingdom		Positive shock	High financial stress	-0.1	0.1	0.3	0.3
						Low financial stress	0.1	0.2	0.2	0.5
					Negative shock	High financial stress	0.1	-0.1	-0.2	-0.2
						Low financial stress	-0.1	-0.2	-0.2	-0.5
			Germany		Positive shock	High financial stress	0.1	0.1	0.1	0.3
						Low financial stress	0.0	0.0	0.1	0.1
					Negative shock	High financial stress	-0.1	-0.1	-0.1	-0.2
						Low financial stress	0.0	-0.1	-0.1	-0.2
			Italy		Positive shock	High financial stress	0.5	0.3	0.1	0.8
						Low financial stress	0.2	0.2	0.1	0.5
					Negative shock	High financial stress	-0.5	-0.3	0.0	-0.9
						Low financial stress	-0.2	-0.2	0.0	-0.5
							1 year (mean)	1 year (max)		

Study	Method	Sample	Country	Variable	Component	Regime	Fixed effects	Max	Cumulative (20 quarters)
Auerbach–Gorodnichenko (2012a)	Smooth-transition VAR	Semiannual data Old members: 1985–2010 Newer members: mid-1990s–2010 1985–	OECD	G		Recession	w/o year fixed effects	0.4	0.5
						Expansion	w/o year fixed effects	−0.1	0.0
						Linear	w/o year fixed effects	0.1	0.2
						Recession	w/ year fixed effects	0.3	0.5
						Expansion	w/ year fixed effects	−0.1	0.1
						Linear	w/ year fixed effects	0.2	0.2
Auerbach–Gorodnichenko (2012b)	Smooth-transition VAR	Quarterly data 1947:1–2008:4	United States	G		Linear		1.0	0.6
					Defense spending	Expansion		0.6	−0.3
						Recession		2.5	2.2
						Linear		1.2	−0.2
					Nondefense spending	Expansion		0.8	−0.4
						Recession		3.6	1.7
						Linear		1.2	1.6
					Consumption spending	Expansion		1.3	1.0
						Recession		1.1	1.1
						Linear		1.2	0.2
					Investment spending	Expansion		0.2	−0.3
						Recession		2.1	1.5
						Linear		2.1	2.4
						Expansion		3.0	2.3
						Recession		2.9	3.4

(continued)

Table A12.1
(*continued*)

Source	Methodology	Data sample	Country	Fiscal shock[a]	Controlling for expectations		Fiscal multipliers	
							Impact	Max
				Total spending	Controlling for expectations with Ramey (2011a) news shocks.	Expansion	0.7	−0.5
						Recession	4.9	3.8
Bachmann and Sims (2011)	(i) Structural linear VAR models, taking into account "confidence" of households and businesses. (ii) Structural nonlinear VAR models with specifications to allow for differential impacts of government spending in "normal" times versus recessions.	Quarterly data	United States	G	Normal times	With consumer confidence	0.7	0.8
						Without consumer confidence	0.8	0.8
						With CEO confidence	1.0	1.2
						Without CEO confidence	1.0	1.0
					Recessions	With consumer confidence	0.4	3.1
						Without consumer confidence	0.3	0.3
						With CEO confidence	1.0	2.5
						Without CEO confidence	0.8	0.8
							1 quarter	4 quarters

8 quarters   (cumulative)

Study	Method	Data	Country		Regime	1.0	0.5	0.0
Batini, Callegari, Melina (2012)	Nonlinear threshold VAR (TVAR), which separates observations into different regimes based on a threshold variable.	Quarterly Data 1975:1–2010:2	United States	G	Linear	1.0	0.3	-0.5
					Expansion	2.0	2.2	2.2
					Recession	0.0	0.0	0.3
				T	Linear	0.0	0.2	0.7
					Expansion	0.0	0.2	0.7
					Recession	0.7	1.2	1.5
		Quarterly Data 1981:1–2009:4	Japan	G	Linear	0.7	1.4	1.1
					Expansion	1.3	2.0	2.0
					Recession	-0.3	-0.3	-0.2
				T	Linear	-0.3	-0.3	-0.1
					Expansion	-0.3	-0.2	0.2
					Recession	0.6	0.8	0.9
		Quarterly Data 1981:1–2007:4	Italy	G	Linear	0.3	0.4	0.5
					Expansion	1.4	1.6	1.8
					Recession	0.1	0.1	0.0
				T	Linear	0.1	0.1	0.1
					Expansion	0.1	0.2	0.2
					Recession	1.5	1.8	2.1
		Quarterly Data 1970:1–2010:4	France	G	Linear	1.4	1.6	1.9
					Expansion	2.6	2.1	1.8
					Recession	0.0	0.0	-0.1
				T	Linear	-0.1	-0.1	-0.2
					Expansion	0.0	0.0	-0.3
					Recession	0.3	0.3	0.3
		Quarterly Data 1985:1–2009:4	Euro area	G	Linear	0.4	0.4	0.1
					Expansion	2.1	2.6	2.5
					Recession	-0.2	-0.5	-0.6
				T	Linear	-0.1	-0.2	-0.1
					Expansion	-0.2	-0.4	-0.4
					Recession			
						4 quarters	10 quarters	

(continued)

Table A12.1
(*continued*)

Source	Methodology	Data sample	Country	Fiscal shock[a]			Fiscal multipliers	
							4 quarters	8 quarters (cumulative)
Baum and Koester (2011)	Threshold structural VAR	Quarterly Data 1976:1–2009:4	Germany	G	Positive shock (2% of GDP)	Linear	0.7	0.7
						Recession	1.0	1.0
						Expansion	0.4	0.3
					Positive shock (5% of GDP)	Linear	...	...
						Recession	1.3	1.3
						Expansion	0.3	0.3
					Negative shock (2% of GDP)	Linear	...	...
						Recession	−0.9	−0.8
						Expansion	−0.6	−0.6
					Negative shock (5% of GDP)	Linear	...	...
						Recession	−0.8	−0.8
						Expansion	−0.8	−0.8
				T	Positive shock (2% of GDP)	Linear	−0.7	−0.7
						Recession	−0.5	−0.5
						Expansion	−0.6	−0.5
					Positive shock (5% of GDP)	Linear	...	...
						Recession	−0.5	−0.5
						Expansion	−0.6	−0.5
					Negative shock (2% of GDP)	Linear	...	...
						Recession	0.5	0.5
						Expansion	0.6	0.5
					Negative shock (5% of GDP)	Linear	...	...
						Recession	0.5	0.5
						Expansion	0.6	0.6

Study	Method	Data	Country		Regime		
Baum, Poplawski-Ribeiro, Weber (2012)	Regime-switching VARs with output growth as the threshold variable.	Quarterly Data 1965:2–2011:2	United States	G	Expansion (positive output gap)	1.3	1.0
					Recession (negative output gap)	1.8	1.3
				T	Expansion (positive output gap)	−0.1	−0.1
					Recession (negative output gap)	0.1	0.1
		Quarterly Data 1970:1–2011:2	United Kingdom	G	Expansion (positive output gap)	0.0	0.0
					Recession (negative output gap)	0.2	0.1
				T	Expansion (positive output gap)	0.4	0.3
					Recession (negative output gap)	−0.2	−0.2
		Quarterly Data 1970:1–2011:2	Japan	G	Expansion (positive output gap)	1.5	1.7
					Recession (negative output gap)	2.0	2.0
				T	Expansion (positive output gap)	−0.4	−0.5
					Recession (negative output gap)	0.7	0.6

(continued)

Table A12.1
(*continued*)

Source	Methodology	Data sample	Country	Fiscal shock[a]	Fiscal multipliers			
					Impact	1 year	3 years	5 year
		Quarterly Data 1976:1–2009:4	Germany	G	Expansion (positive output gap)	0.4	0.2		
					Recession (negative output gap)	1.3	1.2		
				T	Expansion (positive output gap)	0.6	0.4		
					Recession (negative output gap)	0.4	0.3		
		Quarterly Data 1970:1–2010:4	France	G	Expansion (positive output gap)	−0.1	−0.1		
					Recession (negative output gap)	0.2	0.1		
				T	Expansion (positive output gap)	−0.5	−0.4		
					Recession (negative output gap)	−0.7	−0.5		
		Quarterly Data 1970:1–2011:2	Canada	G	Expansion (positive output gap)	−0.9	−0.7		
					Recession (negative output gap)	−1.1	−0.9		
				T	Expansion (positive output gap)	−0.3	−0.2		
					Recession (negative output gap)	0.1	0.1		

Study	Method	Data	Country	Variable	Scenario				
Beetsma and Giuliodori (2011)	Panel Structural VAR	Annual data 1970–2004 1970–2004	14 EU countries	G	Baseline	1.2	1.5	1.2	0.7
					w/o time effects	1.1	1.5	1.2	0.5
					w/ qiadratic time trends	1.2	1.4	0.8	0.3
					In first difference—no trends	1.1	1.5	1.7	1.7
Blanchard and Perotti (2002)	Structural VAR. No explicit control for interest rates or money supply.	Quarterly data 1960:1–1997:4	United States	G, DT	1 quarter / 1 year / 2 years / 3 years	0.8	0.5	0.5	1.1
				G, ST		0.9	0.6	0.7	0.7
				T, DT		0.7	0.7	0.7	0.4
				T, ST		0.7	1.1	1.3	1.3
Bryant et al. (1988)	Comparison of various frameworks (econometric, VAR and model- simulations). Varying assumptions about the interest rate response.		United States	G	1 year / 2 years / 3 years	0.6–2	0.5–2.1	0.5–1.7	
Burriel et al. (2009)	Structural VAR, following Blanchard and Perotti (2004) allowing for nonlinearity.	Quarterly data 1981:1–2007:4	United States	G	1 quarter / 4 quarters / 8 quarters — Baseline	0.8	0.9	0.7	
					With financial stress	0.8	1.1	0.8	
					With fiscal stress	0.8	1.3	1.3	
				T	Baseline	0.0	0.1	0.4	
					With financial stress	0.3	0.6	0.9	
					With fiscal stress	0.0	0.3	0.7	
			EMU	G	Baseline	0.8	0.9	0.9	
					With financial stress	0.7	0.8	0.7	

(continued)

Table A12.1
(*continued*)

Source	Methodology	Data sample	Country	Fiscal shock[a]		Fiscal multipliers		
						1 quarter	**8 quarters**	
				T	With fiscal stress	0.9	1.2	1.5
					Baseline	0.8	0.6	0.5
					With financial stress	0.9	0.8	0.7
					With fiscal stress	1.5	1.4	1.9
Cimadomo and Bénassy-Quéré (2012)	Structural VAR for the United States, and factor-augmented VAR (FAVAR), augmented by "global factors" representing developments in the world economy, for Germany and the United Kingdom (the FAVAR was proposed for monetary policy analysis by Bernanke et al. 2005).	Quarterly data 1971:1–2009:4	Germany	G		0.5	0.1	
				T		0.7	0.7	
			United Kingdom	G		0.3	-0.1	
				T		0.1	-0.1	
			United States	G		1.3	-0.7	
				T		-0.1	-0.2	
Fisher and Peters (2010)	VAR: estimate the dynamic responses of output to a government military spending shock using the information on surprises in the returns of top three military contractors to identify government spending shocks.	Quarterly data 1957:3–2007:4	United States	Government military spending		Cumulative for 5 years		
						1.5		
				G		0.6		
						1940:2– 1941:2	1940:2– 1941:4	

Study	Method	Data	Country/Sample	Variable		1 quarter	1 year	2 years	3 years
Gordon and Krenn (2010)	VAR with Cholesky factorization. Fiscal multipliers are calculated as the marginal effect of G innovations on GDP relative to the marginal effect of G innovations on G itself.	Quarterly data 1920:2–1941:4	United States	G		1.8	0.9		
Ilzetzki and Végh (2008)	Panel VAR: applied to 27 developing and 22 high-income countries. No explicit control for (country-specific) interest rates (only US interest rate included).		High-inc.	G		0.4	0.7	0.9	0.8
			Developing	G		0.6	0.4	0.1	−0.1

Study	Method	Data	Country/Sample	Variable	Category		Impact	Cumulative for 20 quarters
Ilzetzki, Mendoza, Végh (2011)	Bivariate panel structural VAR	Quarterly data 1960:1–2007:4	44 countries (20 high-income; 24 developing)	Government consumption	Income level	High-income	0.4	0.8
						Developing	−0.2	0.2
					Exchange rate regime	Fixed	0.1	1.5
						Flexible	−0.3	−0.4
					Trade openness	Total trades (IM+EX) over 60% of GDP	−0.3	−0.8
						Total trades (IM+EX) below 60% of GDP	0.0	1.3

(continued)

Table A12.1
(continued)

Source	Methodology	Data sample	Country	Fiscal shock[a]	Fiscal multipliers	
				Financial Fragility		
				Total central gov. debt over 60% of GDP	−0.2	−2.3
				Total central gov. debt below 60% of GDP (high-income)	0.7	0.4
				Total central gov. debt below 60% of GDP (developing)	0.1	0.3
				Z		
				Income level		
				High-income	0.4	1.2
				Developing	0.6	0.8
				Exchange rate regime		
				Fixed	0.4	1.4
				Flexible	0.5	0.2
				Trade openness		
				Total trades (IM+EX) over 60% of GDP	−0.2	0.5
				Total trades (IM+EX) below 60% of GDP	0.5	0.7
	Multivariate panel structural VAR			Government consumption		
				Income level		
				High-income	0.4	0.9
				Developing	−0.1	0.5
				Exchange rate regime		
				Fixed	0.0	1.3
				Flexible	−0.1	0.0
				Trade openness		
				Total trades (IM+EX) over 60% of GDP	−0.1	−0.3

						Total trades (IM+EX) below 60% of GDP	0.1	1.3		
					Financial Fragility	Total central gov. debt over 60% of GDP	−0.2	−4.7		
							4 quarters	8 quarters	12 quarters	Max
Mountford-Uhlig (2009)	Quarterly VAR with the method of identifying policy shocks using sign restrictions on impulse responses, which has been introduced and applied to monetary policy in Uhlig (2005).	Quarterly data 1955:1–2000:4	United States	Deficit-financed tax cut			0.9	2.1	3.4	3.6 (qrt 13)
				Deficit-financed spending			0.3	−0.7	−1.2	0.65 (qrt 1)
							1 year	2 years	3 years	
Perotti (2004)	Quarterly VAR. 10-year nominal interest rate included in the VAR. Multipliers reported are cumulative.	Australia: 1960:1 2001:2, Canada: 1961:1–2001:4, Germany: 1960:1–1989:4, UK: 1963:1–2001:2, US: 1960:1–2001:4.	Australia	G			0.6	0.9	0.9	
				Z			−0.3	0.0	0.5	
			Canada	G			0.6	0.7	0.9	
				Z			0.4	−0.2	−0.7	
			Germany	G			0.8	0.8	0.9	
				Z			5.1	4.4	3.8	
			United Kingdom	G			0.6	0.9	1.0	
				Z			0.0	−0.1	−0.1	
			United States	G			1.4	1.9	2.2	
				Z			1.2	0.5	0.2	

(continued)

Table A12.1
(*continued*)

Source	Methodology	Data sample	Country	Fiscal shock[a]	Fiscal multipliers	
					1 year	3 years
Perotti (2005)	Quarterly VAR. 10-year nominal interest rate included in the VAR. Multipliers reported are cumulative.	Australia: 1960:1–2001:2, Canada: 1961:1–2001:4, Germany: 1960:1–1989:4, UK: 1963:1–2001:2, US: 1960:1–2001:4.	Australia	G	-0.1/0.4	1.4/0.7
				T	-1.5/-0.6	-1.7/-0.9
			Canada	G	1.0/-0.3	0.6/-1.1
				T	-0.4/0.4	-0.2/1.6
			Germany	G	0.6/0.5	-0.8/-1.1
				T	-0.3/0.0	0.1/-0.6
			United Kingdom	G	0.5/-0.3	0.0/-0.9
				T	0.2/-0.4	0.2/-0.7
			United States	G	1.3/0.4	1.7/0.1
				T	1.4/-0.7	23.9/-1.6
					Peak	
Ramey (2011a)	VAR: measure fiscal multipliers by controlling for anticipation effects using a narrative method to construct richer government spending (particularly military spending) news.	1939:1–2008:4	United States	G	Post-WWII 0.6–0.8	
					1 year / 2 years / 3 years	
Romer and Romer (2010)	Narrative, single equations, and VARs. Explicit control for interest (federal funds) rates in some specifications.	1945–2007	United States	T	1 year 1.2 / 2 years 2.8	3 years 2.7

a. G: government spending; T: taxes; and Z: government investment.

Table A12.2

Literature survey on the size of fiscal multipliers: Macroeconomic model-based (New Keynesian/DSGE) approaches

Source	Methodology	Country	Fiscal shock[a]	Fiscal multipliers	
				1 year	2 years
Al-Eyd and Barrell (2005)	NiGEM model with one-year shock. Taylor interest rate rule assumed to meet domestic inflation targets.	France	Indirect tax	0.3	0.2
			Corporate tax lump	0.0	0.2
			Corporate tax rate	0.2	0.4
			Direct tax	0.3	0.2
			Transfers	0.2	0.1
		Germany	Indirect tax	0.5	0.2
			Corporate tax lump	0.1	0.6
			Corporate tax rate	0.2	0.7
			Direct tax	0.7	0.2
			Transfers	0.5	0.1
		Italy	Indirect tax	0.2	0.2
			Corporate tax lump	0.0	0.2
			Corporate tax rate	0.2	0.4
			Direct tax	0.2	0.2
			Transfers	0.1	0.1
		Spain	Indirect tax	0.2	0.1
			Corporate tax lump	0.0	0.1
			Corporate tax rate	0.2	0.2
			Direct tax	0.2	0.1
			Transfers	0.1	0.1
				1 year	

(continued)

Table A12.2
(continued)

Source	Methodology	Country	Fiscal shock[a]	Fiscal multipliers
Barrell, Holland, and Hurst (2012)	NiGEM model with one-year shock. Taylor interest rate rule assumed to meet domestic inflation targets.	Australia	Consumption	0.8
			Benefits	0.3
			Indirect tax	0.3
			Direct tax	0.2
		Austria	Consumption	0.5
			Benefits	0.2
			Indirect tax	0.1
			Direct tax	0.1
		Belgium	Consumption	0.2
			Benefits	0.0
			Indirect tax	0.1
			Direct tax	0.0
		Canada	Consumption	0.5
			Benefits	0.2
			Indirect tax	0.1
			Direct tax	0.1
		Denmark	Consumption	0.5
			Benefits	0.1
			Indirect tax	0.1
			Direct tax	0.0
		Finland	Consumption	0.6
			Benefits	0.1
			Indirect tax	0.1
			Direct tax	0.1
		France	Consumption	0.7
			Benefits	0.3
			Indirect tax	0.1
			Direct tax	0.3
		Germany	Consumption	0.5
			Benefits	0.3
			Indirect tax	0.1
			Direct tax	0.3
		Greece	Consumption	1.1
			Benefits	0.4
			Indirect tax	0.2
			Direct tax	0.3

Country	Category	Value
Ireland	Consumption	0.3
	Benefits	0.1
	Indirect tax	0.1
	Direct tax	0.1
Italy	Consumption	0.6
	Benefits	0.2
	Indirect tax	0.1
	Direct tax	0.1
Japan	Consumption	1.3
	Benefits	0.7
	Indirect tax	0.3
	Direct tax	0.6
Netherlands	Consumption	0.5
	Benefits	0.2
	Indirect tax	0.1
	Direct tax	0.2
Portugal	Consumption	0.7
	Benefits	0.2
	Indirect tax	0.1
	Direct tax	0.1
Sweden	Consumption	0.4
	Benefits	0.2
	Indirect tax	0.1
	Direct tax	0.2
Spain	Consumption	0.7
	Benefits	0.2
	Indirect tax	0.2
	Direct tax	0.1
United Kingdom	Consumption	0.7
	Benefits	0.2
	Indirect tax	0.2
	Direct tax	0.2
United States	Consumption	1.1
	Benefits	0.4
	Indirect tax	0.4
	Direct tax	0.3

(continued)

Table A12.2
(*continued*)

Source	Methodology	Country	Fiscal shock[a]		Fiscal multipliers			
					Impact	1 year	2 years	5 years
Canzoneri et al. (2011)	Cúrdia-Woodford New Keynesian model with costly financial intermediation. Credit market frictions are assumed to be countercyclical.	United States	G	Recession	The size of intervention of 1 % of GDP	2.3			
					The size of intervention of 5 % of GDP	1.9			
					The size of intervention of 10 % of GDP	1.7			
				Expansion (origin: financial shock)	The size of intervention of 2.5 % of GDP	0.9	0.7	0.6	0.5
				Recession (origin: financial shock)	The size of intervention of 2.5 % of GDP	2.2	0.9	0.7	0.6
Christiano, Eichenbaum, and Rebelo (2009)	DSGE model with Calvo-style pricing frictions and no capital, incorporating the nonlinearity of nominal interest rates.	United States	G	Standard model without capital	No zero bound is binding	1.1			
					Zero interest bound is binding	3.7			
				Medium-size DSGE based on Altig, Christiano, Eichenbaum, and Lindé (2005)	No zero bound is binding after the discount rate moves from 4% to -10.5% on an annual basis for 10 periods.	0.8			
					Zero bound is binding between 2-10 periods after the discount rate moves from 4% to -10.5% on an annual basis for 10 periods.	3.4			
					No zero bound after the neutral technology shock fall by 4.5 percent for 10 periods.	0.7			
					Zero bound between 3-9 quarters after the neutral technology shock fall by 4.5 percent for ten periods.	1.3			

Study	Description	Country	Instrument	Notes	1 quarter	1 year	2 years	3 years
Coenen et al. (2012)	DSGE: seven structural DSGE models used by policy-making institutions.	United States	Government consumption (2 years)	Fiscal stimulus is assumed to last for 2 years, unless otherwise indicated, with 2-year monetary accommodation.		1.6		
			Government consumption (1 year)			1.2		
			Government investment			1.6		
			Targeted transfers			1.3		
			Consumption taxes			0.6		
			General transfers			0.4		
			Corporate income taxes			0.2		
			Labor income taxes			0.2		
		European Union	Government consumption (2 years)	Fiscal stimulus is assumed to last for 2 years, unless otherwise indicated, with 2-year monetary accommodation.		1.5		
			Government consumption (1 year)			0.9		
			Government investment			1.5		
			Targeted transfers			1.1		
			Consumption taxes			0.7		
			General transfers			0.3		
			Corporate income taxes			0.2		
			Labor income taxes			0.5		
Cogan, Cwik, Taylor, and Wieland (2009)	New Keynesian simulation exercise, based on the model in Smets and Wouters (2007). Varying assumptions about the interest rate response.	United States	T, G		0.96-1.03	0.67-0.89	0.48-0.61	0.41-0.44

(continued)

Table A12.2
(*continued*)

Source	Methodology	Country	Fiscal shock[a]		Fiscal multipliers			
					1 quarter	1 year	2 years	3 years
Dalsgaard et al. (2001)	Based on the OECD INTERLINK model. No monetary policy response (nominal interest rate held constant).	United States	G, country specific			1.1	1	0.5
			G, global shock			1.5	1.3	0.7
		Japan	G, country specific			1.7	1.1	0.4
			G, global shock			2.6	1.9	0.6
		Euro area	G, country specific			1.2	0.9	0.5
			G, global shock			1.9	1.5	0.7
Eggertsson (2006)	DSGE model with assumptions of sticky prices, rational expectations, and the government that cannot commit to future policy.	United States	Real government consumption (hold the budget balanced)	Coordinated policy, Interest rate=0		PV 3.4		
				Interest rate>0		0.5		
				Uncoordinated policy, Interest rate=0		3.4		
				Interest rate>0		0.5		
			Deficit spending (tax cuts and accumulate debts)	Coordinated policy, Interest rate=0		3.8		
				Interest rate>0		0.8		
				Uncoordinated policy, Interest rate=0		0.0		
				Interest rate>0		0.0		
Elmendorf and Furman (2008)	Based on model in Elmendorf and Reifschneider (2002). Interest rates adjust based on a Taylor rule. For rebates: low: 20 percent of rebate spent; high: 50 percent spent.	United States	Income taxes reduction		0.2	0.3 / 0.4		
			Investment tax credit		0.2	0.1 / 0.2		
			G		1.0	1.0 / 1.0		
			Tax rebate (low)		0.3	0.0 / 0.0		
			Tax rebate (high)		1.0	1.0 / 0.2		

				1 quarter	1 year	2 years	3 years
Freedman et al. (2008)	Annual GIMF model simulations. Varying assumptions about the monetary policy response.	United States	Z and transfers	0.5	0.3	-0.1	0.8
		Euro area	Lump-sum transfer	0.2	0.0	-0.2	0.2
			Z and transfers	0.5	0.3	-0.1	0.8
		Japan	Lump-sum transfer	0.2	0.0	-0.2	0.2
			Z and transfers	0.5	0.3	-0.1	0.8
		Emerging Asia	Lump-sum transfer	0.2	0.0	-0.2	0.2
			Z and transfers	0.7	0.4	-0.3	1.1
		Other	Lump-sum transfer	0.4	0.1	-0.3	0.5
			Z and transfers	0.7	0.4	-0.2	1.1
			Lump-sum transfer	0.3	0.1	-0.3	0.4
				1 quarter			
Heathcote (2005)	Calibrated (real) model with distortionary taxation and capital market imperfections. No modeling of monetary policy.	United States	T (temporary proportional income tax reduction)	0.4			
				1 year			
Her Majesty's Treasury (2003)	European Commission's QUEST model. Interest rates respond to meet EU area inflation targets (except Sweden and the UK, which are assumed to target their own inflation rates).	Germany	T	0.2			
			G	0.4			
		Spain	T	0.1			
			G	0.5			
		France	T	0.1			
			G	0.5			
		Ireland	T	0.1			
			G	0.4			
		Italy	T	0.1			
			G	0.5			
		Netherlands	T	0.1			
			G	0.4			
		Portugal	T	0.0 to 0.1			
			G	0.7			

(continued)

Table A12.2
(continued)

Source	Methodology	Country	Fiscal shock[a]		Fiscal multipliers			
					Impact	4 quarters	10 quarters	25 quarters
		Sweden	T		0.3			
			G		0.4			
		United Kingdom	T		0.2			
			G		0.3			
Leeper, Traum, and Walker (2011)	Five nested DSGE models.	United States	Real business cycle model	Lump-sum finance	0.1	0.0	0.0	-0.2
			Real business cycle model	Labor tax finance	0.1	0.1	-0.1	-0.3
			Real business cycle model	Distortionary finance	0.1	0.0	-0.1	-0.5
			Real business cycle model	Real frictions	0.6	0.4	0.2	-0.3
			New Keynesian	Sticky price & wage	1.0	0.7	0.5	0.2
			New Keynesian	Nonsavers	1.2	0.9	0.6	0.3
			Open New Keynesian	Financial integration: G nontraded	1.1	0.8	0.6	0.3
			Open New Keynesian	Financial integration: G traded	0.9	0.7	0.5	0.2
					Year 1	Year 2		
OECD (2009)	Various macro models surveyed for OECD countries (all studies, year 1)	10 OECD countries plus euro area	Purchases of goods and service	low/high/mean	0.6/1.9/1.1			
			Corporate tax cut	low/high/mean	0.1/0.5/0.3			
			Personal income tax cut	low/high/mean	0.1/1.1/0.5			
			Indirect tax cut	low/high/mean	0.0/1.4/0.5			
			Social security contribution cut	low/high/mean	0.0/1.2/0.4			

Source		Model description	Policy		Year 1	Year 2
		Various macro models surveyed for OECD countries (studies with year 1 and year 2)	Purchases of goods and service	low/high/mean	0.9/1.9/1.2	0.5/2.2/1.3
			Corporate tax cut	low/high/mean	0.1/0.5/0.3	0.2/0.8/0.5
			Personal income tax cut	low/high/mean	0.1/1.1/0.5	0.2/1.4/0.8
			Indirect tax cut	low/high/mean	0.0/0.6/0.2	0.0/0.8/0.4
			Social security contribution cut	low/high/mean	0.0/0.5/0.3	0.2/1.0/0.6
		OECD global model	Government expenditure (consumption and investment)	Accommodative monetary policy	0.9	1.3
		OECD global model	Income tax cuts	Accommodative monetary policy	0.6	1.0
Zandi (2008)	United States	Moody's Economy.com macro model. Details of the model are not specified. The two tax rebate multipliers are from nonrefundable and refundable rebates.	Tax rebate		1 year 1.0 / 1.3	
			Payroll tax holiday		1.3	
			Tax cut		1.0	
			Accelerated depreciation		0.3	
			Extend alternative min. tax patch		0.5	
			Bush income tax cuts permanent		0.3	
			Dividend and capital gains tax cuts permanent		0.4	
			Cut corporate tax rate		0.3	
			Extend unemployment insurance benefits		1.6	
			Temporarily increase food stamps		1.7	
			General aid to state governments		1.4	
			Infrastructure spending		1.6	

a. G: government spending, T: taxes, and Z: government investment.

Table A12.3
Literature survey on the size of fiscal multipliers: Other approaches

Source	Methodology	Data sample	Country	Fiscal shock	Fiscal multipliers	
					Contemporaneous	2 years
Barro and Redlick (2009)	Two-stage least-square regression	Annual data 1912–2006	United States	Government defense spending	0.4–0.5	0.6–0.7
				Temporary increase in defense spending		
				Permanent increase in defense spending	0.6	0.8
					1 quarter	
Broda and Parker (2008)	Econometric case study of the 2008 tax rebate. Implicit control for interest rates through fixed effects.	2008	United States	Tax rebate	0.2	
					1 quarter	1 year
Coronado et al. (2005)	Econometric case study of the 2003 Jobs and Growth Tax Relief Reconciliation Act, based on survey data. No explicit control for interest rates.	2003	United States	Increase child credit, reduce withholding T	0.3	0.3
					1 year	3 years
IMF (2008)	Dynamic panel regressions using the Arelloano-Bond estimator.	1970–2007	Advanced (21 countries)	T	0.4 / 0.0	0.6 / 0.4
				G	–0.1 / 0.2	–0.3 / 0.5
			Emerging (20 countries)	T	0.2 / 0.1	0.2 / 0.2
				G	0.2 / 0.1	–0.2 / –0.2
					1 quarter	1 year
Johnson et al. (2006)	Survey data used to study the effect of the 2001 tax rebate. Authors consider household impact responses. Any effect from interest rates would come through household expectations.	2001	United States	Tax rebates	0.2–0.4	0.7

Notes

We thank Thomas Baunsgaard for his contribution to an earlier version of this chapter.

1. The discussion here is based on Blanchard, Dell' Ariccia, and Mauro (2010).

2. There is a widespread perception that the government simply cannot react quickly enough to fine-tune the economy because of the following three types of lags: (1) a lag between the time a change in policy is required and the time that the government recognizes this, (2) a lag between when the government recognizes that a change in policy is required and when it takes action, and (3) a lag between policy is implemented and it actually affects the economy.

3. G20 (2009) indicates that by early 2009 the G20 countries adopted (or planned to adopt) fiscal stimulus measures amounting on average to around 0.5 percent of GDP in 2008, 1.5 percent of GDP in 2009, and about 1.25 percent of GDP in 2010. The stimulus consisted of one-third revenue measures and two-thirds expenditure measures. Revenue measures focused on cuts in personal income taxes and indirect taxes, such as VAT or excises, while increased spending for infrastructure was emphasized on the expenditure side.

4. See Spilimbergo, Symansky, and Schindler (2009) for more discussion.

5. The plausible range excludes the top and bottom 35 percentile in table 12.1 (see the table notes). Full results of the survey are presented in the appendix.

6. There are typically two channels that cause the resulting simultaneity bias: the automatic stabilizers and endogenous fiscal policy (i.e., systematic countercyclical policy).

7. Blanchard and Perotti (2002) indicate that direct evidence on the conduct of fiscal policy suggests that it takes policy makers and legislatures more than a quarter to learn about a GDP shock, decide what fiscal measures to take in response, pass these measures through the legislature, and actually implement them.

8. For example, Favero and Giavazzi (2007) argue that omitting feedbacks from changes in the level of public debt (as a ratio to GDP) in response to a fiscal shock (a tax reduction or a spending increase) to future taxes, spending, and interest rates (the cost of debt services) can result in incorrect estimates of the dynamic effects of fiscal shocks.

9. The approaches are based on the argument that it could be misleading to assume that changes in output in a given quarter are caused solely by actual changes in tax collections or government spending in the contemporaneous quarter. This is because information on fiscal policy, for example, changes in taxes, often becomes available more than a quarter before the implementation, and economic entities likely start adjusting their behavior based on this information, before taxes are actually changed. Regarding the timing of the announcement of changes in fiscal policy, some studies (e.g., Ramey 2011a; Mertens and Ravn 2011) find that changes in taxes tend to be known well in advance to the implementation. Blanchard and Perotti (2002) also indicate that most of the changes in tax and transfer programs are known at least a few quarters before they are implemented.

10. Coenen et al. (2010) indicate that there is no complete consensus on the appropriate structural features and calibration. Feve, Matheron, and Sahuc (2012) demonstrate with a DSGE model that an estimation bias could arise from omitting the combination of Edgeworth complementarity between private spending and government expenditures and endogenous government expenditures (automatic stabilizers), indicating the importance of appropriately structuring a DSGE model.

11. For example, see Dolls, Fuest, and Peichl (2010).

12. Corsetti, Kuester, and Müller (2011) argue that the short-run effect of fiscal measures does not only depend on the exchange rate regime and the monetary strategy more generally but hinges also on the future fiscal mix, therefore one cannot assess fiscal stimulus independently of the exchange rate regime.

13. Corsetti, Meier, and Müller (2012) conducting an empirical analysis using panel data comprised of 17 OECD countries find that net exports decrease in response to a fiscal expansion while the real exchange rate appreciates.

14. Contrary to this statement, Corsetti, Meier, and Müller (2012) emphasize that the typical textbook notion of monetary policy being more accommodative under a fixed exchange rate regime is not a general prediction of standard open economy models. With imperfect credibility about the currency peg, a government spending increase may generate tensions in the currency market, promoting the central bank to defend the currency with an increase in the interest rate.

15. The "open economy relative multiplier" is defined as the effect that an increase in government spending in one region of a currency union relative to another has on relative output and employment.

16. Contrary to this statement, Farhi and Werning (2012) demonstrate with a DSGE model that self-financed government spending multipliers tend to be small—smaller than unity—in a currency union because government spending leads to inflation in domestically produced goods, which lowers the competitiveness of the economy given, the fixed exchange rate, and depresses private consumption. However, they also find transfer-financed spending multipliers large in the short run (when prices have not fully adjusted), as positive transfers from the rest of the world increase the demand for home goods, thereby they argue that the overall government spending multipliers could be larger than unity.

17. This may be partly because compared to a change in government spending a change in taxes tends to take more time to build its impact. For example, Mountford and Uhlig (2009) and Zubairy (2012) suggest that the effects of tax shocks take 12 to 20 quarters to build. Zubairy (2012) indicates, with a DSGE model, that tax changes take time to build up because the primary driver of the buildup is investment, not consumption.

18. In contrast to this statement, IMF (2010) finds that fiscal consolidations based on spending are less contractionary than those based on tax increases. The IMF study explains that this finding is due to different monetary-policy reactions to fiscal consolidation: monetary policy tends to be more accommodative when a government implements a spending-based consolidation than a revenue-based consolidation. This is partly because many tax increases in past fiscal consolidation plans involve increases in the value-added tax, which increases inflation.

19. For example, a temporary cut in distortionary taxes that shifts private consumption from the future to the present would increase real interest rates and crowd out investment.

20. For example, Barrell, Holland, and Hurst (2012) quantitatively analyze the differences in the size of fiscal multipliers between temporary and permanent fiscal measures.

21. The study finds, with a sample of country episodes of high debt for advanced and emerging economies, that the impact fiscal multipliers are close to zero and long-run multi-

pliers become negative during episodes of debt-to-GDP ratios exceeding 60 percent for three or more consecutive years.

22. The study also indicates that the change in short-term fiscal multipliers could be explained by the change in spending composition; a lower share of government investment and a larger wage component in total spending.

23. Barrell et al. (2012) indicate the correlations between country size and the tax and spending multipliers are 40 to 50 percent. They discuss that the impact of a large economy on global interest rates are offset by other features of large economies, such as the less propensity to imports. Furceri and Poplawski-Ribeiro (2009), in turn, show that larger countries have less volatile discretionary and nondiscretionary government spending, which could also increase the spending effectiveness and multipliers.

24. Erceg and Lindé (2010) argue that the size of fiscal multipliers could decline with the level of government spending if the stimulus package is large enough to get the economy out of the liquidity trap, hence pushing interest rates upward. Similarly Fernández-Villaverde et al. (2012) and Rendahl (2012) also find with New Keynesian models that fiscal multipliers decline as the stimulus package expands and closes much of the output gap.

25. Dalsgaard, André, and Richardson (2001) also demonstrate with a multiregion DSGE macroeconomic model (LITERLINK) that a coordinated fiscal stimulus among all OECD countries has a larger impact than a noncoordinated one. Blanchard and Leigh (2013) revisit, extend, and examined the robustness of the analysis done in IMF (2012). They conclude that actual multipliers were substantially above 1 early in the crisis.

26. The simulation indicates that government spending partly crowds out private consumption under the scenario of unemployment is less than the natural rate plus 2 percentage points, while no crowding-out is observed when unemployment exceeds the natural rate by 3 percentage points or more.

27. In this context, several economists, including Parker (2011) and Seidman (2011), argue that it is incorrect to assume the size of multipliers during recessions would be the same as the size of multipliers estimated with data during World War II when the economy was at full employment ("the unemployment rate during 1942 averaged 4.7 percent and was steadily falling, reaching 0.7 percent by 1944"; Parker 2011).

28. A number of studies, including Drautzburg and Uhlig (2011) and Coenen et al. (2010), also indicate the size of fiscal multipliers is large if transfers are targeted to credit-constrained households.

29. This section is based on appendix 1 of the April 2012 IMF *Fiscal Monitor*, and on Baum, Poplawski-Ribeiro, and Weber (2012).

30. As a robustness check, we also compute the estimations using output growth as a threshold variable.

31. Quarterly fiscal data on Italy were not available for a comparable period. Therefore Italy is excluded from the analysis.

32. The data are arranged in increasing order on the basis of the threshold variable. Sequential estimation of linear VARs gives a sequence of OLS regressions, each using the first x ranked observations. For each of these regressions, the one-step-ahead predictive residuals are kept.

33. Caldara and Kamps (2012) show, moreover, that differences in estimates of fiscal multipliers documented in the literature by Blanchard and Perotti (2002), Mountford and Uhlig (2009), and Romer and Romer (2010) are due mostly to different restrictions on the output elasticities of tax revenue and government spending.

34. When large discrepancies are observed between the IMF (2010) "action-based" measure of policy changes and the cyclically adjusted primary balance, the component of revenue and expenditure changes unrelated to output developments and discretionary measures is removed from the quarterly net revenue and expenditure series. This yields a "clean" series, where changes in revenue mainly reflect changes related to output and policy measures.

35. A Cholesky decomposition is applied as a robustness check to account for the vulnerability of our results to the exact identification method; even though this identification methodology does not identify the revenue shocks correctly (it does not account for the effects of automatic stabilizers). The results with respect to spending multipliers, available upon request, remain robust.

36. GIRFs have been employed in several empirical applications. For example, in monetary economics they are applied in Balke (2000) and Atanasova (2003).

37. The results for the Tsay threshold approach can be found in Baum, Poplawski-Ribeiro, and Weber (2012, tab. 3). Apart from the United Kingdom, the threshold value is below the average output gap and negative for all other countries. For most of them, the majority of the observations lie in the upper output gap regime. The threshold values are significant at the 10 percent level for France, at 5 percent for the United Kingdom, and at 1 percent for Canada, Germany, Japan and the United States.

38. See Baum, Poplawski-Ribeiro, and Weber (2012, app. B) for the results using the GIRFs.

39. Using output growth as a threshold variable rather than the output gap yields results that are qualitatively similar. More details are available from the authors upon request.

40. Averages are taken over the fiscal multipliers that are estimated for each country separately. In case of the linear model, the multiplier is estimated in a linear VAR for the entire data sample for each country. The average is taken over the six individually estimated linear multipliers.

41. The effect of interactions between fiscal and monetary policy on multipliers is ambiguous. In periods in which fiscal and monetary policies were not coordinated, the effect of fiscal policy could have been even greater than our model suggests. Conversely, in periods in which there was policy coordination, multipliers might have been overestimated, since monetary policy could have contributed in the same direction to changes in output. However, more recently the zero lower bound on interest rates has been binding, and some studies have argued that fiscal multipliers became much larger than unity once this happened (Woodford 2010; Christiano, Eichenbaum, and Rebelo 2011).

42. There is an argument of "expansionary fiscal contraction." For example, Cogan et al. (2013) demonstrated with an example of the House Budget Resolution of the United States applied to a New Keynesian DSGE model with the assumptions of forward-looking households who adjust their behavior in response to expectations of future tax and spending policy, and price and wage rigidities, that a reduction in government spending increases GDP both in both the short run and the long run relative to the baseline. However, as Barrell et al. (2012) indicate, episodes of expansionary fiscal contractions are exceptionally rare.

43. Ball (1999) notes that countries that came out of the recession of the early 1980s more slowly, such as the United Kingdom and Germany, saw noticeable increase in their natural rates of unemployment, relative to countries that came out more quickly, notably the United States and Canada.

44. Erceg and Lindé (2012b) examine with a two-country DSGE model the effects of fiscal consolidation in a currency union and find the following: (1) given limited scope for monetary accommodation, tax-based consolidation (less inflationary) tends to have smaller adverse effects on output than expenditure-based consolidation in the near term, although it is more costly in the longer term; (2) a large expenditure-based consolidation may be counterproductive in the near term if the zero lower bound is binding, reflecting that output losses rise at the margin; and (3) a mixed strategy that combines a sharp but temporary rise in taxes with gradual spending cuts may be desirable in minimizing the output costs of fiscal consolidation.

References

Afonso, Antonio, Jaromir Baxa, and Michal Slavik. 2011. Fiscal developments and financial stress: A threshold VAR analysis. Working paper 1319. ECB, Frankfurt.

Aiyagari, Rao S., Lawrence J. Christiano, and Martin Eichenbaum. 1990. The output, employment, and interest rate effects of government consumption. Working paper 3330. NBER, Cambridge, MA.

Al-Eyd, Ali, and Ray Barrell. 2005. Estimating tax and benefit multipliers in Europe. *Economic Modelling* 22: 759–76.

Altig, David, Laurence J. Christiano, Martin Eichenbaum, and Jesper Lindé. 2005. Firm-specific capital, nominal rigidities and the business cycle. Working paper 11034. NBER, Cambridge, MA.

Alumnia, Miguel, Agustin Benetrix, Barry Eichengreen, Kevin H. O'Rourke, and Gisela Rua. 2010. Lessons from the Great Depression. *Economic Policy* 25 (62): 220–65.

Atanasova, Christina. 2003. Credit market imperfections and business cycle dynamics: A nonlinear approach. *Studies in Nonlinear Dynamics and Econometrics* 7 (4): 1–22.

Auerbach, Alan J., and Yuriy Gorodnichenko. 2012a. Fiscal multipliers in recession and expansion. Prepared for the NBER conference, "Fiscal Policy after the Financial Crisis," Milan, January.

Auerbach, Alan J., and Yuriy Gorodnichenko. 2012b. Measuring the output responses to fiscal policy. *American Economic Journal* 4 (2): 1–27.

Bachmann, Rüdiger, and Eric R. Sims. 2011. Confidence and the transmission of government spending shocks. Working paper 17063. NBER, Cambridge, MA.

Balke, Nathan S. 2000. Credit and economic activity: Credit regimes and nonlinear propagation of shocks. *Review of Economics and Statistics* 82 (2): 344–49.

Ball, Laurence. 1999. Aggregate demand and long-run unemployment. *Brookings Papers on Economic Activity* (2): 189–251. Available at: http://www.brookings.edu/about/projects/bpea/papers/1999/launch-european-monetary-union-ball.

Barrell, Ray, Dawn Holland, and Ian Hurst. 2012. Fiscal consolidation: Part 2. Fiscal multipliers and fiscal consolidations. Working paper 933. Economics Department, OECD, Paris.

Barro, Robert J., and Charles J. Redlick. 2009. Macroeconomic effects from government purchases and taxes. Working paper 15369. NBER, Cambridge, MA.

Batini, N., G. Callegari, and G. Melina. 2012. Successful austerity in the United States, Europe and Japan. Working paper 12/190. IMF, Washington, DC.

Baum, Anja, and Gerrit B. Koester. 2011. The impact of fiscal policy on economic activity over the business cycle—Evidence from a threshold VAR analysis. Discussion paper 03/2011. Deutsche Bundesbank, Frankfurt.

Baum, Anja, Marcos Poplawski-Ribeiro, and Anke Weber. 2012. Fiscal multipliers and the state of the economy. Working paper 12/286. IMF, Washington, DC.

Baxter, Marianne, and Robert G. King. 1993. Fiscal policy in general equilibrium. *American Economic Review* 83 (3): 315–34.

Beetsma, Roel, and Massimo Giuliodori. 2011. The effects of government purchases shocks: Review and estimate for the EU. *Economic Journal* 121 (February): F4–32.

Bernanke, S. Ben, Jean Boivin, and Piotr Eliasz. 2005. Measuring the effects of monetary policy: A factor-augmented vector autoregressive (FAVAR) approach. *Quarterly Journal of Economics* 113 (3): 869–902.

Blanchard, Olivier. 1985. Debt, deficits, and finite horizons. *Journal of Political Economy* 93: 223–47.

Blanchard, Olivier, Giovanni Dell'Ariccia, and Paolo Mauro. 2010. Rethinking macroeconomic policy. Staff position note 10/03. IMF, Washington, DC.

Blanchard, Olivier, and Daniel Leigh. 2013. Growth forecast errors and fiscal multipliers. Working paper 13/1. IMF, Washington, DC.

Blanchard, Olivier, and Roberto Perotti. 2002. An empirical characterization of the dynamic effects of changes in government spending and taxes on output. *Quarterly Journal of Economics* 117: 1329–68.

Boussard, Jocelyn, Francisco de Castro, and Matteo Salto. 2012. Fiscal multipliers and public debt dynamics in consolidations. Economic paper 460. European Commission, Brussels.

Broda, Christian, and Jonathan Parker. 2008. The impact of the 2008 tax rebate on consumer spending: Preliminary evidence. Unpublished manuscript. University of Chicago Graduate School of Business.

Bryant, Ralph C., Dale W. Henderson, Gerald Holtham, Peter Hooper, and Steven A. Symansky. 1988. *Empirical Macroeconomics for Interdependent Economies.* Supplemental volume. Washington, DC: Brookings Institution.

Burriel, Pablo, Francisco de Castro, Daniel Garrote, Esther Gordo, Joan Paredes, and Javier J. Perez. 2009. Fiscal policy shocks in the euro area and the U.S. Working paper 1133. ECB, Frankfurt.

Caldara, Dario, and Christophe Kamps. 2012. The analytics of SVARs: A unified framework to measure fiscal multipliers. Finance and economics discussion series 2012–20. Board of Governors of the Federal Reserve System, Washington, DC.

Canzoneri, Matthew B., Fabrice Collard, Harris Dellas, and Behzad Diba. 2011. Fiscal multipliers in recessions. Discussion paper 12–04. Department of Economics, University of Bern.

Christiano, Laurence J., Martin Eichenbaum, and Sergio Rebelo. 2009. When is the government appending multiplier large? Unpublished manuscript. Northwestern University.

Christiano, Laurence J., Martin Eichenbaum, and Sergio Rebelo. 2011. When is the government spending multiplier large? *Journal of Political Economy* 119 (1): 78–121.

Cimadomo, Jacopo, and Agnès Bénassy-Quéré. 2012. Changing patterns of fiscal policy multipliers in Germany, the U.K. and the U.S. *Journal of Macroeconomics* 34: 845–73.

Cloyne, James. 2011. What are the effects of tax changes in the United Kingdom? New evidence from a narrative evaluation. Working paper 3433. CESifo Group, Munich.

Coenen, Günter, Christopher Erceg, Charles Freedman, Davide Furceri, Michael Kumhof, Rene Lalonde, Douglas Laxton, et al. 2010. Effects of fiscal stimulus in structural models. Working paper 10/73. IMF, Washington, DC.

Coenen, Günter, Christopher Erceg, Charles Freedman, Davide Furceri, Michael Kumhof, Rene Lalonde, Douglas Laxton, et al. 2012. Effects of fiscal stimulus in structural models. *American Economic Journal: Macroeconomics* 4 (1): 22–68.

Cogan, John F., Tobias Cwik, John B. Taylor, and Volker Wieland. 2009. New Keynesian versus old Keynesian government spending multipliers. Working paper 14782. NBER, Cambridge, MA.

Cogan, John F., Maik H. Wolters, and Volker Wieland. 2013. Fiscal consolidation strategy. *Journal of Economic Dynamics & Control* 37: 404–21.

Coronado, Julia Lynn, Joseph P. Lupton, and Louise Sheiner. 2005. The household spending response to the 2003 tax cut: Evidence from survey data. Discussion paper 2005–32. Federal Reserve Board, Washington, DC.

Corsetti, Giancarlo, Keith Kuester, and Gernot Müller. 2011. Pegs, floats and the transmission of fiscal policy. Discussion paper 8180. CEPR, Washington, DC.

Corsetti, Giancarlo, Andre Meier, and Gernot Müller. 2012. What determines government spending multipliers? Working paper 12/150. IMF, Washington, DC.

Cottarelli, Carlo, and Laura Jaramillo. 2012. Walking hand in hand: Fiscal Policy and growth in advanced economies. Working paper 12/137. IMF, Washington, DC.

Dalsgaard, Thomas, Christophe André, and Pete Richardson. 2001. Standard shocks in the OECD interlink model. Working paper 306. Economics Department, OECD, Paris.

DeLong, J. Bradford, and Laurence H. Summers. 2012. Fiscal policy in a depressed economy. *Brookings Papers on Economic Activity* (spring): 233–97.

Devries, Pete, Jaime Guajardo, Daniel Leigh, and Andrea Pescatori. 2011. A new action-based dataset of fiscal consolidation. Working paper 11/128. IMF, Washington, DC.

Dolls, Mathias, Clemens Fuest, and Andreas Peichl. 2010. Automatic stabilizers and economic crisis: US vs. Europe. Working paper 16275. NBER, Cambridge, MA.

Drautzburg, Thorsten, and Harald Uhlig. 2011. Fiscal stimulus and distortionary taxation. Working paper 17111. NBER, Cambridge, MA.

Eggertsson, Gauti B., 2006. Fiscal multipliers and policy coordination. Staff report 241. Federal Reserve Bank of New York.

Elmendorf, Douglas W., and David Reifschneider. 2002. Short run effects of fiscal policy with forward-looking financial markets. *National Tax Journal* 55 (3).

Elmendorf, Douglas W., and Jason Furman. 2008. If, when, how: A primer on fiscal stimulus. Hamilton Project strategy paper. Brookings Institution, Washington, DC.

Erceg, Christopher J., and Jesper Lindé. 2010. Is there a free lunch in a liquidity trap? International Finance Discussion paper 1003.Board of Governors of the Federal Reserve System.

Erceg, Christopher J., and Jesper Lindé. 2012a. Fiscal consolidation in an open economy. *American Economic Review* 102 (3): 186–91.

Erceg, Christopher J., and Jesper Lindé. 2012b. Fiscal consolidation in a currency union: Spending cuts vs. tax hikes. Discussion paper 9155. CEPR, Washington, DC.

Eyraud, L., and A. Weber. 2013. The challenge of debt reduction during fiscal consolidation. Working Paper 13/67. IMF, Washington, DC.

Farhi, Emmanuel, and Iván Werning. 2012. Fiscal multipliers: Liquidity traps and currency unions. Working paper 18381. NBER, Cambridge, MA.

Favero, Carlo, and Francesco Giavazzi. 2007. Debt and the effects of fiscal policy. Working paper 12822. NBER, Cambridge, MA.

Favero, Carlo, and Francesco Giavazzi. 2012. Reconciling VAR based and narrative measures of the tax multiplier. *American Economic Journal: Economic Policy*, forthcoming.

Favero, Carlo, Francesco Giavazzi, and Jacopo Perego. 2011. Country heterogeneity and the international evidence on the effects of fiscal policy. Discussion paper 8517. CEPR, London.

Fernández-Villaverde, Jesús, Grey Gordon, Pablo A. Guerrón-Quintana, and Juan Rubio-Ramírez. 2012. Nonlinear adventure at the zero lower bound. Working paper 18058. NBER, Cambridge, MA.

Feve, Patrick, Julien Matheron, and Jean-Guillaume Sahuc. 2012. A pitfall with DSGE-based, estimated, government spending multipliers. Working paper 379. Banque de France, Paris.

Fisher, Jonas D.M., and Ryan H. Peters. 2010. Using stock returns to identify government spending shocks. *Economic Journal* 120 (544): 414–36.

Freedman, Charles, Michael Kumhof, and Douglas Laxton. 2008. Deflation and countercyclical fiscal policy. Unpublished manuscript. IMF, Washington, DC.

Furceri, Davide, and Marcos Poplawski-Ribeiro. 2009. Government consumption volatility and the size of nations. Working papers 687. Economics Department, OCED, Paris.

Galí, Jordi, J. David López-Salido, and Javier Vallés. 2007. Understanding the effects of government spending on consumption. *Journal of the European Economic Association* 5 (1): 227–70.

Girouard, Nathalie, and Christophe André. 2005. Measuring cyclically adjusted budget balances for OECD countries. Working paper 434. OECD Economics Department, OECD, Paris.

Gordon, Robert J., and Robert Krenn. 2010. The end of the Great Depression: Policy contributions and fiscal multipliers. Working paper 16380. NBER, Cambridge, MA.

Group of Twenty (G20). 2009. Meeting of the Deputies, January 31–February 1, 2009, London. Note by staff of IMF, February. Available at: http://www.google.com/url?sa=t&rct=j&q=&esrc=s&frm=1&source=web&cd=1&ved=0CCkQFjAA&url=http%3A%2F%2Fwww.imf.org%2Fexternal%2Fnp%2Fg20%2Fpdf%2F020509.pdf&ei=CKBEUpiCNdir4AO4goG4Bg&usg=AFQjCNFpQrXxRq1l_109LYMd2tghQR3uDw.

Hall, Robert E. 2009. By how much does GDP rise if the government buys more output? Working paper 15496. NBER, Cambridge, MA.

Hansen, Bruce E. 1996. Inference when a nuisance parameter is not identified under the null hypothesis. *Econometrica* 64 (2): 413–30.

Hansen, Bruce E. 1997. Inference in TAR models. *Studies in Nonlinear Dynamics and Econometrics* 2 (1): 1–14.

Harding, D., and A. Pagan. 2002. Dissecting the cycle: A methodological investigation. *Journal of Monetary Economics* 49: 365–81.

Hayo, Bernd, and Matthais Uhl. 2014. The macroeconomic effects of legislated tax changes in Germany. *Oxford Economic Papers*, forthcoming.

Heathcote, Jonathan. 2005. Fiscal policy with heterogeneous agents and incomplete markets. *Review of Economic Studies* 72: 161–88.

Her Majesty's Treasury. 2003. Fiscal stabilisation and EMU. Discussion paper. HMTreasury, London.

Ilzetzki, Ethan, Enrique G. Mendoza, and Carlos A. Végh. 2011. How big (small?) are fiscal multipliers? Working paper 11/52. IMF, Washington, DC.

Ilzetzki, Ethan, and Carlos A. Végh. 2008. Procyclical fiscal policy in developing countries: Truth or fiction? Working paper 14191. NBER, Cambridge, MA.

International Monetary Fund. 2008. Fiscal policy as a countercyclical tool. *World Economic Outlook* (October). Washington, DC: IMF, ch. 5.

International Monetary Fund. 2010. Will it hurt? Macroeconomic effects of fiscal consolidation. *World Economic Outlook* (October). Washington, DC: IMF, ch. 3.

International Monetary Fund. 2012b. United Kingdom. Staff report for the 2012 Article IV Consultation. Country report SM/12/168. IMF, Washington, DC.

International Monetary Fund. 2012a. Are we underestimating short-term fiscal multipliers? *World Economic Outlook* (October). Washington, DC: IMF, ch. 1, box 1.1.

Johnson, David S., Jonathan A. Parker, and Nicholas S. Souleles. 2006. Household expenditure and the income tax rebates of 2001. *American Economic Review* 96 (5): 1589–1610.

Kirchner, Markus, Jacopo Cimadomo, and Sebastian Hauptmeier. 2010. Transmission of government spending shocks in the euro area: Time variation and driving forces. Working paper 1219. ECB, Frankfurt.

Koop, Gary, Hashem M. Pesaran, and Simon M. Potter. 1996. Impulse response analysis in nonlinear multivariate models. *Journal of Econometrics* 74 (1): 119–47.

Leeper, Eric M., Nora Traum, and Todd B. Walker. 2011. Clearing up the fiscal multiplier morass. Working paper 17444. NBER, Cambridge, MA.

Mertens, Karel, and Morten O. Ravn. 2011. Measuring fiscal shocks in structural VARs using narrative data. Unpublished manuscript. Cornell University and University College, London.

Mountford, Andrew, and Harald Uhlig. 2009. What are the effects of fiscal policy shocks? *Journal of Applied Econometrics* 24 (6): 960–92.

Nakamura, Emi, and Jón Steinsson. 2011. Fiscal stimulus in a monetary union: Evidence from U.S. regions. Working paper 17391. NBER, Cambridge, MA.

Oh, Hyunseung, and Ricardo Reis. 2011. Targeted transfers and the fiscal response to the Great Recession. Working paper 16775. NBER, Cambridge, MA.

Organisation for Economic Co-operation and Development. 2009. The effectiveness of and scope of fiscal stimulus. *Economic Outlook* (March). Interim report. Paris: OECD, 105–50.

Parker, Jonathan A. 2011. On measuring the effects of fiscal policy in recessions. Working paper 17240. NBER, Cambridge, MA.

Perotti, Roberto. 2004. Public investment and the Golden Rule: Another (different) look. Working paper 277. IGIER, Bocconi University, Milan.

Perotti, Roberto. 2005. Estimating the effects of fiscal policy in OECD countries. Discussion paper 4842. CEPR, London.

Perotti, Roberto. 2011. The effects of tax shocks on output: Not so large, but not small either. NBER Working paper 16786. NBER, Cambridge, MA.

Ramey, Valerie A. 2011a. Identifying government spending shocks: It's all in the timing. *Quarterly Journal of Economics* 126 (1): 1–50.

Ramey, Valerie A. 2011b. Can government purchases stimulate the economy? *Journal of Economic Literature* 49 (3): 673–85.

Rendahl, Pontus. 2012. Fiscal policy in an unemployment crisis. Working paper in economics 1211. Cambridge University.

Romer, Christina, 2011. What do we know about the effects of fiscal policy? Separating evidence from ideology. Speech note at Hamilton College, Clinton, NY.

Romer, Christina. 2012. Fiscal policy in the crisis: Lessons and policy implications. Unpublished manuscript. University of California, Berkeley.

Romer, D. Christina, and David H. Romer. 2010. The macroeconomic effects of tax changes: Estimates based on a new measure of fiscal shocks. *American Economic Review* 100: 763–801.

Seidman, Laurence. 2011. Keynesian fiscal stimulus: What have we learned from the Great Recession? Working paper 2011–11. University of Delaware.

Smets, Frank, and Rafael Wouters. 2007. Shocks and frictions in U.S. business cycles: A Bayesian DSGE approach. *American Economic Review* 97: 506–606.

Spilimbergo, Antonio, Steve Symansky, and Martin Schindler. 2009. Fiscal multipliers. Staff position note SPN/09/11. IMF, Washington, DC.

Tsay, Ruey S. 1998. Testing and modeling multivariate threshold models. *Journal of the American Statistical Association* 93: 1188–1202.

Uhlig, Harald. 2005. What are the effects of monetary policy? Results from an agnostic identification procedure. *Journal of Monetary Economics* 52: 381–419.

Woo, Jaejon, Tidiane Kinda, and Marcos Poplawski-Ribeiro. 2014. Economic recovery from recessions: The role of fiscal policy, and structural reforms. Working paper. IMF, Washington, DC, forthcoming.

Woodford, M. 2010. Simple analytics of the government expenditure multiplier. Working paper 15714. NBER, Cambridge, MA.

Zandi, Mark. 2008. A second quick boost from government could spark recovery. Edited excerpts from July 24, 2008, testimony by Mark Zandi, chief economist of Moody's Economy.com, before the US House of Representatives Committee on Small Business.

Zubairy, Sarah. 2012. On fiscal multipliers: Estimates from a medium scale DSGE model. Bank of Canada, Ottawa.

13

Coordination of Fiscal and Monetary Policies

Mika Kortelainen, Douglas Laxton, and Jack Selody

13.1 Introduction

In this chapter we use the International Monetary Fund's Global Integrated Monetary and Fiscal Model (GIMF) to illustrate the increased effectiveness of expansionary fiscal policy when monetary policy accommodates the shock, such as was the case in the 2008 to 2009 coordinated fiscal expansion. To accomplish this, we introduce simple fiscal policy and monetary policy rules into the model to show the dynamics of policy coordination. We also show how features like financial accelerators affect the dynamics of policy coordination.

The chapter starts with a review of the literature on activist monetary and fiscal policies, describes the key features of the economic model in which the policy rules are imbedded, and finally discusses the simulation results that illustrate the benefits of coordinating fiscal and monetary policy. The chapter ends with a brief conclusion.

13.2 Literature Review

A model-based examination of the dynamic coordination of fiscal and monetary policies requires a macroeconomic model with rigidities so that aggregate demand management policies can help dampen economic cycles.

The literature on activist monetary policy rules is more developed than that for fiscal policy rules. On the model side, the time-dependent price adjustment formulations of Taylor (1980), Rotemberg (1982), and Calvo (1983) made it possible to incorporate price-setting rigidities into rational expectations macroeconomic models with forward-looking optimizing agents. Empirical support for the importance of price-setting rigidities came from evidence showing that monetary policy has significant short-run real effects, such as Christiano, Eichenbaum, and Evans (1996, 1998) and Leeper, Sims, and Zha (1996). On the policy reaction side, the work by Taylor (1993) on the revealed behavior of monetary policy makers, and by Bernanke and Mishkin (1997) on constrained discretion, laid the foundation for simple formulations of activist monetary policy rules that conformed to conventional wisdom about how policy responds to economic cycles.

Although the literature on activist fiscal policy rules is more recent than that for activist monetary policy, fiscal policy has been a variable in macroeconomic models from the beginning. Early on, Philips (1954) included a role for fiscal automatic stabilizers in the Keynesian framework. Musgrave (1959) advocated the systematic use of discretionary fiscal policy; specifically, he promoted a system whereby changes in taxes and spending would be legislated in advance to respond to changes in income. Tobin (1972) makes a similar argument.

However, Keynesian fiscal activism started to be challenged in the 1960s for theoretical and empirical reasons. One of the first theoretical challenges came from Mundell (1963) and Fleming (1962), who extended the Keynesian IS-LM model to the open economy and showed that fiscal policy lost its effectiveness in stimulating aggregate demand under flexible exchange rates. Stronger challenges arose from the neoclassical school. Eisner (1969), based on Friedman (1957), realized that in a permanent income model, temporary changes in taxation would have only minor effects on lifetime income and therefore on consumption demand. Barro (1974) went further by showing that the timing of tax changes has no real effect on infinitely lived representative agents because economic agents change their savings behavior to restore their optimal consumption time path. This is known as the Ricardian equivalence hypothesis. This skepticism about the efficacy of activist fiscal policy, along with the difficulty of meeting the Gramlich (1999) criterion that fiscal policy needs to be delivered in a "timely, targeted, and temporary" manner to be effective in managing the economic cycle, led to the presumption that activist demand management should be left to monetary policy. Legislatures are generally much slower at changing taxation and spending than central banks at changing the policy rate, they may not deliver stimulus where it is most needed but instead where it is politically advantageous, and they may be reluctant to withdraw it sufficiently quickly in good times to preserve fiscal sustainability.

Empirical work has not settled the debate about the effectiveness of fiscal activism as measured by the size of fiscal multipliers, mainly because identifying the discretionary components of fiscal policy entails overcoming serious methodological issues. For further discussion of fiscal multipliers, and what their size depends on, see chapter 12 in this book, "Size of Fiscal Multipliers."

Recent studies have used structural dynamic stochastic general equilibrium (DSGE) models to identify the private sector response to changes in fiscal policy. This approach has been used successfully in the monetary policy literature. The DSGE models are New Keynesian in spirit in that they contain significant nominal and real rigidities, have non-Ricardian properties, and liquidity-constrained households. A key study of this nature is Gali, López-Salido, and Vallés (2007).

But there has been little progress on fiscal rules that manage aggregate demand and maintain a sustainable fiscal policy. Taylor (2000) considers a rule in which the budget surplus depends on the output gap, but he argues that such a rule is unnecessary, and in fact undesirable, because the Fed has been very successful at stabilizing the business cycle and would only suffer from having to forecast the fiscal stance. He therefore argues, along with many other commentators at that time, that the role of fiscal policy should be limited to minimizing distortions and to "letting automatic stabilizers work." Automatic stabilizers describe the channels through which the structure of fiscal policy is countercyclical without discretionary action. Taylor (2000) makes two exceptions to his call for nondiscretionary fiscal policy. The first is in a fixed exchange-rate regime where monetary policy does not have a stabilizing role. The second is a situation where nominal interest rates approach their zero lower bound and monetary policy becomes less effective. Support for activist demand management fiscal policy under fixed exchange rates has been provided by Beetsma and Jensen (2005) and Gali and Monacelli (2008). The latter focuses on understanding the theoretically optimal policy.

Solow (2005) and Wyplosz (2005) support activist fiscal policy by looking at institutions and procedures to make fiscal policy timely, targeted, and temporary. These include either automatically triggered countercyclical rules or a technocrat-run fiscal policy board that decides on the overall budget balance but leaves decisions on the composition of the budget to parliament so as to maintain democratic accountability.

Wyplosz (2005) also provides a list of countries that actually use activist fiscal rules. Apart from the Maastricht criteria of the EU, which include a 60 percent of GDP maximum debt and a 3 percent of GDP maximum deficit, very few countries pursue either a debt rule or a golden rule that limits the deficit to financing public investment over the cycle. Four countries pursue structural surplus rules, including Brazil (4.5 percent primary surplus), Chile (0.5 percent overall surplus), Sweden (2 percent overall surplus), and Switzerland (0 percent overall surplus).

Following Kumhof and Laxton (2009a, b), the analysis in this chapter uses a class of rules for fiscal and monetary policy similar to Taylor rules. For monetary policy, this means a rule that keeps inflation on target in the long run, but responds to disequilibrium aggregate demand (i.e., output gap) in the short run in order to manage the economic cycle. Similarly the fiscal policy rule ensures debt sustainability in the long run but also stabilizes the business cycle in the short run by reacting to the output gap. The monetary policy variable is a very short-term interest rate. The fiscal policy variable is the budget-surplus-to-GDP ratio. The fiscal policy variable is influenced by tax rates and government spending variables. The policy rules are calibrated to reflect the automatic stabilizers in Canada and the United States.

It is important to embed the analysis of fiscal and monetary activist rules in the appropriate macroeconomic model. An obvious candidate is an example of the new generation of open economy business-cycle models, with nominal and real rigidities, that are currently being deployed in central banks and other policy-making institutions. However, most of these models face difficulties in replicating the medium- and longer term effects of fiscal policy.[1] Some also have shortcomings when used to analyze medium- and long-run fiscal issues such as the crowding-out effects of a permanent increase in public debt. These difficulties occur largely because of the absence of non-Ricardian household savings behavior in the model that would make the timing of fiscal interventions nonneutral. In this chapter we use a new generation model with added non-Ricardian behavior. In particular, the model maintains the nominal and real rigidities necessary to generate interactions between monetary and fiscal policies.

The literature contains two candidates for non-Ricardian features to include in the model: an overlapping generations structure following Blanchard (1985) and Weil (1989); and a subset of liquidity constrained agents following Gali, López-Salido, and Vallés (2007). Both agents are subject to a stochastic lifetime which effectively makes their discount rate higher than the government's assumed discount rate. As the liquidity-constrained agents have a higher marginal propensity to consume, this effectively enhances the response to fiscal interventions.

In the model we assume that there is no coordination problem between monetary and fiscal policies, and that monetary policy follows the familiar type of interest-rate reaction function, calibrated to reflect the historical conduct of monetary policy in Canada and the United States.

The rest of the model features endogenous labor supply, endogenous capital accumulation, productive government investment in infrastructure, habit persistence, investment and import adjustment costs, sticky nominal goods prices, and an endowment sector for raw materials that are used as a manufacturing input.

13.3 The Model

The model of the economy used to analyze the coordination of fiscal and monetary policy is the International Monetary Fund's Global Integrated Monetary and Fiscal Model (GIMF). GIMF is a multicountry dynamic general equilibrium model used extensively inside the IMF, and also at a small number of central banks, for policy and risk analysis.[2] The strength of GIMF for this analysis is the inclusion of a range of non-Ricardian features in the model that make not only spending-based but also revenue-based fiscal measures nonneutral. These features have been included in the model to aid the analysis of the short-run effectiveness of fiscal stimulus packages. However, GIMF is also useful when the focus turns from short-run stimulus to long-run sustainability, given its focus on the savings–investment balance. It can answer questions about the link between fiscal deficits and real interest rates, crowding out, and current account deficits. The structure of GIMF can be found in Kumhof et al. (2010), "The Global Integrated Monetary and Fiscal Model (GIMF): Theoretical Structure."

In the version of GIMF used for this analysis the world consists of six "countries": Canada, the United States, the euro area, Japan, Emerging Asia, and the remaining countries of the world. All parameters in the model can differ across countries, except gross population growth and gross technology growth.

Countries are populated by two types of households, both of which consume final retailed output and supply labor to unions. First, there are overlapping generations (OLG) households with finite planning horizons as in Blanchard (1985). Second, there are liquidity-constrained households which do not have access to financial markets, and which, consequently, are forced to consume their after tax income in every period.

Firms are managed in accordance with the preferences of their owners, the myopic OLG households that have finite-planning horizons. Each country's primary production is carried out by manufacturers producing tradable and nontradable goods. Manufacturers buy capital services from entrepreneurs, labor from monopolistically competitive unions, and raw materials from the world raw materials market. Firms are subject to nominal rigidities in price setting as well as real rigidities in labor hiring and in the use of raw materials. Capital goods producers are subject to investment adjustment costs. Entrepreneurs finance their capital holdings using a combination of external and internal financing. A capital income tax is levied on entrepreneurs. Unions are subject to nominal wage rigidities and buy labor from households.

Manufacturers' domestic sales go to domestic distributors. Their foreign sales go to import agents that are domestically owned but located in each export destination country. Import agents in turn sell their output to foreign distributors. When the pricing-to-market assumption is made, these import agents are subject to nominal rigidities in foreign currency. First, facing an adjustment cost in changing the volume of imported inputs, distributors assemble nontradable goods and domestic and foreign tradable goods. This private-sector output is then combined with a publicly provided capital stock (infrastructure) as an essential further input. This capital stock is maintained through government investment expenditure financed by tax revenue and the issuance of government debt. The combined final domestic output is then sold to consumption goods producers, investment goods producers, and import agents located abroad.

Consumption and investment goods producers in turn combine domestic and foreign output to produce final consumption and investment goods. Foreign output is purchased through a second set of import agents that can price to the domestic market, and, here also, changes in the volume of imported goods are subject to an adjustment cost. This second layer of trade at the level of final output is critical for allowing the model to produce the high trade-to-GDP ratios typically observed in small, highly open economies. Consumption goods output is sold to retailers and the government, while investment goods output is sold to domestic capital goods producers and the government.

Consumption and investment goods producers are subject to another layer of nominal rigidities in price setting. This cascading of nominal rigidities from upstream to downstream sectors has important consequences for the behavior of aggregate inflation. Retailers, who are also monopolistically competitive, face real instead of nominal rigidities. While their output prices are flexible, they find it costly to rapidly adjust their sales volume. This feature contributes to generating inertial consumption dynamics.

Asset markets are incomplete. There is a home-country bias toward owning domestic-currency government debt. The only home-country assets traded internationally are foreign-currency bonds. There is also a home bias in ownership of domestic firms. In addition, equity is not traded in domestic financial markets. Instead, households receive lump-sum dividend payments. This assumption is required to support the assumption that firms, as well as households, are myopic.

Fiscal consolidation through higher taxes takes the form of bringing tax payments forward to the near future from the more distant future so as to reduce the debt stock. Taxes cannot be raised permanently without an increase in government expenditures because the government has to respect its inter-temporal budget constraint, which means that the expected present discounted value of its future primary surpluses has to remain equal to the current debt when future surpluses are discounted at the market interest rate. But when individual households discount future taxes at a higher rate than the government, the same tilting of the tax profile represents a decrease in human wealth because it increases the expected value of future taxes for which the household expects to be responsible. This is true for the direct effects of lump-sum taxes and of labor-income taxes on labor-income receipts, and for the indirect effect of corporate taxes on dividend receipts. For a given marginal propensity to consume, these reductions in human wealth lead to a reduction in consumption.

Entrepreneurs and banks are modeled following Bernanke et al. (1999) and Christiano et al. (2010).

The GIMF raw materials sector is constructed primarily with oil in mind, with extremely low demand and supply elasticities. This is the main reason, apart from analytical tractability, why the output of raw materials has been specified as having a zero price elasticity. Firms in the raw materials sector can choose how much they sell in any given period by adding to or drawing down from a storage facility.

Unions buy labor from households and sell labor to manufacturers. They are perfectly competitive in their input market and monopolistically competitive in their output market. Their wage setting is subject to nominal rigidities.

Import agents buy intermediate goods (or final goods) from manufacturers (or distributors) in their owners' country and sell these goods to distributors (intermediate goods) or consumption/investment goods producers (final goods) in the foreign countries. Import agents are perfectly competitive in their input market and monopolistically competitive in their output market. Their price setting is subject to nominal rigidities.

Distributors produce domestic final output. They buy domestic tradable goods and nontradable goods from domestic manufacturers, and foreign tradable goods from import agents. They also use the stock of public infrastructure free of a user charge. Distributors sell their final output composite to consumption goods producers, investment goods producers, and final goods import agents in foreign countries. They are perfectly competitive in both their output and input markets. Investment goods producers buy domestic final output directly from domestic distributors, and foreign final output indirectly via import agents. They sell the final composite good to capital goods producers, to the government, and back to other investment goods producers. Investment goods producers are perfectly competitive in their input markets and monopolistically competitive in their output market. Their price setting is subject to nominal rigidities.

Consumption goods producers buy domestic final output directly from domestic distributors, and foreign final output indirectly via import agents. They sell the final composite good to consumption goods retailers, to the government, and back to other consumption goods producers. Consumption goods producers are perfectly competitive in their input markets and monopolistically competitive in their output market. Their price setting is subject to nominal rigidities.

The consumption good is sold by retailers. Retailers combine final output purchased from consumption goods producers and raw materials purchased from raw materials producers. There are adjustment costs to rapid changes in materials inputs. Retailers sell their output to households. They are perfectly competitive in their input market and monopolistically competitive in their output market. Their price setting is subject to real rigidities in that they find it costly to rapidly adjust their sales volume in response to changing demand conditions.

The government uses consumption goods and investment goods to produce government output. Fiscal policy consists of choosing the level of public investment spending, public consumption spending, transfers from overlapping-generations households to liquidity-constrained households, and lump-sum taxes. Government investment and consumption spending is a demand for government output. Both types of government spending are exogenous and stochastic. Government investment spending augments the stock of publicly provided infrastructure capital. Government consumption spending, on the other hand, is modeled as unproductive. The government's policy rule for transfers partly compensates for the lack of asset ownership of liquidity-constrained households by redistributing a small fraction of the overlapping-generations household's dividend income.

The model makes two key assumptions about fiscal policy. The first concerns dynamic stability and the second relates to the stabilization of the business cycle. Constraining fiscal policy to be dynamically stable ensures a nonexplosive government-debt-to-GDP ratio. This is achieved by adjusting tax rates to generate sufficient revenue, or by reducing expenditure, in order to stabilize the overall interest (inclusive government surplus-to-GDP ratio at a long-run level chosen by policy). In other words, for a given nominal growth rate, choosing a surplus target implies a debt target, which keeps debt from exploding. Constraining fiscal policy to be business-cycle stable ensures that the government surplus-to-GDP ratio can also flexibly respond to the business cycle while satisfying the long-run debt target. Specifically, the deficit responds to the output gap, a tax revenue gap, and a raw materials revenue gap.

Monetary policy uses an interest rate rule that features interest-rate smoothing and which responds to (1) deviations of one-year-ahead year-on-year inflation from the inflation target, (2) the output gap, (3) the year-on-year growth rate of GDP, and (4) deviations of current exchange-rate depreciation from its long-run value. Monetary policy shocks are allowed to persist. Thus, the interest rate rule used to implement monetary policy is very general and similar to conventional inflation forecast based rules, with one minor and one important exception. The minor exception is the presence of exchange-rate depreciation, which is used only to model strict exchange-rate targeting. The more fundamental exception is that the non-Ricardian nature of the model implies that potential GDP and the equilibrium real interest rate are not constant, but are modeled as moving averages of observed values. The inflation rate targeted by monetary policy is a weighted average of current and one-year-ahead inflation.

Finally, combining all market-clearing conditions in the model with the budget constraints of households and the government and with the expressions for firm dividends determines the current account.

13.4 The Simulations

13.4.1 Scenario 1: Expansionary Fiscal Policy When the Monetary Policy Rate Can Move

Scenario 1 is an increase in baseline government consumption of 1 percentage point of GDP forever. After two years, government transfers decrease via the assumed fiscal policy stabilization rule in response to the otherwise unsustainable rise in gov-

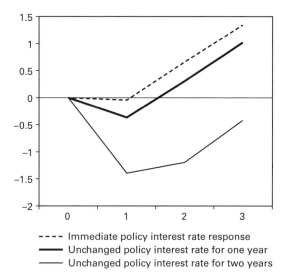

Figure 13.1
Scenario 1: US government debt (percent of GDP deviation from baseline)
Source: GIMF simulations

ernment debt such that the debt-to-GDP ratio stabilizes over time. The shape of the endogenous path for government debt is largely independent of the country undertaking the fiscal expansion because the fiscal policy stabilization rule is assumed to be the same for each country. Actual government spending does not increase by the full shock to baseline government consumption because of the automatic stabilizer component of government spending—essentially, the economy is stronger because of the shock, which reduces the demand for some government programs.

The three lines in figure 13.1 show the effect of different monetary policy coordination strategies.

- The dashed line shows the baseline monetary policy reaction function at work. Here the policy interest rate rises to counteract the increase in aggregate demand in order to more strictly adhere to the inflation target, even in the short run.
- The bold line shows the effect of partially accommodating monetary policy that keeps the policy interest rate unchanged for one year, before returning to the baseline monetary policy reaction function that then returns inflation to target.
- The thin line shows the effect of fully accommodating monetary policy that keeps the policy interest rate unchanged for the full two-year length of the fiscal shock, before returning to the baseline monetary policy reaction function.

The stance of monetary policy—that is, whether monetary policy is easy or tight—depends on whether the policy rate rises less or more than the rate of expected inflation (i.e., the change in the real interest rate). The baseline monetary policy reaction function produces a tightening of the stance of monetary policy to counteract the inflationary effects of the increase in aggregate demand associated with the expansionary fiscal shock. Keeping the policy rate unchanged for a year produces a mild easing in monetary policy for that year, followed by tighter policy. The fully accommodating monetary policy keeps policy easy for two years, followed by a dramatic tightening of policy to contain the inflationary pressure that was created.

The government-debt-to-GDP ratio is lower when monetary policy accommodates fiscal policy because interest rates are relatively lower and the economy is stronger. The economy responds so strongly to the fully accommodating monetary policy that government indebtedness falls temporarily, as can be seen by the thin line falling below its control value.

Scenario 1 shows that fiscal policy is much more effective when monetary policy accommodates the fiscal shock.

Canada

In the results for Canada, the government expenditure multiplier is less than one when monetary policy tightens immediately in response to the inflationary pressure coming from the increase in aggregate demand. In contrast, when monetary policy is fully accommodating, the government expenditure multiplier is greater than 1.

When monetary policy is fully accommodating, the real interest rate, which indicates the stance of monetary policy, falls by over one-half percentage point in the first year of the shock. This easing of policy adds to the initial fiscal shock, producing an increase in GDP of over 1.2 percentage points in the first year. A partial accommodation of the shock would have monetary policy easing in the first year of the shock, but not sufficiently to produce a multiplier greater than one. The reason is that financial markets anticipate that monetary policy will tighten in the second year so the exchange rate appreciates, which crowds out domestic production despite an increase in domestic consumption and investment.

Private consumption rises whether or not monetary policy accommodates the shock because of spillovers from the increase in government consumption on wages and salaries. However, the effect of lower real interest rates on private consumption, which arises from the monetary accommodation, is more significant. The rise in investment is very muted without monetary accommodation, showing the power of real interest rates in stimulating investment in the model. Inflation rises even without monetary accommodation. This owes to interest-rate smoothing in the monetary policy reaction function that prevents the monetary authorities from moving the policy rate sufficiently to fully offset the increase in inflationary pressure from the stimulus to aggregate demand.

United States

Results for the United States are similar in pattern to those for Canada, but there are a few notable differences. Interestingly, the government expenditure multiplier is larger for the United States than it is for Canada, especially when monetary policy is accommodating. Since the United States is more of a closed economy than is Canada, less of the increase in aggregate demand is satisfied by imported goods (i.e., there are fewer import "leakages") and so the impact on domestic production is greater. This makes the economy more inflation prone, with inflation responding more to the fiscal shock and monetary policy responding less aggressively in the baseline monetary policy reaction function. The larger increase in inflation results in lower real interest rates when monetary policy accommodates by holding the nominal interest-rate constant. The stance of monetary policy is therefore easier, which adds an extra boost to GDP (thin line in figure 13.2).

With the greater inflation response, monetary policy needs to respond aggressively when accommodation ends. Indeed, in the case of full accommodation, the nominal policy rate rises to a point where it is double that of the no-accommodation case (dashed line in figure 13.2). This shows that when an economy

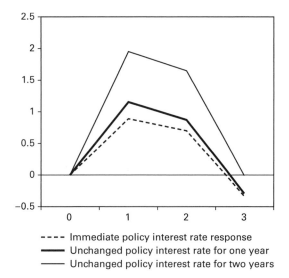

Figure 13.2
Scenario 1: US real GDP (percent deviation from baseline)
Source: GIMF simulations

is inflation prone, any delay in reacting to inflationary pressures is costly in terms of the subsequent amount by which the policy rate will need in order to rise to return inflation to target.

13.4.2 Scenario 2: Expansionary Fiscal Policy When the Policy Rate Is at Its Lower Bound

The monetary policy rate cannot fall in the simulation because the policy rate is at its lower bound. Instead, monetary accommodation in scenario 2 is a purchase of longer maturity government bonds by the central bank, which reduces the interest rate on long-dated government bond by 50 basis points at one year, 75 basis points at three years, and 100 basis points at ten years—essentially, an operation twist to flatten the yield curve on government debt. In addition, monetization of government debt causes an increased perception of inflation risk and results in an increase in the country risk premium by about 25 basis points. The policy is assumed to last two years.

When this unconventional monetary policy is combined with expansionary fiscal policy, the result is a significant increase in inflation expectations which causes the stance of monetary policy to ease dramatically in the case where interest rates are held constant for two years. This creates an expansion in GDP that, when combined with the low interest rates, reduces government indebtedness.

Even if the central bank were to raise its policy rate to counter the expansion in GDP, the stance of monetary policy would ease because of the perception of higher inflation from the unconventional policy. Again, the expansion of the economy is sufficient to reduce government indebtedness slightly in the first year, in contrast to scenario 1 where indebtedness remained unchanged.

As a result fiscal policy expansion with unconventional monetary policy is very effective in the simulation.

Canada

Recall that the expansionary fiscal policy is an increase in government consumption expenditures of 1 percentage point of GDP and unconventional monetary policy is an operation "twist" that flattens the yield curve combined with an increase in the country risk premium. When the policy interest rates remains unchanged for two years, the fiscal multiplier is 2 in the first year, indicating that the economy expands by two dollars for every dollar the government spends. Even in the case where the policy interest rate is held fixed for one year before moving to respond to the building inflationary pressures, the fiscal multiplier is one.

The policy combination stimulates private consumption significantly, which increases by about the same amount as the increase in government consumption when the policy rate is held unchanged for two years. Private investment increases substantially and is up over four percentage points when the policy rate is constant.

The policy combination causes inflation to rise. When the policy interest rate is held unchanged for two years, inflation is up by almost a full percentage point by the second year. It is this increase in inflation that helps explain the effectiveness of the policy as it produces lower real interest rates and a depreciated real exchange rate, which stimulates consumption and investment.

If policy rates rise in the second year to choke off the inflationary pressure, inflation rises by less than one-half of a percentage point by the second year. This monetary policy response maintains a fiscal multiplier greater than one without much threat to achieving the inflation target.

United States

The policy combination of expansionary fiscal policy and unconventional monetary policy is even more effective in the United States, again because inflation reacts more to the shock so that real interest rates decline and the real exchange rate depreciates. When the policy interest rates remain unchanged for two years, the fiscal multiplier is 2.5 in the first year, indicating that the economy expands by two and a half dollars for every dollar the government spends (thin line in figure 13.3). Even in the case where the policy interest rate is held fixed for one year before moving to respond to the building inflationary pressures, the fiscal multiplier exceeds one (solid line).

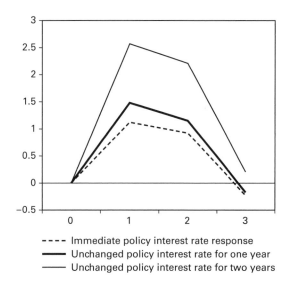

- - - - Immediate policy interest rate response
—— Unchanged policy interest rate for one year
—— Unchanged policy interest rate for two years

Figure 13.3
Scenario 2: US real GDP (percent deviation from baseline)
Source: GIMF simulations

Consumption is stimulated by relatively more than when the same shock is applied to Canada, whereas the increase in investment is similar in the two countries. This reflects the greater sensitivity of investment to the real exchange rate in Canada.

The results in scenario 2 show why Freedman et al. (2009a, b) argued that a global fiscal stimulus is essential to support aggregate demand and restore economic growth when interest rates are at their lower bound and cannot move lower. The results are robust in that simulations for different countries generate similar results, as is the case with the simulations from Canada and the United States shown here. The implication is that coordinated fiscal action will be more effective than a single country working alone. That is indeed what Freedman et al. (2009a, b) show using simulations with GIMF. The simulations also show that monetary policy accommodation is essential to effective fiscal policy, even if that accommodation is unconventional.

Since Freedman et al. (2009a, b), governments and central banks responded to the global slowdown with simulative fiscal policy and accommodative monetary policy. In addition, central banks reduced interest rates to unprecedented levels to offset the increase in private-sector risk premia and to underpin aggregate demand. The simulations here show that fiscal policy would not have been effective had monetary policy not been accommodative, even though some of the accommodation was unconventional.

One important difference between the results in the simulations shown above and the post 2008 outturn is that inflation was not as much a threat as suggested by the simulations. The reason, no doubt, is that the world economy was facing significant deflationary pressures as a result of (1) the sharp decline in stock market and housing wealth, (2) the related desire to rebuild assets and to repay debts, (3) the difficulty of accessing credit in a world of deleveraging, and (4) the much-increased uncertainty surrounding future economic developments. While deflation did not occur, the simulations above suggest that it would have if it were not for the fiscal policy stimulation supported by accommodative monetary policy. The inflationary consequences of the policies were in fact sufficient to offset the disinflationary consequences of the crisis.

Freedman et al. (2009a, b) also focus on the importance of a clear commitment to long-run fiscal discipline by countries wishing to engage in short-run discretionary fiscal stimulus. This commitment is built into the policy rules used in the above simulations. In the absence of such a perceived commitment, expansionary fiscal actions could lead to increases in long-term real interest rates, which could offset the stimulus effects of the fiscal actions on GDP. These negative effects were not part of the simulations shown here.

Like Freedman et al. (2009a) our analysis implies that if fiscal policy and monetary policy work together, they can make a significant contribution to preventing the economy from going into a recession after a financial crisis that forces interest rates to their lower bound. However, it is important to reiterate that while fiscal and monetary policy can help support demand in the short run, these tools have limitations and should not be viewed as a substitute for dealing with financial sector issues.

13.4.3 Scenario 3: Expansionary Fiscal Policy with the Perception of Unsustainable Debt

Scenario 3 shows the negative consequences of perceived unsustainable fiscal policies. The perception of unsustainability is accompanied by a higher country risk premium as investors need an incentive to hold government debt equivalent to the perception of increased risk of default. As a result government indebtedness rises.

Scenario 3 shows how expansionary fiscal policy becomes ineffective as a country becomes increasingly indebted. Moreover it is the perception of unsustainable indebtedness that renders fiscal policy ineffective, since people are forward looking, so demand increases risk premiums above the point at which government becomes unable (or unwilling) to continue to service its debt.

The increase in the risk premium works in the opposite direction of operation twist, the unconventional monetary policy action. Yet, despite the increased risk premium, it is assumed that monetary policy does not raise the nominal policy rate in the first two years of the scenario. An increase in the country risk premium without a corresponding rise in the nominal policy rate means that the stance of monetary policy has effectively eased, but the easing is not enough to offset the effect of the rise in risk premiums.

Canada

The effect of unsustainable indebtedness on the effectiveness of fiscal policy is dramatic. In the most realistic case where all domestic interest rates rise, the government multiplier drops from about 2 (scenario 2, fully accommodating monetary policy) to 0.2. The multiplier drops because the real interest rate rises owing to the higher country risk premium. But even without the rise in the country risk premium, the multiplier is barely back to where it was in scenario 1 without any monetary policy accommodation. In effect, the rise in government risk premiums more than fully offsets the unconventional monetary policy accommodation, also making the economy behave as if monetary policy was reacting to the shock. However, interest rates in the economy are rising not because the policy rate is higher but because the private sector demands greater compensation for the higher probability of government default associated with the increase in government spending.

In the case where both the government and country risk premiums rise, inflation falls because of the economic downturn that is created by the rise in longer term interest rates in response to the fiscal expansion. The economic downturn happens in year two and beyond, but inflation expectations are forward looking and so the decline in inflation starts almost immediately.

Both consumption and investment are affected negatively by the increase in government indebtedness. Investment is hit hardest because it is long-term interest rates that rise the most. As a result of the decline in investment, the weakness in the productive capacity of the economy is likely to be long lasting.

United States
The negative effects of increased government spending when the government is already highly indebted are equally severe for United States. In the most realistic case where all domestic interest rates rise, the government multiplier drops from about 2.5 (scenario 2, fully accommodating monetary policy) to about 0.4 (solid line in figure 13.4). It does not matter whether the economy is open or closed, as domestic investors are just as likely to choose to invest in more sustainable economies as are foreign investors, and so a dramatic rise in real interest rates is still needed to keep investment at home.

Inflation in the United States rises a bit more than in Canada, and the government multiplier is a bit larger, as we saw in scenario 1, again owing to the greater openness of the Canadian economy and hence import leakages damping the direct effect of increased government spending on domestic production. However, this effect is

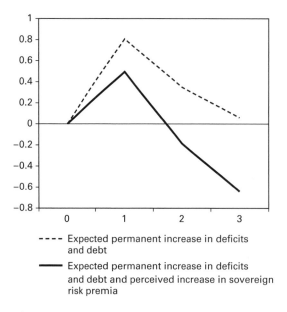

Figure 13.4
Scenario 3: US real GDP (percent deviation from baseline)
Source: GIMF simulations

small in relation to the negative impact of the higher risk premia on the economy in both countries.

The real exchange rate does not depreciate significantly (and actually appreciates when the country risk premium does not rise) despite the weakness in GDP. The higher interest rates necessary to keep investors from fleeing the country puts additional pressure on the currency to appreciate. Thus, the increase in government spending is doubly counterproductive in that it works against the need for the country to increase exports as a way of generating the income to service its increasing debt, as well as adding directly to the interest costs of servicing the debt owing to the higher interest rates that the increase in indebtedness produces.

Again, as with the open-economy case of Canada, investment is hit hardest by the rise in long-term rates caused by the increase in government spending, which is likely to dampen the long-term productive capacity of the economy.

Freedman et al. (2009b) caution that if fiscal stimulus should lead to permanently higher deficits and therefore debt, the consequences can be very unfavorable in the long run even though they may in the short run look favorable for the domestic economy. In scenario 3 we show the effects of fiscal expansion when debt is perceived to be unsustainable. This perception brings forward the negative long-run effects that Freedman et al. (2009b) illustrate in their paper.

13.5 Conclusion

The simulations in this chapter show that fiscal stimulus is significantly more effective in boosting economic output when the higher real interest rates that it can generate are offset by other policy measures. A coordinated expansion of monetary policy, or credible commitment to reverse the fiscal stimulus in the future in order to keep government indebtedness on a sustainable track, could accompany policies and be effective in keeping real interest rates from rising, thereby maximizing the positive impact of the fiscal stimulus.

Notes

1. See Kumhof and Laxton (2009c).

2. Many of the properties of GIMF are similar to other DSGE models. For a discussion of GIMF fiscal multipliers see Anderson et al. (2013), and for a comparison of these multipliers to fiscal multipliers in other models see Coenen et al. (2012).

References

Anderson, D., B. Hunt, M. Kortelainen, M. Kumhof, D. Laxton, D. Muir, S. Mursula, and S. Snudden. 2013. Getting to know GIMF: The simulation properties of the Global

Integrated Monetary and Fiscal Model. Working paper. IMF, Washington, DC, forthcoming.

Barro, R. J. 1974. Are government bonds net wealth? *Journal of Political Economy* 82 (6): 1095–1117.

Beetsma, R. M., and H. Jensen. 2005. Monetary and fiscal policy interactions in a micro-founded model of a monetary union. *Journal of International Economics* 67: 320–52.

Bernanke, B., M. Gertler, and S. Gilchrist. 1999. The financial accelerator in a quantitative business cycle framework. In John B. Taylor and Michael Woodford, eds., *Handbook of Macroeconomics*, vol. 1C. Amsterdam: Elsevier, 1342–90.

Bernanke, B., and F. Mishkin. 1997. Inflation targeting: A new framework for monetary policy? *Journal of Economic Perspectives* 11: 97–116.

Blanchard, O. J. 1985. Debt, deficits, and finite horizons. *Journal of Political Economy* 93: 223–47.

Calvo, G. A. 1983. Staggered prices in a utility-maximizing framework. *Journal of Monetary Economics* 12: 383–98.

Christiano, L. J., M. Eichenbaum, and C. Evans. 1996. The effects of monetary policy shocks: Evidence from the flow of funds. *Review of Economics and Statistics* 78 (1): 16–34.

Christiano, L. J., M. Eichenbaum, and C. Evans. 1998. Monetary policy shocks: What have we learned and to what end? Working paper 6400. NBER, Cambridge, MA.

Christiano, L. J., R. Motto, and M. Rostagno. 2010. Financial factors in economic fluctuations. Working paper 1192. ECB, Frankfurt.

Coenen, G., C. J. Erceg, C. Freedman, D. Furceri, M. Kumhof, R. Lalonde, D. Laxton, J. Lindé, A. Mourougane, D. Muir, S. Mursula, C. de Resende, J. Roberts, W. Roeger, S. Snudden, M. Trabandt, and J. int Veld. 2012. Effects of fiscal stimulus in structural models. *American Economic Journal Macroeconomics* 4 (1): 22–68.

Eisner, R. 1969. Fiscal and monetary policy reconsidered. *American Economic Review* 59: 897–905.

Fleming, J. M. 1962. Domestic financial policies under fixed and floating exchange rates. *IMF Staff Papers* 9: 369–79.

Freedman, C., M. Kumhof, D. Laxton, and J. Lee. 2009a. The case for global fiscal stimulus. Staff position paper 09/04. IMF, Washington, DC.

Freedman, C., M. Kumhof, D. Laxton, D. Muir, and S. Mursula. 2009b, Fiscal stimulus to the rescue? Short-run benefits and potential long-term costs of fiscal deficits. Working paper 09/255. IMF, Washington, DC.

Friedman, M. 1957. *Theory of the Consumption Function*. Princeton, NJ: National Bureau of Economic Research.

Gali, J., J. D. López-Salido, and J. Vallés. 2007. Understanding the effects of government spending on consumption. *Journal of the European Economic Association* 5: 227–70.

Gali, J., and T. Monacelli. 2008. Optimal monetary and fiscal policy in a currency union. *Journal of International Economics* 76: 116–32.

Gramlich, E. M. 1999. Remarks by Governor Edward M. Gramlich before the Wharton Public Policy Forum Series. Philadelphia, PA.

Kumhof, M., and D. Laxton. 2009a. Chile's structural fiscal surplus rule: A model-based evaluation. Working paper 09/88. IMF, Washington, DC.

Kumhof, M., and D. Laxton. 2009b. Simple, implementable fiscal policy rules. Working paper 09/76. IMF, Washington, DC.

Kumhof, M., and D. Laxton. 2009c. Fiscal deficits and current account deficits. Working paper 09/237. IMF, Washington, DC.

Kumhof, M., D. Laxton, D. Muir, and S. Mursula. 2010. The global integrated monetary and fiscal model: Theoretical structure. Working paper 10/34. IMF, Washington, DC.

Leeper, E. M., C. Sims, and T. Zha. 1996. What does monetary policy do? *Brookings Papers on Economic Activity* 2: 1–63.

Mundell, R. A. 1963. Capital mobility and stabilization policy under fixed and flexible exchange rates. *Canadian Journal of Economics. Revue Canadienne d'Economique* 29: 475–85.

Musgrave, R. A. 1959. *Theory of Public Finance*. New York: McGraw-Hill.

Philips, A. W. 1954. Stabilization policy in a closed economy. *Economic Journal* 64: 290–332.

Rotemberg, J. 1982. Sticky prices in the United States. *Journal of Political Economy* 90: 1187–1211.

Solow, R. M. 2005. Rethinking fiscal policy. *Oxford Review of Economic Policy* 21 (4): 509–14.

Taylor, J. B. 1980. Aggregate dynamics and staggered contracts. *Journal of Political Economy* 88: 1–24.

Taylor, J. B. 1993. Discretion versus policy rules in practice. *Carnegie-Rochester Conference Series on Public Policy* 39: 195–214.

Taylor, J. B. 2000. Reassessing discretionary fiscal policy. *Journal of Economic Perspectives* 14 (3): 21–36.

Tobin, J. 1972. *New Economics One Decade Older*. Princeton: Princeton University Press.

Weil, P. 1989. Overlapping families of infinitely-lived agents. *Journal of Public Economics* 38: 183–98.

Wyplosz, C. 2005. Fiscal policy: Institutions versus rules. *National Institute Economic Review* 191: 70–84.

14

Financial Sector Support: Why Did Costs Differ So Much?

Ceyla Pazarbasioglu, Uffe Mikkelsen, and Suchitra Kumarapathy

14.1 Introduction

The global financial crisis continues to impose significant strains on public finances. Extensive public support has been provided to restore confidence in the financial system. As the crisis unfolds its fiscal costs remain uncertain but so far they have differed widely across countries; and differences are likely to remain significant going forward. Crisis management strategies that rely on containment at the expense of upfront restructuring tend to shift fiscal costs into the future, and ultimately increase them. Compared with previous crises, governments to date have relied more on containment (central bank liquidity provision and guarantees of bank liabilities) and less on restructuring banks' assets. This approach has given rise to large contingent liabilities as risks are transferred from private to government balance sheets (see chapters 1 and 16 of this volume), but in most cases has limited the initial fiscal outlays. Importantly, this approach delays the much needed restructuring of banking and corporate sectors, which is critical for their viability and sustainable profitability. This risks transferring the costs of the crisis into the future and extending the economic downturn.

Reliance on guarantees can be particularly costly for the government in countries where guarantees proved not to be credible and were activated. The reach of guarantees relative to fiscal space is key—owing to sovereign weaknesses entering the crisis and the size of the financial sector, or both. Fiscal outlays in these countries have been much larger and put sovereign solvency under pressure.

Financial systems structure is also important. Features that can increase the risk of fiscal strains in the event of crisis include size (relative to GDP), bank complexity and cross border orientation (which make resolution more difficult), and financial diversification (lack of which can deepen the economic downturn when banks are impaired).

The rest of the chapter is organized as follows. Section 14.2 describes the types of central bank and government support provided to the financial sector during the crisis. In section 14.3 we quantify the initially pledged and utilized government support measures in response to the crisis and compare these across countries. Section 14.4 compares the costs of the current crisis interventions with earlier episodes. Section 14.5 concludes.

14.2 Central Bank and Government Measures to Support the Financial Sector

14.2.1 Central Bank Support

After the financial crisis intensified in the fall 2008, the liquidity condition of financial institutions worsened rapidly. Central banks from advanced economies deployed a number of existing—aggressive interest rate cuts—and new tools to provide additional liquidity to both banks and other financial institutions. These included:

- lowering reserve requirements,
- extending the duration of existing liquidity facilities (e.g., the long-term refinancing operations, LTRO, with three-year maturity by the ECB),
- relaxing counterparty and collateral requirements, and
- outright asset purchases (quantitative easing).

These measures expanded central bank balance sheets significantly (see figure 14.1). Central bank portfolios became more risky owing to direct purchases of risky

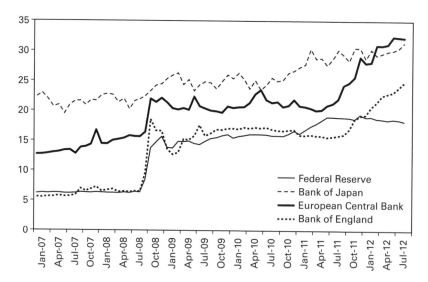

Figure 14.1
Central banks' balance sheets (percent of GDP)
Sources: Bloomberg; Haver Analytics

assets and lower collateral requirements, implying potentially significant contingent liabilities for governments.

14.2.2 Government Support
The global nature of the crisis and the interconnectedness of the global financial system exacerbated contagion risks and the associated uncertainties. As a result government support included extensive guarantees of financial sector assets and liabilities and nationalizations of financial institutions that were deemed "too important to fail" whereas the cleanup of financial institution balance sheets (e.g., government purchases of impaired assets and allowing bank failures) has been more limited.

14.2.3 Guarantees of Bank Liabilities
The initial crisis response was wide-ranging government guarantees of financial sector liabilities. Across the board, countries increased deposit insurance (Claessens et al. 2011). Deposit insurance guarantee limits for the United States increased from $100,000 to $250,000, and in several European countries, deposit insurance was increased to EUR 100,000 (from around EUR 25,000). Other countries went further and provided unlimited coverage.

In addition countries guaranteed other financial sector liabilities such as banks' bonds issuances. The United States guaranteed newly issued senior unsecured debt, United Kingdom guaranteed short- to medium-term debt of financial institutions, Germany guaranteed interbank loans and bank debt, and the Irish government guaranteed most financial liabilities of the ten largest Irish banks. While such guarantees help restore financial market confidence and do not require any initial government outlay, contingent liabilities can potentially be large if guarantees are to be utilized.

14.2.4 Recapitalizations and Nationalizations
The widespread deterioration of bank assets has caused extensive bank recapitalizations during the crisis. Such recapitalizations included specific assistance to institutions judged as systemically important to mitigate contagion fears as well as broad-based capital support. Several advanced economies announced recapitalization programs—United States (TARP), Germany (SoFFin), United Kingdom (Bank Recapitalization Program), Spain (FROB), and France (SPPE). These capital injections were largely done via the issuance of preferred shares to limit the dilution of ownership of shareholders and ease market concerns of significant public sector ownership. For financial institutions with systemic risks or those deemed as too important to fail, governments took on ownership stakes—the purchase of ordinary or preferred shares—evident in Germany, Spain, the United Kingdom, and the United States.

Regulators also took action to assuage concerns about the soundness of banking institutions—attributable to the wide range of uncertainty surrounding asset quality, future losses, and solvency—by undertaking tests of the health of banks in their respective jurisdictions to inform markets about their resilience. In the United States, credible stress tests coupled with policy decisiveness, disclosure, transparency and availability of public backstops allowed the financial institutions to raise capital from private sources. In the case of the EU, markets questioned the severity of the stress tests, the adequacy of coverage in terms of risks and banks included in the exercise, as well as the adequacy of backstops to address capital deficiencies (see Davies and King 2010).

14.2.5 Asset Relief Measures (Asset Purchases and Guarantees)

Asset relief measures can be either the direct sale of impaired assets to the government or asset guarantees where the government insures financial institutions against losses stemming from specific types of assets. The advantage of asset guarantees instead of outright asset purchases is that no initial outlay is required by the government. The United States, the United Kingdom, Spain, and the Netherlands designed asset guarantees to ring-fence selected portfolios of impaired assets of financial institutions. In most of these schemes, the institution bears the first loss and the subsequent losses (of up to 90 percent) are borne by the government.

Asset purchases have been somewhat less used in this crisis when compared with past episodes, such as the Nordic and East Asia crises. Only in about a quarter of the crisis countries (in Ireland and more recently in Spain), asset purchases have been considered (see figure 14.2).[1] Other forms of asset purchases—such as those for private securities and commercial papers purchased by the Fed and the Bank of England—were generally more limited in size than the programs in past crises.

14.3 Pledged and Utilized Government Support

In assessing government support, it is useful to distinguish between *pledged* support (e.g., government guarantees of assets and liabilities and pledges of bank recapitalization) and *utilized* support (e.g., recapitalization, nationalization, and asset purchases). Pledged support has been substantial across countries, whereas utilized support measures (and hence the realized strain on the public) have varied significantly.

14.3.1 Government Pledges

The upfront pledged amounts were significantly higher compared with previous banking crisis. As of end-December 2009, advanced G20 economies had made pledges for capital injections, asset purchases, and guarantees for more than $5,500

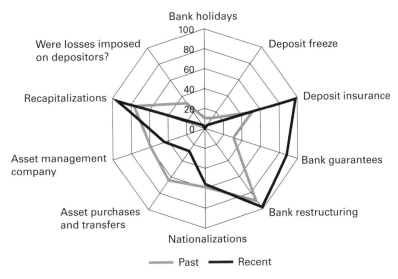

Figure 14.2
Crisis policies in current and past crises. Shown are the share of countries that applied the specific policy during the crisis. Past crises are defined as crises beginning before 2007. For detailed explanation of policy definitions, see Laeven and Valencia (2008).
Source: Laeven and Valencia (2012)

billion equivalent to 17 percent of GDP. Ireland pledged an unlimited guarantee of most liabilities of ten large financial institutions (all deposits, covered bonds, senior debt, and subordinated debt), United Kingdom pledged amount corresponded to more than 40 percent of GDP, and in Germany, France, Spain, and United States pledges exceeded 15 percent of GDP (see figure 14.3). Emerging G20 economies pledges were considerably lower around 1 percent of GDP (IMF 2010).

14.3.2 Utilization of Public Funds

For most countries utilized expenditures have been much smaller than the pledged amounts. This can be attributed to the containment of the crisis and the heavy reliance on guarantees that do not require upfront financing in most cases—although they contribute to a significant buildup of contingent liabilities. Public utilized support to the financial sector has been below 5 percent in most advanced economies so far (including United States, Germany, Italy, France, and Spain—although full-fledged reforms only started in 2H2012 in Spain). In other countries, the size of government guarantees was too large to be credible to the financial markets and utilized public measures have been significantly larger. In countries where pledges were more credible, either because of strong public finances or a lower scale of the financial sector problems, they helped contain the crisis and were not utilized.

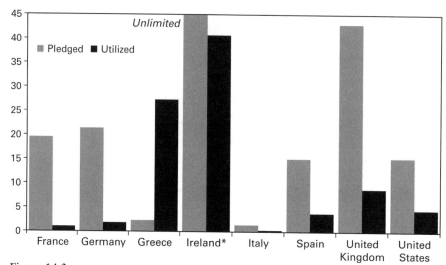

Figure 14.3
Pledged and utilized banking sector support (percent of GDP). In Ireland the government guaranteed all liabilities of ten large banks. Pledged amounts are the amount countries pledged at the onset of the crisis.
Sources: IMF staff estimates; Laeven and Valencia (2012); central banks' websites

14.3.3 Recovery of Fiscal Costs

The financial resources that have been channeled into the financial system will be partially recovered as governments' stakes in financial institutions generate revenue such as dividends or sale of assets. For most countries, recovery rates are still relatively limited owing to the ongoing crisis.

One exception has been the United States where the government has recovered so far more than three-fourths of the support provided to the financial sector. The Treasury has recovered almost all of TARP's bank programs through repayments, dividends, interest, and other income. The relative success of the United States in recovering capital injections under TARP was largely due to the government adopting substantial fiscal and especially monetary and housing support measures that boosted banks profitability which in turn helped to recoup some of the fiscal costs.

The fiscal burden has for some countries been relatively small owing to the lack of comprehensive diagnostic assessments. Even though implicit and explicit central bank support was put in place, a diagnostic assessment through comprehensive and transparent stress testing is imperative. Comprehensive and intrusive diagnostics of firms and associated triage should be undertaken prior to intervention leading to credible recapitalization plans or restructuring of institutions' liabilities without amplifying sovereign debt burdens. Several countries such as Ireland, and more recently Spain, adhered to the sequencing of crisis management: diagnosis, recapitalization, and the removal of nonperforming assets or the creation of bad and good banks.

For some of the other advanced economies (United States and United Kingdom), swift and decisive actions in providing liquidity support and guarantees helped in reducing the fiscal burden of financial crisis. Europe, in contrast, by adopting such an approach, is reeling from a sovereign debt crisis with pronounced implications for the financial sector.

14.4 Comparison with Earlier Episodes of Systemic Crises

14.4.1 Fiscal Costs

The final net fiscal costs cannot yet be assessed as the crisis is ongoing. Gross fiscal outlays since the onset of the crises can be compared with previous episodes, though. Iceland and Ireland emerge as the venues of the costliest banking crises, accounting for more than 40 percent of GDP, but still lower than that of Indonesia during the 1990s. Countries such as the United States and the United Kingdom incurred much smaller fiscal costs (4.5 and 8.8 percent of GDP respectively). If we compare fiscal costs to financial system assets, the costs are much lower in the current crisis (figure 14.4). Hence the reason for the large fiscal costs of the crises in Ireland and Iceland

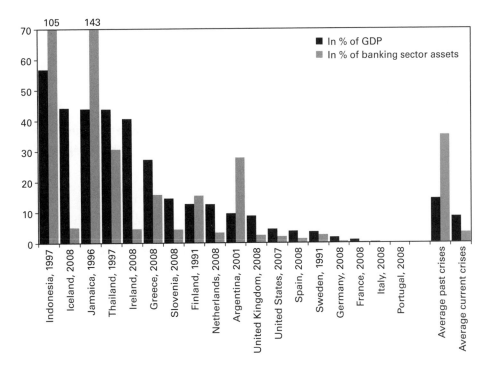

Figure 14.4
Gross fiscal costs of crises
Source: Laeven and Valencia (2012)

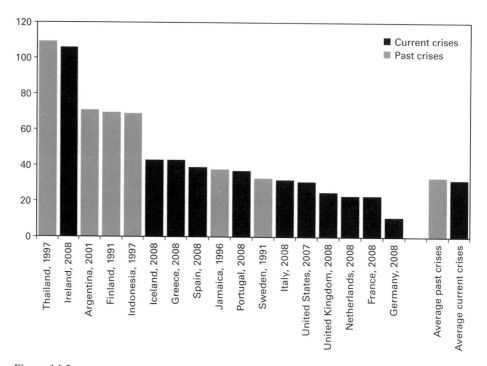

Figure 14.5
Output losses (percent of GDP). Output losses are calculated as the cumulative sum of the differences between actual and trend real GDP from the year of the crisis and the three years after.
Source: Laeven and Valencia (2012)

is not that the impact on the banking system was extraordinarily large but more that banking systems in these countries were several times the size of GDP.

14.4.2 Real Effects of the Crisis

Output losses have been large in most countries and are comparable to previous crises (figure 14.5). The largest decline during the crisis occurred in Ireland (where output losses have been larger than in past crises), Iceland, Greece, Spain, and Portugal (where output losses are comparable to those of past crises).

The initial decline in output faced by advanced economies was lower at 4.2 percent compared to that of emerging economies (7.2 percent). This illustrates that advanced economies had greater financial resources to cushion the blow from the fallout of the financial crisis. The recovery of advanced economies however has lagged that of emerging countries and will be complicated by the second wave of sovereign debt overhang, which would amplify fiscal costs. The impact on unemployment has been more pronounced in advanced economies where unemployment increased from around 6 percent before the crisis to over 10 percent after, whereas in emerging markets unemployment has increased less.

14.4.3 Accommodating Monetary and Fiscal Policies

In the current crises several countries have had the buffers to implement unprecedented policy responses to stave off the crises with the impact on the fiscal burden kept at a moderate level. Monetary policies were critical in supporting banks and asset markets and were relaxed significantly early on by quickly adjusting short-term interest rates to historical lows, with major central banks taking coordinated actions. Several central banks maintained low interest rates for prolonged periods. Those moves were a reversal of the efforts of central banks in many past crises in which nominal rates were kept high or sometimes even raised to support currencies. In the recent crises, the low policy rates and ample liquidity often allowed banks to preserve their intermediation margins in spite of higher costs of other funding. Accommodative monetary policy also helped support overall asset values, reduced the risk of an adverse debt-deflation spiral, and limited nonperforming loans, at least initially, thus protecting some of the banks' profit streams and balance sheets despite losses on traded securities.

Accommodative fiscal policies were also important in maintaining aggregate demand and asset values, thus indirectly supporting financial institutions (see chapter 10 in this volume). By supporting aggregate demand, fiscal stimulus helped reduce expected defaults on bank loans (fiscal policy has a greater effect on firms that are relatively dependent on external finance, see Aghion et al. 2009; Laeven and Valencia 2011) and thus reduced banks' recapitalization needs (Claessens et al. 2011). This approach differs from that of past crises, when fiscal policy was often contractionary. Also fiscal policy responses were more coordinated across countries than in the past, further helping to support economies. In some countries, however, expansionary fiscal policy and the costs of financial sector support measures have caused the financial crisis to transform into a sovereign debt crisis and the expansionary policies have been reversed and replaced by extensive fiscal consolidation.

14.4.4 Public Support and Conditionality

While some public sector support programs imposed restrictions, deeper operational restructuring—such as cost cutting, downsizing, changes in management, forced write-downs of shareholder value—has been imposed less than in past crises (Claessens et al. 2011), except when governments took majority ownership or fully nationalized institutions. The less intrusive conditions than in the past reflect institutions' stronger "reported" solvency positions and continued majority private ownership. More conditions were imposed on institutions receiving state support in EU countries where public liability guarantees came with restrictions on balance sheet growth, dividends, and employee compensation. When recapitalizing institutions and providing asset relief, EU countries included significant balance sheet and operational conditions such as restrictions on acquisitions, refocus on core activities, and divestments of businesses and assets. To avoid back tracking or complacency, EU also imposed a deadline for institutions to restructure their balance sheets. For other institutions, including those that have benefited from government support, market pressures will force many to rebuild balance sheets and restructure operations. Capital assistance under TARP in the United States come with the requirement that banks had to be adequately capitalized which implied that the only restrictions were limits on executives' compensation and the need for approval from the US treasury prior to any issuance of dividends.[2]

14.4.5 Asset Restructuring

While the recent crises broadly exhibit the characteristics of a typical boom–bust cycle (Reinhart and Rogoff 2009), the rise in nonperforming loans for many countries was much less pronounced. For Europe more broadly, impaired assets increased more gradually and have been lower to date than in past crises.[3] This was in part due to the types of assets involved, with the drop in the value of securitized loans occurring earlier than in other crises, before the end of the cycle. Actual defaults followed only when the crisis affected the real economy and corporate sector and household conditions had worsened. Furthermore in most countries corporate sectors were generally not overleveraged. Partly for these reasons, asset restructuring has been far more limited in the recent crises than in the past. In the recent episodes, many countries applied asset restructuring on a case-by-case basis, with public relief provided mainly through guarantees against a large deterioration in asset values—less frequent in the recent crises has been the use of asset management companies or "bad banks." Governments took on higher contingent costs through the issuance of asset guarantees, which minimized further deterioration in asset values of financial institutions but delayed asset restructuring.

Asset guarantees were preferred over asset purchases owing to the size and complexity of nonperforming assets including the many securitized portfolios and mortgages to be restructured. While the reliance on extensive asset guarantees has mitigated some of the anticipated fiscal costs in containing a financial crisis, they imply that the removal of nonperforming from banks' balance sheets have been more limited than in past crises. In the Asian and Nordic financial crises public asset management companies or bad banks removed nonperforming loans from financial institutions' balance sheets to a larger extent than in the current crisis. Leaving nonperforming loans on the balance sheets of financial institutions risks further weakening of banks' profitability, and the delayed restructuring of bank assets can come with large costs as witnessed during the banking crisis of Japan beginning in the mid-1990s.

14.4.6 Structure of the Financial System

The global nature and the speed of contagion in the current crisis make it unusual compared to past crises. Crises in the past were to a larger extent limited to specific regions or types of economies—the Nordic countries in the early 1990s, Latin America in the mid-1990s, Asia in the late 1990s, and the emerging market economies of the early 2000s. In the current crisis, it took on a global nature as it affected countries with a speed and malignancy not witnessed since the Great Depression with advanced economies and countries recently joining the European Union the most affected. This, coupled with their large and complex financial structures, has entailed significant fiscal costs. Also banking crises in the past occurred more frequently among economies that had smaller financial systems, implying lower costs of government support of the financial system.

In the run up to the financial crisis several features of the structure of the financial system implied increased risks of strains to public finances from financial sector support. Financial intermediation had changed from its traditional role where banks take deposits and make loans making a profit from the interest margin. Banks relied more on trading activities, nonbank financial institutions had come to play a larger role, and new innovative products had emerged. These changes implied that more financial intermediation took place in markets instead through traditional bilateral negotiation (IMF 2012). This shift towards more market based financial intermediation caused changes in the structure of financial markets. Banks became larger and more complex, making them more difficult to resolve in the current crisis compared to earlier episodes. The banking industry has thus become more concentrated with few large—and often too important to fail—institutions. The increase in market based financial intermediation implied that banks behaved more pro-cyclically since banks that mark their assets to market increase their demand when asset prices rise and vice versa when they fall. This can induce upward spiraling asset prices in upturns and lead to downward spiraling asset prices and fire sales in downturns. Such boom–bust financial cycles were amplified by the complexity of the innovative financial products on banks' balance sheets—such as US Mortgage Backed Securities (MBS) and Collateralized Debt Obligations (CDOs). With the shift in financial intermediation towards more tradable financial products banks have become more interconnected. While this has brought better diversification and better integrated global financial integration it has also left the financial system more vulnerable to large systemic shocks.

IMF (2012) finds that financial stress from 2008 to 2011 was higher in countries with a high degree of financial globalization (large amounts of foreign bank assets, high global interconnectedness), less traditional bank-based intermediation (e.g., low net interest margin implying less reliance on traditional banking activities), and bigger financial systems.

14.5 Lessons and Conclusions

In the current crisis, extensive containment measures have restored confidence in the financial system and averted a global economic depression. An important element of these containment measures consisted in extensive guarantees to the financial sector. While pledges have been large, fiscal costs have so far been limited in many countries. However, for some countries, pledges were too large to be credible and have placed their sovereign solvency under immense pressure with markets now focused on their sovereign risks. Further, as many countries have not yet undertaken the necessary restructuring of their banking sector, additional costs may be realized going forward. Although we are in the midst of the second phase of the crisis, four main lessons can be drawn.

First, in the current crisis there was a widespread use of government guarantees and less asset purchases compared to earlier crises. Such policies give rise to large contingent liabilities as risks are transferred from the private sector to the sovereign. Markets will most likely recognize these contingent liabilities as sovereign risks. This increases the likelihood of self-fulfilling prophecies where doubt about the strength of the government lowers the value of guarantees which in turn reduces the strength of the banking sector. Further, if the size of the banking sector is large, regulators have to tread carefully when issuing blanket guarantees, as guarantees that are not fully credible may be utilized. In particular, if a government has a high level of sovereign debt, to avoid further increases, governments could assume sufficient ownership of shares of distressed financial institutions in return for public support.

Second, exit from public sector involvement is necessary to minimize the fiscal burden. For those banks having a large public ownership interest, restructuring efforts will directly depend on government actions with the ultimate goal of selling its stake. The United States has been successful in transferring its involvement in the financial sector back into private hands, but the same cannot be said for other advanced economies notably in Europe.

Third, the mix of policies could have transferred the costs to the future in the form of higher public debt and likely slower economic recovery. While the complexity may have justified more emphasis on guarantees to restore confidence and less deep restructuring early on, it precluded thorough due diligence of individual banks and might currently reduce incentives to restructure assets. Past crisis experiences show that prompt corrective action is a key ingredient of successful banking reform. It is important to effectively diagnose the nature and extent of the problems, identify the underlying causes, and design a restructuring strategy to address them systematically. Failing to do so raises the total cost of restructuring. Instead of a policy of targeted, diagnosis-based resolution and early asset restructuring, the current stance is, in many cases, a muddling-through approach that delays addressing nonviable banks and nonperforming assets through a mix of accounting and regulatory forbearance, guarantees, and (implicit) public support. With the crisis entering into its sixth year, it is clear that the public sector support should have imposed stricter conditions and requirements which would have put governments in a position to require banks to clean up their balance sheets. The presumption should therefore remain in favor of deep restructuring early on, even when generally pursuing accommodative policies.

Last, but not least, prompt action and coordination are critical. The United States in dealing with the crisis, though there were several independent agencies involved, acted decisively and quickly with a unified set of messages. For Europe, efforts to act swiftly have been hampered by the multiple country independent agencies, with positions that have not been well coordinated.

Notes

1. The crisis episodes considered throughout the chapter are based on those identified by Laeven and Valencia (2012). Implicit and direct support programs of only a selection of countries are covered.

2. The recent crises followed this pattern through the first phase, but subsequent policy responses have been less forceful, at least for the major countries. Other papers reviewing policy responses in past and recent crises include Claessens, Klingebiel, and Laeven (2003); Ingves and Lind (2008); Ingves et al. (2009); Panetta et al. (2009); and Calomiris et al. (2005).

3. Exceptions have been Ireland and Spain, which experienced a more traditional banking crisis following the collapse of a real estate bubble.

References

Aghion, P., D. Hemous, and E. Kharroubi. 2009. Credit constraints, cyclical fiscal policy and industry growth. Working paper 15119. NBER, Cambridge, MA.

Calomiris, C., D. Klingebiel, and L. Laeven. 2005. Financial crisis policies and resolution mechanisms: A taxonomy from cross-country experience. In P. Honohan and L. Laeven, eds., *Systemic Financial Distress: Containment and Resolution*. Cambridge: Cambridge University Press, ch. 2.

Claessens, S., D. Klingebiel, and L. Laeven. 2003. Financial restructuring in banking and corporate sector crises: What policies to pursue? In Michael Dooley and Jeffrey Frankel, eds., *Managing Currency Crises in Emerging Markets*. Chicago: University of Chicago, 147–86.

Claessens, S., C. Pazarbasioglu, L. Laeven, M. Dobler, F. Valencia, O. Nedelescu, and K. Seal. 2011. Crisis management and resolution: Early lessons from the financial crisis. Staff discussion note 11/05. IMF, Washington, DC.

Davies, M., and M. R. King. 2010. EU bank stress tests: Good for transparency. *BIS Quarterly Review* (September): 4.

International Monetary Fund. 2010. *A Fair and Substantial Contribution by the Financial Sector: Final Report for the G20*. Washington, DC: IMF.

International Monetary Fund. 2012. *Global Financial Stability Report.* Washington, DC: IMF.

Ingves, S., and G. Lind. 2008. Stockholm solutions. *Finance and Development* 45 (4): 21–23.

Ingves, S., G. Lind, M. Shirakawa, J. Caruana, and G. O. Martinez. 2009. Lessons learned from previous banking crises: Sweden, Japan, Spain, and Mexico. Occasional paper 79. IMF, Washington, DC.

Laeven, L. and F. Valencia. 2008. Systemic banking crises: A new database. Working paper 08/224. IMF, Washington, DC.

Laeven, L. 2011. The real effects of financial sector interventions during crises. Working paper 11/45. IMF, Washington, DC.

Laeven, L. 2012. Systemic banking crises database: An update. Working paper 12/163. IMF, Washington, DC.

Panetta, F., T. Faeh, G. Grande, C. Ho, M. King, A. Levy, F. M. Signoretti, M. Taboga, and A. Zaghini. 2009. An assessment of financial sector rescue programmes. *BIS Papers* (48).

Reinhart, C., and K. Rogoff. 2009. *This Time Is Different: Eight Centuries of Financial Folly.* Princeton: Princeton University Press.

United States Department of Treasury, Office of Financial Stability. 2011. *Troubled Asset Relief Program: Three Year Anniversary Report.* Supplement to the *TARP Two Year Retrospective*, October.

15

Impact of the Crisis and Policy Response at the Sub-national Level

Borja Gracia, Jimmy McHugh, and Tigran Poghosyan

15.1 Introduction

The global crisis had an adverse effect on public finances at all levels of government. The impact of the crisis on *general government* finances has been documented widely (e.g., see International Monetary Fund 2010a; International Monetary Fund 2010b; OECD 2009; European Commission 2009), while evidence on *sub-national government* (SNG) finances is scarce. The existing small literature has largely focused on the impact of the crisis on aggregate SNG indicators (OECD 2011; Blöchliger et al. 2010; Dexia 2011; Ter-Minassian and Fedelino 2010), but aggregate data mask substantial regional variation and do not allow disentangling the impact of common and idiosyncratic shocks (Rodden and Wibbels 2010; International Monetary Fund 2012). Systematic analysis of the impact of the crisis on SNG finances is warranted in light of their growing role in public policy-making, driven by rapid decentralization efforts over the last several decades.

The important role played by the central government in stabilizing regional macroeconomic shocks has been documented widely. Sachs and Sala-i-Martin (1992), Von Hagen (1992), and Bayoumi and Masson (1995) showed that the central government cushions the impact of permanent (redistribution) and idiosyncratic (risk-sharing) shocks hitting individual regions in the United States and Canada through a system of intergovernmental transfers. Later studies provided similar evidence for the United Kingdom (Goodhart and Smith 1993), France (Melitz and Zumer 2002), Italy (Decressin 2002), and Sweden (Andersson 2004). However, little empirical evidence is available on the role of SNG finances in coping with macroeconomic shocks.

This chapter provides an empirical assessment of the impact of the crisis on SNG finances using a novel disaggregated dataset for eight large federations—Australia, Brazil, Canada, China, Germany, Mexico, Spain, and the United States. It takes into consideration the regional variation overlooked in most previous studies. We address the following issues: (1) the impact of the crisis on SNG finances, (2) the short-run response of SNGs to the crisis, and (3) the long-run challenges facing SNGs in the aftermath of the crisis.

Our analysis leads to the following conclusions. First, the global crisis had an adverse effect on SNG finances in most countries under consideration, largely through falling revenues. Overall, an average SNG in an emerging economy was less affected than an SNG in an advanced economy. In both advanced and emerging economies, the impact of the crisis was uneven across regions within the same country. Second, the short-run response of SNGs to the crisis was predominantly countercyclical, avoiding a sharp reduction of expenditures in the aftermath of the crisis. This result seems to contradict the theoretical prediction of limited stabilization room at the disposal of SNGs. However, there was a strong policy response by the central government in the form of stimulus packages. Part of this response was channeled through SNGs, allowing them to abstain from expenditure cuts. Finally, given that a considerable part of revenue declines was structural (or permanent) and taking into account current plans of central governments to withdraw the stimulus packages, going forward SNGs should put in place reforms to tackle the long-run structural gap between the high level of expenditures and permanently lower revenues.

15.2 The Institutional Framework Governing SNG Finances

Differences in the institutional frameworks governing SNG and central government finances have important implications for their vulnerability to macroeconomic shocks. Given the highly elastic nature of most taxes, a cyclical downturn automatically results in a decline in government revenues. In order to smooth expenditures over the business cycle, the central government can either use part of its savings accumulated during good times or borrow from credit markets. By increasing (decreasing) spending during cyclical downturns (upturns) the central government performs its macroeconomic stabilization function.

In principle, SNGs should also be able to smooth their expenditure over the regional cycle, contributing to the stabilization of the local economy. However, in practice, differences in the institutional frameworks of SNG and central government finances limit such stabilization.

- *Disproportional expenditure and revenue decentralization.* As expenditures have been decentralized at a faster pace than revenues, most SNGs rely heavily on intergovernmental transfers to finance their activities (Eyraud and Lusinyan 2011).
- *Revenue sharing.* SNGs share tax revenues with the central government, often through complicated revenue-sharing formulas. Typically the terms of these for-

mulas are dictated by the central government, limiting the autonomous ability of
SNGs to react to short-term cyclical fluctuations.

- *Expenditure structure.* SNG expenditures are mostly targeted at non-income-
  related items and investment projects, whereas unemployment insurance and social welfare spending are usually performed by the central government (Buettner
  2009). This makes SNG spending relatively less responsive to the cycle compared to that of the central government. At the same time, SNGs are responsible
  for a large part of public investment, which is easier to adjust during a crisis.
- *Fiscal rules and limitations on borrowing.* SNGs are subject to various fiscal
  rules, such as balanced budget rules and limitations on borrowing, which are often designed and monitored by the central government. Indeed, if the rules were
  strictly applied, fiscal policy in SNGs would be procyclical in the absence of
  increased transfer payments from the central government or "rainy day funds,"
  with spending cuts triggered during downturns owing to falling revenues.

The most common form of SNG fiscal rule is a balanced budget requirement
(Sutherland et al. 2006).[1] Virtually all US states except Vermont have statutory limitations on their ability to run budget deficits (Bohn and Inman 1996; Liu 2010).
During the 1990s many Australian state governments adopted explicit rules requiring balanced cash budgets (Robinson 2002). In Spain, the Fiscal Stability Law came
into force in 2003, requiring SNG budgets to be in balance (Sutherland et al. 2006).
In Germany, the 2009 amendment to the constitution introduced a (structural) balanced budget provision for SNGs (not binding until 2016), and before that, they
were obliged to operate on a "golden rule" limiting borrowing to gross investment
(Seitz 1999; Koske 2010). Balanced budget restrictions are common among Canadian provinces, although in some cases surpluses can be carried over to finance a
deficit in a subsequent year (Tapp 2010). There is a similar deficit carryover provision in many Australian states (Robinson 2002). In Brazil, the Fiscal Responsibility
Law and the Fiscal Crimes Law require balanced budgets for SNGs (Santos de Souza
2008).

There are also widespread constraints on SNG borrowing. According to the 1994
Budget Law, Chinese provinces need State Council approval to borrow, although it is
possible for provinces to establish special purpose vehicles to finance capital projects
through borrowing (Ahmad et al. 2004). In Mexico, states require the permission of
the central government to borrow in foreign currency. The central government also
obliges Mexican states to obtain at least two credit ratings before borrowing (Liu
and Webb 2011; Sutherland et al. 2006). Australia has a unique cooperative arrangement, where a national loan council coordinates borrowing by the Commonwealth
and the SNGs (Grewal 2000). In the United States, many states limit borrowing
to short-term financing needs. Moreover in most countries SNG borrowing is not

explicitly guaranteed by the central government. A notable exception is Germany where a constitutional court ruling in 1992 established a requirement for the central government to provide support to highly indebted SNGs in times of economic distress (Seitz 1999).

The SNG institutional framework in most countries is characterized by weak enforcement mechanisms. In the United States, there is generally no explicit legal enforcement mechanism, although in many states fiscal rules are embodied in the state constitutions (Mullins and Wallin 2004). Australia, China, and Mexico do not have any formal sanctions for SNGs that break debt rules. Even though Spain requires offending SNGs to develop a fiscal consolidation plan and make up the difference in the following year, it lacks a credible enforcement procedure. A notable exception is Brazil, where violating public officials in noncomplying governments are potentially liable to criminal sanctions (Santos de Souza 2008). Brazil also has a comprehensive requirement for SNGs to have fiscal responsibility legislation. In other countries, medium-term fiscal frameworks and fiscal responsibility laws are relatively rare and in some cases (e.g., Australia and Canada) were introduced only recently (Liu and Webb 2011).

15.3 Data and Empirical Analysis

In this section we provide an empirical assessment of the impact of the crisis on SNG finances in Australia, Brazil, Canada, China, Germany, Mexico, Spain, and the United States.

15.3.1 Data

Appendix A gives a description of the variables used in our analysis and their sources. Given some small definitional differences, adjustments were made to homogenize variables across countries, giving broadly comparable indicators for own-revenues (disaggregated by tax and other revenues),[2] total expenditures, overall balances, and transfers from central government. The dataset also includes macroeconomic indicators (GDP, population, and, whenever possible, also CPI) at the state level. The sample period starts in the mid-1990s and extends through 2010 for most countries (with the exception of China and Spain, where it ends in 2009).

Using these variables, we arrived at the following SNG-level balance sheet identity:

$$E_{i,t} - OR_{i,t} - T_{i,t} = OB_{i,t},$$

(15.1)

where i and t denote SNG and time, respectively, E_t represents SNG total expenditures, OR_t denotes SNG own-revenues, T_t is central government transfers to SNG budgets, and OB_t is the SNG overall balance.

15.3.2 Impact of the Crisis

We use two complementary approaches to gauge the impact of the crisis. First, we estimate annual percentage changes of SNG-level real per capita total expenditures, own-revenues, and transfers from the central government (variables entering the left-hand side of equation 15.1). We compare the dynamics of these percentage changes with state-level real per capita GDP growth rates during three years before (2005–2007) and after (2008–2010) the crisis. In order to smooth out annual fluctuations, we examine three-year medians for each of these periods. Second, we take the ratios of all four variables entering specification (15.1) in nominal terms with respect to nominal state GDP. Similar to the first approach, we smooth out annual fluctuations by examining three-year medians for the periods before and after the crisis.

Figure 15.1 shows that the global crisis led to a sharp deceleration in median SNG real per capita growth rates across all countries in our sample. This slowdown was more pronounced for advanced economies (e.g., Germany, Spain, and the United States have recorded a decline in median GDP growth) compared to emerging economies, where median growth remained positive albeit at a considerably lower level than in the pre-crisis period. The distribution of growth rates indicates notable heterogeneity across states within a country, with some states continuing to grow rapidly even in countries with a negative median growth rate. In fact heterogeneity increased substantially during the crisis shown in figure 15.1 by a large widening of the distributions.

- *Own-revenues.* In some advanced economies (e.g., Spain), the own-revenue decline in the aftermath of the crisis for the median state outpaced that of output, pushing own-revenues to GDP ratios marginally lower. By contrast, in some emerging economies (notably, China) the deceleration in own-revenues growth was not as pronounced as that of output growth, leading to a modest increase in own-revenues to GDP ratios.

- *Total expenditures.* Unlike own-revenues, real per capita total expenditure was either unaffected or increased despite the output growth slowdown in the aftermath of the crisis. The diverging dynamics of own-revenue and total expenditure growth rates suggests a countercyclical response by SNGs, which seem to go against the popular view that SNGs have a limited ability to conduct stabilization policy in light of institutional and borrowing constraints. As discussed in the next paragraph, this short-term countercyclical response was largely supported by transfers from the central government.

- *Transfers from the central government.* Similar to total expenditures, growth of transfers from the central government has stayed unchanged or increased in response to the output growth slowdown. Not surprisingly, the increase was particularly pronounced in countries where central governments put in place

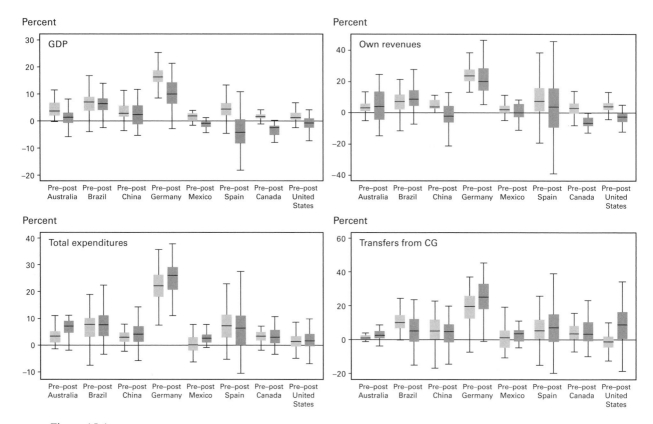

Figure 15.1
Real per capita growth rates of state GDP and other SNG fiscal variables. Each graph shows the distribution for the pre-crisis period (2005–2007) and post-crisis (2008–2010) for the relevant variable. Each vertical line represents the distribution around the median, with the box representing the out-turns between the 25th and 75th quartiles. The central horizontal line represents the median.
Source: IMF staff calculations

sizable stimulus packages following the crisis (e.g., China and the United States). Given that the global crisis represents a common shock hitting all states simultaneously (although some more than others), a coordinated response from the central government helped SNGs to limit procyclical expenditure cuts.

Own-revenue to GDP ratio remained unchanged in most countries following the output slowdown (figure 15.2), implying that the own-revenue elasticity with respect to output was close to one. By contrast, the total expenditure to GDP ratio increased in almost all countries in the aftermath of the crisis. As a consequence a sizable gap between own-revenue and expenditure emerged; this gap was largest in advanced countries. Moreover the increase in the transfers to GDP ratio was not sufficient to

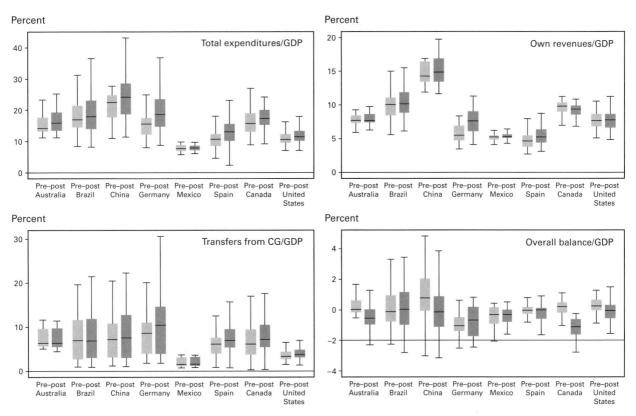

Figure 15.2
SNG fiscal variables as a share of GDP. Each graph shows the distribution for the pre-crisis period (2005–2007) and post-crisis period (2008–2010) for the relevant variable. Each vertical line represents the distribution around the median, with the box representing the out-turns between the 25th and 75th quartiles. The horizontal line represents the median.
Source: IMF staff calculations

fully cover this gap in most countries, including those with sizable stimulus packages, resulting in a deterioration of SNG deficit ratios.

Despite the deterioration in SNG deficits after the crisis, their level was not that large compared to deficits run by the countries as a whole. The main reason for this divergence is a surge in intergovernmental transfers after the crisis, which helped reduce SNG deficits at the cost of increasing central government deficits. On balance, this intervention resulted in much higher general government deficits compared to SNG deficits.

Overall, the analysis above suggests that the global crisis has had an adverse impact on SNG finances, resulting in deteriorating deficits. The slowdown in own-revenues was partially mitigated by the increase in transfers from the central government triggered by countercyclical stimulus packages. The latter helped SNGs to smooth out expenditure in the short run.

15.3.3 Policy Response

Analysis Based on Fiscal Impulses

In this section we conduct a more formal analysis of SNG policy countercyclicality. Previous studies analyzing SNG fiscal policy countercyclicality in the United States (Sorensen and Yosha 2001), Brazil (Arena and Revilla 2009), and a panel of federations (Rodden and Wibbels 2010; IMF *Fiscal Monitor* 2012) have adopted an approach focused on panel regressions between expenditure and GDP growth rates. Our analysis is based on fiscal impulse methodology outlined in IMF (2008) and Blanchard (1993).

Appendix B describes the methodology employed in our analysis. An expenditure impulse represents the discretionary (or policy induced) component of SNG expenditures as opposed to the cyclical (or automatic stabilization) component. To identify the expenditure impulse, we estimate expenditure movements driven by changes in the economic environment between t and $t-1$. The part of movements not explained by changes in the economic environment is assumed to be driven by discretionary policies. This latter component is the expenditure impulse, which we estimated for the three-year periods before (2005–2007) and after (2008–2010) the crisis. A positive (negative) value of the impulse indicates expansionary (contractionary) fiscal policies. As in the previous section, we smooth out annual fluctuations by focusing our analysis on three-year medians for both periods.

Figure 15.3 presents comparative analysis of fiscal policy cyclicality in the three-year periods before and after the crisis. For both periods, the scatterplots are divided into four quadrants, two of which represent procyclical policies (a combination of expenditure impulses and output gaps with the same sign), while the other two represent countercyclical policies (a combination of expenditure impulses and output gaps with the opposite signs).

- *Pre-crisis.* As shown in the top scatterplot, in the pre-crisis period SNG expenditure policies were predominantly procyclical. This finding is in line with the evidence from previous empirical studies.

- *After the crisis.* As shown in the bottom scatterplot, during the short period following the crisis, SNG policies in all countries (except Germany) turned countercyclical. This finding differs from the results obtained in previous empirical studies. The main reason is that the previous studies covered only samples that preceded the global crisis. In those samples, states did not experience common shocks of a comparable magnitude and did not benefit from as massive national stimulus packages as they did recently.

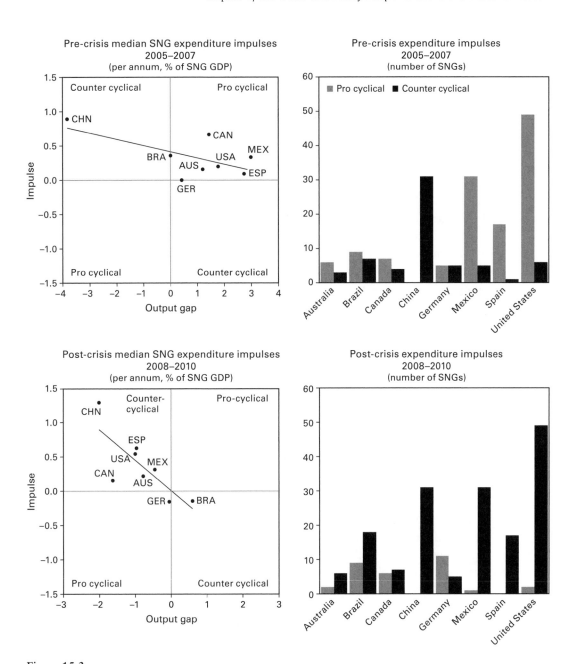

Figure 15.3
Response to the crisis: Comparison of SNG expenditure impulses before (2005–2007) and after (2008–2010) the crisis.

The bar charts in the same figure show the number of SNGs with positive and negative expenditure impulses in both periods. The charts suggest that following the crisis, a predominant number of SNGs were running a countercyclical expenditure policy in all countries (except Germany). This contrasts with the pre-crisis period, when a predominant number of states were running a procyclical fiscal policy. A notable example is the United States where almost all states running procyclical policies before the crisis switched their stance to countercyclical in the aftermath of the crisis.

Factors Contributing to Countercyclical SNG Fiscal Policy after the Crisis

The countercyclical response of SNG expenditures to the crisis documented in the previous section seems to contradict the theoretical prediction that SNGs should have a limited role in economic stabilization. SNG countercyclical response was supported by measures introduced by the central government in response to the common shock hitting all states. These temporary measures can be grouped into two broad categories: (1) national stimulus packages channeled through SNGs and (2) temporary relaxation of fiscal rules/borrowing constraints. Below we describe each of these measures in detail.

Support through Stimulus

As shown in figure 15.1, in the aftermath of the crisis transfers from the central government increased for most countries of our sample. The extent of the increase depended on the specificities of national stimulus packages. In China, Mexico, the United States, and to a lesser extent Canada and Spain, a considerable portion of the stimulus package was directed through SNGs. In the case of Australia, Brazil, and Germany, the direct role of SNGs in national stimulus efforts was more limited.

- *Australia.* SNGs played a central role in managing the stimulus efforts but received little direct budgetary support (Leigh 2009). Out of a total stimulus package of AU\$49 billion, around AU\$2.1 billion were allocated directly to states under the Nation Building and Jobs Plan (Swan 2009). This direct allocation understates the role of Australian states in stimulus efforts. The Council of Australian Governments established a National Partnership Agreement to facilitate the "rapid and cooperative delivery of the plan" (Australian Government 2009). As such, much of the package was implemented by agencies managed by the Australian states rather than by the state governments directly.

- *Canada.* The Economic Action Plan of 2008 envisaged a limited supporting role for provinces. From a total stimulus package of C\$60 billion, around C\$14 billion were directed toward "leveraged provincial and territorial actions," which required an element of provincial co-financing. As part of the action plan, an infrastructure stimulus fund was established, providing up to 50 percent in federal funding for provincial investment projects. Canada's stimulus plan also offered SNGs the option of accelerating transfers under the already existing Provincial-Territorial Base Fund.

- *China.* The stimulus package was designed to maximize its impact at a regional level, with a strong emphasis on public investment rather than tax cuts (Cova et al. 2010; Fardoust et al. 2012). A large share of the stimulus was earmarked for investment managed by the provinces, particularly in the transport and energy sectors.

- *Germany.* Two stimulus packages focused on tax cuts and labor market measures to cushion the fall in economic output and employment. There was little direct budgetary support for SNGs. Nevertheless, an agreement was reached whereby struggling SNGs would receive additional support amounting to €800 million, financed jointly by the federal government and other SNGs.[3]

- *Spain and Brazil.* A key objective of their stimulus packages was to avoid a decrease in SNG infrastructure investment (OECD 2010). In Spain, a State Fund for Local Governments was established and received an allocation of €8 billion to help sustain public investment. In Brazil, the focus of the stimulus was on tax reductions rather than expenditure increases. However, Brazilian federal government utilized the growth acceleration program (Programa de Aceleração do Crescimento) to maintain public investment levels in SNGs and municipalities. With the onset of the crisis, the program was used to accelerate transfers to municipalities and special credit lines for long-term investment by SNGs (Allain-Dupré 2011).

- *The United States.* The stimulus package envisaged a key role for SNGs. A large component of the American Recovery and Reinvestment Act (ARRA) of 2009 provided direct budgetary support for SNGs. The plan earmarked US$286 billion for state and local administrations through infrastructure expenditure and social spending. The Act also established a State Fiscal Stabilization Fund, which received an allocation of $53.6 billion to help state and local governments avert budget cuts. The bulk of these funds were targeted toward protecting education expenditures.

Relaxing Fiscal Rules/Borrowing Constraints

At the onset of the crisis, SNG fiscal rules—in particular, borrowing constraints—were eased in a number of countries. This provided some limited opportunities for SNGs to cover part of the rising gap between own-revenues and expenditures by borrowing.

- *Australia and Spain.* In both countries the central government offered explicit guarantees to facilitate sub-national borrowing. Spain also allowed municipalities to borrow and finance their 2008 operational deficit, including payments owned to suppliers (OECD 2010).

- *Brazil.* The federal government established credit lines for SNGs through the national development bank. A degree of forbearance was given to those SNGs that were not in compliance with the requirements of fiscal responsibility legislation (Canuto and Liu 2010).

- *China.* Provincial borrowing restrictions were relaxed. The central government issued bonds on behalf of provinces, although this debt will eventually become the responsibility of provinces. Provincial governments also established off-budget special purpose vehicles to borrow funds and finance public investment.

- *Germany.* Unlike the above-mentioned countries, there has been a move toward tightening sub-national fiscal rules.[4] In 2009 the Constitution was amended to include a structural balance rule for SNGs. Moreover SNGs will be only permitted to engage in cyclically adjusted net borrowing. These reforms come into force in 2011 and should be fully operational by 2020. Nevertheless, a sizable part of the additional post-crisis SNG expenditures was covered by additional borrowing by the states.

- *The United States.* The central government did not have the power to modify the self-imposed balanced budget requirements of states, which remained in place following the crisis. Nevertheless, the ex post median overall deficit deteriorated by 0.6 percent of state GDP. This broadly matched the increase in current expenditures, indicating that there was some implicit relaxation of ex post policies relative to ex ante balanced budget rules. The US states also mitigated revenue shortfalls by drawing on the reserves accumulated in "rainy day funds" (Bernanke 2010).

The impact of the more lax fiscal rules and borrowing constraints was partially offset by a worsening in SNG borrowing conditions, which might have constrained the rise in post-crisis SNG borrowing. Canuto and Liu (2010) reported that between October 2008 and January 2010, Moody's initiated 72 ratings actions on SNG debt, representing about a quarter of the "rated universe outside the United States" of which 96 percent of the actions were in a downward direction. Canuto and Liu also reported that in 2009 Fitch ratings of European SNGs were experiencing a "general shift towards negative outlooks." Similarly S&P's negative ratings actions for European SNGs largely exceed positive ones in 2009 and 2010. Reflecting this deterioration in borrowing conditions, the Spanish government established a liquidity facility for regional governments.

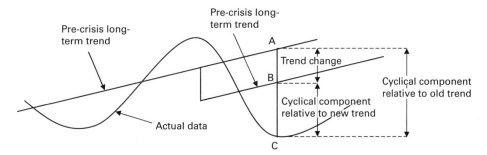

Figure 15.4
Decomposition of the changes into cyclical and structural components

Long-Term Fiscal Implications of the Crisis

Due to their highly elastic nature, SNG own-revenues closely followed the regional growth developments. As a result the adverse output shock experienced by most countries in our sample has pushed down SNG own-revenues. A natural question arising here is whether this output shock was temporary or permanent. Figure 15.4 illustrates this point graphically. If the shock was temporary (or cyclical), then own-revenues should recover to their pre-crisis trend when the output recovers. If the shock was permanent, then own revenues will recover to a new trend level that would fall short of the pre-crisis trend, having long-run implications for the structural adjustment in expenditures to cover the revenue gap.

In order to assess the long-run impact of the crisis, we estimated the pre-and post-crisis trends for real per capita output, own-revenues, and expenditures using the following regression for each state:

$$\log(X_{it}) = a_{0i} + a_{1i}trend_t + a_{2i}trend_t^2 + \beta_i crisis_t + \varepsilon_t , \qquad (15.2)$$

where i and t indexes denote state and time, respectively, $\log(X_{it})$ is the logarithm of the variable of interest (real per capita GDP, own-revenue, and total expenditure), *trend* and *trend²* are linear and squared trends, respectively, *crisis* is the dummy variable that takes the value of 1 for the period 2008 to 2010 and 0 prior to the crisis, and ε is the i.i.d. error term. The coefficients a_{0i}, a_{1i}, and a_{2i} identify the pre-crisis trend. The coefficient β_i is the parameter of interest: it captures the shift in the post-crisis trend variable. Given that the dependent variable is expressed in logarithm, the magnitude of the coefficient β_i indicates the percentage deviation of the post-crisis trend in state i relative to its pre-crisis level.

Table 15.1 shows country-level weighted averages of state-specific estimates β_i for real per capita GDP, own-revenue, and expenditures, where weights represent the share of respective state variable in the national aggregate. In all countries

Table 15.1
Estimated level shift of trend relative to the pre-crisis level

	GDP	Total expenditures	Own-revenues
Australia	−2.5	−0.5	−3.4
Brazil	1.2	4.2	3.6
Canada	−3.7	1.2	−2.8
China	−4.8	3.0	−2.7
Germany	−0.9	0.5	−1.0
Mexico	−5.2	3.0	−8.0
Spain	−4.8	0.1	−5.3
United States	−4.4	0.9	−3.2

Note: Reported data are weighted averages of state-specific estimates of coefficients β_i from specification (15.2).

(except Brazil), trend output was shifted down following the crisis, with the magnitude of the shift ranging from −0.9 percent in Germany to −5.2 percent in Mexico. This permanent shift resulted in a permanent loss of SNG own revenues, ranging from −1 percent in Germany to −8 percent in Mexico, suggesting that the structural loss of own-revenues closely matched the structural decline in trend GDP (see figure 15.5, right panel). In contrast, structural expenditures have increased following the decline in structural GDP; in some cases by a wide margin (see also figure 15.5, left panel).

The bottom panels of figure 15.5 decompose deviations of real per capita own-revenues and total expenditures for the last year of the sample (2010 for most countries). The chart shows that in all countries (except Brazil and China), own-revenues at the end of the sample are lower compared to their pre-crisis trend. A bulk of this difference is explained by the downward structural shift in own-revenues caused by a permanent decline in output (distance between points *A* and *B* in figure 15.4), while the rest of the decline is cyclical. By contrast, total expenditures in all countries exceed their pre-crisis trend. The contribution of the structural shift to this increase is sizable, creating a structural gap between post-crisis total expenditures and own-revenues.

15.4 Conclusions

Motivated by the ongoing decentralization efforts and growing role of SNGs in public policy-making, this chapter analyzes the impact of the global crisis on SNG finances. Using disaggregated data on eight large federations over the most recent period starting from the mid-1990s, we find that:

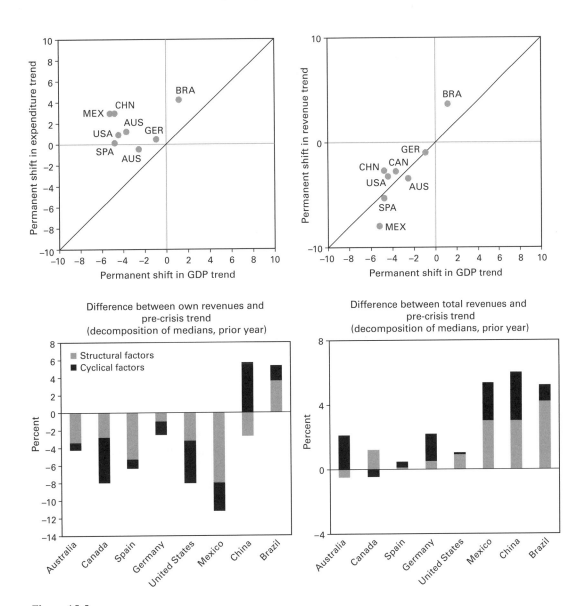

Figure 15.5
Permanent and transitory impact of the crisis on SNG finances

- The global crisis has had an adverse effect on SNG finances in most countries under consideration. The impact of the crisis was largely transmitted through lower own-revenues in response to a permanent and cyclical decline in state outputs. In general, SNGs in advanced economies, where the crisis originated, were more affected than those in emerging economies. The strength of the adverse impact was uneven across individual SNGs within a country.

- The short-run response of SNGs to the crisis was predominantly countercyclical. In most SNGs, total expenditures held ground or even increased following the crisis, helped by the support from the central government. This support was provided through two main channels: (1) by an increase in transfers from the central government through national stimulus packages and (2) by relaxation of SNG budget rules and borrowing constraints.

- The crisis unveiled long-run sustainability challenges facing SNGs due to a permanent loss of own-revenues triggered by a downward shift in the level of trend output. Given that the temporary stimulus measures put in place by central governments were withdrawn in many countries and will be withdrawn over the next few years in the remaining countries, SNGs have to implement structural reforms to fill out the structural gap between permanently lower own-revenues and persistently high expenditures.

Overall, moving from stimulus to consolidation will require close coordination between SNGs and central governments. In order to be successful, consolidation efforts will require a coherent medium-term framework that encompasses both central and sub-national levels of government. This will provide SNGs with sufficient time to incorporate stimulus withdrawal plans into their medium-term budgetary frameworks in order to minimize the possible disruption caused by the eventual decline in transfer flows from the central government.

Appendix A: Database

The database covers revenues, expenditures, debt and GDP at the state government level. Municipal data is not included. The database includes eight countries (Australia, Brazil, Canada, China, Germany, Mexico, Spain, and the United States). Our sample countries have broadly similar expenditure responsibilities, covering law and order, education, transportation, and infrastructure development. Revenue assignments are more heterogeneous. In some countries, for example, SNGs have the authority to raise income tax. In other countries, revenues from headline taxes are shared between federal and state level entities, as in the case of general sales tax in Australia.

The data for Australia were taken from the *Australian Bureau of Statistics*. Revenue, expenditure and public debt data range from 1999 to 2010, while GDP data range from 1990 to 2010. Revenue data are broken down into 12 variables including total revenue, tax revenue, sales of goods and services, and interest income and current grants and subsidies. Expenditure data are broken down into 11 variables and includes subsidies and transfers, personal services, goods and services, financial investment, public works, and other services.

The data for Brazil were taken from the *Institute of Applied Economic Research* (IPEA Data) and the *Ministry of Finance*. Data from IPEA range from 1985 to 2005, while the data from the Ministry of Finance span from 1995 to 2010. The Brazil data set includes revenues, expenditure and GDP data. Revenue data are broken down into 17 variables including total revenue, tax revenue, current and capital revenue, while expenditure is broken up into 30 variables including expenditure by function and capital and current expenditure.

State level data for Canada were taken from the *Department of Finance*. Revenue, expenditure and net public debt data are available from 1988 to 2010, while GDP data are available from 1980 to 2010; however, the breakdown available for revenues and expenditure data is limited including just total revenues and federal cash transfers, and debt charges and other expenditures, respectively.

Data for China were collected from the *CEIC China database*. The CEIC database includes macroeconomic, industry and financial time series for global emerging and developed markets. Revenue and expenditure data are available from 1999 to 2009, while GDP data are available from 2004 to 2011. Revenue data include a breakdown of 29 variables (mainly tax revenue variables), while expenditure data are broken up into expenditure by function (40 variables).

Revenue, expenditure, public debt, and GDP for Germany have been taken from the *Federal Statistics Office*. Data are available from 1995 to 2010. Revenues and expenditure data are broken down by broad capital budget and administrative budget categories.

Revenues, expenditure and GDP data for Mexico have been collected from the *CEIC Non-Asia Database* and from the *National Institute of Statistics and Geography (INEGI)*. Revenues and expenditure data taken from INEGI range from 1989 to 2010, and are broken down in to 12 and 13 categories, respectively. GDP data from the CEIC Non Asia Database are from 2003 to 2009.

State-level data for Spain have been collected from the *Ministry of Finance*. Revenue, expenditure, and public data range from 1984 to 2009, while GDP data range from 1980 to 2009. Revenue and expenditure data are broken down into 14 variables each, including totals, different taxes, capital and current spending, and expenditure by function.

The data for the United States have been collected from the *US Census Bureau*. Revenue, expenditure and debt data range from 1958 to 2009, while GDP data have been collected from 1995 to 2009. Data for 2010 are expected to be available by December. The database includes a breakdown for revenues (140 variables), expenditures (350 variables), including different type of tax revenues, and expenditure by function.

Appendix B: Estimation of Regression-Based Fiscal Impulses

We adopt the IMF (2008) methodology for assessing fiscal impulses at the state level. The SNGs fiscal balance (excluding CG transfers) in period t can be expressed as $B(P_t, E_t) = Rev(P_t, E_t) - Exp(P_t, E_t)$, where P_t and E_t stand for the discretionary fiscal policy and economic environment, respectively, and Exp_t and Rev_t for total expenditures and own-revenues, respectively (both measured in real per capita terms).

The change in the fiscal balance can be decomposed as follows:

$$\Delta B_t = B(P_t, E_t) - B(P_{t-1}, E_{t-1})$$
$$= [B(P_t, E_t) - B(P_t, E_{t-1})] + [B(P_t, E_{t-1}) - B(P_{t-1}, E_{t-1})] = \Delta B_t^E + \Delta B_t^P.$$

The first element, ΔB_t^E, represents the *automatic stabilizers* or the fiscal effects of changes in the economic environment between t and t-1. The second element, ΔB_t^P, represents the *fiscal impulse* or changes in the fiscal balance due to discretionary policies.

Following IMF (2008), we assume that real per capita GDP growth is a good proxy for the economic environment and start by estimating the following equations:

$$Rev_t = a_0^R + a_1^R growth_t + a_2^R trend_t + u_t,$$

$$Exp_t = a_0^E + a_1^E growth_t + a_2^E trend_t + e_t,$$

where *trend* is a time trend and u and e are the i.i.d. residuals. The growth-adjusted revenue, indicating what the revenue would have been in period t if the growth rate remained unchanged from the previous period, is computed as

$$Rev_t(growth_{t-1}) = \hat{a}_0^R + \hat{a}_1^R growth_{t-1} + \hat{a}_2^R trend_t + \hat{u}_t.$$

Similarly the growth-adjusted expenditure is computed as

$$Exp_t(growth_{t-1}) = \hat{a}_0^E + \hat{a}_1^E growth_{t-1} + \hat{a}_2^E trend_t + \hat{e}_t.$$

The measure of the balance that would have prevailed in period t if the growth rate remained at the $t-1$ level $B(P_t, E_{t-1})$ can be calculated as

$$Rev_t(growth_{t-1}) - Exp_t(growth_{t-1}).$$

The fiscal impulse measure then can be derived as

$$FI_t = [Rev_t (growth_{t-1}) - Exp_t (growth_{t-1})] - [Rev_{t-1} - Exp_{t-1}].$$

FI_t captures changes in the fiscal balance that are attributed solely to discretionary policies in period t.

Impulses can be procyclical, neutral or countercyclical, depending on the change of output gap. If the output gap is negative and the own-revenues are also negative then this signifies a countercyclical response. Discretionary taxes being reduced as output has fallen below trend. For transfers and expenditures, a positive impulse is countercyclical when the output gap is negative. Expenditures are increasing and the central government is transferring more resources to the sub-national entities, while the economy is operating below trend.

Notes

1. Revenue rules are rare and include some US and Canadian states that require voter approval for new taxes (Lutz and Follette 2012; Tapp 2010). Expenditure rules exist in Brazil in the form of a cap on salary costs (Liu and Webb 2011), the United States (and more recently Spain) in the form of limits on SNG total expenditure (Waisanen 2008).

2. We consider shared revenues with the central government as part of SNG own revenues.

3. Berlin, Sachsen-Anhalt and Schleswig-Holstein will each receive €80 million per year, Saarland will receive €260 million per year, and Bremen will receive €300 million per year (Koske 2010).

4. Incidentally, Germany is the only country in our sample that did not exhibit countercyclical policy response following the crisis (see figure 15.3) as tighter borrowing constraints may have limited the ability of SNGs to increase expenditures.

References

Ahmad, E., R. Singh, and M. Fortuna. 2004. Toward more effective redistribution: Reform options for intergovernmental transfers in China. Working paper 04/98. IMF, Washington, DC.

Allain-Dupré, D. 2011. Multi-level governance of public investment: Lessons from the crisis. Regional Development working paper 2011/05. OECD, Paris.

Andersson, L. 2004. Regional risk-sharing provided by the fiscal system: Empirical evidence from Sweden. *Regional Studies* 38 (3): 269–80.

Arena, M., and J. Revilla. 2009. Pro-cyclical fiscal policy in Brazil: Evidence from the states. Policy research paper, 5144. World Bank, Washington, DC.

Australian Government. 2009. National partnership agreement on the nation building and jobs plan: Building prosperity for the future and supporting jobs now. http://www.coag.gov.au/node/149.

Bayoumi, T., and P. Masson. 1995. Fiscal flows in the United States and Canada: Lessons from Monetary Union in Europe. *European Economic Review* 39: 253–74.

Bernanke, B. 2010. Challenges for the economy and state governments. Speech to the Annual Meeting of the Southern Legislative Conference of the Council of State Governments, Charleston, SC.

Blanchard, O. 1993. Suggestions for a new set of fiscal indicators. Working paper 79. OECD, Paris.

Blöchliger, H., C. Charbit, J. Campos, and C. Vammale. 2010. Sub-central governments and the economic crisis: Impact and policy responses. Working paper 752. Economics Department, OECD, Paris.

Bohn, H., and R. Inman. 1996. Balanced-budget rules and public deficits: Evidence from the U.S. states. *Carnegie-Rochester Conference Series on Public Policy* 45 (1): 13–76.

Buettner, T. 2009. *Fiscal Policy, Grants, and Sub-national Government Budget Balance*. IEB World Report on Fiscal Federalism. Barcelona: Institute d'Economia.

Canuto, O., and L. Liu. 2010. Sub-national debt finance: Make it sustainable. In The Day after Tomorrow—A Handbook on the Future of Economic Policy in the Developing World. Edited by Otaviano Canuto, Marcelo M. Giugale, Washington: World Bank, 219–37.

Cova, P., M. Pisani, and A. Rebucci. 2010. Macroeconomic effects of China's fiscal stimulus. Working paper IDB-WP-211. IDB, Washington, DC.

Decressin, J. 2002. Regional income redistribution and risk-sharing: How does Italy compare in Europe? *Journal of Public Economics* 86: 287–306.

Dexia. 2011. Sub-national public finance in the European Union. Available at: http://www.dexia.com/EN/news/in_short/Documents/NDCE_july_2011_EN.pdf.

European Commission. 2009. *Economic Crisis in Europe: Causes, Consequences and Response*. Brussels: DG Economic and Financial Affairs.

Eyraud, L., and L. Lusinyan. 2011. Decentralizing spending more than revenue: Does it hurt fiscal performance? Working paper 11/226. IMF, Washington, DC.

Fardoust, S., J. Yifu Lin, and X. Luo. 2012. Demystifying China's fiscal stimulus. Policy Research working paper 6221. World Bank, Washington, DC.

Goodhart, C., and S. Smith. 1993. Stabilization. In The Economics of Community Public Finance, European Economy Reports and Studies, vol. 5. Brussels: European Commission, 417–55.

Grewal, B. 2000. Australian Loan Council: Arrangements and experience with bailouts. Working paper R-397. Inter-American Development Latin American Research Network, Washington, DC.

International Monetary Fund. 2008. *World Economic Outlook*. Washington, DC: IMF, October.

International Monetary Fund. 2010a. *Navigating the Fiscal Challenges Ahead. Fiscal Monitor*. Washington, DC: IMF.

International Monetary Fund. 2010b. *Taking Stock: A Progress Report on Fiscal Adjustment. Fiscal Monitor*. Washington, DC: IMF.

International Monetary Fund. 2012. *Balancing Fiscal Policy Risks. Fiscal Monitor.* Washington, DC: IMF.

Koske, I. 2010. After the crisis—Bringing German public finances back to a sustainable path. Working paper. Economics Department, OECD, Paris.

Leigh, A. 2009. How much did the 2009 fiscal stimulus boost spending? Evidence from a household survey. CAMA working paper series 22/2009. Australian National University, Canberra.

Liu, L. 2010. China: Strengthening subnational debt financing and managing risks. Policy note. Worldbank, Washington, DC. Available at: http://documents.worldbank.org/curated/en/2010/08/13159499/china-strengthening-subnational-debt-financing-managing-risks-policy-note.

Liu, L., and S. Webb. 2011. Laws for fiscal responsibility for sub-national discipline: International experience. Policy Research working paper 5587. World Bank, Washington, DC.

Lutz, B., and G. Follette. 2012. Fiscal rules: What does the American experience tell us? Finance and Economics discussion paper 2012/38. Federal Reserve Board, Washington, DC.

Melitz, J., and F. Zumer. 2002. Regional redistribution and stabilization by the centre in Canada, France, the U.K. and the U.S.: A reassessment and new tests. *Journal of Public Economics* 86 (2): 263–84.

Mullins, D., and B. Wallin. 2004. Tax and expenditure limitations: Introduction and overview. *Public Budgeting and Finance* 24: 2–15.

OECD. 2010. Fiscal policy across levels of government in times of crisis. OECD Network on Fiscal Relations, Paris. Available at: COM/CTPA/ECO/GOV/WP(2010)12.

OECD. 2011. *Dealing with Sub-national Finances under Strain.* OECD Regional Outlook. Paris: OECD, ch. 2.

Robinson, M. 2002. National and state fiscal rules in Australia: An outline and critical analysis. *Fiscal Rules* (February). Rome: Banca d'Italia.

Rodden, J., and E. Wibbels. 2010. Fiscal decentralization and the business cycle: An empirical study of seven federations. *Economics and Politics* 22 (1): 37–67.

Sachs, J., and X. Sala-i-Martin. 1992. Fiscal federalism and optimum currency areas: Evidence for Europe from the United States. In Matthew Canzoneri, Vittorio Grilli, and Paul Masson, eds., Establishing a Central Bank: Issues in Europe and Lessons from the U.S. Cambridge: Cambridge University Press, 195–219.

Santos de Souza, Saulo. 2008. Fiscal rules in Brazil: The limits of fiscal stabilization for poverty reduction. *Delaware Review of Latin American Studies* 8 (2).

Seitz, H. 1999. Sub-national government bailouts in Germany. Working paper B20. Center for European Integration Studies, Bonn.

Sorensen, B., and O. Yosha. 2001. Is state fiscal policy asymmetric over the business cycle? *Economic Review of the Federal Reserve Bank of Kansas City* 86: 43–64.

Sutherland, D., R. Price, and I. Joumand. 2006. *Fiscal Rules for Sub-central Governments; Design and Impact,* vol. 1. Paris: OECD. Available at: COM/CTPA/ECO/GOV?WP(2006)/1

Swan, W. 2009. *Fact Sheet: 2009 Updated Economic and Fiscal Outlook: Household Stimulus Package.* Media Release, February 13, 2009, Parliament of Australia.

Tapp, S. 2010. *Canadian Experiences with Fiscal Consolidations and Fiscal Rules*. Ottawa, Canada: Canadian Parliament.

Ter-Minassian, T., and A. Fedelino. 2010. *The Impact of the Global Financial Crisis on Sub-national Governments' Finances*. IEB World Report on Fiscal Federalism. Barcelona: Institute d'Economia.

Von Hagen, J. 1992. Fiscal arrangements in a Monetary Union: Evidence from the U.S. In Don Fair and Christian de Boissieux, eds., Fiscal Policy, Taxes, and the Financial System in an Increasingly Integrated Europe. London: Kluwer, 1–2.

Waisanen, B. 2008. State tax and expenditure limits. National Conference of State Legislatures, Washington, DC.

Part IV
Post-crisis Fiscal Outlook

16

Fiscal Outlook in Advanced and Emerging Markets

Laura Jaramillo and Pablo Lopez-Murphy

16.1 Introduction

The financial crisis left many countries, especially advanced economies, with a dangerous combination of high debt to GDP ratios not seen since World War II (figure 16.1) and overall deficits unheard of in at least thirty years (figure 16.2). While overall balances are expected to improve over the medium term as economic activity recovers and countries implement ambitious structural reforms, this improvement is expected to make only a small dent in the debt stock, as countries struggle to address the enduring legacies of the crisis. These legacies include a tepid recovery of revenues as potential GDP is not expected to recover to its pre-crisis trend and rising expenditure pressures are linked to debt service and entitlement spending. The crisis also left countries facing greater risks to debt dynamics owing to greater macroeconomic volatility, uncertainty related to policy implementation, and large contingent liabilities.

The chapter is organized as follows. Section 16.2 takes stock of the fiscal positions of advanced and emerging economies following the financial crisis and analyzes the main challenges countries face over the medium term—including those arising from the crisis—that constrain their ability to recoup their pre-crisis fiscal positions. Section 16.3 identifies ongoing risks—some of which are also remnants of the crisis—that that are likely also to weigh negatively on the fiscal outlook, in particular those risks related to uncertainty with respect to macroeconomic performance, policy implementation, and contingent liabilities. Section 16.4 concludes.

16.2 Baseline Outlook: Subdued Revenues amid High Spending

Even as stimulus measures are unwound, headline deficit to GDP ratios are not expected to return to pre-crisis levels as the recovery in revenues to GDP is not enough to offset the higher share of expenditures to GDP. To a large extent, this comes as a

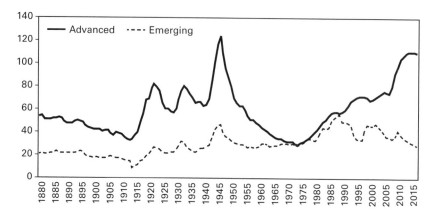

Figure 16.1
Historical public debt (percent of GDP). The "world" public debt-to-GDP series is based on debt-to-GDP data for a constant sample of 68 countries, weighted by PPP GDP. Debt data were drawn from the Historical Public Debt Database, which has almost full data coverage from 1880 to 2011 for all advanced and some emerging economies. Gaps for earlier years in both the PPP GDP and debt data series were populated through back-extrapolation using the debt and PPP GDP growth rates of countries for which data were available. Data for 2012 to 2017 are from the IMF *Fiscal Monitor*, April 2012. Sources: IMF Historical Public Debt Database; IMF, *Fiscal Monitor*, April 2012

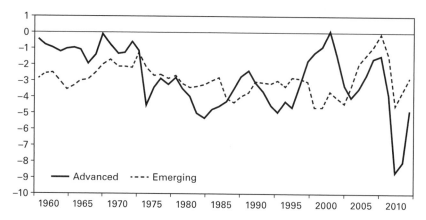

Figure 16.2
Overall balances, 1960 to 2011 (percent of GDP)
Source: Mauro et al. (2013)

result of an expected permanent loss in the level of potential GDP as a consequence of the global crisis.

Based on analyses of previous crisis episodes, several studies argue that output is not likely to recover to its pre-crisis trend.[1] IMF (2009) finds that following banking crises, the path of output tends to be depressed substantially and persistently, with no rebound on average to the pre-crisis trend over the medium term as a result of enduring losses of capital and employment relative to trend. European Commission (2009) also finds that a crisis can reduce potential output in the short and medium term through its adverse impact on investment due to credit constraints—which would not only depress capital accumulation, but also slow the process of industrial restructuring and limit spending on research and development, curtailing total factor productivity—and on the labor force through hysteresis effects.[2] DeLong and Summers (2012) and Romer (2012) also underscore the risk of hysteresis effects in the recent crisis in light of the share and persistent increase in unemployment rates. With this in mind, medium-term forecasts by IMF staff typically expect potential output to remain below its pre-crisis trend, especially among advanced economies (figure 16.3). Output losses associated with the crisis—calculated as the difference between the level of potential per capita GDP in the baseline and the level that would have

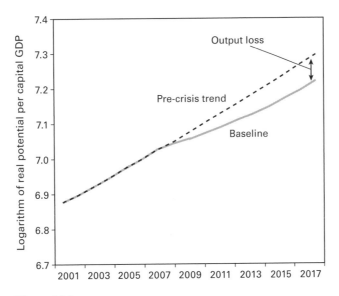

Figure 16.3
Advanced economies: Potential per capita GDP, baseline and pre-crisis trend. The pre-crisis trend is estimated as the average over 2000 to 2006, and extrapolated linearly thereafter, based on methodology in IMF (2009).
Sources: *World Economic Outlook (WEO)*, October 2012; authors' estimates and projections

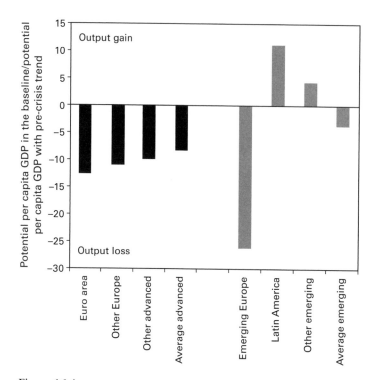

Figure 16.4
Output loss by region (percent). Output loss associated with the crisis is the difference between the level of potential GDP in the baseline and the level that would have been expected based on the prevailing pre-crisis trend. The pre-crisis trend is estimated as the average over 2000 to 2006, and extrapolated linearly thereafter, based on methodology in IMF (2009).
Sources: *World Economic Outlook (WEO)*, October 2012; authors' estimates and projections

been expected based on the prevailing pre-crisis trend—are estimated at 8.5 percent of GDP for advanced economies and 3.66 percent of GDP for emerging economies, though the loss is especially high for emerging Europe (figure 16.4).

Over the medium term, even as revenue to GDP ratios are expected to recover to their pre-crisis levels, revenues in nominal terms would remain subdued by weaker potential GDP. The ratio of revenues to GDP is indeed expected to return to its pre-crisis level in most advanced economies by 2014, and even earlier in the case of emerging economies (figure 16.5). This reflects in part an improvement in the cyclical position, as tax collections would improve as real GDP returns to its potential. However, in light a lower expected level of potential GDP, revenue losses—estimated as the difference between the level of revenues in the baseline and the level that would have been expected if potential GDP had remained on the pre-crisis trend—would amount to close to 4 percent of GDP in advanced economies, 2 percent of GDP in emerging economies, and significantly higher for countries in Europe (figure 16.6).

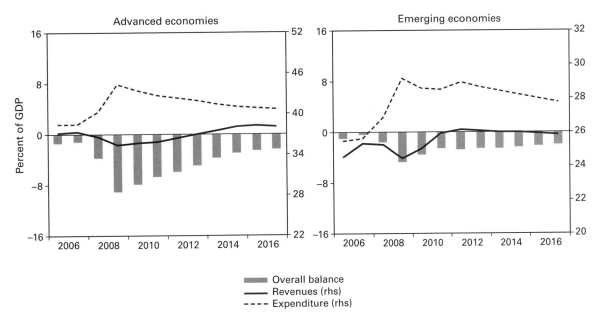

Figure 16.5
Revenue, expenditure, and overall balance (percent of GDP)
Source: IMF, *Fiscal Monitor*, October 2012

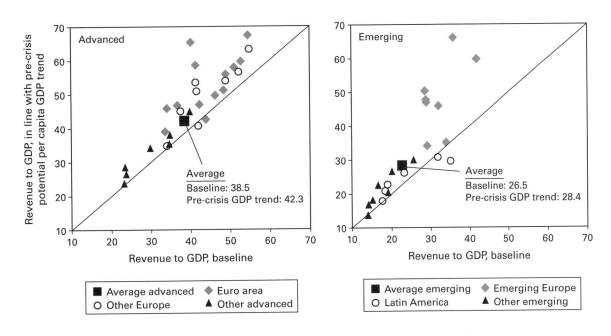

Figure 16.6
Baseline revenue forecast versus revenues in line with pre-crisis potential GDP trend (percent of GDP). The pre-crisis potential GDP trend is estimated as the average over 2000 to 2006, and extrapolated linearly thereafter, based on methodology in IMF (2009).
Sources: IMF, *Fiscal Monitor*, October 2012; authors' estimates and projections

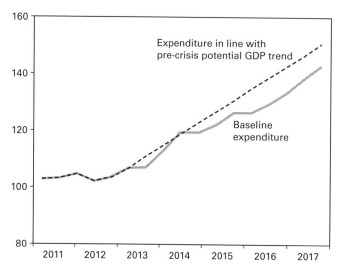

Figure 16.7
Expenditure in line with baseline potential GDP versus expenditure in line with pre-crisis potential GDP Trend (index 2006 = 100). The pre-crisis potential GDP trend is estimated as the average over 2000 to 2006, and extrapolated linearly thereafter, based on methodology in IMF (2009).
Sources: IMF, *Fiscal Monitor*, October 2012; authors' estimates and projections

Furthermore expenditure is expected to remain high in terms of GDP, despite the implementation of sizable expenditure cuts over the medium term, owing to a combination of lower expected potential GDP and new spending pressures. Most of the expansion in outlays during the crisis is expected to be reversed as temporary stimulus measures expire and countries embark on fiscal consolidation, with expenditure falling by about 3 percent of GDP in advanced and 1 percent of GDP in emerging economies, between 2010 and 2017.[3] In the absence of measures to curb spending, expenditure could indeed be higher by about 5 percent in advanced economies over the medium term if it is allowed to continue to grow in line with the pre-crisis potential GDP trend (Figure 16.7). Nevertheless, spending to GDP in 2017 is still expected to remain more than 2 percent of GDP above the pre-crisis ratio in both advanced and emerging economies. Of this, about 1 percent of GDP is explained by the gradual increase of entitlement spending over the next years (which is expected to continue to rise considerably over the long term). In the case of advanced economies, interest expenditure to GDP is also expected to remain elevated from servicing a larger debt stock, even as real interest rates are expected to remain broadly in line with pre-crisis levels. In emerging economies, the increase in public investment during the crisis is not expected to be rolled back (figure 16.8).

These revenue and expenditure trends in advanced economies imply that overall balances are expected to narrow only gradually over the medium term, and will

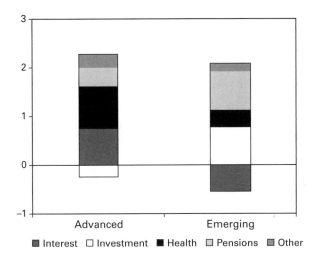

Figure 16.8
Change in expenditure by component, 2007 to 2017 (percent of GDP)
Sources: IMF, *Fiscal Monitor*, October 2012; authors' calculations

therefore continue to add to the debt stock.[4] Between 2011 and 2017, debt to GDP in advanced economies is expected to rise by about 7 percentage points, keeping debt at close to peak levels. Primary balances are expected to contribute about 5 percent of GDP, and stock flow adjustments (in some cases linked to financial sector support measures) another 5 percent, while a favorable interest-rate–growth differential helps contain debt accumulation (figure 16.9). In several large advanced countries, debt to GDP ratios would remain above 80 percent (figure 16.10), which could take a toll on potential growth through crowding out effects on private investment. [5]

In contrast, in emerging economies, debt is expected to decline by close to 8 percent of GDP, with strong GDP growth as the most important contributor. Emerging economies are also expected to maintain primary surpluses (favored by relatively strong growth prospects), which would also help bring debt ratios down. On average, debt ratios are expected fall below 30 percent of GDP, but will remain above 40 percent of GDP in some large emerging economies, a level associated with greater vulnerability.[6]

16.3 Risks to the Outlook: Macroeconomic and Political Uncertainty

Underlying the baseline debt path over the medium term are relatively benign assumptions regarding interest rates and growth trends. Some sensitivity analysis

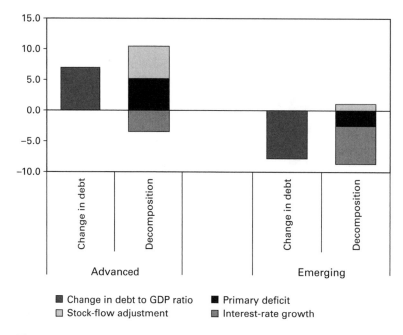

Figure 16.9
Decomposition of debt accumulation, 2011 to 2017 (percent of GDP)
Sources: IMF, *Fiscal Monitor*, October 2012; authors' calculations

is warranted to gauge the impact alternative macroeconomic assumptions and to quantify some fiscal risks.[7] For example, real interest rates are expected to be below those before the crisis, with growth also lower (figure 16.11). However, market volatility since the start of the crisis implies that there is considerable downside risk that lower real interest rates will not materialize. On the upside, growth prospects could be stronger than currently anticipated. Table 16.1 provides a risk assessment matrix with the relative likelihood that alternative sources of risk materialize and impact of such risks on debt sustainability.

16.3.1 Implementation Risk

Several countries have announced ambitious consolidation plans to improve fiscal positions over the medium term. Assuming that such plans are implemented fully, the baseline scenario of the October 2012 *Fiscal Monitor* forecasts that debt in advanced economies would stabilize by 2014. While in many cases these measures have already been incorporated into law, there is a nonnegligible risk that policy measures are not fully executed, owing to lack of public support or shortcomings in implementation capacity. Debt in advanced economies would be on a steeper trajec-

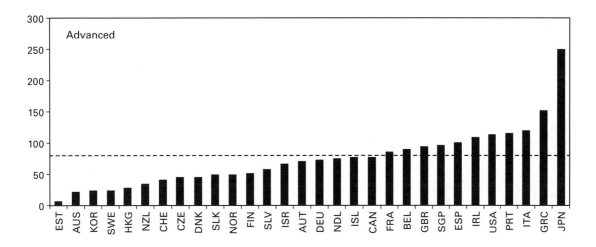

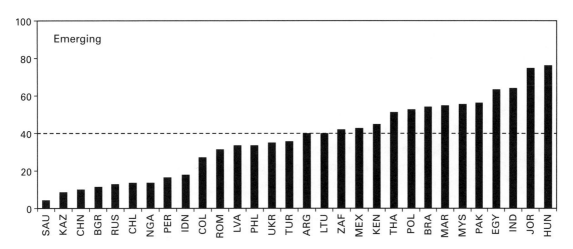

Figure 16.10
General government gross debt (percent of GDP)
Source: IMF, *Fiscal Monitor*, October 2012

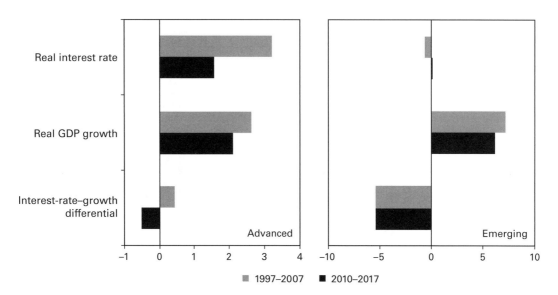

Figure 16.11
Difference between interest rate and growth (percent)
Sources: IMF, *Fiscal Monitor*, October 2012; authors' calculations

tory if, owing to policy slippages and/or a slower recovery, the primary balance gets stuck at its 2011 level (figure 16.12). Debt would reach close to 130 percent of GDP by 2017. If the primary balance remains instead at its 2012 level, where some adjustment is expected to have taken place, debt would reach just above 120 percent of GDP in the medium run. And if it is fixed at its 2013 level, it would be 118 percent of GDP.

In contrast, emerging economies as a group are not expected to implement large fiscal adjustment over the medium term. As noted earlier, changes in the primary balance are playing almost no role in explaining the debt reduction that is projected in the baseline scenario. The debt path in emerging economies as a group would be almost invariant if the primary balance remains constant at its 2011 level (figure 16.13), with the exception of countries with relatively high debt (e.g., Jordan, Poland, Morocco, and Malaysia).

16.3.2 Increase in Financing Cost
The crisis brought about a structural change in the way markets perceive credit risk among advanced economies, in particular in the euro area. Prior to the crisis, there tended to be little discrimination among bond spreads across advanced economies in Europe. With the crisis, markets started to price in more credit risk, introducing greater volatility into sovereign bond markets and greater differentiation across sov-

Table 16.1
Debt sustainability: Risk assessment matrix

	Relative likelihood		Impact if realized	
	Advanced	Emerging	Advanced	Emerging
Slippage in implementation of fiscal consolidation	*Medium* Many consolidation measures have already been incorporated into legislation. However, the negative impact of austerity on growth and equity could wither public support for adjustment.	*Low* Many countries have not announced sizable fiscal consolidation measures, and in many cases fiscal adjustment needed to bring debt down over the medium-term is relatively small.	*High* Debt ratios would continue rising without sufficient fiscal adjustment. Also, lack of progress in implementing fiscal adjustment could trigger loss of market credibility.	*Low* Debt ratios would continue on a downward path, supported by beneficial debt dynamics.
Higher interest rate	*Medium* Ongoing market uncertainty could push interest rates up for some countries. However, in countries with monetary policy, central banks are expected to maintain easy monetary conditions until growth is on firm footing.	*Medium* Risk is contained by relatively low global interest rates. However, capital markets in emerging economies are thin and less liquid, and are vulnerable to sudden shifts in market sentiment.	*High* Debt ratios would continue rising, in particular in the context of subdued growth.	*Medium* Interest-rate shock would have to be significant to put debt ratios on an upward path. However, if higher interest rates make a dent on growth, then debt dynamics could worsen.

(continued)

Table 16.1
(*continued*)

	Relative likelihood		Impact if realized	
	Advanced	Emerging	Advanced	Emerging
Lower growth	*Medium* Medium-term growth forecasts are already subdued. However, fiscal consolidation could weaken growth further if fiscal multipliers are larger than expected.	*High* Growth in these countries has been above historical trends over the past decade or so, supported in part by financial deepening and rapid credit growth, which may well have generated overly optimistic expectations about potential growth.	*High* Implementing fiscal adjustment and reducing debt to GDP ratios with tepid growth is very challenging.	*High* Debt reduction in the baseline hinges on robust growth. Many countries continue to run primary deficits notwithstanding years of strong growth. A slowdown would compromise debt reduction.
Exchange-rate depreciation	*Low* Most debt is in domestic currency	*High* Shifts in global risk aversion could lead to sudden capital outflows. For commodity exporters, a fall in commodity prices could affect sustainability of public finances for those that followed procyclical policies.	*Low* Most debt is in domestic currency	*High* Many countries have a significant share of debt denominated in foreign currency.
Banking sector recapitalization	*High* Financial sector reform has not been fully implemented. Some countries continue to be exposed to contagion from further escalation of financial stress in the euro area.	*Medium* Sharp credit expansion in some countries during recent years raises concern about asset quality if growth were to underperform.	*High* Banking sector liabilities in advanced economies are high. Compared to the direct cost of financial sector support in previous crises, the cost of the recent crisis has been relatively small so far.	*Medium* Banking sector liabilities in emerging economies are relatively lower than in advanced economies.

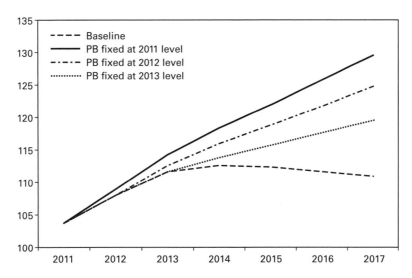

Figure 16.12
Advanced economies government gross debt (percent of GDP)
Sources: IMF, *Fiscal Monitor*, October 2012; authors' calculations

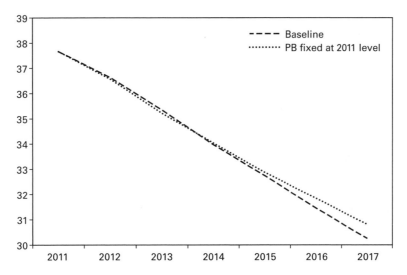

Figure 16.13
Emerging economies government gross debt (percent of GDP)
Sources: IMF, *Fiscal Monitor*, October 2012; authors' calculations

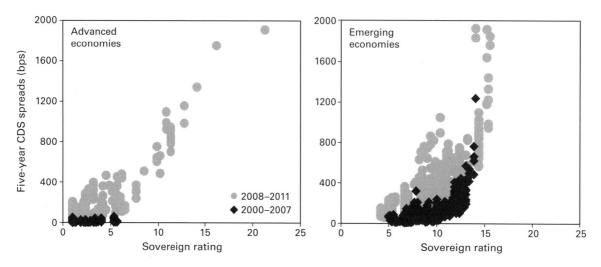

Figure 16.14
Sovereign CDS spreads and ratings. CDS: credit default swap. Sovereign credit ratings and outlooks from Fitch Ratings, Moodys Investor Services, and Standard & Poor's are converted into a linear scale, and then averaged across the three agencies, with AAA equal to 1.
Source: IMF, *Fiscal Monitor*, April 2012

ereigns (figure 16.14). Mirroring sovereign bond markets, rating agencies have also altered their behavior, in particular toward advanced economies. Before the crisis, upward revisions were common place, but since the crisis, downgrades seem to be the norm (figure 16.15).

If high interest rates faced by some countries now become more permanent, debt dynamics would become severely affected. Debt accumulation in advanced economies would in fact accelerate if interest rates over the medium term were higher than in the baseline scenario (figure 16.16). For example, if interest rates were 100 basis points higher than in the baseline every year between 2011 and 2017, and all else remains equal, debt-to-GDP ratios would climb by 6 percentage points to reach 117 percent by 2017, and would fail to stabilize. If interest rates each year were 200 basis points higher than the baseline, then debt ratios would reach 125 percent of GDP in the medium term, an even more worrisome scenario.

Debt reduction in emerging economies would continue, even if at a slower pace, if interest rates picked up (figure 16.17). Even if interest rates increase 300 basis points each year compared to the baseline, debt ratios would be, on average, slightly lower in 2017 than in 2011, given the strong growth assumptions incorporated in the baseline.[8] However, this shock would imply an explosive path for debt in some countries with relatively high initial debt (e.g., Hungary, Jordan, and Malaysia).

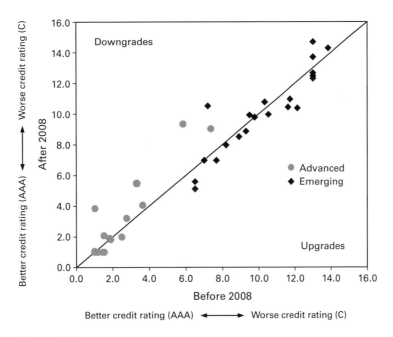

Figure 16.15
Sovereign ratings
Sources: Fitch Ratings; Moody's Analytics; Standard & Poor's; authors' calculations

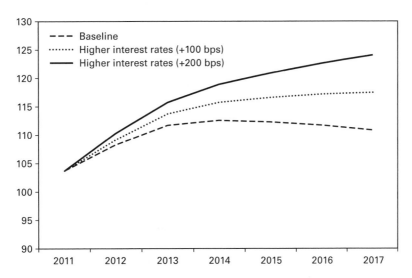

Figure 16.16
Advanced economies government gross debt (percent of GDP)
Sources: IMF, *Fiscal Monitor*, October 2012; authors' calculations

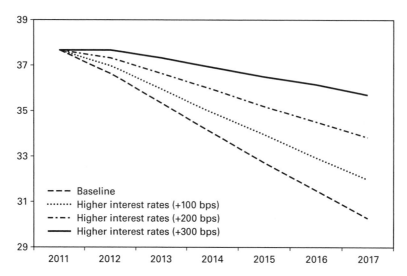

Figure 16.17
Emerging economies government gross debt (percent of GDP)
Sources: IMF, *Fiscal Monitor*, October 2012; authors' calculations

16.3.3 Worsening Growth Outlook

There is a considerable amount of uncertainty regarding the path of real growth in coming years. On one hand, if the potential GDP trend were not as negatively affected by the global crisis as currently assumed in the baseline (and were to return to its pre-crisis trend), economic recovery could take place at a much faster pace than currently envisaged facilitating deleveraging.[9] On the other, as mentioned earlier, high debt stocks could also depress growth prospects, making them lower than current assumptions (see chapter 5 in this volume). The fiscal landscape in advanced economies could be significantly different under alternative growth scenarios (figure 16.18). A permanently lower growth (−1 percentage point each year) in the case of high debt countries would imply an increase in debt of more than 15 percent of GDP in the medium term. In contrast, lower growth in low debt countries would imply lower debt reduction in the medium term. This highlights the importance of growth for high debt countries.

Only a dramatic reduction in growth could jeopardize the envisaged deleveraging in emerging economies (figure 16.19). In the case of high-debt countries, a 1 percentage point lower growth each year coupled with the resulting lower primary balances would imply an increase in debt by 1 percent of GDP in 2017. In the case of low-debt countries, public debt would still go down more than 5 percent of GDP with 1 percent lower growth. Two percentage points lower growth each year would result

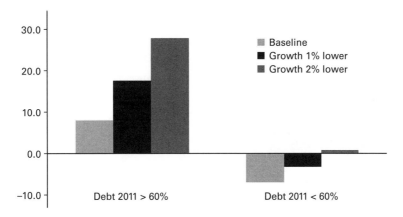

Figure 16.18
Advanced economies increase in debt, 2012 to 2017 (percent of GDP)
Sources: IMF, *Fiscal Monitor*, October 2012; authors' calculations

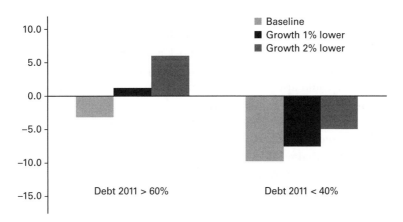

Figure 16.19
Emerging economies increase in debt, 2012 to 2017 (percent of GDP)
Sources: IMF, *Fiscal Monitor*, October 2012; authors' calculations

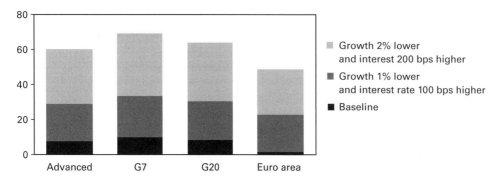

Figure 16.20
Advanced economies increase in debt, 2012 to 2017 (percent of GDP)
Sources: IMF, *Fiscal Monitor*, October 2012; authors' calculations

in a significant increase in public debt in the case of high-debt countries raising fiscal sustainability concerns. Low-debt countries would still look good.

16.3.4 Increase in Financing Cost Combined with Worsening Growth Outlook
So far we analyzed an interest-rate shock and a growth slowdown in isolation. However, in practice, both such shocks are likely to hit a country simultaneously. Moreover there could also be interactions, as slower growth leads to a higher debt stock, which results in higher interest rates and thus still slower growth and higher debt.[10]

Figure 16.20 shows that a combination of lower growth (1 percentage point) and higher financing costs (100 bps) in advanced countries could result in an increase in public debt of almost 30 percent of GDP in the medium term, with the debt ratio continuing on an upward trend over the medium term. The increase would be more dramatic if growth is 2 percentage points lower and interest rates are 200 bps higher since public debt would increase 60 percent of GDP in the medium term.

Figure 16.21 shows that a combination of lower growth (1 percentage point) and higher interest costs (100 bps) would bring to an end the deleveraging process envisaged in emerging economies. The public debt-to-GDP ratio would in fact increase slightly in the medium term. Not surprisingly, public debt would increase by 10 percent of GDP in the medium term in a more pessimistic scenario.

16.3.5 Exchange Rate Risk
An additional source of risk over the medium term is related to exchange rate volatility, especially in emerging economies.[11] An exchange rate shock might materialize as a result of a financial turmoil in some advanced economies that could lead to an increase in global risk aversion and capital outflows from emerging economies, or as a result of rising monetary policy rates in advanced economies over the medium term

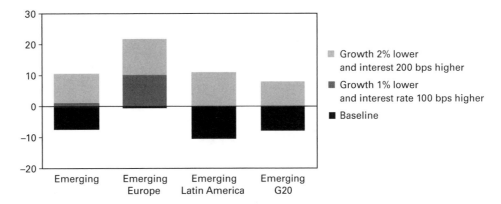

Figure 16.21
Advanced economies increase in debt, 2012 to 2017 (percent of GDP)
Sources: IMF, *Fiscal Monitor*, October 2012; authors' calculations

as central banks unwind monetary stimulus. Another driver could be a fall in commodity prices that could raise questions about the sustainability of public finances in countries that followed procyclical policies. The projected downward trend in public debt in emerging economies with a significant share of foreign currency debt (at least 20 percent of total debt in 2010) would be reversed in the event of an exchange rate shock (figure 16.22). In the most extreme case, where the exchange rate depreciates by 30 percent, the debt ratio in the medium term would be 24 percent of GDP higher than in the baseline. An exchange rate shock is less relevant in the case of advanced economies since only a couple of them issue foreign currency denominated debt.

16.3.6 Risks from Financial Sector

Financial sector weaknesses that led to the global crisis have not been fully resolved. Therefore countries continue to face significant risks if an unexpected shock was to force governments to step in once again to support the financial sector. Compared to the direct cost of financial sector support in previous crises, the cost of the recent crisis has been relatively small so far: the average net fiscal outlay is below 5 percent of GDP, and one-third of the support has already been repaid. However, explicit contingent liabilities in guarantee schemes are, in some cases, much larger than the direct support itself. Implicit contingent liabilities could also arise if the economic outlook deteriorates further, weakening private sector balance sheets.[12] Therefore debt accumulation in advanced economies could skyrocket if contingent liabilities from the rescue of the financial system were to materialize, given that banking sector liabilities in advanced economies were, on average, around 55 percent of GDP in 2011 (figure 16.23).[13]

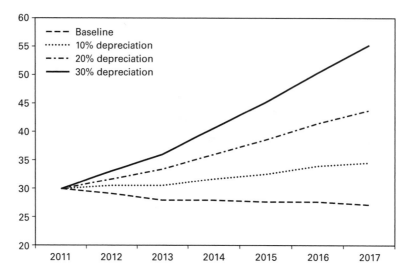

Figure 16.22
Emerging economies government gross debt (percent of GDP)
Sources: IMF, *Fiscal Monitor*, October 2012; authors' calculations

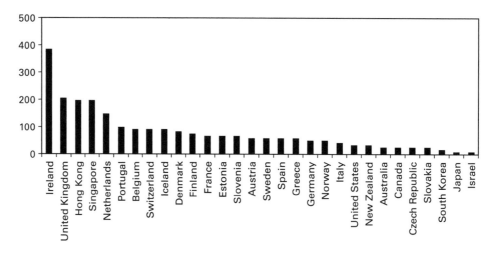

Figure 16.23
Advanced economies banking sector liabilities, 2011 (percent of GDP)
Sources: Bank of International Settlements; authors' estimates

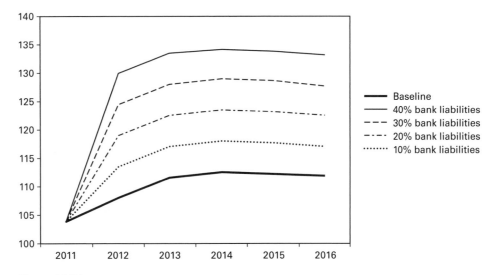

Figure 16.24
Advanced economies government gross debt (percent of GDP)
Sources: IMF, *Fiscal Monitor*, October 2012; authors' calculations

The scenarios illustrate the debt path assuming that the government has to support banks to meet a certain fraction of its liabilities. In countries where the size of the banking system is significant (e.g., Ireland, United Kingdom, Greece, Singapore, and Netherlands), the impact on public debt is higher (figure 16.24). In emerging economies, the liabilities of the banking system were, on average, around 10 percent of GDP, making the analysis of this shock less interesting.

16.4 Conclusions

Fiscal positions worsened dramatically with the global crisis, especially in advanced economies, as revenues contracted and expenditures claimed a higher share of GDP. While fiscal positions are expected to improve as temporary factors unwind and countries implement adjustment packages, many countries are not expected to recover to their pre-crisis fiscal position over the medium term. Revenues as a percentage of GDP are expected to recover, but to a lower overall nominal level as potential GDP is not expected to recover to its pre-crisis trend. The rise in expenditure to GDP during the crisis is not fully reversed, owing to lower expected potential GDP and new spending pressures, in particular the increase in debt-servicing costs and the upward trend in health and pension spending linked to an aging population.

The crisis left countries facing important risks that could derail their consolidation plans. Medium-term debt sustainability is now subject to greater uncertainty stemming from macroeconomic volatility—of interest rates, growth, and the exchange rate—policy implementation, and large contingent liabilities.

Until debt is solidly on a downward trend, advanced economies need to remain committed to medium-term consolidation. While the appropriate pace of adjustment in the short run is country specific (depending on market access and the risks to growth), there is much to be gained from strengthening medium-term plans that include both revenue enhancing measures and expenditure reforms that address rising age-related spending pressures.

While medium-term debt dynamics in emerging economies are more favorable than in advanced economies, they hinge on sustained strong growth over the medium term. These countries should therefore aim to rebuild their fiscal policy buffers (pacing adjustment as necessary in the short run) to address potential negative shocks down the road.

Notes

1. A debate is ongoing about the impact of the crisis on potential output, with some authors more skeptical about the negative impact of the crisis on potential growth (e.g., see Paul Krugman's post at http://krugman.blogs.nytimes.com/2010/05/15/misimformation/?_r=0).

2. Hysteresis effects can occur when long unemployment spells cause a permanent destruction of human capital, leading to an irreversible rise in the nonaccelerating inflation rate of unemployment (NAIRU).

3. Note that the October 2012 *Fiscal Monitor* assumes sizable expenditure cuts as part of fiscal consolidation plans in 2012 and 2013.

4. Fiscal forecasts in the October 2012 *Fiscal Monitor* assume no further policy action beyond 2013 and therefore could overestimate the size of fiscal deficits over the medium term.

5. Kumar and Woo (2010), Reinhart and Rogoff (2010), and Cecchetti et al. (2011) all find that beyond a certain threshold (about 80 to 90 percent of GDP) higher public debt lowers potential growth. However, Panizza and Presbitero (2012) find no evidence of an effect of public debt on medium-term growth. For further discussion, see chapter 3 in this volume.

6. IMF (2002) suggest that the probability of a debt crisis in emerging economies is much higher when total external debt (public and private) exceeds 40 percent of GDP. Reinhart and Rogoff (2010) find that beyond 60 percent of GDP, external debt has a significant negative effect on growth.

7. IMF (2011b) presents a useful framework in which to think about these issues.

8. Escolano et al. (2011) document that emerging economies have benefited for some time from negative interest rates. However, as financial markets become more developed this situation is unlikely to persist, which means that interest rates are likely to be underestimated in the baseline.

9. Irons and Bivens (2010) emphasize the key role of GDP growth in reducing the public debt-to-GDP ratio in United States economic history. IMF (2011b) and Abbas et al. (2011) also find that in post–World War II nondefault debt reductions were associated with notice-

ably large growth–interest differential components (arising from 4 to 5 percent growth and negative real interest rates).

10. See Cottarelli and Jaramillo (2012) for a discussion of the feedback loops between fiscal policy and growth in the short and long run.

11. Large emerging economies and smaller emerging economies in Asia tend to have undervalued exchanged rates according to IMF (2012b). However, several emerging economies in Europe and Latin America may have overvalued exchange rates and therefore exchange rate shock may be relevant.

12. See IMF (2012a).

13. Laeven and Valencia (2008) find that the fiscal costs, net of recoveries, associated with banking crisis management can be substantial, averaging about 13.3 percent of GDP, and can be as high as 55.1 percent of GDP.

References

Abbas, S. M. A., N. Belhocine, A. El-Ganainy, and M. Horton. 2011. Historical patterns and dynamics of public debt—Evidence from a new database. *IMF Economic Review* 59: 717–42.

Cecchetti, S. G., M. S. Mohanty, and F. Zampolli. 2011. The real effects of debt. Working paper 352. BIS, Basel.

Cottarelli, C., and L. Jaramillo. 2012. Walking hand in hand: Fiscal policy and growth in advanced economies. Working paper 12/137. IMF, Washington, DC.

DeLong, J. B., and L. Summers. 2012. Fiscal policy in a depressed economy. Spring 2012 Conference on the Brookings Papers on Economic Activity (BPEA), available at: http://www.brookings.edu/~/media/Files/Programs/ES/BPEA/2012_spring_bpea_papers/2012_spring_BPEA_delongsummers.pdf.

Escolano, J., A. Shabunina, and J. Woo. 2011. The puzzle of persistently negative interest rate–growth differentials: Financial repression or income catch-up? Working paper 11/260. IMF, Washington, DC.

European Commission. 2009. Impact of the current economic and financial crisis on potential output. Occasional paper 49. EC, Brussels.

International Monetary Fund. 2002. Assessing sustainability. Available at: http://www.imf.org/external/np/pdr/sus/2002/eng/052802.htm.

International Monetary Fund. 2009. *World Economic Outlook, October 2009: Sustaining the Recovery, World Economic and Financial Surveys*. Washington, DC: IMF.

International Monetary Fund. 2011b. Modernizing the framework for fiscal policy and public debt sustainability analysis. Available at: http://www.imf.org/external/np/pp/eng/2011/080511.pdf.

International Monetary Fund. 2012a. *Fiscal Monitor October 2012: Taking Stock: A Progress Report on Fiscal Adjustment, World Economic and Financial Surveys*. Washington, DC: IMF.

International Monetary Fund. 2012b. Pilot external sector report. Available at: www.imf.org/external/np/pp/eng/2012/070212.pdf.

Irons, J., and J. Bivens. 2010. Government debt and economic growth: Overreaching claims of debt "threshold" suffer from theoretical and empirical flaws. Briefing paper 271. EPI, Washington, DC.

Kumar, M., and J. Woo. 2010. Public debt and growth. IMF Working paper 10/174. IMF, Washington, DC.

Laeven, L., and F. Valencia. 2008. Systemic banking crises: A new database. Working paper 08/224. IMF, Washington, DC.

Mauro, P., R. Romeu, A. Binder, and A. Zaman. 2013. A modern history of fiscal prudence and profligacy. Working paper 13/5. IMF, Washington, DC.

Panizza, Ugo, and A. F. Presbitero. 2012. Public debt and economic growth: Is there a causal effect? Working paper 168. POLIS, Brussels.

Reinhart, C., and K. Rogoff. 2010. Growth in a time of debt. Working paper 15639. NBER, Cambridge, MA.

Romer, C. 2012. Fiscal policy in the crisis: Lessons and policy implications. Available at: http://emlab.berkeley.edu/~cromer/Lessons%20for%20Fiscal%20Policy.pdf.

17

Escaping High Debt: The Narrow Path Ahead

Lorenzo Forni and Marialuz Moreno Badia

17.1 Introduction

Previous chapters have highlighted the challenges faced by advanced economies with gross public debt increasing by more than 30 percent of GDP in the wake of the financial crisis. Although progress has been made since 2010 in adjusting fiscal balances, weak growth and downside risks restrict the room for maneuver of policy makers. Moreover some countries have been subject to market pressures leading to spikes in sovereign risk premia. Market confidence in these economies is indeed being currently sapped by what is perceived as an unsustainable level of public debt. In these countries the path to fully restore market confidence appears to be narrow. However, it is also a challenge for countries enjoying very easy financing conditions but still having large imbalances (e.g., the United States and Japan).

This chapter analyzes what should be the goal of fiscal adjustment and to what extent other nonconventional measures can help in restoring and maintaining market confidence in advanced economies. Section 17.2 addresses the reasons why fiscal adjustment cannot be delayed, and section 17.3 quantifies the size of the challenge. Section 17.4 focuses on the role of fiscal policy and, in particular, the speed and composition of adjustment. Section 17.5 explores whether other policies (beyond the fiscal arena) can support consolidation efforts, and section 17.6 concludes.

17.2 The Effects of Fragile Fiscal Positions

Advanced economies can be broadly divided into two groups based on the market assessment of sovereign risk. On the one hand, countries with high sovereign spreads tend to have high debt and deficit levels (figure 17.1). On the other, there is a group of countries that enjoy low borrowing costs—the two most notable examples being the United States and Japan—despite having high debt and deficits as well. In the particular case of the United States and Japan, markets have so far absorbed large

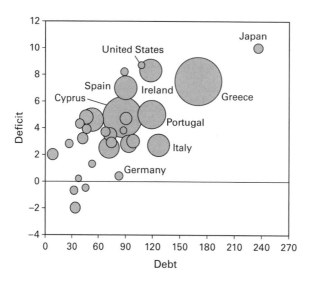

Figure 17.1
General government deficit, debt, and spreads, 2012 (percent of GDP). Bubble size represents five-year credit default swap spreads as of August 2012.
Sources: Markit; IMF staff estimates and projections

increases in public debt with ease thanks to a very accommodative monetary stance and amid expectations that fiscal adjustment will eventually take place.

Overall, the differences in yields between countries such as the United States and Japan, on one side, and the peripheral European countries on the other are related to a range of factors. First, the former have the status of reserve currency and have a monetary policy authority that intervenes heavily in the sovereign debt market. By contrast, the latter do not enjoy monetary sovereignty and therefore their bond market can suffer from runs that significantly reduce market liquidity (De Grauwe and Ji 2012). Also sovereign yields of advanced countries like the United States and Japan tend to be low if assessed against their historical relationship with fundamentals, while based on the same criteria those of peripheral euro area members seem to be too high (Di Cesare et al. 2012; Poghosyan 2012). Capital flight out of peripheral European countries into "safe havens" has indeed been the norm since the onset of the financial crisis, partly driven by uncertainties regarding the overall European governance and, despite recent improvements, the yield differentials and credit default swap (CDS) spreads between the two groups of countries remain large (figure 17.2).

A central bank can always step in and buy government bonds in order to maintain the market liquid and yields contained—thereby decreasing the likelihood of sovereign default. However, it is unclear how such a script would play out in the medium

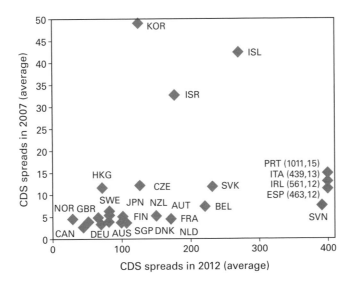

Figure 17.2
Sovereign CDS spreads, 2007 to 2012 (basis points). Data for 2012 represent the average from January until October 2012.
Source: Markit

to long run. The fiscal theory of the price level, for example, argues that when the central bank passively accommodates the development of fiscal policy, inflation expectations become guided by the fiscal authority. At that stage it might become very difficult for the central bank to steer inflation. In such a context, nominal rates can easily increase more than expected inflation, as market participants would ask for a premium due to higher inflation uncertainty and possibly exchange rate volatility. Thus monetary policy can buy some time for the fiscal authority to adjust, but cannot be the solution.

17.3 What Should Be the Goal?

The standard neoclassical theory of debt (Barro 1979) derives a very clear result about the optimal long-run level of debt: there is no such a thing. On the one hand, optimal taxation requires that tax rates should be kept as smooth as possible over time, which means debt must act as a shock absorber. When national income is unusually high, the government should run a surplus and decrease its debt, and vice versa. Under this optimal fiscal policy, the debt level drifts over time with no tendency to return to any particular long-run level. Tax rates, on the other hand, vary but just enough to pay for the change in interest payments.

Crucially, Barro's model disregards some aspects that seem to be particularly relevant at the current juncture. In particular, excessive debt levels are associated with slower growth and higher borrowing costs in the medium term. The effect on growth has been discussed in chapter 5 in this volume. Higher borrowing costs are due to the classical crowding out of private capital from government borrowing (Ardagna, Caselli, and Lane 2007; T. Laubach 2009; Baldacci and Kumar 2010; Alper and Forni 2011). If we allow for the possibility of sovereign default, high debt levels will also increase sovereign spreads and possibly bring a country to a sudden stop in foreign financing. Therefore reducing excessive indebtedness should be a priority. Box 17.1 discusses the trade-off between the costs related to the fiscal contraction necessary to bring down the debt level and the long-term benefits of permanently reducing it.

In general, the crisis has reinforced the view that the current debt levels can be dangerous and that countries should make all efforts to bring public debt to a

Box 17.1
Is reducing public debt beneficial?

An assessment of the macroeconomic effects of permanently reducing the debt level needs to take into account both the short-term cost of the fiscal adjustment and the long-term benefits of having a lower level of debt. The latter brings about smaller levels of interest payments—which frees resources that can be used for tax cuts or spending increases—as well as lower long-term interest rates reflecting the increase in domestic savings. Tax cuts coupled with a reduction in long-term interest rates can, in turn, support economic activity.

To quantify the long-term gains of reducing public debt, Leigh et al. (2010) use the global integrated monetary and fiscal model (GIMF) and assume that the decrease in interest expenditures translate into a reduction in labor income taxes. Their simulations suggest that GDP would be lower than in the baseline for three years before rising above the baseline forever. Using a similar general equilibrium model, Forni et al. (2010) show that tax distortions can be significant (especially in some European countries) and that cuts to public expenditures that are large enough to allow for reductions in both tax rates and debt ratios can have limited negative effects on GDP. In particular, reductions in tax rates boost households' disposable income and ease distortions, leading to an increase in private consumption and investment that partly offsets the drag on GDP due to the expenditure cuts.

Although, on the one hand, these models suggest that permanent reductions in public debt are beneficial in the long term, short-term costs may be underestimated given the current constraints in the conduct of monetary policy and the fact that many countries have to implement fiscal consolidation at the same time. On the other hand, these studies may not fully capture the increased resilience of the economy to shocks after a reduction in the debt level.

safe level.[1] The latter can be defined as the one that the tax authority can reasonably sustain even in the face of significant adverse shocks. Nevertheless, assessing what is a "safe" level of debt is not straightforward in practice. First of all, the safe level will depend on a variety of country-specific characteristics. One important of such characteristics is the starting level of debt. Countries with a very high level will have to trade off the cost of adjusting with the benefit of having a lower level. Second, countries are subject to different types and magnitude of shocks (see chapter 1 in this volume). Third, the size of the automatic stabilizers and preferences over how much to use discretionary fiscal policy as a countercyclical tool vary across countries. In this regard countries that, ceteris paribus, intend to use fiscal policy more heavily as a countercyclical tool should aim for lower levels of debt. Finally, the exposure to contingent liabilities, especially in the banking sector, will be different from country to country. It is beyond the scope of this chapter to recommend a specific debt target. However, it is clear from the above discussion that many advanced countries should aim at reducing substantially their current debt level.

Table 17.1 presents some benchmarks that can help guide our thinking on this issue. The first one is the primary balance that countries would need to reach just to stabilize the debt at the current (2013) level (column 5). This is a sort of lower bound on the adjustment effort. The second benchmark is the primary balance that would be needed to bring the debt ratio to 60 percent by 2030 (column 4). This should be considered an ambitious target. In particular, it might require an improvement in the primary balance difficult to achieve over the medium term, also considering the weak cyclical position.[2] A reasonable target for the cyclically adjusted primary balance (CAPB) would likely be in between these two values. In this line, there is an increasing focus in the policy debate on attaining some given fiscal balance (e.g., a budget balance) that would lead to a decline of the debt ratio over time rather than targeting a specific debt level (IMF 2013a).[3]

According to these benchmarks, a number of countries should adjust their primary balance by more than 2 percentage points as compared to the 2013 CAPB level in order to stabilize their debt. Among these, Japan is an outlier requiring an adjustment of over 10 percentage points of GDP. The required adjustment to reduce the debt to 60 percent is even more demanding. But what is most striking is that the level of primary balance that these countries have to attain (and maintain) exceeds the best historical performance. In particular, since the 1950s the distribution of the maximum ten-year moving average primary surpluses shows a median of 3.25 percent of GDP among advanced economies (IMF 2013b) while the required CAPB for those countries with debt above 90 percent is close to 5 percent of GDP on average. These figures give a sense of the dimension of the challenge.

Table 17.1
Advanced economies: Illustrative adjustment needs (percent of GDP)

	2013			Illustrative fiscal adjustment strategy to achieve debt target in 2030			
	Gross debt[a]	CAPB[b]	Age-related spending, 2013–2030	CAPB in 2020–2030[c]	Required adjustment 2013–2020	Required adjustment and age-related spending, 2013–2030	Debt stabilizing CAPB[d]
	(1)	(2)	(3)	(4)	(4) - (2)	(4) + (3) - (2)	(5)
Austria	74.4	0.5	4.1	1.3	0.8	4.9	0.4
Belgium	100.9	1.1	6.4	4.0	2.8	9.3	1.7
Canada	36.5	-2.3	3.6	0.5	2.8	6.5	0.0
Denmark	47.1	2.3	1.6	0.0	-2.3	-0.8	0.1
Finland	58.0	0.2	4.2	-0.1	-0.3	3.9	-0.2
France	93.5	-0.7	1.0	3.0	3.7	4.7	0.7
Germany	80.4	2.2	2.1	1.2	-1.0	1.1	0.6
Greece	175.7	4.8	1.2	6.8	2.1	3.3	-0.9
Iceland	93.2	2.8	1.4	2.6	-0.3	1.2	1.3
Ireland	123.3	-0.3	1.5	6.0	6.3	7.7	2.8
Italy	132.3	4.7	0.0	6.8	2.1	2.2	3.3
Japan	139.9	-8.6	1.6	6.7	15.3	16.8	1.8
Netherlands	74.4	1.9	6.3	1.8	-0.1	6.2	0.4
Portugal	123.6	1.1	1.2	6.0	4.9	6.1	2.5
Spain	93.7	-1.4	1.4	4.7	6.1	7.5	1.5
Sweden	42.2	-0.2	0.9	-0.2	0.0	0.8	-0.3
Switzerland	48.2	1.2	5.8	-0.5	-1.7	4.1	0.0
United Kingdom	92.1	-1.0	2.0	4.0	5.0	7.0	1.0
United States	106.0	-1.3	6.7	3.7	5.0	11.7	0.6

Sources: IMF, April 2013 *Fiscal Monitor,* and authors' calculations.
Note: The CAPB required to reduce debt and its comparison to the 2013 CAPB is a standardized calculation, and policy recommendations for individual countries would require a case-by-case assessment.
a. Gross general government debt, except in the cases of Canada and Japan, for which net debt ratios are used.
b. Cyclically adjusted primary balance (CAPB) is reported in percent of nominal GDP (in contrast to the conventional definition in percent of potential GDP). CAPB is defined as cyclically adjusted balance (CAB) plus gross interest expenditure, except in the cases of Canada and Japan, for which CAPB is defined as CAB plus net interest payments. Structural balances are used instead of CAB for Sweden and the United States.
c. CAPB needed to bring the debt ratio down to 60 percent in 2030, or to stabilize debt at the end-2013 level by 2030, if the respective debt-to-GDP ratio is less than 60 percent. For Japan, a net debt target of 80 percent of GDP is assumed, which corresponds to a target of about 200 percent of GDP for gross debt. The CAPB is assumed to change in line with *Fiscal Monitor* projections in 2011–14 and adjust gradually from 2015 until 2020; thereafter it is maintained constant until 2030. These calculations assume that the initial country-specific interest rate–growth differentials (based on *Fiscal Monitor* projections) converge over time to model-based country-specific levels with the speed of adjustment based on empirical estimates of the effect of public debt on the interest rate (Poghosyan 2012) and growth rates obtained from *Fiscal Monitor* projections for 2018. The assumption on interest rate–growth differentials for countries with IMF/EU supported programs and without market access (Greece, Portugal) is drawn from their debt sustainability analyses. The interest rate–growth differential is assumed to follow the endogenous adjustment path determined by debt levels from 2019 in the case of Portugal.
d. The cyclically adjusted primary balance (CAPB) needed to stabilize debt at 2013 levels.

17.4 The Role of Fiscal Policy

In this section we discuss how policy makers should approach these significant fiscal challenges. Specifically, we lay down six important principles that a successful fiscal consolidation strategy should follow. The first three are focused on the short-run challenges, while the second three refer to the long run.

1. *In the current weak economic environment, fiscal policy has to walk a fine line, proceeding with gradual but steady adjustments except in the presence of market pressures.* Fiscal multipliers tend to be high in recessions and in the presence of a liquidity trap (see IMF 2012a; also box 17.2). Thus large fiscal contractions can undermine growth and lead to short-run increases in the debt-to-GDP ratio, which may raise markets' concerns. In fact, recent evidence shows that large fiscal tightening can lead to an increase in spreads (see appendix in Cottarelli and Jaramillo 2012). On the other hand, fiscal adjustments cannot be too timid as promises of future adjustment are unlikely to be sufficient to ensure fiscal credibility. Moreover countries under market pressure do not have the luxury of choice and they will need to proceed at a faster pace.

2. *Fiscal targets should be set in cyclically adjusted terms within a clear medium-term plan.* Commitments expressed in terms of headline deficit-to-GDP risk giving way to vicious cycles where fiscal contraction reduces output and in turn calls for more retrenchment. Leaving aside short-term considerations, a budget deficit, even if due to a recession, will add up to the public debt. Therefore it is essential that the upward pressures on the debt be compensated in good times in order to avoid introducing upward biases in debt dynamics. For example, the German debt-brake rule aims exactly at avoiding this upward bias and it's a good reference of how rules can support an effective use of fiscal policy.

3. *In terms of composition, fiscal adjustment in advanced economies should rely primarily on reducing high levels of expenditures rather than on tax increases* (for a detailed discussion, see IMF 2010). In most advanced countries the level of taxation is high and the medium-term goal should be to reduce tax distortions. This can be achieved by broadening the tax bases (i.e., reducing deductions and tax expenditures) and decreasing tax rates or moving toward less distortionary taxes. A thorough revision of spending will also be necessary. In some countries, especially in Europe, this will provide an opportunity to reduce some of the spending increases approved before the crisis, especially related to public employees and pensions (see figure 17.3).

The three principles above are important elements to navigate in the short term, but it is essential to look beyond the immediate challenges. No success can be expected if policy makers do not build a medium-term course that is sound, fair, and

Box 17.2
Key features of past fiscal adjustments: Some lessons for the future

Recent episodes of large fiscal adjustments can provide some lessons on what are the factors contributing to a successful fiscal consolidation.

IMF (2012b) looked at eight large consolidation plans in European countries (Greece, Iceland, Ireland, Latvia, Lithuania, Portugal, Romania, and Spain) developed in 2009. Given the large size of the government and the collapse of revenues in the aftermath of the global financial crisis, the adjustment in these countries focused on spending. Nevertheless, the original plans experienced slippages due to three factors: first, growth proved to be lower than expected; second, in some countries large contingent liabilities materialized; and third, the initial fiscal position proved to be worse than initially estimated due to statistical revisions of past data. Mauro (2011) finds similar conclusions looking at the experiences of fiscal consolidation among G7 and European countries over the last twenty years.

Several factors explain the growth underperformance in recent adjustment plans. First, consolidation efforts have been large and concentrated on expenditure. The short-run effects of expenditure cuts tend indeed to be larger than those of equivalent revenue increases. Second, evidence suggests that short-run fiscal multipliers are larger in recessions than in expansions (Baum et al. 2012). This is because during periods of weak economic activity, monetary policy is constrained by the fact that interest rates are at the zero lower bound and therefore cannot be further reduced to accommodate the fiscal contraction; at the same time a larger number of firms and households might be liquidity constrained and be more dependent on government support and transfers; moreover some of the countries implementing the fiscal consolidation could not rely on devaluations, as they are part of a monetary union. Therefore the current state of the economy suggests caution in implementing fiscal consolidations. At the same time there is evidence that adjustments tilted toward expenditures rather than revenues have a higher likelihood of not being reversed and tend to be followed by higher economic activity in the medium term (Alesina and Ardagna 2010), and that tax increases can be very harmful to growth (Romer and Romer 2010).

This evidence suggests that given current circumstances, the speed of the adjustment should be moderate. Adjusting on the spending side seems to be the right course of action for countries with big governments, whereas part of the adjustment should come from revenues in those countries that have lower levels of taxation. In any case, fiscal adjustments should be designed and implemented with a view to minimize the negative effects on economic activity. First, reforming entitlement spending, especially pension and health, allows containing future expenditures without affecting too heavily private consumption in the short run. Similarly better targeting of social expenditures and of tax deductions in order to make sure that needy are receiving most support, it is not only the right thing to do from an ethical point of view, but it should also lead to a restraint in expenditures that has moderate effects on growth. Containing expenditures should also create space to reduce some taxes. Tax distortions can be reduced without leading to revenue losses by broadening the tax bases (i.e., reducing deductions and tax expenditures) and decreasing tax rates, or moving toward less distortionary taxes, for example, indirect and property levies.

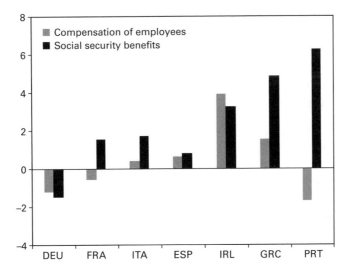

Figure 17.3
Spending increase in selected euro area countries, 2000 to 2008 (percent of GDP). Social security benefits are payable in cash and in kind to households by social security schemes, and include, for example, sickness, maternity, unemployment, retirement, and survivor's pension, death benefits. The dynamic of compensation of employees reflect also reclassifications. For example, Portugal in 2006 and 2007 has reclassified some hospitals outside the general government. This partly explains the drop in compensations shown in the figure.
Sources: IMF, *World Economic Outlook*; authors'calculations

sustainable. Here are three other important factors of a successful fiscal adjustment strategy.

4. *Reform efforts on age-related spending to make it more equitable and targeted should continue.*[4] The adjustment needs reported in table 17.1 account for age-related spending. Although reforms have been widespread in the last few years (IMF 2012b), more has to be done. Improving targeting can be a way of containing cost while preserving the level of services. Moreover particular care should be used to protect the most vulnerable, as fiscal adjustments that are seen as unfair are unlikely to be sustainable.

5. *Reviving growth is essential and fiscal policy can contribute to improve activity and employment.* The effect of growth on fiscal sustainability is increasingly recognized as essential, by providing resources to accommodate some of the structural increases in expenditures and to reduce the burden of high debt levels. Product market and employment reforms remain the key to sustain growth and employment. There are many ways in which also fiscal policy can support economic activity and employment (Cottarelli and Keen 2012).

6. *Reforms to create credible fiscal institutions are important.* Evidence shows that fiscal prudence and fiscal institutions complement each other (see chapter 18 in this volume). Moreover good fiscal institutions can enhance the credibility of medium-term fiscal plans, creating fiscal space in the short run when it is needed. However, institutional changes take time, and therefore it is important that the reform momentum be maintained.

These six principles are surely not exhaustive and by any means they represent a challenging agenda. It will require hard work and persistence on the part of the policy makers to implement them even partially. But they are essential steps in order to set advanced economies on a sounder ground.

17.5 The Role of Other Policies

What contributions can other policies bring to the fiscal adjustments process? This section explores other tools (some more conventional than others) that have been used in the past to support fiscal adjustment.

17.5.1 Asset and Liability Management

The first standard tool to consider is the asset and liability management. The overall objective is to minimize the risk of the government being unable to service its obligations without unrealistically large adjustments in its revenues and expenditures (Rawdanowicz et al. 2011). In practice, it means choosing the size and structure of government assets and liabilities taking into account asset yields and debt servicing costs.[5] This can support fiscal consolidation through two channels: first, asset management can help provide liquidity and reduce the stock of debt (through disposals); and second, by choosing the appropriate debt instruments, liability management can lead to lower debt service. Variations in strategy across countries can be justified given different assessment of trade-offs and market conditions. However, from the data it appears that there is scope to manage government balance sheets more actively in some countries, particularly on the asset side. Let's look at each component in turn.

Asset Management

On the asset side, one should distinguish between financial and nonfinancial assets:

- *Financial assets* (FAs) include currency and deposits, loans granted by the government, securities other than shares, shares and other equity, insurance and technical reserves, and other accounts receivable. In some cases there has been a substantial increase in FAs since 2008 as a result of the recapitalization or takeover of financial institutions during the crisis—for example, in Germany and the Netherlands (Hartwig Lojsch et al. 2011, sec. 3.3).[6] In any case, the level of

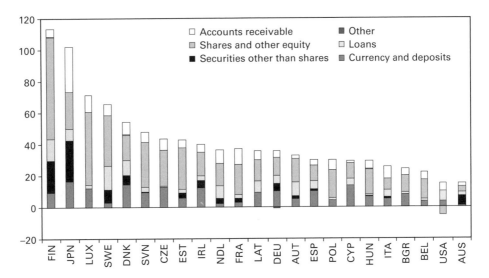

Figure 17.4
General government financial assets in 2012 (percent of GDP). For Japan, data as of 2010; France and Germany, data as of 2011. For all other countries, stock as of end of third quarter of 2012 (percent of GDP). "Other" includes monetary gold and Special Drawing Rights, financial derivatives, and insurance technical reserves.
Source: IMF, Government Finance Statistics

FAs differs considerably among advanced countries. The asset ratios are high in Finland, Japan, and Luxembourg (above 70 percent of GDP) while in most of the other countries they are below 40 percent of GDP (figure 17.4). In terms of composition, total securities are the largest category for most advanced countries, accounting for nearly half of financial assets on average.

- *Nonfinancial assets* (NFAs), in contrast, are stores of value that are used in the production of goods and services or that provide property income (System of National Accounts 2008). They are generally divided into produced assets (mostly inventories, valuables, and fixed assets; e.g., buildings) and nonproduced tangible (e.g., land and subsoil resources) and nontangible (e.g., leases and licenses) assets. Notwithstanding data shortcomings,[7] it appears that produced assets—mostly buildings and structures—account for more than 65 percent of NFAs, and nonproduced assets consist almost entirely of land (Bova et al. 2013). Where data are available, it shows that NFAs are large and have grown over time. Moreover, in most countries, NFAs are larger than FAs on average by a ratio of 1.2 to 1.3 (figure 17.5).

If assets are held together with debt, it means that they are effectively debt financed. With the exception of Sweden and Norway, gross debt exceeds financial

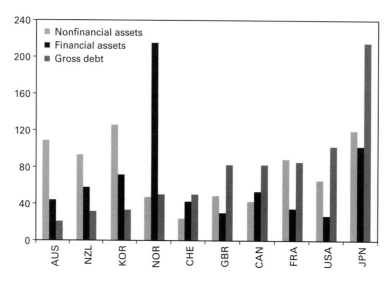

Figure 17.5
Key indicators of the general government balance sheet, 2010 (percent of GDP). Data for Switzerland are for 2009; data for France, the United Kingdom, and the United States are for 2011.
Sources: Eurostat; Organisation for Economic Co-operation and Development; IMF, Government Finance Statistics; IMF staff estimates and projections

assets by a relatively high margin. This bears the question of whether it makes sense for governments to have a higher gearing in order to finance those assets. A key parameter to look at in order to answer that question is the implicit rate of return on financial assets, but given data constraints, we focus on the general government interest revenue instead.[8] On average, interest receipts in advanced economies amounted to about 1 percent of GDP in 2012 or an implicit interest rate of about 2 percent. This compares to an implicit rate above 3 percent on government debt, suggesting that, in some cases, the cost of debt could be higher than the returns from financial assets. Thus, from a purely financial point of view, there might be a case for divestment or at least for increasing the risk-adjusted return of those assets.[9] Three options should be considered for that purpose:

• *Privatization.* The sale of government assets can be used more actively than currently is the case to help reduce gross debt. This would also boost economic growth provided that the regulatory framework addresses potential market failures. The argument is that public firms may distort relative prices and competition. Indeed empirical evidence points to divested firms being more efficient than public ones particularly in competitive industries (e.g., see Megginson and Netter 2001). Nevertheless, under current market conditions it may not be feasible to unwind equity participations in the short term. First, given its own deleverag-

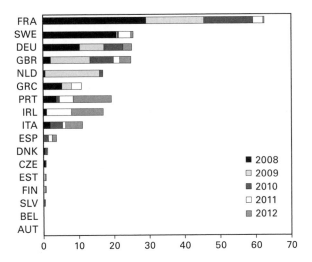

Figure 17.6
Privatization revenues (US$ billion)
Sources: Megginson and Bortolotti (2011); Megginson (2013); Privatization Barometer

ing needs, the private sector may not be in a position to absorb large privatizations without significant discounts. Second, disposing of stakes in banks can only happen after the restructuring of the financial sector is well underway and this may take some time. Finally, liquidating assets may be politically challenging given that subnational governments and social security funds own a large share of assets in some countries (e.g., Canada, Germany, and the United States). Even with these constraints, privatization may ultimately be the best course of action as it could reduce transfers to unprofitable enterprises and eliminate quasi-fiscal operations that end up increasing public debt (see Davis et al. 2000). This is in fact an important pillar in some recent IMF-supported programs. For example, Ireland was the leader among EU countries in privatization during 2011 (figure 17.6).

- *Securitization.* This avenue does not involve the disposal of a government asset but allows to immediately cash in a stream of revenue pledges (e.g., securitization of lottery receipts or future payments of employers' social security contributions). This option has been used in the past by countries facing financing difficulties or unable to access the market. However, securitization could give rise to an increase in the cost of funding as it implies a future revenue loss, and thus higher deficits down the road. Nevertheless, some argue that it can improve the governance and efficiency of the asset used to back the issue as the new creditor may be more aggressive to recoup costs (see UBS Investment Research 2011).

Also securitization puts a price on the government asset, which can be used as a benchmark to decide on whether it is worthwhile to sale that asset in the future. But, for the full benefits of securitization to be realized, the accounting of the transaction should be transparent so that there is not a perception that deficits/debt have been artificially reduced without an underlying improvement.

- *Leaseback.* In most countries public administrations occupy state-owned buildings for which the rents are far from market rates if set at all. There are several alternatives to exploit these real estate assets. The simpler option is to sell the asset but the government can also lease the property itself. The idea is to rent buildings in prime locations and relocate government offices to less expensive areas. Another option is to securitize the rents from a real estate portfolio either through a bond (with coupons paid by rents) or a private company (holding and managing real estate assets) issuing debt. This approach is a way of revealing asset prices, forcing the government to undertake better valuations. However, as with securitization, the accounting of these operations should appropriately capture the transfer of value and other nontransactional economic flows.

Liability Management

It is now generally accepted the objective of debt management should be to contribute to reduce fiscal vulnerability by providing insurance against budget shocks so as to support optimal taxation or to stabilize the debt-to-GDP ratio.[10] However, the fiscal insurance approach does not give precise guidelines on the type of bonds to be issued or their maturity and, in practice, debt managers focus on minimizing costs subject to an acceptable level of liquidity risks. The risk-cost profile of debt is largely determined by (1) its maturity distribution, (2) the use of indexed debt instruments, and (3) the investor base. Under current conditions, however, the scope to reduce debt servicing costs by managing the debt profile may be limited.

- *Term structure of debt.* At the onset of the financial crisis, many advanced economies shortened their public debt in an attempt to raise additional funds quickly at the lowest possible cost.[11] Since then, the average maturity has increased somewhat (figure 17.7). As gross financing needs are quite large and the yield curve has steepened for some countries in the last years, it may be tempting to exploit the short end of the yield curve by reducing the maturity structure. A counterargument is that heightened debt rollover risks (figure 17.8) could lead to a sudden significant deterioration in the fiscal position. In addition, assets may not provide much buffer in the short term (as discussed above). Thus it may be desirable to extend maturities to the extent possible. This would also help lock in long-term interest rates, which are at historical lows in some countries and would likely rise in the medium term as monetary policy moves to a neutral stance.

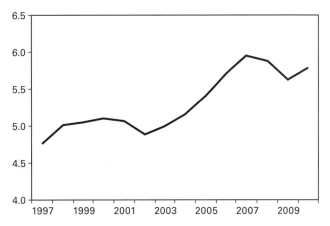

Figure 17.7
Advanced economies: Average term-to-maturity (years). Data refer to central government debt. Countries included in the sample are Australia, Belgium, Canada, Denmark, Czech Republic, Finland, France, Germany, Greece, Iceland, Ireland, Italy, Japan, Korea, Luxembourg, Netherlands, New Zealand, Norway, Portugal, Slovak Republic, Slovenia, Spain, Sweden, and United States.
Source: Organisation for Economic Co-operation Development

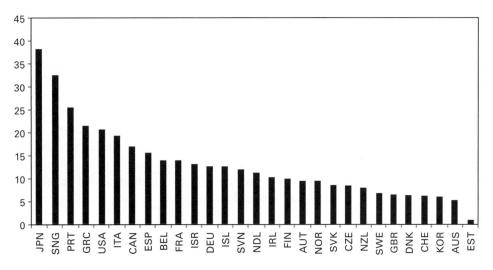

Figure 17.8
Debt to maturity, 2013 (percent of GDP). Gross debt to average maturity is an indicator of the rollover risk.
Sources: Bloomberg; authors' calculations

- *Indexed-debt instruments.* In principle, indexed instruments could provide a hedge against macroeconomic shocks that could be valuable for governments in the current economic environment. For example, a debt instrument indexed to the rate of growth of GDP would help insure against economic slowdowns and allow countries to avoid procyclical fiscal policies (Borensztein and Mauro 2004). However, how well these instruments perform depends on the type of shocks. On the one hand, inflation-indexed bonds (or GDP indexed) provide a good insurance in the case of negative demand shocks (Missale 2012). On the other hand, if the economy is prone to supply shocks, with inflation and growth moving in opposite directions, nominal debt would be better than GDP indexing for hedging purposes. In any event, the use of this type of instruments is hampered by (1) thin or nonexistent markets and (2) lagged data releases and revisions. Given these obstacles, it is unlikely this type of instruments would be beneficial in the short term unless several countries develop a market of a significant scale.

- *Investor base.* Since the onset of the crisis, the trend toward nonresident investors has stalled and, in some cases, the investor base has shifted back toward domestic holders. First, central banks have become important players as a result of quantitative easing programs. Also domestic commercial banks have increased their holding of government bonds, partly to obtain collateral. These swings may not be entirely optimal as the link between domestic banks and the sovereign may create adverse feedback loops. Also a more diversified base can reduce vulnerabilities by pooling investors with different degrees of risk aversion. At the same time there is increasing evidence that the entry of foreign investors may lead to lower yields (see Peiris 2010; Andritzky 2012). By the same token, countries with too high concentration of foreign investors are more susceptible to financial crises given that they are less committed to these assets (Das et al. 2010). Overall, debt managers should strive to issue instruments that attract a large and stable investor base (to the extent possible) as this would provide for lower yields and reduced rollover risks.

17.5.2 Central Banks

What role, if any, should monetary policy—and more broadly central banks—play in the face of fiscal consolidation? Theoretical analyses have not yet provided a clear answer. At the heart of the discussion is the game of chicken described in Sargent and Wallace (1981), whereby the first mover constrains the actions of the follower. In this world, if the fiscal authority moves first (fiscal dominance), it can ultimately force the central bank to generate inflation in order to satisfy the government's intertemporal budget constraint. But, assuming that the fiscal authorities were tempted by this route, exactly how much inflation would be needed to wipe out the debt problem?

Higher inflation could help reduce public debt through three main channels. First, governments can capture real resources by base money creation (*seigniorage*). Second, inflation can erode the real value of the debt. Finally, inflation can affect the primary balance, including if brackets are not indexed under a progressive income tax. Akitoby et al. (2013) simulate the effect of the first two channels for the Group of Seven (G7) countries if inflation were to average 6 percent annually over 2012 to 2017—compared to an average inflation of 1.6 percent over the same period in the baseline *World Economic Outlook* projections. Given the relatively low levels of base money in most advanced economies, the cumulative seigniorage over five years under that scenario would be about 2.5 percentage points of GDP. The debt erosion channel would have a stronger impact. In particular, the same increase in inflation under assumptions of a constant debt maturity structure, no impact of inflation on economic growth, and a one-for-one adjustment to inflation of nominal interest rates on newly issued debt (full Fisher effect) would reduce the average net debt-to-GDP ratio by less than 10 percentage points by the end of the period for most countries (other than Japan and Italy, where the effect would be larger) (figure 17.9).[12] The erosion effect would drop rapidly after five years, because an increasingly large share of securities would have been issued at higher interest rates, including to replace maturing debt that had been issued at lower rates.

Thus, although inflation could help lower public debt, it could hardly solve the debt problem on its own and would raise significant challenges and risks. First, it might be difficult to create higher inflation in the current economic environment, as

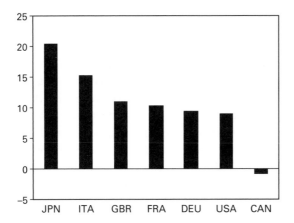

Figure 17.9
Impact of inflation on net debt reduction, 2017 (percent of GDP). The scenario depicted in the figure implies an increase in inflation by 4.4 percentage points over the projected average inflation of 1.6 percent.
Source: Akitoby et al. (2013)

evidenced by Japan's experience in the last decades. But, more important, for inflation to erode debt, the monetary authorities would have to overshoot their goal persistently, and thus expectations would not be anchored around the inflation target. This would undermine the credibility of the framework built over the past three decades to control inflation. Introducing some form of financial repression would keep interest rates low and enhance the effectiveness of this policy on debt reduction, but cause additional collateral damage to the economy (see the discussion below).

In view of these findings, it is difficult to see how "fiscal dominance" could be a dominant strategy, particularly in the absence of financial repression that prevented nominal rates to adjust to higher inflation. But this does not mean that monetary policy should pursue price stability without reference to fiscal policy (monetary dominance). As we discussed earlier in this chapter, fiscal consolidation is likely to have short-run contractionary effects on output and inflation, though multipliers and lags will vary. Thus, to the extent that fiscal policy is credibly expected to tighten with an impact over the central bank's time horizon for policy making, interest rates should be cut and/or remain low taking into account the lags of monetary and fiscal policy implementation. This argument is further strengthened considering that many countries are undertaking consolidation simultaneously with negative spillover effects (Leigh et al. 2010).

The empirical evidence actually shows that reductions in interest rates support output during episodes of fiscal consolidation, increasing the likelihood of success. For example, Hellebrandt et al. (2012) look at a sample of 17 advanced countries for the period 1978 to 2009 and find that successful consolidations tend to be preceded or accompanied by greater monetary loosening than unsuccessful consolidations, particularly as the size of consolidation increases. Simon et al. (2012) review the historical experience of six advanced countries and find similar conclusions.[13]

But beyond implementing an accommodative monetary policy, is there anything else central banks can do to facilitate fiscal consolidation? After all, policy rates are already at historical lows in many advanced economies and the scope for further cuts is small. Still, in some cases, it would appear the monetary transmission mechanism remains impaired and further measures would be justified. With that view, several central banks have announced/implemented unconventional policy measures. On the one hand, in the United States there have been three rounds of quantitative easing (QE). While QE1 was undertaken to intervene in dislocated segments of the market (credit easing), QE2, Operation Twist, and more recently QE3 targeted the long end of the yield curve.[14] The Bank of Japan, on the other hand, has recently adopted a new quantitative and qualitative easing (QQE) in an effort to achieve 2 percent inflation within two years. Meanwhile the Bank of England has launched the Funding for Lending Scheme to ease bank credit conditions for households and businesses. Finally, the European Central Bank (ECB) introduced the Security Market

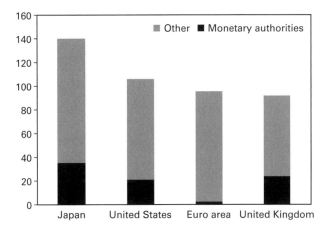

Figure 17.10
General government debt by holders (percent of GDP). Gross government debt except for Japan, which is net. Data as of 2013 Q3. US debt includes holdings of agency debt and mortgage-backed securities. Sources: Bank of England; Bank of Japan; European Central Bank; Federal Reserve; IMF, *World Economic Outlook*

Purchases (SMP) and, more recently, the Outright Monetary Transactions (OMT), with the aim of addressing distortions in the government bond market. Although the design and rationale of unconventional policies varies across countries, all major central banks have intervened in the sovereign debt market to a greater or lesser extent (figure 17.10).

Purchases of sovereign debt in the secondary market are, however, not without controversy and some see them as a form of fiscal dominance that could jeopardize price stability.[15] Nevertheless, the increased interlinkages between the government and financial sector balance sheets may justify this policy as a last resort. This is particularly the case in the euro area where monetary financial institutions hold a large share of domestic government paper—25 percent of GDP on average (figure 17.11).[16] As a result declines in government bond prices have contaminated the financial sector creating a vicious feedback loop between the pressure to deleverage and lower asset prices, hindering the necessary balance sheet repair. These dynamics have ultimately led to financial sector fragmentation within the euro area (as capital flowed from the periphery to the core and outside the euro area), and threatens financial stability and growth prospects.

The analysis above suggests that an active role of central banks in stabilizing the demand for sovereign bonds can avoid adverse tail scenarios of self-defeating deleveraging. In the absence of intervention in government bond markets, the central bank may be forced into providing exceptional support to banks that may not

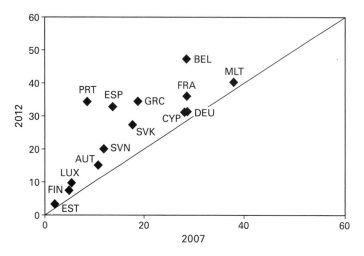

Figure 17.11
Sovereign debt held by domestic financial institutions (percent of GDP). Data for Greece refer to 2011.
Sources: European Central Bank; IMF, *World Economic Outlook*; authors' calculations

otherwise have been necessary. That option is likely to require more resources than a bond market intervention, and it does not directly address the balance sheet damage done by valuation losses stemming from the sovereign.

A supporting argument is that central bank intervention should not necessarily lead to higher inflation when the financial sector is deleveraging, its demand for liquidity is high, and fiscal adjustment is proceeding. Indeed, international experience also shows that large-scale balance sheet increases are a viable monetary policy tool provided the public believes the increases will be appropriately reversed (Anderson et al. 2010). This makes a credible fiscal adjustment path a critical component of the strategy. Finally, to avoid time inconsistency, last resort lending could arguably be conducted at penalty rates but below levels that would suggest a self-fulfilling default. In practice, the cost of central bank borrowing should not be higher than the level consistent with debt sustainability under conservative growth projections and full implementation of planned consolidation.

17.5.3 Financial Repression
With public debt at historical highs, financial repression has been suggested (or seen as inevitable) by some as an alternative way to lower public debt. In simple terms, financial repression occurs when governments interfere with free-market activity to channel funds to themselves. Financial repression can take many forms, including directed lending, caps on interest rates, controls of cross-border capital flows, and public ownership of banks or moral suasion. But regardless of the form it takes, its

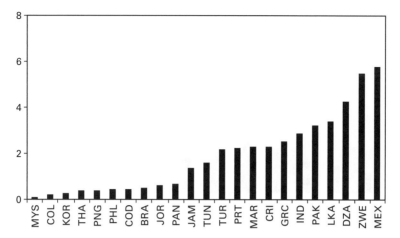

Figure 17.12
Revenue from financial repression 1972 to 1987 (percent of GDP). Annual revenue from financial repression estimated as the difference between the foreign and domestic cost of funds times the domestic stock of government debt.
Source: Giovannini and De Melo (1993)

primary goal is to keep real yields below market-clearing levels. From that perspective, financial repression is most effective in liquidating debt when it is accompanied by inflation.

Some argue that financial repression is indeed making a come-back: Reinhart et al. (2011) talk about financial repression emerging under the disguise of prudential regulation, while Magud et al. (2011) note an increasing trend to introduce capital controls. But, what is the evidence regarding its effectiveness? The empirical literature initially focused on the use of financial repression in emerging markets prior to the financial liberalization of the 1980s. For example, Giovannini and De Melo (1993) estimated that the average annual government revenue from financial repression for a sample of 22 countries over the period 1972 to 1987 was 2 percent of GDP—but with substantial variation across countries (figure 17.12). More recently Reinhart and Sbrancia (2011) have looked at the post–World War II experience in advanced economies. During this period tight capital controls and interest rate ceilings resulted in low nominal rates, which delivered consistently negative real rates with the aid of inflation. The amount of debt reduction brought by financial repression was quite substantial with estimates of the annual liquidation effect ranging from about 1 percent of GDP in Sweden to more than 5 percent of GDP in Italy (figure 17.13).

Given these experiences, it is natural to ask whether financial repression could help this time around. Several factors suggest that this might not be the case. First,

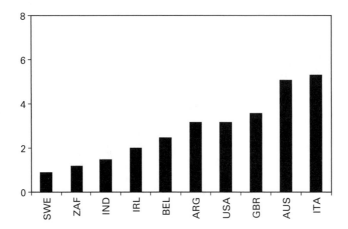

Figure 17.13
Liquidation effect of financial repression, post–World War II (percent of GDP). Average annual liquidation effect reflects the savings to the government from having a negative real interest rate on government debt.
Source: Reinhart and Sbrancia (2011)

global capital mobility was limited at the time, making it easier to capture and retain capital through repressive policies. However, in the current economic and financial environment it would be much more difficult to introduce a set of controls and regulation to effectively stop leakages.[17] This would probably require an almost universal policy (with attendant coordination problems), leading to a much less financially integrated world. One difficulty is that the public debt challenge is not equally strong in all advanced economies, let alone emerging economies. So the incentives for a coordinated action will not be high. Second, persistent inflation surprises were tolerated relatively well by the markets in the postwar era, which is unlikely to be the case this time around. Finally, financial repression becomes more challenging as the scale and the scope of repression required increases.

Even if one was to successfully introduce some form of financial repression, there are costs and risks associated with it. First and foremost, financial repression can inhibit growth over the medium to longer term because it tends to promote inefficient capital allocation crowding out productive investment.[18] While growth prospects were bright in advanced economies after World War II (because of global rebuilding and favorable demographics), partly offsetting the distortions and loss of output associated with financial repression, at present advanced economies can no longer afford the reduction of an already meager potential growth.[19] More important, financial repression can lead to market distortions like asset booms/busts, sudden stops, and capital flight, setting the stage for the next big crisis.

17.5.4 Debt Restructuring

The final measure in the toolkit is default and/or debt restructuring.[20] From the outset, it is important to point out that there is a wide range of possible default/ restructuring modalities and that the actual outcomes will largely depend on their characteristics (the size of the creditor losses, whether the default/restructuring is negotiated with creditors or not, the investor base of government bonds, and so on). In any case, some economists maintain that, given the scale of the adjustments in advanced economies, it is only a matter of time before some countries are forced into this option (e.g., see Buiter 2010; Buiter and Rahbari 2010). The main argument is that debt may not be sustainable; that is, the outstanding stock of debt exceeds the present discounted value of current and future expected primary surpluses.[21] Moreover, even if governments were able to generate sufficiently large surpluses, there is still the potential for self-fulfilling debt crises if markets do not believe the governments are able to generate those surpluses.

In order to assess how successful this strategy can be to reduce debt burdens, one has to look at past experiences. However, debt restructuring has not been a common event among advanced economies in the last six decades. Furthermore, one should be careful to assess the viability of this option by focusing on the experiences in emerging economies. The main reason is that domestic residents hold a large share of government debt in advanced economies (Andritzky 2012), while in many instances of default among emerging markets, foreign holdings were prevalent. This matters because default (or restructuring) is essentially a *one-off wealth tax*. Therefore, if the tax is imposed on foreign residents it leads to an increase in the net wealth of the country, while if it is imposed on domestic agents is equivalent to a large and sudden fiscal adjustment.

A restructuring also affects the reputation of the country as a reliable borrower, and it is generally accepted that it weights on the country's *borrowing costs* and access to international financial markets. Recent empirical evidence suggests that market access can be severely restricted upon default depending on the size of creditor losses (Cruces and Trebesch 2013). In particular, a 20 percentage point increase in haircuts is associated with about 120 bps higher borrowing costs even in years four to seven after the restructuring.

In addition, sovereign default can result in substantial *output losses*. Indeed, the empirical literature finds a drop in output between 2 and 5 percent of GDP in the face of a debt restructuring (Das et al. 2012b). Forni and Pisani (2013) find even higher losses in a dynamic equilibrium model where a small economy belonging to a monetary union restructures its debt.[22] Their results suggest that the sovereign restructuring implies a persistent and large output, consumption, and investment drop, in particular if the share of domestically held debt is high.

In the specific case of the euro area, where there are large cross-border holdings of government debt, large *spillovers* from a restructuring can also occur. The reason is that, to the extent to which the wealth tax is imposed on residents in other countries of the union, this has negative effects that can reverberate easily into the domestic economy. Furthermore sovereign debt restructuring can affect the financial sector via two channels: (1) on the asset side, banks will take a hit from the loss of restructured assets; and (2) on the liability, banks can experience deposit withdrawals and the disruption of credit lines. The empirical evidence suggests there is indeed a correlation between sovereign default and banking crises (Borensztein and Panizza 2009). There is also evidence that private sector access to credit can be reduced up to 40 percent in the face of a debt restructuring (Das et al. 2012b).

Finally, the empirical evidence is not clear on whether debt restructuring can ultimately help restore sustainability and regain market confidence. On the one hand, Das et al. (2012a) look at 18 restructuring episodes during the period 1998 to 2010 and find the public debt-to-GDP ratios declined from a median of over 50 percent of GDP to about 35 percent of GDP. On the other hand, Benjamin and Wright (2009) look at 90 default episodes during the period 1989 to 2006 and find that the creditor losses average roughly 40 percent but the average debtor exited default with a debt-to-GDP ratio 25 percent higher than before default.

Despite the arguments above, there are some circumstances when debt restructuring may be unavoidable. If the primary surplus needed to make the fiscal path sustainable is too large (in terms either of adjustment or of the level that would have to be maintained over time) to be sustained by a country without unbearable economic costs, debt restructuring may become inevitable. Still, two considerations should be taken into account. First, restructuring is not a substitute for fiscal consolidation. As defaults are usually partial, a defaulting country needs to run a primary surplus in order to finance the payment on the interest bill of the restructured debt in any case (Cottarelli et al. 2010), while primary deficits are still large among advanced economies (around 4 percent of GDP on average). Thus, even with a large haircut, fiscal adjustment would be required. Second, a restructuring with large haircuts may become a source of systemic instability in the financial sector. Thus it is important to take appropriate remedial actions in advance.

17.6 Concluding Remarks

This chapter has documented the fiscal challenges facing the advanced economies over the next years. Although considerable adjustment has already occurred, many countries still have a long way to go as deficit reductions have not yet made a dent on debt ratios. Given the unprecedented size of adjustment, however, it would be naive to expect a quick turnaround. Thus it is essential to calibrate the pace of adjustment for the long haul, taking into account the state of the economy and funding pressures.

While fiscal consolidation should proceed in a sustained and gradual manner, central banks also have a role to play. Not only should they provide a supportive monetary policy environment (as long as inflation expectations are well anchored and fiscal adjustment is proceeding), but in some cases there is a scope for a more active role to repair the monetary transmission mechanism as access to funding at reasonable costs is essential to allow economies to adjust successfully.

Even financial repression (with or without inflation) is unlikely to have large payoffs as a captive domestic investor base may be difficult to achieve in a globalized world. The privatization of nonfinancial assets, by contrast, have a larger potential to reduce the debt burden although it may be difficult to materialize in the short term given volatile market conditions and some assets may not be "salable" altogether.

Finally, there might be cases where debt levels are such that debt restructuring cannot be avoided. Still it should be recognized that this option is not a panacea as orthodox fiscal adjustment is likely to be needed after default, and the ensuing cost of restructuring could be very large, particularly if public debt is domestically held. Moreover spillover effects (within and outside the country) from debt restructuring can be large, thereby reducing its potential benefits.

Notes

1. The Great Recession has brought debt to historically unprecedented levels, indeed putting into question the repayment capacity of some sovereigns.

2. These illustrative scenarios are based on the assumption that the cyclically adjusted primary balance improves smoothly from the level in 2013 until 2020 and remains constant thereafter until 2030.

3. Focusing on the overall fiscal balance rather than a specific debt objective has political and economic appeal. First, it can usefully focus the attention of policymakers. But also, once a certain fiscal balance has been achieved, the debt decline will be determined by the nominal GDP growth rate, allowing for a certain element of cyclicality (i.e. debt will decline faster in periods of faster growth).

4. See chapter 20 in this volume for a discussion on the fiscal challenges related to population aging.

5. Government balance sheet management is usually fragmented among the public debt management office, public sector entities, and the central bank, and this raises the risks of coordination failures. Thus there is a potential for efficiency gains on that front. However, this topic will not be discussed here as it is beyond the scope of this chapter.

6. These transactions are thought to be temporary as governments plan to divest the acquired assets once market conditions allow it.

7. Data on nonfinancial assets are limited (partly because they are difficult to value) and are not fully comparable across countries.

8. To make a proper comparison, one would need to calculate the rate of return on financial assets using property income (which includes not only interest but also dividends and rents) and valuation changes and compare that to the yield on debt.

9. However, to the extent that holding financial assets serves other purposes (e.g., providing a buffer against refinancing risks, particularly when assets are liquid), it is not necessarily optimal to divest all government assets—even if their returns are lower than the cost of debt.

10. Nevertheless, Faraglia et al. (2008) look at a sample of OECD countries and find limited evidence that debt management has actually helped to insulate policy against unexpected fiscal shocks. They argue that achieving better fiscal insurance will require either holding more extreme portfolio positions than is actually the case, issuing new forms of contingent securities, or magnifying existing positions through the use of derivatives.

11. This was possible because many of these countries entered the crisis with relatively long maturities.

12. If maturity were to shorten in response to the inflation shock, the debt erosion effect would be somewhat smaller.

13. For example, in Belgium, Canada, and Italy, on the one hand, the monetary environment during the 1980s was tight because of disinflationary efforts by the central banks. As a result debt continued to increase despite tight fiscal policy and only when real rates fell (after disinflation) they were able to reduce debt. In the United States, on the other hand, monetary policy was exceptionally supportive after World War II and this, coupled with tight fiscal policy and a financial repression, resulted in a significant reduction of debt.

14. Many studies have found that the Fed's first two purchase programs lowered yields below what would otherwise have prevailed (e.g., see D'Amico and King 2010; Hamilton and Wu 2011; Gagnon et al. 2011).

15. See Bogenberg Declaration (2011), De Grauwe (2011), Stark (2011), and Weidman (2011) for discussions on this point.

16. Interestingly, countries with high public debt also have larger holdings of domestic government bonds as percentage of bank capital (Committee on the Global Financial System 2011).

17. Prudential regulations may catalyze credit flows into safe assets but they mainly serve the purpose of financial stability, and it is unlikely they can alone expand the boundaries of public debt sustainability in the long run.

18. For example, Fry (1980) estimated that for each percentage point by which the real deposit rate is below the market equilibrium rate in a sample of developing countries, half a percentage of growth is forgone.

19. Lower growth prospects stem not only from the simultaneous deleveraging in the private sector but also from an aging population.

20. Default is the failure of a government to make a principal or interest payment on time. In most cases restructurings occur after default, and they involve a debt rescheduling (lengthening maturities, possibly lowering interest rates) and/or debt reduction (reduction in the face of nominal value of old instruments).

21. According to the IMF (2002), debt sustainability is defined as a situation where a borrower is expected to be able to continue servicing its debts without unrealistically large future correction to the balance of income and expenditure. Underpinning this argument is the idea that there is a maximum level of primary surplus that a country could attain given social, political, and economic constraints.

22. In their model, sovereign debt is held by domestic agents and by agents in the rest of the monetary union, and after the restructuring, the sovereign borrowing rate increases.

References

Akitoby, B., T. Komatsuzaki, and A. Binder. 2013. Inflation and debt reduction in advanced economies. Working paper. IMF, Washington, DC, forthcoming.

Alesina A., and S. Ardagna. 2010. Fiscal adjustments: Lessons from recent history. Paper prepared for the ECOFIN meeting, Madrid, April 15.

Alper, C. E., and L. Forni. 2011. Public debt in advanced economies and its spillover effects on long-term yields. Working paper 11/210. IMF, Washington, DC.

Anderson, R. G., C. S. Gascon, and Y. Liu. 2010. Doubling your monetary base and surviving. *Federal Reserve Bank of St. Louis Review* 92 (6): 481–505.

Andritzky, J. 2012. Government bonds and their investors: What are the facts and do they matter? Working paper 12/158. IMF, Washington, DC.

Ardagna, S., F. Caselli, and T. Lane. 2007. Fiscal discipline and the cost of public debt service: Some estimates for OECD countries. *B.E. Journal of Macroeconomics* 7 (1).

Baldacci, E., and M. S. Kumar. 2010. Fiscal deficits, public debt, and sovereign bond yields. Working paper 10/184. IMF, Washington, DC.

Barro, R. 1979. On the determination of public debt. *Journal of Political Economy* 87 (5): 940–71.

Baum, A., M. Poplawski-Ribeiro, and A. Weber. 2012. Fiscal multipliers and the state of the economy. Working paper 12/ 286. IMF, Washington, DC.

Benjamin, D., and M. L. J. Wright. 2009. A theory of delays in sovereign debt renegotiations. Unpublished manuscript. University of California, Los Angeles.

Borensztein, E., and P. Mauro. 2004. The case for GDP-indexed bonds. *Economic Policy* (April): 19 (38): 165–216.

Borensztein, E., and U. Panizza. 2009. The costs of sovereign default. *IMF Staff Papers 56* (4): 683–741.

Bova, E., R. Dippelsman, K. Rideout, and A. Schaechter. 2013. Another look at governments' balance sheets: The role of nonfinancial assets. Working paper 13/95. IMF, Washington, DC.

Buiter, W. 2010. Sovereign debt problems in advanced industrial countries. *Citi Economics, Global Economics View*, April 26.

Buiter, W., and E. Rahbari, 2010. Is sovereign default "unnecessary, undesirable, and unlikely" for all advanced economies? *Citi Economics, Global Economics View*, September 16.

Committee on the Global Financial System. 2011. *The Impact of Sovereign Credit Risk on Bank Funding Conditions*. Basel: BIS.

Cottarelli, C., L. Forni, J. Gottschalk, and P. Mauro. 2010. Default in today's advanced economies: Unnecessary, undesirable, and unlikely. Staff position note 10/12. IMF, Washington, DC.

Cottarelli, C., and L. Jaramillo. 2012. Walking hand in hand: Fiscal policy and growth in advanced economies. Working paper 12/137. IMF, Washington, DC.

Cottarelli, C., and M. Keen. 2012. Fiscal policy and growth: Overcoming the constraints. In Otaviano Canuto and Danny Leipziger, eds., Ascent after Decline: Regrowing Global Economies after the Great Recession. Washington, DC: World Bank, 87–133.

Cruces, J., and C. Trebesch. 2013. Sovereign defaults: The price of haircuts. *American Economic Journal: Macroeconomics*, 5(3): 85-117.

D'Amico, S., and T. King. 2010. Flow and stock effects of large-scale treasury purchases. Discussion series 2010–52. Federal Reserve Board Finance and Economics, Washington, DC.

Das, U. S., M. Papaioannou, D. Grigorian, and S. Maziad. 2012a. *A Survey of Experiences with Emerging Market Sovereign Debt Restructurings*. Washington, DC: IMF.

Das, U. S., M. Papaioannou, G. Pedras, F. Ahmed, and J. Surti. 2010. Managing public debt and its financial stability implications. Working paper 10/280. IMF, Washington, DC.

Das, U. S., M. Papaioannou, and C. Trebesch. 2012b. Sovereign debt restructurings 1950–2010: Literature survey, data, and stylized facts. Working paper 12/203. IMF, Washington, DC.

Davis, J., R. Ossowski, T. Richardson, and S. Barnett. 2000. Fiscal and macroeconomic impact of privatization. Occasional paper 194. IMF, Washington, DC.

De Grauwe, P. 2011. The European Central Bank: Lender of last resort in the government bond markets? Working paper 3569. CESifo, Munich.

De Grauwe, P. and Yuemei Ji. 2012. Mispricing of sovereign risk and multiple equilibria in the eurozone. Working paper. CEPS, Brussels.

Declaration, Bogenberg. 2011. Sixteen theses on the situation of the European Monetary Union (October). Available at: http://www.cesifo-group.de/ifoHome.html.

Di Cesare, A., G. Grande, M. Manna, and M. Taboga. 2012. Recent estimates of sovereign risk premia for euro-area countries. Occasional paper 128. Bank of Italy, Rome.

Faraglia, E., A. Marcet, and A. Scott. 2008. Fiscal insurance and debt management in OECD economies. *Economic Journal* 118 (527): 363–86.

Forni, L., A. Gerali, and M. Pisani. 2010. The macroeconomics of fiscal consolidations in euro area countries. *Journal of Economic Dynamics & Control* 34 (9): 677–708.

Forni, L., and M. Pisani. 2013. Macroeconomic effects of a sovereign restructuring in a monetary union: A model based approach. Working paper 13/269. IMF, Washington, DC.

Fry, M.J. 1980. Saving, investment, growth and the cost of financial repression. *World Development* 8 (4): 317–27.

Gagnon, J., M. Raskin, J. Remasche, and B. Sack. 2011. The financial market effects of the Federal Reserve's large-scale asset purchases. *International Journal of Central Banking* 7 (1): 3–43.

Giovannini, A., and M. De Melo. 1993. Government revenue from financial repression. *American Economic Review* 83 (4): 953–63.

Hamilton, J., and J. C. Wu. 2011. The effectiveness of alternative monetary policy tools in a zero lower bound environment. Working paper 16956. NBER, Cambridge, MA.

Hartwig Lojsch, D., M., Rodríguez-Vives, and M., Savík. 2011. The size and composition of government debt in the euro area. Occasional paper 132. ECB, Frankfurt. Available at: http://www.ecb.europa.eu/pub/pdf/scpops/ecbocp132.pdf.

Hellebrandt, T., A. S. Posen, and M. Tolle. 2012. Does monetary cooperation or confrontation lead to successful fiscal consolidation? Policy brief PB 12–8. Peterson Institute for International Economics, Washington, DC.

International Monetary Fund. 2002. Assessing sustainability. Available at: http://www.imf.org/external/np/pdr/sus/2002/eng/052802.pdf.

International Monetary Fund. 2010. From stimulus to consolidation: Revenue and expenditure policies in advanced and emerging economies. Policy paper. IMF, Washington, DC.

International Monetary Fund. 2012a. Balancing fiscal policy risks. Fiscal Monitor, April. IMF, Washington, DC.

International Monetary Fund. 2012b. Taking stock: A progress report on fiscal adjustment. Fiscal Monitor, October. IMF, Washington, DC.

International Monetary Fund. 2013a. Taxing times. *Fiscal Monitor* (October). Washington, DC: IMF.

International Monetary Fund. 2013b. Fiscal adjustment in an uncertain world. *Fiscal Monitor* (April). Washington, DC: IMF.

Laubach, T. 2009. New evidence on the interest rate effects of budget deficits and debt. *Journal of the European Economic Association* 7 (4): 858–85.

Leigh, D., P. Devries, C. Freedman, J. Guajardo, D. Laxton, and A. Pescatori. 2010. Will it hurt? Macroeconomic effects of fiscal consolidation. In *World Economic Outlook* (October). Washington, DC: IMF, ch. 3.

Magud, N. E., C. M. Reinhart, and K. S. Rogoff. 2011. Capital controls: Myth and reality—A portfolio balance approach. Working paper 11–7. Peterson Institute for International Economics, Washington, DC.

Mauro, Paolo, ed. 2011. Chipping away at Public Debt—Sources of Failure and Keys to Success in Fiscal Adjustment. Hoboken, NJ: Wiley.

Megginson, W. L. 2013. Privatization trends and major deals in 2012 and 1H2013. Report 2012, 5–25. PB, Milan.

Megginson, W. L., and B. Bortolotti. 2011. Privatization trends and major deals in 2011. Report 2011, 7–22. PB, Milan.

Megginson, W. L., and J. M. Netter. 2001. From state to market: A survey of empirical studies on privatization. *Journal of Economic Literature* 39 (2): 321–89.

Missale, A. 2012. Sovereign debt management and fiscal vulnerabilities: In "threat of fiscal dominance? Paper 65. BIS, Basel.

Peiris, S. 2010. Foreign participation in emerging markets' local currency bond markets. Working paper 10/88. IMF, Washington, DC.

Poghosyan, T. 2012. Long-run and short-run determinants of government bond yields in advanced economies. Working paper 12/271. IMF, Washington, DC.

Rawdanowicz, Lukasz, Eckhard Wurzel, and Patrice Ollivaud. 2011. Current issues in managing government debt and assets. Working Paper 923. Economics Department, OECD, Paris.

Reinhart, C. M., J. F. Kirkegaard, and M. B. Sbrancia. 2011. Financial repression redux. *Finance and Development* 48 (1): 22–26.

Reinhart, C. M., and M. B. Sbrancia. 2011. The liquidation of government debt. Working paper 16893. NBER, Cambridge, MA.

Romer, C. D., and D. H. Romer. 2010. The macroeconomic effect of tax changes: Estimates based on a new measure of fiscal shocks. *American Economic Review* 100 (3): 763–801.

Sargent, T. J., and N. Wallace. 1981. Some unpleasant monetarist arithmetic. *Federal Reserve Bank of Minneapolis Quarterly Review* 5 (3): 1–17.

Simon, J., A. Pescatori, and D. Sandri. 2012. The good, the bad, and the ugly: 100 years of dealing with public debt overhangs. In *World Economic Outlook* (October). Washington, DC: IMF, ch. 3.

Stark, J. 2011. Economic situation and fiscal challenges. Speech before Forecasters' Club of New York, December 2.

UBS Investment Research. 2011. How can governments sweat their assets? UBS, London.

Weidman, J. 2011. The crisis as a challenge for the euro area. Speech before Verband der Familienunternehmer (Association of Family Enterprises), Cologne, September 13.

18

Institutional Reforms and Fiscal Adjustment

Xavier Debrun and Andrea Schaechter

18.1 Introduction

As current debt dynamics call for significant fiscal retrenchment over the medium term, present governments must credibly anchor future fiscal policy in some trajectory deemed consistent with a sustainable debt. Absent credibility, a vicious cycle of large frontloaded consolidations followed by financial market bets on the self-defeating nature of these adjustments is a real possibility (IMF 2012a). This is where a central lesson from the 2008 to 2009 crisis meets the precondition to a successful exit from crisis policies: sound fiscal governance must ensure that fiscal policy is predictable, stabilizing, and financially sustainable.

Clearly, the institutional arrangements governing fiscal policy prior to the crisis could not prevent some of the imbalances that magnified its effects. In particular, in many EU and euro area countries, fiscal buffers had not been built up as envisaged during the relatively prosperous pre-crisis years owing to weak implementation of the Stability and Growth Pact obligations. Exceptions were largely those EU countries that followed national fiscal rules that complemented the supranational rules. Outside the European Union, the disciplining role of fiscal institutions was also mixed, although pre-crisis institutional reforms had helped a number of emerging economies to create sufficient space to stabilize the economy.

Thus strengthening fiscal institutions has naturally emerged as an essential element to address the fiscal legacy of the crisis. This applies to governance reforms at the national level as well as the supranational level in the euro area and the EU, where implementation of the reformed Stability and Growth Pact is aimed to close the pre-crisis gaps. Outside the European Union, many countries have started or are considering reforms by anchoring fiscal policy over the medium term, strengthening budgetary planning, reporting, analysis, and execution, and improving risk management. In addition to specific measures in public financial management, reforms center on rules-based fiscal frameworks and nonpartisan fiscal agencies, which will be at the center of this chapter.

The rest of this chapter is structured as follows. Section 18.2 analyzes pre-crisis shortcomings of fiscal governance, in particular in the European Union. It also reviews the limits of fiscal institutions that were exposed by the crisis. Sections 18.3, 18.4, and 18.5 summarize key aspects of recent institutional reforms related to numerical fiscal rules, nonpartisan fiscal agencies, and major public financial management features, respectively. All three sections cover also governance reforms at the EU level. Section 18.6 concludes and summarizes several governance challenges.

18.2 Fiscal Institutions before and during the Crisis

We use the term fiscal institutions to designate processes or arrangements intended to favor the conduct of sound fiscal policies, through adequate constraints on policy discretion, including measures that enhance transparency and democratic accountability. At the macroeconomic level they aim at addressing the deficit and procyclicality biases that often affect discretionary fiscal policies. Two institutional approaches have frequently been advocated: the first approach sets policy boundaries, the second relies on self-discipline by raising transparency and reputational costs. In particular, fiscal rules impose long-lasting constraints through numerical limits on budgetary aggregates. External surveillance arrangements, including fiscal watchdog bodies, foster democratic accountability through analysis, information, and advice. These two approaches are increasingly used in combination. Effective implementation of fiscal rules is supported by sound public financial management systems, including reliable, comprehensive, and timely reporting systems, good forecasting and medium-term planning capacity (including through medium-term fiscal frameworks), top-down budgeting, and strong budget execution.[1]

In the past, institutional fiscal reforms often followed episodes of fiscal stress, allowing many of the countries that implemented such reforms to face the current crisis with better starting positions. As regards the adoption of national numerical fiscal rules, a first surge occurred in advanced economies in the early and mid-1990s. This was in part in response to bank and debt crises of the 1990s (e.g., Finland and Sweden) as well as consolidation needs to qualify for the euro area (e.g., Belgium). In emerging economies, fiscal rules spread from the early 2000s. Many adopted rules-based fiscal frameworks in response to experience with fiscal excesses and overhauled budget procedures, often reflected in the adoption of fiscal responsibility laws (e.g., Brazil, Colombia, Panama, Peru, and Sri Lanka). Before the crisis more emerging than advanced economies had national fiscal rules in place, often combined with relatively strong fiscal positions (figure 18.1).

Despite supranational budgetary limits, many EU countries entered the crisis with insufficient fiscal buffers. In the pre-crisis years, public finances improved in

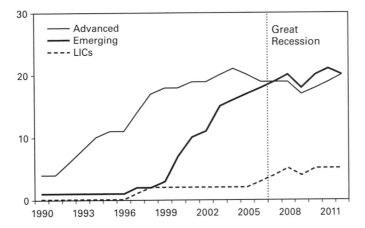

Figure 18.1
Number of countries with national fiscal rules. Based on fiscal rules in effect by end-March 2012.
Source: Schaechter et al. (2012)

most EU economies such that all excessive deficit procedures were abrogated (except in Hungary and the United Kingdom). However, these improvements came on the back of strong economic growth and asset price booms in some economies which pushed overall balances below the 3 percent deficit threshold, while structural deficits remained high in many economies and considerably above the country-specific medium-term budgetary objectives. The focus of the Stability and Growth Pact (SGP) on its corrective arm (the headline deficit limit) with no enforcement of the preventive arm (the structural deficit) and the debt limit, combined with a lack of governance and policy convergence outside the fiscal area, emerged as considerable weakness of EU fiscal governance which left many EU economies ill-prepared for the crisis. In contrast, EU countries with strong national rules in place fared better. For example, the Netherlands and the Nordic countries, with their traditions of rules-based medium-term fiscal policy-making, realized small structural deficits or surpluses on average in the six pre-crisis years and were among the few to meet their medium-term budgetary objectives (figure 18.2).

While financial markets did not differentiate euro area sovereign risk in the run up to the crisis, countries with stronger fiscal institutions—and especially fiscal policy rules—largely escaped the panic sell-offs that followed the Greek debt crisis. Although a careful econometric analysis would be required to identify causation, figure 18.3 depicts the dramatic contrast between the government bond yields in countries with strong national fiscal rules and those with weaker or no rules.

While rules can help anchor medium-term expectations, the crisis has exposed their limits when faced with extreme shocks. The ability to provide countercyclical

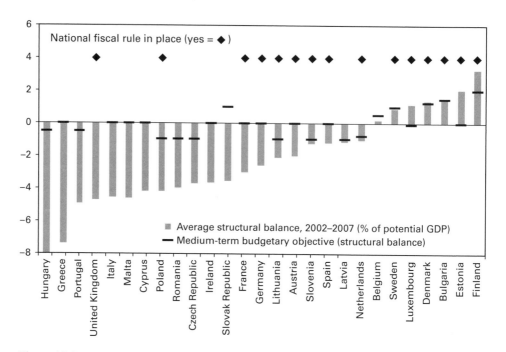

Figure 18.2
EU countries: Pre-crisis fiscal performance and national fiscal rules
Sources: IMF, *Fiscal Monitor*; IMF staff assessment

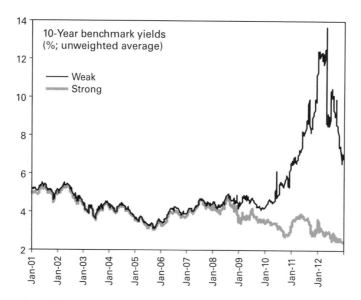

Figure 18.3
Euro area economies: Evolution of yields and strength of national fiscal rules. Countries classified as "strong" are those where the fiscal rule strength index from Schaechter et al. (2012) is above the pre-crisis (2007) median (Austria, Finland, France, Germany, Netherlands, and Spain); in countries classified as "weak" the index is below the median (Belgium, Greece, Ireland, Italy, Portugal, and Slovenia). Sources: Bloomberg; IMF staff estimates

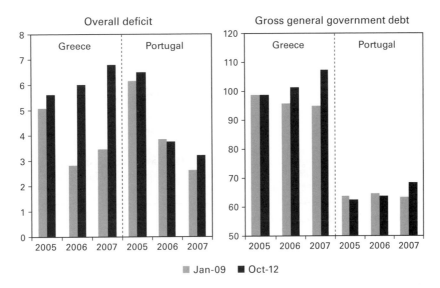

Figure 18.4
Revision of historical fiscal variables over time: Greece and Portugal (percent of GDP)
Sources: IMF, *World Economic Outlook*, January 2009 and October 2012

policy support within the rules-based framework was notable in those national rules that account for the cycle (e.g., Australia and Switzerland) or include escape clauses (e.g., Brazil and Spain). The supranational arrangements in monetary unions all have the option to extend the time frame for adjustment in case of deviations from the rule for the case of severe recessions. Most national rules, however, did not have this flexibility built in and were thus put into abeyance during the crisis. Experiences with formulating transition paths back to the rules' budgetary limits differ across countries, often linked to the capacity for formulating medium-term plans and the degree of economic uncertainty.

Other fiscal institutional weaknesses were revealed by the crisis. Reporting short-comings led to significant upward revisions of key fiscal variables (figure 18.4). The Greek budget deficit for 2007 turned out to be nearly twice as large as reported earlier and was revised up from 3.5 percent (reported in January 2009) to 6.8 percent of GDP (in the October 2012 WEO). At the same time, accounting stratagems have sometimes been used to meet fiscal targets—thereby sidestepping the need for true adjustment (see Irwin 2012). Examples include currency swaps to hide a debt build-up (e.g., Greece), assumption of long-term pension obligations in exchange for short-term revenue (e.g., Portugal, Hungary, and other Eastern European countries), and use of public-private partnerships to defer the recognition of investment spending (e.g., Portugal).

Table 18.1
Type of recently adopted national fiscal rules since 2010

Type of rule	Countries
Budget balance rule[a]	Austria, Colombia, Croatia, Italy, Jamaica, Portugal, Serbia, Spain, United Kingdom
Pay-as-you-go rule[b]	Japan, United States
Debt rule	Croatia, Hungary, Serbia, Slovak Republic, Spain, United Kingdom
Expenditure rule	Croatia, Ecuador, France, Israel, Japan, Namibia, Poland, Romania, Russia, Spain, United States
Revenue rule	France

Sources: National authorities; IMF staff assessments.
Note: Rules include those that have been adopted but have not yet taken effect. See table 18.2 for more details.
a. All of these budget balance rules account for the economic cycle, except in Jamaica.
b. The pay-as-you-go rules are considered procedural rather than numerical rules and thus not counted in the dataset.

18.3 "Next-Generation" Fiscal Rules

18.3.1 National Fiscal Rules

Many countries adopted new rules or overhauled existing ones in response to the crisis (tables 18.1 and 18.2). Multiple motivations were typically behind these decisions: reassuring markets about the sustainability of fiscal policy and public finances; committing to and locking in sustained adjustment efforts; guiding expectations about the medium-term fiscal stance.

While many reforms concern European countries hardest hit by the crisis, the trend is broader as the below examples show (table 18.2).

- A few countries could build on their pre-crisis institutional reform efforts. Germany enshrined a structural budget balance rule in its constitution in 2009. After a transition period, starting in 2011, the structural deficit ceiling of 0.35 percent of GDP for the federal government will take full effect in 2016, and the states will need to maintain structurally balanced budgets from 2020. France sets binding multiyear expenditure ceilings and minimum targets for the net impact of new revenue measures legislated in its Multi-Year Public Finance Planning Act.

- Most other EU member states for which new rules already took effect are transition economies (Poland, Romania, and Slovakia), while others have adopted a transition period.

Table 18.2
New fiscal rules adopted since 2010

Country	Description of rules
Austria	Parliament passed in December 2011 an amendment to the federal budget law stipulating that, from 2017 onward, the structural deficit at the federal level (including social insurance) shall not exceed 0.35 percent of GDP. Operational details are still being prepared in separate laws and regulations. This includes a general government structural deficit limit of 0.45 percent of GDP (split into 0.35 percent of GDP for the federal level and 0.10 percent of GDP for states/municipalities).
Colombia	A structural budget balance rule for the central government was approved by Congress in June 2011. It sets a path that lowers the structural deficit to 2.3 percent of GDP by 2014 and provides a ceiling of 1 percent of GDP effective in 2022. The rule allows for fiscal expansion when the expected output growth rate is at least 2 percentage points lower than the long-term rate and creates a sovereign wealth fund.
Ecuador	A new expenditure rule was adopted in 2010 and took effect in 2011, but the existing budget balance and debt rules were dropped. The expenditure rule states that current expenditure cannot be higher than permanent income including oil revenue. External financing and oil revenues are to be used only to finance public investment.
France	The Multi-Year Public Finance Planning Act from December 2010 sets binding expenditure ceilings and minimum targets for the net impact of new revenue measures for 2011–14. It expands the ceilings from the 2009–12 framework and the "zero volume rule" for central government expenditure introduced in 2004.
Germany	A new structural balance rule (0.35 percent of GDP for the federal government and structurally balanced budgets for the Laender) was enshrined in the constitution in June 2009. After a transition period, starting in 2011, it will take full effect in 2016 for the federal government and 2020 for the states.
Hungary	A debt rule, included in the constitution, will come into effect in 2016 and require cutting the government debt-to-GDP ratio annually until it falls to below 50 percent of GDP. Debt reduction can be suspended when real GDP contracts.
Italy	A constitutional amendment was approved in April 2012 that introduces the principle of a balanced budget in structural terms with details and implementation principles to be specified in secondary legislation by end-February 2013.
Japan	The Fiscal Management Strategy, which includes a pay-as-you-go rule, was adopted in 2010 (by cabinet decision). The rule implies that any measure that involves increases in expenditure or decreases in revenue needs to be compensated for by permanent reductions in expenditures or permanent revenue-raising measures. A Medium-Term Fiscal Framework, including a limit on expenditure, was also introduced.[a]
Namibia	An expenditure rule took effect in 2010 that caps the ratio of expenditures to GDP at 30 percent.
Poland	A new expenditure rule (from 2011) limits the increase in central government discretionary spending and all newly enacted spending to 1 percent in real terms (based on consumer price index inflation) (defined in 2011 budget law).

(continued)

Table 18.2
(*continued*)

Country	Description of rules
Portugal	The new budgetary framework law (May 2011) approved a fiscal rule establishing that the general government structural balance cannot be less than the medium-term objective in the Stability and Growth Pact. It also includes requirements for a correction of the multiannual plan whenever deviations from the target occur. The rule will come into effect in 2015.
Romania	From 2010 general government expenditure growth should not exceed projected nominal GDP for three years until the budget balance is in surplus. Moreover, personnel expenditure limits are binding for two years.
Serbia	In October 2010, fiscal responsibility provisions were introduced in the budget system law from 2009. These include numerical fiscal rules and the adoption of a fiscal council. The fiscal rules comprise a budget balance rule that corrects for past deficit deviations and allows a partial operation of automatic fiscal stabilizers. A debt rule provides a ceiling on general government debt of 45 percent of GDP.
Slovak Republic	In December 2011, a constitutional bill was adopted, taking effect March 1, 2012, that caps public debt at 60 percent of GDP. Automatic adjustment mechanisms take effect when the debt-to-GDP ratio reaches 50 percent. The bill also calls for setting up a Fiscal Council to monitor and evaluate fiscal performance.
Spain	A constitutional amendment (2011) and its corresponding organic legislation (2012) require that the structural deficit for all levels of government stay within the limits set by the European Union, and set debt limits for each level of government. The rules will enter into force from 2020, with transition rules in effect until then. The amendment also introduces expenditure ceilings and constrains growth in expenditure for all levels of government.
United Kingdom	The new cyclically adjusted budget balance rule, from 2010, aims to achieve cyclically adjusted current balance by the end of the rolling five-year forecast period (currently by FY2016/17). The new debt rule (from 2010) targets a falling public sector net-debt-to-GDP ratio by FY 2015/16.
United States	Statutory pas-as-you-go rules for revenue and mandatory spending were reinstate in February 2010 but are subject to important exemptions. In August 2011, Congress enacted discretionary spending caps, saving about $900 billion over the next decade. If Congress does not take legislative action, additional spending cuts (sequesters) are scheduled to take effect from March 2013 to produce savings of roughly US$1.2 trillion over a decade, with one half coming from defense spending and the other half from domestic nondefense programs, excluding Social Security, Medicaid, parts of Medicare, and certain other entitlement programs.[a]

Source: National authorities; IMF staff assessment
a. The pay-as-you-go rules are considered to be procedural rather than numerical rules.

- In Spain the constitutional amendment of September 2011 and its corresponding organic legislation (2012) require that the structural deficit for all levels of government stay within the limits set by the European Union and set debt limits for each level of government. The rule will enter into force in 2020.
- Portugal's new budgetary framework law (May 2011) establishes that the structural budget balance cannot be less than the medium-term objective in the Stability and Growth Pact.
- Austria passed an amendment to the federal budget law stipulating that, from 2017 onward, the structural deficit at the federal level (including social insurance) shall not exceed 0.35 percent of GDP.
- Italy approved a constitutional amendment (April 2012) introducing the principle of a balanced budget in structural terms with details and implementation principles to be specified in secondary legislation by end-February 2013.
- Outside the European Union, for example, Colombia adopted a structural budget balance rule with a 1 percent of GDP deficit limit, taking effect in 2022. Serbia introduced balanced budget rules, which correct for past deficit deviations and allow for a partial operation of automatic fiscal stabilizers, and a debt ceiling.

These "next-generation" fiscal rules explicitly combine the sustainability objective with more flexibility to accommodate economic shocks. Following the examples of earlier adopted rules in Chile,[2] Germany, and Switzerland, many of the new rules set budget targets in structural terms (e.g., Austria, Colombia, Germany, Italy, Portugal, Spain, and Switzerland), cyclically adjusted terms (e.g., United Kingdom), or accounted for the cycle in other ways (e.g., Panama and Serbia); see figure 18.5. Some also correct automatically for past deviations with a view to avoiding the "ratcheting-up" effects of debt (e.g., Serbia, and the so-called debt brakes of the structural budget balance rules in Germany and Switzerland).[3] Others combine new expenditure rules with new or existing debt rules, thereby providing operational guidance as well as a link to debt sustainability (e.g., Poland).

At the same time the design features of fiscal rules are becoming more encompassing, and supporting arrangements are being strengthened. This includes, for example, enshrining rules in legislation (away from political agreements), adopting explicit escape clauses and provisions for the transition path in case of deviations, and formulating medium-term expenditure frameworks. This evolution is captured by the summary fiscal rules index presented in figure 18.6, which also accounts for the number of rules per country that increased since the crisis in advanced and emerging economies. Figure 18.7 shows the main driving forces: the use of supporting arrangements, in particular expenditure ceilings, independent monitoring of

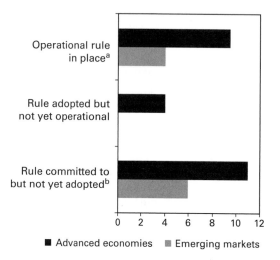

Figure 18.5
Number of countries with budget balance rules accounting for the cycle. (a) Includes countries with a clearly specified transition path. (b) Includes EU member states that have signed the Fiscal Compact but have not yet adopted a rule that accounts for the cycle.
Sources: National authorities; IMF staff assessments

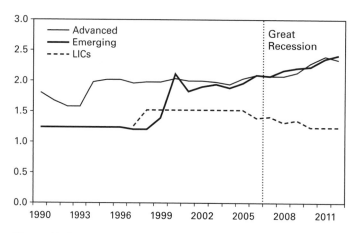

Figure 18.6
National fiscal rules index (index ranging from zero to five)
Source: Schaechter et al. (2012)

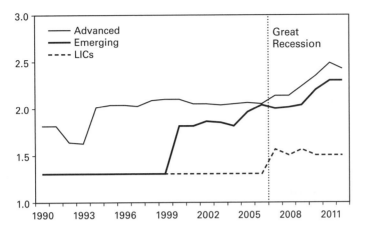

Figure 18.7
Fiscal rules sub-index: Supporting arrangements (index ranging from zero to five). Includes expenditure ceilings, fiscal responsibility laws, independent projections and monitoring.
Source: Schaechter et al. (2012)

rules, independent macroeconomic projections for budget assumptions, and fiscal responsibility legislation.

But the greater complexity of the rules frameworks also creates new challenges. The increased number of rules, their interaction, and sophistication can complicate implementation and make compliance more difficult to explain and monitor. To address the first challenge, several countries are reforming their budgetary procedures and medium-term budgetary framework (e.g., Austria, Greece, Ireland, and Portugal) (section 18.5). Nonpartisan fiscal agencies can potentially play an important role in dealing with the second challenge and a number of countries have set up, or adopted, plans for such institutions (see section 18.4).

18.3.2 Reforming the EU Fiscal Governance Framework

The European Union has taken steps to enhance both the prevention and management of sovereign debt crises. To reduce the main loopholes that were exposed by the crisis, governance reforms have focused on (1) setting more comprehensive limits on fiscal aggregates, (2) tightening enforcement at the national and supranational level, (3) improving coordination, (4) strengthening budgetary procedures, (5) enhancing transparency, and (6) broadening governance beyond the fiscal area. At the same time a crisis management apparatus was created with the EFSF and the ESM. These reforms are captured predominantly in the "six pack" of five new EU regulations and one EU directive, which took effect in December 2011, as well as an intergovernmental treaty signed in March 2012 (the Treaty on Stability, Coordination and

Governance in the Economic and Monetary Union), which incorporates broad guidance for the reform of national fiscal frameworks (the so-called Fiscal Compact; see European Commission 2012a), and the Treaty Establishing the European Stability Mechanism (signed in February 2012).

To foster greater fiscal discipline, in particular in good economic times, the array of numerical budget limits has been broadened (table 18.3). The reforms mandate the adoption in legislation of a national structural budget rule with a maximum deficit limit of 0.5 percent of GDP,[4] and give more prominence to debt and expenditure developments in supranational rules. First, in the corrective arm of the SGP, the debt criterion has been made operational. The failure to reduce the debt-to-GDP ratio by the benchmark 1/20th of the distance between the observed level and the 60 percent threshold on average for three consecutive years can now trigger an excessive deficit procedure even if the headline Maastricht deficit is below the 3 percent threshold. Second, in the preventive arm, expenditure growth is to be used alongside the structural budget balance to assess progress toward the medium-term budgetary objectives (MTOs). Specifically, countries exhibiting an annual growth of primary expenditure—excluding unemployment benefits and subtracting revenue discretionary increases—above long-term nominal GDP growth and therefore not making significant progress to reaching their MTOs can face financial sanctions and fines (for euro area members).

Several avenues have been pursued to tighten enforcement of the new commitments, though shortcomings remain. A key novelty is to give greater role to enforcing requirements at the national rather than the EU level. This is particularly reflected in the obligation to adopt nationally binding structural budget balance rules combined with legally enshrined automatic mechanisms for correcting deviations from the rule.[5] Moreover the most recent reform initiative ("two pack," enacted in May 2013) advocates the creation of independent bodies at the national level that would assess compliance with the rules and thereby raise reputational costs for deviations (see section 18.4 for more details). Enforcement at the supranational level has advanced by operationalizing the debt criterion and introducing new fines and sanctions in the preventive and corrective arms of the pact. These can be triggered more automatically as they would be proposed by the Commission and implemented unless a qualified Council majority blocks the proposal (so-called reverse qualified majority).

Broader policy coordination is now based on the "European semester" with enforcement procedures still to be established, however (figure 18.8). So far the key new element is a revised timetable that aims to allow assessing all macroeconomic developments and policies together. In addition to raising awareness of spillovers, the new procedure permits timely feedback for the preparation of national budgets. An ex ante peer review and recommendations, including on how to reduce macro-

Table 18.3
EU fiscal rules from Maastricht to the Fiscal Compact

Type	Rules				Level of enforcement and legal basis	Action following violation[a]
	Maastricht (SGP1)	2005 Reform (SGP2)	2011 "Six Pack" Reform (SGP3)	Fiscal compact		
Debt Rule	Debt/GDP is reduced to below 60 percent		Annual reduction in debt/GDP equal to 1/20th of distance between current level and target		Maastricht Treaty	Excessive deficit procedure (Council's decision by qualified majority); fines and sanctions
Deficit Rule	Deficit/GDP below 3 percent at any time				Maastricht Treaty	Excessive deficit procedure (Council's decision by qualified majority); fines and sanctions
Structural Budget Balance Rule	Medium-term budget positions "close to balance or in surplus"	Structural deficit/GDP to remain below 1 percent		... below 0.5 percent deficit	Stability and Growth Pact (SGP) regulations; National legislation (2014)	Fines and sanctions; European Court of Justice fines and National enforcement
Expenditure Rule			Primary expenditure (excluding unemployment benefits and tax discretionary increases) grows less than medium-term GDP		Stability and Growth Pact (SGP) regulations	Fines and sanctions

Source: Anderson et al. (2012)

Note: Sanctions typically refer to interest or non-interest-bearing deposits of 0.2 percent of GDP. Fines can range from 0.1 to 0.5 percent of GDP. They apply differently to euro area and non–euro area member states.

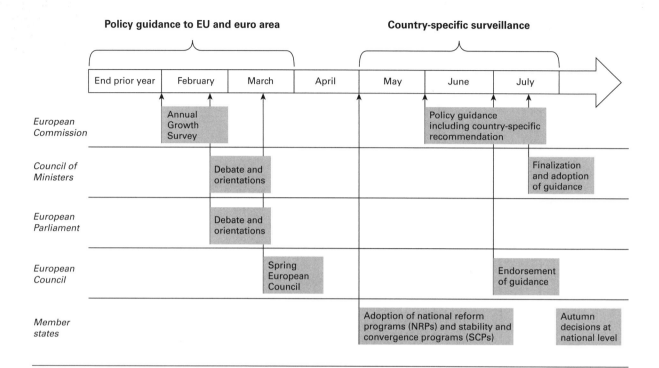

Figure 18.8
European semester
Source: European Commission

economic imbalances, financial sector issues, and growth-enhancing structural reforms, are however not binding at this stage. But the above-mentioned "two-pack" mandates also a common timetable to prepare national budgets, and, in case they are in noncompliance with the obligations of the Stability and Growth Pact, to allow the European Commission to request their revision.

A new excessive imbalances procedure (EIP) recognizes that unsustainable public debts may be rooted in nonfiscal problems. Macroeconomic imbalances, such as private sector financial excesses, may lead to sudden adjustments that result in the realization of implicit or contingent liabilities. The new surveillance mechanism aims to prevent and correct such divergences by establishing an alert system, consisting of a scoreboard of indicators and in-depth country studies, making country-specific recommendations for adjustments, and allowing for sanctions and fines in the case of noncompliance (European Commission 2012b). In the first assessment round in 2012, the European Commission found that 12 EU member states "experience macroeconomic imbalances, which are not excessive but need to be addressed."

With the European Stability Mechanism (ESM) a new crisis management institution has been created. The ESM essentially makes permanent the existing, strictly conditional assistance scheme (European Financial Stabilization Facility), expands its instruments (bond purchases in the primary market and direct recapitalization of banks under discussion), and links assistance to the adoption of stronger national fiscal rules. It will help prevent liquidity stress, including a potential degeneration into a full-blown solvency crisis through adverse market reactions.

These reforms are important steps to encourage fiscal responsibility and address any procyclical bent. A strengthened framework for fiscal rules, budgetary institutions, and crisis resolution mechanism should help prevent a recurrence of fiscal distress if the reforms are implemented coherently.

18.4 Nonpartisan Fiscal Agencies[6]

18.4.1 Rationale

Fiscal Authorities versus Fiscal Councils

Fiscal policy rules have historically been the institutional response of choice to the deficit and procyclical biases of discretionary policies. However, as documented in section 18.2, experience has revealed serious limitations related to three interdependent causes: the lack of political commitment (often reflected in weak budget procedures and controls), the rules' inflexibility in the face of adverse circumstances, and the absence of credible enforcement mechanisms. Typically weak commitment and procedures prevent the accumulation of sufficient buffers in good times, when a rigid rule (i.e., noncontingent on the state of the economy) does not bind. This makes the rule vulnerable to even a mild slowdown, when compliance would require procyclical adjustments that policy makers are reluctant to enact. Absent credible enforcement, the rule is ultimately circumvented, suspended or even eliminated. The European Council's decision to put the Stability and Growth Pact (SGP) in abeyance in November 2003 is a vivid illustration of this interaction between weak commitment, inflexible quantitative limits, and flawed enforcement. The subsequent reform of the SGP in 2005 largely addressed the inflexibility problem, but did not correspondingly strengthen enforcement procedures, undermining the effectiveness of the entire system (Beetsma and Debrun 2007) and sowing the seeds of the fiscal crisis experienced today in some euro area countries.

These difficulties have led some analysts to argue that other solutions should apply to eliminate fiscal policy biases. Since the mid-1990s, a number of academics have proposed to "depoliticize" certain dimensions of fiscal policy in the same way as monetary policy was delegated to unelected policy makers. Specifically, they argued that the authority to set the annual deficit or borrowing levels should be delegated to independent institutions with a clear mandate to devise a policy stance consistent with long-term debt sustainability and short-term macroeconomic stability (e.g., for a survey of the early literature, see Wyplosz 2005; Debrun, Hauner, and Kumar 2009). The limits set by those institutions would not only tie the hands of elected policy makers ex ante, but many proposals envisaged automatic adjustments in certain tax levers to ensure ex post compliance in case slippages occurred during the budget year (e.g., see Ball 1996; Blinder 1997; Eichengreen, Hausmann, and von Hagen 1999; Gruen 1997; Wren Lewis 2002).

The case for these Independent Fiscal Authorities (IFAs) has since been dismissed on both normative and positive grounds. From a normative angle, most aspects of fiscal policy are distributive in nature, which precludes delegation to unelected policy makers. This includes the deficit, which directly affects intergenerational equity. Alesina and Tabellini (2007) have formally modeled this generalization of the no-taxation-without-representation principle. From a positive perspective, the fact that fiscal biases are likely rooted in the genes of the political system—rather than in a pure time-inconsistency problem—implies that the system itself cannot credibly delegate fiscal policy to an IFA. The problem is indeed fundamentally different from that of delegating monetary policy to independent central banks because, in that case, elected policy makers fully understand ex ante the benefits of low inflation and the futility of exploiting the Phillips curve to lower structural unemployment (Debrun 2011).[7]

Experience in a handful of advanced economies suggests that another class of independent fiscal institutions could still play a role in promoting more sustainable and more stabilizing fiscal policies even if no policy-making power is delegated to them. These "fiscal councils," as they are best known, would influence the conduct of fiscal policy through independent analysis, assessments, forecasts, and possibly, recommendations driven by well-specified objectives set by elected policy makers.

Effectiveness of Fiscal Councils

The effectiveness of fiscal councils depends on two main transmission channels. The first is increased transparency fostering democratic accountability. By raising voters' awareness about the consequences of certain policy paths, a fiscal council could help them reward desirable options and sanction bad ones, effectively encouraging policy makers to deliver more viable and more countercyclical policies. One could even envisage a more direct contribution of these councils to democratic accountability by providing nonpartisan analyses of electoral platforms, as in the Netherlands (see Bos and Teulings 2011), Australia, and to some extent the United States, where the Congressional Budget Office evaluates the impact of major policy proposals. The second channel is direct inputs to the budget process, including the provision of unbiased macroeconomic and budgetary forecasts, and the costing of individual legislation tabled in parliament.

Proponents of fiscal councils are often keen to emphasize that these bodies could help shape an adequate policy response in practically any circumstances without risking the loss of the fiscal anchor that the demise of a rigid rule could entail. Hence an effective fiscal council could significantly relax the trade-off between credibility and flexibility central to the determination of the desirable pace of fiscal adjustment.

A natural question is whether a fiscal council should be viewed as a substitute for or as a complement to rules. There are at least two reasons to consider that fiscal councils may not necessarily be perfect substitutes for rules. First, the effectiveness of these institutions critically depends on the way the public debate constrains fiscal discretion, which is itself highly contingent on fundamental features of a country's political system, including the intensity of checks and balances between the executive and the legislative branches, and the type of electoral rule in place (proportional vs. majority voting). Second, the design of any incentive scheme—be it a rule or a fiscal agency—aimed at discouraging undesirable policies has to balance the space given to the proper exercise of policy discretion with the need to ultimately impose binding constraints when discretion is misused (Beetsma and Debrun 2007). Given that trade-off, exclusive reliance on a fiscal agency would point to establishing an agency that could in well-specified circumstances supersede elected policy makers. Such a council would arguably be too close to an IFA for comfort.

When fiscal rules are already in place or envisaged, it might therefore be worth exploring how a fiscal council could work with rules rather than how it could replace them. Specifically, a council could ease the enforcement of the more sophisticated fiscal rules described in section 18.3 by contributing to a better balance between flexibility and binding constraints on policy. We can think of three ways this could work. First, through continuous monitoring and analysis, the fiscal council could issue early warnings that compliance with the rule might be at risk. These could be particularly useful in good times, when confusion between permanent and transitory revenue gains may feed complacency and hamper a sufficient build-up of fiscal buffers, even if the rule sets quantitative limits in structural terms. Second, mandating a fiscal council to produce independent macroeconomic and revenue forecasts and to score policy initiatives could lessen the risk of optimistic bias in budget assumptions. This would reduce the likelihood that plans compliant with the rules systematically lead to outcomes at odds with them (Beetsma et al. 2011; Frankel and Schreger 2012). Third, a fiscal council could play a direct role in the enforcement of a rule through the formulation of a motivated opinion about the activation of an escape clause, or the calculation of fiscal indicators particularly vulnerable to manipulations, such as the structural budget balance. Finally, one should also note that the complementarity between rules and councils goes both ways: a simple and transparent fiscal rule can facilitate the council's work by providing an unambiguous and easily monitorable benchmark for assessing fiscal performance (Debrun, Hauner, and Kumar 2009).

Contributing to the implementation of fiscal rules is central to the remit of most existing fiscal council (see below) as well as of many academic proposals (e.g., Fatás et al. 2003; European Commission 2004; Ubide 2004; Jonung and Larch 2006). In the European Union, the Fiscal Compact assumes (Article 3, par. 2) that independent agencies will monitor compliance with national fiscal policy rules in each euro area member state, as now mandated by the "two pack".

In the remainder of this section, we clarify the concept of fiscal council, and map existing fiscal councils along a number of key aspects of their remit, tasks and institutional form.

18.4.2 Fiscal Councils in Practice

What Qualifies as a Fiscal Council?

In principle, any organization seeking to inform the public and foster the quality of the public debate on fiscal policy in a nonpartisan way could fit the concept of a fiscal council as discussed above. This includes specialized think tanks or research institutes—for example, the Institute for Fiscal Studies in the United Kingdom, or the Austrian Institute of Economic Research (WIFO) in Austria.

However, the literature generally focuses on a much narrower set of institutions. First, only institutions with an official mandate from elected policy makers qualify as fiscal councils. The existence of a mandate is more likely to generate significant reputational costs when the council has to report and comment on undesirable policy developments or bias. In principle, an official mandate also implies public funding commensurate to the tasks of the council and some form of legal guarantee against partisan influence. Thus the mandate criterion excludes private bodies, such as think tanks and self-proclaimed watchdogs or whistle-blowers. Intergovernmental agencies are also excluded. Their surveillance responsibilities are arguably too broad to generate the large reputational effects a national body with a well-defined remit can deliver; they lack the local anchorage and the deep understanding of political customs needed to effectively influence the national policy debate through continuous interaction with policy makers and the media; and last but not least, they are not expected to fully internalize the country-specific preferences regarding the objectives assigned to fiscal policy and therefore cannot be held accountable before national parliaments. In sum, the official mandate criterion crystallizes the full ownership of the institution required to effectively shape the national public debate and foster accountability, a point theorized by Debrun (2011) and emphasized by Kopits (2011) as part of best practice.

Also audit institutions are generally not considered as fiscal councils. Although they contribute to democratic accountability and transparency, their approach is in most cases backward-looking and legalistic, as opposed to the mostly forward-looking and economic work of fiscal councils. That said, some audit bodies perform tasks that are of a prospective and economic nature—the French *Cour des Comptes* is a case in point. One potential problem with that approach is that ex ante assessments are likely to constrain ex post analyses. For instance, if the audit body was tasked to assess the costs and economic impact of budget plans and policies, reputational concerns would likely taint the ex post evaluation of these policies, especially if they ended up having unforeseen consequences.

The question as to whether strict formal guarantees against any type of interference by elected officials must exist to qualify as a fiscal council is less clear-cut than in the case of central banks. Experience with long-standing watchdogs is that incomplete *de jure* independence does not exclude considerable *de facto* autonomy. Since fiscal councils are not expected to impose binding constraints on policy choices, the immediate reward for politicians to interfere with their activity is unclear. Of course, de facto independence is unlikely to survive repeated and public divergences of views between elected officials and the fiscal council, especially if the latter has some leverage on the conduct of fiscal policy through high-impact normative analysis and recommendations, or the provision of forecasts. The experience with the High Council of Finance (HCF) in Belgium is very telling in that respect (Coene and Langenus 2011).

In the remainder of this section, we review key features of actual institutions that have been commonly classified as fiscal councils. We identified 24 councils in 22 countries (Belgium and Slovenia have two separate fiscal councils, according to our definition), most of them in Europe. The sample includes two defunct institutions: the original Hungarian Fiscal Council and the Parliamentary Budget Office of Georgia. As Debrun and Takahashi (2011), we distinguish between the "veterans" and the new generation of fiscal councils.

Role and Main Features: Veterans and the New Generation[8]
The universe of institutions qualifying as fiscal councils is limited, albeit expanding rapidly (figure 18.9). Nonetheless, the population of fiscal councils is also extraordinarily diverse, making it difficult to establish robust trends that would point to obvious best practice. As a first step, it is useful to distinguish between veteran institutions with a well-established reputation and newcomers with little or no track record. In 1960, only two fiscal councils were in operation; Belgium's High Council of Finance, created in 1936 to advise the Ministry of Finance, and the Dutch Central Planning Bureau, established in 1945 to provide forecasts and economic analysis supporting the design of fiscal policy. By 1995, only six new fiscal councils had

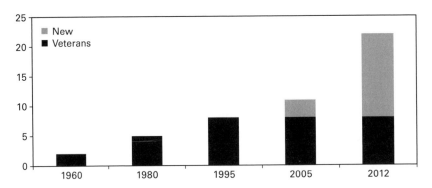

Figure 18.9
Number of active fiscal councils
Source: IMF staff assessment based on publicly available information

emerged, including those in Denmark, Germany, and the United States—the Congressional Budget Office, created in 1974. The number of fiscal councils then doubled between 2005 and 2012 to reach 22 active institutions at the time of writing. These new institutions include the Swedish Fiscal Policy Council, the United Kingdom's Office for Budget Responsibility, the Parliamentary Budget Offices in Australia and Canada, and other fiscal councils in Portugal, Ireland, and emerging Europe (Bosnia-Herzegovina, Hungary, Romania, Serbia, the Slovak Republic, and Slovenia). Overall, only two fiscal councils were dismantled (Georgia in 2008) or reduced to insignificance (Hungary in 2010).

The distinction between veterans and newcomers is useful because the design of new institutions could have been influenced by the intensifying academic debate on their potential role in improving the conduct of fiscal policy (with the most prominent contributions by von Hagen and Harden 1995; Eichengreen, Hausmann and von Hagen 1999; Calmfors 2003; Fatás et al. 2003; Wyplosz 2005) and by the experience with politically independent agencies in other policy areas such as central banking or the regulation and supervision of specific sectors (banking, energy, and media). Based on publicly available information, a few notable differences emerge between the two groups.

Looking at the remit, all the fiscal councils are mandated to provide nonpartisan positive assessments of fiscal policy (figure 18.10). A large majority of them are also required to analyze long-term sustainability and to either assess the quality of macroeconomic and/or budgetary forecasts, or to prepare such forecasts themselves. However, only a few countries (Belgium, the Netherlands, and Slovenia) generally (or are obliged to) use these forecasts for budget preparation.[9] Only a minority of fiscal councils is expected to provide normative assessments and policy recommen-

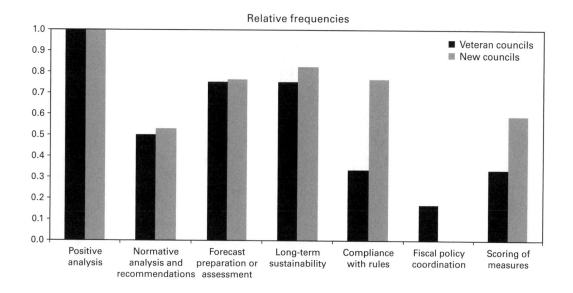

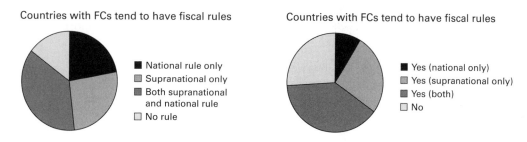

Figure 18.10
Tasks of fiscal councils
Source: IMF staff assessment based on publicly available information

dations (regardless of the group), and fiscal councils are rarely involved in coordinating policy among government entities. Newly established councils are more often mandated to score specific policy initiatives than the veteran agencies, perhaps reflecting a growing awareness of the importance of transparency in policy-making. And in contrast to veterans, new institutions are also more frequently tasked to monitor compliance with national or supranational fiscal policy rules, pointing to a growing perception that rules and councils are complements rather than substitutes, as discussed above. The mid and lower panels of figure 18.10 confirm that most countries with fiscal councils have fiscal rules and that among that subgroup, about three-quarters of fiscal councils monitor compliance.

The channels through which councils can influence fiscal performance vary widely, ranging from informal or technical advice to public communications and formal procedures specifically aimed at magnifying the reputational and political costs of deviations from ex-ante commitments. In line with theory, which rules out delegation and direct constraints on discretion, relatively "soft" channels of influence—public reports, analyses, communication—seem preferred to "harder" channels whereby the council's activity creates an obligation for the government, including requiring public explanations of policy slippages or biased forecasts, the compulsory use of council's projections for budget preparation, and the possibility for the council to access elected representatives through formal hearings in Parliament. The latter feature is more prominent in recent councils, possibly to compensate for the lack of pre-existing reputation and the correspondingly lower visibility of (and lesser public trust in) their work. Indeed, veteran councils generally enjoy significant media impact which helps them influence the public debate on fiscal policy (figure 18.11).

Still reflecting a revealed preference for soft influence, the new councils are rarely tasked to provide binding forecasts for budget preparation and governments are in general not compelled to formally respond to the council's assessments. Of course, such an obligation need not be enshrined in law and can emerge spontaneously, as the council's work progressively gains traction in the public. It is important to note

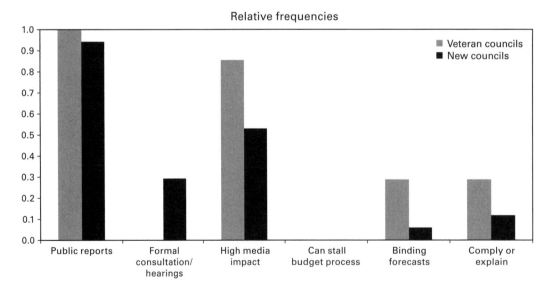

Figure 18.11
Fiscal councils' channels of influence
Source: IMF staff assessment based on publicly available information

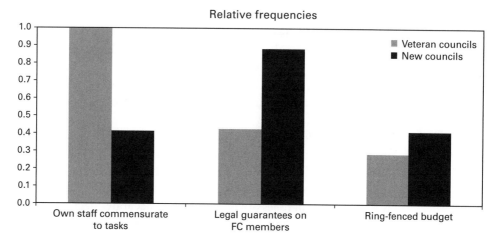

Figure 18.12
Fiscal councils: Determinants of independence
Source: IMF staff assessment based on publicly available information

that no fiscal council is allowed to block the budget process in case a draft budget violates objectives or constraints the council is mandated to monitor.[10]

Turning to the degree of political and operational independence, three dimensions are relevant: (1) legal guarantees similar to those in place for central banks (e.g., long, nonrenewable tenures for the council's management, prohibition of political activities prior to the appointment), (2) the appointment and retention of professional staff commensurate in skills and number to the tasks of the council, and (3) secured financing (figure 18.12). The latter dimension is particularly important because, unlike central banks, fiscal councils cannot generate significant own income. And it is through financial starvation that certain governments—most egregiously in Hungary—have attempted to curtail (or virtually eliminate) their fiscal council. Interestingly, only a minority of fiscal councils enjoy some form of safeguard on the financing of their activities. This could be viewed as another manifestation of elected policy makers' instinctive reluctance to permanently cede influence on the power to tax and spend.

Regarding the other dimensions of independence, there appears to be a sharp contrast between the veterans and the new generation. The latter rely more on legal safeguards similar to those preserving the management of central banks from political influence. However, based on our own assessment of publicly available data on staffing and budget, many new fiscal councils do not appear to have adequate resources to perform their duties. The opposite applies to the group of veterans which do have significant resources in terms of expertise and size of their staff. This is in line with our conjecture above that *de facto* independence acquired through reputable analyses is perhaps as important as *de jure* independence. And the reliance of new councils on the latter is only understandable given the absence of preexisting reputation. Of course, this stylized fact is a reflection of history based on the total population of fiscal councils; it is not the manifestation of an ex ante trade-off between adequate staffing and legal guarantees of independence. Clearly, the two should go hand in hand.

A key question is whether certain combinations of those features are more likely to contribute to better fiscal performance than others. Assessing the effectiveness of fiscal councils is clearly beyond the scope of this paper and existing attempts are rather unconvincing. The only solid evidence regarding the impact of fiscal councils is that they prepare less biased and more accurate macroeconomic and budgetary forecasts (Jonung and Larch 2006; Frankel and Schreger 2012). Testing other aspects of the influence of fiscal councils on fiscal performance remains vexingly difficult. Not only the small size of the population severely impedes a rigorous statistical analysis aimed at unveiling causalities, but the subtle and varied ways in which a fiscal council can shape policy outcomes dramatically complicates attempts to quantify its influence on the conduct of fiscal policy. Of course, as more fiscal councils are likely to emerge, the universe of potentially interesting case studies will expand significantly.

18.5 Improving Public Financial Management

Effective implementation and monitoring of fiscal rules should be supported by strong public financial management arrangements. These arrangements play an important part in the formulation of overall fiscal policy; supporting the design of specific policies that are consistent with the overall fiscal rules; and helping delivering and implementing budgets in line with what is intended. Reforms are underway in many countries, in particular in those where significant institutional weaknesses compounded the imbalances of public finances during the crisis.

The *budget formulation and execution cycle* should be well-integrated with fiscal rules to form a cohesive public financial management. In particular, a top-down budgeting process, where the aggregate expenditure limit is decided before the distribution of expenditures helps alleviate the common pool problem (i.e., the conflict between unlimited spending demands from line ministries and a finite budget constraint) at the root of excessive deficits. For example, in Germany as of 2012, the federal budget is being drawn up using a top-down approach so as to better accommodate the requirements of the structural budget balance rule.

Medium-term budget frameworks (MTBF) can reinforce fiscal rules and can in turn be strengthened by the adoption of a numerical fiscal rule. MTBFs enable governments to demonstrate the impact of current and proposed policies over the course of several years, set future budget priorities, and ultimately achieve better control over public expenditure. Presenting the budget over a multiyear horizon, demonstrates ex ante whether government policy is consistent with the fiscal rule, and what policy actions are necessary to bring it into line in the event that it is not. In countries with high budget deficits, MTBFs can also serve as a transition regime toward a meeting the requirements of a fiscal rule. Greece, Ireland, and Portugal are moving toward setting up MTBFs. Greece has adopted a medium-term fiscal strategy, Ireland has established three-year expenditure ceilings for each ministry, and Portugal's Stability Program now includes indicative ceilings on program level expenditures.

Good technical forecasting capacity, both of the fiscal aggregates and of the key macroeconomic variables is needed to ensure that the budget is developed on a realistic basis—particularly so when combined with MTBF, where the potential for errors is much greater. This should include quantifying the impact of new policy measures from the baseline forecast on the fiscal and macroeconomic environment as well as the risks around the baseline forecasts, through sensitivity analysis. This allows identifying policy adjustments needs to ensure compliance with fiscal rules. Since overly optimistic forecasts in some countries with weak or pro-cyclical public finances pre-crisis were not so much a result of limited technical capacity but rather a lack of independence, a response is to mandate independent agencies with this task (see section 18.4).

Effective budget execution systems, such as commitment controls, arrears monitoring, and cash management systems are essential to ensure that budget outcomes are in line with budget appropriations and that hidden liabilities that can endanger the overall fiscal rules are not being accumulated outside of the budgetary systems. To be effective, these systems need to be comprehensive in coverage, as many problems have emerged outside of the immediate budgetary central government, where systems tend to be stronger. For example, Portugal is in the process of strengthening and broadening its budget execution system to cover the whole general government and control expenditure at the point of commitment rather than payment, thereby preventing the accumulation of arrears.

Budget reporting systems should be comprehensive in terms of aggregates covered, able to produce reports on a consistent basis, and sufficiently developed to produce in-year and timely end-year reports to allow monitoring adherence to rules-based requirements. Given that fiscal strategies and budgets are typically prepared and approved before the start of the financial year, timely information on the state of public finances for the current year is critical in establishing the baseline for new fiscal settings. This is particularly true in the case where fiscal rules relate past fiscal performance to future fiscal policy setting and require adjustments in case of deviations as, for instance, in Germany's debt brake system and as requested for the new structural budget balance rules in the EU. A number of south eastern European countries, such as Croatia, have strengthened their fiscal reporting systems in order to meet EU accession requirements. Other countries have taken steps to improve the consistency of the reporting between budgets and outturns, through initiatives such as the "alignment project" in the United Kingdom.[11]

Internal and external audit systems are also important to ensure accountability and credibility of fiscal rules. Fiscal data—consistent with the budget reporting system—should be publicly released in line with a pre-announced calendar to allow external monitoring. In addition, externally audited financial statements are needed to scrutinize budget performance, to understand the extant position, and to provide a basis for the budget process. Development of external audit capacity in the public sector has been a key reform area for all new EU member states though further strengthening is needed in many cases. The internal audit function should provide support and assurance to the managers of public sector agencies on the adequacy and effectiveness of internal control systems. Again new EU member states and EU candidate countries, for which improvements in internal audit and internal control systems are a prerequisite for EU membership, have been active in developing capacity in this area in recent years.

Guidance to strengthen national budgetary institutions and procedures as well as accounting practices is also provided through the EU governance reforms ("six pack").[12] This includes, for example, broad recommendations to make medium-term budget frameworks more binding, prepare budgets in a more top-down sequence, report more frequently, timely, and comprehensively on fiscal developments and risks. While minimum benchmarks are provided, they miss some important elements—for example, statistical coverage of the public sector, rather than the general government, and certain elements of budgetary institutions—and provide little operational details. Progress in the areas for which guidance is provided is currently being assessed in an EU peer review with progress underway in many countries.

18.6 Conclusion

From a macroeconomic perspective, good fiscal institutions provide incentives at all levels of government to plan and execute fiscal policies that preserve the long-term financial sustainability of the public sector, deliver public services in an efficient way, and contribute to stabilizing the economy. While countries have generally understood the importance of getting the incentives right, institutional reforms have often suffered from the intrinsic reluctance of elected officials to directly limit their discretionary power to tax and spend. The result was partial reforms that often failed the test of time. A typical example is the adoption of fiscal policy rules that do not bind in good times—such as caps on headline deficits—and cannot be enforced in bad times, when fiscal adjustment is even more politically and economically unpleasant than otherwise. Incomplete and ineffective institutional arrangements are partly to blame for the fiscal vulnerabilities revealed by the crisis.

The discussion in this chapter nevertheless points to encouraging developments in the aftermath of the crisis, suggesting efforts to find a better balance between preserving policy discretion when needed, while establishing fiscal institutions that can effectively constrain such discretion in a legitimate and transparent manner when fending off undesirable trends is required. A first interesting development is the preference for fiscal rules that account for cyclical factors, and are therefore more likely to bind in good as well as in bad times, delivering greater macroeconomic stability. The need for a credible enforcement of the rules is also part of recent reforms, with the adoption of automatic correction mechanisms that reduce the risk of political interference when the implementation of the rule mandates difficult measures. Second, the rapid increase in the number of fiscal councils suggests that countries are prepared to envisage other forms of constraints on fiscal behavior, involving a better operation of checks and balances in the political system and greater awareness of the electorate. Fiscal councils could also play a formal role in facilitating the implementation of the new rules. Finally, public financial management reforms aimed at a stronger medium-term orientation of the budget should provide a supportive environment for the elimination of the deficit and procyclicality biases.

While welcome, these developments are no magic bullets. First, there will always be circumstances where political commitments will be tested to an extent that could threaten the very existence of good fiscal institutions. Second, the more sophisticated macroeconomic frameworks implied by the new rules, and the design and operation of fiscal councils and full-fledged MTBFs pose important implementation challenges. Many essential questions remain open. How can we implement an effective structural budget balance rule for the general government in a highly decentralized or federal context? How can we set up an effective fiscal council in a fractious political environment? How can limited administrative capacities be overcome when establishing full-fledged MTBFs and fiscal councils? The answers to these questions are highly country-specific, and pragmatism will be at a premium, as it will take some time for a robust set of best practices to emerge.

Notes

Jason Harris provided input for section 18.5 (Public Financial Management).

1. A comprehensive review on the design options of public financial management tools is provided in Cangiano, Curristine, and Lazare (2013).

2. The fiscal rule in Chile not only accounts for the economic cycle but also for deviations of copper and molybdenum prices from their long-term trends.

3. Automatic corrections of ex post deviations from the deficit or debt rule can raise their enforceability. They require policy makers to "undo" past fiscal excesses and determine the path back to the fiscal rule. For example, Germany and Switzerland use notional accounts in which ex post deviations (positive or negative) from the structural budget balance rule are stored. When the accumulated deviation exceeds a threshold, improvements in the structural balance are required within a predefined time frame to undo these deviations.

4. One percent of GDP for countries with debt levels below 60 percent and low sustainability risks.

5. The European Court of Justice (ECJ) will verify the transposition of structural balanced budget rules to national legislation; it will, however, not verify compliance with the rules.

6. This section draws on Debrun and Takahashi (2011) and Debrun et al. (2013).

7. In contrast, governments have an ex ante incentive to delegate monetary policy to independent central banks because the inflationary bias under discretion reflects a pure time-inconsistency problem where ex ante and ex post incentives are not aligned.

8. This section updates and expands Debrun and Takahashi (2011).

9. Jonung and Larch (2006) and Frankel and Schreger (2012) show that independent forecasts reduce the risk of an optimistic bias.

10. This was a feature of a first proposal of the Hungarian fiscal council. According to the proposal, the council would have had the right to prevent—through a ruling of the Constitutional Court—that a draft budget deemed inconsistent with the overarching principle of budget responsibility be tabled in parliament.

11. The UK government previously used three different methods for preparing its budget, presenting the expenditure estimates for parliamentary approval, and producing its end-of-year resource accounts, resulting in significant misalignment of up to around 4 percent of GDP. The Alignment Project has reduced and clarified the discrepancies and brought the three reports closer to the International Financial Reporting Standard (IFRS).

12. Council Directive 2011/85/EU on "Requirements for Budgetary Frameworks of the Member States."

References

Alesina, A., and G. Tabellini. 2007. Bureaucrats or politicians? Part 1: A Single policy task. *American Economic Review* 97: 169–79.

Anderson, A., M. Moreno Badia, E. Perez Ruiz, S. Snudden, and F. Vitek. 2012. Fiscal consolidations under the SGP: Some illustrative simulations. Country report 12/182. IMF, Washington, DC.

Ball, L. 1996. A proposal for the next macroeconomic reform. *Victoria Economic Commentaries* 14: 1–7.

Beetsma, R., B. Bluhm, M. Giuliodori, and P. Wierts. 2011. From first release to ex-post fiscal data: Exploring the sources of revision errors in the EU. Discussion paper 2011–080/2. Tinbergen Institute, Amsterdam.

Beetsma, R., and X. Debrun. 2007. The new stability and growth pact: A first assessment. *European Economic Review* 51 (2): 453–77.

Blinder, A. 1997. Is government too political? *Foreign Affairs* 6: 115–26.

Bos, F., and C. Teulings. 2011. Evaluation election platforms: A task for fiscal councils? Scope and rules of the game in view of 25 years of Dutch practice. Paper 31536. MPRA, Munich. Available at: http://mpra.ub.uni-muenchen.de/31536/.

Calmfors, L. 2003. Fiscal policy to stabilize the domestic economy in the EMU. *CESifo Economic Studies* 49: 319–53.

Cangiano, M., T. Curristine, and M. Lazare, eds. 2013. *Public Financial Management and Its Emerging Architecture*. Washington, DC: IMF.

Coene, L., and G. Langenus. 2011. Promoting fiscal discipline in a federal country: The mixed track record of Belgium's High Council of Finance. *Wirtschaftspolitische Blätter* 58 (1): 11–36.

Debrun, X. 2011. Democratic accountability, deficit bias, and independent fiscal agencies. Working paper 11/173. IMF, Washington, DC. Available at: http://ideas.repec.org/p/imf/imfwpa/11-173.html.

Debrun, X., D. Hauner, and M. Kumar. 2009. Independent fiscal agencies. *Journal of Economic Surveys* 23 (1): 44–81.

Debrun, X., and K. Takahashi. 2011. Independent fiscal councils in continental Europe: Old wine in new bottles? *CESifo Dice Report* 9 (3): 44–50. Available at: http://ideas.repec.org/a/ces/ifodic/v9y2011i3p44-50.html.

Debrun, X., T. Kinda, T. Curristine, L. Eyraud, J. Harris, and J. Seiwald. 2013. The functions and impact of fiscal councils. Policy Paper. IMF, Washington, DC. Available at: http://www.imf.org/external/pp/longres.aspx?id=4791.

Eichengreen, B., R. Hausmann, and J. von Hagen. 1999. Reforming budgetary institutions in Latin America: The case for a national fiscal council. *Open Economies Review* 10: 415–42.

European Commission. 2004. *Strengthening Economic Governance and Clarifying the Implementation of the Stability and Growth Pact*. Communication from the Commission to the Council and the European Parliament. Brussels: EC.

European Commission. 2012a. 2012 Report on public finances in EMU. European economy paper 4/2012. EC, Brussels. Available at: http://ec.europa.eu/economy_finance/publications/european_economy/2012/pdf/ee-2012-4.pdf.

European Commission. 2012b. Scoreboard for the surveillance of macroeconomic imbalances. European Economy occasional paper 92. EC, Brussels. Available at: http://ec.europa.eu/economy_finance/publications/occasional_paper/2012/pdf/ocp92_en.pdf.

Fatás, A., J. von Hagen, A. Hughes Hallett, R. Strauch, and A. Sibert. 2003. Stability and growth in Europe: Towards a better pact. *Monitoring European Integration* 13.

Frankel, J., and J. Schreger. 2012. Over-optimistic official forecasts in the eurozone and fiscal rules. Working paper 18283. NBER, Cambridge, MA.

Gruen, N. 1997. Making fiscal policy flexibly independent of government. *Agenda (Durban, South Africa)* 4: 297–307.

International Monetary Fund. 2012a. *Fiscal Monitor*, April. IMF, Washington, DC.

Irwin, T. 2012. Accounting devices and fiscal illusions. Staff discussion note 12/02. IMF, Washington, DC. Available at: http://www.imf.org/external/pubs/ft/sdn/2012/sdn1202.pdf.

Jonung, L., and M. Larch. 2006. Improving fiscal policy in the EU: The case for independent forecasts. *Economic Policy* 21: 491–534.

Kopits, G. 2011. Independent fiscal institutions: Developing good practices. Paper presented at 3rd Annual Meeting of OECD Parliamentary Budget Officials.

Schaechter, A., T. Kinda, N. Budina, and A. Weber. 2012. Fiscal rules in response to the crisis—Toward the "next-generation" rules: A new dataset. Working paper 12/187. IMF, Washington, DC. Available at: www.imf.org/external/pubs/ft/wp/2012/wp12187.pdf.

Ubide, A. 2004. Just reinforce the pact. *Finance and Development* (June): 26–28.

von Hagen, J., and I. J. Harden. 1995. Budget processes and commitment to fiscal discipline. *European Economic Review* 39: 771–79.

Wren Lewis, S. 2002. Fiscal policy, inflation, and stabilization in EMU. Unpublished manuscript.

19

Long-Term Fiscal Challenges

Baoping Shang and Mauricio Soto

19.1   Introduction

Reforming age-related spending, including both pension and health care spending, will be a key policy challenge in both advanced and emerging economies over coming decades. A large share of government budgets is devoted to public pension and health care systems. Spending in these two areas has been growing rapidly, driven by population aging and excess cost growth[1] in health care spending, and is projected to increase by 3.5 percentage points of GDP in advanced economies and by 2 percentage points of GDP in emerging economies over the next two decades, with a greater contribution coming from projected increases in health care spending.[2]

Many countries already face a need for large fiscal adjustment because of high deficits and debt-to-GDP ratios, and the continued rise in age-related spending will make this adjustment even more challenging over the long run. This long-term fiscal challenge requires structural reforms of both public pension and health care systems.

This chapter first presents projections for spending in both public pensions and health care for 28 advanced and 22 emerging economies,[3] and then discusses reform options to improve the long-term sustainability and performance of public pension and health care systems while safeguarding the most vulnerable. Pension and health care systems differ greatly across countries. For example, some pension systems include mandatory, privately funded individual retirement account schemes while others rely solely on public pensions financed on a pay-as-you-go basis; some health systems are financed by payroll contributions while others are financed by general tax revenues. The projections and reform options in this chapter are based on the existing pension and health care systems, assuming these systems would remain in place in the foreseeable future. In addition there is evidence that while the types of systems may matter for spending efficiency, the details in the design of each individual system appear to be more important (IMF 2011b; Joumard, Andre, and Nicq 2010).

516 *Baoping Shang and Mauricio Soto*

19.2 The Evolution of Public Pensions and Health Care Spending

Public pension and health care systems have gone through substantial expansion in the last several decades and are currently two of the most important items in government budgets, accounting for, on average, 40 percent of primary spending in advanced economies and 30 percent in emerging economies in 2010. For example, more than 80 percent of the increase in primary spending to GDP ratio in G7 countries between 1960 and 2007 is due to the increase in public pension and health spending (Cottarelli and Schaechter 2010).

19.2.1 Public Pensions

In advanced economies, public pension spending on average increased from 5 percent of GDP in 1970 to 9.5 percent in 2010. The four drivers behind the change in public pension spending as a share of GDP are aging, eligibility rates (the number of pensioners as a proportion of the population 65 and older), replacement rates (the ratio of average pension to average wages), and labor force participation rates (figure 19.1). During 1970 to 1990, increases in spending reflected a combination of higher replacement rates, aging, and increased eligibility—the average statutory retirement age declined by one year over this period. Increasing female labor force participation offset some of the increase in spending by raising output and thus reducing pension spending as a share of GDP. Pension spending growth was more contained over the past two decades. The impact of aging and benefit increases was partly offset by both tighter pension eligibility rules (including increasing statutory

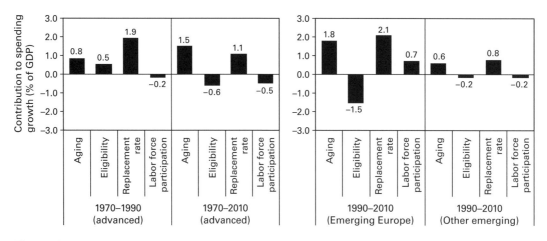

Figure 19.1
Evolution of public pension expenditures in advanced and emerging economies, 1970 to 2010
Sources: OECD; Eurostat; International Labor Organisation (ILO); UN; IMF staff estimates

retirement ages and restricting early retirement) and further increases in labor force participation rates.

Over the past two decades, increases in public pension spending in emerging economies have been larger than those in advanced economies, but from a much lower level in emerging economies outside Europe. Between 1990 and 2010, spending in all emerging economies increased on average by 2 percentage points of GDP. In emerging Europe, spending increased from about 7.5 percent of GDP in 1990 to 10 percent in 2010, with rapid increases in the 1990s in Poland, Romania, Turkey, and Ukraine. This increase was due mainly to higher replacement rates (average pensions increased relative to wages during the 1990s) and population aging. Declining labor force participation rates also played a role. In other emerging economies, spending increased from 2 to 3 percentage points of GDP over the same period, owing to increases in replacement rates, albeit from relatively low initial levels.

Today the variation in current public pension spending across countries and regions reflects mainly differences in old-age dependency ratios, generosity of benefits, and coverage rates. On average, spending is very similar in advanced economies and emerging Europe—at 9.5 and 10 percent of GDP, respectively—but is substantially lower in other emerging economies at 3 percent. However, there is substantial variation in spending among advanced economies, with spending ranging from less than 5 percent of GDP in countries with relatively younger populations and low replacement rates (Australia, Canada, Iceland, and Korea), to more than 12 percent in countries with relatively high replacement rates and older populations (Austria, France, Greece, Italy, and Portugal). In contrast, no emerging European economy has spending below 6 percent of GDP. Most advanced and emerging European economies have replacement rates of between 40 and 60 percent, old-age dependency ratios above 20 percent, and nearly universal coverage. The relatively low spending in emerging economies outside Europe reflects a combination of relatively low coverage (generally only those in the formal sector are eligible and receive pensions that are high relative to the average wage) and younger populations.

19.2.2   Public Health Care

Total health expenditures have risen sharply in recent decades, particularly in advanced economies (figure 19.2). Since 1970, real per capita total health spending has increased fourfold in advanced economies, while spending as a share of GDP has increased from 6 to almost 12 percent. Two-thirds of this increase has been due to greater public health spending, with its share of total health spending rising from 55 to 60 percent. In emerging economies, the increase in total health spending has been more moderate over the same period—from below 3 percent of GDP to about 5 percent—and public spending on health has increased from around 1.5 to 2.5 percent of GDP, about the same as the increase in private spending.

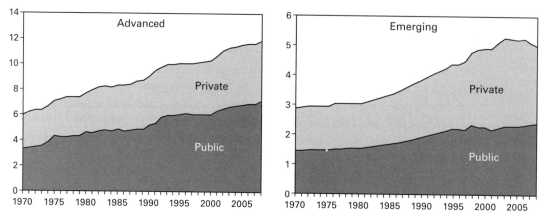

Figure 19.2
Evolution of public health care expenditures in advanced and emerging economies, 1970 to 2012. Average spending is weighted on the basis of GDP at purchasing power parity. For advanced economies without 2008 data (five countries), 2006 or 2007 data were used. The final year for spending data for the emerging economies is 2007.
Sources: OECD Health Database; WHO; Sivard (1974–96); IMF staff estimates

Public health spending in advanced countries has been characterized by short periods of accelerated growth followed by periods of cost containment.[4] The rapid increase in spending during 1971 to 1975 (1 percentage point of GDP) reflected the expansion of health insurance coverage in most countries. This was followed by a longer period of relative cost control as many countries introduced health reforms as part of broader fiscal consolidation efforts. Public health spending increased by less than 1 percentage point of GDP over the fifteen-year period from 1975 to 1990. Expenditures again began to accelerate in the early 1990s, before another period of containment in the second half of the decade. The slowdown in spending growth reflected reforms in both the United States and Europe as part of a broader restraint of total government spending. The growth of public health spending picked up after 2000, with outlays rising one percentage point (to 7 percent of GDP) by 2010.

Public health care spending levels and increases have been relatively low in the emerging economies. During 1971 to 1995, public health spending increased by 0.5 percentage point of GDP, to 2 percent. Spending accelerated after that with an additional 0.5 percentage point of GDP in the following decade. Public spending ratios are substantially higher in emerging Europe and Latin America than emerging Asia with no evidence of convergence in ratios across emerging economies over time. Since 1995, the largest increases in spending have been in Romania, Saudi Arabia, Thailand, and Turkey (1 to 1.5 percentage points of GDP), while spending ratios have fallen in Estonia, Hungary, India, Latvia, Russia, and Ukraine. Since 2000— when average public health spending to GDP ratios started to rise—only six countries have had increases of more than 0.5 percentage point (Brazil, Bulgaria, Chile, Poland, Thailand, and Ukraine).

The literature has identified income, aging, technology, and health policies as the key factors behind rising public spending-to-GDP ratios. On the demand side, health care spending tends to rise as a share of GDP as countries develop. In addition elderly people consume, on average, more health services than their younger counterparts. On the supply side, technological change has expanded the scope of what is medically possible by improving treatments and diagnostics. This has increased the cost of medical services, reflecting improvements in quality (e.g., the diffusion of angioplasty or the use of MRIs instead of X rays). Additionally health costs have been driven upward by the relatively low productivity growth of services relative to other sectors of the economy (the so-called Baumol effect). Among these drivers, nondemographic factors dominate. On average, approximately one-fourth of the increase in public spending-to-GDP ratios between 1980 and 2008 is explained by changes in the age distribution of the population ("aging"). The rest—known as excess cost growth (ECG)—is attributable to the combined effect of nondemographic factors, including rising incomes, technological advances, the Baumol effect,[5] and health policies and institutions. Of course, positive ECG should not be interpreted to mean that the costs of public spending have exceeded its benefits, because technological advancements—the main driver of higher health care costs—have yielded enormous improvements in health status and well-being (Cutler and McClellan 2001). This said, the benefits of higher health spending would also need to be weighed against their costs.

Inefficiencies in public health spending are believed to be large. While higher spending can help, improving the efficiency of these outlays while maintaining the same level of spending is even more critical for improving health outcomes. This can be illustrated by examining the gains from reducing the "efficiency gap" for countries, which provides an estimate of the difference between the life expectancy they achieve—taking account also of the effects of socioeconomic and lifestyle factors—and that of the best-performing country at similar levels of spending.[6] Cutting the efficiency gap of OECD countries in half, for example, would increase life expectancy by over one year. Achieving this same gain in life expectancy through higher spending, by contrast, would require a spending increase of over 30 percent. Countries where spending has been identified as the most efficient include Australia, Korea, and Switzerland, while Hungary, the Slovak Republic, and the United States are among the least efficient. In developing and emerging countries, health spending is also an important determinant of health outcomes (Baldacci et al. 2008). As in the advanced economies, the efficiency of their outlays varies widely (Gupta and Verhoeven 2001; Gupta et al. 2008), again suggesting ample room to improve health outcomes without raising spending.

Table 19.1
Public pension and health spending in advanced and emerging economics, 1970 to 2010

Country	Public pension expenditure (percent of GDP)			Public health expenditure (percent of GDP)		
	1970	1990	2010	1970	1990	2010
Advanced economies						
Australia	2.6	4.1	4.7	3.0	4.4	6.2
Austria	10.0	12.8	14.5	3.9	6.1	8.4
Belgium	6.5	9.9	10.9	—	6.2	7.9
Canada	2.4	4.7	4.9	4.9	6.3	8.1
Czech Republic	—	7.3	9.8	—	3.9	6.3
Denmark	5.1	6.7	8.1	6.9	7.2	9.4
Estonia	—	—	14.5	—	—	5.0
Finland	6.1	9.4	12.0	3.3	5.1	6.6
France	6.7	11.1	14.3	4.7	7.4	8.9
Germany	8.8	9.5	10.9	4.4	6.3	8.9
Greece	5.4	10.5	13.9	2.3	3.5	6.1
Iceland	2.6	2.9	3.3	2.8	6.2	7.5
Ireland	4.0	4.3	8.1	4.5	4.4	6.4
Italy	6.7	10.9	15.6	—	6.1	7.4
Japan	1.1	5.2	10.0	3.3	4.7	7.6
Korea	—	0.8	1.7	—	1.5	4.1
Luxembourg	4.9	9.9	7.9	2.6	4.7	6.6
Netherlands	6.2	10.9	6.8	4.2	5.5	10.3
New Zealand	4.0	8.0	5.5	4.2	5.7	8.4
Norway	5.6	7.9	7.3	4.3	6.7	8.0
Portugal	1.4	6.5	13.4	1.6	4.1	7.0
Slovakia	—	—	7.7	—	—	5.8
Slovenia	—	—	11.1	—	—	6.6
Spain	3.1	8.9	10.8	2.6	5.9	6.8
Sweden	4.9	9.6	9.2	5.9	7.5	7.8
Switzerland	3.6	6.4	8.2	—	4.0	7.4
United Kingdom	4.9	5.9	7.2	3.6	4.6	8.0
United States	4.9	6.3	6.8	2.6	4.8	8.5
Emerging economies						
Argentina	—	5.2	7.4	—	—	4.4
Brazil	—	5.1	9.1	—	—	4.2
Bulgaria	7.0	8.6	8.2	—	—	3.7
Chile	2.7	8.5	5.5	—	—	3.9
China	—	1.0	3.4	—	—	2.7
Hungary	4.6	8.5	11.4	—	—	5.1
India	—	0.2	1.0	—	—	1.2

Table 19.1
(*continued*)

Country	Public pension expenditure (percent of GDP)			Public health expenditure (percent of GDP)		
	1970	1990	2010	1970	1990	2010
Indonesia	—	0.5	0.7	—	—	1.3
Latvia	—	—	9.4	—	—	4.1
Lithuania	—	—	8.4	—	—	5.2
Malaysia	0.7	1.6	3.0	—	—	2.4
Mexico	—	0.5	1.5	—	1.8	2.9
Pakistan	—	0.0	0.6	—	—	0.8
Philippines	—	0.5	1.7	—	—	1.3
Poland	4.9	7.1	11.5	—	4.4	5.0
Romania	—	4.9	9.5	—	—	4.4
Russia	—	—	8.9	—	—	3.2
Saudi Arabia	—	1.4	2.2	—	—	2.7
South Africa	—	—	1.9	—	—	3.9
Thailand	—	—	1.0	—	—	2.9
Turkey	0.4	2.4	6.3	—	1.6	5.1
Ukraine	7.4	14.2	17.7	—	—	4.4

Sources: OECD; WHO; IMF staff estimates

19.3   Outlook for Public Pensions and Health Care Spending

Projected increases in age-related spending are substantial in many advanced and emerging economies. Spending in public pensions and health care is projected to increase by 3.5 percentage points of GDP in the advanced economies and by 2 percentage points of GDP in the emerging over the next two decades, in large part owing to projected increases in health care spending.[7]

The cumulative fiscal cost of these projected spending increases is large. The average present discounted value (PDV) of age-related spending increases over 2010 to 2050 is 142 percent of 2010 GDP in advanced (44 percent from pensions and 98 percent from health) and 61 percent for emerging economies (29 percent from pensions and 32 percent from health).[8]

19.3.1   Public Pensions

Pension spending is projected to increase by 1.5 percentage points of GDP over the next two decades in advanced economies and less than 1 percentage point in emerging economies, but substantial variation exists across countries. Among advanced

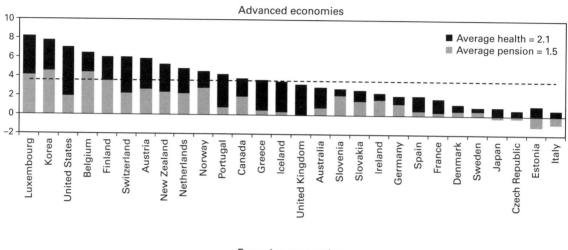

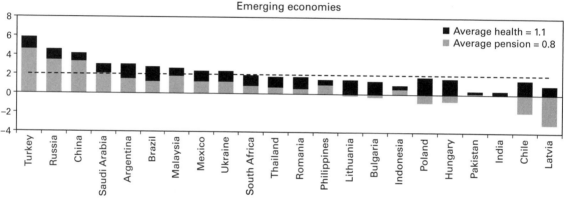

Figure 19.3
Increase in public health and pension spending, 2011 to 2030
Sources: OECD; ILO; WHO; UN; IMF staff estimates

economies, increases in spending in excess of 2 percentage points of GDP are projected in Austria, Belgium, Finland, Korea, Luxembourg, the Netherlands, New Zealand, Norway, Slovenia, and Switzerland, while spending is projected to decrease in the Czech Republic, Estonia, Italy, and Japan. Among emerging countries, spending increases are projected to exceed 3 percentage points of GDP in China, Russia, and Turkey; and to decrease in Bulgaria, Chile, Hungary, Latvia, Lithuania, and Poland.

Pension reforms enacted over the past two decades have been crucial in containing the impact of population aging on spending. In the absence of reforms, these demographic changes would increase public pension spending by 4.5 percentage points of GDP in the advanced economies, 4 percentage points in emerging Europe, and 2 percentage points in other emerging economies. If implemented as planned, as assumed by the above projections, enacted reforms will lower average pension spending in 2030 by 3 percentage points in the advanced economies, 3 1/2 percentage points in emerging Europe, and 1 percentage point in other emerging economies.

There is considerable uncertainty with respect to these pension spending projections, but risks are on the upside for a number of countries. First, the impact of aging is directly related to demographic assumptions—fertility rates and longevity—for which past projections have proven relatively optimistic. Second, projected spending in a number of countries is based on relatively optimistic macroeconomic assumptions, involving, for example, high productivity growth. Third, official projections are also subject to risks of reform reversal. In response to substantial aging challenges, legislated reforms often imply ambitious reductions in pension spending. As these reforms take effect, political pressure to reverse them could mount. To reduce the risk of reform reversal, replacement rate reductions should not undermine the ability of public pension systems to alleviate poverty among the elderly. For example, in Greece and Italy, recent reforms have reduced benefits while protecting low-income pensioners.

19.3.2 Public Health Care

Public health spending in advanced economies is projected to rise, on average, by 2 percentage points of GDP over the next twenty years. Spending is projected to increase by over 2 percentage points of GDP in 14 of the 27 advanced economies. Around one-third of the increase would be due to the effects of population aging, a slightly higher share than in the past. The remaining two-thirds would be due to excess cost growth, reflecting technological change, income growth, the Baumol effect, and health policies.

The projections suggest that the outlook is grim in the United States, but also in Europe, where the fiscal challenge posed by health spending is sometimes underestimated. In the United States, public health spending is projected to rise by about 5 percentage points of GDP over the next twenty years, the highest of the advanced economies. Spending increases are expected to be driven by continued high rates of excess cost growth. In Europe, public health spending is also expected to rise substantially, by 2 percentage points of GDP, with spending expected to rise by over 3 percentage points of GDP in seven countries.

Recent health care reforms in most advanced countries are unlikely to alter long-term public health spending trends. In the United States, a sweeping reform expanding coverage was introduced and is expected to reduce the budget deficit primarily because of higher payroll and excise taxes on health. The envisaged expenditure savings, however, are small and remain highly uncertain because the revenue and spending measures would largely offset each other, and because past efforts to curtail health spending increases had been overridden by Congress before taking effect. In Europe, fiscal adjustment plans affecting general government employment and compensation could have an effect on health spending in the near term, but their long-term effect on excess cost growth is uncertain. Recent reforms have also addressed spending on pharmaceuticals, which constitutes about 15 percent of public health spending. In the United Kingdom, a broader effort to contain spending increases is envisaged, with real health spending budgeted to rise by less than 0.5 percentage point over the next four years as part of the government's fiscal adjustment efforts. In Germany, health reforms include the reversal of the reduced health care contribution which was approved in November 2010, but spending reductions are expected to be small (0.1 percentage point of GDP). In any case, these reforms in advanced economies, including those being undertaken in Greece as part of its fiscal adjustment program, have not been incorporated into the projections because these reforms are still evolving. The impacts of these reforms on the growth of public health spending, however, are expected to be limited.

Public health spending in emerging economies is projected to rise by 1 percentage point of GDP over the next twenty years, a third of the increase projected for the advanced economies. This is consistent with the assumption that excess cost growth in these countries will follow the average level observed in advanced countries over 1980 to 2008, and is also consistent with the lower initial health expenditure ratios in emerging economies. In most countries, the increase would range between 0.5 to 1.5 percentage points of GDP. Aging would account for about 0.5 percentage point of GDP increase in this spending and would have the largest effect on spending in Brazil, Chile, and Poland.

Spending pressures in emerging Europe and Latin America are expected to be higher than in emerging Asia. On average, spending would rise by 1.5 percentage point of GDP in both emerging Europe and Latin America, with all countries projected to raise spending by at least 1 percentage point of GDP. In emerging Asia, spending increases would be about half this amount, reflecting the low initial spending levels in these countries. The modest increases projected across all regions suggest that rising health spending is unlikely to pose a heavy fiscal burden in emerging economies over the next twenty years, which is consistent with the view that the primary challenge for these countries is to improve the efficiency of this spending and quality of services.

Health spending projections are also subject to considerable uncertainties. Similar to pension spending projections, demographic assumptions, including fertility and longevity, could be overly optimistic. There are large uncertainties regarding the advances of medical technologies in the future. Moremore demographic and technological assumptions could interact with each other and manifest the uncertainties even further. For example, breakthroughs in medical technologies could save lives and extend life expectancy, and at the same time the types of medical advances could also be related to the demographic profiles of the populations.

19.4   Reform Options

Reforms are necessary for the long-term sustainability and performance of the public pension and health care systems in many countries. For countries with large projected spending increases and limited fiscal space, the challenge is to contain the growth of public pension and health spending without adversely affecting the social objectives of these programs; for countries where coverage is still limited and with available fiscal space to increase spending, the challenge is to expand coverage while keeping the systems in a fiscally sustainable path.

19.4.1   Public Pensions

There are a number of considerations that should guide pension reform. First, the basic objective of public pensions is to provide retirement income security within the context of a sustainable fiscal framework. Many economies will need to achieve significant fiscal consolidation to lower their debt-to-GDP ratios over the next two decades (IMF 2010a, 2011a). Related, countries could consider strengthening their overall fiscal positions and reducing public debt in anticipation of age-related spending pressures. Pension reform could potentially play an important role in this. Second, the importance of providing income security, especially for low-income groups, suggests that equity should be a key concern of pension reforms. Third, the design of public pensions could potentially have an impact on economic growth through its effect on the functioning of labor markets and national savings.

Pension reforms that curtail eligibility (e.g., by increasing the retirement age), reduce benefits, or increase contributions can help countries address fiscal challenges. The trade-offs across these choices are illustrated in figure 19.4. Beyond what is already legislated, with no increases in payroll taxes and no cuts in benefits, average statutory ages would have to increase by about another 2.5 years on top of what is included in the baseline to keep spending constant in relation to GDP over the next twenty years in advanced economies. Relying only on benefit reductions would require an average 16 percent across-the-board cut in pensions. Relying only on contributions would require an average payroll rate hike of 3.5 percentage points. To keep pension spending as a share of GDP from rising after 2030, additional reforms would be needed: for each decade, retirement ages would have to increase by about one year and three months, benefits cut by about 8 percent, or contribution rates increased by about 1.5 percentage points.

The appropriate combination of reforms depends on each country's circumstances. Nevertheless, raising statutory retirement ages has clear advantages. First, it

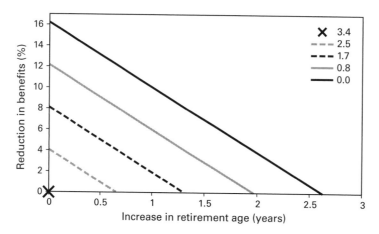

Figure 19.4
Trade-offs across reform options to stabilize spending, 2010 to 2030
Sources: OECD; EC; ILO; UN; IMF staff estimates

would promote higher employment levels and economic growth, while increases in social security contribution rates could decrease labor supply. By increasing lifetime working periods and earnings, raising the retirement age can also boost the growth of real consumption, even in the short run (Karam et al. 2010). Second, raising retirement ages would help avoid even larger cuts in replacement rates than those already legislated, thus reducing the impact of reforms on elderly poverty. Third, increases in retirement ages could also be easier for the public to understand in light of increasing life expectancies. Increases in the statutory retirement age would need to be accompanied by steps to limit early retirement, for example by decreasing (financial) incentives to do so (Queisser and Whitehouse 2006) and by controlling alternative pathways to retirement such as disability pensions (OECD 2006). Furthermore, they should also be accompanied by measures that protect the incomes of those that cannot continue to work. In the United States, for example, about a quarter of all workers in their sixties may find continued work difficult on account of disabilities or reduced health status (Munnell, Soto, and Golub-Sass 2008). Older workers should be protected fully by disability pensions where appropriate and social assistance programs to ensure that increases in retirement ages do not raise poverty rates. To ensure that higher life expectancies do not erode the progressivity of pension systems, consideration could be given to offsetting measures, such as reducing replacement rates for upper income households.

In emerging Europe, priority should be given to putting public pensions on a sound financial footing. Countries in emerging Europe look closer to the advanced economies than to other emerging economies in terms of public pension spending and the importance of aging. Although fiscal adjustment needs are not as large as in advanced economies (IMF 2011a), fiscal conditions are weaker than in other emerging economies and gross financing needs remain above 10 percent of GDP in several economies. In this light, pension reforms could help support fiscal adjustment over the medium to long term. Public pension spending is projected to rise sharply in some countries that have not reformed their systems, including Lithuania, Russia, and Ukraine. In these countries parametric reforms are needed to contain the growth in pension spending. For countries that have introduced mandatory private pensions, the priority should be to stabilize spending in the pay-as-you-go component before further expanding their mandatory private pension systems.

In other emerging economies, increasing pension coverage in an affordable way remains a key challenge. On average, coverage rates are particularly low in emerging Asia, somewhat higher in Latin America, and still higher in Middle Eastern and African countries. This partly reflects the high degree of economic informality in these countries. Assuming the same replacement rates and eligibility rules of current systems, relatively modest expansion in pension coverage would raise pension spending substantially. Over the next two decades, increasing coverage from 26 to 32 percent—the projected increase in coverage taking into account the projected growth in GDP per capita—would increase spending by 0.5 percentage points of GDP in emerging Asia. Similarly, in other emerging economies outside Europe, increasing coverage from 69 to 78 percent would increase spending by 1 percentage point of GDP. Parametric reforms to existing public pension schemes, including raising retirement ages and lowering replacement rates, will be required to contain these costs. In addition, for countries with very low coverage rates, "social pensions" that provide a flat pension aimed at poverty reduction could be considered. However, the cost of social pensions can be substantial (around 0.5 percent of GDP) (Holzmann, Robalino, and Takayama 2009). To contain fiscal costs, these schemes should be means-tested to target only the needy. In addition the design of such programs should aim for benefits that are sufficient to alleviate poverty but low enough to minimize incentives to remain outside of the formal pension system.

19.4.2 Public Health Care

Past reform experiences in advanced economies show that health care reforms could help slow the growth of public health spending. Econometric analysis of the relationship between key indicators of health care systems (Joumard, Andre, and Nicq 2010) and the growth of public health spending identifies health reform measures that can be effective in containing public health spending. These reform measures are also supported by country case studies and event analysis of reform episodes. The impact of particular reforms on the growth of public health spending is then simulated by changing a country's score on these indicators.

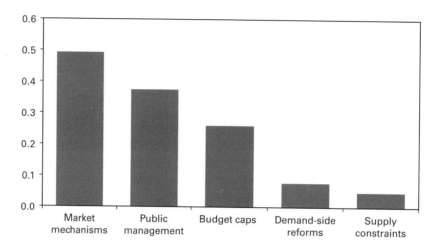

Figure 19.5
Average impact of reform components on health spending, 2030 (decrease relative to the baseline; percent of GDP)
Sources: OECD Health Database; IMF staff estimates

Figure 19.5 shows the average impact of raising countries to the mean score in these indicators on public health spending-to-GDP ratios in 2030, grouped in five categories: budget caps (including budget constraints and central government oversight), public management and coordination (including "gatekeeping" processes that require referrals for accessing specialized care and subnational government involvement), market mechanisms (including choice of insurers and providers, private provision, and the ability of insurers to compete), demand-side reforms (including expansion of private insurance and cost-sharing), and supply controls (including regulation of the health care workforce). Reforms of market mechanisms can be powerful, yielding a reduction in spending of about 0.5 percentage point of GDP. The exercise also underscores the importance of budget caps, which can reduce spending by 0.25 percentage point of GDP. The simulated impacts of demand-side reforms and supply constraints are small, but not negligible.

It is important to note that the possible savings under reforms is subject to uncertainty. Simultaneous reforms across different aspects of the health system may be undesirable or counterproductive. Thus, the effect of the reforms across categories may not necessarily be aggregated. Some reforms, however, could be complementary, implying that the savings under any particular reform may be understated.

The impact of the simulated reforms might still fall short of what would be needed in some countries to stabilize public health care spending-to-GDP ratios at current levels. Thus additional efforts would be needed to achieve this target, or fiscal adjustment might need to rely more on cuts in other areas or additional revenue increases.

This is especially important in some advanced European economies with relatively high projected growth in public health spending, such as Austria, Portugal, Switzerland, and the United Kingdom. In the United States the challenge would be even larger. The illustrative savings from an assumed increase to the mean in the category of budget caps would yield savings of about 1 percentage point of GDP. Other options to reduce spending in the United States, beyond those captured in the econometric analysis, include the extension of health information technology, which would yield savings of 0.25 percent of GDP.[9] Curtailing the favorable tax treatment of health insurance contributions (which involves tax expenditures amounting to about 2 percent of GDP) could potentially yield large savings, and recent proposals in this area would yield savings of an additional 0.5 percentage point of GDP on an annual basis.[10] All told, these reforms, including those simulated in the econometric analysis, would reduce spending (including tax expenditures) by about 2 percentage points of GDP. Even with the reforms, however, health spending would still be rising by 3 percentage points of GDP.

Reform options and the appropriate mix of reforms will depend on country characteristics and the projected outlook for the growth of public health spending. The reform impacts simulated above focus on strengthening cost-containing characteristics of health systems on which countries score below the OECD mean. Of course, all the identified reforms using this methodology may not necessarily apply to every country. Box 19.1 provides an assessment of options using this approach.

For emerging economies, the challenges is to improve health outcomes in a fiscally sustainable matter, as average life expectancy is about nine years lower than in advanced economies and infant mortality rates are significantly higher.

In emerging Europe, health spending is relatively high by emerging economy standards, as coverage of the population is nearly universal and disease patterns mirror those of advanced economies. Given limited fiscal space,[11] most of emerging Europe will need to rely on additional micro-level reforms to improve health outcomes, rather than on increasing spending. Most of these countries (including Estonia, Hungary, Latvia, Russia, and Ukraine) have successfully contained spending, in some cases implementing reforms similar to those of the advanced economies. Estonia and Hungary, for example, implemented a single insurance fund and a global budget, which helped contain spending growth and reduced transaction costs.

In most emerging economies of Asia and Latin America, the main challenge remains to expand basic coverage to a larger share of the population without generating undue fiscal pressures over the medium term as incomes rise and these systems expand. In these economies, increased public spending could not only improve health indicators but also catalyze economic growth (Baldacci et al. 2008). These economies should aim to expand their systems in a way that avoids the inefficiencies and resulting high costs of health systems in the advanced economies.

Box 19.1
Potential reform strategies to contain the growth of public health spending

Countries Relying on Market Mechanisms
In Canada, the Czech Republic, France, Germany, Japan, and the Slovak Republic, staying the course with marginal reforms would be enough to contain excess cost growth, although bolder reforms could still be needed to offset the effects of demographics on health spending.

In Australia, Austria, Belgium, and the Netherlands, possible strategies include tightening budget constraints, strengthening gatekeeping (such as by requiring referrals to access secondary care), and increasing cost-sharing.

Greece, Korea, Luxembourg, Switzerland, and the United States are projected to have relatively high spending growth, indicating the need for future reforms, especially for Greece and Luxembourg, which score low on efficiency measures.[a] These countries tend to have less stringent budget constraints, minimal central oversight (Korea and Luxembourg), lax regulations of the workforce and equipment, and little gatekeeping. Future efforts to contain spending growth in these countries should address these weaknesses.

Countries That Rely More Heavily on Public Insurance and Provision
Denmark and Ireland could focus on efficiency-enhancing reforms to reduce spending growth. Italy and Sweden, both of which score high in efficiency, could improve priority setting in the area of health (for example, by better monitoring public health objectives and the composition of the public health package).

In Norway and Spain, containing the growth of spending could require tightening macro controls (including central oversight), broadening private insurance for care beyond the basic health package (Norway), and improving priority setting (Spain).

Finland, Iceland, New Zealand, Portugal, and the United Kingdom have relatively high projected spending growth. Countries in this group could strengthen supply constraints on the workforce and equipment (e.g., by rationing high-technology equipment). In addition these countries could benefit from extending the role of private health insurance for over-the-basic care and increasing choice among providers (especially in Finland, New Zealand, and the United Kingdom).

a. The assessment does not take into account reforms in Greece since 2010.

Emerging economies in Latin America and Asia have more scope to increase spending but will need to avoid putting health systems on a fiscally unsustainable path as they expand coverage. In many of these economies, the public system provides coverage for only a small share of the population, and in some cases the benefit package, even for those covered, is insufficient to protect against all key health risks. Thailand and Chile have successfully expanded basic coverage at a low fiscal cost and provide valuable lessons for other countries. By extending benefits to a wide share of the population, health risks can be pooled for much of the population. This can lead to a substantial improvement in aggregate social welfare and equity, as it helps reduce the burden of catastrophic health events on low-income groups.

19.5 Conclusion

Age-related spending is projected to increase by 3.5 percent of GDP over the next two decades in advanced economies. These increases will occur at a time when countries need to undertake large fiscal adjustments to reduce public debt ratios in the wake of the global financial crisis. Lowering the general government debt-to-GDP ratio will require both revenue increases and expenditure reductions in many countries. On the expenditure side, stabilizing age-related spending to GDP ratios, including on both pensions and health by containing its growth, could constitute an important pillar of this strategy in advanced economies. Pension reforms that curtail eligibility (e.g., by increasing the retirement age), reduce benefits, or increase contributions can help countries address fiscal challenges while involving apparent trade-offs. Nonetheless, raising the retirement age is the preferred option. Containing public health spending requires a mix of macro-level controls, such as imposing budget caps, and micro-level efficiency enhancing reforms, such as strengthening market mechanisms.

In emerging economies, the projected increase is smaller than in advanced economies, with an average of 2 percent of GDP. In some emerging economies, the challenge ahead is to expand basic coverage for pensions and health to a larger share of the population in a fiscally sustainable manner while avoiding the inefficiencies and resulting high costs of the pension and health systems of advanced economies; in others, where coverage is already extensive, the challenge is to enhance the efficiency of public spending and limit its increase as a share of GDP. In these countries the needed reforms are broadly similar to those for advanced economies.

Notes

The authors would like to thank Lilla Nemeth for excellent research assistance.
1. Excess cost growth is defined as the excess of growth in real per capita health expenditures over the growth in real per capita GDP after controlling for the effect of demographic change.

2. All country group averages are unweighted unless otherwise noted.

3. The advanced economies in this study comprise some 28 countries: Australia, Austria, Belgium, Canada, Czech Republic, Denmark, Estonia, Finland, France, Germany, Greece, Iceland, Ireland, Italy, Japan, Korea, Luxembourg, the Netherlands, New Zealand, Norway, Portugal, Slovakia, Slovenia, Spain, Sweden, Switzerland, the United Kingdom, and the United States. The 22 emerging economies are Argentina, Brazil, Bulgaria, Chile, China, Hungary, India, Indonesia, Latvia, Lithuania, Malaysia, Mexico, Pakistan, Philippines, Poland, Romania, Russia, Saudi Arabia, South Africa, Thailand, Turkey, and Ukraine.

4. The public health spending data have been adjusted for statistical breaks to ensure comparability over time.

5. The Baumol effect refers to the rising unit labor costs in sectors where it is difficult to achieve productivity gains, usually in services. Because salaries tend to rise in these sectors in line with economywide averages, while productivity does not, unit labor costs rise in relative terms. For evidence of the Baumol effect in health spending, see Pomp and Vujic (2008).

6. The efficiency results cited here from Joumard, Andre, and Nicq (2010) control for the effects of these nonspending inputs on life expectancy. Although life expectancy is only one dimension of health status, it is highly correlated with other widely used health status indicators.

7. See IMF (2010c) and IMF (2011b) for details of the projection methodologies.

8. The estimates assume a growth-adjusted discount rate of 1 percent.

9. See Hillestad et al. (2005) and US Congressional Budget Office (2008).

10. See US Senate Joint Committee on Taxation (2008). A proposal to replace the employer-sponsored health insurance tax exclusion in the United States with a credit indexed to the consumer price index would save a little over 5 percent of GDP cumulatively over a ten-year period (Committee for a Responsible Federal Budget 2010).

11. This can be assessed with reference to the adjustment required for them to reduce debt to an illustrative target of 40 percent of GDP over the next twenty years.

References

Auerbach, Alan. 2011. Long-term fiscal sustainability in major economies. Working paper. University of California, Berkeley.

Baldacci, Emanuele, Benedict Clements, Sanjeev Gupta, and Qiang Cui. 2008. Social spending, human capital, and growth in developing countries. *World Development* 36:1317–1341.

Cottarelli, Carlo, and Andrea Schaechter. 2010. *Long-term trends in public finances in the G-7 economies. Staff position note SPN/10/13.* Washington, DC: IMF.

Committee for a Responsible Federal Budget. 2010. Principle #5: Continued vigilance in health reform. CRFB, Washington, DC.

Congressional Budget Office (CBO). 2008. *Evidence on the Costs and Benefits of Health Information Technology. Publication 2976.* Washington, DC: Government Printing Office.

Cutler, D., and M. McClellan. 2001. Is technological change in medicine worth it? *Health Affairs* 20 (5): 11–29.

Gupta, Sanjeev, Gerd Schwartz, Shamsuddin Tareq, Richard Allen, Isabell Adenauer, Kevin Fletcher, and Duncan Last. 2008. *Fiscal Management of Scaled-up Aid*. Washington, DC: IMF.

Gupta, S., and M. Verhoeven. 2001. The efficiency of government expenditures: Experiences from Africa. *Journal of Policy Modeling* 23:433–467.

Hillestad, Richard, James Bigelow, Anthony Bower, Federico Girosi, Robin Meili, Richard Scoville, and Roger Taylor. 2005. Can electronic medical record systems transform healthcare? An assessment of potential health benefits, savings, and costs. *Health Affairs* 24 (5): 1103–1117.

Holzmann, Robert, David A. Robalino, and Noriyuki Takayama, eds. 2009. Closing the Coverage Gap: The Role of Social Pensions and Other Retirement Income Transfers. Washington, DC: World Bank.

International Monetary Fund. 2010a. From stimulus to consolidation: Revenue and expenditure policies in advanced and emerging economies. Departmental paper 10/03. IMF, Washington, DC. Available at: http://www.imf.org/external/np/pp/eng/2010/043010a.pdf.

International Monetary Fund. 2010b. *Addressing fiscal challenges to reduce economic risks*. Washington, DC: Fiscal Monitor, September. IMF.

International Monetary Fund. 2010c. Macro-fiscal implications of health care reform in advanced and emerging economies. Policy paper, December. IMF, Washington, DC. Available at: http://www.imf.org/external/np/pp/eng/2010/122810.pdf.

International Monetary Fund. 2011a. Addressing fiscal challenges to reduce economic risks. *Fiscal Monitor*, September. IMF, Washington, DC. Available at: http://www.imf.org/external/pubs/ft/fm/2011/02/pdf/fm1102.pdf.

International Monetary Fund. 2011b. The challenge of public pension reform in advanced and emerging economies. Policy paper, December. IMF, Washington, DC. Available at: http://www.imf.org/external/np/pp/eng/2011/122811.pdf.

Joumard, I., C. Andre, and C. Nicq. 2010. Health care systems: Efficiency and institutions. Working paper 769. Economics Department, OECD, Paris.

Joumard, I., C. Andre, C. Nicq, and O. Chatal. 2008. Health status determinants: Lifestyle, environment, health care resources and efficiency. Working paper 627. Economics Department, OECD, Paris.

Karam, Philippe, Dirk Muir, Joana Pereira, and Anita Tuladhar. 2010. Macroeconomic effects of public pension reforms. Working paper 10/2. IMF, Washington, DC. Available at: http://www.imf.org/external/pubs/ft/wp/2010/wp10297.pdf.

Munnell, Alicia H., Mauricio Soto, and Alexander Golub-Sass. 2008. Would people be healthy enough to work longer. Working paper 2008–11. Center for Retirement Research at Boston College. Available at: http://crr.bc.edu/images/stories/Working_Papers/wp_2008-11.pdf.

Organization for Economic Cooperation and Development. 2006. *Live Longer, Work Longer*. Paris: OECD. Available at: http://www.oecd-ilibrary.org/employment/ageing-and-employment-policies-vieillissement-et-politiques-de-l-emploi_19901011.

Pomp, M., and S. Vujic. 2008. Rising health spending, new medical technology, and the Baumol effect. Discussion paper 115. CPB, The Hague.

Queisser, Monika, and Edward Whitehouse. 2006. Neutral or fair? Actuarial concepts and pension-system design. Working paper 40. Social, Employment and Migration, OECD, Paris. Available at: http://www.oecd.org/dataoecd/2/42/37811399.pdf.

Sivard, R. 1974–1996. *World Military and Social Expenditures,* various editions. Leesburg, VA: WMSE Publications.

US Senate, Joint Committee on Taxation. 2008. *Tax Expenditures for Health Care. Hearing before the Senate Committee on Finance, July 30, (JCX-66–08).* Washington, DC: GPO.

20

Fiscal Adjustment, Growth, and Global Imbalances

Mika Kortelainen, Douglas Laxton, and Jack Selody

20.1 Introduction

Over the medium term, significant fiscal consolidation seems inevitable in much of Europe and the United States in order to counter rising public-sector indebtedness. Fiscal consolidation is usually associated with shrinking current-account deficits and a slowdown in growth as demand for foreign goods falls along with demand for domestically produced goods. In this chapter we illustrate how combining fiscal consolidation with structural reform and coordinated fiscal policy can result in lower public-sector indebtedness, stronger growth, and a lessening of global imbalances for all participating countries.

The chapter starts with a high-level discussion of the virtuous circle that can be generated when fiscal consolidation is accompanied by productivity-enhancing structural reform and monetary easing. The chapter then goes on to describe the specifics of the hypothetical policy actions put into the model and the key features of the model in which the coordinated policy actions are embedded, followed by a brief review of previous studies of the macroeconomic effects of fiscal consolidation. The chapter then discusses the simulations results and ends with a brief conclusion.

20.2 Coordinating Fiscal Consolidation with Structural Reform

Four basic elements contribute to the virtuous circle created by coordinating fiscal consolidation with structural reform. The coordinated policy creating a virtuous circle is illustrated in figure 20.1.

Structural and fiscal reforms create the potential for the world economy to grow, which helps fiscal consolidation by contributing to higher tax revenues with a lower increase in tax rates than would otherwise be needed. Reform also contributes to increasing domestic demand relative to foreign demand, for example in China, which lessens global imbalances. Fiscal consolidation lessens global imbalances by reducing the need for public borrowing from abroad, but it results in reduced government

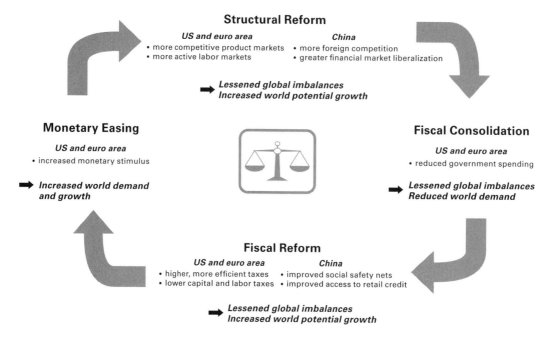

Figure 20.1
Coordinating fiscal consolidation with structural reform

consumption, lowering demand for world output. Monetary policy easing creates increased demand for world output, which offsets the reduction in demand from fiscal consolidation and helps the world economy reach a new and higher potential growth path.

For the euro area, the reforms are of the type envisioned by Cacciatore et al. (2012) and Bouis et al. (2012). Examples of such reforms are (1) a decline in product market regulation, (2) a reduction in barriers to entry for new firms, (3) a decline in the amount and duration of unemployment benefits, (4) a decline in job protection, (5) an increase in spending on training, (6) an increase in employment incentives, (7) an increase in the minimum retirement age, (8) a decline in payroll taxes, (9) a decline in capital taxes, and (10) an increase in value-added taxes. From the macroeconomic perspective, the net effect of these reforms is to increase labor and total-factor productivity, which is the way these measures are introduced into the macroeconomic model. The United States could improve the efficiency of its economy by selectively introducing some of these reforms—for example, increased training—but US product and labor markets are already relatively competitive compared to markets in the euro area.

For China, the reforms are of the type needed to transform an emerging economy reliant on export-led growth to a mature economy reliant on growth balanced between domestic demand and export demand. Such reform consists of opening Chinese markets to more foreign competition so as to supply more goods to stimulate Chinese consumer demand and greater financial market liberalization that will equate the availability and cost of credit in China to that in the developed world. From a macroeconomic perspective, the net effect of these reforms will be to transfer resources from satisfying foreign demand to satisfying domestic demand in China.

Fiscal consolidation is required only in those countries running large public-sector deficits. The net effect of the consolidation is to reduce deficit-to-GDP and debt-to-GDP ratios. Monetary easing is implemented in those countries that pursue fiscal consolidation. It is implemented by positing that the monetary authorities announce their tolerance for inflation temporarily to exceed the inflation target, and then engaging in quantitative easing. With sufficient monetary easing, the net result is an increase in the demand for domestic and foreign goods in the consolidating economies.

The virtuous circle is illustrated in two parts. First the structural and fiscal reforms are combined with fiscal consolidation in deficit countries to show that even without monetary policy easing the result of coordinated policy action is positive for participating countries. Then fiscal consolidation is combined with monetary easing to show that coordinating these actions is positive for the world economy and does not generate inflation in the major developed economies, even in the absence of increased potential growth from structural and fiscal reforms.

20.3 Specifics of Country Measures

20.3.1 United States

Structural Reform
• In the scenario, the US structural reforms consist of an increase in productivity consistent with what might be expected from product-market reforms and an increase in active labor-market policies as estimated by Cacciatore et al. (2012) and Bouis et al. (2012). The level of productivity in the traded-goods sector is increased by 3 percent over five years, with productivity in the nontraded-goods sector increasing by 1 percent over the same time period. Thereafter, the productivity growth rate stabilizes at one-half of a percentage point annual growth above the baseline growth rate in the tradable sector, and at one-quarter of a percentage point above baseline in the nontradable sector for the next ten years. Active labor-market policies are assumed to increase labor supply by almost 1 percent spread out over fifteen years.

Fiscal Reform
• The US fiscal reform shock consists of a change in the tax code toward taxes with a less distorting effect on the incentives that drive the supply side of the economy. Specifically, value-added taxes are increased to 1.5 percent of GDP over a number of years. This allows lower labor and capital taxes, each of which is posited to fall by 0.75 percent of GDP. These changes are constructed to be revenue neutral in that government revenue is unchanged in the long run. The resulting reduction in distortions to supply-side incentives does, however, have a positive effect on economic growth.

Fiscal Consolidation
• The shock that results from US fiscal consolidation produces a reduction in the government deficit of 3 percentage points of GDP in the long run. The increase in the surplus is achieved by lowering government consumption by over 2 percentage points of GDP gradually over the first four years of the simulation. Taxes are increased starting in 2015, with the increase cumulating in about 1 percentage point of GDP by 2020. Four years into the simulation, entitlement spending is significantly reduced by lowering general transfers to achieve and to maintain the approximate 3 percentage point of GDP increase in the government surplus. The improvement in the fiscal stance also lowers the debt-to-GDP ratio, which gradually brings down the interest-expense-to-GDP ratio.

20.3.2 Euro Area

Structural Reform
• Structural reform in the euro area scenario consists of a combination of product-market reforms and a broad range of labor-market reforms targeted at adding flexibility to European labor markets and increasing European labor force participation. The net effect is to increase productivity and potential output in the euro area. The level of productivity in both the tradable and nontradable sectors is assumed to increase by 3.5 percent over fifteen years. In addition, the labor supply is assumed to increase by 0.4 percent over fifteen years owing to increased labor force participation. These gains are assumed to be permanent.

Fiscal Reform
• The euro area fiscal reform shock consists of shift toward taxes that distort the supply-side of the economy less. Specifically, value-added taxes are increased gradually by 0.9 percent of GDP. The resulting increase in revenue is used to lower both labor and capital taxes, which both fall by 0.45 percent of GDP. As a result, the tax changes are revenue neutral, such that the government revenue does not change as a percentage of GDP in the long run. Nevertheless, taxes distort the supply-side

of the economy less, which has a positive effect on the potential of economy in the long run.

Fiscal Consolidation
• The fiscal consolidation shock in the euro area results in a reduction in the government deficit of 0.8 percentage points of GDP spread out over a number of years. The increase in the surplus is achieved by positing that government consumption is reduced gradually by a total of over 0.3 percentage points of GDP in the long run. As an offset, value-added taxes are increased over the first four years of the simulation by a cumulative total of about 0.15 percent of GDP. Moreover entitlement spending is cut by lowering general transfers over the first four years of the simulation by an additional 0.15 percent of GDP. The fiscal consolidation results in a lower debt-to-GDP ratio, which gradually brings down interest-expense payments.

20.3.3 China
In the scenario the contribution to coordinated action from China includes reforms to reduce underlying distortions, which shift the economy toward domestic demand-led growth and away from export-led growth. These reforms are summarized as follows:

Product Market Reform
• The scenario includes measures to (1) level the playing field between tradable and nontradable sectors of the Chinese economy, (2) open the economy further to foreign competition, (3) further reduce restrictions on service-sector producers, (4) strengthen corporate governance, and (5) increase R&D spending. The measures are assumed to increase productivity in the nontradable sector of the economy by 2 percentage points over five years.
• The scenario also includes measures to improve the quality of the nontraded and domestically produced traded goods and services, as well as making the goods and services produced in China conform better to the preferences of Chinese households for them. This change is implemented in the model as an exogenous increase in the demand for domestically produced nontraded goods and services in the final consumption basket of Chinese consumers.

Financial Market Liberalization
• The scenario includes greater financial market liberalization that equates the availability and cost of credit in China to that in the developed world. The net result is lower credit costs for Chinese households and a rise in the cost of capital for manufacturing firms. We implement the shock via an increase in the external finance premium of firms in the tradable sector by 100 basis points.

Financial Liberalization and Fiscal Reform
• Complementing the financial-market liberalization shock, the scenario also includes financial liberalization reforms to increase access to credit for households and small and medium enterprises (SMEs) in China. The posited fiscal reform in China aims to improve the social safety net by augmenting social insurance in areas such as pension, health care, and the education system. It also includes improving public infrastructure in rural areas. The financial liberalization shock is implemented as an increase in the share of households with access to credit institutions by 10 percentage points spread out over twenty years, with an assumed reduction in the level of household savings as a percent of GDP by 10 percentage points over ten years. The fiscal reform shock is implemented as an increase in government spending on health and education of 2 percentage points of GDP over five years (0.4 percent per year). The increase in expenditures is financed through an increase in labor taxes of 4 percent of GDP over ten years that matches the ten-year reduction in private savings.

Labor Market Reform
• The scenario includes an assumed reform of the Hukou system aimed at increasing the mobility of rural workers and enhancing the efficiency of labor-market turnover. The shock is implemented with a permanent 1 percent increase in the labor force participation rate every year for five years.

20.4 Base Model

The base model used to analyze the two coordination scenarios is global integrated monetary and fiscal model (GIMF). The model is flexible in that it can be configured to model a variable number of regions of the world. With the six-region version of the model used here, we can show the benefits of coordinating structural-reform and aggregate demand-management policies, on the one hand, and fiscal and monetary policies on the other. GIMF is a multicountry dynamic general equilibrium model used extensively inside the IMF, and at a small number of central banks, for policy and scenario risk analysis. The strength of GIMF for addressing fiscal policy coordination issues is the inclusion of a range of non-Ricardian features in the model that make both spending-based and revenue-based fiscal policy measures nonneutral. The nonneutralities give a more realistic rendering of the short-run effectiveness of fiscal policy changes. GIMF's rich structure also captures the longer run determinants of savings and investment behaviors, making it useful when the focus of analysis turns from short-run stimulus to longer run sustainability issues and the resolution of global savings-investment imbalances. GIMF has been constructed to answer questions about the relationships among fiscal deficits, real interest rates, crowding out, and current account deficits. A complete description of the structure of GIMF can be found in Kumhof et al. (2010).

The six regions included in the version of GIMF used for the simulations in this chapter are the United States, euro area, China, emerging Asia, Japan, and remaining countries. This setup contrasts the need for fiscal consolidation in the United States and the euro area versus the other countries, and the global imbalances between the same two entities and China. All regions explicitly identified in the model follow inflation-targeting regimes.

20.5 Literature Review

The simulation results presented below are similar to those in previous studies. Coenen et al. (2012) look at fiscal consolidation in seven structural models used by policymakers and find that GDP multipliers from fiscal consolidation can be large if the effects originate from spending cuts, and that those effects are even stronger if monetary policy accommodates the change in fiscal policy. Although this study looked at the effects of a coordinated fiscal/monetary expansion where the effect of fiscal expansion was larger when accompanied by expansionary monetary policy, the results are consistent with the simulation shown above where the effects of a contractionary fiscal policy are offset by coordinating it with expansionary monetary policy. Freedman et al. (2009, 2010a, b) find similar results in simulations that coordinate fiscal and monetary policy in the IMF's GIMF model.

Kumhof and Laxton (2009c) look at a combination of fiscal policy and supply shocks, and find that effective fiscal policy requires increased tolerance for inflation deviating from target in the short run. Clinton et al. (2010) find that globally coordinated fiscal policy can effectively reduce global imbalances.

20.6 Simulation Results of Coordinated Implementation of Country-Specific Measures

The simulated scenario in this section illustrates the benefits of coordinating structural reform and aggregate demand-management policies. The simulations are run with countries in emerging Asia following flexible exchange-rate policies. Monetary policy is held neutral in the simulation to show the extent to which structural change can endogenously generate aggregate demand that offsets the short-run contractionary effects of fiscal consolidation.

20.6.1 United States
Figure 20.2 shows the effect of the structural reform under the fiscal consolidation coordination scenario as a deviation from a baseline scenario. The shock illustrates the fact that fiscal consolidation in the United States can have an immediate and

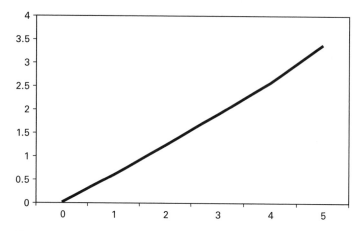

Figure 20.2
Coordinated implementation of country-specific measures: United States—fiscal balance (percent of GDP deviation from baseline)
Source: GIMF simulations

positive effect on the government-balance-to-GDP ratio provided it is combined with a productivity-enhancing structural reform. The current account also immediately improves and the improvement grows over time. The shock is having the desired effect on the United States with government balances improving and global imbalances diminishing.

The effect of the policies on the US economy is not quite so positive in the short run, even though the gain from the structural reform starts almost immediately as real interest rates fall in anticipation of the improvement in economic efficiency from the structural reform. The fiscal consolidation does create a small loss of GDP in the United States that lasts for about three years (figure 20.3). The loss occurs despite the increase in potential output from structural reforms. Essentially, the full gain from the structural reforms takes time to impact the economy, and without a source of additional demand in the short run, there is nothing to offset the reduction in demand coming from fiscal consolidation. Over time, however, investment rises significantly above baseline as firms respond to the rise in productivity. The investment contributes to demand but also puts in place the capital to create additional GDP that displaces slowing imports from China. By year five the US economy has more than made up for the output lost in the first three years of the simulation. The United States has effectively grown its way out of its fiscal problem and global imbalances have improved.

The US real interest rate is stubbornly high in the first year as monetary policy is not very accommodating despite the slowdown in the US economy. Eventually, however, the real interest rate falls in response to the slowdown of GDP, but the move is

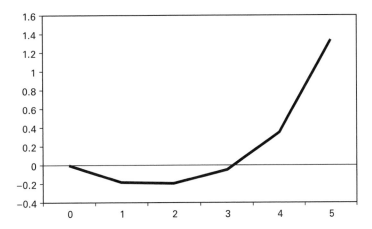

Figure 20.3
Coordinated implementation of country-specific measures: United States—real GDP (percent deviation from baseline)
Source: GIMF simulations

small reflecting the modest size of the slowdown. In effect the real interest rate is not contributing much to the dynamics of the simulation.

The US real effective exchange rate does the heavy lifting in the scenario. It depreciates significantly, which boosts foreign demand for the goods and services produced by the more productive American economy. It is the resulting increase in exports of American-made goods that lies behind the significant improvement in the American current account surplus seen in the earlier panel.

20.6.2 Euro Area

Fiscal consolidation in the euro area also results in improved fiscal and current account balances. However, the improvement is not so dramatic as for the United States owing to less assumed fiscal consolidation and stickier prices resulting in less depreciation of the real effective exchange rate. The improvement in the current account surplus is indeed significantly less than it is for the United States.

The euro area does not suffer a loss of GDP from the fiscal consolidations, unlike the United States, as the fiscal consolidation is smaller (figure 20.4). Nevertheless, the increase in real GDP after five years is similar to that in the United States, showing the effectiveness of productivity-improving structural reforms in Europe. The increase in investment in the euro area is less than that in the United States reflecting the relative bias toward reforms that improve labor force participation.

The real interest rate in the euro area rises only slightly in the scenario as monetary policy does not accommodate the shock. The real effective exchange rate

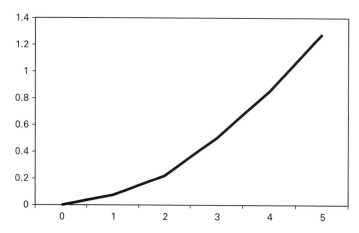

Figure 20.4
Coordinated implementation of country-specific measures: Euro area—real GDP (percent deviation from baseline)
Source: GIMF simulations

depreciates, raising foreign demand for European goods and services, but the depreciation is not as large as that in the United States owing to greater product market rigidities compared to those in the US economy. This explains why the current account balance in Europe did not improve as much as in the United States.

20.6.3 China

Fiscal reform in China has little effect on the Chinese fiscal balance as the policy was aimed at stimulating domestic demand and therefore had a significant increase in government expenditures that offset increased tax revenues. Global imbalances improve with the increase in domestic demand, resulting in a reduction in the Chinese current account surplus. The reduction in the current account surplus as a proportion of Chinese GDP is larger than that in the United States or the euro area as those economies are larger than the Chinese economy.

Despite reduced exports, China does not suffer any loss of GDP as increased domestic demand more than makes up for the lost foreign demand. Indeed, after five years the increase in Chinese GDP is proportionally greater than that in either the United States or the euro area (figure 20.5). This result illustrates the potential power of coordinated fiscal consolidation and structural reform policies in that all participating countries can be made better off. China also experiences a slowdown in investment spending as nontraded goods and services tend to be less capital intensive than traded goods and services.

The real interest rate rises significantly in China illustrating that the increase in GDP is not the result of easing monetary policy. In addition the real effective ex-

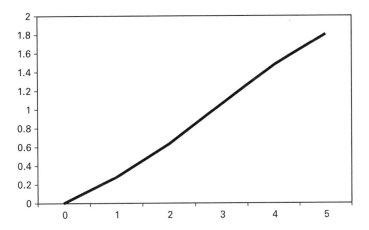

Figure 20.5
Coordinated implementation of country-specific measures: China—real GDP (percent deviation from baseline)
Source: GIMF simulations

change rate appreciates illustrating that the increase in GDP is also not the result of increased exports. Rather, the growth comes from increased domestic demand for consumption goods resulting from improved access to retail credit and the greater attractiveness of domestically produced goods to Chinese consumers. The rise in real interest rates and the appreciation of the real exchange rate reflects the improvement in the welfare of Chinese consumers.

20.7 Simulation Results of Coordinated Monetary and Fiscal Actions

The simulated scenario in this section illustrates the advantages of the international coordination of fiscal and monetary policies in avoiding the risk of deflation that could result from a fiscal consolidation that is not accompanied by offsetting policies to stimulate aggregate demand. The analysis uses the same six-region version of the GIMF used in the simulation above, but without the structural reform measures that stimulate aggregate demand but also increase potential output. Rather, the offsetting increase in aggregate demand is achieved by easier monetary policy.

The easing in monetary policy addresses two vulnerabilities associated with undertaking extensive and coordinated fiscal consolidation at a time when interest rates are already very low: (1) the high risk of deflation and (2) limited scope for a further easing in monetary policy by the traditional means of lowering the policy interest rate, in an environment where policy interest rates in the G3 economies have been near the zero lower bound over an extended period.

In the scenario the G3 monetary authorities implement easier monetary policy with two key measures. First, they simultaneously signal that to close output gaps more quickly they will tolerate paths for inflation that exceed their inflation targets over the near term. They do this by publishing inflation forecasts that exceed their inflation target for a period of time. Second, they pursue monetary policy quantitative easing by buying bonds from the government with the government then spending the newly created money via fiscal transfers.

The success of this strategy will depend on the ability of the central banks to effectively communicate that they are serious about raising the rate of inflation in the near term and that the higher rate of inflation is temporary and unacceptable in the longer run. With this assumed credibility, the stimulus to domestic demand from the monetary injection starts to eliminate output gaps quickly and reverses the downward momentum in inflation from fiscal consolidation. With the nominal policy rate at zero, the rising inflation reduces real interest rates providing additional stimulus to domestic demand.

An important point to note is that the G3 currency depreciation in the scenario helps close output gaps, but does not imply a loss in GDP below baseline in other countries. The increase in incomes in the G3 countries from the easing monetary policy results in an increase in demand for foreign goods that more than offsets the reduction in demand from the higher price of foreign goods owing to the depreciation. GDP growth in the world outside the G3 also increases, leaving all regions of the global economy better off.

20.7.1 United States

In figure 20.6 the solid line represents the baseline case before fiscal consolidation coordinated with monetary policy easing action. The dashed line represents the case with fiscal consolidation and monetary policy action. The simulation starts in 2012, which is a period of extremely low interest rates in the United States, so the monetary policy action takes the form of announcing a reduction in the weight on the goal of containing inflation in the short term and quantitative easing.

The tightening of fiscal policy has an immediate effect of bringing down the debt-to-GDP ratio in the United States. Surprisingly, the output gap closes faster with fiscal consolidation than without. Part of the reason for the relatively stronger economy is that the easing in monetary policy gives an additional boost to aggregate demand. But the simulation also shows that the high debt levels in the United States are becoming a drag on economic activity. And the higher inflation from the easier monetary policy reduces real debt burdens. The simulation shows that in a situation of high indebtedness, readjusting aggregate demand-management policy away from debt-augmenting fiscal policies and toward real debt-reducing monetary policies helps the economy find its maximum potential equilibrium more quickly.

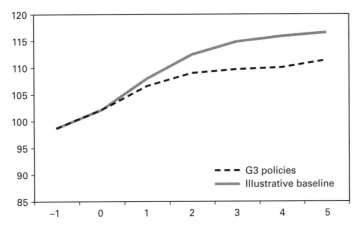

Figure 20.6
Coordinated monetary and fiscal actions: United States—debt-to-GDP ratio (percent of GDP deviation from baseline). The results in this section are created by developing an illustrative baseline scenario and then adding additional policies. Obviously these additional policies would need to be recalibrated if the baseline changes in response to new information about the economy or any new policies that are implemented. (For examples of applications using GIMF, see Kumhof and Laxton 2009a, b, c.)
Source: GIMF simulations

The increase in inflation from the easier monetary policy is noticeable but not dramatic. Inflation comes down from 2011 rates but does not drop below 2 percent per year, and it rises in the outer years of the simulation. In contrast, in the baseline scenario, inflation decelerates through 2013, reaching a low of about 1 percent per year, before rising toward 2 percent per year in the outer years of the simulation. This persistent, but short-term, higher rate of inflation reduces the real debt burdens of Americans, thereby reducing a drag on consumption.

20.7.2 Euro Area
The decline in the debt-to-GDP ratio in the euro area owing to fiscal consolidation is similar to that in the United States. The debt ratio in the euro area is not as high as that in the United States at the start of the simulation, and it starts to decline in the baseline owing to the fiscal consolidation that is already taking place, which means that public-sector indebtedness is on a clear downward track by the end of the fiscal consolidation simulation.

The coordinated policy combination of tighter fiscal policy and looser monetary policy closes the output gap in the euro area very rapidly. In part this is because the output gap in the euro area closes more quickly than that in the United States, since its gap is smaller to begin with. But also the inflation rate is higher in the euro area with this policy combination, so the real reduction in the debt burden is greater, which has a greater effect on reducing the drag on consumption coming from a heavy indebtedness burden.

With the easier monetary policy, inflation in the euro area falls little in the near term and rises to just under 3 percent per year by 2015. This results in inflation persisting about its target level for a number of years, which could damage ECB credibility if not explained well.

20.7.3 Japan

Fiscal consolidation in Japan of a size suitable for the United States and the euro area barely makes a noticeable dent in their debt-to-GDP ratio, given that the debt-to-GDP ratio is initially high. Nevertheless, the easier monetary policy has the effect of closing the Japanese output gap within two years and sends the economy into a slight excess demand.

The effect on Japanese inflation is noticeable in that it rises to 2 percent per annum by 2014, when it stabilizes.

20.7.4 Remaining Countries

In the scenario the policy of coordinated fiscal consolidation and monetary expansion is limited to the United States, euro area, and Japan. The remaining countries of the world do not change their aggregate demand-management policies. Growth in the remaining countries is not much affected by the policy change as the increase in aggregate demand in the G3 regions is largely a short-term increase in the level of GDP. Inflation, however is persistently above what it is in the base case as inflation expectations around the world rise in response to the purposefully easier monetary policy in the G3 region.

20.7.5 World

The increase in GDP in the G3 region is sufficient to lift world GDP growth for two years. Subsequently some of the growth is given back as the increase in GDP is a level shift upward that has but a transitory effect on world growth.

20.8 Conclusion

The simulations in this chapter show that fiscal consolidation need not depress world growth, provided that it is accompanied by a package of significant fiscal reform, productivity-enhancing structural reform, and monetary policy easing. Such a policy mix can generate a virtuous circle that increases the potential of the economy and stimulates aggregate demand sufficiently to offset the negative short-run effects on growth of reduced government expenditures and higher taxes.

References

Bouis, R., O. Causa, L. Demmou, R. Duval, and A. Zdzienicka. 2012. The Short-term effects of structural reforms: An empirical analysis. Working paper 949. Economics Department, OECD, Paris.

Cacciatore, M., R. Duval, and G. Fiori. 2012. Short-term pain or gain? A DSGE model-based analysis of the short-term effects of structural reforms in labour and product markets. Working paper 948. Economics Department, OECD, Paris.

Clinton, K., M. Kumhof, D. Laxton, and S. Mursula. 2010. Budget consolidation: Short-term pain for long-term gain. Working paper 10/163. IMF, Washington, DC.

Coenen, G., C. J. Erceg, C. Freedman, D. Furceri, M. Kumhof, R. Lalonde, D. Laxton, J. Lindé, A. Mourougane, D. Muir, S. Mursula, C. de Resende, J. Roberts, W. Roeger, S. Snudden, M. Trabandt, and J. int Veld. 2012. Effects of fiscal stimulus in structural models. *American Economic Journal: Macroeconomics* 4 (1): 22–68.

Freedman, C., M. Kumhof, D. Laxton, and J. Lee. 2009. The case for global fiscal stimulus. Staff position paper 09/04. IMF, Washington, DC.

Freedman, C., M. Kumhof, D. Laxton, and D. Muir. 2010a. Policies to rebalance the global economy after the financial crisis. *International Journal of Central Banking* 6 (1): 215–52.

Freedman, C., M. Kumhof, D. Laxton, D. Muir, and S. Mursula. 2010b. Global effects of fiscal stimulus during the crisis. *Journal of Monetary Economics* 57 (June): 506–26. Available at: http://www.sciencedirect.com/science.

Kumhof, M., and D. Laxton. 2009a. Simple, implementable fiscal policy rules. Working paper 09/76. IMF, Washington, DC.

Kumhof, M., and D. Laxton. 2009b. Chile's structural fiscal surplus rule: A model-based evaluation. Working paper 09/88. IMF, Washington, DC.

Kumhof, M., and D. Laxton. 2009c. Fiscal deficits and current account deficits. Working paper 09/237. IMF, Washington, DC.

Kumhof, M., D. Laxton, D. Muir, and S. Mursula. 2010. The global integrated monetary and fiscal model: Theoretical structure. Working paper 10/34. IMF, Washington, DC.

21

Policy Lessons from the Crisis and the Way Forward

Carlo Cottarelli, Philip Gerson, and Abdelhak Senhadji

The analysis in previous chapters makes clear that the global financial crisis has reshaped our understanding of the role of fiscal policy and has refocused the attention of the economics profession on fiscal sustainability issues. Had such a focus existed prior to the crisis, many countries might have been better prepared to deal with its impact than has turned out to be the case: fiscal policy, particularly in advanced economies, was far from optimal prior to the crisis due in part to gaps in fiscal frameworks. As a result many advanced economies' fiscal position was relatively weak even before the crisis and worsened significantly thereafter, leading to open fiscal crises in some countries and subjecting others to the vagaries of financial market jitters. The crisis has also affected our thinking about the role of fiscal policy in responding to shocks. Fiscal policy was given a more prominent stabilization role during the crisis, and the question is whether this was just the appropriate response due to the exceptional circumstances that prevailed at the onset of the crisis, or whether the experience of the last few years has implied a paradigmatic shift regarding the role fiscal policy should play in offsetting cyclical fluctuations. This crisis has exposed important structural and institutional weaknesses in the eurozone that can only be addressed through deep reforms. A path to full recovery and long-term fiscal sustainability exists, but it is likely to be a long and bumpy one. While it is too early to write a definitive history of the crisis, it is not, however, too early to begin drawing lessons from it to provide guidance for fiscal policy makers as they continue to deal with its effects. The goal of policy makers should be not just to recover from the current crisis but to minimize the likely costs of the next one.

Policy Lessons from the Crisis

This section presents ten preliminary conclusions from the post-crisis experience, a long list and yet certainly one that is neither complete nor final.

Lesson 1: No Country Can Defy Fiscal Gravity, at Least Not Forever

Prior to the global crisis a false sense of security had settled among advanced countries supported by a benign global economic environment (see chapter 6). A conventional fiscal risk threshold for public debt in emerging economies was believed to be in the 40 to 50 percent of GDP range. There was no well-established equivalent threshold for advanced economies because they had not experienced severe fiscal crises over the past few decades, perhaps contributing to complacency. But reality settled in with the recent experience of Cyprus, Greece, Iceland, Ireland, Italy, Portugal, and Spain, reminding us that advanced economies too can run into trouble if markets perceive countries' fiscal policy to be unsustainable. Admittedly, the experience of advanced economies has been more diverse than that of emerging economies. For instance, Japan and the United States have run debt ratios of 100 percent of GDP or more while facing record low borrowing costs thanks to the idiosyncratic nature of their investors' base (the unusually strong home bias of Japanese investors and the reserve currency status of the dollar). But, ultimately, equilibria based on the attitude of investors to finance lenders at low interest rates are precarious. Indeed, also, sovereign spreads for economies of the eurozone seemed disconnected from their economic fundamentals during the period leading up to the crisis. And, yet, recent events in Europe have shown how rapid and abrupt financial market responses to fiscal fundamentals can be.

Lesson 2: In Good Times, Prepare for Bad Times

Fiscal balances should be stronger in good times, so that their deterioration in bad times will not be seen as worrisome. While this principle is well understood and generally accepted, its application is far from universal. Deviations from this principle stem from two main reasons. First, political economy considerations tend to confer to fiscal policy a deficit bias. In other words, policy makers face popular pressure to increase spending or cut taxes when growth slows, but receive little political reward for tightening the purse strings when output recovers. Second, the tools for measuring the cyclical position of the economy have been deficient, meaning that policy makers may not always have been able to separate structural from cyclical factors that were affecting fiscal outturns. While the traditional focus has been on GDP cycles, fluctuations in asset markets, commodity prices and the sectoral composition of output are also relevant in determining the underlying state of public finances (see chapter 6). For instance, the United Kingdom benefited from high tax revenue during the period leading up to the crisis as a result of the high profitability and high labor incomes in the financial services industry. Similarly Ireland's tax revenue was buoyed by transactions-based taxes in the property sector and by capital gains taxes during the rapid asset price appreciation of the pre-crisis period. More generally, high asset prices can amplify tax revenues directly through capital gains and wealth taxes and indirectly through wealth and balance sheet effects. Accordingly, the underlying state of the fiscal accounts cannot be assessed just by looking at the output gap. Well-designed fiscal rules built around a notion of structural fiscal balance (which would correct for transitory fiscal revenue related to the output gap, asset or commodity price movements, and output composition shifts) along with independent fiscal monitors (such as fiscal councils) could help avoid procyclicality and enhance macroeconomic and financial stability. In this context, more research is needed to address the challenges in operationalizing such rules.

Lesson 3: Fiscal Policy Can Be an Effective Stabilization Tool in Some Cases

Before the crisis there was broad agreement among macroeconomists and policy makers that short-run stabilization was almost exclusively the domain of monetary policy while fiscal policy was given a more medium-term focus. While practice sometimes deviated from this paradigm, monetary policy was regarded as the main tool for countercyclical policy because it was more flexible, less prone to political pressures, and more easily delegated to independent experts. In addition monetary policy was thought to be a potent instrument in most, if not all, cases of weak aggregate demand. While economists were aware of the zero-bound problem, it was regarded simply as a peculiar textbook case. However, the size of the shock during the great recession was so large that many countries hit, or came close to, the lower bound for the policy interest rate and had to resort to both fiscal stimuli and unconventional monetary policy. In fact, as shown in chapter 10, almost every major country adopted a substantial fiscal stimulus after the crisis. While a broad consensus on the role of fiscal policy has not yet emerged, it is clear that fiscal policy is now regarded with much more interest as a tool to regulate the economic cycle. This more pragmatic approach is a positive development, although the risk of excessive fiscal activism remains a significant one. We do not advocate a more activist role for fiscal policy in general. Monetary policy should remain the primary stabilization tool. However, there may be circumstances such as the ones that prevailed during the current crisis that would warrant a more activist role for fiscal policy. This point is also supported by the reassessment of the size of fiscal multipliers discussed next.

Lesson 4: Fiscal Multipliers Could Be Relatively Large When Output Gaps Are Sizable and Monetary Policy Is Constrained

The comeback of fiscal activism during the crisis has sparked a great deal of work on the short-run effects of fiscal policy, particularly on fiscal multipliers. As Robert Solow stressed in his remarks in a recent IMF conference, it is futile to try to find "the" multiplier since the effects of fiscal policy are highly regime dependent—a central feature of chapter 11. Recent research at the IMF and elsewhere has indeed documented important asymmetries of fiscal policy over the cycle with significantly higher multipliers during recessions than periods of expansion. To some extent, this is obvious. On the one hand, when the economy is running at full potential, boosting aggregate demand through a fiscal expansion will result primarily in higher inflation (and/or a larger external current account deficit). On the other hand, if there is spare capacity a surge in demand will be met by higher output. Fiscal multipliers seem indeed to have been relatively large (greater than one) at the onset of the crisis when aggregate demand collapsed while many central banks had no further room left for lowering policy interest rates and the credit channel was impaired by heightened uncertainty and the weak state of the financial sector. High fiscal multipliers also have implications on the pace of fiscal consolidation underway. The adjustment needs to be gradual, to the extent made possible by market conditions, to limit the potential drag on growth by postponing a large portion of the fiscal adjustment until the recovery has taken hold and multipliers are lower.

Lesson 5: Growth Can Greatly Facilitate Fiscal Sustainability

Faster growth helps bring debt ratios down more rapidly though denominator effects (as shown in chapter 2). In addition faster growth helps because the data show that countries with faster growth rates typically also run stronger primary balances (according to the results of chapter 4). Indeed consider a country with an initial debt ratio of 100 percent and a revenue-to-GDP ratio of 40 percent, not too far from the average ratios in advanced European countries. If such a country manages to raise its potential growth rate by one percentage point and saves all the additional revenue, its debt-to-GDP ratio will fall to about 70 percent within ten years. Faster growth can also help reduce the social costs of fiscal consolidation and enhance its political sustainability, at least as long as the benefits of growth are fairly distributed. Thus, fiscal consolidation in advanced economies could be significantly less painful if they implement rapidly the necessary structural reforms in goods, labor, and financial markets to boost potential growth.

Lesson 6: Credibility Is Essential in Explaining Why Some Countries Can Sustain Higher Debt Ratios More Easily Than Others

This fact is also a direct consequence of the simple debt dynamics equation mentioned above. More specifically, the debt stabilizing primary balance (i.e., the primary balance that would keep the debt ratio constant) is equal to the debt stock times the difference between interest rate on public debt and the growth rate. A doubling of the growth-adjusted interest rate, say from 1 to 2 percent due to a loss of fiscal credibility, thus has the same effect on the debt stabilizing primary balance as a doubling of the debt ratio from 50 to 100 percent. Countries that are punished by financial markets through huge sovereign spreads are precisely those that have lost their fiscal credibility. Of course, maintaining credibility is much more important and difficult when the debt ratio is high. This underscores the importance of having a reliable medium-term consolidation plan with clear policy intentions, the fiscal institutions to support the adjustment, and a good communication strategy.

Lesson 7: Political Economy Considerations and an Appropriate Mix of Revenue Increases and Spending Cuts Are Essential for the Success of Fiscal Consolidation Plans

In advanced economies a substantial consolidation effort is in progress which will have to be maintained over the medium term to bring debt levels to more appropriate levels. The success of this effort hinges critically on the consolidation plans being perceived by all stakeholders as fair and equitable. This will require a delicate balancing act in the design of such plans and an effective communication strategy to ensure buy in by all interested parties. Countries with already high tax rates (as in many European countries) will have to act primarily on the spending side, while countries with relatively low revenue ratios (as is the case of the United States and Japan) will need to act also on the revenue side.

Lesson 8: A Monetary Union Cannot Be Sustained without Adequate Fiscal Integration

The crisis has underscored that the interplay of fiscal and banking risks, together with deep financial linkages across countries, can turn country-specific shocks into systemic ones. Avoiding a recurrence of these problems over the medium term will require a much deeper degree of fiscal integration than the one existing in the euro area before the crisis. There has been much concern in the past about the difficulty of having countries that could be subject to large idiosyncratic shocks in the same currency area. But many of the shocks that hit euro area member countries since 2007 reflected policy mistakes and lack of coordination, including with fiscal policy, rather than idiosyncratic shocks. The proper working of the euro area requires that fiscal policies become less fragmented. This recognition has been reflected in the new Fiscal Compact. More integration is needed in other policies too, particularly those affecting productivity growth and competitiveness. This said, countries will still be affected by sizable (and genuine) idiosyncratic shocks and the euro area as a whole should provide adequate insurance mechanisms against these shocks to avoid that they lead to problems for the whole area.

Lesson 9: Budget Institutions Need Strengthening in Most Countries

The global crisis has underscored the importance of strengthening fiscal institutions. To support the consolidation effort and enhance policy credibility, many countries have started or are considering reforms to better anchor fiscal policy over the medium term; strengthen budgetary planning, reporting, analysis, and execution; and improve risk management. In addition to specific measures in public financial management, reforms center on rules-based fiscal frameworks and independent fiscal agencies. However, a lot of work remains to be done. In particular, while most advanced and emerging market economies have basic fiscal reporting, limited coverage and reporting delays reduce its impact on policy-making. Similarly an increasing number of countries report multiyear macroeconomic and fiscal forecasts but only a few countries report risk assessments around the baseline scenario. Fiscal consolidation plans need to be supported by more comprehensive and binding medium-term budget frameworks with clear objectives, a more rigorous top-down approach to budgeting, more robust contingency arrangements, and greater independent scrutiny. Defining those plans in cyclically adjusted terms can provide some flexibility to respond to cyclical fluctuations.

Lesson 10: Financial Sector Risks Warrant Particular Attention due to the Devastating Effects of Financial Crises on Fiscal Accounts and More Generally on the Economy

In the past, fiscal risk analysis had focused too much on contractual obligations arising for the public sector, including guarantees. We now have clear evidence that non contractual obligations can be even more important. The financial sector is too important to fail, and therefore governments have no choice but to support it, potentially at a huge cost during a crisis. How should fiscal policy respond to these risks? Lowering public debt in good times is necessary but insufficient to address these risks: in fact Ireland had a debt ratio of 20 percent of GDP before the crisis. The solution is to minimize risk through appropriate financial regulation and supervision.

Conclusion

The global crisis has severely shaken the world economy as well as our understanding of fiscal policy. Some of the widely held fiscal principles in the economics profession have been challenged by facts, including those related to the size of fiscal multipliers, the interaction of monetary and fiscal policies, and more generally the role of fiscal policy itself. What has not changed, however, is the fact that sound fiscal accounts are a necessary condition for macroeconomic and financial stability and sustainable growth. The magnitude of the fiscal challenge ahead requires a multiyear adjustment effort, putting a premium on the credibility and equity of the process.

We hope that this book contributes to efforts to identify the challenges ahead for fiscal policy and begins to chart a course toward full economic recovery and fiscal sustainability.

Contributors

S. Ali Abbas

Nathaniel Arnold

Aqib Aslam

Thomas Baunsgaard

Nazim Belhocine

Dora Benedek

Carlo Cottarelli

Petra Dacheva

Mark De Broeck

Xavier Debrun

Asmaa El-Ganainy

Julio Escolano

Lorenzo Forni

Philip Gerson

Borja Gracia

Martine Guerguil

Alejandro Guerson

Laura Jaramillo

Jiri Jonas

Mika Kortelainen

Manmohan Kumar

Suchitra Kumarapathy

Douglas Laxton

Pablo Lopez-Murphy

Thornton Matheson

Jimmy McHugh

Uffe Mikkelsen

Kyung-Seol Min

Aiko Mineshima

Marialuz Moreno Badia

John Norregaard

Ceyla Pazarbasioglu

Iva Petrova

Tigran Poghosyan

Marcos Poplawski-Ribeiro

Anna Shabunina

Andrea Schaechter

Jack Selody

Abdelhak Senhadji

Baoping Shang

Mauricio Soto

Bruno Versailles

Anke Weber

Jaejoon Woo

Li Zeng

Index